HENRY VIII

J. J. Scarisbrick was educated at John Fisher School and at Christ's College, Cambridge, where he took a Ph.D. in 1954. Until 1969 he was Lecturer in History at Queen Mary College, London. He has travelled extensively in Africa and America, and went as a Visiting Lecturer to Ghana in 1959. He has contributed to a number of scholarly periodicals including the *Journal of Ecclesiastical History* and the *Cambridge Historical Journal*.

In 1969 J. J. Scarisbrick was appointed Professor of History at the University of Warwick.

J. J. SCARISBRICK

Henry VIII

PENGUIN BOOKS

Penguin Books Ltd, Harmondsworth, Middlesex, England
Penguin Books Australia Ltd, Ringwood, Victoria, Australia
Penguin Books (N.Z.) Ltd,
182–190 Wairau Road, Auckland 10, New Zealand

—

First published by Eyre & Spottiswoode 1968
Published in Penguin Books 1971
Reprinted 1972, 1974

—

—

Made and printed in Great Britain
by Richard Clay (The Chaucer Press) Ltd,
Bungay, Suffolk
Set in Linotype Georgian

Contents

Preface

THIS book is neither a 'private life' of Henry VIII nor a comprehensive study of his life and times. Rather, it is something in between. I have tried to see the whole of Henry and to discuss the more personal, domestic events of his life as well as the vast range of diplomatic, political and ecclesiastical affairs in which he was involved. But because he is at the centre of the canvas, there is little here concerning the economic and social life of Henrician England, little about such matters as the history of governmental institutions during the reign. Moreover, I have analysed the state of the Church in England on the eve of the Reformation only in sufficient detail (as I hope) to provide a background to Henry's actions, and discussed events of such capital importance as the dissolution of the monasteries and the Pilgrimage of Grace only in relation to him, not in their own right. Had I done otherwise, this book would have been much longer than it already is and would have ceased to be a biography.

I do not apologize for producing a life of a king – and a life cast in traditional form – at a time when academic historians are rightly much concerned with exploiting the techniques of socio-economic analysis and the like. Biographies of monarchs still have their place, as well as their limitations. Nor do I apologize for producing the biography of seemingly so well-known a figure as Henry VIII. It is now sixty-five years since A. F. Pollard's celebrated life of the king appeared, and none of the surprisingly few subsequent biographies has gone significantly beyond the limits of that pioneer work. In the meantime, a great deal has been written about the reign, not least by Pollard himself, which throws new light on the king; some new material has come to hand in the British Museum; the calendaring of state papers relating to England in foreign archives has gone forward. Pollard's primary concern was to digest the immense wealth of material contained in the *Letters and Papers ... of Henry VIII* – an enterprise not complete when he wrote. Of course, this monumental collection has been the centrepiece of my work, but I have tried to consult the originals of all the more important documents which I have used therein; and I have been able to explore some of the large areas of manuscript sources in the Public Record Office which the editors of *Letters and Papers* did not penetrate and which Pollard did not use.

The preface of a first book provides a welcome opportunity to acknowledge help received in the course of one's academic career. My warmest thanks go to Professor J. H. Plumb for guiding me through my undergraduate days; to Professor M. D. Knowles for launching me on my research and for his benevolent patronage ever since; to Dr G. R. Elton for supervising my thesis work and for constant kindness thereafter; to the Central Research Fund of the University of London for enabling me to undertake study abroad on two occasions, some of the fruit of which is contained in this book. Finally, I must record an especial debt to Professor S. T. Bindoff of Queen Mary College, University of London. It has been my great privilege to be a member of his Department for thirteen years; and what I owe to him is incalculable.

I must also thank those who have helped me with this book: Professor David C. Douglas, the most patient and encouraging editor of the series to which it belongs; Professor A. G. Dickens, who gave me extremely valuable, painstaking aid; Mr R. J. Knecht and Dr D. S. Chambers, who, among many other things, have endured a great deal of talk about Cardinal Wolsey; Mr M. H. Merriman, who tried hard to steer me through the intricacies of Scottish affairs in the 1540s; the members of Professor S. T. Bindoff's postgraduate seminar, held at the Institute of Historical

Research, who listened to various portions of this book from time to time and commented upon them to very good effect; to Professor Bindoff himself – once more – for all manner of assistance and unwearying encouragement.

Finally, I should explain that I have modernized the spelling and punctuation of all original documents which I have quoted.

J. J. SCARISBRICK

Queen Mary College
(University of London)
June 1967

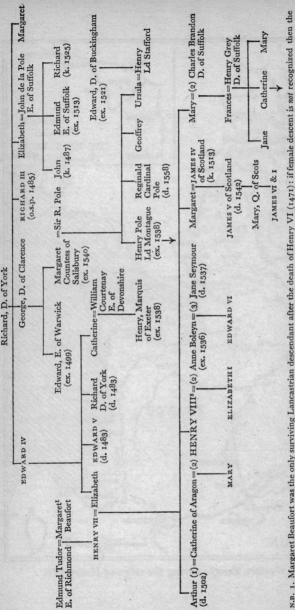

GENEALOGY

N.B. 1. Margaret Beaufort was the only surviving Lancastrian descendant after the death of Henry VI (1471): if female descent is *not* recognized then the Lancastrian claim to the throne ended with Henry VI.
2. Henry VIII's other wives were (4) Anne of Cleves; (5) Catherine Howard (ex. 1542); (6) Catherine Parr.

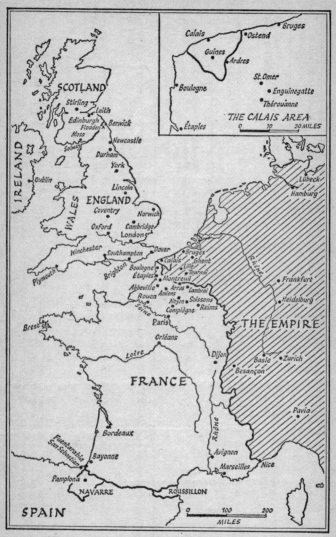

Western Europe during the reign of Henry VIII

Abbreviations

B.I.H.R.	*Bulletin of the Institute of Historical Research.*
B.M.	British Museum, London.
Burnet	*The History of the Reformation of the Church of England*, ed. Pocock, Oxford, 1865.
Cavendish	*The Life and Death of Cardinal Wolsey*, ed. Sylvester, E.E.T.S., 1959.
C.H.J.	*Cambridge Historical Journal.*
E.E.T.S.	Early English Text Society.
E.H.R.	*English Historical Review.*
Ehses	*Römische Dokumente zur Geschichte des Ehescheidung Heinrichs VIII von England, 1527–1534*, Paderborn, 1893.
Fiddes	*The Life of Cardinal Wolsey*, 1724.
Foxe	*The Act and Monuments*, ed. Pratt, 1874.
Hall	*The union of the two noble and illustre famelies York and Lancaster*, ed. Ellis, 1809.
Hughes and Larkin	*Tudor Royal Proclamations. 1. The Early Tudors (1485–1553)*, New Haven and London, 1964.
L.P.	*Letters and Papers, Foreign and Domestic, of the Reign of Henry VIII, 1509–47*, ed. Brewer, Gairdner and Brodie, 1862–1910, 1920.
Martene-Durand	*Veterum Scriptorum et Monumentorum . . . Amplissima Collectio*, Paris, 1724–33.
Migne, P.L.	*Patrologiae Cursus Completus etc.*
Mil. Cal.	*Calendar of State Papers, Milan (1385–1618)*, ed. Hinds, 1912.
Pastor	*History of the Popes*, trans. Antrobus and Kerr, 1891–1933.

Pocock	*Records of the Reformation. The Divorce 1527–1533*, Oxford, 1870.
P.R.O.	Public Record Office, London.
Rymer	*Foedera, Conventiones, Litterae etc.* (edn 1704–35).
S.P.	State Papers (P.R.O.).
Sp. Cal.	*Calendar of State Papers, Spanish*, ed. Bergenroth, Gayangos and Hume, 1862– .
Sp. Cal. F.S.	*Further Supplement to the Calendar of State Papers, Spanish*, ed. Mattingly.
Sp. Cal. S.	*Supplement to the Calendar of State Papers, Spanish*, ed. Bergenroth.
St.P.	*State Papers of the reign of King Henry the Eighth*, 1830–52.
T.R.H.S.	*Transactions of the Royal Historical Society.*
Ven. Cal.	*Calendar of State Papers, Venetian*, ed. Rawdon Brown, 1864– .
Wilkins	*Concilia Magnae Brittaniae etc.*, 1737.

Unless otherwise stated, all references to *Hughes and Larkin*, *L.P.*, *Mil. Cal.*, *Sp. Cal.*, *Sp. Cal. F.S.*, *Sp. Cal. S.* and *Ven. Cal.* relate to documents, not pages.

HENRY VIII

[1]

The New King

HENRY was born on 28 June 1491 in the royal palace at Greenwich. He was the third child of his parents, Henry VII and Elizabeth of York, the second of their four sons and the only one to achieve adulthood. He was baptized by Richard Fox, then bishop of Exeter, in the near-by church of the Observant Franciscans,[1] a group of religious upon whom his hand was to fall with particular violence before his life was out.

Not least because he was the second son of his father and inevitably overshadowed by his elder brother Arthur, we know very little about his early life. We hear of his nurse, one Anne Luke, to whom he granted an annual pension of £20 when he became king,[2] but for the rest of his infancy and early youth can only catalogue the succession of titles and honours which were bestowed upon him, or catch occasional mention of him and his household in the state papers. On 5 April 1493 he received his first office, that of constable of Dover Castle and warden of the Cinque Ports.[3] Soon afterwards he became earl marshal of England and, on 12 September 1494, lieutenant of Ireland.[4] On 30 October of the same year the three-year-old boy was brought from Eltham to Westminster to undergo the elaborate ceremony of admission to the Order of the Bath, which ended next day when the young Henry was carried in the arms of the earl of Shrewsbury to the king, who bade the duke of Buckingham place a spur on the child's right heel and then

1. As Fox himself later recalled. *L.P.*, iv, 5791.
2. *L.P.*, i, 132 (39).
3. *Calendar of Patent Rolls, 1485–1494*, 423.
4. *Letters and Papers ... of Henry VII*, ed. Gairdner (1861–3), ii, 374.

dubbed him and his companions.[5] On the following day,
Henry VII came into the Parliament Chamber in full regalia
and, before a large company of nobles and prelates, the
mayor and aldermen of London and many others, heard his
son proclaimed duke of York.[6] In December of the same
year the new duke was appointed warden of the Scottish
Marches; on 17 May 1495 he received the Garter.[7]

Of course, the duties attached to the high offices conferred on the duke were performed by deputies. But at
Windsor, on 21 September 1496, the five-year-old boy seems
to have carried out his first public act, namely, witnessing a
royal grant by charter to the abbot and convent of Glastonbury to hold two annual fairs.[8] If this was his début, it was
an ironical one; for, forty-three years later, he had reduced
that abbey to ruins and had its last abbot hanged for
treason on Tor Hill near by. Then, on 14 November 1501,
Duke Henry took part in the ceremonies for the marriage
of his brother Arthur to the princess who had newly arrived
from Spain to be his bride. He was to head the procession
which led Catherine of Aragon from Baynard's Castle to
St Paul's, and to lead her out of the cathedral after the
wedding; and in the ten days of festivities which followed,
the young Henry was much to the fore, dancing with
Margaret, his elder sister, with a grace and ease which delighted his parents.[9]

According to the well-known tale of Lord Herbert of
Cherbury, Henry VII had originally intended that his second
son should enter the Church and occupy the primatial see
of Canterbury.[10] There is no evidence for this, and it is as
difficult to assess the worth of Herbert's statement as it is
to resist wondering what would have happened to Henry
and to the Church in England if the father's designs for his

5. *L.P.*, i, 388 ff.   6. ibid., 403.   7. ibid, ii, 57.

8. *Calendar of Patent Rolls, 1494-1509*, 72.

9. *Letters and Papers ... of Henry VII*, i, 413.

10. Herbert, Lord Edward (of Cherbury), *The life and raigne of
King Henry the eighth* (1672), 2.

son had come to pass. The latter (and Canterbury), however, were spared, when death suddenly carried off Arthur prince of Wales, his elder brother and heir to the throne. Immediately after his marriage Arthur had departed with his bride to Ludlow, to preside over his principality and the council in the Marches of Wales. In April 1502, four months after his arrival there, the fifteen-year-old prince died of consumption which had long racked his sickly body. Arthur's tragic death transformed Henry's condition – translating him from the dynastic and political limbo of the second son to the limelight of heir apparent, sweeping aside any plans there may have been for a career in the Church and bringing yet more honours upon him. After some doubt had been set aside as to whether the title of duke of Cornwall belonged only to the first-born son or could pass to the *filius primogenitus existens*, Henry succeeded his brother to this dukedom in October 1502.[11] Four months later, on 18 February 1503, he was created prince of Wales and earl of Chester.

Details of his education are sparse. The poet laureate John Skelton seems to have been his first tutor, probably beginning his work in the mid 1490s and ending it in 1502. It was he who taught Henry, so he claimed, 'his learning primordial',[12] that is, the rudiments. After this

> The honour of England I learned to spell
> I gave him drink of the sugared well
> Of Helicon's waters crystalline,
> Acquainting him with the muses nine,

he wrote.[13] Whether the bitter-tongued Skelton was an entirely wholesome influence on his pupil may be debated, though it is true that in 1501 he wrote for him a *Speculum Principis*, a ponderous (if highly virtuous) handbook of princely perfection of a kind which was a familiar literary

11. G. E. C[okayne], *Complete Peerage*, iii (1913), 442.
12. Skelton, *Works*, ed. Dyce (1843), i. 129.
13. ibid.

exercise, full of earnest advice which his charge was to show little sign of having taken to heart – including the recommendation to keep all power in his hands and entrust little to his servants, and to 'choose a wife for yourself; prize her always and uniquely'.[14] Skelton's intentions were doubtless admirable; his pedagogy, however, seems to have been defective.

Henry's elder brother underwent a strenuous course of classical studies. By the time he was fifteen, so his mentor, the laureated poet Bernard André, wrote proudly, Arthur 'had either committed to memory or read with his own eyes and leafed with his own fingers' the standard works on grammar, a selection of Homer, Virgil, Ovid, Terence and others, a good deal of Cicero and a wide span of history, including works by Thucydides, Caesar, Livy and Tacitus.[15] Presumably Henry endured a similar regime, though whether this was under the guidance of Skelton or his rather misty successor, one William Hone, later tutor also to Henry's sister Mary,[16] is not clear. Lord Herbert believed that Henry received the beginnings of a clerical education, as befitted one who was destined for an ecclesiastical career. But there is no evidence for this; and it is not easy to guess what specifically clerical content could have been given to the education of a boy who was not yet eleven years old when it became clear that he would ascend the throne of England rather than that of Canterbury. Nor do we know exactly how Henry acquired his linguistic skills or learned music. It is likely that Henry VII's mother, Lady Margaret Beaufort, had surveillance of her grandson's upbringing, perhaps presiding over the royal nursery in much the same way as Catherine Parr was to do four decades later.[17] Possibly it was she who brought Skelton and Hone from her beloved Cambridge to teach Henry, his sister Mary and their

14. Nelson, *John Skelton Laureate* (New York, 1939), 75.
15. ibid., 15. 16. *L.P.*, i, 2656 (5).
17. See *V.C.H. Beds.*, iii, 41 for an interesting inscription in Bletsoe parish church on the monument of Sir John St John, Lady Margaret's nephew, who is said there to have been educated by her together with her grandson.

companions in the royal school; possibly she chose these
tutors on the advice of her friend John Fisher; and doubtless
it would have been easy enough to find in Henry VII's interesting and talented court several folk well qualified to
teach the prince languages and music. What influence the
Lady Margaret exerted on her protégé and what she thought
of him are unanswerable questions. But on her deathbed
she bade him follow the counsel of John Fisher, now bishop
of Rochester, in all things:[18] an injunction which has
scarcely less irony about it than the maxims from Skelton's
Speculum Principis.

Though much information about Henry's childhood and
adolescence is lacking, two very telling facts remain. First,
the son was apparently never given any responsibility, however circumscribed, for state affairs during his father's life-
time, or any taste of independence. At the age of fifteen,
Arthur was despatched to Wales, presumably because his
father wished him to be about a prince's duties and to
acquire political experience in the tough world of the
Marcher lordships. But either because the experiment had
apparently cost him his first son and he dared not risk losing
his second, or because he had serious doubts about the latter's
proficiency, Henry VII provided no such apprenticeship for
Henry prince of Wales. Henry VIII ascended the throne of
England – so it seems – unseasoned and untrained in the
exacting art of kingship. Worse, until the moment when he
came to the throne, he had led a severely restricted life.
According to a Spanish envoy called Fuensalida, who came
to England in early 1508, the prince of Wales was kept under
such strict supervision that he might have been a young
girl. He could not go out except through a private door
which led into a park, and then only in the company of
specially appointed persons. No one dared to approach him
and speak to him. He spent his time in a room the only
access to which was through the king's chamber and was so

18. So Pole recalled in his *Apologia ad Carolum Quintum*. See *L.P.*,
xiv, i, 200. Pole was writing twenty years after the event – but his
mother might well have been an eye-witness to the scene.

cowed that he never spoke in public except to answer a
question from his father.[19] Fuensalida had come to England
to clinch the marriage between Henry and his brother's
widow, Catherine, and Henry's father may have had good
reason for making it especially difficult for the ambassador
to have access to his son. Moreover, the same ambassador
was soon reporting how the young Henry spent day after
day at Richmond in his favourite, boisterous sport, tilting.
True, even then his father was an onlooker – at least on
occasion. But the prince may not have been so thoroughly
shut in as Fuensalida first supposed. Nonetheless, it may
well be that he was kept under rigorous supervision by a
severe father for the same reasons which perhaps prevented
him from following his elder brother to Wales or to a post
of responsibility somewhere else. A son and heir – as this
son would soon discover – was a precious possession; and the
rather gaunt Henry VII, who had now lost five out of eight
children as well as his wife, may also have judged that his
only living son was a colt who badly needed disciplining
under his own, and Lady Margaret's, eye. Whatever the
truth of the matter, a modern may well shake his head over
this story of evident repression of an ebullient youth and
conclude that it explains a good deal of the flamboyance
and waywardness of the grown man.

  Nor had his father provided him with a wife. Royal offspring, as Henry's sisters and his own children were to discover, could rarely hope to be anything but pawns in the
incessant, most serious game of international match-making.
Royal marriage-treaties were the very stuff of diplomacy –
long had been, and long would remain so – and the parties
concerned were neither expected nor allowed to have any
say in the bartering. Marriage, it was contended, came first,
love afterwards. But by any standards, Prince Henry's experience of the ways of parents in this commerce was unfortunate. In 1501 his father had begun, very tentatively, to

19. *Correspondencia de Gutierre Gomez de Fuensalida*, etc., ed.
Duque de Berwick y de Alba (Madrid, 1907), 449.

negotiate on his behalf for the hand of Eleanor, a daughter
of Philip duke of Burgundy and a niece of that Catherine
of Aragon whom his brother was to marry.[20] When Arthur
died, however, it was decided that his brother should inherit his young widow. The suit for Eleanor was therefore
set aside and her aunt, Catherine of Aragon, substituted –
though not before Henry VII, widowed early in 1503, had
fleetingly proposed that he might take on his dead son's
widow himself.[21] On 23 June 1503 a treaty was signed for
the marriage of Prince Henry and Catherine. Henry was
then almost twelve, Catherine seventeen. The treaty provided that the marriage should be solemnized as soon as the
prince reached his fifteenth year, which would be on 28
June 1505, by which time Catherine's parents were to have
delivered another hundred thousand crowns, in plate and
jewels as well as coin, as a marriage portion.[22] Furthermore,
since Catherine had been married to Arthur, a papal dispensation would be necessary before she could be united to
his brother. Catherine herself and her fiery duenna, Doña
Elvira, insisted that that first marriage had never been consummated, in which case a dispensation from the so-called
impediment of public honesty was required; but not least
in order to secure the princess's dower rights, the Spanish
ambassador in London at the time, Dr Puebla, thrust
Catherine's protests aside and agreed with the English that
a dispensation should be sought from the impediment of
affinity in the first degree collateral, an impediment which
could have arisen only from physical union of the parties.
Hence, shortly afterwards supplication was made to Rome
for the fateful dispensation whereby Henry might wed
Catherine despite the affinity which stood between them.[23]
Two days after the marriage treaty was signed, the pair

20. *Letters and Papers . . . of Henry VII*, i, 167.
21. Mattingly, *Catherine of Aragon* (edn 1950), 52 f.
22. *Sp. Cal.*, i. 364.
23. On the impediments of public honesty and affinity, and the
problems associated with Julius's bull, see Chapter 7, below.

were solemnly betrothed. As soon as the papal dispensation arrived (and it was to be delayed for many months), Catherine would be, as Henry called her in April 1506, 'my most dear and well-beloved consort, the princess my wife'.[24]

Re-marriage ended Catherine's bleak and impecunious widowhood, but did not deliver her from unhappy confinement at Durham House in the Strand amidst a squabbling household, a discomfort made worse by the egregious Dr Puebla and, at one point, King Henry's withholding the monthly allowance of £100 which he had allocated to her. She saw little, probably, of Prince Henry and, since she had apparently still not mastered English, would not have been able to communicate much to him when she did. She fell ill more than once; and there was no sign of the missing half of her marriage portion still due from her father. 28 June 1505 came and went, but the money did not arrive; as a result, there was no solemnization of her nuptials.

While Catherine waited, lost and rather beleaguered, Prince Henry was involved in two curious incidents. On 27 June 1505 he made a solemn protest before Bishop Fox disowning the marriage contract which he had entered some two years previously and stating that he would never validate or ratify that contract.[25] Many years later this protest would be brought out to prove that Henry had never wanted to marry Catherine and be offered as further proof that his marriage was null and void.[26] But certainly the prince had spoken this piece at his father's behest. What King Henry's purpose was is far from clear. Perhaps he really wanted to offer his son elsewhere; perhaps he wanted to hasten the dispatch from Spain of the second instalment of the marriage portion; perhaps he wanted to disconcert the Spaniards in return for their having offered him, who was still a roving widower, the hand of the widowed queen of Naples who, on inspection, turned out to be a lady without either material

24. *Letters and Papers . . . of Henry VII*, i, 285.
25. Printed in *Burnet*, iv, 17 f., and elsewhere.
26. See below, p. 242.

resources or prospects.[27] But, if the match between the prince and the princess was in jeopardy at this moment, then it is even more difficult to deal with a second incident which must have begun shortly after this protest was uttered. On 20 October 1505, and in response to a request presumably made three or four months previously, Pope Julius II wrote to the prince of Wales empowering him to restrain his wife from persevering in excessive religious observances which were injurious to her health. He had been told, wrote the pope, that Catherine wished to bind herself by vow to a rigorous life of prayer, fasting, abstinence and pilgrimage, that she did so without her husband's permission, that her zeal might harm her body, imperil the '*maritalis consuetudo*' and endanger her ability to bear children. Mindful, there-fore, of the fact that she should be subject to her spouse, her head, and that procreation is among the chief purposes of marriage, Julius authorized the suppliant to forbid his spouse to undertake any such vows in the future contrary to his command, and to oblige her to commute them into such other, less arduous acts of piety as her confessor directed.[28]

Such was the pope's response to an allegedly anxious hus-band. Perhaps it was true that Catherine was embarking on severe asceticism which would spoil her young body, though she herself attributed her undoubted ill-health, which prob-ably owed most to her low spirits, to tertian fever. Perhaps the prince's supplication, like his protest shortly before, had some ulterior motive – though what this might have been is not easy to guess. Julius's brief is a curious document, both for having been asked for and for having said what it said. It is curious for yet a third reason. The only extant copy of it lies in a register of briefs in the Vatican Archives. Though certainly dated 20 October 1505, it is addressed to Arthur

27. This last is Mattingly's suggestion (op. cit., 58). It is, perhaps, a little too colourful.

28. Vatican Archives, Arm. xxxix, 23, fol. 689. It is printed, with some corrections, in *Ehses*, xliii f.

prince of Wales, who had been dead three and a half years. Presumably an absent-minded clerk mis-read the supplication and addressed the reply to the wrong prince. Whether the brief that came to England bore the same unfortunate flaw we cannot know; if it did, Catherine may well have gone about her works of penitence unimpeded.

At the very moment when the pope was bidding Catherine, via her prince, to keep herself young and nubile, Henry VII was seriously considering the possibility of casting her out of the family and giving his son, after all, to that Eleanor, daughter of Philip of Castile, who had been ear-marked for him some four years previously. Eleanor was nearer the prince's age than was her aunt Catherine and she was the grand-daughter of an emperor; another aunt of hers, Margaret, might suit Henry VII himself very well; her brother Charles, the future emperor, would make an admirable match for Mary, the youngest Tudor child.[29] Plans for this triple liaison with the Habsburgs were afoot by October 1505. Moreover, this programme so well served the tortuous interests of the head of the Habsburg clan, the Emperor Maximilian I, that by 1507 an Imperial ambassador had come to England and made considerable progress in his negotiations. It was in response to this threatening counter-move that Ferdinand of Aragon dispatched Fuensalida to England with urgent instructions to hold off the Habsburgs and to rescue the union of Prince Henry and Catherine. But the newcomer found the situation almost hopeless. The king of England was now hostile towards his master; in the English Council some pressed for the young prince to be given a Habsburg bride (either Eleanor or the daughter of the duke of Bavaria, whom Maximilian had himself offered as a replacement for the former), and some urged that he should be given a French bride, Margaret of Alençon. None, apparently, had much thought for Catherine of Aragon. Such being the case, Fuensalida judged that the only thing

29. *Sp. Cal.*, i, 354 ff.; *Letters and Papers . . . of Henry VII*, i, 134 ff., 189 ff.; ii, 106 ff.

to do was to rescue the unwanted princess and as much of her dowry as could be recovered, and to abandon the English to their obscure fate.[30] The closely guarded Prince Henry probably knew little of these machinations by his seniors and would doubtless have acquiesced obediently in them if he did. His spouse, however, was a twenty-three-year-old of very different mettle and one whom seven years in England, many of them spent in lonely penury at Durham House, had turned into a steadfast, mature woman. Long ago she had declared that she would rather die in this foreign land than return, disowned, to Spain, and she now roundly denounced her fellow-countryman's defeatism as traitorous. 'Recall him at once,' she wrote to her father of Fuensalida, 'and punish him as he deserves.'[31] But the ambassador may well have been right. If Henry VII had lived and continued in his recent revulsion against Spain, his heir might well have finally been given to Eleanor or Margaret, not Catherine. But on 22 April 1509 the old king lay dead in Richmond Palace. His son was at his bedside. Next day Henry VIII was proclaimed king and left Richmond to go to the Tower. On Wednesday 9 May his father's embalmed body was taken by chariot to St Paul's, where John Fisher preached the funeral oration. On the following day it was buried in Westminster Abbey, beside Queen Elizabeth, in the matchless chapel named after him.

Doubtless many reigns have begun amidst an atmosphere of jubilant expectation; but this beginning had an especial lustre. For the new king, accession to the throne brought deliverance from a long, probably oppressive subjection to a stern father and grandmother, and released him into the bright, cloudless warmth of gaiety, freedom and power. He stood now on the brink of manhood, suddenly clad with the full panoply of kingship. He ascended a throne which his father had made remarkably secure, he inherited a fortune which probably no English king had ever been bequeathed,

30. Mattingly, op. cit., 90 f.   31. ibid., 91.

he came to a kingdom which was the best governed and most obedient in Christendom. Shortly before his death, his father had granted a general pardon to his people. The new king confirmed this – in ampler form.[32] His father left him a body of accomplished ministers, most of whom would continue to serve him. But those two men, Richard Empson and Edmund Dudley, who had served Henry VII's money-gathering and law-enforcement so assiduously, and whose 'unreasonable and extort doing noble men grudged, mean men kicked, poor men lamented, preachers openly at Paul's Cross and other places exclaimed, rebuked and detested' – these would be cast aside.[33] Within a few hours of his accession Henry had been so roused to wrath by tales of their wrong-doing that, even as he came to the Tower amidst the trumpets and rejoicing on that 23 April, the second day of his reign, they were seized and brought thither as prisoners, where they languished until their execution sixteen months later.

'Heaven and earth rejoices; everything is full of milk and honey and nectar. Avarice has fled the country. Our king is not after gold, or gems, or precious metals, but virtue, glory, immortality.' So wrote Lord Mountjoy to Erasmus in a celebrated, and, as it proved, somewhat inaccurate, outburst of enthusiasm.[34] There had come to the throne the very perfection of Christian kingship – gracious, gifted and enlightened – and with his coming, it seemed, bleak days must give way to bounteous prosperity.

The new king quickly married; and, after all, he married Catherine. He himself said that he did so in obedience to his father's dying wish,[35] but it may well be that his story of Henry VII's deathbed change of heart was invented shortly afterwards to placate the Habsburgs whose daughter,

32. *Hughes and Larkin*, nos. 59, 60.
33. *Hall*, 503.
34. *Opus Epistolarum Des. Erasmi Roterodami*, ed. 6. S. and H. M. Allen (Oxford, 1906), i, no. 214.
35. Henry to Margaret of Savoy, 27 June 1509. *L.P.*, i, 84.

Eleanor, had just been jilted. Fuensalida believed that it
was the young king himself who brought about the change
of plan, and this may be the truth. Five days after Henry
VII died, the ambassador was still convinced that Catherine's
cause was lost and quoted two members of the Council to
the effect that the dying king had assured his son that he
was free to marry whomsoever he chose. Then the situation
changed radically. Fuensalida was suddenly called before
the Council and, to his astonishment, not only assured of
the king's fervent goodwill towards the princess, but told by
the bishop of Durham, Thomas Ruthal, who had at that
moment emerged from a meeting with Henry in a near-by
room, that such matters as Catherine's dowry were trifles
and that the king looked to him to settle quickly all the
details concerning the marriage; whereupon he withdrew in
some bewilderment and set about recovering the possessions
of the princess which he had already begun to transfer to
Bruges.[36] Six weeks later, on 11 June, the marriage between
Henry and Catherine was solemnized in the Franciscan
church at Greenwich. A little while before there had been
some talk of a possible scruple about his marrying his dead
brother's widow,[37] and many years later Bishop Fox recalled
that the archbishop of Canterbury, William Warham, had
disapproved of the union, apparently because he doubted
the sufficiency or validity of the now six-year-old bull of
dispensation – though on what ground he did so we are not
told.[38] Warham's qualms were to be of consequence nearly
two decades hence when the lawfulness of this marriage be-

36. *Correspondencia de . . Fuensalida*, 518 ff.; Mattingly, op. cit.,
93 f.
    37. Mattingly, op. cit., 93, quoting Fuensalida.
    38. So Nicholas West, bishop of Ely, deposed many years later when
the divorce was afoot. See B.M. Vit., B xii, fol. 123 v (*L.P.*, iv, 5774).
West said that Warham and Fox had disagreed about the permissi-
bility of the union, the former, apparently, arguing against it. But it
may well be that Warham had voiced his doubts before the papal
dispensation was issued, i.e. in 1503, and that by 1509 he had abandoned them.

came a matter of impassioned debate; but for the moment
any doubts there may have been were brushed aside as a
proud king undid the protest he had made at his father's
command three years before and finally (and freely) ratified
his union with a princess who, though five years his senior,
was probably still beautiful and certainly of a quality of
mind and life which few queens have seriously rivalled.

At least outwardly, her husband was, and had been since
childhood, immensely striking. Ten years before, Erasmus
had strolled over to Eltham in the company of Thomas
More to meet the royal children and been much impressed
by the grace and poise of the eight-year-old Duke Henry.[39]
By the time he came to the throne he had burgeoned into a
full-blooded seventeen-year-old, upon whom Nature had
showered apparently every gift. 'His majesty', wrote a
dazzled Venetian shortly after the new reign began, 'is the
handsomest potentate I ever set eyes on.' He was tall and
splendidly built, with glowing auburn hair 'combed short
and straight in the French fashion' and a pink round face
so delicately cut 'that it would become a pretty woman'.[40]
He was 'extremely handsome. Nature could not have done
more for him,' one said a few years later, in 1519. 'He is
much handsomer than the king of France, very fair and his
whole frame admirably proportioned.'[41] His was a superlative
body. He was a capital horseman who could stay in the
saddle for hour after hour and tire out eight or ten horses;
he exulted in hawking, wrestling and dancing; he excelled
at tennis, 'at which game it is the prettiest thing in the
world to see him play, his fair skin glowing through a shirt
of the finest texture'.[42] He could throw a twelve-foot spear
many yards, withstand all comers in mock combat with
heavy, two-handed swords, draw the bow with greater
strength than any man in England. In July 1513, while at
Calais on his first campaign, he practised archery with the
archers of his guard and 'cleft the mark in the middle and
surpassed them all, as he surpasses them in stature and per-

39. *Opus Epistolarum etc.*, i, no. 1.   40. *L.P.*, ii, 395.
41. *Ven. Cal.*, ii, 1287.   42. ibid.

sonal graces'.[43] Above all, he delighted in prowess in the ring
and at the barrier, the sovereign sport of princes. Through
the summer of 1508 the prince of Wales, still only just
seventeen, had hurled his keen, tireless body into the fury
of the tournament and excelled all his opponents,[44] and his
accession to the throne would inaugurate a festival of
apparently endless jousting and tilting, at which the king
ever carried away the prizes.

When Erasmus first met him on that day in 1499 – standing with his sisters Margaret and Mary and his infant
brother Edmund, soon to die – he 'sent me a little note,
while we were at dinner, to challenge something from my
pen'; whereupon Erasmus, unable to perform *extempore*,
spent three anxious days composing an ode entitled 'A
Description of Britain, King Henry VII and the King's
Children' and a eulogy of Skelton (who had doubtless been
the true author of the boy's message), to which he added
some odds and ends scraped together from the bottom of
his trunk to form a literary nosegay worthy of the young
duke.[45] Seven years later Erasmus wrote to Henry and received so accomplished a reply that he was convinced that
someone else had had a large hand in its composition. But
Lord Mountjoy, his patient patron, showed him a number of
letters from the prince to various people in which there were
so many signs of corrections and additions that Erasmus
was forced to abandon his scepticism.[46] Presumably Skelton
and Hone pushed Henry's pen to paper, for in later life
Henry was never an industrious letter-writer – except during those months twenty years or so later when romantic
passion got the better of sluggishness and drew from him
some rather heavy sighings for his absent beloved, Anne
Boleyn. But Henry was undoubtedly a precocious, nimble-
minded pupil. He knew Latin and French and some Italian.
He is said to have acquired some Spanish, and about 1519

43. *L.P.*, i, 2391.
44. Gairdner, *Memorials of King Henry the Seventh* (1858), 116, 124.
45. *Opus Epistolarum etc.*, i, no. 1.
46. ibid., v, 241 (*L.P.*, iv, 5412).

had a sufficient (if passing) interest in Greek to receive instruction in this fashionable language from Richard Croke, a minor English humanist who had hitherto been at Paris, Louvain, Cologne and Leipzig, and was now to teach at Cambridge. His grasp of theology may have been less assured than he supposed, but it was remarkable for a king; he showed himself an apt student of mathematics, and it was his custom to take Thomas More 'into his private room, and there some time in matters of astronomy, geometry, divinity and such other faculties, and some time in his worldly affairs, to sit and confer with him, and other whiles would he in the night have him up into the leads [i.e. the roof] there to consider with him the diversities, courses, motions and operations of the stars and planets'.[47]

Above all he was a gifted, enthusiastic musician. He had music wherever he went, on progress, on campaign. He scoured England for singing boys and men for the chapels royal, and even stole talent from Wolsey's choir, of which he was evidently jealous.[48] Sacred music in the Renaissance style – the work of Benedict de Opitiis and Richard Sampson, later bishop of Chichester – was introduced into the royal chapel in 1516 and sung by a choir judged by an Italian visitor to be 'more divine than human'; and between 1519 and 1528 the king acquired a collection of French and Netherlandish music. Henry had many foreign musicians at court, like the violinist Ambrose Lupo, the lutenist Philip van Wilder from the Netherlands, as well as trumpeters, flautists and two Italian organists, de Opitiis and the famous Dionisio Memo, organist of St Mark's, Venice, who was lured to England in 1516 and would sometimes perform for four hours at a stretch before the king and court.[49] There were twenty-six lutes in Henry's collection of instruments,

47. Roper, *The Life of Sir Thomas More*, E.E.T.S. (1935), 11.
48. *L.P.*, ii, 410, 4024.
49. ibid., 2401, 3455; *Ven. Cal.*, ii, 780; Hughes and Abraham, *Ars Nova and the Renaissance*; *Oxford History of Music*, iii (Oxford, 1960), 304 f.; Reese, *Music in the Renaissance* (1954), 769 ff., 842, 850.

together with trumpets, viols, rebecs, sackbuts, fifes and drums, harpsichords and organs. The king himself played the lute well; he could manage the organ and was skilled on the virginals (which perhaps John Heywood, his virginalist, taught him). He had a strong, sure voice, could sight-read easily, and delighted to sing with a courtier like Sir Peter Carew 'certain songs they called "freeman's songs", as "By the banks as I lay" and "As I walked the wood so wild" '. His court was a generous patron to composers, headed by the great Dr Fairfax, if not Henry himself – for the king wrote at least two five-part Masses, a motet, a large number of instrumental pieces, part songs and rounds. 'Pastime with good company', 'Helas, madam' and perhaps 'Gentle prince' are his work; so too the motet 'O Lord, the maker of all thing' – no mean achievement for a monarch.[50] Henry has traditionally been seen, alongside James IV of Scotland or the colourful, versatile Emperor Maximilian I, as the archetype of resplendent Renaissance monarchy; and the praise which Erasmus and other humanists heaped upon the zeal for learning and the arts of this king who had been so generously endowed in mind and body seemed to justify this picture of him. But, though Erasmus could speak stern words about monarchy and wealth, he was a shameless flatterer of kings and the wealthy, and we should treat his outpourings with caution. If anything, Henry was the last of the troubadours and the heir of Burgundian chivalry: a youth wholly absorbed in dance and song, courtly love and knight-errantry.

He was to grow into a rumbustious, noisy, unbottoned, prodigal man – the 'bluff king Hal' of legend – exulting in his magnificent physique, boisterous animal exercise, orgies of gambling and eating, lavish clothes. 'His fingers were one mass of jewelled rings and around his neck he wore a gold

50. For Henry's compositions (and collection of instruments) see Lady Mary Trefusis, *Ballads and Instrumental Pieces composed by King Henry the Eighth etc.*, Roxburghe Club (1912). On Henry's singing with Carew, see Reese, op. cit., 769.

collar from which hung a diamond as big as a walnut', wrote
the Venetian ambassador, Giustinian, of him.[51] He loved to
dress up and his wardrobe, ablaze with jewels of all description and cloth of gold, rich silks, sarcenets, satins and highly-
coloured feathers, constantly astounded beholders. He was
a man who lived with huge, extroverted ebullience, at least
in the earlier part of his life, revelling in spectacular living,
throwing away money amidst his courtiers on cards, tennis
and dicing, dazzling his kingdom. Many readers will have
their chosen picture of him – Henry, cock-sure and truculent,
astride one of Holbein's canvases; Henry, dressed in
dazzling richness and with a huge gold whistle, crusted with
jewels, hanging from a gold chain, dining with his queen
aboard *Henry Grace à Dieu* on the occasion of its launching;[52] Henry walking up and down More's garden at Chelsea
for an hour with his arm round More's neck;[53] Henry showing the Venetian ambassador his fine calf and demanding to
know whether it was not a finer one than the French king
boasted;[54] Henry, at Hunsdon, over twenty years later, holding his precious son Edward in his arms and bringing him
proudly to a window 'to the sight and great comfort of all
the people'.[55]

He was a formidable, captivating man who wore regality
with splendid conviction. But easily and unpredictably his
great charm could turn into anger and shouting. When (as
was alleged) he hit Thomas Cromwell round the head and
swore at him,[56] or addressed a lord chancellor (Wriothesley)

51. *Four Years at the Court of Henry VIII etc.*, ed. Rawdon Brown,
i, 85 f.

52. *L.P.*, ii, 1113. This was in October 1515.

53. Roper, op. cit., 20 f.

54. *Four Years at the Court of Henry VIII etc.*, i, 90 f.

55. So Richard Cromwell in a letter to his father of 16 May 1538.
L.P., xiii, i, 1011.

56. 'the king beknaveth him twice a week and sometimes knocks
him well about the pate; and yet when that he hath been well pum-
melled about the head and shaken up as it were a dog, he will come
out of the Great Chamber shaking off the bush with as merry a

as 'my pig',[57] his mood may have been amiable enough, but More knew that the master who put his arm lovingly round his neck would have his head if it 'could win him a castle in France'.[58] He was highly strung and unstable; hypochondriac and possessed of a strong streak of cruelty. Possibly he had an Oedipus complex: and possibly from this derived a desire for, yet horror of, incest, which may have shaped some of his sexual life.[59]

Eighteen days after his marriage, and as custom demanded, Henry came from Greenwich to the Tower of London in preparation for his crowning. 'If I should declare,' wrote the chronicler Edward Hall, whose appetite for the details of Tudor pageantry, one would have thought, was insatiable, 'what pain, labour and diligence the tailors, embroiderers and goldsmiths took both to make and devise garments for lords, ladies, knights and esquires and also for decking, trapping and adorning of coursers, jennets and palfreys, it were too long to rehearse; but for a surety, more rich, nor more strange nor more curious works hath not been seen than were prepared against this coronation.'[60] On Saturday 23 June the king came with his queen through the City to Westminster. He travelled along streets hung with tapestries and cloth of gold, and was himself studded with a riot of diamonds, rubies, and other precious stones. Next day he and Catherine processed from the palace to the abbey under canopies and along a carpet of cloth which

countenance as though he might rule all the roost'; the king 'hath called my lord privy seal villain, knave, bobbed him about the head and thrust him from the Privy Chamber' – so, in 1538, George Paulet, a commissioner in Ireland and brother of the famous William, is said to have said about Cromwell. The reader must judge for himself the reliability of this testimony, to be found in *St.P.*, ii, 551 f. n.

57. So Foxe says he liked to call him. *Foxe*, v, 564.

58. Roper, op. cit., 21.

59. Flügel, 'On the Character and Married Life of Henry VIII', in *Psychoanalysis and History* (Englewood Cliffs, N.J., 1963), 124 ff.

60. *Hall*, 507.

'was cut and spoiled by the rude and common people immediately after their repair to the abbey'. There, before the great of the realm, he was anointed and crowned by the archbishop of Canterbury. After the ceremony, all retired to Westminster Hall for a banquet 'greater than any Caesar had known', which opened with a procession bearing the dishes into the assembly, led by the duke of Buckingham and the lord steward on horesback; and once the immense feast was over the company adjourned to take part in a tournament which lasted until nightfall.[61]

Jousts and feasting filled the following days, and when the coronation celebrations were over the Court settled into an almost unbroken round of festivities – revels and disguisings, maying, pageants, tilts and jousts, interspersed with long days in the saddle or following the hawks and long nights banqueting, dancing and making music. Gathered around the young king were such as Lord Henry Stafford, the earl of Essex and Edward Neville,[62] Thomas and William Parr, Thomas Boleyn, Edward and Henry Guildford, and the Carews and William Compton – gay courtiers and companions of the king. Now, in January 1510, Henry burst into the queen's chamber at Westminster one morning with ten fellows dressed as Robin Hood's men in short coats 'of Kentish kendal' for dancing and pastime with the abashed ladies; now, on the following Shrove Tuesday, he disappeared in the midst of a banquet in honour of foreign ambassadors given in the Parliament Chamber and returned with the earl of Essex dressed 'in Turkey fashion', laden with gold decoration and with two scimitars hanging

61. Hall, 509.
62. Neville resembled Henry not only in tastes, but also in looks – so much so that an impossible legend had it that he was an illegitimate son of the king. The rumour was revived jokingly by Queen Elizabeth when, on her first progress in Berkshire, she met Neville's son Henry and greeted him with the words, 'I am glad to see thee, brother Henry.' See *Notes and Queries*, 1st ser. ii (1850), 307. Edward Neville was executed in 1538 as an accomplice to the Exeter conspiracy.

from his waist. Six others were dressed as Prussians, the torch-bearers as Moors. After this mummery was over, Henry reappeared with five others disguised in a short suit of blue and crimson slashed and lined with cloth of gold, and danced with the ladies, including his sister Mary. There were revels and pageants on New Year's day, Epiphany and Shrovetide and at the return of the Court from summer progress. Each 1 May the king went a-maying, and scarcely a month, it seems, passed without some festivities, such as the prodigious celebrations for the birth of the king's first (and short-lived) son in February 1511 or the Epiphany revels two years later, when the king, with eleven others, took part in a disguising 'after the manner of Italy called a mask, a thing not seen afore in England'.[63] And over and above all this, there was an unceasing round of jousting and tilting. Apparently not until 12 January 1510 did Henry enter his first joust as king, when he took part incognito with Sir William Compton, a gentleman of the Privy Chamber, in a private joust at Richmond.[64] Though Compton was nearly killed, the two strangers won great praise for skill, and thereafter the king was an untiring devotee, challenging all comers to combat on horse or on foot, revelling in the elaborate ceremonial of knightly exercise, passing hour after hour with men like Charles Brandon, the earl of Essex or the marquis of Dorset, contending for ladies' favours.

The royal regime was astounding. In the course of a progress in 1511, Henry exercised himself 'in shooting, singing, dancing, wrestling, casting of the bar, playing at the recorders, flute and virginals, and in setting of songs, making of ballads and did set two godly Masses, every of them of five parts, which were sung oftentimes in his chapel and afterwards in divers other places. And when he came to Woking, there were kept both jousts and tourneys. The rest

63. *Hall*, 526. For these stories of court revels etc., see ibid., 513 ff.
64. ibid., 513. Cf. *L.P.*, i, 98, 112, 156, 400, 467, 477, 671, 698 etc. for accounts of the endless jousting and tilting which marked the first months of the reign.

of his time was spent in hunting, hawking and shooting.'[65]
The rest of the time – though it is difficult to see that there
was much of it – might also have been spent playing cards,
tennis and dice, the last two of which cost him a good deal
of money when 'crafty persons ... brought in Frenchmen
and Lombards to make wagers with him' and to profit from
his carefree bounty, until 'he perceived their craft' and sent
them away.[66] Money flowed easily: £335 to Jacques Maryn
a jeweller of Paris; 10s. for a midsummer bonfire; thirty
marks for a new pair of organs at Richmond; ten marks for
the 'lord of misrule' at the New Year celebrations of 1511; £5
to the keeper of the king's instruments, William Lewes; £566
for a thousand pearls and other jewels; over £800 for New
Year presents; £40 for a friar who gave the king an instrument; £20 to Dr Fairfax for a pricksong book[67] – not to mention the scores of pounds in the traditional offerings to the
shrines of Our Lady of Pew, Walsingham, Missenden and
Doncaster, of St Thomas of Canterbury, of Edward the Confessor, of St Bridget of Sion, or spent on court preachers,
Maundy money, Requiem Masses and tapers. Hundreds of
pounds would be spent on clothing the monarch, feeding his
court and paying his servants; thousands of pounds on
repairs and additions to the royal palaces.[68]

He was a prodigy, a sun-king, a *stupor mundi*. He lived in,
and crowned, a world of lavish allegory, mythology and
romance. Soon the great state occasions would be marked by
pageants and triumphs full of political meaning, but early in
the reign the mood was lighter. Court pageants portrayed the
roses and pomegranates of England and Spain growing out
of a golden stake, standing on a hillock from which came
morris dancers; or an artificial forest of hawthorn, maple,
hazel and birch amidst which wandered maidens in distress,

---

65. *Hall*, 515.   66. ibid., 520.
67. I.e. a book of 'pricked' (that is, printed – as distinct from mem-
orized) part-song or accompanied vocal music.
68. I have taken these facts and figures at random from the King's
Book of Payments for the first years of the reign in *L.P.*, ii, 1446 ff.

foresters and men-at-arms; or the 'golden arbour in the arch-
yard of pleasure'.[69] Above all, this was a world of chivalry –
of Fame, Renown, Hardiness, of Sir Gallant and Cœur Loyal.
Henry had proclaimed himself as the 'very perfect', valorous
knight, and the joust and tourney led directly to that serious
business of kingship in which the new king's abundant
energy would find perfect release, namely, war.

69. See P.R.O., E.36/217 (Richard Gibson's Accounts of Revels),
fols 15, 38, 41.

The Renewal of
the Hundred Years War

ON ascending the throne of England, the young king had to decide, if he had not decided already, to what end he would put his kingship. In effect, he had to decide whether he would be content to imitate a father remarkable for the extent to which he had withdrawn from foreign entanglements and given himself to the unspectacular, civilian business of money-making and law-enforcement. Henry VII had been more interested in winning commercial advantage than bits of France and preferred the receipt books of the treasury of the Chamber to the old-fashioned luxuries of war and flamboyant diplomacy. He had looked to the problem of how England might live at peace with Scotland by marrying his daughter Margaret to the Scottish king; he had looked, albeit fitfully, to the new world which Spanish ships were opening up across the Atlantic. The choice before his son was, therefore, not just between being a quiet working monarch and a martial hero, not just between peace and war, but, in a real way, between new and old.

He chose the latter. Henry VIII would lead England back into her past, into Europe and its endless squabbles, into another round of that conflict misleadingly defined as merely a Hundred Years War. He would reject his father's notion of a king's function, quickly dissipate his inherited treasure, set Scotland once more at violent odds with England and pay so little attention to the Americas and Asia that, when overseas exploration was resumed over forty years later, his country would find that Iberian ships had meanwhile gained an advantage which it would take her generations to rival. Furthermore, like the French invasion of Italy at the end of

the fifteenth century, England's return to a 'forward' continental policy was not in pursuit of any vital ends, such as
Lebensraum, natural frontiers, or political or commercial
advantage. On the contrary, it was occasionally clearly
opposed to at least the last-mentioned. Neither did it go
uncriticized. Perhaps one of the boldest things which the
Christian humanists of the Renaissance did was to protest
against bootless, pestilential and scandalous war among
European states. Erasmus, Vives, More, to name but the
most conspicuous, had already dedicated themselves, or were
soon to do so, to denouncing the bloodshed which national
pride and prejudice brought in their train. Their passionate
call for pacifism had already condemned the policy upon
which Henry was about to embark and approved the way
that his father had followed the 'arts of peace alone, without
sword and bloodshed'.[1]

But Henry ignored all this. He could so do, in the first
place, because the society over which he ruled was, in its
higher ranks, one still largely geared to war. However
civilian in many of their functions they might have become,
the English upper orders still held their fighting as a major
raison d'être, prowess in arms was still a mark of aristocracy,
a quasi-feudal military retinue still a concomitant of landed
wealth. The nobility and those immediately beneath them
were not only the natural leaders of civil society; they also
supplied the natural leaders of the army and navy.

If fighting remained for some, who happened to be those
who mattered, an evident function of their estate, then fighting in France was probably still the most obvious manner
in which to exercise it. Not many decades before, war in
Gascony, Guienne and Normandy had at times been the
classic way to adventure, honour and quick money. A French
prince's ransom could set an English family squarely on the
road to prosperity; there were booty and spoil to be won,

1. So Bernard André, court poet and minor humanist, in his
Annales Henrici Vii. See *Memorials of King Henry the Seventh*,
ed. Gairdner, Rolls Series (1858) 91.

an heiress perhaps, a knighthood on the field of battle, offices
and lands in the Pays de Conquête, and fame. The memory
of the glorious campaigns in France of the Black Prince and
Henry V was probably still green; the Hundred Years War
still a living issue. Until Renaissance writers had made
ground with their plea for a Platonic society ruled by an
elite trained in the humanities and the arts of citizenship,[2]
the English aristocracy retained the character, essentially, of
an hereditary military caste nourished on the cult of war
and chivalry. The world of Malory's *Morte d'Arthur*,
Caxton's *Kyng Arthur*, Stephen Hawes's *The Passetyme of
Pleasure* (published in 1509) and Lord Berners's translation
of Froissart (produced in 1523), a world of chauvinism,
knight-errantry and militarism – or, as Ascham preferred to
say, of 'open manslaughter and bold bawdry' – praised the
heroism of the tiltyard and the cannon's mouth rather than
the asceticism of the philosopher-ruler; and it doubtless
made it easier for England to burst back into Europe.[3]

Much of this is true also of the king. Whatever else an
English king may have been – and he was much else – he
was still a leader in war. He must still 'venture' himself in
battle, to use an old formula, and blood himself.[4] For him,
too, war would bring ransoms and booty, fame and perhaps
titles, not to mention taxable conquests. If Henry ever felt
the pull of the ideal Christian prince, the man of peace and
justice, he felt, too, the call of the chivalrous and spectacular.
As we have seen, before and after he came to the throne he
spent much of his time in the tiltyard and tournament ring,
playing at war according to the elaborate code of chivalry.
His abundant energy found full outlet in the idealized world
of valorous knighthood (did he not commission Lord Berners

2. See Caspari, *Humanism and the Social Order in Tudor England*
(Chicago, 1954).

3. Cf. Ferguson, *The Indian Summer of English Chivalry* (Durham,
N. Carolina, 1960).

4. Thus Polydore Vergil could observe that Henry was 'not un-
mindful that it was his duty to seek fame by military skill'. *Anglica
Historia*, ed. Hay, Camden Soc., 3rd ser. lxxiv (1950), 161.

to translate Froissart?); and besides, he grew up among fellow-monarchs, like Charles VIII of France or the gifted, impulsive Emperor Maximilian, much of whose lives was absorbed in war-making. More than anything else, he would be one of them. Though perhaps he would not find the hazards and discomfort of real war so agreeable, just as the English did not like paying for it, he probably saw himself (albeit erratically) as a military leader who would lead his people back to war and emulate the great captains of a not-so-distant past. It is damaging historical surgery that cuts him off from his ancestry – Edward I, Edward III, Henry V – for they, surely, were his models. There were men at his side whose grandfathers fought at Agincourt; it was only some eighty years since Henry VI was crowned king of France at Paris; he himself commissioned the translation of an early life of Henry V.[5] Patriots at his side, as well as his own instincts, urged him to take up where that hero, or a Bedford, had left off and lead his chivalry back across the Channel, professedly at least, in search of a lost kingdom and throne. And if he did not seek fame in France, then he might even toy with the idea of a crusade. Fighting Islam may have become the plaything of cynical Christian diplomacy, but it still mattered to the kings of Spain and Portugal and, indeed, as the sixteenth century wore on would become increasingly necessary. More than once Henry would feel the claim of an ideal that was a close bedfellow of a perhaps revived chivalry. He began his reign as a warrior, therefore, bent on the splendid and heroic. Later he would take on other parts, of peacemaker, theologian, Supreme Head of the Church. But when he had dealt with what some may have regarded as but an interlude in his career (and which we take as its

5. By Titus Livius. It was anonymously translated into English in 1513. The translator says that the work was commissioned by Henry, and in return calls upon him to emulate Henry V. See edn by C. L. Kingsford (Oxford, 1911), 4. For similar calls from other quarters, see *Ven. Cal.*, ii, 24, and (later) *L.P.*, ii, 982, 1265 – remarkable jingoism by the English ambassador with the emperor, Sir Robert Wingfield.

centre-piece), namely, the matters ecclesiastical of the 1530s, he was able to resume what had once been for him the principal business of his reign and end his life as he had begun it, at war.

Immediately after his accession he made his intentions clear, swearing publicly that he would soon assault the king of France.[6] A few weeks later he insulted an envoy from France whom he had received in audience at Westminster by hurling contemptuous words at his king and then walking out of the meeting to attend a tilt.[7] Meanwhile he had written to find out whether King Ferdinand of Spain, his father-in-law and likeliest ally, would be ready to join the attack.[8] In short, the new, virile policy was promptly declared.

But there were two obstacles which had to be overcome before that policy could be executed. The first was a major one: there was no ally for him. It was an axiom throughout his reign that England could not enter the continent single-handed, and in 1509 all the great powers, with the exception of the victim whom France and her friends were devouring, were in alliance with France. Spain, the emperor Maximilian and the pope were parties to the league of Cambrai, concluded in 1508, and the only friend of worth whom Henry could find was the very state whose neck that powerful league was apparently about to wring, namely, Venice. Henry may have given honest sympathy to the Venetian ambassador for his republic's plight, for there were many threads, not the least being commercial, which bound Venice to England; but there was no gainsaying the advice which his inquiry to Ferdinand elicited – that he should restrain himself and pretend to be friendly to France, as his father had been, until a more propitious moment for picking a quarrel occurred.[9] Henry wrote to France on behalf of Venice and received an uncivil reply; he wrote to the emperor Maximilian offering himself as peacemaker and to the pope asking him to lift

6. *L.P.*, i, 5 (ii).   7. *Ven. Cal.*, ii, 11.
8. *L.P.*, i, 162 – the reply to his letter, which alone is extant.
9. *Sp. Cal.*, ii, 27.

the interdict which he had laid on his enemy.[10] But for the rest, he must wait. However, in late 1509 he despatched to Rome one Christopher Bainbridge, archbishop of York, to be his resident envoy at the Holy See. Bainbridge, a bellicose jingoist full of animosity towards the French, and a man as much after the heart of that warrior-pope, Julius II, as he was Henry's, was sent now to announce and prepare the way for his king's programme.[11] Shortly afterwards a proclamation was issued warning all those able to bear arms to be ready in the new year,[12] and as this was prepared Henry was exploring the possibility of a secret treaty with Ferdinand, Venice and Maximilian.[13]

Apart from the unfavourable diplomatic situation, there was another impediment in the way of the 'forward' policy. In the early years of his reign, until well into 1512 and, in a sense, until Wolsey finally achieved primacy of place in mid 1514, Henry was not the master of his own house, but had to work with a council chosen for him by his father. There is evidence that the young, impetuous and inexperienced king was not wholly in step with at least some of his councillors, who were men of a very different stamp. Warham, Fox and Fisher, for example, were products of the old regime and had seen it end with England on reasonably good terms with France and somewhat gruff, but far from hostile, ones with Spain. The son wanted to turn this about in order to make war. They, it seems, did not. There was a group, perhaps a small group, in the Council who were not at ease with the new policy, with Fox, if we can put weight on the remorse which he later expressed for having meddled with war-mongering,[14] probably leading the way. Several interesting incidents give substance to this suggestion. In the summer

10. *Ven. Cal.*, ii, 17, 22, 39. *Sp. Cal.*, ii, 23, 25, 26.

11. Chambers, *Cardinal Bainbridge in the Court of Rome, 1509 to 1514* (Oxford, 1965), 22 ff.

12. *Hughes and Larkin*, no. 61.

13. *L.P.*, i, 325; *Sp. Cal.*, ii, 27; *Ven. Cal.*, ii, 33.

14. *Letters of Richard Fox*, ed. P. S. and H. M. Allen (Oxford, 1929), 93.

of 1509 an envoy arrived from France saying he had come
in response to a cordial letter of friendship from Henry himself. When the latter heard this, he said, 'Who wrote this
letter? I ask peace of the king of France, who dare not look
at me, let alone make war?' and so saying rose and would
hear no more[15] – a splendid scene which lacked only the contemptuous dismissal of a derisory casket of tennis balls from
across the Channel to give it final panache. Perhaps he was
simply showing off, but perhaps the letter had been sent by
the Council without his knowledge or with only his reluctant
consent. Then, in March 1510, an Anglo-French treaty was
signed, exactly as that letter had suggested. Maybe a motive
for it was to lull France into unpreparedness; but the Spanish
ambassador in England, Luis Caroz, reported on the authority of some of the councillors themselves that Henry had
opposed the treaty and had only agreed to it after earnest
pleading. Some of the Council were mortal enemies of
France, he said; but there were others of different persuasion.[16] When he first met Henry, he found the king eager
to conclude a treaty with Spain, yet, when the matter was
handed over to Fox and Ruthal and others, discussions went
very slowly. However, that treaty was concluded in May 1510
– and virtually annulled the one just entered into with
France. Thus the two wings of Council (if this is a correct
diagnosis) had each won a point. Some time later Henry
presided over a Council meeting to discuss proposals for
war with France. After a long debate, he invited all present
to give their opinions in turn and found many opposed to
the idea, arguing that England should stand aloof from continental squabbles which did not concern her, and save herself
expense.[17] This was reasoning of the kind which Henry VII
would have approved. But his son paid it no heed.

Meanwhile, despite everything, Henry had publicly kept

15. Sanuto, *Diarii etc.* (Venice, 1879–), ix, 149 (*L.P.*., i, 156).
16. *Sp. Cal.*, ii, 44.
17. Polydore Vergil, op. cit., 161.

up his anti-French posture.[18] By the middle of 1510 it was beginning to make sense. The league of Cambrai was breaking up as Julius prepared a 'holy' league to unite Europe against his former ally, France, and drive her out of Italy. In reply to thus having a dagger plunged into his heart, as he described this diplomatic turn-about, the king of France, Louis XII, called a local council of the French Church to utter traditional Gallican anti-papalism. Then, backed by a group of dissident cardinals, Louis took the further steps of summoning a schismatic General Council of the Church to meet at Pisa in May 1511, which would have on its agenda nothing less than the deposition of Julius himself. Even by contemporary standards this was drastic action and expanded what had hitherto been a purely military and diplomatic clash into a major spiritual contest. The threat of calling a schismatic Council was an old one, but now it would be implemented and with it might begin a new chapter in the history of conciliarism. But Louis's violent counter-attack played into Julius's hands, for now his league could be a holy one indeed, and it certainly played into Henry's, for nothing could rouse an aggressively orthodox country better, or sweep aside more certainly the opposition to war – probably largely clerical – which he had hitherto encountered in his Council. Henry had now been provided with the sovereign *casus belli* and the prospect of allies in abundance.

True enough there was the embarrassment of that Anglo-French treaty which he had been elbowed into by some of his Council. When Julius heard of it he was just beginning to marshal the league against France and, encouraged by Bainbridge (whose francophobia he would soon reward with a red hat), had counted on England's support. 'You are all rascals,' he shouted angrily at some English[19] – Bainbridge having wisely absented himself and gone hunting. But Julius did not despair and spent the next months building up his league, wooing his intended allies, including England. Henry

18. See, e.g., *Ven. Cal.*, ii, 66; *L.P.*, i, 355.
19. *Ven. Cal.*, ii, 56.

– to whom the pope would send a golden rose, a hundred Parmesan cheeses and barrels of wine[20] – was easily won and readily helped the pope with his work, especially with an emperor who was so intent upon destroying Venice that he saw no reason to be distracted from his purpose by a suspect papal alternative.

Auspiciously enough, on New Year's Day 1511 Queen Catherine was safely delivered of a child – a boy, and live. Guns, bells and bonfires welcomed the news. Henry rode to Walsingham to give thanks and returned to Westminster to a splendid tournament and pageant. Dressed in clothes covered with golden 'Hs' and 'Ks', he was mobbed by excited groundlings who ripped off these ornaments and then set about his courtiers and the ladies. However, all was taken in good part. Henry's gladness, and Catherine's, 'turned all these hearts to laughing and game'.[21] But alas, seven weeks later the son, Henry prince of Wales, was dead and recent joy changed to sorrow. From this disappointment he would turn all the more eagerly to the prospect of war.

He was ready to make war, but not to make it alone. So, while the allies were assembling, he indulged his appetite for international display with two minor military ventures. First, a small force of archers was dispatched to the Low Countries to help the emperor against that perennial rebel, the duke of Gelders – a handsome gesture, intended not only to win prestige but perhaps to wean a grateful Maximilian off French friendship and towards the incipient papal league. Then, in May 1511, Lord Darcy was sent with a thousand men, largely at his own expense, to Cadiz to accompany Ferdinand on an expedition to North Africa against the Moors, another gesture but also, perhaps, a faint symptom of a crusading instinct. Fortunately for England's military reputation, the force sent against Gelders met some success. Darcy's expedition was a fiasco. Henry was said to have thought of going with it, but happily, he did not. Arrived at Cadiz, Darcy found that Ferdinand had aban-

20. *L.P.*, i, 842.   21. *Hall*, 519.

doned the idea of an expedition across the straits of Gibraltar and was therefore told curtly that the English had better go home. Sixteen days after their arrival they did so. But in their short stay they at least made a mark on their ungrateful colleagues when some of them went ashore, promptly became drunk and ran amok. Within a few hours, the troops intended to conquer in Africa and kill infidels had broken down Spanish hedges, vines and orange trees, provoked a fracas when one of them accosted a local girl and killed several Christians in the subsequent brawl.[22]

But all this was peripheral. France was the focal point of activity and at last, in October 1511, the Holy League was signed at Rome. By an oversight, Bainbridge had not received sufficient powers to pledge his master to it at once, so England did not join until some five weeks later. But when she did so she stood henceforth amidst a phalanx of allies, poised for war. Henry was on the move. He had just sent an envoy to France to demand that Louis abandon the schismatic Council and make peace with the pope – which, of course, was refused. When he heard this, Henry summoned his Privy Council. Now its mood was different. It agreed unanimously to war.[23] Louis's actions and the urgent papal appeals to punish him had made it possible for Henry to mobilize a united country against him. Over two decades later, when he was about to follow very closely in Louis's steps, Cuthbert Tunstal, by then bishop of Durham, would boldly remind him of how, in bygone days, he had taken up the sword against a schismatic king in defence of the papacy – to which Henry replied that then he was young and in-

22. *Hall*, 520 ff. Ferdinand met some of the expense of the expedition and Henry converted a loan of £1,000 to Darcy into a free gift (*L.P.*, i, 880). But Darcy was still badly out of pocket. Cf. *L.P.*, i, 2576.

23. Polydore Vergil, op. cit., p. 163. I have altered his chronology somewhat. He places the two Council meetings (in the first of which war was opposed and in the second accepted) close together in time. It seems more reasonable to space more widely by putting the first back to, say, late 1510.

experienced, and evil councillors had led him by the nose.[24] But the truth is rather different. He himself had led England to war, fulminating against the 'great sin of the king of France' and against those who 'lacerate the seamless garment of Christ', who 'would wantonly destroy the unity of the Church', who are guilty of 'the most pernicious schism' and stop at nothing, however 'cruel, impious, criminal and unspeakable'.[25]

In November 1511 it was agreed between England and Spain that, as their part in the Holy League, a joint Anglo-Spanish army should attack Aquitaine and conquer it for Henry. The winter and spring of 1511–12 were busily spent in preparations, gathering the troops, ships, food, bows and staves, and the rest. At the end of April 1512 Lancaster herald arrived at the French court to deliver the English declaration of war. By the end of the month an English fleet, carrying an army-by-sea[26] six thousand strong under the command of Edward Howard, had put out, and in early June the army-by-land, twice that size and commanded by the marquis of Dorset, set sail from Southampton for Gascony, mightily encouraged, said Henry, by a papal indulgence.[27] After over three years of patient waiting and manoeuvring the young king's ambition had been realized, though, interestingly, he was not accompanying his men; and after a lapse of twenty years, an English army was on its way to France once more.

The campaign was a wretched failure. The allies' plan was that a combined English and Spanish army should attack Aquitaine from the south, but once the English had disembarked at San Sebastian and made, as agreed, for the

---

24. See below, p. 424.   25. Sanuto, op. cit., xiv, 425 f.
26. I.e the naval fighting-force – as distinct from the army which, having been shipped across the Channel, would then fight on land. Until the major changes in naval architecture and tactics (discussed below, pp. 644 ff). had taken place, sea warfare was soldiers' warfare, consisting in in-fighting (grappling, boarding and taking), and the man on board essentially a soldier rather than a sailor.
27. *L.P.*, i, 1182; *Sp. Cal.*, ii, 131.

town of Fuentarrabia, they found that the Spanish had prepared none of the promised ordnance or horses. Then, when
Dorset proposed that Bayonne should be captured first, to
act as a base for advance into the duchy of Aquitaine, he met
refusal. It is clear that Ferdinand was never interested in
winning anything for his son-in-law and had always intended
to use the English troops to cover the seizure by his own
army of the independent kingdom of Navarre, upon which
he had ancient predatory designs. Accordingly, when Dorset
proposed the move against Bayonne, Ferdinand insisted that
Navarre should be the first objective and that the English
should therefore march towards his camp. Angry messages
passed to and fro, but neither side would accept the other's
plan. Eventually Ferdinand decided to attack alone, sent his
troops into Navarre and quickly lost interest in the war.
Meanwhile Dorset and his men waited forlornly at Fuentarrabia for their Spanish allies to arrive. Their morale
quickly disintegrated. They were short of tents and drenched
in heavy rain; most of their bows proved useless; two hundred mules bought locally at exorbitant prices 'would neither
bear nor draw, for they were beasts which were not exercised
afore';[28] food was scarce, beer scarcer; local cider made the
men sick and the wine was too 'hot'; their numbers were
being drained fast by illness and desertion; the remainder
were near mutiny for better pay and soon took to looting and
pillaging the locals; in nearly two months only one letter
from Henry had reached them, and worst of all, perhaps, the
council of officers was rent by quarrels.[29] Clearly the situation was out of hand. According to the chronicler Edward
Hall, and his story is not the only one, in late August, when
the officers decided to strike camp and withdraw to a near-by
village, the rank and file refused to obey, hired ships and
took themselves and their officers homewards. But probably
it was the officers themselves who decided to cut losses and

28. *Hall*, 528.
29. For all this, see ibid., 528 ff.; *L.P.*, i, 1326–7, 1422. Polydore
Vergil, op. cit., 177 ff.

depart, having sent one Dr Knight on ahead to break the
news to Henry. Just after they had set sail, a letter came
from the King ordering his army to join Ferdinand's forces
after all;[30] but Dorset was now so ill and his men so dispirited
that, even if Henry's command had arrived in time, it would
probably have been disobeyed. Henry had sent to Fuentarrabia an apparently crack fighting force; four months later
there came back from Fuentarrabia a half-mutinous
shambles.[31] And to make matters worse, despite the fact that
all this was largely his fault, Ferdinand quickly made capital
out of the English departure and publicly accused his allies
of being slow, unused to war, uncooperative, 'French' and so
on. Then, arguing that he had been left exposed to great
danger by their retreat, he came to terms with France, leaving Henry stranded.[32]

This final reversal was yet in the future. For the moment,
Henry had to recover from this military fiasco: the second
into which the Spanish king had led him. Soon after the
army returned, in mid November, the officers were brought
before the king, the Council and the Spanish ambassadors,
and declared guilty of grave misconduct; whereupon the
Spaniards were invited to name condign punishment – a
humble submission indeed to Ferdinand's stinging rebukes.[33]
Furthermore, within a few days of this public abasement of
England's military reputation, a plan was being drawn up
for a second and more ambitious assault on France in the
new year. Henry would yet prove his mettle to his father-
in-law. Dorset might not have won an inch of France, but
the large French army had recently met reverses across the
Alps and, by the end of 1512, been largely driven from Italian

30. *L.P.*, i, 1458.
31. And naval affairs had not fared much better. Henry had sent
his fleet to Brittany to intercept a large French force and lost one of
his capital ships, *Regent*, by fire. For the story of this escapade, see
Wolsey's vivid letter to Fox in *Letters of Richard Fox*, pp. 57 f.
32. *Sp. Cal.*, ii, 68, 70; *L.P.*, i, 1511.
33. *Sp. Cal.*, ii, 72. Their reply was that Ferdinand sought no punishment.

soil; and it could plausibly be argued that this owed something to the presence of English troops on the edge of south-
west France and justified a return to the fight next year.
Julius was still bent on punishing France and, most encouragingly, the Emperor Maximilian had at last put an end
to indecision and decided to join the fray. Once this had
happened, Henry was able confidently to plan a major venture for the next spring which would efface the humiliation
of this recent preliminary campaign.

In late December 1512, probably, he and the Council proposed to the Spanish ambassador a two-pronged invasion of
France, in which the Spanish army, heavily subsidized by
Henry, would attack Aquitaine and, as had been undertaken
before, conquer it for England, while Henry himself set out
on his first campaign and led an army into Picardy or Normandy. Since Maximilian, and therefore the Low Countries,
had now befriended his cause, Henry could attack France
from the north, leaving Ferdinand to deal with the distant
duchy in the south and avoiding a repetition of last summer's
disastrous attempt at a combined operation. In the meantime
Parliament had been summoned and had granted Henry
supplies for the campaign.

Indeed, English ambition did not halt there. During the
early months of 1513 English envoys in the Low Countries
wrestled with the emperor in an attempt to lure him into
active support of the Anglo-Spanish *impresa*. It was enormously taxing to win him, but at length, after Henry had been
committed to subsidizing him generously, Maximilian entered the new league in defence of the Church towards
which he had recently been openly disobedient, and against
a France with whom he had been prepared to do a deal up to
the very last minute. The new, larger league was concluded
at Malines on 5 April and formally sworn at a ceremony at
St Paul's on 25 April, binding the pope, the emperor, Ferdinand and Henry to war. Now there would be a massive
quadruple attack upon France: by Henry from the north;
Ferdinand from the south; Maximilian from any direction he

might choose; the pope through Provence and Dauphiné.[34] After years of effort, Henry had apparently assembled all that could be desired to provide for brilliant, swift conquest.

At home, preparations for war went ahead briskly. Thousands of suits of armour were bought in Italy and Spain; from Germany and Flanders came the ordnance, headed by a dozen great cannons named 'the twelve apostles' – as befitted the artillery for a holy war. The bows and arrows, pikes and bills were ready. Henry, it was said, went daily to the docks to hearten his fleet and watch ships, especially *Great Harry*, being built. Other ships had been requisitioned, transports and hoys bought or hired abroad to transport the English army of 40,000 to France. The victuals, including, this time, enough beer to avoid mutiny, the draught horses, tents in plenty and gorgeous pavilions were nearly ready.[35]

There were two more matters to attend to at home before the expedition could set sail. First, before he dared quit the realm, Henry must dispatch the traitor and pretender, Edmund de la Pole, the son of a sister of Edward IV and the last but one of a family which had lived under the shadow of violence ever since William de la Pole, duke of Suffolk, had been done to death in 1450. Edmund had been in the Tower since 1506; recently his brother Richard had taken up arms with France against England, and this sealed the other's fate. In the spring of 1513, Edmund was brought out of the Tower and beheaded. Later on, Richard would cause some anxiety to Henry when Louis recognized him as king of England, and then Francis I thought of sending him at the head of an army to invade his motherland. However, this was in the future. For the moment, the White Rose had been crushed and Henry would go to France secure, but with blood on his hands. He would also go thither having silenced a last, belated protest against war. On Good Friday 1513 none other than John Colet preached before Henry and the Court at Greenwich, exhorting his hearers to follow Christ rather than false heroes like Caesar or Alexander and

34. *Sp. Cal.*, ii, 73, 97; *Rymer*, xiii, 354; *L.P.*, i, 1750, 1884.
35. *Ven. Cal.*, ii, 225; *L.P.*, i, 1568, 1572, 1629, 1726, etc.

declaring an unjust peace preferable to a just war. Even as he poured out his plea to cast aside vainglorious war-mongering, Henry's ships were gathering on the Thames close by and his troops making ready to set forth for France. After the service was finished, and fearful lest Colet's words might have struck doubt into his captains, Henry summoned the preacher to his presence. Colet was staying in the Observants' house near by. On hearing this, the king strode over to the friary and met Colet in the garden. He dismissed his attendants, announced to his companion that 'I have come to discharge my conscience, not to distract you from your studies', and thereupon entered into a discussion with him. Either because Colet had never meant to condemn the campaign in defence of the Church which Henry was about to undertake, or because he lost his nerve in the face of his king, the latter emerged from the encounter with his conscience at rest and his spirits high. He called for wine and jovially dismissed Colet with the toast, 'Let every man have his own doctor. This is mine.'[36] The illustrious dean of St Paul's had declared his cause a just and holy one.

To perfect his confidence, Henry had a final, and remarkable, feather in his cap. In a brief dated 20 March 1512 and written in the grand manner of popes of the golden age, Julius II had stripped the schismatic King Louis of his title of Most Christian King of France and of his kingdom, and had conferred both upon Henry of England. At the latter's request, which Ferdinand supported, Julius invested him and his heirs with the 'name, glory and authority' of the king of France 'for as long as they shall remain in faith, devotion and obedience to the Holy Roman Church and Apostolic See'.[37] Moreover, the brief not only bestowed on Henry a forfeited kingdom, but also promised him coronation as king

36. All this story comes from Erasmus, *Opus Epistolarum, etc.*, iv, 525 f.

37. For the text see Ferrajoli, 'Un breve inedito di Guilio II per la Investitura del Regno di Francia ad Enrico VIII d'Inghilterra', *Arch. della R. Società Romana di Storia Patria*, xix (Rome, 1896), 425 ff. Julius deprived Louis in a consistory on 1 April 1512 (Sanuto, op. cit., xiv, 292).

of France, perhaps, as Julius was reported to have suggested, at the hands of the pope himself, who would come to Paris to perform the ceremony. However, there was one important condition attached to this astonishing papal grant: Louis must be defeated before it would take effect. Until Henry had conquered, so Julius prudently ruled, the brief would be in the safe-keeping of two cardinals and unknown to the outside world.[38] Clearly it was a bribe to secure England's adhesion to the Holy League; but for Henry it was also a supreme prize waiting to be claimed from the hands of the sovereign ruler of Christendom once the allied armies had brought France to the ground – as now they seemed well set to do. These, then, were months of dashing diplomacy, and feverish hustle and bustle, driven forward by the prospect of a success as brilliant and resounding as any that had ever befallen an English king.

Of course, not everything went well. About three weeks before the Spanish ambassador swore to the new war-treaty at St Paul's, his master had concluded a truce of one year with France. For the second time, Ferdinand had let Henry down disgracefully, not only unilaterally making friends with an enemy on which, at almost the same instant, he was contracting to wage war, but also including Henry in the truce without the latter's knowledge. Moreover, he then returned the English charge of duplicity with angry complaints that Henry had bullied a wanton fool of an ambassador into acting without his knowledge and that now no one would trust Spain's word.[39]

But Henry, though much aggrieved, would not be deterred by Spanish defection. By mid March an English fleet under Edward Howard, such as 'was never seen in Christendom', had set out to harry the coast of Brittany around Brest. By

38. Ferrajoli, loc. cit. Chambers, op. cit., 39.

39. *L.P.*, i, 1736, 2006; *Sp. Cal.*, ii, 91, 105, 106. Ferdinand continued to try to justify himself and eventually made the claim that when he signed the truce with France he had been *in articulo mortis* and wanted to make peace with his enemies before he faced judgement. *Sp. Cal.*, ii, 118.

25 April it had fought two unsuccessful engagements, during
the second of which Howard had been pinned against the
rails of a French galley which he and his men had boarded
and thrown into the sea to his death. By the end of April
the remains of his leaderless fleet were back in Plymouth.
Within a short while another naval force was being prepared
by Edward's brother, Thomas Howard, to return to Brittany,
though this, like its companion force in the Thames, would
be held in port for weeks by contrary winds.[40] However, the
army-by-land was ready. By the end of June, the van and
rearguard were across, commanded by the earl of Shrewsbury and Lord Herbert respectively. At 7 p.m. on 30 June
Henry himself, clad in armour, landed at Calais with the
remainder of the army. Hundreds of ships – a sight such as
Neptune had never seen before, an eye-witness said – had
filled the sea and, as the vast fleet hove into Calais, it received a tumultuous welcome from those who had already
arrived. As soon as he landed, Henry rode on his magnificent
charger to the church of St Nicholas to dedicate himself to
God and war. With him had come a huge personal entourage – his almoner (Thomas Wolsey), 115 members of his
chapel, minstrels, players, heralds, trumpeters, clerks of the
signet and privy seal, over three hundred other members of
the Household, two bishops, a duke and a score of other
nobles, together with an abundance of royal clothing and
jewellery, and a huge bed.[41]

For three weeks Calais was the scene of pageantry and
bustle as Henry received ambassadors from the emperor and
planned details of the campaign, and the army, wearing
white and green colours and swollen by foreign mercenaries,
made ready. On 21 July the main force set out to do battle.
It moved its cumbersome self three miles on the first day and
was drenched in heavy rain. That night the king would not
put off his clothes, but rode round the camp (as, we are told,

40. *L.P.*, i, 1844, 1851, 1875, 1885, 1905, 1898; *Letters of Richard Fox*,
61.
    41. *L.P.*, i, 1939, 1950, 2065, 2053 (2); *Hall*, 539; *Ven. Cal.*, ii, 250, 252.

did another Henry almost a hundred years before) encouraging his sodden men. Next day the army set out again in search of the French and Thérouanne. The latter, a small town in Artois which the English had taken after Crécy, and which Maximilian, then archduke, had taken in 1479 and since lost, was the agreed first objective for the English. The vanguard had already set about it and knocked down some of its houses. By a very hot 1 August, eleven days after it had set out from Calais, the royal army had covered some forty miles and reached Thérouanne. There had been several mishaps on the way, one or two skirmishes and, one misty morning, a false alarm that a French force was about to attack – whereupon Henry drew up his men in battle array. But the French had had orders not to fight and so Henry had resumed his march. Now he had placed the whole weight of his forces against this small town. His ample tents with cloth of gold hangings were set up, with sideboards, gold goblets and his big, carved bed within. A few days later, after the full siege had begun, Maximilian rode into the English camp. So far he had studiously avoided mounting the full-scale campaign which was required of him by treaty. Instead, he flatteringly offered to place himself and the small force he had brought with him under the standard, and in the pay, of Henry in order to lend a hand in overpowering a citadel whose capture would serve Habsburg interests well and English little. Henry agreed, shifted his men as Maximilian suggested and tightened the siege.[42]

This was an unspectacular affair. But in the middle of it occurred the sole open engagement of the campaign, and one which, ironically, Henry missed. On the morning of 16 August a French cavalry force which had come to succour the besieged town suddenly found itself opposite the allied army, whose position it had misjudged. Repelled by the latter's artillery, it turned and fled, with English and Burgundian horse in hot pursuit. There was no pitched battle – only a hurtling gallop across the fields at Guingates (today

42. *L.P.*, i, 2173. Polydore Vergil, op. cit., 213.

Enguingattes) to the east of Thérouanne. The main French force escaped but left behind six standards and a handsome body of prisoners, including a duke, a marquis and the vice-admiral of France. This was enough to give the skirmish the aura of an heroic victory – the so-called Battle of the Spurs – and to allow Henry to describe it in grandiose terms.[43] A week later the garrison of Thérouanne succumbed, and on 24 August Henry and Maximilian made triumphant entry into the town, halting at the church for a *Te Deum* sung by the king's choir. Three days afterwards, this, his first prize of war, was handed over by the king to Maximilian, who alone had any real strategic interest in it and promptly ordered his troops to raze all, save the church, to the ground.

Flushed with victory, Henry and the emperor went to Lille, some forty miles away, to meet the regent of the Netherlands. Lille's folk gave the king a lavish reception, and for three days he danced and sang in the castle, delighting the ladies with his skill with pipes, the lute and cornet. When this gay respite was over, he returned to his army and to the siege of a second French citadel, Tournai – which, like Thérouanne, menaced Artois and had been besieged long ago by Edward III. Then the English had failed. This time they met success. Unnerved by the terrible penalty inflicted on Thérouanne for stubbornness and hammered by English artillery, Tournai surrendered after an eight-day siege. The day after the formal capitulation, that is on 24 September, Henry entered the city in magnificence. Tournai was a handsome prize – an episcopal see, girt with double walls, a ring of great towers and seven gates, boasting fine bridges across the Scheldt and renowned for its wine and carpets. '*La pucelle sans reproche*' was its motto, which Henry ostentatiously ordered should now be erased. Unlike Thérouanne, Tournai was to remain intact in English hands, garrisoned and governed by the English; a second Calais and a second spring-board from which to launch the reconquest of lost possessions in France. After about three weeks of feasts and

43. *L.P.*, i, 2170, Henry to the Archduchess Margaret.

tilts and tournaments, revels and balls, Henry left Tournai
to return to Lille. Thence he made his way to Calais and
England. He was anxious to get home now that the campaigning season was nearly over.[44]

So ended the first royal campaign. In truth, though certainly impressive compared with Dorset's wretched expedition to Spain in the previous year, it had not achieved much
militarily and was trivial compared with the momentous victory which had been won at home during the king's absence.
When he left Dover earlier in the year, Henry had proclaimed Catherine governor of the realm and captain-
general of the forces, and given her a handful of councillors
to manage the kingdom while he was away. As there could
be little doubt that the Scots would observe ancient practice
and exploit Henry's absence, Catherine and her council
were especially concerned with the northern borders. Even
as she was immersed in maintaining the flow of supplies to
France and setting her servants to sew standards and badges,
or worrying about a husband liable to get overhot or lack
clean linen, the northern counties were being mustered
against a Scottish invasion. The blow soon fell. On 11 August
a Scottish herald arrived at the English camp outside
Thérouanne to deliver his master's defiance to Henry, who
sent him away with rough words. Despite repeated warning
from Julius that he and his whole kingdom would be ana-
thematized if he attacked England while she was engaged in
her holy war, James IV crossed the Tweed at the head of
a large army to do battle with the English, under Surrey.
On 9 September the two armies met at Flodden in a fearful,
bloody encounter which ended after about three hours with
the English absolute masters of the field. Most of the Scottish aristocracy, including twelve earls, the archbishop of St
Andrews, two bishops, two abbots and, finally, the king himself, were killed. This was a shattering defeat. Beside so

44. For much of the preceding, see John Taylor's account of the
campaign in B.M. Cleo. C, v, fols 64 ff. (*L.P.*, i, 2391). Also *L.P.*, i,
2208, 2227, 2302.

immense and consequential a victory, Henry's exploits on the continent and the Battle of the Spurs seemed slender indeed. It had been doubtful wisdom anyway to take a large English army across the Channel and expose the homeland to an assault from the north, and doubtful wisdom too, to have allowed the continental campaign to prevent full exploitation of the great victory at home. In philandering in Lille and gaining Tournai, Henry perhaps lost Scotland. Catherine wrote to Henry fulsome praise for the victory of the Spurs, but the praise was due elsewhere. Henry sent her his leading French prisoners, a duke included; but Catherine could send him the blood-stained coat of a king whose unburied body now lay in the Carthusian house at Sheen.[45]

Partly because the army had landed in France rather late in the year and partly because Henry had been manipulated by Maximilian into serving the latter's purposes, no great conquests in Picardy or Normandy had yet come his way. But if his tangible successes were meagre, they were at least the first which English arms had won from the French for some seventy-five years and had done something to redeem England's military reputation, and something to persuade the casual Ferdinand that perhaps there was a new and growing power in Europe. Henry had tasted war, had ventured himself, had cut a martial figure. He had wheeled his army through rain and mud, set it to siege, fired cannon, seen his cavalry charge. He had dubbed knights and held councils of war on the battlefield, ridden in triumph to a *Te Deum*, and been acclaimed by the grandees of Lille. He had taken a clutch of fine prisoners, released some, with a hearty gesture, at a reduced ransom and sent the rest home to embellish his Court. He had been mightily flattered by an emperor (which was only justice, considering that Henry had not only to subsidize his campaign but fight it as well) who called him now son, now brother, had allowed him to ride ahead

45. Polydore Vergil, op cit., 221. Henry later secured papal permission to bury the excommunicated king in Westminster Abbey, *L.P.*, i, 2355, 2469.

into Thérouanne and taken second place in the church
there. When Tournai fell, again Henry entered first, with
Maximilian modestly following some days later. It was gratifying for a young king thus to be handled by an emperor.[46]
Nor had Julius's brief been forgotten. As soon as news of
Henry's alleged triumphs reached Rome, that unsleeping
patriot, Bainbridge, had demanded that the document
should be handed over to its intended recipient and called
upon the pope to be ready to go to Rheims to crown the new
king of France. But though one of the cardinals who had
the brief in his keeping could absentmindedly write to Henry
as 'Most Christian King', it was not forthcoming. Henry and
Bainbridge continued to pester for it; but the king had
apparently not yet earned his reward.[47]

He might next year. This first expedition had been but a
beginning. Henry had returned home for the winter, to deal
with the Scots and to meet Parliament; not because the war
had come to an end. While at Lille, he had agreed with the
emperor, in the person of the regent, that the campaign
should be renewed before 1 June next. At Tournai he had
also agreed with Maximilian that the latter's grandson,
Charles duke of Burgundy (later king of Spain and Holy
Roman Emperor), should marry his sister Mary Tudor at
Calais before 15 May next. The military alliance was to be
sealed with a marriage compact, therefore, and the emperor
and king, having met at Calais to celebrate the union of
grandson and sister, would then ride forth to divide France.[48]
Even this was not the whole of the plan. Despite the fact that
he had twice openly played Henry false, Ferdinand was also
to be party to the new scheme. Once again it was provided
that a Spanish army should strike from the south at Guienne,

46. So John Taylor in his diary. For reference see note on page 60.
47. See Ferrajoli, art. cit., 437 ff., and Chambers, op. cit., 50 ff. In a
letter to Pace, then in Rome, Brian Tuke referred to Henry as
'*Christianissimus rex noster*'. Tuke was then (i.e., September 1513) in
France with the king. *Ven. Cal.*, ii, 316.
48. *L.P.*, i, 2355, 2366, 2768 (ii), 2815.

while English troops went into Picardy; and once again England would act as pay-master for any who cared to fight her battles, such as the Spanish and the emperor's 6,000 German mercenaries: to all of which Ferdinand eventually agreed, even though he probably had no intention of being distracted from his real concern – building a kingdom in Italy.[49]

Apparently, therefore, the strategy of the past expedition had not been misjudged. It had brought Maximilian into enthusiastic partnership and caused Ferdinand to take Henry more seriously. Next spring Henry would return to the continent well set to make irresistible his demand for Julius's brief of investiture.[50] Probably shortly after Christmas 1513 he succumbed to an attack of small-pox, but soon rose undaunted from his bed to resume preparations for the new season.[51] On 1 February Thomas Howard was restored to the dukedom of Norfolk, and Charles Brandon created duke of Suffolk; and the elevation to the highest degree of these two war-lords was as much a sign for the future as a reward for past services. Men and equipment were being assembled once more and shipped to Calais. The plans for the royal marriage due to take place there were going ahead, even though Prince Charles had been overheard saying ungraciously of his bride-to-be, who, if a few years his senior, was still an indisputably beautiful girl, that he wanted a wife, not a mother.[52] Mary herself was already styled princess of Castile, carried about a portrait of her betrothed and sighed for him dutifully. Meanwhile the elaborate protocol surrounding the visit of the emperor and the regent of the Netherlands who would come with him had to be settled,

49. Ferdinand jibbed at the title of king of France with which Henry was credited in the treaty – though this was, of course, already part of his style. *Sp. Cal.*, ii, 146, 148.

50. Had he not told a council anxious about his personal safety that 'his ambition was not merely to equal but to exceed the glorious deeds of his ancestors'? So Polydore Vergil, op. cit., p. 197.

51. *L.P.*, i, 2610, 2634.

52. *Ven. Cal.*, ii, 295.

food and furnishings provided for the distinguished guests
and their suites, oats and hay for their horses – as well as for
the English army that would be passing through the port at
the same time.[53] All this was well in hand in early 1514. All
was to be a waste of effort. Within a year Mary Tudor would
be about to marry, not Charles Habsburg, but the very king
of France whose kingdom Henry was now aspiring to receive
from the pope's hands; and England would not go to open
war again for eight years.

53. E.g. *L.P.*, i, 2544, 2572, 2656, 2737, 2759, 2809, 2812, etc.

[3]

The Coming of Wolsey

It is not possible to establish the exact moment when primacy of place, above Warham, Fox and, indeed, Catherine, passed to the minister who stands almost as large as, perhaps even larger than, his master during the first twenty years of Henry's reign – Thomas Wolsey. Although he had been at court, on the edge of power, since 1505, it was the accession of the new king in 1509 which marked the beginning of real advancement when, though still only royal almoner, he acted as informal royal secretary and provided the regular channel of communication between the king and ministers like Fox, who, perforce, were often away from Court on government business. His position was a powerful one, for he was attendant on the king and had ready access to everyone and everything of moment. Years later, when Wolsey had long since climbed to the highest office, Thomas More would occupy much the same position at the king's side; and like him, More was to find that it yielded good fruit.

If Wolsey mattered, as he did, by 1512, he mattered still more by the end of 1513. It was his firm hands which had largely shaped the campaign in France of that year, providing Henry with a well-fed, remarkably healthy, disciplined and well-equipped army. By the standard of the previous year, at any rate, this was an efficient expedition and some of the credit for this must go to the almoner who rode to war alongside Henry and was with him throughout, worrying about tents, setting the troops to building wooden huts with chimneys against the winter, and so on.[1] The war both proved his competence and provided a new bond, that of

1. For a dated, over-enthusiastic (but useful) study of all this, see Law, *England's First Great War Minister* (1916).

comradeship in arms, between him and the king. By the
end of 1513 he held sway at least equal to that of Fox; by
mid 1514 he probably outstripped him – and he had some
time ago overhauled the archbishop of Canterbury, William
Warham. Furthermore, political ascent was mirrored by
ecclesiastical advancement. In 1513 he acquired the see of
Tournai, then Lincoln, and within a few months had exchanged this for the archbishopric of York. Thus in a year
he had been raised – at royal instance – from a mere dean to
archbishop, *legatus natus* and primate of England. But as
yet he held no secular office. He would have to wait until the
end of 1515 before the chancellorship would be his and his
mastery complete.

Three things explain his swift rise to power and his long
enjoyment of it. In the first place, he undoubtedly possessed
an enormous appetite for hard work, swift judgement, a most
acute eye for detail and overflowing confidence – qualities
that had commended him to Henry VII and made his claim
to power in the next reign irresistible. Secondly, he had the
right patronage. It was Bishop Fox, above all, who nursed
him to prominence[2] and he, with Warham, who willingly
made way for him by retirement. It has sometimes been
implied that these two men, Fox and Warham, were thrust
aside by the aggressive ambition of Wolsey and more or
less forcibly sent home by him to the quiet obscurity of their
dioceses. But the truth is that both were anxious to escape
from secular affairs and turn to other things. Warham was
an ageing man whose palmy days had been in the last reign
and who was probably never at ease in the new. He had not
approved of Henry's marriage with his dead brother's wife;[3]
he was immersed in another round of the long-standing
quarrel with some of his suffragans in the province of Canterbury concerning tsetamentary jurisdiction, a dispute in

2. Thus Polydore Vergil says Fox advanced Wolsey to counter
Surrey's influence, and calls him Fox's *alumnus*. See *The Anglica
Historia*, etc., 195 ff.
3. Above, p. 29.

which the king, to his evident irritation, had become involved during his campaign in France in 1513.[4] We have the clear testimony of More that Warham was anxious to abandon politics[5] and we have it from Fox's own pen that the same was true of him. These two English bishops, like the Frenchman Claude de Seyssel, bishop of Marseilles, and, a little later, Gian-Matteo Giberti, bishop of Verona, wanted to go to their dioceses not, as Fox said, 'to hunt nor to hawk, nor to take none worldly pleasure, nor for ease of my body, nor yet for quietness of mind', but, rather, to 'do some satisfaction for xviii years' negligence'.[6] Far from being elbowed out by him, it is possible that these two, certainly Fox, brought Wolsey forward as a protégé and gratefully stood down once he was established. Moreover, though relations between Wolsey and Warham, and perhaps also between Wolsey and Fox, were not always happy later on, the latter watched much of the younger man's subsequent progress with evident pride and approval. He praised his doings, spoke to him earnestly about the dangers of overwork, advised him to adopt a sensible horarium and not to work after 6 p.m. For his part, Wolsey turned to him for guidance – on one occasion, for example, entreating him to undo his resolve to leave aside worldly affairs if only to help with the business of rebuilding the fortifications of Calais.[7]

But ministers of the crown were the crown's and nobody else's, and neither the wisdom of Solomon nor the patronage of angels would have availed Wolsey if the king had not wanted him to be his leading servant. Cavendish[8] tells us how shrewdly Wolsey judged the young king and, seeing him irked by the tedium of Council meetings, would en-

4. *L.P.*, i, 2019, 2312.
5. Rogers, *The Correspondence of Sir Thomas More* (Princeton, 1947), 86.
6. *Letters of Richard Fox*, 83, 82.
7. ibid., 82 ff., 92 ff., 96 ff.
8. Wolsey's gentleman usher and biographer.

courage him to cast off the cares of state and leave him, a
mere almoner, to look after them: a suggestion to which
Henry easily acquiesced. As fast as other councillors urged
Henry to look to the affairs of the realm 'so busily did the
almoner persuade him to the contrary: which delighted
him much and caused him to have greater affection and
love for the almoner.... Who was now in high favour, but
Master Almoner? And who ruled all under the king, but
Master Almoner?' wrote Cavendish.[9] But Wolsey was bound
to the king not only because he relieved him of work. He
and Henry had a good deal in common: both were vigorous,
extroverted men, both intelligent, both greedy for the flamboyant and vainglorious; indeed, so akin were they that the
envious and imaginative could attribute Wolsey's intimacy
with the king to witchcraft. Wolsey's was the keener mind,
probably, and certainly the firmer will – with the result that
for about a dozen years Henry's dependence upon him,
though erratic, was often childlike; and in return Henry
would receive years of unstinted, though sometimes self-
opinionated, service. If hitherto the young king had ruled
with ministers inherited from his father, men who may
not have relished his forward foreign policy and who expected him to be a working monarch like his predecessor
(which he was not prepared to be), now at last he had found
one who was apparently precisely what was required. The
new reign thus had a new beginning – and with it there
opened the first of two great partnerships between the king
and a minister.

For much of the time, as, week after week, Henry hawked
and hunted, jousted and tilted, diced and bowled, played
tennis and made music, danced and banqueted, it must have
seemed that an indolent, self-indulgent king had wholly
surrendered the cares of state into the cardinal's hands.
While Wolsey bore the heat of the day at Westminster or
Hampton Court, dividing his time between incessant diplomacy and the Star Chamber and Chancery, Henry might

9. *Cavendish*, 13.

be in the saddle day after day, from dawn to dusk, miles from the chancellor – and miles, too, from the Privy Council which was attendant upon him. Then ambassadors would have to ride into the country, or wait for days in London, to have audience of him; letters would receive no answer; the smallest decision be left to Wolsey. And even when Henry was more accessible, on a leisurely progress, or at Greenwich, he would often give only the minimum time to affairs of state. Wolsey was to receive letters addressed to the king and send him digests, or to annotate the text to spare him having to listen – for he did not like to read these letters himself – to long-winded screeds. He would send him 'extracts' of news from, perhaps, Italy or Germany; and summaries of treaties, because 'it should be painful to your grace to visit and overread the whole treaty'.[10] If a letter were required of Henry, then Wolsey would send a 'minute' thereof or a full draft for him merely to sign – and, even so, royal correspondence was often in arrears. Urgent letters would be left unsigned while the king ate or looked at his horses, or would be laughingly set aside for tomorrow; and by tomorrow harts and hinds would have called the king away.

On one occasion, in order to persuade Henry to sign or, better still, copy draft letters to Margaret, the regent of the Netherlands, which had waited a long time for signature, Wolsey could write, 'I beseech your grace, though it shall be to your pain to do somewhat therein, [to bestir yourself]', and added encouragingly, 'Ye know well enough that women must be pleased'[11] – a piece of plodding humour of the kind that not infrequently adorned his letters. Now Henry would send to Wolsey a letter he had received from Francis I and for which he wanted a reply in French drafted for him, but it must be 'some short letter'; now, after postponing the effort

10. *St.P.*, i, 118. References for all the statements made in this paragraph would run to excessive length. Some will be substantiated in later pages of this work. The doubtful reader may verify my statements quickly by perusal of *St.P.*, i.

11. *St.P.*, i, 11 f.

overnight, he was unable to add the opening greeting to two (short) letters to the same Francis which had been drafted for him, and had to imitate the form which the French king had used in addressing him; now Wolsey had to take over a correspondence with the earl of Surrey, then leading the king's forces in France, which Henry had begun but could not carry further.[12] Though Wolsey sent him a daily stream of letters, messages and documents for his perusal and approval, he rarely replied in his own hand. He would debate his reply with the secretary, leave it to the latter to put pen to paper and perhaps have the finished article read to him before despatch – but no more. 'I have received your letters', he wrote in one of the very few extant royal holographs addressed to the cardinal, 'to the which, because they ask long writing, I have made answer by my secretary,'[13] which was at least an honest admission of weakness. But, if Henry was not eager with the pen, this fact should not be used in evidence against him. No man of consequence – let alone a king – either wrote, or was expected to write, his own letters. However, a king could be expected to pay more attention to routine business than he did.

For much of his career as chancellor, it was Wolsey who alone guided English affairs. His quick, strong hands grasped everything because Henry seemed unable, or unwilling, to make the smallest decision himself. Who shall attend upon the Princess Mary? What shall he reply to the regent of the Netherlands' request to visit England? Shall the law courts be closed because of the outbreak of sweating-sickness?[14] and so on. All these Wolsey had to decide for him, for they were problems which this apparently helpless man, for all his bluster and swagger, could not resolve. Wolsey must be servant yet master, creature yet impresario; he must abase himself and yet dominate, playing a part which only a man of superlative energy, self-confidence and loyalty could have endured.

12. *St.P.*, 14, 25; *L.P.*, iii, 2526.
13. *St.P.*, i, i.   14. ibid., 70 f., 141.

Yet the king who so often seemed to want nothing more than to dance and to hunt, and to have only the feeblest grip on royal duties, was also the man who, time and again, could show a detailed grasp of foreign affairs and hold his own with, if not outdo, foreign ambassadors; who could suddenly put off his supper until he had dealt with a stack of business;[15] who could pounce on something Wolsey had missed, cut a proposal to ribbons with a few swift strokes, assess a situation exactly, confidently overrule his minister, correctly predict that a plan could not work, demand the recall of this ambassador, order that undertaking. There is no doubt that, at times, Henry was furiously involved in public business and in commanding partnership with Wolsey, and that he could break into his minister's conduct of affairs with decisive results. There is no doubt that he had intense interest in certain things – in ships, in war, in what Francis I was doing, for example. That he was the true source of the really important events of his reign – the wars, the divorce, the breach with Rome – is scarcely disputable; and by the mid 1520s he seems to have acquired much more confidence and control (which he never wholly surrendered thereafter). But in the earlier years, at least until about 1521–2, his undisciplined life was filled with an assortment of projects which were enthusiastically begun, sometimes quickly abandoned and not often brought to fruition.

The first twenty years of Henry's reign were dominated by foreign affairs, for it was there that – albeit erratically – the king looked for his fulfilment; and it was to foreign affairs that Wolsey gave most of his time and energy, not merely because of Henry's predilection but also because his own ambition led him there. On the whole, and especially recently, Wolsey has had terrible judgement passed against him for having squandered power that was greedily amassed, for having mishandled, violated, corrupted or neglected most of what was in his charge. But perhaps it might be said in

15. ibid., 96 (*L.P.*, iii, 2130).

his defence that his critics have not always perceived that,
since the bulk of his energy was given to foreign policy,
ambitious designs for the domestic life of the country, to
which he none the less gave some attention, had perforce to
be set aside until the first call on his time had been answered.
A reputation is not easy to make with a foreign policy,
especially if that policy was a failure, as Wolsey's was; and
it is even less easy if that policy is misrepresented.

To the eminent Tudor historian, A. F. Pollard,[16] the meaning of Wolsey's diplomacy was clear: it entirely hitched
England to the Holy See. If Rome sought peace, so too did
England; if Rome made war on France, so too did England;
if Rome made war on the emperor, so too did England. Anywhere that Leo X or Clement VII went, England, thanks to
the cardinal of York, was sure to go.[17] Furthermore, England
was tied to the papacy not out of any loyalty to a divine
institution but because Wolsey was always wanting something from it – now a red hat, now a legacy, now a more
fulsome legacy – and even hoped to become pope himself,
and above all because his own precious authority as legate
a latere was sustained by Rome. Thus England was cast
into the vortex of papal, and hence often merely local Italian,
politics, without regard for her true interests and in response
only to his own devouring ambition.

But there are difficulties with Pollard's thesis. It assumes
that English foreign policy was wholly Wolsey's and never
Henry's, which is not true. Secondly, one of the striking facts
about at least the early years of Wolsey's career is the way in
which he persistently failed to show even a modicum of
solicitude, indeed, of mere good manners, towards Rome.
Time and again there came complaints from Leo X and
Silvestro Gigli, the English agent at Rome, that Henry and
Wolsey were failing lamentably in their filial duties. They

16. In his *Wolsey* – his final verdict on the reign of Henry VIII
and his finest work.

17. '*Ubi Petrus, ibi Anglia*' is Philip Hughes's neat summary of
Pollard's thesis, *The Reformation in England*, i, 113.

did not write regularly, as did other princes, it was said,
except for their own personal advancement or appointments
to English sees; they left Rome uninformed about their
policies; urgent letters to them were not answered; they
promised money and it never came; they did not even
bother to reply to the proposal for the reform of the calendar for which the Fifth Lateran Council called, and so on.[18]
Leo X and Adrian VI were clearly baffled and exasperated
by this insouciance. And the English not only failed to write,
but were content with a representation at Rome which was
meagre compared with that of other countries and depended
mainly on *ad hoc* missions and Italian agents.[19]

If Wolsey was really so obsessed with Rome, it is strange
that he should have been chided for silence so often by an
exasperated pope or, for example, begged by Gigli to send a
letter once a month, even if he had nothing to say. If Rome
was the key to his career, would he have failed so conspicu-
ously to ingratiate himself with the Curia or to build up the
English presence there? Moreover, as we shall see, it is
questionable whether Wolsey seriously aspired to the
papacy;[20] and, if he did not, an important part of Pollard's
thesis must be discarded. Finally – and this is the most
serious objection of all to it – though there is certainly a
coincidence between English and papal policy when they
are seen from a distance, at closer sight this often disappears.
England and Rome were frequently out of step, sometimes
seriously so; and when there was an identity of purpose, the
identity was often accidental.

Then what did Wolsey seek? The answer would seem to
be: peace. Wolsey's career as an international figure, it will
be argued here, was a serious search for the deliverance of
England and Western Europe from the discord which in

18. E.g. *L.P.*, ii, 1928, 2580, 2649, 3352, 4068 (especially), 4084;
iii, 533, 791, 945, 2714. See D. S. Chambers, 'Cardinal Wolsey and the
Papal Tiara', *B.I.H.R.*, xxxviii (1965), 20 ff.
19. Cf. Chambers, art. cit.
20. Below, pp. 148 ff.

recent decades had been their constant affliction. The search failed, but it was probably earnestly undertaken.

The earliest extant letter of Wolsey's, apart from mutilated scraps from Henry VII's reign, is one written to Fox in late September 1511, when Wolsey was informal middle-man between him and the king. In it he complained of the way in which 'the king's money goeth away in every corner', as a result of Darcy's expedition to North Africa and the trouble on the Scottish border, largely caused by Surrey's aggressiveness, 'by whose wanton means his grace spendeth much money and is more disposed to war than peace.... Your presence [i.e. here with the king]', he goes on, 'shall be very necesssary to repress this appetite.'[21] Curiously, it was in another part of this letter that Pollard found the first sign of what he claimed was the *Leitmotiv* of his career, namely, Wolsey's preoccupation with the papacy.[22] But perhaps it is not that passage with its casual reference to the pope so much as the one just quoted which throws the first light on the meaning of Wolsey.

He sought peace for the severely practical reason, which he constantly repeated, that war was the quickest way to lose money. Wolsey, it must be remembered, had served his apprenticeship under Henry VII and he remained throughout his life a disciple of that king's school of thrift. But perhaps he also thought in loftier terms. When he praised peace as a good and holy thing – as he often did – and deplored war between Christians as scandalous, it is easy to dismiss his words as the jargon of a cynical diplomat who was merely paying lip-service to convention. But Wolsey was sympathetic to contemporary humanism, as his educational projects, for example, show. There was more of the 'New Learning' in him, probably, than in the king, and it is at least possible that he was touched by the desperate cry of the humanists to contemporary kings and statesmen to cast off amoral diplomacy and put an end to disgraceful war among Christians. Of all the humanists, none indicted

21. *Fiddes*, 9.   22. Pollard, *Wolsey* (1929), 16.

nationalistic pride, militarism, diplomatic chicanery and
perfidy more severely than Erasmus and More – the latter,
especially, in his *Utopia*. But Erasmus more than once hailed
Wolsey as one of his own, for perhaps more than flattery's
sake, and within a short while of damning contemporary
politics for its manifold wickedness and its power to corrupt
those who dabbled therein, that is a few months after writing *Utopia* – in which he certainly tried to resolve a personal *crise de conscience* as he faced the call of service to his
prince – More, to the puzzlement of some, then and now,
himself accepted public office. Perhaps what put an end to
his doubt and led him to accept office was the belief that,
with Wolsey to lead the way, things might be different and
public service less likely to sully his hands. Perhaps More
already saw the undeniable flaws in Wolsey's character, but
hoped that his qualities would overlay them; or, perhaps,
disillusion came later. Whichever it was, for the moment
he could have believed that Wolsey's instinct for good, for
seeking peace and giving justice, made it possible for him
to enter government.

Wolsey's policy was a peace policy and for about fifteen
years he struggled to make it work. It is true that he had
taken his final step to power in 1513 as a war minister. This
is an incongruity that cannot be escaped. But it is fair to
remark that the war in which he proved his organizational
genius by handling the commissariat so ably was not of his
own making but something which, as a lesser servant of the
king, he was required to support. It cannot be denied either
that, between 1514 and 1529, when Wolsey was master of
the realm, England was on the brink of war often and at
war twice – and this too must be explained. The explanation is that Wolsey's policy failed. It failed because it was
unrealistic and perhaps even self-contradictory. Henry had
deliberately led England back into involvement in Europe
and Wolsey was eager to keep her there. But as long as
England was bound to the continent by elaborate treaty
systems (intended to enforce peace) she could only have that

peace if her allies wanted it, and they, above all France, did not. France, led by a belligerent king with an appetite for adventurism and fearful of encirclement by the Habsburgs, was the constant irritant of the European comity. And Charles V must also carry some of the blame for Europe's upsets. His later claim that he had never been guilty of aggression may be true, but his preoccupation with his family and Habsburg claims made him peculiarly susceptible to French provocation. As long as Francis I and Charles V were there the chances of peace for Europe were slim; and as long as England was knitted by diplomacy into the fabric of such a Europe there could be no peace for her either. The choice for England was between withdrawal from Europe and peace on the one hand, and a continental policy with its inevitable entanglement in endemic European war on the other. Wolsey chose the latter, believing that he could master Europe by dexterous employment of his own and England's weight – weight which he easily overestimated – and he chose thus because he wanted the flamboyant role of arbiter of Europe. He wanted peace *and* glory. He won little of either.

He failed as a peacemaker because Europe would not submit to his designs. But it is also possible that these were not always in accord with his master's instincts. The evidence will not support the statement that, between 1514 and 1529, England possessed two foreign policies rather than one; but, as we shall see, there were certainly moments when the royal urge for war was at least tempered by the minister's quest for peace and there seem to have been moments when the king's belligerence finally broke the cardinal's designs. Wolsey, of course, was not a pacifist in the strict sense of the term. He allowed the possibility of the just war (which may also help to explain his enthusiasm for the campaign of 1513 against a schismatic king of France) and regularly rattled the sabre in order to intimidate the belligerent. Nor was he prepared to die for peace. He was probably not prepared to die for any save natural reasons. When it was evident that all attempts to preserve peace must fail, he was ready to throw his talents and energy into waging war.

His programme required that, if Europe's peace could not survive, then force might be used, provided that others did the fighting first; that if this failed, England might threaten, but not take, military action herself; that, if this failed, England might declare war but, if possible, not fight; that, if this too failed to win peace, England should embark on hot war in the shape of a swift, decisive stroke rather than a long, sprawling campaign. Such was Wolsey's *schema*. It was not always and exactly Henry's.

In the early months of 1514 Henry, more intent than ever upon a dazzling forward policy, was preparing to lead his army back to Calais to take part in a new, triple offensive against France and to see England and the Habsburgs united by three royal marriages.[23] But by the time these plans were ready to materialize the international situation had changed radically. In the first place France made her peace with Rome, abandoning the schismatic Council at Pisa and formally submitting to the pope and his Council at the Lateran – thus removing the basic justification for Henry's intervention – and, in the second, there had come to the papal throne in March 1513 a new pope, Leo X, who, as far as his chronic indecisiveness would allow, was set upon turning France into a friend and using her as a counterweight to Spanish influence in Italy.[24] So it was that, about the same time as Henry returned home like a hero from his first campaign, Leo decided to try to disperse the anti-French league which his predecessor had assembled and bring the combatants to peace. No less a person than Gian-pietro Caraffa, a founding-father of the Theatines and, later, Pope Paul IV, was sent to England to propose the papal

23. *L.P.*, i, 2705, 2822–3 etc. *Ven. Cal.*, ii, 371.
24. See Nitti, *Leone X e la Sua Politica* (Florence, 1892) for an excellent analysis of the pope's diplomacy.

plan,[25] while Leo went on to revive a rather obscure scheme
whereby the English Cardinal Bainbridge should go to the
emperor, accompany him to a meeting with Henry at Calais
and there preside over a full peace conference.[26]

Leo's appeals alone would not have moved Henry. It was
only a few months since another pope had solemnly commanded him to enter the war which Leo was now trying to
halt, and Henry, having tried to prevent Caraffa's coming,
ignored him when he came.[27] But Rome's was not the only
influence at work. Once again Ferdinand was at the root of
trouble. By early January French bribery had won him over
and he had effectively abandoned both the league and a
plan ratified but a few weeks before whereby he, Henry and
the emperor were to conquer and divide France. And having secretly defected himself, he set about corrupting Maximilian, who was easy prey.

Henry first suspected Spanish treachery towards the end
of February 1514. John Stile, his ambassador in Spain, sent
suspicious news about Ferdinand, and then Thomas Spinelly
in the Low Countries heard disturbing stories, from the
other side of the league.[28] But in England preparations for
war went ahead – until it was suddenly learnt that Ferdinand
had signed a new truce with France, once again not only in
his name but also in Henry's and the emperor's.[29] Ferdinand
had defected a third time. On a previous occasion he had
justified a truce on the ground that he was on his death-bed;
now he produced an elaborate story about a conspiracy by
the pope and others to drive him and Maximilian out of
Italy, which forced him to come to terms with France. Indeed, he added, it was Maximilian who had pressed this
truce and given authority to his ambassador to act in Henry's
name. Tell Henry, Ferdinand instructed Caroz, his ambassa-

25. *L.P.*, i, 2448, 2658, 2820 etc.
26. B.M. Vit. B, ii, fol. 63; iv, fols 104 ff. (*L.P.*, i, 2512, 2611). Also
L.P., i, 2559–60.
27. *L.P.*, i, 2610.   28. *L.P.*, i, 2678, 2694, 2743.
29. *Sp. Cal.*, ii, 164.

dor in England, that he was quite sure that Maximilian had Henry's approval when his name was put to the truce. Tell Henry that France could be attacked later. Tell Henry that England and Spain would never fall apart. Tell him anything. But Henry must sign the truce – and the ambassador burn his copy of the treaty of Lille by which Spain was to join the invasion of France that year.[30]

Thus Ferdinand contracted out of the league, with Maximilian following suit, to England's bitter chagrin, soon after. Nevertheless, Henry stated categorically that he would press on with the campaign against France without his allies.[31] Troops were being mustered, ships hired and put to sea, and flour, meat, bacon and other supplies sent to Calais.[32] It would be, he said, 'a very great dishonour' to halt now. There remained the Swiss and with them as sole support he would bravely go ahead. Five envoys had been sent to Zürich and a Swiss delegation received lavishly in England. By early August a ten-year league had been concluded at Berne binding the Swiss to put a large army into the field against France, at English expense, whenever Henry should require.[33] Meanwhile, in the middle of June, an English army-by-sea had landed three miles west of Cherbourg and ravaged an area of some fourteen square miles – in revenge for a recent French raid on Brighton.

Yet, within a few weeks, England and France had come together in a treaty of peace. This was a *volte-face* which is difficult to explain. Perhaps Henry had suddenly perceived that to fight with only the Swiss support was impracticable and had lost his nerve. Perhaps the earlier war preparations had never been any more than a deception. But it does seem probable that Fox and Wolsey were particularly concerned with bringing England and France together. They had

30. *Sp. Cal.*, ii, 159, 170; *L.P.*, i, 2743.
31. *Lettres de Roy Louis XII etc.* (Brussels, 1712), iv, 312 ff. (*L.P.*, i, 2817).
32. *L.P.*, i, 2759, 2812, 2883, 2842 etc.
33. *Mil. Cal.*, 686, 708–9 (*L.P.*, i, 2997).

responded warmly to Leo's peace initiative,[34] even if they argued against the cumbersome plan of sending Bainbridge to a conference at Calais. True enough, Wolsey was at this moment trying to persuade Leo to reduce the tax on his newly-acquired see of Lincoln, but this could hardly explain why not only Wolsey, but Fox too, would have risked the charge of sizeable hypocrisy by playing with Leo, nor perhaps wholly account for the latter's praise for the dexterous way in which the two of them had dealt with Henry to bring him to peace (and Leo would have known from Caraffa, then in England, just what they had been about).[35] These two did not do anything behind Henry's back, though there is more than a hint that they had colleagues who were not of their persuasion.[36] But it does seem that they were occupied with ending Anglo-French hostilities; and it was to Wolsey that the French particularly looked when they began putting out peace-feelers. Maybe he was telling the truth when he later boasted 'I was the author of this peace', despite 'those members of the Council who were averse to it' and who thought him 'more anxious for peace with France than for the honour of his king'. As Henry later told the pope, 'no one laboured and sweated' for that peace as did the bishop of Lincoln.[37]

Papal pressure on Henry to come to terms was heavy. In mid May an emissary arrived bringing a sword and cap of maintenance for Henry – a mark of papal esteem for secular rulers. They were delivered to the king at St Paul's on

34. See B.M. Vit. B, iv, fols 107 ff. (*L.P.*, i, 2611). In this letter Fox and Wolsey declared themselves to be 'unius animi, unius mentis et concordiae' in all things, including 'hac sanctissima causa', i.e. peace. ibid., fol. 107v.

35. B.M. Vit. B, ii, fols 105 ff. (*L.P.*, i, 2928). This was a letter from Gigli, English orator in Rome, to Fox and Wolsey.

36. See *L.P.*, i, 2811, a mutilated letter of Fox and Wolsey in which there is cryptic mention of 'some folks' who may carp at what they are doing.

37. *Ven. Cal.*, ii, 635, 695. B.M. Add. 15,387, fol 25 (*L.P.*, i, 3140) for Henry's statement that Wolsey '*laboravit et sudavit*'.

Sunday 21 May. Kneeling before the high altar, he was girded with the sword and had the large, ornate cap placed on his head – though, since it was not intended to be worn, it produced the rather comical effect of completely engulfing his face and making the subsequent procession hazardous.[38] Some weeks later there arrived a third papal envoy, who had come via France to join Caraffa in persuading Henry to accede to Leo's plans. Hedged about by intense papal diplomacy, by French offers of terms and the efforts of his two leading ministers, Henry yielded. In early August vigorous bargaining came to an end, and France and England swore a treaty of peace that was to last until one year after the death of whichever of the two monarchs died first. Louis was to pay the arrears on the pension due to Henry under the treaty of Etaples of 1492 and, by a third instalment, Henry's sister Mary, who had been due until now to marry Charles of Burgundy, was given in marriage to the king of France, now a decrepit specimen of manhood many years her senior.[39]

Thus the two enemies came together in what was advertised as a peace that would long endure, and thus closed the first chapter in Henry's life. Its final pages had taken an ironical turn – with the young king who had called upon his nation to return to its past and launch a splendid war of conquest against the traditional enemy now casting aside his ruined plans and accepting the enemy into brotherhood. The Henry V *redivivus* had made a somewhat unconvincing entry into martial history, though this was not entirely his own fault. War with a refurbished France that had broken independent Burgundy was a very different affair from that in which earlier Henrys had indulged. Further, it had been found almost impossible to create any long-lived, reliable offensive alliances. The pope, emperor and Venetians were ready to take English money, but England's interests could never be anything but peripheral to their own. For her

38. *Ven. Cal.*, ii, 445.
39. *Rymer*, xiii, 413 ff. *L.P.*, i, 3101, 3171.

to exploit others was difficult; for others to exploit her easy. She had been manipulated and milched, and had nothing to show for her efforts save emptied coffers. Henry's wars and rumours of wars had been stunningly expensive. Between his accession and 12 June 1513 the treasurer of the Chamber, the major financial office, paid out a little over a million pounds, of which some two thirds went on war and nearly half in the single week of 5-12 June 1513.[40] The cost of mounting campaigns across the Channel and of her allies' demands were crippling her finances so fast that peace was urgent. That continental war was shockingly expensive was the supreme lesson to be learned from the king's first essay in military adventuring and it was put with exquisite cynicism by Silvestro Gigli, England's agent at Rome, who is said to have remarked loyally, 'let the barbarous people of France and England every one kill other. What should we care therefore, so we have their money to make merry withal here?'[41]

Henry's treaties with France offended at least one of his former allies, namely the Archduchess Margaret who, it was said, could not 'appease herself' at the loss of English friendship and the marriage of Charles and Mary Tudor. So aggrieved was she that she threatened to publish a document drawn up by Wolsey and signed by Henry during the interview at Lille in the previous autumn in which the latter had given his royal word that he would never deal with France unilaterally. To Margaret's entreaties and threats he had an easy retort. If it were a question of broken promises let his accusers peruse their own conduct. All in turn had dishonoured undertakings.[42] Henry was rightly angry, for the first breach of honour had not been his.

40. P.R.O., *King's Book of Payments*, 1–9 Henry VIII (E.36/215), fol. 257, etc.

41. B.M. Vit. B, ii, fol. 87 – in which Bainbridge reported this conversation to Henry.

42. *L.P.*, i, 3208, 3210. Cf. ibid., 2707. Gigli blasphemously observed that Maximilian and Ferdinand had used a perfidy worse than that of Judas, ibid., 2928.

Towards Margaret and Maximilian – who, the Council said, had treated Henry like a child – the king felt a grievance. But towards Ferdinand he felt something stronger, and understandably so. Three times in twenty months Ferdinand had been guilty of perfidy and on this final occasion had undermined the whole diplomatic structure that Henry had painfully erected. Three times, Henry could believe, victory had been in his grasp, only to be denied him by his father-in-law. Ever since he entered the tough game of European power politics as a mere stripling five years ago he had taken one blow after another from the accomplished Ferdinand. But now he was a more hardened, fiery young man of twenty-three and insults of the size which he had just endured would not go unrequited.

As we have seen, a variety of motives led Henry to abandon his campaign against France, but probably not the least was a desire somehow to hit back at Ferdinand. Now, in 1514, Henry first displayed that instinct for revenge which was to be an increasingly demanding constituent of his character the older he became. He must strike back at Ferdinand. But how? The only practicable way was to engineer a *volte-face* of the kind at which the king of Spain was himself so adept and persuade the recent enemy, Louis, to join him in an act of vengeance. For the moment, francophobia was swamped by the lust to retaliate, and within a few weeks of signing the treaty with France he was talking of turning what was in theory a union of defence into an offensive alliance against Spain.

In October 1514 the duke of Suffolk, Henry's *alter ego* and comrade in belligerence, was sent over to Europe, nominally to witness the coronation of Mary Tudor in St Denis, but really to propose a meeting between Henry and Louis in the next spring to explore the possibility of some action against Ferdinand. He was either to suggest that England should help in the recovery of Navarre (which Ferdinand had seized in 1512), or to broach an intriguing alternative

which ran thus: since the kingdom of Castile belonged to
Ferdinand's wife, Isabella, and not to her husband, that
kingdom had properly descended to her daughters, one of
whom was, of course, Catherine of Aragon; Suffolk was
therefore to ask Louis what aid he would give Henry if the
latter set about the recovery of his wife's inheritance. Henry
VII had talked of a claim to Castile soon after Isabella's
death ten years ago, when he began to think of Catherine's
sister, Joanna, as a possible wife. Now this idea recurred in
wild and, one would think, wholly impracticable form,
though how absurd it seemed then is another matter. Certainly Henry so thirsted for revenge that he asked Suffolk
to devise any concerted scheme which would bring the king
of Spain the greatest mischief, and it is quite possible that
the meeting which was planned with Louis could have had
a sizeable item like this on its agenda. To Suffolk's proposals
the French made polite replies, pretending to be impressed;
but in truth they were interested only in an expedition to
Milan the following March.[43] So Henry's desire for vengeance went unsatisfied. But Ferdinand's ambassador in
England wrote that he was being treated not like an ambassador, but like 'a bull, at whom everyone throws darts',
and Henry was saying that he would hurt Ferdinand somehow, somewhere, and that the time had come to put a bridle
on this colt before he became impossible to handle.[44] Moreover, there was a rumour abroad that he might put away his
Spanish wife.[45]

On 1 January 1515 Louis XII died. Mary Tudor had been
his wife only eleven weeks when, wonderfully soon after she
had been sacrificed on the altar of diplomacy to a gouty,
toothless man three times her age, she was suddenly free at
last to marry her true love, none other than Suffolk himself.
Louis's death brought to the French throne a twenty-year-
old prince who lusted for the heroic and martial as much as

43. For all this, see *Sp. Cal.*, ii, 192; *L.P.*, i, 3472, 3476.
44. *Sp. Cal.*, ii, 201.   45. See below, p. 203.

did Henry, who was reported to resemble the Devil and would inevitably give new and violent impetus to French aggressiveness. Here was a man before whom the peace of Europe would quickly collapse, as would the fragile, artificial Anglo-French *entente* which had just been created. For, not only had the union by royal marriage been cut short, but France had now been given a king towards whom Henry would feel an intense rivalry which quickly eclipsed his recent violent feelings towards Ferdinand. England's alliance with France would probably have collapsed had Louis launched a new expedition across the Alps, but with Francis at the head of a petulant expansionism it was bound to do so. Though talk of a meeting between the two kings survived Louis's death and in April 1515 the recent Anglo-French peace, which would have expired in January 1516, that is, one year after the demise of Louis, was renewed, Henry could write of 'the ambitious mind and insatiable appetites' of the French king and the need to 'bridle' him too;[46] while Francis had no illusions about the neighbour who would spring at him as soon as his back was turned. He would quickly try to block Henry's path by binding the Netherlands closely to himself and, to make doubly sure, by exploiting the complicated affairs of Scotland where Margaret Tudor, widowed at Flodden, struggled to control a country torn by English and French factions. After James IV was killed, the French king had claimed, against Henry, the title of protector of Scotland during the royal minority. In the course of the recent negotiations, the English had asked that this claim be surrendered, but Louis had demanded in exchange the first-fruits of Henry's military captaincy, the solitary flower of his reign, namely, the citadel of Tournai. The price was too cruel, so France kept the protectorship and a useful excuse to meddle in the

46. B.M. Galba B, v, fols 7v, 8 (*L.P.*, ii, 539). Henry told the Venetian ambassador that no Frenchman was to be trusted; and there was strong francophobia in the Council. See *Ven. Cal.*, ii, 594, 635.

affairs of England's nearest neighbour.[47] Then, shortly after the Anglo-French peace was renewed, Francis sent to Scotland a man who was to cause frequent trouble for England, John Stuart, duke of Albany, prince of the blood royal and heir presumptive to the Scottish throne. Hitherto resident in France, Albany arrived in Scotland in the early summer of 1515 and immediately set about strengthening French influence there.

Anglo-French relations were deteriorating fast, and new sources of ill-will arrived daily. First there were complaints on both sides of privateering; then, just as Henry was planning a useful marriage for his sister with the duke of Bavaria, Mary Tudor – still at the French court – married the uxorious Charles Brandon, duke of Suffolk. Francis had encouraged the match because he was keen to keep her out of the international marriage-market; and to make matters worse, having seen her off on the arm of an English nobleman, refused to hand over much of the jewellery and plate which Louis had given her, saying that they would serve to meet some of his predecessor's debts. All in all this affair was more than vexing to Henry and, had not Wolsey intervened, might have harmed Suffolk when he came home. Finally, as the dispute over Mary's jewels, especially one known as 'the mirror of Naples', became increasingly acrimonious, the pugnacious Albany seized Margaret and her children and put them away in Stirling Castle, from which she later escaped to England – to be delivered of a daughter shortly after she had arrived. Thanks to all this, Henry forgot his recent burning malevolence towards Ferdinand and thought only of the provocations which Francis had heaped upon him. However, for his part, the king of France calculated that he had now placed enough trip-wires across England's path to halt her if she should aspire to take advantage of his absence in Italy; and if Albany and the Scots were not enough, there was still at hand in France a member of the de la Pole family, a somewhat forlorn pretender

47. *Ven. Cal.*, ii, 596.

to the English throne, who could be released against the potential enemy. With England thus in toils, he reckoned, she could be ignored.[48] Henry's view of the situation was different. Far from being hamstrung, he saw himself as Europe's puppet-master. He told the Venetian ambassador that he could make the pope do what he chose, that the English liaison with the Swiss held Francis at bay, and so on. 'If I choose he will cross the Alps,' he said magnificently of Francis, 'and if I choose he will not cross.'[49] Both monarchs were therefore confident of their grip on the other. Both were wrong, but Henry more so than Francis. Within a few weeks the French army was in the plain of Lombardy and within another few weeks Leo X was making a treaty with Francis at Bologna; and neither event had taken place by Henry's leave. On 14 September the French army routed the Swiss at Marignano, nine miles from Milan, shattering their military reputation, knocking to pieces an anti-French league before it had begun to move and bringing the duchy of Milan once more into the grasp of France; and it was a few days before this that Margaret had bolted from Stirling Castle, apparently leaving Scotland in French control. Clearly a sun had risen in the firmament that was far brighter than Henry's.

For some time Ferdinand, unabashed by his past inadequacies, had been wooing his son-in-law in the hope of reviving the old idea of a joint Anglo-Spanish attack on France – the strategy which he had thrice ruined – and had sent a new ambassador to England to try to mend relations with her. Stung by French success and Albany's deeds in Scotland, Henry proved easy to bait.[50] By the end of October the man who not many months before had sent Suffolk to France to plot some savage blow against Ferdinand had signed a new treaty with Ferdinand and protested love for

48. For the above, see esp. B.M. Add. 19,469, no. 3; Calig. D, vi, fols 240 ff. (*L.P.*, i, 926, 827).

49. *Ven. Cal.*, ii, 633.

50. On Henry's belligerence, see *Ven Cal.*, ii, 659, 664; *L.P.*, ii, 1113.

him that sought nothing but his prosperity. After eighteen
months of uneasy peace, an interlude largely forced on him
by circumstances, Henry was preparing to return to his first
love and reopen the ancient conflict with France.

A few days after Henry wrote to Ferdinand affirming his
complete reconciliation, one Richard Pace was dispatched
to Switzerland on an errand whose success would finally
commit England to a new enterprise across the Channel.
Pace, a humanist of some repute, had visited the Swiss
in 1514 and hired them to launch an attack on France
that was to coincide with an English invasion from the
other side, a plan which fell through when England came
to terms with France. Now, in the autumn of 1515, the idea
of employing the Swiss was revived, probably initially by the
Swiss Matthew Schiner, cardinal of Sion, a friend of Bainbridge and like him a warrior-clerk of strong anti-French
hue, and by the dispossessed duke of Milan. Neither
Schiner nor the duke had, apparently, to press very hard,
and by the end of October Pace was secretly on his way to
Switzerland to offer 120,000 crowns for a force of 20,000 to
fight as Henry directed.[51] England's treaty with Ferdinand
(and probably despite him) was a defensive one only, which
was sound enough in view of his past performance, and may
have been designed only to provide some aid for a war
against Scotland planned or mooted for the spring of 1516.[52]
Pace, however, had been sent to Zürich to raise a force
which, combined with an Imperial and perhaps a papal
army, would expel the French from Milan and cross the
Alps to invade France herself. Furthermore, said Wolsey, 'I
doubt not but that the king of England for his part will and
shall forthwith, either in his own person or with his lieutenant, invade France with an army royal.'[53] Thus another
grand design – which prudently omitted the Spaniards –

51. *L.P.*, ii, 1053; B.M. Nero B, vi, fol. 36v (*L.P.*, ii, 1065).
52. *L.P.*, ii, 1113.
53. ibid., 1095. These instructions by Wolsey to Pace make it clear
that the Swiss were to invade France once Milan had been freed.

was on hand to unhorse Francis. A new double invasion of France by the English and the Swiss, and perhaps others, was to take place and be accompanied by an English attack on Scotland. We are back in the bold days of 1513.[54]

By the end of January 1516, Pace was writing home full of optimism for the success of his mission. Maximilian, he reckoned, was ready to join in an attack on Milan. Despite French intrigues, Pace had met the Swiss diet at Zürich and was confident that their support would be forthcoming as soon as they caught sight of English cash, which had just arrived in his wake at Augsburg.[55] Hitherto he had been able to offer '*sola spes*'; now he could begin the serious work of gathering the footsoldiers for whom Maximilian was to supply cavalry and artillery. By 18 February Schiner reported to Wolsey that recruiting was going so well that he feared the allies would be swamped; that the army would soon set out; that within a month Wolsey would hear how the French had been driven out of Italy; that Maximilian would even join the invasion of France himself, and so on. Pace, Schiner and others had worked with remarkable industry – as also, it must be added, had the English ambassador with the emperor, Sir Robert Wingfield, an unconscionable jingoist of whom Pace soon fell foul.

True enough, the Swiss entered Italy quickly and, true enough, Maximilian followed hard in their wake towards Milan. By the end of March they had reached the walls of Milan itself and seemed to be within sight of their objective, the expulsion of France from North Italy. But at the moment when English efforts seemed to be on the brink of success, Maximilian suddenly retreated. Why he did so is not clear. He spluttered a long list of excuses and headed back for Trent, leaving his guns behind. The Swiss remained pressing against Milan, but the spine had been taken out of

54. But with this difference – that France was now, on paper, the pope's good friend. See *L.P.*, ii, 1729.

55. *L.P.*, ii, 1466. See *Wegg, Richard Pace* (1932), 65 ff. for a full account of this mission.

their enterprise. Moreover, they were demanding more money from England. Pace's original instructions implied that Henry would pay their wages only after they had entered France, but, in obedience presumably to later instructions, he had distributed one month's pay when they first assembled at Chur; and a second became overdue when they reached Milan. If the money did not come, he said, his life would be in peril. At last it arrived, only to be largely pilfered by Imperial troops. A third consignment was now on its way and Pace was acutely worried lest it be intercepted by the emperor as it crossed his domains. The Swiss grew increasingly anxious until, dispirited and sullen, they too abandoned the campaign and went home as soon as their final salary had been paid.[56]

What had begun rosily had thus dissolved into quarrelsome disarray. An opportunity bright enough to move an ass, said Pace,[57] let alone an emperor, had been thrown away. Pestered and bullied from all sides, even thrown into prison for a short while by the Swiss and then driven to bed by illness, Pace struggled on, determined to rebuild what had collapsed and to galvanize the so-called allies into combined action once more against France. For such was still the English plan; Henry would even yet join the Swiss in a double invasion of France. But then English policy suddenly changed. All at once Pace was told that there would be no English invasion after all and that the Swiss were on no account to chase the French across the mountains into their homeland – as, until now, he had been trying to persuade them to do. That enterprise had been hastily called off.

Though both the king and Wolsey sponsored Pace's mission, it seems that the plans for the double invasion of France by English and Swiss troops were the king's, and his alone. In a letter to Gigli of 22 May 1516, a letter in which he had no particular motive to mislead, Wolsey said that, though the king himself was ready to invade France, all his coun-

56. For Pace's account of this, see *L.P.*, ii, 1817, 1877, 1896.
57. ibid., 1754.

cillors had opposed the plan on the ground that it would be better to postpone attack until England could overwhelm France single-handed, rather than to campaign now with allies who would doubtless leave England in the lurch as they so often had done before.[58] This was written before the Swiss had abandoned the attack on Milan and made off for home; it was good sense and is the first piece of evidence that king and minister were not in accord. Then, at the end of May, letters were sent to Pace informing him of the change of plan just noted and of how his master had indeed thought again. As Wolsey put it, the king 'is minded not to prepare any army or make actual voyage into France' after all, but wanted the French merely to be driven out of Milan by Imperial and Swiss troops. The double invasion of France, from the north-west and south-east, was impracticable because, in the first place, England would have to pay for both armies, which 'is not feasible'; and, in the second, the fickle Swiss would probably abandon their friends as soon as they entered France; and besides, England could not bear the burden of mustering, transporting and feeding her own army of invasion. For these reasons then, said Wolsey, the plan in its original bold form was off.[59]

But as well as telling him this, Wolsey had a request to make of Pace which throws a precious beam of light on English policy-making and Wolsey's relations with Henry. 'By good [policy and] wise drifts', he said, Pace was to persuade the emperor and the Swiss to 'make instance to you to be a mean unto the king that they proceed no further but only into the [duchy of] Milan' and that they may be 'discharged of the persecuting of the Frenchmen into France'.[60] Pace was therefore to squeeze out of the allies a request, addressed to himself, that he should ask Henry to excuse them a major part of their undertaking. If Henry was already

58. *Martene-Durand*, iii, 1274 (*L.P.*, ii, 1928). For further evidence that Henry was intent on invasion, see L.P., ii, 1244, 1863.

59. B.M. Vit. B, xix, fols 98 ff. (*L.P.*, ii, 1943).

60. ibid., fol. 100v.

in full accord with the decision to abandon the joint invasion of France, why should Wolsey have now thought it
necessary to concoct this circuitous plan to persuade him to
accept it? It can only have been because the king had not
fully agreed to this decision, because it was something being
pressed on him, because it was hoped by this device to press
him more successfully.

It would seem, therefore, that it was Henry who proposed
the renewal of large-scale war against France and the return
of an English army across the Channel, that the plan met
hostility from the Council, including Wolsey, for reasons
just rehearsed; and that, instead, the plans for a complicated
major war were laid aside – at least until next year. Though
Wolsey could write to Pace that the king was 'right well
contented' that the Swiss should go no further than Milan,
he thereby stretched the truth.[61] So strenuously did he have
to wrestle to prevent the royal plan that he even bade Pace
fabricate an appeal from the allies that that plan be set
aside.[62]

That Wolsey opposed the king from the start of this
liaison with the Swiss is possible; that he opposed him now,
in May 1516, is very probable. But we must not overstate the
cleavage between king and minister. Wolsey was against an
invasion of France, or at least argued that it should not take
place now, adding, rather vaguely, that if all went well it
might be mounted next year. He opposed the invasion because it must be a rash and costly affair, but he was not
against hiring the Swiss to fight the French in Italy. On the

61. B.M. Vit. B, xix, fol. 231v (*L.P.*, ii, 1965).
62. It is interesting that in the letter quoted in the previous note,
Wolsey has corrected the draft in such a way that the first part, which
records all the plans for supporting the Swiss and attacking the
French next year, is written in the king's name, 'we' having been
crossed out and replaced by 'the king's grace', etc. In the second part,
'we' and 'us' are changed to 'I' and 'me'. This second half concerns
immediate arrangements for the Swiss (and only the Swiss) in their
campaign this year – all of which may be further indication of a
cleavage between Henry and Wolsey.

contrary, this was very necessary. His plan was to send back 'this Gaul into his kingdom of France' and to 'diminish the authority, strength and puissance of the said Frenchmen' by denying them Swiss support and using it to release Milan; but no more than this. He wanted the *status quo* restored and France contained – not by the direct use of English arms but, more cheaply, by Swiss. He was acting on the principle, already noted, that if peace could only be secured by fighting for it, then it was better to have the fighting done by others.

Accordingly, showing a zeal and optimism that approached the heroic, Pace went about the work of stirring the allies to 'resume their hearts and eftsoons valiantly set forth for the exterminating of the French out of Italy'.[63] More money was sent to him to distribute once the Swiss were on the move and, as ever, Pace was confident that the new campaign would be successfully launched.[64] Meanwhile English diplomacy was trying to widen its foundations by conscripting the pope, the emperor and Charles (now king of Spain) into a new league which would guarantee the Swiss an annual pension of 40,000 angels in return for their services against France.[65] The pope was nominally France's friend, but might be won over to this project; Maximilian, variable as a weather-cock, as Pace observed, was obviously susceptible to bribery; Charles would not say yes, but did not say no. English pressure upon him mounted and included an offer of cash to cover the cost of his first visit to Spain, but still he did not succumb.[66]

Instead, he suddenly wrecked Wolsey's plan for an anti-French confederacy by secretly concluding a strict treaty with Francis at Noyon in northern France – where, seven years previously, John Calvin had been born. French diplomacy thus outbid England and snatched a key figure in

63. As Wolsey said, B.M. Vit. B, xix, fol. 181 (*L.P.*, ii, 2082).
64. *L.P.*, ii, 2100.
65. B.M. Vit. B, xix, fols 181 ff. (*L.P.*, ii, 2082); *L.P.*, ii, 2087, 2151.
66. *L.P.*, ii, 2082, 2099, 2269, 2322.

Wolsey's scheme from under his nose. What was more, with Charles having defected, the pope might well decide to stand by his agreement with France, and the Swiss and Maximilian prefer discretion to valour. Charles's action, therefore, threatened to wreck English plans thoroughly. But Wolsey was brave in the moment of defeat and, running his sensitive fingers over the treaty of Noyon, quickly found flaws in it. France, he believed, had overreached herself. The anti-French league to which he aspired might yet come about; and English diplomacy went to work to create it with a will.[67] Suspiciously eager Imperial plans were taken up whereby Maximilian, now suddenly cooperative, would come to meet Henry at Calais to plot action against France, with England meeting the cost of his 'descent' into the Low Countries, as it was called;[68] in mid September that great Swiss patriot, Matthew Schiner, came to England once more to negotiate the new league and, it was said, to propose all manner of plans for war against France on three fronts, in Italy, Burgundy and Picardy, and was warmly received by Henry. Whether or not Schiner placed the mirage of a new concerted attack on France before Henry's eyes, whether, if he did, Henry liked what he saw, we cannot know. Nor can we know what Wolsey thought, though we are told that, for some reason or other, he returned home from one interview with Schiner more angry and upset than he had ever been seen before.[69]

What exactly was afoot is not clear. But in late October a league designed to contain France and provide for the maintenance of the Swiss, for which Wolsey had been working for months, was signed in London.[70] Maximilian's support had been bought at a high price; his debts to England had been wiped out, large sums of money were to be sent to him

67. B.M. Vit. B, xix, fols 267 ff. (*L.P.*, ii, 2387); B.M. Galba D, v, fol. 410 (*L.P.*, ii, 2415).

68. B.M. Vit. B, xx, fol. 9 (*L.P.*, ii, 2631); *L.P.*, ii, 2632.

69. *Ven. Cal.*, ii, 791, 793, 795.

70. *Rymer*, xiii, 556 f.

to pay both for his 'descent' and a private war of his own around Verona.[71] Smelling cash, the emperor played his part admirably. He ratified the treaty on 9 December, wearing his Garter at a splendid ceremony, and then apparently began to move towards the rendezvous which he had proposed with Henry, arriving at Trêves on 6 January 1517.[72] All this was most encouraging. So far the pope and Charles had refused to join the league against France, but if the emperor held fast they might yet fall into line.

But, if Wolsey thought that success was at hand, he was mistaken. Ignoring the plans for their 'entertainment' by the opponents of France, the Swiss quickly accepted French counter-offers, leaving Pace (and Wolsey) empty-handed. The day on which, at Hagenau, Maximilian swore on the four Gospels to observe Wolsey's new league, he received a messenger from Francis offering him at least 60,000 florins if he would enter the treaty of Noyon[73] – to which he soon agreed. He assured a Henry perplexed and 'marvellously anguished' by news of his dealings that it was the French whom he was double-crossing and that, when he and the king should meet, the whole world would see what was written on his heart and what he thought of the 'detestable' treaty of Noyon – and did this so successfully that, even as he was striding ever deeper into fraud, Henry confidently described his doings as 'drifts and inventions publicly devised by the emperor' to deceive the enemy.[74] Suddenly the crushing truth fell upon the king. On 12 February English ambassadors in the Low Countries reported that the emperor had utterly betrayed him and would certainly join the treaty of Noyon, which Charles was about to confirm and amplify. The 'descent' into the Netherlands to undo Noyon, punish Charles's 'French' ministers, meet Henry

71. *L.P.*, ii, 2501, 2652, 3106.
72. *L.P.*, ii, 2647–8, 2663, 2685, 2754–5.
73. *L.P.*, ii, 3090.
74. *L.P.*, ii, 2662, 2678, 2702, 2765, 2792; B.M. Galba B, vi, fol. 116 (*L.P.*, ii, 2719).

and plan war had been turned inside out and, instead, Noyon had been amplified, those ministers strengthened, and Maximilian pledged to meet Francis and marry a French bride. He who had been paid by Henry to come as an avenging angel against France had been turned by her into a brother-in-law with prospects of a large French dowry; and, as a final insult, by the terms of his new engagement, he was to hand over Verona to the Venetians for the sum of 20,000 florins, having a few weeks before received 40,000 florins from Henry for the defence of that city against the same Venetians.

As Wolsey had written shortly before this, the emperor 'doth play on both hands using the nature of a participle which taketh *partem a nomine et partem a verbo*'.[75] When he discovered once more the emperor's 'brittleness' and 'of what promptitude he is to sudden mutations', he was full of bitter complaint, lashing Schiner for his part in the plot and then sending the emperor so fierce a letter that the English ambassadors thought it better not to deliver it.[76] Meanwhile the villain of the piece showed no sign that his conscience troubled him. Maximilian was soon talking amiably of meeting Henry, say, at Gravelines or even Dover, and yet more remarkably, began to put out feelers for a new English loan. It is difficult to know which to admire the more: the thoroughness of his deceit or the ease with which he overlooked it. However, the emperor's blandness was not without rival. Though the latter had tricked and humiliated the king of England and made him the laughing-stock of Europe, Wolsey wrote to the ambassadors with Maximilian that they were to say that all this had left Henry merely 'somewhat pensive'.[77] This was indeed a modest reaction for a man who had failed to launch a new enterprise

75. B.M. Galba B, vi, fol. 109v (*L.P.*, ii, 2700). Cf. Knight's comment to Wolsey: 'he selleth his blood and honour for money, *L.P.*, ii, 2930.

76. *L.P.*, ii, 2958, 3106, 3126.

77. B.M. Galba B, vi, fol. 364v (*L.P.*, ii, 2958).

against France, failed to supervise the expulsion of the French from North Italy, failed to rally the great powers to an anti-French treaty, failed to halt a landslide of his friends into the French camp, failed to secure anything but transient initiative in European affairs, and failed to find a place in the sun any more distinguished than that of paymaster of the emperor, and the forgivably, but inexhaustibly, venal Swiss.

[4]

The Quest for Peace

THE Europe which England was unwilling to ignore, she was also unable to control. As a result she had been worsted and isolated by the treaty of Noyon. But Wolsey was energetic in the moment of reverse and quickly set about making up lost ground.

Before this, however, a domestic upset occurred. On 1 May 1517, henceforth known as Evil May Day, several hundred Londoners, many of them apprentices, ran amok. Stirred by preaching, mere xenophobia and what was thought to be excessive economic influence wielded by foreigners, they stormed London's streets throwing stones and sacking aliens' houses. The mob insulted the Spanish and also the Portuguese ambassador (who had arrived only that day), threatened death to the mayor and aldermen, and death also to Wolsey, whose London palace was promptly fortified. The riot was over by the evening. None, apparently, was killed, but there were many injured; and soon there were hundreds in prison.[1]

Swift punishment came upon this treasonous breach of peace with the rest of Christendom, and the quartered bodies of the ringleaders were soon on view throughout the City. Over four hundred remained in detention, some mere youths, some clerics, some women – until the queen intervened on their behalf. On bended knees before her husband (not the last time she would find herself thus) she obtained their pardon, which was later announced at Westminster Hall, at a splendid public ceremony. The hall was hung with cloth of gold and filled with the great of the realm. Wolsey opened proceedings with a long speech, to which Henry replied. Then the prisoners paraded past him,

1. *Hall*, 588 ff.; *Ven. Cal.*, ii, 876, 881–2, 887.

handcuffed and with chains about their necks, and shouting 'Mercy!' Wolsey and others now knelt before Henry, whereupon he ordered the prisoners' release.[2]

Shortly after this gracious ceremony there came another, of rather different character. Despite their recent setbacks, Henry and Wolsey continued to work for a defensive league against France. On 5 July, after England had promised a good deal of money to all her friends, that league was concluded and celebrated in London with Masses, jousts and pageants. Henry appeared throughout in astounding magnificence, now in Hungarian style, now in Turkish, now in a robe embroidered with Tudor roses of rubies and diamonds, now with a feathered hat coated with jewels, now in cloth of gold and accompanied by twenty-four trumpeters and forty gentlemen on white horses. On the last day of the celebrations, he began with a huge tournament and then proceeded to a seven-hour banquet in which almost every kind of meat and fish, and jellies galore, were eaten; and after this ordeal, which would have stunned a modern, he danced with the ladies till day-break.[3]

Wolsey had been ill in June, so ill that his life was despaired of at one time;[4] but he was up for these festivities. Shortly afterwards a very hot summer set in, following an extreme winter which saw the Thames frozen, and with it came a vicious outbreak of sweating sickness, a fever of the influenza variety. It carried off victims so quickly that, in Hall's vivid phrase, one might be 'merry at dinner and dead at supper'.[5] Henry and the court immediately sped into the country. But then a few of the Council fell ill and some pages who slept in the king's bedchamber died. Now really afraid, Henry kept on the move and admitted none to his presence save his physician, his musician and three other favourites. Wolsey remained behind in London, which wore

2. *Ven. Cal.*, ii, 887.
3. *L.P.*, ii, 3437; *Ven. Cal.*, ii, 913; *L.P.*, ii, 3446 gives the seating-plan for the feast.
4. *Ven. Cal.*, ii, 908.   5. *Hall*, 592.

the face of a dead city. Many of his household fell ill and he himself, but recently risen from sickness, survived no less than four bouts of the sweat in a few weeks.[6] He must have been a sturdy man. Then in September he did something not usually associated with him: he went on pilgrimage to Walsingham, in fulfilment of a vow – perhaps made recently when he faced death.[7]

Pope Leo X seriously desired a crusade; or rather, the pope's desire for a crusade, when it came, was serious; but it tended to come and go. It had come a few years before and it came again in 1517 when a conference of cardinals and ambassadors produced a sanguine plan for universal peace in Christendom and an all-out attempt to recover Constantinople.[8] The initial programme was circulated to heads of state for their comments. Francis gave conventional (and tardy) approval. Maximilian, who had recently had a lunatic idea to become pope and canonized saint at one blow, replaced the papal plan with a grandiose design for a huge crusade against Islam which the emperor of Abyssinia, the king of Georgia and the shah of Persia should join[9] – a plan which made Henry laugh and say 'that this should be only an expedition of money',[10] but which Leo took as encouragement. On 6 March 1518 a five-year truce was proclaimed in Rome, and on the following *Laetare* Sunday the crusade solemnly preached. Four legates had already been nominated to announce the crusade in western Europe; no less than Cajetan, for instance, to Germany, and Thomas Campeggio – who now made his début in English affairs – to this country. On 15 April he set out for England to rouse the king and nation to the holy cause.

Whatever Leo intended by all this, he probably assumed that England would be docile enough. But she was not.

6. *L.P.*, ii, 3571, 3603; *Ven. Cal.*, ii, 944, 950, 953, 958, 987.
7. ibid., 966.
8. *Pastor*, vii, 213 ff.   9. *L.P.*, ii, 3815–17.
10. P.R.O. S.P. 1/13, fol. 173v (*L.P.*, ii, 4023).

Henry proved difficult from the start, protesting that 'it was not the manner of this realm for to admit *legatos a latere*' and saying that Campeggio could enter only if his authority were strictly confined to treating of the crusade.[11] Then some further conditions were laid down. Campeggio might come in if Wolsey, too, were made a legate to act as the Italian's equal[12] – a demand which probably came from Wolsey (an exactly similar one was made on behalf of Cardinal Lang, the Imperial chancellor, and one whose career Wolsey's followed very closely, before Cajetan was permitted entry into Germany). In view of later history, it is worth noting how the king approved Wolsey's ambition. 'The king's grace,' wrote Pace, now back from Switzerland and attendant on Henry, 'hath repeated unto me again how well he is contented for the provision that your grace may be joined in commission with the legate ... and have with him equal authority.'[13] As far as Henry was concerned, Wolsey's plan did two agreeable things at once: it took the sting out of Campeggio's coming and it brought honour to a prized servant. Accordingly, when he arrived at Boulogne in early June, Campeggio had to wait while Wolsey pressed for all that he wanted from Rome. Leo succumbed at last and after some six weeks of delay, Campeggio was allowed to cross the Channel to join his brother legate.

Further humiliation awaited him. Wolsey did not intend to cooperate in the papal plan at all if he could help it. He did not intend to do so because he thought the plan worthless, or, in the more restrained contemporary language, full of 'inconvenience';[14] and because he had what he thought was a much better plan which would win back for him the initiative in European diplomacy.

The papal plan was a mirage because the machinery for

11. B.M. Vit. B, iii, fol. 245 (*L.P.*, ii, 4034). It seems from this letter that this was Henry's unprompted reaction.

12. *Martene-Durand*, op. cit., iii, 1283 (*L.P.*, ii, 4073).

13. P.R.O. S.P. 1/16, fol. 206 (*L.P.*, ii, 4055).

14. *L.P.*, ii, 4137.

keeping peace in Europe during the crusade, in particular the machinery for keeping France in restraint, was insufficient. As Henry observed, one ought to be 'more apprehensive of a certain other person than the Great Turk, of one who devises worse things against Christendom than Sultan Selim', by which he meant the king of France.[15] It was a mirage also because the powers of Europe were not really interested in a crusade. France was not; Venice was not (her commercial interest shivered at the mention of the word and she had refused the prayers ordered by Rome); England was not, because, Wolsey said, the Turks were so remote that they did not affect her.[16]

For the moment England delayed. Henry had agreed to Wolsey's plan for 'entertaining the said pope's holiness' with words which expressed enough filial loyalty to secure Wolsey his legacy without committing England to anything; and with this Leo had to be content.[17] Meanwhile Wolsey pursued his separate plans, though with his usual prudence he had ready a draft ratification by England of the five-year truce called for by the pope if his own course of action failed.[18]

Since the accession of Henry VIII, England had tried four policies towards France. She had tried fighting and this had profited nothing. She had tried to live at peace, but had failed, for a variety of reasons. She had tried fighting her indirectly through the emperor and the Swiss, and been cheated by her employees. She had tried to hem her in with a league of several powers, only to see that league collapse. The moral clearly was that she should either forget the whole matter or think again. Wolsey was already doing the latter.

15. *Martene-Durand*, iii, 1277 ff.; *Ven. Cal.*, ii, 1015.

16. *Ven. Cal.*, ii, 1072, 1086, 1111.

17 P.R.O. S.P. 1/13, fol. 173 (*L.P.*, ii, 4068); *Martene-Durand*, iii, 1277 ff., 1292 ff. (*L.P.*, ii, 3973, 4073).

18. P.R.O. S.P. 1/13, fols 162 ff. (*L.P.*, ii, 4003).

His aim was a complete Anglo-French *rapprochement* – as an initial step – that would settle the fate of Albany, Margaret of Scotland, Mary Brandon's jewels, Tournai and so on in one sweeping treaty, and be fortified with a marriage alliance – of Henry's young daughter, Mary, to the dauphin. If his plans had gone no further than this they would have been both conventional and unlikely to succeed. But this Anglo-French treaty was to be embedded in a much larger entity, namely, a treaty which all the great powers were to swear and thereby commit themselves collectively to guaranteeing peace[19] – the outlines of which had begun to take shape in Wolsey's mind by January 1518.[20]

Then, a few weeks later, came the news of Leo's scheme. This was both a threat, because an alternative, and an opportunity, because it prepared the stage for something grandiose and gave Wolsey the chance of acquiring the new authority of a legate *a latere* to place behind his own plans. Thus through 1518 he played a skilful game, appearing to follow when he was in fact leading, to cooperate when he was in fact twisting the papal design to his own prepared pattern.

On 29 July Campeggio made his solemn entry into London amidst orations, hymns and salvos of artillery. Five days later he and his brother-legate were received by the king at Greenwich and announced the purpose of their coming, to call up a crusade; to which appeal Henry replied in elegant Latin.[21] But behind all this studied grandeur, surreptitious negotiations for a different purpose were going on between Wolsey and the bishop of Paris, who had arrived in England incognito. Towards the end of September these two had made enough progress to warrant the coming of a

19. See *L.P.*, ii, 4137 and P.R.O. S.P. 1/17, fols 13 f. (*L.P.*, ii, 4357) for first sketches of the grand design.

20. The draft of the general league referred to in the previous note was headed '*Pro foedere arctiore ex quo indubitanter sequetur pax universalis*'. P.R.O. S.P. 1/17, fol. 13. Its appearance can partly be dated by a reference he apparently made to it in conversation with Giustiniani in January 1518. See *Ven. Cal.*, ii, 1002.

21. *L.P.*, ii, 4333, 4348, 4362; *Ven. Cal.*, ii, 1052–3.

formal embassy from Francis I[22] and meanwhile Wolsey had
written to the pope, the emperor and the king of Spain to
prepare for the programme which he was about to realize.[23]

On 2 October 1518 representatives of England and France
swore to his new plan for Europe – a treaty binding all the
great powers to perpetual peace and including over twenty
lesser powers, from Denmark, Portugal and the Swiss to the
dukes of Gelders and Urbino. It provided that, should any
signatory suffer aggression, the victim was to appeal to the
others, who would collectively demand the aggressor to withdraw; that, should the latter then refuse, within one month
all were to declare against him, within two months make
war by land on his nearest possessions and, within three,
make war by sea – until peace was restored and recompense
made. All were to allow the movement of others' troops
across their territories and none to permit his subjects to be
hired for use against a fellow-contrahent. Finally, any existing treaty in conflict with this was to be annulled, and this
new undertaking ratified by the principals in four months,
by the rest in eight.[24]

The remaining great powers swore to this treaty, the treaty
of London, later. Meanwhile, on 4 October, subsidiary
treaties were signed between England and France which
restored Tournai at the price of 600,000 crowns, arranged
for Mary's marriage to the dauphin and settled old privateering claims.[25] But these agreements lay below the first, the
treaty of London. This was to be the master-document,
committing Europe to a new principle in her diplomatic life,
namely, that of collective security. Europe knew well the
peace treaty between several powers, usually former combatants, but had never seen an attempt to create a treaty of
universal peace by which all the powers, in advance, swore
to punish any breach of the peace by any country. This was
a plan which Italy had tried in the second half of the

22. *L.P.*, ii, 4356, 4401; *Ven.* Cal., ii, 1074.
23. *L.P.*, ii, 4440–1, 4462.
24. *Rymer*, xiii, 624 ff.   25. ibid., 632 ff.

fifteenth century and which had been suggested for Europe
as a whole by the king of Bohemia in the 1460s – though
his scheme had gone even further and asked for a permanent European assembly, secretariat and court of justice.[26]
Wolsey did not venture as far as this, but it is possible that
his plans derive from the earlier project.

With few exceptions,[27] historians have brushed them aside
as insignificant, flamboyant verbiage. This is unjust. There
were flaws in the construction, certainly, and these showed
clearly in the following years, but they are not in themselves
evidence of dishonesty so much as of the extreme size of the
problem. Nor does Wolsey's evident desire to parade himself, nor his use of dubious methods, prove that the whole
project was fraudulent. The main treaty included such
powers as Venice, Gelders and Urbino – all trouble-makers
in the recent past. It banned hiring the Swiss, of which
England, among others, had been guilty. To secure French
friendship Wolsey had handed over Tournai, a prize that
meant a good deal to English *amour propre*, even if it was
very expensive to maintain. More important, he earnestly
tried to make his plan work. 'Nothing pleases him more than
to be called the arbiter of the affairs of Christendom,' the
Venetian ambassador declared shortly afterwards.[28] It was
true. But the failure of this vainglorious, grandiose man to
impose a new order on Europe does not mean that the
treaty of London was not a sincere attempt to banish war.
The urgent call of the Christian humanists for an end to
internecine conflict in Europe had come to a climax in recent
years and this treaty was the first practical response to it.
On 3 October 1518, to celebrate the inauguration of the new

26. Mattingly, 'An Early Non-aggression Pact', *Journal of Modern History*, x (1938), 8 f.
27. *Viz.* Busch, *Drei Jahre englischer Vermittlungspolitik* and Mattingly, art. cit. I have leaned heavily on the latter for this and previous paragraphs. Cf. his *Renaissance Diplomacy* (1955), 167 f.
28. *L.P.*, iii, 125.

programme, the king, the two cardinal legates, ambassadors and the lay and spiritual peers gathered at St. Paul's for solemn High Mass sung by Wolsey in unusual splendour. In the evening he entertained the company to a banquet which ended with a mummery in which two participants turned out to be Henry and his sister, Mary. More celebrations took place at Greenwich where Princess Mary was betrothed to the dauphin. Jousts followed – and a banquet and pageant, heavy with political meaning.[29]

Wolsey had had his way. What had begun as a plan for a five-year truce under papal auspices, to be followed by a crusade, had ended as a multilateral treaty of universal peace organized by a cardinal and concluded in London, with peace in Christendom as its objective. The crusade was given a brief, conventional mention in the preamble, and the pope named as mere '*comes*' of the contrahents, not their master. The somewhat insulting metamorphosis was the climax of Wolsey's rough handling of the papacy and, if it is too strong to describe it as a 'great blow ... struck at the international position' of Rome,[30] it was certainly disrespect for it. As the future Clement VII observed, 'from it we can see what the Holy See and the pope have to expect from the English chancellor'.[31] But on 3 December Leo meekly confirmed the treaty. By the following March, both Spain and Venice had ratified it.[32] Some while before, Bishop Fox had written to his protégé of the treaty: 'undoubtedly, my Lord, God continuing it, it shall be the best that ever was done for the realm of England; and after the king's highness, the laud and praise shall be to you a perpetual memory'.[33] Wolsey was the author of this peace, with Henry in full approval and readily wearing the guise of peacemaker of Europe.

29. *Ven. Cal.*, ii, 1085, 1088.
30. Creighton, *History of the Papacy, etc.*, iv, 253.
31. Quoted by *Pastor*, vii, 243.
32. *L.P.*, iii, 128; *Ven. Cal.*, ii, 1178, 1180, 1207.
33. *Letters of Richard Fox*, p. 112 (*L.P.*, ii, 4540).

In the Anglo-French peace of 1514, plans had been laid for a meeting between the English and French kings as the final act of reconciliation between their two realms. The proposal had survived the death of Louis XII, only to fall victim of the deterioration of relations which Francis I's accession caused. It reappeared in 1518. Included in the clutch of treaties settling particular Anglo-French questions was one providing for a meeting of Henry and Francis in the early summer of 1519.[34] However, when the time came, pressure of other business, especially the Imperial election, forced the postponement of the interview – though not before Henry, to soften the blow, had promised not to shave until the two had met (a promise which Francis quickly reciprocated).[35] Alas, this amiable vow was frustrated by Henry's wife, Catherine, who never liked her husband with a heavy beard, and in the past had 'daily made him great instance and desired him to put it off for her sake'. She apparently intervened again now. The beard came off and Anglo-French relations trembled – until it was gallantly decided that the love between Henry and Francis was 'not in the beards but in the hearts'.[36] By January 1520 Wolsey had been empowered by both kings to begin preparations for their meeting, with or without hirsute ornament.

The projected meeting not only raised problems of protocol and of transporting the king and a huge entourage across the Channel, feeding and housing them (and this was little less than the equivalent of mounting a moderate military expedition), it required the leaders of perhaps Europe's oldest enemies to come together in a solemn and public way and, surrounded by the chief of the realm, who still felt contempt and hostility for one another, to embrace and pledge their people to brotherhood. For the warrior-king of England, heir to Edward III and Henry V, to kiss Francis on the cheek was a significant act. Moreover, as if this were

34. In April 1519 Henry was reported as saying that he was about to cross the Channel. *Ven. Cal.*, ii, 1193.

35. *L.P.*, iii, 416.   36. ibid., 514.

not enough, plans for meetings multiplied. By early 1520, when Henry was due to set out for his interview with Francis, the newly-elected emperor Charles V would be returning by sea to the Low Countries from his first visit to Spain, and this opened up the possibility of a meeting *en route* between him and Henry to match that between Henry and Francis, or, indeed, even of a meeting between all three monarchs, at which the 1518 treaty could be reaffirmed – with Wolsey presiding, no doubt.[37]

This last was too ambitious and was never seriously discussed. But a meeting with Charles, before or after the meeting with Francis, was practical politics and would have the additional advantage of demonstrating England's impartiality. Both Charles and Francis disliked the idea of Henry meeting the other, but Wolsey went ahead with his plans. Moreover, Wolsey intended that, if this first experiment proved successful, the device of the personal interview by heads of state should become a regular event. Such provision was to be made for the comfort and honour of the two princes, Francis and Henry, and such care taken to avoid any jealousy between the two nations that, Wolsey said, all concerned might be 'encouraged thereby to repair to such meetings hereafter'.[38] Perhaps he thought that the treaty of London should be crowned by a 'Congress system'.

In the early autumn of 1519, probably, an invitation was made to the emperor to visit England on his return from Spain. The first plan, proposed by the English, was that he should land at Southampton, travel overland to a Kentish port and take ship to Calais in company with Henry, who would then be on his way to meet Francis. But Charles suggested instead that he should land at Sandwich in the middle of May 1520, spend a few days with Henry near by and return to the Continent independently. He was particularly

37. *L.P.*, iii, 637, 728; *Ven Cal.*, ii, 1279.
38. P.R.O. S.P. 1/19, fols 206v–7. He also noted that 'superfluous triumphs' were to be avoided for the same reason. He hardly had his way.

anxious that his meeting with Henry should precede Henry's with Francis, and thus perhaps prevent the latter taking place at all; but if he could not do this he was content to take up a suggestion of Wolsey's that he should meet Henry a second time after the Anglo-French encounter and thus, as he hoped, nullify it.[39]

By the middle of April Charles was at Corunna waiting for a wind to take him to Sandwich. Four weeks later he was still at Corunna, locked in by a strong north-easter which refused to shift. The date was 13 May and he was due at Sandwich on 15 May. Henry had consented to wait for him until the 26th – the very latest he could delay before crossing to meet Francis. Charles was busy with letters of apology, warning Wolsey against French trickery and promising him, and others of the Council, Spanish cash in the hope of preventing mischief.[40] Then suddenly the wind changed and the Imperial fleet slipped out of its prison. Late on 26 May Charles was met offshore by Wolsey, landed at Dover and repaired to the castle there. Henry sped down to meet him and arrived well into the night. He went straight to the emperor's bedroom and embraced him. Next day, which was Whit Sunday, king and emperor rode to Canterbury where Charles was magnificently received and, for the first time in his life, met his aunt, Queen Catherine, standing at the top of the marble staircase in the archbishop's palace. Henry and Charles were together less than three days, and much of this time was spent banqueting and dancing – in the latter of which Henry, but not the emperor, took part. Serious business was done one afternoon (29 May), and that evening the emperor left Canterbury. Five miles outside the city he parted company from Henry to make for Sandwich, while Henry continued on his way towards Dover and his rendezvous with the French king.[41]

Preparations had been going ahead fast for this meeting since March, so that when Charles eventually landed at

39. *L.P.*, iii, 551, 689, 728; *Sp. Cal.*, ii, 274; cf. *Ven. Cal.*, iii, 41.
40. *L.P.*, iii, 787–8, 803.   41. *Ven. Cal.*, iii, 50, 53.

Dover he ran into a huge expedition, composed of the flower
of the nation, male and female, now being marshalled towards France and the Field of Cloth of Gold. That the
emperor's visit, in doubt until the moment it happened and
requiring swift provision of accommodation and state banquets, did not de-rail the other operation is another measure
of Wolsey's capacity for organization and of the competence
of early Tudor administration.

Over five thousand persons made up the suites of Henry
and his queen. Hundreds of pounds' worth of velvet, sarce-
net, satin, cloth of gold and doublets, bonnets, shirts and
boots were supplied for them. They had to be gathered at
Dover, shipped over the water, given lodgings at Calais and
then Guines. Hundreds of tents and pavilions were sent over,
together with enough food for men and beasts, and mountains of plate, cutlery and glass. Six thousand men were busy
preparing the English quarters. At least two thousand from
England and Flanders – masons, carpenters, glaziers, etc. –
were at work converting Guines Castle and building a summer palace next to it of fairy-tale magnificence for the main
entertainments. They had started work on 19 March. Tim-
bers so long that no ship could carry them were lashed together and floated to Calais from Holland. The foundations
of the palace were of brick, above was timber and canvas.
Within lay the banqueting hall, pantry, cellar, chapel and so
on – elaborately furnished with Tudor roses and king's
beasts. Outside, like a fleet in full sail, stood the tents and
pavilions for the rest of the English company. Exactly half-
way between Guines and Ardres, in the palm of a shallow
dip called Val d'Or (which may have helped to name the
meeting), was the spot where Anglo-French commissioners
had carefully agreed that the two kings should meet. The
sides of the valley, from which they would first see each
other, were re-shaped so as to give neither side the advantage
of height or width. Near by, a sumptuous pavilion was set
up, as well as lists and galleries for the chivalrous enter-

tainment which was to follow the meeting and for which a field surrounded by a nine-foot rampart had been prepared.[42]

Wolsey's hands guided all this. He compiled the programme of events and drew the plans for the tournament field. He dealt with all the queries concerning the buildings, worried whether it would be cheaper to buy the flour in England or at Calais, whether there would be enough beer and wine, green geese, rabbits, storks, quails and cheese, enough fuel for the kitchens. As well as all this he had to prepare for Charles's visit and satisfy him that nothing prejudicial to him would come from Henry's visit to France, while assuring Francis that Charles's visit to England would not impair Anglo-French relations.[43] Two days after Charles and Henry parted, the twenty-odd miles of sea between Dover and Calais were filled with a great concourse of ships carrying the king and queen and their suites to France – leaving England emptied of most of its nobility, hierarchy, courtiers, precious stuffs, jewels and high-born women. All were shipped to France.

Shortly after Henry arrived at Calais, which was now in near-pandemonium as folk from round about flocked in to see the sights and get drunk on free wine, Francis came to the small town of Ardres, a few miles from Guines and just inside the French frontier. There, too, workmen had been busy refurbishing the castle and putting up pavilions, including one for the king that was so vast that it shortly succumbed to a high wind. Wolsey came quickly to Francis to make last-minute plans for the interview and an embassy from Francis arrived at the same time in Calais. On 5 June Henry set out for Guines, on the edge of the English pale.

42. *L.P.*, iii, 702, 704, 869, 870, etc.; *Ven. Cal.*, iii, 53, 57 ff.; *The Chronicle of Calais*, Camden Society (1846), 18; Anglo, 'Le Camp du Drap d'Or et les Entrevues d'Henri VIII et de Charles Quint', *Fêtes et Cérémonies au Temps de Charles Quint* (Paris, 1959), 116 ff.

43. *L.P.*, iii, 685, 747, 821, 851. See *L.P.*, iii, 919, for a list of food provided by the English – including 700 conger eels, 2,014 sheep, 26 dozen heron, 4 bushels of mustard and £1 os. 10d.-worth of cream for the king's cakes.

Two days later, *Corpus Christi* day, cannon sounded at the appointed hour on both sides to announce to each king the other's departure, and Henry and his company rode off to the edge of the Field of Cloth of Gold. When he reached the slight eminence on his side of the field he stopped. Francis was halted at the other side. The two kings stood still and silent, with their suites drawn up around them as if in battle array. Then trumpets sounded. Both kings spurred their horses, galloped forward to the agreed point – marked by a spear stuck in the ground – and embraced two or three times, still in the saddle and bonnets in hand. Then they dismounted, embraced again and went into the pavilion. After they had spoken a little they signalled their lords to come forward and embraced each other's graciously.[44]

In the following days there was much good cheer. Henry and Francis set out from Guines and Ardres respectively to dine with the other's queen, they jousted and tilted without a break for nearly a fortnight, apart from one day when high winds made tilting impossible and instead they wrestled and danced. In all this Henry took superlative pleasure, except at that anxious moment when Francis threw him at wrestling. At last, on Saturday 23 June, the sport came to an end. An open-air altar was set up and, before the two kings and numerous ambassadors, Wolsey sang Solemn High Mass. Two choirs took part, one English, one French, each accompanied by the other's organist. The sermon was on peace. On the following day came the last banquets, the exchange of presents and farewells. The two kings vowed to build a chapel to our Lady of Peace on the spot where they had met, and parted.[45]

Henry now returned to Calais for another state function. Before the emperor parted from Henry nearly a month before it had been decided that, because of the shortness of this first encounter, the two sovereigns should meet a second time immediately after the Field of Cloth of Gold.

44. *L.P.*, iii, 869, 870; *Ven. Cal.*, iii, 68, 69.
45. *Ven. Cal.*, iii, 95.

Accordingly, about a fortnight after he had left Francis, Henry was riding to Gravelines to meet Charles and the Archduchess Margaret. He stayed there forty-eight hours and then, on 12 July, came back to Calais with Charles and Margaret to a palace recently built on a site specially cleared of its houses.[46] Charles stayed two days, was most handsomely entertained in a splendid circular banqueting hall within the palace (until, like the French king's pavilion, this too was damaged by wind) and did some serious talking. He left on 14 July. Henry returned to England soon after, with Wolsey following behind. Six weeks of intense activity left both in the mood for quieter things. For the rest of the summer Henry hunted from dawn to dusk in the West Country; Wolsey went on another pilgrimage to Walsingham – leaving London to the plague and those who could not afford to leave.[47]

It is easy to dismiss the Field of Cloth of Gold as vain posturing, as a huge, expensive game, as a Renaissance folly. But this is probably wrong. What contemporaries extravagantly described as the eighth wonder of the world and what has often since been discounted as mere play-acting was designed to bring the chivalries of two nations together to joust and tilt, feast and dance – instead of to fight. Anti-French feeling was deeply embedded in some Englishmen, including Henry. 'These sovereigns', said a Venetian, 'are not at peace ... they hate each other cordially' – and on his return to England from this meeting a brother of the marquis of Dorset was heard to say to a fellow that, if he had a drop of French blood in his body, 'he would cut himself open and get rid of it'; to which the other replied 'so would I'.[48] This was the kind of animosity against which Wolsey strove. A start had been made. Old enemies had mingled and despite anxious moments – when, for instance, the two columns of English and French

46. Anglo, art. cit., 127 f. for a description of this pavilion.
47. *Ven. Cal.*, iii, 115.   48. ibid., 108, 119.

approached for their first meeting and there were fears
that the French intended an ambush, or when they stood
facing one another in tense silence across the Field – they
had tasted friendship and taken part in a solemn act of
reconciliation. With some justice the lords of the Council
left behind to govern England in Henry's absence wrote
of this meeting that 'the like whereof heretofore have not
yet been brought to effect and purpose by any other of your
noble progenitors'.[49]

More than once it has been said that for Henry to have
met both Charles and Francis was deceitful. But to balance
the meeting with one by meeting the other was to observe,
not offend, the spirit of the treaty of 1518. It has been
further suggested that, when he met Charles, Henry committed himself to betray the French king whom he had
recently embraced. But at neither meeting did Henry do
anything that was contrary to the treaty of 1518 or secretly
engage to disown one whom he had just met. With Francis
he ratified a marriage treaty concluded in 1518. With
Charles he agreed that neither side should conclude any
closer matrimonial alliance with France than now existed,
that deputies should meet at Calais to discuss Anglo-
Imperial matters and ambassadors be exchanged.[50] But this
was not to infringe any previous understanding and, what
was more, Charles's subsequent attempts to lure England
into close alliance against France met with rebuff.

England studiously observed the spirit and letter of her
treaty. Charles was told that if France invaded Naples all
the confederates would rally to his defence. When Charles
asked a little later if England would help against Gelders
he was told that this matter was already provided for by
the treaty. When Leo suggested a league with France
against Charles he was refused, and when, later, he suggested an exactly opposite course of action, namely, a com-

49. *L.P.*, iii, 896.
50. ibid., 914. At the Canterbury meeting Henry and Charles had
apparently reaffirmed the treaty of 1518.

bined assault on France, he was refused again – and emerged from all this an angry man.[51]

But it was the Emperor Charles who most felt the firmness of England's new policy. Within a short while of entering the treaty of universal peace (which he had not sworn with any enthusiasm) he was trying to draw England into an explicitly anti-French alliance against the day when Francis would break loose again. He probably attempted this at Canterbury; he certainly did so at Calais. But Henry refused to listen 'to any such exhortation tending to the violation of his said promise'.[52] On both occasions Henry was urged to break the marriage contract between Mary and the dauphin, and refused; and until the end of 1521 pressure was continually being applied on England to side openly with the emperor, but to no effect.[53]

Indeed, her policy during these months acquired a new clarity and simplicity of aim, thanks, curiously, to the coming of Charles V to the Empire. Before this event there were four major powers in western Europe – France (the most formidable), Spain, the Empire and England. Following the union, in 1519, of Spain and the Empire in the person of Charles, there were three. Of these three, two appeared to be of roughly equal weight, namely, France and the newly-formed Habsburg colossus. The third was therefore in a peculiarly influential position, or could easily believe herself to be. Her alliance would bestow dominance, while her neutrality could, in theory, guarantee peace. If she were committed to fighting either of the other two who was guilty of breaking the peace, she could make aggression an act of insanity. As Wolsey never tired of pointing out, although Henry was bound to Charles 'by good peace,

51. *L.P.*, ii, 4553; iii, 344; *Sp. Cal.*, ii, 283, 288, 289. When Henry heard in late 1520 of a papal plan to overcome Ferrara he protested that he had included Ferrara in the treaty of 1518. *Ven. Cal.*, iii, 141.

52. P.R.O. S.P. 1/21, fol. 23v (*L.P.*, iii, 936).

53. *L.P.*, iii, 922, 1213; P.R.O. S.P. 1/21, fol. 258 f. (*L.P.*, iii, 1214); *L.P.*, iii, 1150, 1162, etc.

fraternal love and consanguinity', yet there were 'such
great concordances ... in personages, appetites and manners' between Henry and Francis that friendship with
France was for Henry 'the most principal and imprinted in
his heart and affection'.[54] If Henry was Charles's kinsman
and 'uncle' he was also Francis's brother and ally, and so
on.[55] England was the real, whole-hearted friend of both,
but in virtue of the treaty of 1518 she was the potential
enemy of either, if either broke the peace. Her policy was
not, therefore, to create a balance of power, for a balance
seemed already to exist; but rather to act as a third party
who would be prepared to upset that balance and swing
it heavily against either of the other two great powers. If
anything, this was a policy of imbalance[56] and, since it was
thought that neither of the others would risk incurring
such a heavy penalty for aggression, it seemed that England
had it in her grasp to impose peace, albeit the peace of
stalemate, upon Europe, and to acquire that dominance
to which her chancellor unceasingly aspired.

Wolsey saw how kind fate had been to his plans and to
England, and quickly tried to exploit the influence thrust
upon, as well as constructed by, him. During 1520 relations
between France and the Empire worsened. France was
clearly provoking war and Charles inevitably replied with
counter-threats. England's part was clear. As the two combatants crouched to spring – to 'be at a pick', as Wolsey
said – Henry must 'pass between and stay them both'.[57]
Accordingly, Charles was implored to hold his hand and
not to march to Rome 'with puissance', as somewhat pro-

54. B.M. Calig. D, vii, fol. 150 (*L.P.*, iii, 416).

55. *Ven. Cal.*, iii, 135. For words exactly similar and addressed to
Charles's ministers, see *L.P.*, iii, 403, 689.

56. Busch's term *'Vermittlungspolitik'* exactly describes it. We
might translate this as 'middlemanship'. For good evidence of English
impartiality, see the reply to Francis that English ambassadors would
only appear with his in public in Rome if the Imperial ambassador
was in their company. P.R.O. S.P. 1/21, fol. 27v (*L.P.*, iii, 936).

57. *L.P.*, iii, 1213.

vocatively he planned to do, in order to receive his crown, but to use 'peaceable and politic ways, without hostility'.[58] To France, a rapid succession of embassies was sent to try to cure her king of his wantonness, begging him not to provoke the emperor and not to go to Italy, as he also provocatively intended, save 'for his pastime'. Francis was reminded of the huge dangers of war; Charles that his problems in Spain and Germany were sufficient problems for the moment. Each was urged, with equal force, to keep off the plain of Lombardy and each was repeatedly and solemnly warned that whoever broke the peace would *ipso facto* draw upon himself the hostility of England. 'The king will not fail to give aid and assistance to the French king against the emperor if he invade him, according to the treaty [*sc.* of 1518]; so must his grace be driven of necessity to assist the said emperor against the French king's invasion.' Thus Francis was informed in March 1521. A few weeks later Charles was told that if war broke out Henry would be bound 'to give aid and assistance either to the one party or the other'.[59]

But although England's policy was unambiguous, it was unsuccessful. Border incidents multiplied and, stung by undoubted French aggression, Charles prepared to strike back in Italy, the Pyrenees and Flanders. European peace was crumbling like a sand-castle in a swift-advancing tide, and it was only a matter of weeks, apparently, before it would be finally engulfed. Moreover, Charles had called upon England to discharge her treaty obligations against an obvious aggressor.[60]

For three years Henry had diligently praised and preached peace.[61] His actions – above all on the Field of

58. P.R.O. S.P. 1/21, fol. 24 (*L.P.*, iii, 936); fols 255 f. (*L.P.*, iii, 1212).
59. ibid., fols 256 f.; P.R.O. S.P. 1/22, fol. 31 (*L.P.*, iii, 1212, 1270). For other statements of the same policy, see *L.P.*, iii, 922, 936, 1283; *Ven. Cal.*, ii, 1259; iii, 195; *Sp. Cal.*, ii, 288.
60. *L.P.*, iii, 1315, 1318, 1326, etc.
61. For typical examples, see *L.P.*, iii, 689; *Ven Cal.*, iii, 60, 184.

Cloth of Gold – had proclaimed the new man yet more loudly. We may brush aside his many effusive utterances in praise of peace as *vox et praetera nihil*, and to do so seems realistic; but it is also to fly in the face of the evident zeal on the speaker's part and the conviction of professional diplomats who heard him that he spoke from the heart.[62] For three years he had played the part of peacemaker with earnest energy. There was nothing insincere or half-hearted in his performance of this role, or indeed of any of the other roles which he would play; its only defect was its inevitable instability. By instinct and by treaty, Henry was embroiled in Europe's affairs, and now that the continent was plunging back into war the erstwhile devotee of peace must be irresistibly drawn into the mêlée.

When he first heard of open hostility between Francis and Charles, and that the latter was backed by the pope, he 'did utterly determine himself to join with his holiness and the emperor'.[63] So the pope was categorically informed by the English agent in Rome, John Clerk, who added that when the matter was discussed by Henry and his Council 'therein there was some difficulty' found, such as the huge cost of the expedition which would be needed, the lateness of the year and so on. All this was probably a specially prepared account of what happened, designed to assuage a pope who was urgent that England should join the fray on his side; though it may be true, as the letter suggests, that Henry had wanted war and that he was advised against it by the Council. We cannot be sure. However, Clerk goes on to say what happened next. 'The king's grace with his Council had further devised' that Henry should offer to mediate between the disputants, thus postponing England's entry into the war 'until a more convenable season', and that a new treaty should be concluded with the emperor to

62. E.g. *Ven. Cal.*, ii, 1259, 1271, 1279, 1298.
63. B.M. Vit. B, iv, fol. 180v (*L.P.*, iii, 1574). This passage is in code, which I have deciphered with a key of my own devising. The date of the letter is 14 September 1521.

give England greater security for this enterprise. Hence it had been decided that Wolsey should go to Calais, nominally as the king's lieutenant to mediate, in fact to conclude an offensive alliance with Charles against France.[64]

If Henry spoke as Clerk reported, then, technically, he was in the right. Francis had manifestly broken the peace and England was bound to take up arms against him – after the prescribed warning had been given. But apparently the Council had set aside this fact and persuaded Henry to pretend to mediate and thus win extra time. The idea of English arbitration was not new. Since the middle of 1520 Wolsey had been talking about converting England's *de facto* position of mediator of Europe into something more precise by persuading the great powers to commission him to preside over some sort of international court with power to settle disputes – rather as the blue-print which he may have followed had envisaged.[65] How far he had gone with this ambitious plan is not clear. But by May 1521, to prevent 'the effusion of Christian blood ... the consuming of treasure, subversion of realms, depopulation and desolation of countries and other infinite inconveniences', a firm offer was made by England to mediate between Francis and Charles.[66] However, what was proposed now by the Council was a scheme for violence, not arbitration. Seemingly Wolsey was prepared to pervert his plans and, under the cloak of mediation, cynically plot war. He did go to Calais. He went, as he said, to mediate. Within a few days he had left the conference to visit Charles at Bruges where he concluded the secret treaty against France which the Council had asked for. He then returned to Calais in order, as he said, that the French should not suspect that the English had joined hands with Charles. When the negotiations had failed or, as some would say, a sufficient amount

64. ibid., fols 180v–181v. Cf. Wolsey's letter in *St.P.*, i, 17 (*L.P.*, iii, 1383).
65. *Sp. Cal.*, iii, 285, 288; *Ven. Cal.*, iii, 98. See above, p. 105.
66. P.R.O. S.P. 1/22, fol. 32v (*L.P.*, iii, 1270).

of time had been wasted, he returned home with the most complete deceit of his life accomplished, and a farcical, Machiavellian conference behind him.

But can this be so? Would Wolsey have thrown away so much so quickly?[67] If England simply wanted a new treaty with Charles there was no need for the elaborate subterfuge (which would have deceived no one) of the conference at Calais, and no need for Wolsey to return to it after concluding the treaty with Charles. If that treaty had to be secret, as it did, it would have been far more efficiently done by swift, inconspicuous embassies than by a cardinal legate publicly travelling to Bruges to negotiate it. If the conference was held merely for the sake of prestige it is incredible that it should have been allowed by its author to cost him so much of his time, his health and money. If Wolsey's aim was entirely base then, it must be said, he went to extraordinary and inept lengths to secure it. The French ambassadors at Calais believed that his purpose was sincere and confidentially informed their king that Wolsey was his friend, even after his visit to Bruges; and the papal envoy at the conference, Contarini, was similarly convinced.[68] Wolsey took with him to Calais several councillors, including Tunstal and More. It is not easy to believe that the latter would have been an accessory to an unblushing diplomatic fraud of this kind which he belaboured so indignantly a few years before in his *Utopia*.[69] There was vainglory and deceit in this story, but not the villainy often alleged. Wolsey fought to preserve what he had built, and failed; but he failed because others never seriously intended that he should succeed, not because he did not try.

Wolsey would have agreed with the reasons which, according to Clerk, were presented in the Council against the

67. As he himself observed. *L.P.*, iii, 1556.

68. *L.P.*, iii, 1467, 1513, 1555 (cf. *Sp. Cal.*, ii, 368); *Ven. Cal.*, iii, 302.

69. A culpable accessory, too, since, in conversation with Contarini, More said that peace between Francis and the emperor was England's purpose. *Ven. Cal.*, iii, 302.

king's plan for immediate military intervention, even if he did not put them forward himself. With the time thus gained he set about persuading the combatants to 'compromit' their dispute to the diet, as it will be called, or conference. Francis eventually agreed, very grudgingly and in deference, he said, to his mother.[70] Charles proved equally intractable and argued that England's duty was to declare here and now for the Imperial cause, not to act as arbiter.[71] But so urgent was it to win his consent that Wolsey at last entered into a desperate bargain. In return for the presence of Imperial commissioners at the diet, Wolsey agreed that, while at Calais, he would go to the emperor and conclude the new military alliance which had been in the offing for months. As far as Charles was concerned, the conference would be a formality, with his commissioners merely going through the motions of negotiation. The plot was Charles's suggestion and Wolsey accepted it.[72] He had no alternative.

In that the Imperial presence at the diet had thus been bought, there was now a slight chance of its success. Wolsey therefore went to Calais knowing that the emperor and the pope regarded it as a game which had to be played to gratify the author and mislead the king of France, knowing also that, sooner or later, he must conclude the Anglo-Imperial treaty, and yet still hoping that he might succeed. He let Charles think that he was a whole-hearted accomplice to his plot. He let the pope think so.[73] He was probably deceiving both and hoping to outwit both, as well as to coax France into obedience to his arbitration. To secure all this he carried to Calais an omnibus collection of commissions from his king: one to mediate between the combatants, another to conclude a treaty with the emperor against Francis, another to treat for a closer amity with France

70. *L.P.*, iii, 1338, 1347, 1357, 1382, 1385, etc.

71. ibid., 1352, 1371, 1395, etc.

72. ibid., 1340, 1362. Cf. ibid., 1421, 1422 and *St.P.*, i, 21 (*L.P.*, iii, 1439).

73. B.M. Vit. B, iv, fols 181v–182 (*L.P.*, iii, 1574).

against the emperor, a fourth to treat for a confederation of
the pope, emperor and the king of France.[74]

Though Henry had publicly agreed that English intervention should be withheld until the new Anglo-Imperial
treaty was concluded, he was anxious to prepare for war at
once and awaited the offensive treaty with Charles eagerly.[75]
When Charles asked for several thousand archers from
England, Wolsey would not let them go, for, as two councillors said to Henry, 'it were a manifest derision to treat
of peace and to send men, at the same time, to make
actual war'. At first, Henry, who was then trapped indoors
at Windsor by violent summer storms, agreed, saying of
Charles's request for immediate English military action,
'*beati qui audiunt et non intelligunt*'.[76] But then he changed
his mind and was persuaded by Imperial pressure to send
six thousand archers to Calais (presumably) to wait there
until Wolsey had conducted his negotiations with Charles
– whereupon a sharp, intriguing squabble developed between Henry and Wolsey over who should lead this contingent: a marquis or an earl, as, typically, Henry wanted,
or someone of lesser and cheaper rank, a mere knight like
the treasurer of Calais, as Wolsey, equally typically, preferred. And while this squabble was afoot, others grew up
alongside. Henry complained that it was now too late in
the year for the archers to be put to good use – implying
that Wolsey had been dilatory – and then produced the
curious argument that so large a body, as he knew from
experience in the last war, could never 'shoot together unless one should slay another' – a judgement which was
presumably as valid when he first agreed to send the men as

74. *L.P.*, iii, 1443.

75. So Pace to Wolsey in *St. P.*, i, 23 (*L.P.*, iii, 1440). Henry was here
reported as hoping that Wolsey would bring everything between him
and the emperor to 'the desired effect and conclusion . . . considering
the great towardness of the said emperor thereunto'. There was only
one thing that Charles wanted, and which Henry is here said to want
also, namely, the Anglo-Imperial treaty.

76. *St.P.*, i, 16 f. (*L.P.*, iii, 1429).

it was now; and, as well as this, he made difficulties about transporting them and supplying them.[77] In short, he found all manner of things to complain about and complained so tenaciously that it is difficult to avoid the impression that he was arguing for the sake of arguing, because Wolsey had somehow crossed or defeated him. This is the first recorded fracas between the two – a first flicker of mistrust.

By now, Henry had washed his hands of the whole idea of an expeditionary force of archers – despite his early enthusiasm for it[78] – and toyed instead with another project. If there were to be no campaign by land, let there be one by sea. Let his ships destroy the French navy as it lay in harbour, thus clearing the way for next year's expedition. Now it was Wolsey's turn to object. The project was far beyond England's resources. She had not the ships for it. The king must stay his hand. And he did. Moreover, as a preliminary to this renewal of the 'forward' policy, Henry had apparently told Wolsey to recall the English ambassador in France. Wolsey did not do so, and again, it seems, Henry acquiesced.[79]

Henry spoke openly of his intended campaign to recover his rightful inheritance in France, saying that French aggression left him free to declare war whenever he pleased.[80] He rejoiced to hear that France was short of money and, when he heard that Charles wanted powder, swore by St George that he would not lack it.[81] But Wolsey reined him back. And when he could not restrain directly, he seems to have parried. On the one hand, he countenanced the king's belligerence, approving 'your intended enterprise', maybe only to humour him, though insisting that

77. *St.P.*, i, 23, 30, 32 ff.; P.R.O. S.P. 1/23, fols 17 ff. (*L.P.*, iii, 1440, 1462, 1474, 1488).
78. It is worth noting that Wolsey had looked on the archers as a way 'to cause outward princes the rather to condescend to peace'. P.R.O. S.P. 1/23, fol. 19 (*L.P.*, iii, 1488).
79. ibid. Cf. *L.P.*, iii, 1448, 1454.
80. *St.P.*, i, 23, 36 (*L.P.*, iii, 1440, 1474).
81. *L.P.*, iii, 1519, 1536.

nothing overt be done until next year; on the other, he
went to Calais bent on pacifying Europe so that the new
Anglo-Imperial treaty would be a dead letter and next year
there would be no fighting to be done. On one occasion he
certainly let Henry think that the Calais conference was a
mere charade; and yet, having nominally gone there to
promise military aid to Charles in the king's name, he
could also say, to the English ambassadors in France, 'I
doubt not but, by the means thereof [i.e. Francis's coopera-
tion] and other good persuasions, to put over the giving of
the said assistance.'[82] There is no question of Wolsey having
deceived the king, but it is quite clear that he and Henry
were not moving in the same direction and that Wolsey
was partly working behind his master's back – as he had
done in 1516.[83]

It was remarkable that Wolsey should dare to do this.
But he was now at the height of his powers and confidence,
and, furthermore, Henry was not difficult to manoeuvre.
A few days after his aggressive talk about invasion and
smashing the French fleet at anchor, he was lost to state
business. The summer had recovered; Henry was hunting
at Windsor;[84] and the silence of the king was the liberty of
the minister. But Henry's defeat must not be made larger
than it was. Wolsey's subtleties were neither entirely unnoticed nor challenged. The squabble mentioned above
was born of discontent or suspicion and it was followed soon
after by another, in which Henry showed that he sensed
the differences of intention between himself and the chancellor, and doubted the latter's judgement.

Wolsey landed at Calais on 2 August 1521, bringing with
him the great seal of England and about a dozen of the
more effective privy councillors. Having thus taken the
main-spring out of English government and set it down in
Calais, he plunged into the business of the diet which he

82. *St.P.*, i, 27, 46; vi, 75 f., 86 (*L.P.*, iii, 1462, 1523, 1393, 1515).
83. Above, p. 91.   84. *L.P.*, iii, 1459.

had convened. The Imperial embassy, led by the chancellor, Gattinara, soon arrived, demanding as they came that England should declare against France at once and Wolsey go straight to Charles to conclude the promised treaty.[85] Shortly afterwards the French deputation, headed by du Prat, another chancellor, arrived, and then the papal nuncio, Contarini. Even now the war was getting into its stride, in northern France, Navarre and Milan. Wolsey had hoped for an abstinence from war during the conference, but the Imperial ambassadors had no power to conclude this and it was clear that the diet would be a fiasco unless the lack were remedied. Hence, after stiff bargaining had settled most of the details, Wolsey at last succumbed to the Imperial demand that he should set out for the emperor and clinch the treaty. He arrived at Bruges, where Charles had been waiting for several days, on 14 August, having told the French envoys whom he left behind at Calais that he went to persuade the emperor to agree to peace talks and send his chancellor, and the others, sufficient powers to conclude a truce. He wrote to Henry that he had sold this story to the French 'for a colour', to allay their suspicion, and that he had found them agreeably easy to deceive.[86]

Eleven days later he had negotiated the new Anglo-Imperial treaty. Charles had made his last effort to secure the immediate entry of England into the conflict. But, by the terms of this treaty, he would have to wait until May 1523 for the double campaign led by Henry and Charles to be mounted – that is, some twenty-two months hence. Provided that present hostilities had not ended by the coming November, England must declare war on France and launch a small naval campaign against her in 1522.[87] Charles had largely had his own way, for England was now pledged to war; but so too had Wolsey, for the pledge was not to be redeemed for nearly two years, and between now and then a good deal could happen. There was still a chance

85. *St.P.*, i, 27 ff. (*L.P.*, iii, 1462).   86. *L.P.*, iii, 1480, 1493.
87. *L.P.*, iii, 1493. *Sp. Cal.*, ii, 355 for text of treaty.

that the Calais conference would succeed because, in return
for Wolsey's concessions, Charles had agreed to give powers
to his representatives at Calais to treat for a truce. At
Bruges, therefore, Wolsey had made another bargain and,
for the price of an obligation to be discharged in a remote
future, frantically bought yet more time. The treaty destroyed England's mediatory position, which is why it was
kept secret, but it was a hollow victory for the Imperialists.
Moreover, it was not signed until 24 November, that is,
until after the conference had failed.[88]

On 26 August Wolsey was back at Calais to resume the
conference. Discussion proceeded in two directions – in
search of a maritime armistice for the sake of merchants
and fishermen; to discover which of the combatants broke
the peace first and which should therefore sue for an abstinence. Both, especially the last, provoked intricate debate,
occupying the delegates for session upon session – until the
whole discussion had grown so heated and involved that
Wolsey put a stop to plenary meetings and dealt with the
two sides separately.[89]

It was while he was at Calais that his altercation with
Henry occurred concerning the archers to be sent to the
emperor. It ended when Henry heard the news of the
treaty concluded at Bruges, which drew from him a lavish
flow of praise for the minister's good judgement, reliability
and application, as well as some shrewd amendments of the
text of the treaty.[90] Within a few days, however, another,
and more bitter, dispute was brewing. Suit had been made
to the king, we are told, by the English merchants who
sailed each autumn to Bordeaux to ship back wine, 'for to
know his mind and pleasure whether they shall do so or not'
this autumn in view of the danger of French privateers.
Henry professed himself unable to decide and passed the
matter to Wolsey, pointing out as he did so that these
English merchants had considerable assets at Bordeaux

88. See *L.P.*, iii, 1816, 1802.   89. *L.P.*, iii, 1816–17.
90. *St.P.*, i, 45 (*L.P.*, iii, 1519); *St.P.*, i, 49 (*L.P.*, iii, 1539).

which they would do well to get home before news of the
Anglo-Imperial treaty reached French ears, that, were the
ships not to sail, the French would get suspicious and that,
on the other hand, the ships' loss would be a blow to
English naval power. Wolsey was 'maturely to examine and
debate the foresaid doubts', and then tell him what to say.
A long reply was soon on its way from Wolsey urging that
the ships should sail as usual, on the grounds that Francis
was so occupied in Italy, Navarre and Picardy that he would
not want to acquire new enemies and that the English
would surely be well treated by the French. The letter went
on to say that, to make doubly sure, the French chancellor
had been persuaded to issue a placard, or proclamation,
that no one should touch English goods or ships under pain
of death. Wolsey was confident that the merchants would
be safe, but suggested that the number and size of their
ships might be restricted, and the Englishmen be licensed
to import wine in strangers' holds. Such was his reply, made,
it should be noted, in the midst of a gruelling conference.[91]
As soon as he received it Henry disapproved, though he
did not bring himself to writing personally to Wolsey, being
prevented yesterday, as Pace mischievously observed in a
letter to Wolsey, by the 'saying of his matins *in honorem
Divae Virginis;* and this day by harts and hounds'. Instead,
Henry communicated through Pace that he would regard
any French promises, proclamations, placards and the rest
as worse than valueless – as 'lures and allectives to bring
his said navy and subjects into danger' – and that to restrict
trade as Wolsey suggested would 'raise a murmur' among
his subjects. He also complained that the English ambassador in France had reported that Francis had promised to
give battle to the Imperial army shortly and had not done
so – as if this was the ambassador's fault.[92] To all this Wolsey

91. *St.P.*, i, 47 (*L.P.*., iii, 1533); *L.P.*, iii, 1544.
92. *St.P.*, i, 51 (*L.P.*, iii, 1558). The letter was written on 9 September, the day after the feast of the Immaculate Conception. Hence
Henry's distraction.

replied firmly. 'In vain shall it be further to study other
remedies' in the matter of the Bordeaux vintage; he could
only ask the king to trust his judgement. But, he added
rather tartly, if, after the proclamation had been granted,
Henry should order the ships to stay away, 'distrust and
jealousy shall follow'; and when 'good faith shall be once
excluded and taken away, I see no more remedy'. As for the
ambassador's slight lapse, 'I verily believe that . . . as a faithful gentleman he reported no less than the French king
spoke'; and so on.[93]

Henry's reply came back swiftly. He has 'groundly
pondered' Wolsey's last letter, as well he might, and does
'somewhat marvel' at its contents. If Wolsey accuses *him*
of lack of trust, let him know that the king has his full
measure of this virtue, indeed is inclined 'to trust where
other men hath great diffidence'. Wolsey has underesti-
mated the dangers to the English ships, the cruelty of the
French and their perfidy. Anyway, the merchants have
decided of their own will to stay at home. Wolsey claims
that Francis does not suspect England, but the evidence
points to the contrary. Restitution by the French for acts
of piracy is not (as he claims) proof of goodwill but the
result of having the guilty parties brought before Wolsey
himself and compelled to make reparation; and nevertheless the king has suffered loss of customs thereby. And so
the letter goes on, accusing and liverish.[94]

Clearly there was more involved here than the particular
issue of the merchants and their wine. While Wolsey wanted
to avoid anything which suggested international tension,
Henry did not wish to pretend that all was normal and was
impatient with Wolsey's methods, convinced that England
was falling a victim of French guile and that Wolsey was
misleading him. He mis-read Wolsey's letters, but he was
right in sensing that something was out of joint at Calais.
It was as though he had caught a trusted servant, to whom

93. *St.P.*, i, 55 (*L.P.*, iii, 1577).
94. *St.P.*, i, 58 ff. (*L.P.*, iii, 1594).

he had granted remarkable freedom of action, in the midst of some dubious transaction. Probably he could not frame a precise charge against him but, smelling disingenuousness, struck out petulantly with any stick that came to hand.

To Henry's cutting remarks Wolsey replied with a long, firm letter in which he set out his case in detail.[95] It entirely silenced its recipient. Six days after it was written Pace could write laconically to Wolsey, 'It was lately the king's pleasure to dispute with your grace, and now it is his pleasure to hold his peace.'[96] The ships will go to Bordeaux, the French king's placards are welcome, the king is upset to hear that Wolsey is sick and begs him take care of himself, and he asks for help in the appointment of a new lieutenant in Ireland.[97] The storm had inexplicably blown over, as suddenly as it arose.

Meanwhile the Calais conference dragged on exhaustingly. Wolsey had been ill during the recent exchange with the king and handed over negotiations to deputies who struggled hard to compose differences between the parties and persuade them to a truce of eighteen months or two years. But negotiations had reached deadlock. By the middle of October special embassies were sent from Calais, one to Francis and the other to Charles, with a final, personal appeal from Wolsey to yield. This was his last despairing heave to make Charles accept 'more sober' conditions and Francis agree to a truce during which the whole English effort would be given to turning it into 'unity, peace and concord'. The envoys were to 'exhort, stir and move by all means and ways to them possible' and so on; and those sent to France were to turn specially to the French dowager queen, 'the mother and nourisher of peace', as Wolsey several times called her.[98]

It is impossible to read these secret instructions without

95. *St.P.*, i, 62 ff. (*L.P.*, iii, 1611).   96. *L.P.*, iii, 1629.
97. *St.P.*, i, 68 (*L.P.*, iii, 1630).
98. B.M. Vit. B, xx, fols 269 ff.; B.M. Calig. D, viii, fols 125 ff. (*L.P.*, iii, 1694, 1696).

being moved to accept their author's sincerity – not least
because it is only this which makes them really explicable.
True, Wolsey talks of the 'Great Enterprise' against France
and promises Charles that England will join him if mediation fails. But he was bound to this by treaty; and he also
told Francis that Henry would join him if Charles were
obstructive. This may have been duplicity – but it was
duplicity for the sake of a truce which could open the way
to peace.

At first it seemed that the embassies might succeed.
Francis was encouraged by a judicious mixture of 'fair
words and threats' to accept exactly what Wolsey wanted.
But Charles was intransigent. 'The more towardly disposi-
tion I find in the French party,' Wolsey cried, 'the more
sticking and difficulty be showed' by the imperialists.[99] He
had no rest, night or day, because all stood 'always in am-
biguities', and was condemned to 'obstinate dealing' and
frustrating delays.[1] Charles would not yield what, by
Wolsey's reckoning, the situation demanded. Worn out by
interminable conference and brought to the point of frenzy
by others' inconstancy and obstinacy, harried by a king
who depended on him for the smallest decision in domestic
affairs, who had repeatedly called him home and now started
arguing with him about the proposed truce,[2] stricken by ill-
health which he attributed to the 'unwholesome air of
Calais' but which was probably due to sheer pressure of
work, Wolsey must have been on the edge of collapse. He
had until the end of November to win his point. The truce
was already drafted and ready to be published at a moment's
notice. All that was lacking was the emperor's consent –
and despite further pushing from Wolsey, this was not to

99. B.M. Calig. D, viii, fols 130v, 137 (*L.P.*, iii, 1707, 1724). Cf. *L.P.*,
iii, 1736.

1. *L.P.*, iii, 1728.

2. *St.P.*, i, 85 ff. (*L.P.*, iii, 1762). Henry objected that the truce would
bind him by oath to a course of action at variance with that sworn
at Bruges. Wolsey settled this royal scruple by assuring him that the
truce required no oath.

come. The war was now burning fast. A papal army had just captured Milan and soon the French were on the run as, one after another, the citadels of the plain of Lombardy opened their gates to Imperial and papal troops. Meanwhile Tournai had been captured by Charles's army from the Low Countries. It was almost absurd to think that one man at Calais could halt all this. On 28 November Wolsey crossed back to England, after months of bitter and expensive struggle.[3] Indeed, Henry reckoned that the conference had cost Wolsey £10,000 and therefore gave him St Alban's Abbey in recompense.[4] It was disgraceful pluralism thus to unite the richest abbey in England to a primatial see, but there was some justice in the reward. The recipient had brought back neither a truce nor peace, but 'I have as effectually laboured the same by all the politic ways and means to me possible as ever I did any cause in my life'.[5] Moreover, though the treaty of Bruges was now in force, both Francis and Charles had agreed to send envoys to England for another attempt to find concord. The diet had not therefore been dissolved in failure, 'but only put in train and respite'.[6] It would soon be resumed in England. So Wolsey said. He was nothing if not tenacious.

But things were going from bad to worse. Just before Wolsey came back to England, Albany, that bird of ill-omen, returned to Scotland with a small armed escort. To England this could mean only one thing – that France looked for a belligerent renewal of the Auld Alliance. Anglo-French relations were declining fast, so much so that Henry could overcome catarrh and a headache to write, or at least sign, a letter of ardent friendship to Charles protesting that he would avenge the insults the emperor had suffered and that he loved him as though he were sprung of his own body.[7]

This was in December 1521. Wolsey had about five months

3. *St.P.*, i, 85 (*L.P.*, iii, 1762).   4. *L.P.*, iii, 1759.
5. B.M. Calig. D, viii, fol. 137 (*L.P.*, iii, 1724).
6. *St.P.*, i, 90 (*L.P.*, iii, 1762).   7. *L.P.*, iii, 1882.

left before England must declare war. He had not forgotten
that the Field of Cloth of Gold was intended to be the first
of a series and now proposed that Henry and Francis should
meet again. It seems he even thought that Francis might
come to England at the same time as Charles and take
part in a triple 'summit' of the kind that had been mooted
two years previously. But this was too ambitious for the
moment,[8] and instead, throughout the spring of 1522, urgent
appeals continued to go forth from England to Francis (and
Louise of Savoy) and Charles to settle their disputes and
resume the peace conference.[9]

The treaty of London had provided that the victim of
aggression should call upon his fellow-contrahents to warn
the aggressor and threaten war within a month if he did
not desist. Through the winter and spring of 1521–2 Charles
besought England to discharge this duty against France.
But Wolsey even refused to accept the letters of requisition
in which Charles made his demand.[10] Then Charles asked
for some money and met no success. Suddenly Wolsey
offered half the amount – but on condition that England
should not declare war until it had been repaid.[11] Having
used the treaty of Bruges to forestall the operation of the
treaty of London, Wolsey now tried to use a loan to forestall
the operation of the treaty of Bruges. No wonder the
emperor was enraged.

But politics is the art of the probable as well as of the
possible and it was undeniably probable that, sooner or
later, England would have to fling herself at France. Prudence required that ships and men be gathered, if not for
France then for Scotland, against which a massive campaign was talked of for that year. Hence commissioners set
out to discover the nation's military strength and prepare

8. B.M. Calig. D, viii, fols 215v, 230v (*L.P.*, iii, 2036, 2139). Also
L.P., iii, 2092.

9. E.g. *L.P.*, iii, 1946, 1992, 2129.

10. *L.P.*, iii, 1838; *Sp. Cal. F.S.*, pp. 2, 33 f., 38 f., 46 ff., 53, 56.

11. *Sp. Cal. F.S.*, p. 41.

the way for huge war taxation; and meanwhile William Knight went to the Swiss, and Richard Pace, once more, to Venice to win them over to the cause and leave France naked of friends.[12]

Thus in the early months of 1522 English policy displayed every colour of the spectrum – from missions for peace and talk of 'summitry' to plans for grand campaigns. It was Wolsey who directed this many-sided policy, with Henry apparently in approval, especially of the preparations for war.[13]

By the terms of the treaty of Bruges, the emperor was due to visit England soon and this must be the inescapable signal for England's entry into the war. He arrived at Dover on 28 May 1522 on a visit that was to be longer and more splendid than his first two years previously. From Dover – where he had to wait seventy-two hours for his wardrobe to arrive – he came to Greenwich and Windsor, and a round of hunting and banquets, tournaments and pageants, as well as hard talking. By the time he left, he had concluded two more treaties with England binding her to a detailed plan for combined assault on France.[14] Meanwhile an English herald had formally delivered to Francis the English declaration of war. On 6 July Charles embarked for Santander, having achieved all that he had worked for during the previous eighteen months.

Wolsey had been overpowered by forces too great for a chancellor of England and papal legate to contain. Though he had secured eight years of peace for England, his elaborate mechanism of collective guarantees of peace and the device of 'summitry' had proved powerless to protect European peace against princes bent on war. In the event, France

12. England tried to make Venice declare war in the name of that treaty of 1518 which Wolsey would not allow to govern English policy. Venice replied that Leo X's death nullified it. *Sp. Cal.*, ii, 473, 478.

13. See his angry outbursts against France, in which he announces that his patience is at an end – e.g. *Sp. Cal. F.S.*, pp. 16, 121.

14. *L.P.*, iii, 2333, 2360. The treaties were concluded at Windsor and Waltham Cross.

had not been intimidated by the prospect of radically up-
setting the balance of power against herself and had pushed
on regardless of the enormous odds against her. The sound-
ness of Wolsey's reckoning was to be proved in the immense
débâcle which awaited Francis at Pavia. It was the misfortune of Wolsey and Europe that the French king paid
no attention to the cardinal's calculations.

So began the wars of the 1520s. It was from them that
the civilization of Renaissance Italy received a savage
wound: it was in part thanks to them that the Turks were
able to pierce into south-east Europe, seize much of Hungary and wreck its Church, and the Habsburgs and Valois
to enter a new stage in their conflict which would eventually
bring bankruptcy to both; it was in no small measure thanks
to them that Lutheranism was able to take root and grow
into a broad-spanning tree. The stakes for which Wolsey
played were high.[15] During these months an incalculable
amount had hung on a single thread; and had the treaty of
London succeeded, had Wolsey been able to effect some
diplomatic alchemy during the royal meetings in 1520, or
at Calais in the next year, then he might have given Europe
a greater blessing than have a score of chancellors and a
legion of legates. There is one final point to note. It was in
the course of the war which Wolsey tried to halt that the
siege of Pampluna occurred, and it was in the course of that
siege that Ignatius Loyola received the wound which turned
him away from war to other things.

15. As Mattingly noted in 'An Early Non-aggression Pact', pp. 28 f.

5

The Virtuous Prince

HENRY had begun his reign as a warrior, but had probably found war-making less sweet than he had expected. *Capax pugnae nisi pugnasset*, perhaps. The resumption of the Hundred Years War had proved cruelly expensive, had been constantly frustrated by the bewildering instability of European power-politics and had yielded 'ungracious dogholes', as Cromwell would later say, rather than another Agincourt or a rival to Marignano. Hence, willingly or unwillingly, the king changed his persona. The change was complete by 1517 and received final ratification in the treaty of London of October 1518 when, on a stage prepared by Wolsey, he stood forth as the peacemaker of Europe, amidst a blaze of high diplomacy, banquets, revels and pageants.

But the new man was no less vainglorious and competitive, had no less animal energy and appetite for the magnificent than the old. The years of peace, simply because they lacked the heroics of war, left him restless, if not aimless, and seem to have directed his overflowing vitality into some unusual paths.

In 1513, probably, during Henry's first campaign in France, the Emperor Maximilian had made a startling offer to the king – nothing less than to resign the Empire to him or alternatively to secure his election as king of the Romans with right of succession to the Imperial throne. Maximilian was given to spectacular ideas, especially if they brought him material advantage, and presumably this offer was intended to prepare the way for a large loan or something similar. It met no success. The young king, who was ill at the time, cautiously replied that the matter would have to be carefully weighed by him and his Council, where, appar-

ently, it was found lacking and quietly buried, leaving
Maximilian ruefully (and obscurely) observing that, when
a gift of a casket of gold was refused by one, the donor was
free to offer it to another.[1]

Three years later the matter was reopened. Now a most
elaborate plan was outlined. Henry was to accept adoption
as the emperor's son and then, with an army of 6,000, cross
Europe via Tournai to Trèves, where Maximilian would
resign the Empire to him and invest him also with the
duchy of Milan – which was yet to be conquered and which
the emperor had just failed dismally to secure. From Trèves,
Henry was to march to Como and pass by boat to Milan,
there to wait 'a season' until Maximilian joined him, when
the two would go to Rome for Henry's coronation, the ex-
emperor-elect – for Maximilian had not been crowned himself – accompanying emperor-elect. Meanwhile the duke of
Suffolk or a similar would have crossed to France with an
army to begin a conquest which the new emperor would
complete on his return from Rome. Thus would Henry not
only gain an imperial crown but also recover his inheritance.[2]

Such was Maximilian's plan, set out with disarming unconcern for the difficulties which stood across its path. It
was almost certainly made to smooth English tempers after
the recent débâcles in Lombardy and to coax more cash out
of Henry. It did not receive much attention. It was repeated,
fleetingly, in 1517, and again not taken up.[3] Though these
incidents may only be notable for the light they throw on
Maximilian, possibly they sowed a seed in Henry's mind;
for, two years after he was last offered, and had refused,
the Imperial crown he suddenly took the initiative in seeking it.

Shortly after Maximilian's final attempt to inveigle Henry

1. *Lettres du Roy Louis XII* (Brussels, 1712), iv, 323 (*L.P.*, i, 2992).
2. B.M. Vit. B, xix, fols 71 ff., 82; P.R.O. S.P. 1/13, fols 169 ff. (*L.P.*,
ii, 1878, 1902, 1923).
3. *L.P.*, ii, 3724.

with his wild proposal, that is, in the spring of 1518, it was clear that the emperor would soon be dead. It was also clear that his Habsburg heir, the Archduke Charles (Maximilian's grandson), would face a rival in the person of Francis I of France, of whom it was already written that he 'goeth about covertly and layeth many baits to attain the Empire'.[4] But, for the moment, while the two candidates jostled for position, England's attitude was unequivocal. Henry would take no part in the competition, but looked for Charles's success. So the king said to Wolsey and so Wolsey wrote some months after.[5] On 12 January 1519 the wayward, versatile emperor died and, even as his body was being carried off to splendid burial in Innsbruck, the contest between Charles and Francis came into the open. Though Henry's wishes, like Wolsey's, were clear-cut, official English policy was one of complete impartiality, as the treaty of 1518 required. Each candidate, therefore, was promised support, each was secretly informed that encouragement given to the other was verbiage and, at the same time, it was often asserted by Henry that no third candidate would be supplied by England.[6]

But this policy of masterly neutrality suddenly ended. In early May, or perhaps a little before, Henry decided to plunge into the election. Perhaps he was moved by reports that Francis's chances were improving fast and that he already boasted of his coming triumph;[7] certainly he was moved by the pope. Hitherto Leo, fearful of the success of either candidate and guided only by local interests, had wobbled from one policy to another until he had recently decided to support Francis openly. Very probably he did this in order that stalemate might result and the electors be forced to offer the Imperial crown to a third, lesser candidate – one of themselves, or some other prince. A single stone would thus bring several birds to earth and

4. *L.P.*, ii, 4160.   5. ibid, 4257; iii, 50, 70, 137.
6. *L.P.*, iii, 70, 88, 100, 121, 137, etc.
7. E.g. *L.P.*, iii, 100, 170.

leave the pope much more secure.[8] On 19 February there
arrived a letter from Rome to Campeggio, then in England,
explaining the pope's point of view, rebuking Wolsey for
failing to see that the success of either candidate would be
harmful to Christendom and stating that Leo looked for a
third.[9] The latter was not named, but Wolsey took this last
remark as an invitation to Henry to go to the polls. A
very cautious reply was made which, while arguing that
to encourage both of the known candidates and aid neither
was the sanest policy, appeared to toy with the idea of
Henry's candidature.[10] Probably Wolsey gave the papal
proposal (if it were such) little credence and entertained it
either out of courtesy or because it could be a lever to prise
out of Leo's hand an addition to his own legatine power.

However, when Henry studied the pope's letter, or when
he heard a second appeal from Rome which has since disappeared,[11] he reacted differently. By 11 May he had evidently decided to try to do what no other English monarch
had ever succeeded in doing and only one other had
attempted: to become Holy Roman Emperor. On that day
letters were written to the college of electors urging them
to give credence to Richard Pace whom the king was about
to send to them to explain his mind touching the Imperial
election.[12] The campaign had been launched.

We shall never know if Henry was in serious pursuit of
this prize. Doubtless his primary purpose was to win prestige by being paraded as a candidate in this august election
and by demonstrating to Europe that there was nothing

8. On all this, see Nitti, op. cit., 113 ff.

9. Guasti, 'I manoscritti Torrigiani donati al R. Archivio Centrale
di Stato di Firenze', *Arch. Storico Italiano*, 3rd ser., xxv (1887), 383 f.

10. *Martene-Durand*, iii, 1285 ff. (*L.P.*, iii, 137). Cf. Busch, op. cit.,
38 ff.

11. See Nitti, op. cit., 194 n. Reference may have been made to such
a letter in Pace's instructions later on, in which there is talk of a
letter recently sent by Gigli containing a statement of the pope's
electoral policy. B.M. Vit. B, xx, fol. 170 (*L.P.*, iii, 241).

12. *L.P.*, iii, 216.

that Francis did which he could not do equally well; perhaps he also hoped that he might so split the voting that he, Charles and Francis would all emerge empty-handed and the Imperial crown pass to a fourth party. But perhaps, when he suddenly changed his mind and entered the lists, there was a flicker of hope that he himself might be victorious. At the time, his chances would probably not have seemed as bleak as they do in retrospect. Habsburg succession was not yet inviolable and both Charles and Francis were as much strangers to Germany as he was. A last-minute dash by an outsider from England might have seemed to have a chance of success, especially if this outsider had the support of the papacy.

Accordingly, Richard Pace, that much-travelled ambassador-extraordinary and agent of lost causes, was instructed to visit all the electors in turn to discover, and report, their allegiance. To any who were susceptible he was to explain 'the manifold gifts of grace, fortune and nature as be in the king's grace, with the aptitude that he is of to take upon him so great a dignity', and to make handsome offers of cash. He was to explain to the electors that his king was 'of the Germany tongue', whatever that might mean, look for particular help from the cardinal of Sion, Matthew Schiner, and conscript the aid of the papal envoy by showing him the letters which Wolsey had recently received from Rome. But there was a note of caution in his instructions. The true purpose of the mission was not to be publicized. Whenever Pace met convinced supporters or ambassadors of the other candidates he was to assure them that Henry was on their side and to entertain both parties with 'pleasant words founded upon indifference'. England's relations with her fellows were not to be needlessly damaged. Furthermore, if it was clear that the electors would not have Henry, then the next best solution would be for them not to have Charles or Francis either, but to choose one of their own number. Thus, while publicly professing enthusiasm for both the known candidates, Pace and the papal ambas-

sador were furtively to advance the cause of the king of
England or, if this were hopeless, that of a German prince.
Henry's view of things probably ran thus: that Charles's
election was very likely but not particularly desirable;
Francis's election less likely and thoroughly undesirable; a
German's election no more likely but much more acceptable; his own election the least likely but the most acceptable. Pace was to do all in his power to arrange matters
according to this complicated tariff. But a final, important
restriction was placed upon him. In order that money
should not be wasted and in order, as the English judged,
that it should do its work more efficiently, any bond or
instrument in favour of a friendly elector was to contain
an important saving clause. Unlike the agents of the other
candidates, Pace was to make only promises of money – to
be honoured when his master was elected.[13]

By 9 June Pace had travelled through the Low Countries
to Cologne, and thence up the Rhine via Frankfort to
Mainz (for custom required that no stranger should stay
in the electoral city of Frankfort during the election itself).
Despite cruel heat and pestilence he had interviewed as
many of the electors as he could find. The archbishop of
Cologne was less French than had been supposed and,
though his Latin was so bad that he could not cope with
Henry's and Wolsey's letters, he might well, Pace wrote, be
turned into a supporter if judiciously handled.[14] Moreover,
though the cardinal-archbishop of Mainz, like the elector
Palatine, laboured for Francis, his brother, the marquis
of Brandenburg, was open to different ideas. Better still,
the archbishop of Trêves had given his spontaneous
opinion that Henry had as good a chance as any – whereupon Pace was able, for the first time, to unleash the speech
in commendation of the king set out in his instructions,
and apparently impressed the archbishop. Then, next day,
a confidant of the archbishop of Mainz came to him to

13. B.M. Vit. B, xx, fols 165, 170 (*L.P.*, iii, 240, 241).
14. *L.P.*, iii, 283.

promise that he would move his master to favour Henry. Were this to happen, Cologne would follow, and thus all three spiritual electors would be won for Henry. The king's case was beginning to take shape, and Pace had still to interview the electors of Saxony and Bohemia.[15] Four days later he could write that Henry would undoubtedly be proposed and that he, Pace, should immediately be sent a commission to receive the Empire in Henry's name. The French cause was as good as lost; the papal legate and apostolic nuncio had received orders to press Henry's suit and thus Pace expected to hear of Henry's election at any minute.[16] Ten days afterwards he was still waiting, confidently but now rather apprehensively because, he said, the people were so keen for Charles that, were Henry to succeed, they would assault him; and besides, the electors would bind the new emperor to reside in Germany.[17] Four days later the suspense and the badgering came to an end. At seven o'clock on the morning of 28 June Charles king of Spain was elected emperor. Thus there came to the Imperial throne one of the greatest of its occupants, now an uncertain youth of nineteen but soon a confident man with the most exalted view of his place as co-guardian, with the pope, of Christendom and with a prodigious empire at his command which embraced Spain, Naples, Germany and the Low Countries, already overflowed into North Africa and had only just begun to enter upon an uncharted world in the Central Americas. If Charles himself was of a rare cast, his empire was something which had not been seen since ancient Rome, and in some ways mightier than the work of the first Caesars. His election may have been a rebuff to Francis, but it left Henry further outclassed than ever. Compared with Charles he could well appear as no more than a petty potentate whom the might and range of this new empire must outdistance even more obviously than did the kingdom of France.

Henry failed because, in the last resort, he could never

15. *L.P.*, iii, 296, 297.   16. ibid., 307, 308.   17. ibid., 326.

match the claims of a Habsburg heir. This was the root
cause, but not the whole cause. To make matters worse, his
campaign was not competently organized. Wolsey failed
to send his commission to Pace before he left England and
then left him stranded for nearly a month without writing
to him, so that Pace approached despair. A tactical error,
not serious, but significant, was made in opening Henry's
campaign with a common letter to the electors as a body
instead of addressing them singly. Next, as Pace said, he
certainly embarked on his errand weeks too late. He
should have arrived on the scene well before the electors
had begun to gather at Frankfort; and furthermore, as
ever, all-important communications with Rome were so
neglected that papal support was never really behind
Henry's candidature.[18] But the greatest error was English
parsimony. As everybody knew, Charles and Francis spent
lavishly before the election, and beside the torrent of hard
cash from these two (or rather their creditors) Pace's
cautious promises were faint incentives. He could not even
point to royal letters backing the banker, Herman Rynck,
who would produce the cash if Henry succeeded. Eight
days before the cataclysm, Pace wrote that had he had as
much money as Charles disbursed, some 420,000 gold
crowns, Wolsey would already 'have songen *Te Deum
laudamus* for the election of King Henry the VIII *in im-
peratorem omnium Christianorum*'.[19]

Perhaps the apparent carelessness and the financial
caution were merely marks of prudence. Perhaps they were
also signs that the man who had the oversight of Henry's
candidature, namely, Thomas Wolsey, was not enthusiastic about it. Certainly there is one indisputable scrap of
evidence that king and minister were not wholly in accord
over the venture. On 12 June, shortly after Pace had
arrived at Mainz and a few hours before the first votes
were expected to be cast, Wolsey sent John Clerk, his

18. For all this, see *L.P.*, iii, 222, 297, 308, 318, 354, 393.
19. ibid., 318.

chaplain and dean of the Chapels Royal, to Henry at Windsor. His errand was urgent. He was to plead with Henry not to do something. What that was we do not know, except that it was something 'touching his [Henry's] enterprise of the Empire'. At one o'clock next morning, Clerk wrote despairingly, 'Your grace may be assured that I have reasoned as deeply as my poor wit would serve me, not varying from your instructions . . . but his grace, as me thinketh, considereth no jeopardies.' His debate with the king had been inconclusive. Henry had cut it short, saying that he 'would sleep and dream upon the matter and give an answer upon the morning'. He would 'sleep and dream upon' it.[20]

We do not know what was at issue, or what were the 'jeopardies' which Henry brushed aside. Nor do we know the upshot of the incident, for Clerk was to deliver Henry's decision orally when it came. But the matter was serious enough to warrant Clerk's dispatch to the king, to prompt him to write an interim report at 1 a.m. and, presumably, to keep Wolsey up, or to get him up, to receive it. The evidence clearly cannot support the categorical statement that Wolsey was opposed to the whole affair,[21] though this is possible. It may be that the caution which pervades Pace's instructions derived from his desire to rein back an impetuous king, and that the incident just described was provoked by Henry's desire to throw that caution to the winds. Or it may be that only a tactical point was at stake. All that can be said is that, on some matter connected with the election, Henry wanted to go faster or further, or both, than Wolsey.

A few days after the election, Pace set out for home,

20. *St.P.* i, 2 f. (*L.P.*, iii, 302). In the earlier part of the letter Clerk said that Henry was very agitated by news that Pace was ill and 'liketh nothing' Wolsey's suggestion that no substitute should be sent out until more information on Pace's condition was received, for by then, he said, it would be too late. Is this further evidence of Wolsey's lack of enthusiasm?

21. As Busch argues (op. cit., 51 ff.).

leaving Frankfort in a riot of pillage and banditry at the
hands of the citizens and the electors' soldiery. Meanwhile
Wolsey was busy repairing the damage done to his diplomacy by recent events, assuring Francis that Henry had
laboured for his election until it became hopeless[22] and
Charles that Pace had never spoken *openly* against him,
which was true enough;[23] and though the Spanish ambassador's attempts to celebrate his king's success by bonfires
about the city of London were 'disappointed' by the
authorities, who feared that the crowds of strangers might
try to avenge the Evil May Day, Charles's election was
accorded a High Mass at St Paul's soon afterwards. When
Henry's defeat was known, Wolsey wrote to Rome to say
how hard he had worked to remove the indignation at
papal indifference from the king's heart – a roundabout
way of trying to earn gratitude, which misfired, and instead
produced the retort (a just one) that neither he nor Pace
had told the pope how Henry's case could be aided.[24]

Francis and Charles were thus partly placated; so too
Henry. On 11 August Pace was back in England and on
his way to report to the king, then taking his ease at Penshurst. Presumably in anticipation of some hot words, Pace
had been carefully briefed by Wolsey. He found Henry
playing (tennis, perhaps) with some of the Frenchmen who
had newly arrived as hostages for the money due for
Tournai. Pace was received 'lovingly'. He spoke his piece
exactly as Wolsey had taught him, and so successfully that,
'when the king's highness had well perceived and pondered the great charges and profusion of money expent by
the said king of Romans [Charles] for the obtent of that
dignity, his grace did highly wonder thereat and said that
he was right glad that he obtained not the same'. Henry
turned to the duke of Suffolk and told him so. He was
pleased that Pace had been so honourably received in Ger-

22. B.M. Calig. D, vii, fol. 148 (*L.P.*, iii, 416).
23. *L.P.*, iii, 403.
24. *Martene-Durand*, iii, 1301 ff. (*L.P.*, iii, 393).

many and called his host, the duke of Buckingham, to tell
him all about the mission. He agreed with Pace that the
pope's orators at Frankfort had been corrupted by the
French king, punctuating his account of this with the cry
'by the Mass'. This done, Pace spoke of his journey and
took supper with the king, who 'spake of me many better
words than I have or can deserve'. He then withdrew.[25] Not
only had an anxious interview passed off very well, but
the whole affair had apparently been forgotten and all
concerned forgiven. The king was merry. Miraculously, he
was 'right glad that he had not obtained' the Empire.
Perhaps for a moment, however, he had wanted it.

It was about a week later that Henry announced his
readiness to go on a crusade. He did so in an extraordinary
letter to the pope which he may even have dictated verbatim.[26] It is written in the first person and is one of the
longest extant letters hitherto written in his name. It is a
torrent of superlatives and excited generosity. It runs thus:
God will bear witness that we have no cause more dear
than service to man and religion. To strike a blow for
Christendom has ever been the summit of our ambition.
'Miro affecto et toto pectore', *'ardenti animo'* do we respond
to the call to a crusade which you made through Campeggio. We gird ourselves for this most holy expedition,
and dedicate our whole kingdom, our wealth, our goods, our
prestige to it; yes, our very blood and body we offer and
dedicate to Christ and his vicar. Whenever the call is made
we will be ready. If our longed-for heir shall have been
granted before the expedition sets out to do battle with the
Infidel, we will lead our force in person. We promise an
army of 20,000 foot fully equipped with all machines of
war; a navy of 70 ships; an army-by-sea of 15,000. To this

25. *St.P.*, i, 8 f. (*L.P.*, iii, 412).
26. It is undated. Since it refers to Campeggio's imminent departure
(and he left Dover on 24 August) it must have been written about
the middle of August 1519.

will be added private contingents of those many gentlemen
and nobles of England who will hasten to this holy expedition out of zeal for the Christian religion. We will
raise a tenth from the clergy and a fifteenth from the laity
to meet the cost of the expedition. We hope that others
will follow our example and we urge you to stir the rest
of Christendom. We have discussed all this with Wolsey
and Campeggio, at his departure from here. He will explain our mind fully when he arrives. We look for a mighty
triumph for the faith of Christ and will not spare one drop
of blood for Him who, to rescue us from our sins, did not
spare His son.[27]

Of course this outpouring was designed to placate an
indignant pope who for years had been asking for, and had
been promised in a half-hearted way, some cash from the
English clergy, but had never been paid it. More certainly,
it must have been intended to serve the purposes of
Thomas Wolsey. Now that Campeggio had completed his
mission and was about to depart, Wolsey faced the agonizing prospect of losing the legatine authority which had
been acquired so painfully and which he was determined
to keep and, indeed, to expand. Leo had already reluctantly
agreed to empower him to visit and reform English monasteries, whereupon, on 1 August, Wolsey had demanded
that the legacy be conferred on him for life. Doubtless
Henry's letter of a few days later was a much-needed, long-
overdue sop to a pope who was being besieged by an importunate cardinal. And yet one wonders whether this is
the whole explanation of the affair. The letter was so detailed, so enthusiastic, so unlike the conventional replies
to papal calls for a crusade which princes, including Henry,
always had at hand, a good example of which was Henry's
own response to such an appeal made by Leo X in 1515: a
wet blanket trimmed with time-honoured pieties.[28] Campeggio had arrived in the previous year to announce the

27. *Martene-Durand*, iii, 1297 ff. (*L.P.*, iii, 432).
28. B.M. Add., 15,387, fols 33 ff. (*L.P.*, ii, 712).

papal plan for a crusade and been ignored. He was sent home now not to report a few willing words from Henry but to announce England's readiness to ratify the papal five-year truce and 'several other things which, we hope, will please your holiness'; that is, the king's sudden and burning desire for a crusade.[29] We cannot know the whole truth, but perhaps this letter was more than a diplomatic device. Perhaps it represented a momentary, but sincere, impulse of an impetuous and maybe bored man.

The project never went very far. No reply is extant to Henry's offer. Campeggio took months to reach Rome and seems to have forgotten it by the time he had audience of the pope; and anyway Leo had long since lost his enthusiasm for crusading. In early December 1519, Henry once more wrote eagerly about the holy cause and promised to persuade Francis to join him.[30] But this was the end of the affair. By the new year it had been cast into the limbo of lost causes nearly as rapidly, perhaps, as it was acquired, for the king's attention and enthusiasm had now been turned to plans for meetings with Charles V and Francis. The prestige for which Henry thirsted was not to be found in the Holy Land or the Holy Roman Empire but in the panoply of the Field of Cloth of Gold, and when this and a subsequent meeting with the new emperor were over and the thirst had returned there were other things to be done. He might have Wolsey elected pope; he might do what no other English king since Alfred had done, and write a book (against heresy – rather than make war against the Infidel); he might receive from the hands of the pope some new title – all of which would occupy him in the next year, and all of which, it may be noted, pointed in the same direction, the direction earlier marked (per-

29. This in his letter of commendation of Campeggio, ibid., fols 28 f. (*L.P.*, iii, 427).

30. *L.P.*, iii, 537. In a speech to the Spanish ambassador in March 1520, Henry could speak of his desire to strike a blow against the Infidel, ibid., p. 689.

haps) by the project for a crusade: Henry had apparently
become a *dévot*, or, at any rate, an enthusiastic papalist.

It may have been Charles who first planted the idea that
Wolsey might become the second English pope.[31] He made
the suggestion some time in 1520 and repeated it, promising his support at the next papal election, when he met
Wolsey at Bruges in the autumn of 1521. As well as this
he discussed the matter with Henry in person, in England
and at Calais.[32] Thus was the idea sown – or it may have
sown itself. But whatever the agency, it seems that it was
sown in Henry's rather than Wolsey's mind and that it
now became the king's ambition to have his chancellor
become pope; a plan to which Wolsey acceded but which
he did not initiate.

When Charles first broached the idea to Wolsey alone,
in 1520, he met plain refusal.[33] When he met Henry later
on, however, the plan began to take shape.[34] On 1 December 1521 Leo X died, and in a remarkably short time Pace
was sent off to represent his country's interests at another
election. We know that Henry was all enthusiasm for
Wolsey's cause, saying that, in sending Pace, it was 'as if
he had sent his very heart'. In the Imperial ambassador's
presence Wolsey protested to Henry that he would accept
this honour only if the emperor and the king required
him, to which Henry answered that they did so require
him.[35] Wolsey was Henry's candidate and, once dispatched
by the king, would work for success energetically; but he
did so with little hope of success.[36]

A non-Italian (the last) was indeed elected, but he was
not an Englishman. Charles's promise of support had been
merely cards to be played in the diplomatic game, as

31. The first being Nicholas Brakespear (Adrian IV), who reigned
from 1154 to 1159.
32. *L.P.*, iii, 1876, 1877, 1884, 3389.
33. ibid., 1884.   34. ibid., 3389.
35. *Monumenta Habsburgica, etc.*, 506 f. (*L.P.*, iii, 1884).
36. As the same ambassador noted (ibid.). For what follows, cf.
Chambers, art. cit.

Wolsey must have known. It was the emperor's former
tutor, an austere Dutchman, and not Wolsey who won the
tiara. But only twenty months after his election, just as the
Church was beginning to feel his healing hand, Adrian VI
died. Wolsey had another chance.

As soon as news of the pope's death reached England,
Wolsey drew up the necessary instructions and commissions for the English agents at Rome to present his candidature. He did so protesting that he was unworthy of so
great a dignity and would prefer 'to demore, continue, and
end my life with your grace for doing of such poor service
as may be to your honour and wealth'. But since, when the
Holy See was last vacant, it had been Henry's 'mind and
opinion ... to have me preferred thereunto', an intention
the king had not since shed, he was now drawing up documents similar to those prepared for Pace, to be sent to
Henry for him to decide whether or not they should be
used in a second attempt by Wolsey to win the papal
throne.[37]

The documents were soon ready and, apparently,
approved. Their instructions to the agents in Rome were
complex. If it were clear that Cardinal de Medici must
succeed they were to support him, but if it were clear that
he was not in the lead then they were to produce letters
naming Wolsey as Henry's candidate. The cardinals were
to be told of his many virtues and assured that, happily,
he was not given 'to rigour and austereness', like Adrian;
that he was a man of peace who would bring 'final rest,
peace and quiet' to all Christendom; that he promised –
as so many popes promised – to launch a crusade and would
be joined by Henry, who would come to Rome to take part;
that he would arrive in Rome within three months of his
election and would never have the papacy moved to
another place, as once before it had moved – and so the
letter rolled on.[38]

If it is difficult to be moved by Wolsey's frequent pro-

37. *Fiddes, Collections*, 80 f. (*L.P.*, iii, 3372).
38. ibid., 83 ff. (*L.P.*, iii, 3389).

tests of unworthiness for this high honour and his desire
to stay at home rather 'than now, mine old days approaching, to enter into new things', it is no less difficult to believe
that he seriously expected to be successful. But one thing
seems beyond doubt. 'First ye shall understand,' the letter
went on, 'that the mind and entire desire of his highness,
above all earthly things, is that I shall attain to the said
dignity.' Henry was committed. Would Wolsey have dared
to report Henry's promise to come to Rome and join a
crusade unless Henry had been in complete accord? Was
not this magnificent vision of English pope and English
king leading Christendom against Islam – a revival, perhaps, of a recent enthusiasm – just the kind of extrava-
ganza that Henry would have been most ready to suggest?
Wolsey ended his instructions with a postscript written in
his own hand for one of the agents in particular, John
Clerk. It said that the king himself had willed him write
that Clerk should spare no effort or promise of money or
benefice to bring the matter to the desired end, paying
especial attention to younger men, for they would give
good ear to fine offers. 'The king willeth you neither to
spare his authority or his good money or substance.' The
situation was, surely, as the letter implies: that the real
thrust and enthusiasm for Wolsey's candidature came
from Henry. Wolsey took no long-term practical steps to
secure his election in advance, persistently neglected the
Curia and was probably neither very eager nor optimistic,
but, once placed on that course by his master, obediently
trod it with as much energy as he could muster. The surest
proof that this is the truth comes, however, in early 1522,
when Clerk wrote to Wolsey after the election of Adrian
VI to excuse himself of any blame for his patron's failure.
He explained to Wolsey that, when Adrian died, he had
taken few steps on his behalf and seen the cardinals go
into conclave without raising his name for election because,
before Clerk set off for Rome some time before, Wolsey
had told him 'precisely that [he] would never meddle there-

with' – so much so that when, almost incredibly, instructions arrived in Rome suddenly reversing this decision it was too late for Clerk to take effective action.[39] Clerk was very close to Wolsey. What they said to one another in private correspondence like this must be taken as truth. Wolsey had not intended to stand for election in the conclave of 1521. If he changed his mind it is only reasonable to assume that he did so at Henry's behest – especially when much other evidence points to this conclusion. And likewise in 1523 he entered the lists largely under the impetus of Henry's enthusiasm.

Had Wolsey succeeded, he would have brought acclaim and honour to England and its king, and perhaps compensated the latter for his own defeat in another place. Further, as Wolsey wrote, it would have been 'to the honour, benefit and advancement of your affairs in times coming', words that have much irony in them.[40] Instead, as Wolsey had expected, Cardinal de Medici won the election. On hearing of the new pope's success, he wrote that 'I take God to record I am more joyous thereof than if I had fortuned upon my person',[41] and a little later bade Clerk speak of Henry's inexpressible joy at the news that 'so great, so faithful, constant and perfect a friend' had been elected and promise that Henry would 'concur with him in all things which may sound to his honour, weal and surety, the tranquillity, quiet and repose of Christendom; offering his grace's authority, puissance, realm and blood for the furtherance thereof to the uttermost' – words no less ironical.[42]

Henry first tried his hand at writing in the early months

39. Ellis, *Original Letters, etc.*, 3rd ser., i, 308 (*L.P.*, iii, 1960).
40. *Fiddes, Collections*, 81 (*L.P.*, iii, 3372).
41. *Fiddes, Collections*, 82.
42. *St.P.*, vi, 22 f. (*L.P.*, iii, 3659). Cf. his letter of congratulation to Clement on his election saying that he voted for him, praising his peace policy, and declaring Henry and England utterly devoted to the Holy See. Vat. Arch., *Lettere di Principi*, ii, fol. 81.

of 1518. We know little about the product except that it was finished by June of that year, that Wolsey had at first contested what Henry had written and then, to the author's delight, joined in the chorus of praise and declared the reasoning 'inevitable', and that, doubtless because the author soon tired, it never passed beyond manuscript stage.[43] But it is a reasonable guess that, three years later, the piece was rescued from the oblivion that some may think it deserved and used to form the first two chapters of Henry's famous book – the chapters entitled 'Of Indulgences' and 'Of the Pope's Authority'. Henry's first piece, therefore, was a very swift contribution to the controversy occasioned by Luther's attack on indulgences in late 1517, was set aside as soon as it was written and then emerged as the somewhat incongruous opening chapters of a work in defence of the seven sacraments. Such, at any rate, is a possible account of what happened.

His printed book, the *Assertio Septem Sacramentorum*, a lengthy treatise against Luther's *De Captivitate Babylonica* of 1520, appeared in the summer of 1521. By then, of course, Luther had been excommunicated and outlawed, but his creed was spreading fast and had begun to penetrate England. Several calls had come to Henry from Rome to exert himself against what was called a 'wicked pestilence',[44] though probably few expected that he would produce a book. But such it was to be. On 7 April 1521 Pace reported to Wolsey that the king had not had time until that day to deal with recent affairs of state because he was otherwise occupied *'in scribendo contra Lutherum,* as I do conjecture'.[45] Nine days later he was said to be within sight of finishing.[46] On 12 May there was an elaborate ceremony at Paul's Cross, that is, outside the cathedral, when John

43. B.M. Vit. B, xx, fol. 98v (*L.P.*, ii, 4257).
44. E.g. *L.P.*, iii, 1193.
45. ibid., 1220. Cf. a similar report from the Venetian ambassador to the Signory on 23 April. *Ven. Cal.*, iii, 195.
46. *L.P.*, iii, 1233.

Fisher preached against the new heresy before Wolsey and a large concourse of dignitaries, and some of Luther's works were solemnly burned. At that ceremony Wolsey held a copy of Henry's book in his hand – a manuscript copy, presumably.[47] A few days later, the king wrote to the pope to announce his intention of dedicating his work to him.[48] It was printed in July. On 25 August Wolsey told John Clerk, then in Rome, that nearly thirty copies were on their way to him, one a luxurious presentation volume adorned at the end with verses specially chosen by Wolsey and written by Henry himself, the others for the cardinals.[49]

The Defence of the Seven Sacraments is not a piece of theology of the highest order. Estimates of it have varied enormously, but the truth surely is that its erudition is unremarkable (though it makes telling use of the Old Testament in particular), its grasp of Lutheranism defective, its exposition of Catholic teaching on the sacraments sometimes unimpressive and undoubtedly shot through with that semi- or crypto-Pelagianism against which, essentially, Protestantism protested. It left gaps which John Fisher, in a lengthy defence of the king's book against Luther's riposte, would later patiently, and tactfully, fill.[50] Above all, it ran too easily into mere assertion and the jeering that is to be found in so many anti-Protestant works by Catholics, especially those of More and, to a lesser degree, of Fisher. In short, it is unlikely to have moved many convinced, informed Lutherans. Reading its rather conventional discourse on the sacraments and their all-too-mechanical operation (more wrong in tone than content, erring by omission rather than mis-statement), one pines for the sweep and fire of the *Babylonish Captivity* to which it was intended to reply.

But this is not to say that it was an ineffective book. On the contrary, it was one of the most successful pieces of

47. *Ven. Cal.*, iii, 210.   48. *L.P.*, iii, 1297.   49. *L.P.*, iii, 1450, 1510.
50. In his *Defensio Assertionis regis Angliae de fide Catholica adversus Lutheri Captivitatem Babylonicam* (1524).

Catholic polemics produced by the first generation of anti-
Protestant writers. Simply because it was short and often
unfair it would have engaged a wider audience than a
ponderous professional work. It was a skilful piece of writing which made full use of the easy retort to Luther that
one Augustinian hermit was neither likely suddenly to
have discovered truth after centuries of darkness nor empowered by any authority to proclaim it. Henry's ecclesiology was not very strong, but the fundamental issue at
stake, namely, the nature of the Church which Christ
founded, comes out squarely. Finally, the book's greatest
strength was the fact that its author was a notable king.
Today it is its affirmation of the papal primacy, the condemnation of schism and the defence of the indissolubility
of marriage which are remarked most obviously; but to so
monarchical an age as his, Henry's book would have struck
home even before it was read, simply because it was his.
It could scarcely have been better calculated to bolster the
humbler, perhaps uninformed, uncommitted Catholic –
especially the lay Catholic – who fell away so easily. Wolsey
was right to say that it should be sent not only to Rome
but to 'France and other nations';[51] and Luther was right
to reply to it violently.

But did Henry write it? This is yet another question
which will never be answered completely.[52] He did not
write it entirely independently or with his own hand.
Others gathered the materials and helped him throughout
its composition. But he probably at least guided it through
its final stages, when the time came to give shape to the
whole work and place the pieces which others had made
ready. In this limited sense it was his book. Much later,
More spoke about 'the makers' of the book, who must have
been the team that did the preliminary work – not Fisher,[53]
let alone Erasmus, as some thought; not Pace, for the letter

51. Ellis, op. cit., 2nd ser., i, 287 (*L.P.*, iii, 1233).
52. For a discussion of the various theories, see O'Donovan's edition
of the *Assertio* (New York, 1908), Introduction.
53. As Reynolds shows in his *St John Fisher* (1955), 91 n.

quoted above implies that he did not know what the king was about; perhaps Wolsey, though he could scarcely have had the time; perhaps John Longland, royal confessor and almoner, and (maybe significantly) elevated to the see of Lincoln in May 1521; perhaps Edward Lee, as Luther thought; and probably others whom we shall never identify. Thomas More entered the story after their work was done, 'as a sorter-out and placer of the principal matters contained therein',[54] and at this point, presumably, with the donkey-work completed and willing hands available to help him, Henry took over and finally assembled the raw materials.

The book was an act of piety and perhaps of other things also. Henry wrote it because, doubtless, he believed wholly in the cause, because it would do good, because it would bring him acclaim and set him apart from his fellow kings, past and present. But the immediate reason why he wrote it was that Wolsey suggested that he should. We have the direct testimony of the king that he never intended any such thing 'afore he was by your grace moved and led thereunto'.[55] Wolsey had sent him the copy of the *Babylonish Captivity* against which the king's book was aimed; he showed keen interest in its progress and carefully stage-managed its début; he was regarded by the pope as its architect;[56] and later on, when the book was an embarrassment to him, Henry himself would say that he wrote it not of his free will, but at the instance of Wolsey and other bishops.[57] Wolsey may well have been the prime mover for the same kind of reasons that Henry was the author. But had he an additional motive – to provide the king with an occupation which would help him endure the hardships of peace?

54. Roper, *Lyfe of Sir Thomas More*, E.E.T.S. (1935), 67 f.
55. *L.P.*, iii, 1772.
56. *L.P.*, iii, 1233, 1450. Leo later said he thought Wolsey 'to have been a diligent comforter and stirrer that the king's grace should this [sic] employ his time'. B.M. Vit. B, iv, fol. 175v (*L.P.*, iii, 1574).
57. *Sp. Cal.*, v, 9.

Henry's book was something of a best-seller. It went through some twenty editions and translations in the six-teenth century, in Antwerp, Rome, Frankfort, Cologne, Paris and Würzburg (among other places), besides England; and around it there quickly grew a sizeable corpus of polemical writings.

By early 1522, two German translations had appeared – one by Hieronymus Emser (made at the request of Duke George of Saxony, Luther's persistent opponent), the other by Thomas Murner, at Strasburg. When the royal book thus penetrated his homeland, Luther quickly took up the pen and wrote a notoriously virulent reply, 'full of railing' and giving Henry about as thorough a lambasting as Henry had just aimed at him. The king's jeers that Luther had been wildly inconsistent in his theology and his attempt to dismiss him as 'a venomous serpent ... infernal wolf ... detestable trumpeter of pride, calumnies and schism' and the like, stung the latter to reply in kind and to trounce the king as 'deaf adder', 'miserable scribbler', 'fool', and worse. Henry himself made no response to this broadside, which took the form of a book in Latin and a slightly different version in German, but, instead, John Fisher and Thomas More took up the cudgels on his behalf: Fisher with a long defence of Henry's book which elaborated the latter and replied to the counter-attack point by point; More, under the pseudonym of William Ross, with an extremely vituperative harangue. In the same year, Thomas Murner came back into the story with a short tract, in German, cast in dialogue form and entitled *Whether the King of England or Luther is a Liar* – which, in turn, evoked a counter-blast from an anonymous Lutheran hand. Meanwhile Dr John Eck, already well known to Luther, had also written a defence of Henry's work, published in Rome in 1523.[58]

There the contest rested until, in September 1525, Luther

58. For the contents of these last two paragraphs, see Doernberg, *Henry VIII and Luther* (1961), 35 ff.; O'Donovan, loc. cit.

unexpectedly wrote a long letter to Henry in which he begged pardon for the abuse which he had poured on his head some three years before and offered to publish a full recantation. But this offer of an olive branch sprang from a complete misapprehension of what was really afoot in England. Luther had been persuaded by a false report passed on to him from Christian II, the exiled king of Denmark, that Henry had swung towards Reformation, that Wolsey had tumbled and that it was now known that the *Assertio* was the work, not of Henry, but of 'that monstrous beast, hated by man and God ... that pernicious plague and desolation of your majesty's kingdom', the cardinal of York, abetted by his fellow 'cunning sophists'. Armed with this false information, Luther penned his humble letter in which he offered his apologies and prepared to welcome Henry into the household of true believers.[59]

He was, of course, rebuffed – with a long letter mocking him and his creed, decrying his marriage to the ex-nun Catherine von Bora, his attack on monasticism, his contemptuous remarks about Wolsey, and so on. But the reply took a curiously long time to be dispatched. First, so it was said, it was delayed because Henry was on progress when Luther's letter arrived; then the latter was inexplicably mislaid and, though Henry wanted his reply to be sent to the prince of Germany at once, Wolsey held up its dispatch until a copy of Luther's piece could be appended to the king's screed.[60] Hence it was not until late December 1527 that the reply reached Germany, over two years after Luther had opened the correspondence. Luther received a copy of Henry's response about Christmas time, via Duke George of Saxony, and was reported as saying that he had nothing further to say.[61] But his opponents, especially Emser, quickly seized on his ill-judged letter and made full

59. Doernberg, op. cit., 49 ff.
60. *L.P.*, iv, 2420; Rogers, *Correspondence of Sir Thomas More*, 368.
61. *L.P.*, iv, 3697.

play both of his offer to recant and of Henry's firm rejection of him, with the result that he was driven to write another tract defending himself against their insinuations.[62]

There the story of Henry's book and its aftermath effectively ended – in a rather desultory, inconclusive way. Three years later, however, Henry took the initiative and opened communications once more with the Lutheran world, when he turned thither for support for the divorce and began to discuss the possibility of a liaison with the Protestant princes. But, by then, times had changed.

When the *Assertio* was presented to Leo X in October 1521 it earned its author a new and resounding title. However, contrary to what has sometimes been alleged, the book was not the sole reason for the title, nor did it beget the desire for the title. The *Assertio* was only the final motive for Leo's *beau geste*, and the quest for a papal title had a lengthy history before the book was written or even thought of.

For as long as Henry and Wolsey had been badgering Rome for ever more extensive honours for Wolsey, indeed longer, they had also been badgering Rome for honours for Henry to match the titles of Most Christian King of France and Catholic King of Spain enjoyed by his rivals. As we have seen, in 1512 Julius II had been asked to confiscate Louis XII's title and confer it on Henry and had come near to doing so.[63] In 1515 another request was made for an addition to the royal style of a different kind. First 'Protector of the Holy See' and then 'Defender' were suggested, but refused because the former belonged to the emperor and the latter to the Swiss. Then some in Rome proposed 'King Apostolic', others 'Orthodox', but neither pleased the pope.[64] Next year the very title which was eventually granted, *viz.* 'Defender of the Faith', was suggested, but, to Henry's chagrin, met nothing but silence

62. Doernberg, op. cit., 57 f.   63. Above, pp. 55 ff.
64. *L.P.*, ii, 887, 967, 1418, 1456.

from Leo.[65] There the matter rested until May 1521, when Wolsey wrote to the pope once more to ask that some suitable title be bestowed on his master. At a Consistory on 10 June Leo put the matter to the cardinals. Various formulae were offered: *'Rex Fidelis'*, *'Orthodoxus'*, *'Ecclesiasticus'*, *'Protector'* and, rather feebly, *'Anglicus'*. Some of the cardinals cuttingly observed that they would find it easier to act if good reason could be shown for paying honour to Henry, whereupon it was recalled that Henry had once fought for the Holy See against a schismatic Louis XII and been conceded the latter's title of *'Christianissimus'*, and now fought manfully against Luther. Eventually it was decided that the pope should draw up a short list of titles and, when the cardinals had approved it, send it to Henry for him to make the final choice.[66] The *Assertio*, therefore, for it must have been this that was referred to, though not yet distributed in Rome, had tipped the scales.

The presentation copy of the *Assertio*, magnificently bound in cloth of gold, together with the volumes destined for the cardinals, arrived in Rome in early September 1521. As bidden by Wolsey, Clerk went privately to the pope to show him his copy and arrange for the ceremony of presentation. Leo responded warmly. As soon as the book was in his hands he began to read it eagerly, nodding and muttering approval as he went along and expressing marvel that a king could have written thus. When Clerk offered to spare the pope's eyes and recite to him the dedicatory verses at the end which Henry had written in his own hand, Leo would have none of the suggestion and struggled through the lines thrice. A few days later he had finished the book and, said Clerk, commended it *'super sidera'* ['to the skies'] – as, the ambassador added, did all who had read it. The formal presentation would be held as soon as the cardinals, whom the summer heat had driven out of

65. *L.P.*, ii, 1928.
66. Creighton, *A History of the Papacy, etc.* (1901 edn), vi, 374 f.

Rome, were returned.[67] It eventually took place on 2 October. Kneeling before the pope, Clerk kissed his foot and both cheeks, made a florid oration and then presented the book.[68]

Meanwhile Henry had answered Leo's inquiry about a title. He chose the one which had been proposed six years before – '*Defensor Fidei*'. After the recent ceremony, Leo could hardly resist much longer. On 11 October, six long weeks after the presentation of the *Assertio*, he at last gave way, though without allowing to be added to the title the flourish of '*Orthodoxus*', or '*Gloriosus*', or '*Fidelissimus*' which some cardinals had proposed at the last minute.[69] In a bull of that day bestowing the title on Henry, as in his reply to Clerk in the ceremony some weeks ago, Leo spoke golden words of praise and affection for Henry.[70] But the latter had had to fight hard to win what he wanted. The pope's gift was a reluctant concession, a reward for persistence as much as virtue. Moreover, though the recipient believed it had been made to him and his heirs for ever, the grant was intended for Henry personally, not as the hereditary title which it became.[71] It was an act of parliament of 1543, repealed by Mary but restored by Elizabeth, which joined the title in perpetuity to the English crown.[72]

Thus did Henry secure his first unequivocal success and give to English monarchy one of the few additions to its style which has stood the test of time, even if, since 1534, and yet more since 1559, it has been an incongruous one. 'King of Ireland', 'Emperor of India' and so on have vanished, but this one lives on, regardless of the fact that the

67. Ellis, op. cit., 3rd ser., i, 256 (*L.P.*, iii, 1574).
68. ibid., 262 (*L.P.*, iii, 1654); *L.P.*, iii, 1656.
69. Creighton, op. cit., vi, 375.   70. *Rymer*, xiii, 756.
71. See Mainwaring-Brown, 'Henry VIII's book ... and the Royal Title of "Defender of the Faith" ', *T.R.H.S.*, 1st ser., viii (1880), 242 ff. But Henry seems to have considered it hereditary, saying that the pope's bull did honour to him 'and all his successors' (*L.P.*, iii, 1659).
72. 35 Hen. VIII *c.* 3; 1 & 2 Philip and Mary *c.* 8; 1 Eliz. *c.* 1. The last act repealed the act of repeal (the second in the list) and thus restored the first.

faith concerned was the faith of the popes and that the
supporting act of Parliament must be suspect at least to the
successors of the original donor, if not to others.

In May 1519 there was a minor purge of the Court. Some
half-dozen of the most boisterous of those courtiers with
whom Henry had romped and diced and tilted in the past
were expelled, including Nicholas Carew and the one-eyed
Francis Bryan, who had recently been in the French Court
and, in the company of other English bucks and the king
of France himself, had ridden 'daily disguised through
Paris, throwing eggs, stones and other foolish trifles at the
people', and returned home 'all French in eating, drinking
and apparel, yea, and in French vices and brags, so that all
the estates of England were by them laughed at; the ladies
and gentlewomen were dispraised, so that nothing by them
was praised but it were after the French turn'.[73] Apparently
the whole Council came to the king and told him that these
young men of his Privy Chamber were not suitable companions. They were too 'familiar and homely', Hall observes, 'and played such light touches with him that they
forgot themselves'. At first Henry was reluctant to part
with them, but the Council instructed the lord chamberlain
to call Carew and the others before him and the miscreants
were forthwith dispatched to Calais and elsewhere, an exile
which 'grieved sore the hearts of these young men'. Maybe
it grieved the king too to part with those who had been his
'minions' and 'his very soul', all the more so when they
were replaced by sober, middle-aged gentlemen like Sir
Richard Weston and Sir William Kingston.[74] But, we are

73. *Hall*, 597.
74. ibid., 598; *L.P.*, iii, 246–50; *Ven Cal.*, ii, 1220, 1230, As long ago
as March 1518 Pace had recorded his disapproval of Carew when
writing to Wolsey to tell of the courtier's return to court (with his
wife) after a brief absence. He had come back 'too soon, in mine
opinion', Pace said (*L.P.*, ii, 4034). Others involved in this purge were
Sir John Peachy, Sir Edward Poyntz, Sir Edward Neville and Sir
Henry Guildford.

told, Henry himself had decided to mend his ways. He had resolved, said the duke of Norfolk,[75] to lead a new life, eschew dubious company and, so we may presume, give himself to godlier purposes than roistering with high-spirited courtiers.

It may have been shortly after his episode that three papers were drawn up which bear eloquent testimony to the depth of the royal conversion.[76] The first, entitled 'A Remembrance of such things as the king's grace will have to be done and hath given in commandment to his cardinal to put the same in effectual execution as hereafter ensueth', provided for a wide range of changes in financial administration. £10,000 per annum was to be delivered into the king's hands by the treasurer of the Chamber for 'extraordinary expenses'; £6,000 was to be set aside for royal building. Next, 'like a noble, wise and politic prince', the king announced his intention to keep henceforth a close supervision of all the royal revenues. He would 'view' all expenditure on the royal plate, the great wardrobe, ordnance and artillery, ships, the armoury and stable, tents and toils. The treasurer of the Chamber was to present accounts to him every month; once a year the chancellor of the Duchy of Lancaster, the treasurer, under-treasurer and barons of the Exchequer were likewise to report to him 'in his own person', together with the master of the wards. Most remarkably of all perhaps, once a quarter the chancellor of England and the judges were to report 'to his own person' the 'whole state of the realm and order of every shire', and give an account of the administration of justice throughout the kingdom. Finally, this 'remembrance' stated the king's desire that the royal household

75. So Giustinian said. *Ven. Cal.*, ii, 1220.
76. They are to be found in B.M. Titus, B, i, fols 188–90 (*L.P.*, iii, 576). For a full discussion of their meaning, see Elton, *Tudor Revolution in Government* (Cambridge, 1953), 37 ff. They are undated, but, as Dr Elton says, 'there is no reason to doubt' that the editor of *L.P.* placed them in early 1519 correctly.

should undergo thorough reform 'without any further delay'.

The second paper was scarcely less lofty. It listed those matters which the king 'intendeth in his own person to debate with his Council and to see reformation done therein' – matters such as 'equal and indifferent administration of justice', a radical overhaul of the Exchequer machinery, improvement of the government of Ireland, the better use of 'the commodities of this his realm' and 'how the idle people ... may be put in occupation', and the fortification of frontier towns. The third paper, headed a 'Privy Remembrance', began 'That the king's grace do devise to put himself in strength with his most trusty servants in every shire for the surety of his royal person and succession, and resisting of all manner bandings' – an intriguing proposal – and then fell away to discuss the humbler topics of 'the occupation of the king's ships in the feat of merchandises' and the payment of annuities: a curious medley.

The details of these papers, especially the first two, doubtless owed most to Wolsey; but they are so explicit in stating that this is the king's command, the king's pleasure, and repeat so often that the king 'in his own person' intends to debate this or to oversee the other that Henry must have been in accord with the plans even if he was not their prime mover. Had these ambitious reforms been executed, the administration might have been given much new efficiency and centralization, and Henry himself turned into a benevolent, hard-working monarch. Alas, royal zeal was short lived. Other claims on his time – the Field of Cloth of Gold, perhaps, or the rigours of book-writing – snuffed out this brief, bright flame of enthusiasm for good governance and, as a result, except for the plans for household reform contained in the so-called Eltham Ordinances of 1526, nothing came of these grandiose designs.[77]

77. 'There is not the faintest sign that any of them were ever put into practice.' So Elton, op. cit., 38.

Moreover, Carew and most of the others seem to have
come back to Court very quickly. They were much to the
fore at the Field of Cloth of Gold, jousting and revelling
as of yore. By 1521 their exile, such as it was, had long
since been ended.

The purge of May 1519 had almost certainly been innocent of any political implication and brought no more than
temporary displacement of a few courtiers. Two years later
something far more serious was afoot which at first sight
had seemed to involve a large faction of the aristocracy and
ended with the execution of a duke. Probably some time
in 1520 or early 1521 Henry did a rare thing: he wrote a
letter in his own hand. He wrote it to Wolsey – confessing
as he did so that 'writing is to me somewhat tedious and
painful', but that it could not be avoided on this occasion.
The king had a matter to broach to which a messenger
could not be made privy, 'nor none other but you and I,
which is that I would you should make good watch on the
duke of Suffolk, on the duke of Buckingham, on my lord
of Northumberland, on my lord of Derby, on my lord of
Wiltshire and on others which you think suspect to see
what they do with this news. No more to you at this time,
but *sapienti pauca*', he wrote mysteriously.[78] Why and
when these five and 'others which you think suspect' had
come to be doubted, what the ground of the doubt was,
who alerted the king, what 'this news' was which could be
so important to them we are not told. But it is a reasonable
guess that somehow this letter is to be placed at the beginning of the story which came to its conclusion with the
death of Edward Stafford, duke of Buckingham, in May
1521.

Polydore Vergil and the acid-tongued poet John Skelton
had no doubt that the great duke was relentlessly pursued
to his death by Wolsey. Little love was ever either exchanged or lost between these two men, it is true. The

78. *L.P.*, iii, 1. This letter bears no date. It is calendared in early
1519. I propose that it belonged to a later date.

arrogant, hot-tempered Buckingham, a man given to
'fumes and displeasure' and prone to 'rail and misuse himself in words', disapproved of England's friendship with
France and had bitterly resented the Field of Cloth of Gold
because of its expense to him, because it had been devised
by Wolsey without, he said, the consent of the Council,
because it would be nothing but an affair of empty speeches
and gallivanting.[79] But before all else, he loathed Wolsey
for his base birth, his overweening ways and his authority
in the land. On one occasion he had been astounded to see
Wolsey dare to wash his hands in water that the king had
just used. Outraged, he picked up the basin and threw its
contents at Wolsey's feet. The latter turned on him and
swore he would 'sit upon [his] skirts'; so, next day, the duke
appeared at court in a short dress, explaining to the king
that he did so in order to cheat the cardinal of his revenge.[80]
There may have been acrimony between them. Wolsey
may indeed have banished his son-in-law, the earl of
Surrey, to Ireland and had his father-in-law, the earl of
Northumberland, prosecuted for filching a royal ward, but
it is unlikely that he either wanted or would have been able
to bring the duke to his destruction.

Buckingham was a noble in the grand manner – a bluff
patriot, companion in arms of the king, one who had been
much at court to joust and play tennis with Henry, who
had entertained the king at his home at Penshurst, a great
Welsh Marcher lord (the last of his kind) whose possessions
straddled much of England, a magnate who rode with a
large retinue and could seat a huge company at dinner in
his castle, as yet unfinished, at Thornbury in Gloucester-
shire. His mother was a sister of Edward IV's queen, his
wife was a Percy, his son had married a Pole, his sons-in-
law were the earl of Surrey, the earl of Westmorland and

79. Polydore Vergil, *The Anglica Historia*, etc., 262 ff.; *L.P.*, iii,
1283, 1293.
80. So *Fiddes*, 277 f.

Lord Burgavenny; and over and above this there ran in his veins the blood of that fecund sire, Edward III.

Any king would have been anxious about such a subject, however docile that subject might have been. But Buckingham drew disaster upon himself with reckless thoroughness. It was from his surveyor, one Charles Knyvet, who had been dismissed from his post shortly before, that the story of the duke's folly reached Wolsey, and what Knyvet began was completed by interrogation of other servants, especially his confessor and chancellor. Buckingham, it transpired, had been lured by the prior of the Carthusian house at Henton, a man called Nicholas Hopkins, into dabbling in treasonous prophecy of the most damaging kind. As long ago as 1514, the prior had told him that he would one day be king, that he should 'have all', that he should strive to gain the affection of the commons against the moment when he would come into his own, that Henry would have no heir. When, on another occasion, the duke thought that he had so offended the king that he might find himself facing dispatch to the Tower, he declared that, were this to happen, he would do what his father wanted to do to Richard III, that is, kneel before him and then stab him; and as he spoke these words his hand went to his dagger and he swore by the blood of the Lord that this was his purpose. At Bletchingley in February 1520 he had boasted of how he would wait for a more opportune time to carry out his design, talked of those nobles who would support him and said that all that Henry had done was done unjustly. He had accused Wolsey of heinous vice and of procuring for the king, and declared that the death of Henry's son was divine vengeance.

At least, that is what he was said to have said.

Haughty ways had cost him protection at Court; stern landlordism had cost him the support of his tenantry – so much so that he did not dare to enter his Welsh Marcher lordships without a strong escort. When, in late 1520, he asked to be allowed to visit his lands on the borders in strength (as he had asked several times since 1517), he was refused. His purpose was innocent enough: to collect much-needed cash. But to those who remembered his father's rising in 1483, it sounded like the beginnings of a plot to raise rebellion.[81]

In a sense, Buckingham destroyed himself. What he had said, the treasonous words he had heard, the sinister plans he had apparently entertained were enough to bring a score of men to the scaffold. Whether he was really a threat to the kingdom, whether he really intended to usurp the throne, is perhaps largely beside the point. What he had said and done were manifest treason. What he was said to have said and done were manifest treason and would have cost anyone his life in early Tudor England. Indeed, if he had done, or been said to have done, no more than to note that there was no heir to the throne, and state that there never would be, he would have been in jeopardy; for, as early as 1521, the king's failure to beget an heir was probable already a sufficient cause of anxiety to make it dangerous for such as he to remark the fact.

Even as he was occupied, however, tenuously, with the compilation of the *Assertio*, Henry was unravelling the story of the duke's treason. When his letter to Wolsey, quoted above, was written we cannot know. It may have been some months before the full story broke, at a time when Buckingham was under suspicion and, with him, the whole of the powerful aristocratic connection which he dominated. There must have been good reason for Henry to have taken up the pen. If half a dozen and more of the nobility were thought to be conspiring against him, he had it.

Shakespeare has Henry interrogating Knyvet in person. Maybe this is what happened. Alas, the state papers tell

81. For all this, see *L.P.*, iii, 1283; Polydore Vergil, op. cit., 278 f.; *The Marcher Lordships of South Wales 1415–1536*, ed. Pugh (Board of Celtic Studies, Univ. of Wales History and Law Series, no. xx, Cardiff, 1963), 239 ff.

very little, but it is clear from a letter from Pace to Wolsey,
dated 16 April 1521, telling him that the king wanted to
keep Ruthal with him at Greenwich for certain matters connected with Buckingham's servants, that Henry was keenly
interested in the affair.[82] In truth, he had no alternative but
to strike. Eight days before Pace sent this message, the
duke, then at Thornbury, received a summons to London.
Unaware of what was afoot, he made his way there. As he
came down the Thames on the last lap of his journey, the
captain of the guard boarded his barge and arrested him.
He was taken ashore and escorted thence to the Tower.
On 13 May he was tried by his peers at Westminster, found
guilty and sentenced by the lord high steward, the duke of
Norfolk, whose eyes poured tears as he delivered himself
of his terrible words against his son's father-in-law.

1521, therefore, saw Henry write a book, acquire a title,
destroy a duke and secure the throne. It also saw the first –
and, in effect, the last – serious attempt of the reign to push
forward the work which Henry VII had begun by sponsor-
ing a major expedition across the Atlantic. Once again, it
was almost certainly Wolsey who was the inspiration for
this – and it is a measure of the cardinal's vision and
(probably) of the extent to which he remained a creature
of the previous reign that this should be so.

It was in 1517 that three Londoners, of whom the chief
was John Rastell, husband of Thomas More's sister and,
among other things, a printer, dramatist and military
engineer, projected the first recorded overseas voyage of
this reign. Under the direction of the same Sebastian Cabot
who, with his father, had led the earliest English expeditions to the New World in Henry VII's time, Rastell proposed to venture forth not only in search of fish but also
for the purpose of colonization. His voyage was essentially
a private undertaking, though he was armed with royal
letters of commendation addressed to any potentates he

82. *L.P.*, iii, 1233.

might encounter. It began at Gravesend on 1 March 1517. It miscarried badly – reaching no further than Waterford.[83]

Three years later a much larger, and official, plan was afoot to have Sebastian Cabot lead a major expedition to North America to find the North-West Passage around the American land-mass (whose full extent was, of course, not yet known) and thence to follow the sea-route to the spices and jewels of exotic Cathay, the land which Marco Polo had visited over two and a half centuries ago and which had been the objective of Christopher Colombus and the Cabots themselves on their previous voyages. Wolsey, then, would resume the quest for the northerly route to Asia which was to occupy English (and not only English) seamen for generations to come; and he offered Cabot, then in Venice, a handsome reward if he would return to England to be captain of this enterprise.[84] However, for various reasons, Cabot would not agree. Undeterred by this setback, the cardinal pressed ahead with his plans – with Henry evidently in eager accord – to launch what would have been perhaps the largest English maritime venture of the sixteenth century.

In early 1521 the merchant companies of London were invited to finance a fleet of five sail which, accompanied by a royal ship and others from the chief ports of the land like Bristol, would seek to outflank the Spanish and Portuguese and establish direct commercial relations with China and the East Indies. But the London merchants were as diffident as Cabot. Cathay was remote and unknown, the peril attached to challenging the Iberian monopolies great, the existing English commerce with Antwerp booming. Wolsey's bold design met refusal. The lord mayor of London, who had presided over the meeting of the recalcitrant merchants (in the Drapers' Company hall), was summoned

83. On this episode, see Williamson, *The Voyages of the Cabots and English Discovery of North America under Henry VII and Henry VIII* (1929), 85 ff., 244 ff.
84. *Ven. Cal.*, iii, 607.

to the royal presence and urged to cooperate. 'His grace
would have no nay therein, but spake sharply to the mayor
to see it [*sc.* the expedition] put in execution to the best of
his power.' Some ships and money were collected, but the
fleet never sailed.[85] The king's subjects would not be moved.
Six years later (in May 1527) two English ships sailed from
Plymouth to North America. One was lost; the other
reached Hudson's Straits or Frobisher's Sound and came
back. Meanwhile, one Robert Thorne, a Bristol merchant
then in Seville, had urged Henry to return to the search
for the North-West Passage, but his words drew no response. In 1536 a Master Hore of London, doubtless stirred
by the deeds of the Frenchman Cartier who had begun to
open up the St Lawrence estuary two years before, set out
from Gravesend with two ships for Newfoundland and
Labrador. But this was a private venture, apparently quite
without royal backing. In 1541, it was reported by the Imperial ambassador in England that the Privy Council was
thinking of returning to the quest for the North-West
Passage, but nothing came of whatever plans there were.[86]
Though there had been a flicker of former interest in 1527,
after the episode of 1521 Henry turned his back on the
Americas and Asia, so much so that a request by the mercurial Sebastian Cabot in 1537 to enter royal service once
more went unheeded. Cabot would one day return to England (from Spain) and spend the rest of his life here – but
in 1548, shortly after Henry's death.

The years 1519–21, the years when Wolsey stood at the
crest of his career and had seemingly brought western
Europe under his sway, were a wholly remarkable interlude in Henry's life – a second spring full of ambitious
plans and new beginnings. For a moment it appeared that,
under the influence of Wolsey and perhaps More and his
circle, Henry had turned his back on his past and was

85. See Williamson, op cit., 94 ff., 248 ff., for an account of this
affair and transcripts of the documents thereof.
86. *Sp. Cal.*, vi, 163.

preparing to become an industrious, working monarch bent on high purposes. Never had he looked so like his father. And had the expedition of 1521 been mounted, or had Henry and Wolsey taken up the idea with greater persistence soon afterwards, the history of the reign – and of England's evolution – might have been radically different. But this sudden outburst of royal enthusiasm was defeated by the reluctance of the king's subjects; and perhaps more fatally, England was about to be embroiled once more in the squabbles of the Continent; whereupon Henry shed his zeal for maritime venturing and returned to old-style expeditions across the Channel.

As we have seen, by May 1522 England was at war with France again and about to resume continental campaigning. Within a few weeks, Surrey had pillaged the westerly tip of Brittany and then led an Anglo-Imperial force out of Calais which served little military purpose, brought misery to hundreds of innocent peasants and consumed a good deal of money. By 16 October he was back at Calais and the year's fighting over. The truth was that England's heart was not yet in the war and that Charles could scarcely have found a less enthusiastic, generous or gracious ally. At Bruges, Wolsey had committed England to a full-scale invasion of France in early 1523; but, at Windsor nine months later he and Henry forced a postponement of the 'Great Enterprise', as it will be called, until 1524 and urged that, in the meantime, there should be a truce with France for one year.[87] Charles was told that such a truce would leave the allies readier to strike when the time came for the invasion but Wolsey's real purpose was that 'such a truce once had, God may inspire in the minds of Christian princes to condescend into a further peace'.[88] Through the winter of 1522–3, therefore, as the emperor repeatedly called upon England to overlook her treaties and mount some campaign in the coming year, he met the reply that

87. *Sp. Cal. F.S.*, pp. 195 ff.   88. *St.P.*, vi, 117 (*L.P.*, iii, 2764).

she wanted only a truce. Charles, much incensed, continued
to press. In early April Wolsey appeared to have changed
his mind and to have carried the king with him, when,
after all, it was agreed to send a small body of English
troops to the continent again this year. But stinging conditions were attached to this concession: one that the
Great Enterprise itself was to be postponed another year
until 1525 and others making it so easy to delay this year's
minor foray that it would probably never be mounted.[89]
The only difference in England's position, therefore, was
that she was intent on doing nothing for longer.

She was mistrustful of her ally, in constant anxiety about
the expense of the war and fearful of Scotland. In November 1521 Albany had returned to that country to cause
trouble at England's backdoor and, as the French king had
calculated, when England declared war on France, she
was already thinking of little else save Scotland.[90] She would
not risk again the near folly of 1513. She would turn to
Scotland first, then France.

So Henry dallied and haggled, evaded and postponed.
In September 1522, just when trouble from the north
seemed imminent, the English warden, Lord Dacre, concluded a short truce with an oncoming Scottish force (as
it was assumed to be) – a truce on his own initiative, without royal commission. As a result, Albany's army melted
in a few days, leaving its leader with nothing to do but slip
back to France to plead for aid. Henry was angered at
Dacre's action.[91] He was apparently ready to vindicate his
rights in Scotland by force of arms. But to Wolsey the news
of Dacre's *'felix culpa'*, as he called it, was sweet music. A
serious threat had been 'turned *in fumum*' and since the
great lords might now abandon France there was a chance
of a permanent settlement with Scotland – a truce of sixteen

89. *Sp. Cal. F.S.*, pp. 212 ff.

90. E.g. ibid., pp. 175, 202, 259 f.; *L.P.*, iii, 2755, 2764, 2768, 2907,
2922, 2939, etc.

91. So Wolsey said. *L.P.*, iii, 2574.

years, a marriage between Mary and the young James V.
As well as this, the collapse of the Auld Alliance might
compel Francis 'to seek the ways of peace and to make
honourable and reasonable offers for the same'.[92] But the
cardinal was optimistic. The war dragged on. In June and
September 1523 Surrey, Dacre and Dorset made raids across
the border on Kelso and Jedburgh and there was still talk
of a raid into Scotland to settle the matter once and for all.
In October Albany returned from France with 5,000 men
and tried to lead a force into England. Though he could
not persuade his men to cross the Tweed and turned back
in disarray, Scotland was still a good reason for England's
stalling.

In the middle of 1523, however, English policy had suddenly changed. Though not required by treaty to act and
in defiance of the calendar (for the fighting season was well
advanced), the England that had been so sluggish and
cautious suddenly changed her tune, thanks, primarily, to
the emergence of a powerful traitor in the enemy's camp. In
the spring of 1521 the wife of Charles, duke of Bourbon, and
constable of France, died, whereupon the French king and
his mother claimed the extensive lands which his wife had
held and which he himself quickly entered. By the end of
1522 the constable had been driven to the edge of rebellion
by the attack and had turned to France's enemies for aid.
Furtive negotiations with Charles and Henry quickly began, in which each side played for high stakes – Bourbon for
his all, the allies for an incipient rebel who might bring
with him a powerful clientele of lesser noblemen into their
camp and tip the scales decisively against France. He would
be an Albany, and more than an Albany, to France.[93]

Hitherto, despite initial enthusiasm, England had been
wary of him. Indeed, the lack of confidence in him which
Henry had felt was the final reason for that reluctance for
foreign war which we have noted and, for Charles, final

92. *St.P.*, i, 107 ff. (*L.P.*, iii, 2537).
93. See Lebey, *Le Connétable de Bourbon* (Paris, 1904), livre ii.

evidence of England's inadequacy and myopia.[94] Then the
change came. At the end of June 1523 the English ambassador in the Low Countries was ordered to go to Bourbon in
disguise and offer him terms,[95] and a month later a treaty
was signed between Henry, Charles and Bourbon committing all three to a joint invasion of France. The English
army was to attack before the end of that month (August);
English money to be poured into Bourbon's pocket.[96] A few
days before this Henry and Wolsey had agreed over the
dinner-table to send Sir John Russell, disguised as a merchant, to Bourbon to clinch the bargain. He arrived at
Bourg, where Bourbon was, on the night of 6 September,
worked very quickly and set out immediately for home.
Thus, despite the Scots, despite the lateness of the year,
despite her thrift, the England which had refused so many
Imperial demands to launch herself against France was
committed to war across the Channel forthwith.

It was not, as has sometimes been argued, Wolsey's desire
to conscript Imperial support in the next papal election
which precipitated this change, for not even he could pay
as high a price as this for aiding his ambition. England
went to war now because war now seemed suddenly to offer
huge profits. The Swiss and the Venetians had swung to
the allies and pinned down a large army south of the Alps;
Charles was ready to strike at Guienne from the other side
of the Pyrenees; and now Bourbon was an open traitor
prepared to throw himself against Francis.

Since June of the last year (1522) Henry had been talking
once more about his claims to the French crown and kingdom, saying that he trusted in God that he would soon be
'governor' of France and that Francis would 'make a way
for him as King Richard did for his father', that is, that he
looked to another Bosworth Field somewhere across the
Channel.[97] In the terms first offered to Bourbon and, Wolsey

94. *Sp. Cal. F.S.*, pp. 216 ff., 244, 249.
95. *St.P.*, vi, 131 ff. (*L.P.*, iii, 3123).   96. *L.P.*, iii, 3225.
97. *Ven Cal.*, iii, 467. *St.P.*, i, 110 (*L.P.*, iii, 2555). The last are
More's words in a letter to Wolsey.

said, drafted by Henry himself, Bourbon had been required
to acknowledge Henry as lawful king of France and his
liege lord, and to publish this declaration in order to encourage other nobles to follow suit.[98] But Charles had jibbed
at this and the final terms taken to Bourbon by Russell
required the constable to make a full, but private, profession of allegiance which Charles should not know about, or a
qualified public one.[99] Clearly the claim to France, the old
ambition, was coming to the fore again. Recent French
provocation had reawakened it and Bourbon stirred it further. The battle of Pavia would bring it to high heat.

At the end of August 1523 a fine army of 10,000, led by
Suffolk, crossed from the shores of Kent to Calais, exactly
ten years since Henry had embarked on his first campaign. Henry's second major war, which Charles had so
persistently demanded and Wolsey so resolutely tried to
prevent, had finally begun. Wolsey had been hoping to
restrain both Charles and Henry up to the last moment,[1]
but now accepted the inevitability of large-scale war and
threw himself vigorously into the business of campaigning.
But there was a difference between king and minister about
strategy. Suffolk's purpose was the capture of Boulogne,
and no more. By gaining a second Channel port a better
platform would be prepared for the Great Enterprise which
was still due next year, in 1524. Wolsey had hitherto expressed agreement with all this. But about three weeks after
the English army had landed at Calais he changed his mind
and started urging that Henry should send his troops in
a headlong dash towards Paris at the same time as Charles
and Bourbon struck from the south and east respectively.[2]
England, therefore, was to set aside her own separate enterprise and join in a triple thrust into the heart of France.

98. *L.P.*, iii, 3123, 3154; *Sp. Cal. F.S.*, p. 259.
99. *St.P.*, i, 163, 165. Bourbon, however, refused to acknowledge
himself to be anything more than Henry's ally.
1. See the Imperial ambassador's remarks in *Sp. Cal. F.S.*, pp. 230,
250, 259.
2. *St.P.*, i, 135 ff. (*L.P.*, iii, 3346).

Several things may have changed his mind, one of them an
urgent appeal from Bourbon, brought back by Russell,[3] to
accept this strategy, another the fear of crippling expense.
The siege of Boulogne could be very costly. It was very
important not to get caught up in a 'dribbling war', as he
called it, or a war 'of small prickings' which would eat up
money and yield little. There must be a single, coordinated,
assault on France, made 'with great puissances', which
would settle the matter in one blow, perhaps stun the enemy
into peace and save England the expense of mounting a
huge campaign next year.[4] Wolsey had consistently said
that the only reason for fighting France was to drive her
quickly into offering advantageous terms. 'There is no good
war commenced or continued but only to the extent to
conduce and bring once a good peace', he would write later.[5]
With luck, if England abandoned the king's strategy and
toop part in a swift, all-out attack, the war could end in a
few weeks.

But Henry would not agree. The year was too old for
such a campaign. The towns that lay across the English
path were not the trifles that Wolsey supposed and, if they
were easily won, could be easily lost. The difficulties of
victualling a fast-moving army would be huge and, faced
with this sudden assault, Francis would probably recall his
army from Italy and fall upon the invaders in strength.
Finally, so the king argued, if the English troops were
denied the profit of spoil, they would have 'evil will to
march forward and their captains shall have much ado to
keep them from crying Home! Home!'[6] His words were
prophetic. But Wolsey held to his conviction and, by 26
September, that is, six days after the argument had begun,
had won.[7] The siege of Boulogne was called off and Suffolk
told to lead his men towards Paris.

At first they were astoundingly successful. In three weeks
they made about seventy-five miles and crossed the Somme.

3. *Sp. Cal. F.S.*, p. 275. *L.P.*, iii, 3281.
4. *St.P.*, vi, 159, 160 (*L.P.*, iii, 3135).   5. ibid., 243 (*L.P.*, iv, 61).
6. ibid., 135 ff. (*L.P.*, iii, 3346).   7. *L.P.*, iii, 3371.

By the end of October they were only fifty miles from Paris. English troops had not been so near the French capital for generations and, as news of successes reached him, Henry grew highly excited and began to think that there was now 'good likelihood of the attaining of his ancient right and title to the crown of France, to his singular comfort and eternal honour'.[8] There was some truth in Wolsey's assertion 'there shall be never such or like opportunity given hereafter for the attaining of France'.[9] On the strength of all this, Henry decided to throw in reinforcements to keep the campaign going through the winter and himself hurried back from Woodstock to London in order to save time hitherto lost in communicating with Wolsey by letter.[10] It seemed that Wolsey's argument in favour of his strategy had been wholly vindicated.

Then the bubble burst. As ever, the allies' elaborate plans had demanded too much. The Spanish troops had crossed the Pyrenees but were in wretched spirits when the French commander Lautrec found them and contained them easily. Next, Bourbon's expedition collapsed ludicrously. He had scarcely got out of Besançon (where he started) when he turned tail and bolted to Genoa. Meanwhile Suffolk was in acute distress. His Burgundian contingents had melted away, then merciless cold killed men and beasts, and was followed by a thaw that turned all to mud and made it impossible to shift a gun or pitch a tent. Miles from home, scourged by the weather and the news of Bourbon's defection, the English troops did exactly what Henry had predicted and turned back to Flanders.[11] Even as they retreated fast, reinforcements with which to smash through the walls of Paris were being made ready for dispatch from the south coast.

Henry was mortified by the news of this débâcle. At first

8. Rogers, *Correspondence of Sir Thomas More*, 300 (*L.P.*, iii, 3485).
9. *St.P.*, i, 143.
10. Rogers, op. cit., 301; *St.P.*, iv, 60.
11. See *St.P.*, vi, 221 ff., 233 ff. (*L.P.*, iii, 3659; iv, 26), etc. for accounts of the campaign.

he refused to accept it, insisting that his demoralized army
should return to action at once and devised all sorts of
schemes for carrying on the attack.[12] Gradually he accepted
the fact that the war was over, at least for the moment. But
only for the moment. A way had been found 'for entering
the bowels of France without besieging any strong places';
the allies were solid, he thought; and he himself was of 'firm
and constant mind ... to prosecute and follow these good
commencements'. He would launch a new attack in the
spring to recover what belonged to him 'by just title and
inheritance'. The new pope, Clement VII, must throw in
his lot with the allies and Bourbon, wherever he might be,
brought to England to plan the new campaign.[13]

Such was Henry's mood at Christmas 1523, as reported
by Wolsey. A fortnight later the plan had been refined:
Bourbon would command the remains of Suffolk's army,
which was stranded across the Channel, and with his own
missing lanzknechts march on Paris or Normandy. Another
force, led perhaps by Henry. would join the attack, 'pre-
cipitating a clear and new revolution through all that realm
of France'.[14] The fight was still afoot, therefore. It was a
question simply of *reculer pour mieux sauter*. Said the
Spanish ambassador, Henry was confident 'that he can
conquer all the frontier provinces, and even Paris'.[15]

But this belligerence cooled. By the spring, England was
saying that she would indeed launch an attack, but only if
Charles and Bourbon had already done so successfully and,
until then, she would not lend a penny. Moreover, she was
undoubtedly ready for a truce or, better, a peace treaty with
France, provided that the initiative did not appear to come
from her.[16]

12. So Wolsey said. *St.P.*, vi, 201, 234 (*L.P.*, iii, 3601; iv, 26).
13. *St.P.*, vi, 221 ff. (*L.P.*, iii, 3659).
14. ibid., 233 ff. (*L.P.*, iii, 26).
15. *Sp. Cal. F.S.*, p. 318.
16. ibid., *passim*, esp. pp. 309, 311 ff., 347, 359, 376, etc.; *St.P.*, vi,
242 ff., 261 ff., 278 ff.

During the first months of 1524, therefore, English policy assumed a double aspect. On the one hand she welcomed peace moves by Clement VII and, most remarkably, received one John Joachim, a Cistercian and maître d'hôtel of the queen mother of France, who came secretly to discuss terms.[17] On the other hand she repeatedly stated that, if her allies could topple France, she would swoop into attack, with Henry probably leading his forces. Richard Pace was off again, with Sir John Russell, to conclude a new treaty with Bourbon for a double invasion on condition that he first swore fealty to Henry, which he had still avoided doing.[18]

Wolsey could write that this new double-headed policy was judged expedient by 'the king's highness and his council',[19] but there is strong evidence that he had imposed it on a king who was straining to fight. John Clerk, whom we have used before to distinguish king's intentions from minister's, told the pope that Wolsey had laboured hard to persuade the king and Council to listen to the papal plea for peace, 'they now being fixed upon matters of war'.[20] Would Clerk have dared or wanted to say this if it were wholly untrue? The English ambassadors in Spain were told by Wolsey in strict confidence, in a ciphered passage at the end of a long letter of instructions, that 'it is more than necessary to lean unto the peace'.[21] This does not prove that Wolsey alone thought thus. But on the same day (25 March) letters went to Rome in the king's name which called upon Clement to attack France and then, in the second half, which was written by Wolsey in the first person singular, gave detailed and enthusiastic plans for peace. This second half contained what '*in my conceit* may be

17. *L.P.*, iv, 271, 360; *Sp. Cal. F.S.*, 335 f., 355.
18. B.M. Vit. B, vi, fols 69 ff. (*L.P.*, iv, 365); *St.P.*, vi, 288 ff. (*L.P.*, iv, 374).
19. *St.P.*, vi, 243 (*L.P.*, iv, 61).
20. B.M. Vit. B, vi, fol. 116v (*L.P.*, iv, 446).
21. *St.P.*, vi, 277 (*L.P.*, iv, 186).

thought upon or imagined for to conduce everything to best purpose' and was advanced now with as much vigour 'as may stand with my duty to my sovereign lord and master'[22] – which certainly seems to be another example of Wolsey dissociating himself from the king and working somewhat against him.[23] Wolsey was still sceptical about Bourbon and anxious to save money, while Henry, as the Imperial ambassador thought, was readier for war.[24] Wolsey insisted that Bourbon should not be given any cash until he had taken the oath of allegiance, but it was Henry's 'mind and pleasure' that it might be handed over even if he refused.[25]

When Pace came upon Bourbon in a small town a few miles south of Turin, he found him impressive. His forces amounted to over 20,000 and were growing. He was ready to cross into Provence and make for Lyons or Marseilles, while Henry followed the route which Suffolk had marked out last year to Paris. After considerable hedging, he eventually swore allegiance to the king of England, though he declined homage for the duchy he hoped to recover. He would 'spend his blood like a nobleman for the recovery of the king's right', he said and, after communicating, declared, 'I promise unto you, upon my faith, that I will, by the help of my friends, put the crown of France upon the king our common master's head, or else my days shall be cut off.' Said Pace proudly, if Henry will not fetch the French crown for himself, 'we will bring the same unto you'.[26]

Pace had fallen under Bourbon's spell and through the early summer months sent a spate of letters homewards begging Henry to put his men and money into the fray. England, he argued, must exploit this golden chance and back Bourbon to the full. 'Sir', Pace wrote to Wolsey, 'to speak to you boldly, if you do not regard the premises, I

22. *St.P.*, vi, 278 ff. (*L.P.*, iv, 185). My italics.
23. See above, p. 91,   24. *Sp. Cal. F.S.*, pp. 318, 320.
25. *St.P.*, vi, 291 (*L.P.*, iv, 384).
26. B.M. Vit. B, vi, fols 94v, 95, 100v (*L.P.*, iv, 420, 421).

will impute to your grace the loss of the crown of France.'[27]
Bold talk indeed, as was a later summons, recalled by
Wolsey, 'to lay my cardinal's hat, cross, maces and myself'
as pledges for the English invasion.[28] At the same time
letters and an envoy came from Bourbon himself to reinforce the Englishman's barrage. His army and navy had
begun to move; by the end of July he was in Provence and
preparing to throw a hoop of guns about Marseilles.

But in England Pace's excited pleas had fallen on stony
ground. The Great Enterprise, he was curtly informed,
could not take place until next year; Bourbon would be
more impressive if he had turned his army towards Lyons
instead of Marseilles, if he had conquered not in his own
'but in the king's name and to the king's use', and if he
demanded less money; Pace must guard his language in
addressing a cardinal and a chancellor and remember that
Henry would not fight until he saw that he might 'facilely,
without any great resistance, attain the said crown or some
great part of his inheritance'; before that time 'it were small
wisdom' to dispatch an army.[29] So Wolsey wrote – and,
even as he wrote, secret peace talks with France were going
on in London and Calais.

Towards the end of August, news of Bourbon's remarkable successes reached England, whereupon it was suddenly
decided that, if he turned his forces across the Rhône to
Lyons, an English army would be sent to France at once.[30]
Henry had been swept back onto the warpath. But only for
a moment. Neither his army nor Charles's was ready for
such quick action. Wretched liaison between the allies made
a joint attack yet more difficult and left Wolsey swearing
'a great oath that he wished he had broken his arms and
his legs when he stepped on shore to go to Bruges' – the
place where, three years previously, much of the present

27. *St.P.*, vi, 314 (*L.P.*, iv, 442).
28. ibid., 334 (*L.P.*, iv, 605).
29. *L.P.*, iv, 510, 589.
30. *St.P.*, iv, 120 f. (*L.P.*, iv, 615). *Sp. Cal. F.S.*, pp. 376, 378, 380, etc.

troubles had begun.[31] Then Bourbon collapsed. His siege of
Marseilles was suddenly abandoned and his army sent
scuttling across the Alps to Milan. The constable talked
boldly of a new campaign next year, but for the moment
it was all up with him. As Clerk observed, had his men
'made as good speed outwards as they have made homewards, they might have been at Calais long afore this time'.[32]

What Wolsey had felt recently was clear. Several times,
the Spanish ambassador reported, he had said that, for the
sake of peace, Charles ought to abandon his claim to Milan
and Henry his claim to France.[33] If he spoke sincerely he
spoke remarkably and, what is more, in the second part of
this remark, he spoke against the mind of the king.

31. *Sp. Cal. F.S.*, p. 392.
32. *St.P.*, vi, 355 (*L.P.*, iv, 724).
33. *Sp. Cal. F.S.*, p. 417.

6

The Repudiation of the Habsburgs

SHORTLY after Henry and Francis I met on the Field of Cloth of Gold, the two monarchs were standing in a tent listening to Wolsey reading out the Articles relating to the meeting. When the cardinal came to the words 'Henry, king of England and France', his king cried out laughingly. 'Expunge this title!' He then turned to Francis and said, 'They are titles given me which are good for nothing.'[1] But these were words spoken in a moment of chivalrous amity. When, on other occasions, Henry trumpeted his claims to lost English possessions in France he was probably doing more than observing diplomatic formality or invoking what seems today to have been an archaism with which to disguise mere belligerence with the trappings of righteousness. Though English claims had been commuted into an annual (and erratic) pension from France, and though Henry could several times embrace the French monarch in cordial friendship, the ancient ambition to recover at least part of a lost empire was probably still alive in the very core of the man, and his bold talk about his 'true inheritance' and 'just title' to France not much less serious than they had been when an Edward III or Henry V uttered them. We who know that this would-be warrior-king never achieved any brilliant, large-scale conquest or won himself coronation in Paris should remember that this was despite his efforts, and that there was a moment when the wind seemed to be standing fair for England as never before. On 14 February 1525, the twenty-fifth birthday of Charles V, an overwhelming defeat was inflicted on the French outside the walls of Pavia, the citadel of central Lombardy. In a few hours the French army was shattered – thousands of its men, including cap-

1. *Ven. Cal.*, iii, 45.

tains like the king of Navarre and White Rose (the earl
of Suffolk) were killed, and with final, crushing humiliation,
the French king taken prisoner. An apparently indomitable
France, with whom Wolsey had been carrying on secret
peace talks for months, now lay before her opponents without an army, money or a king to defend her from dis-
memberment. Moreover, a whole fighting season lay ahead.
Wolsey had been right. As he had intended, and as Francis
had refused to see, major war had become suicidal.

Charles received the news of his victory with extraordinary calm, withdrawing from his courtiers to pray alone. The
news reached Henry on early 9 March and found him in
bed. He rose, pulled on some clothes and read the messenger's letter, crying out with joy and then falling on his
knees in thanksgiving. 'My friend,' he is reported to have
said to the messenger, 'you are like Saint Gabriel who
announced the coming of Christ,' and after this unseemly
simile called for wine. 'Did you see the king of France in
the hands of the viceroy of Naples, as this letter testifies?'
he asked. 'I helped to disarm him,' the messenger replied.
'He was on the ground. His horse was on top of him. . . . The
viceroy ran up and kissed his hand. The king of France
gave him his sword and the viceroy gave his own sword to
the prisoner. He was wounded in the cheek and in the hand,
but only slightly. As he lay on the ground, everything that
could be taken from him was taken by his captors, every
plume of his helmet.' Henry then heard of the massacre of
the French army. 'And Richard de la Pole?' he asked. 'The
White Rose is dead in battle. . . . I saw him dead with the
others,' he was told. 'God have mercy on his soul!' Henry
cried. 'All the enemies of England are gone. Give him more
wine.'[2]

A Henry V or a Bedford had never been more advantage-
ously placed; nor certainly had Henry VIII. 'Now is the
time,' he would say to an embassy from the Low Countries,

2. Macquereau, *Histoire Générale de l'Europe, etc.* (Louvain, 1765),
231. The source of this story is not given.

'for the emperor and myself to devise the means of getting full satisfaction from France. Not an hour is to be lost.'[3] The Great Enterprise, so often discussed but never executed, could now go forward, Henry himself leading an army in a joint invasion with Charles and Bourbon. Meanwhile, bonfires blazed and Wolsey sang High Mass in St Paul's. The English army was being marshalled, an embassy was on its way to the regent of the Netherlands to organize the hoys, the guns and gunners, the horses and the wagons for Henry's use. On 21 March commissioners were appointed to raise another levy from the country, the so-called Amicable Grant, the climax of three years' heavy fiscalism, with which, so the populace would be told, Henry would exploit this God-given chance to recover his rightful inheritance.

An embassy was soon sent to Spain to arrange the campaign. Its instructions show the extent of Henry's appetite. It is 'for his high orgule, pride and insatiable ambition' that Francis has received this divine punishment and unless the allies seize this opportunity to suppress France 'it is to be feared that God should take high indignation against them, executing his terrible sword of correction and dreadful punishment upon them for the same'. It would be culpable folly to allow Francis to be ransomed and restored, even to a reduced kingdom; rather 'his line and succession ought to be abolished, removed and utterly extinct'. Let the two allied forces march on Paris – where Henry will be crowned and enter into all that is his 'by just title of inheritance'. Henry is not only ready to provide cash for the emperor's army, but will even accompany him to Rome for his coronation and then help him recover his rights in Italy. Let Charles remember that, if he marries Mary, as he is bound to do by treaty, he may thereby add England, Ireland and a title to Scotland, as well as France, to his existing possessions and thus become 'lord and owner . . . of all Christendom'. If the emperor will not invade personally let him subsidize Bourbon (provided Bourbon swears allegiance to

3. *Sp. Cal.*, iii, 82.

Henry, as king of France). If Charles refuses this then Henry will offer 100,000 or even 150,000 crowns towards the cost – and so on.

It is not Henry's intention to claim all that Francis once ruled. Charles will receive Provence, Languedoc and Burgundy; Bourbon will recover his patrimony; Henry will take the rest. Perhaps Charles will not agree to this. If the ambassadors meet absolute, impenetrable refusal they are to present, in turn, a graduated list of demands. If Henry cannot have the crown of France and the whole of the Angevin empire then, very reluctantly, he will settle for the latter only; if he cannot have the whole of this he will give up Guienne; if this is still too much he will accept Picardy, Normandy and Brittany – and so the list descends to England's last, least demand: either Normandy or Picardy plus Boulogne and some other towns. But this is only if Charles is quite unmovable. England's object is all she ever had – an empire and a crown.[4]

We cannot know how much Henry really expected. But that he did expect something large, that this sudden upsurge of ambition was serious, seems beyond doubt. The month or two that followed the arrival of the news of Pavia was a period of bustle and preparation with few equals in his reign. Unfortunately the sources are parsimonious with information on Henry himself. We know that he wanted to lead an army into France without delay but that Wolsey restrained him, and it was decided that Norfolk should go ahead with a van- and rear-guard of 20,000 while Henry waited at the head of the middleward until all the allied forces were on the move.[5] We catch glimpses of the king during the commotion caused by the Amicable Grant and in diplomatic reports. But little else comes to hand. Instead we have to tell how his hopes were dashed.

Charles snubbed Henry's grand plans. He was penniless and anxious for peace. He was not ready radically to redraw the map of Europe or to inflate Henry's power. The victory

4. *St.P.*, vi, 412 ff. (*L.P.*, iv, 1212).   5. *L.P.*, iv, 1249, 1261, 1301.

he had already won was sufficient. And if Mary's hand enticed him so too did the prospect of a Portuguese wife, for whom he was already negotiating.[6] As a result, the ambassadors sent to him from England could only report to Henry that the emperor intended 'little or nothing ... to your commodity, profit or benefit'.[7] Wolsey had made matters worse. Since last summer he had been furtively dealing with his old friend and confidante, the French queen mother, despite Charles's protests. He had met an Imperial request for cash with a harangue in which Charles was dubbed a liar, Margaret of Savoy a ribald and Bourbon a traitor – words ill-designed to ease the return of a prodigal ally, let alone commend his vaulting ambition.[8] About the same time he had insulted the Imperial ambassador by having a letter to him seized by the night watch of the City of London and compounded the offence by rating the ambassador before the Council because of unflattering remarks about himself contained therein. He went on to forbid him communication with the outside world and to demand his recall.[9] Wolsey was being consistent, if outrageous. He had never had confidence in the allies; and now made it certain that Charles would feel little amity in return.

Next, the Amicable Grant was a failure. As the commissioners went about the business of gathering money for the invasion they met raucous resistance. Three years ago there had been heavy loans; in 1523 a lay and clerical subsidy of unprecedented size – most of it quickly anticipated and already spent. The demand now for one sixth of lay and one third of clerical income came upon lambs already close-shorn. There were widespread portents of insurrection and, in places, open opposition to the war – as in Kent, where people protested that, were the king to conquer France, he would spend his time and their money there; that they were sorry Francis was taken captive; that Henry had never yet won a foot of land across the Channel

6. *L.P.*, iv, 1379, 1380.   7. *St.P.*, i, 160 (*L.P.*, iv, 1371).
8. *L.P.*, iv, 1380.   9. *Sp. Cal.*, iii, 51 ff., 62 ff.

(which was not quite true).[10] And in the face of fierce hostility Henry retreated.

He did so with some *sang froid*. He stated that he 'never knew of that demand', i.e. the Amicable Grant, and, we are told, when he heard of the furore it had caused, converted it into a so-called benevolence. It is incredible that he should have been entirely ignorant of it, though he may not have known the rate. Probably, as Wolsey said, the plan was originally devised by the Council independently of the king and without his knowing the full details. We need not accept Wolsey's subsequent claim that he (Wolsey) never assented to it. This was surely as disingenuous as Henry's claim to complete ignorance. But he may not have been keen about it. Moreover, it does seem clear that, having taken the measure of the opposition, it was Wolsey who persuaded the king – on bended knees (he said) – to relent and to pardon those who had resisted.[11] We have the testimony of Warham to give partial support to Wolsey here.[12] The people 'cursed the cardinal' and he accepted the odium to allow the benevolent image of the king, conjured up by Hall, to be presented to the people. But Wolsey observed, concerning the true site of responsibility 'the eternal God knoweth all'.[13]

Charles's disdain for the English plan to carve France into pieces, following hard on the heels of this rebuff, wrecked the Great Enterprise, and hence, after much persuasion by the Council, Henry reluctantly allowed Wolsey to resume negotiations with France in the summer of 1525. An anonymous monk had come to Wolsey in May 1524 – that is, months before Pavia – to explore the terrain and he was quickly followed by one John Joachim, who came to Wolsey from the French queen mother in the guise of a merchant and was kept out of sight in the house of his chaplain, Thomas Lark, at Blackfriars. By March 1525 it seemed that Anglo-French peace was in sight. Wolsey had

10. *L.P.*, iv, 1243, 1260, 1266, etc.   11. *Hall*, 694 ff.
12. Ellis, 3rd ser., ii, 9 (*L.P.*, iv, 1332).   13. *Hall*, 700.

received a third emissary from Louise and an interview with the king was at hand. But on the day that the French were due to meet Henry news of Pavia arrived and with it the sudden upsurge of English belligerence. The French envoys heard the ghastly news as they were riding down Holborn to court; whereupon they turned about and made swiftly for home.[14]

But eleven weeks later the situation had changed so radically that they were back. Their former host, Lark, had received a message to urge Wolsey to resume his work for peace and he readily agreed.[15] Joachim returned to London on 22 June to take up the threads of former negotiation for an Anglo-French entente, and on 30 August 1525 a solemn treaty was signed at The More[16] which put an end to three years of confused and wretched war between England and France.

By the late summer of 1525, English policy possessed considerable complexity. Henry had been humiliated and disappointed by his former ally, against whom he now had a formidable list of grievances. Charles owed him large sums of money, had cast aside an offer of marriage to Mary and, above all, had refused to exploit the massive success of Pavia and to share the fruits of victory. Accordingly the king had come to terms with the very enemy whom, but a few weeks before, he had been hoping to carve into pieces; though this did not stop him continuing to argue, after the Anglo-French treaty had been signed at The More, that Francis was 'our subject or our rebel', who 'ought to be delivered to us'.[17] Henry still hoped that Charles would decide to break France and dismember that kingdom. But this Charles utterly refused to do. When it was clear that he was quite unmovable, England would probably have

14. See Jacqueton, *La Politique Extérieure de Louise de Savoie* (Paris, 1892), 46 ff.

15. Jacqueton, op. cit., 316 ff.; *L.P.*, iv, 1233.

16. I.e. the house at Moor, by Rickmansworth in Herts – one of Wolsey's residences.

17. See *St.P.*, vi, 476 ff., esp. 482 f. (*L.P.*, iv, 1628).

been well advised to extricate herself entirely from European affairs, for recent events had given final proof – if this were needed – that she could not dominate the policies of continental powers. But Wolsey (and Henry) would not relent. Years later, More would recall that there had often been a party in the Council anxious for England to disentangle herself from Europe's affairs, whom Wolsey thrust aside by telling the fable of the men who sheltered in caves from the rain, which, they believed, would make all whom it wetted fools, in the hope that they would thereafter rule over the fools.[18] The cardinal would not make their error. Far from retreating into the caves himself, this overweeningly ambitious, self-confident man would make another attempt to control the destiny of Europe, and one which involved a sudden diplomatic revolution. The treaty of The More, which England would have been ready to break if Charles had agreed, after all, to a joint invasion of France, had been intended not only to protect her and buttress her prestige if Charles should emerge from recent events with quite overwhelming new power, but also to provide the spine of an active anti-Habsburg formation. Partly because of English grievances against him and partly because this was true, Wolsey quickly judged that the emperor would now be the menace to European peace. Hence, even as England was cautiously pursuing a double policy of stirring Charles to strike France and wooing France lest Charles should suffocate her, the self-styled arbiter of Europe was also feeling his way towards restoring that balance of power on the continent which had been created in 1519 and which would give him, as third party, the position of mastery. To this end, Wolsey set to work to encourage a league of Italian powers, clustered around the pope, which, when joined by France, might hold its own with Charles and allow England to recover her former role of *tertius gaudens*, able to tip the balance decisively against an emperor who threatened to make peace unattainable.

18. *L.P.*, vii, 114.

It was Wolsey who swung England into this anti-Imperial stance, though he did so with Henry's knowledge. Albeit the king's bitter discontent with Charles helped, Wolsey had to struggle with him to divert him from making war on France after Pavia and still more to win him over to the peace terms offered by France – which included no cession of land.[19] If it is stretching evidence too far to say that king and minister were working in opposite directions, it seems that Wolsey was ahead of him. The cardinal had lost confidence in Charles and Bourbon long since, had begun negotiations with France months before, been lukewarm (possibly) about the Amicable Grant, slow to want to exploit Pavia and, if the incident concerning the Imperial ambassador's correspondence may be so interpreted, ready to use foul means as well as fair to disrupt relations with the emperor. The English plan to dismember France does not invalidate the thesis that Wolsey believed in a kind of balance of power, because such evidence as there is suggests that the plan did not come from Wolsey. Moreover, as soon as circumstances permitted, he replaced the plan with a new form of that policy which he had worked out painfully in former years. If he brought England out of the war empty-handed, he had at least been consistent.

By the beginning of 1526 his schemes began to bear fruit. Francis I was liberated from captivity in January, having paid dearly for his freedom and only after agreeing to leave his sons in Charles's hands as hostages for the payment of his ransom. At first sight Charles's power seemed handsomely advanced by the treaty (of Madrid) which he had imposed on his captive; but in reality the latter had no intention of abiding by it. 'As soon as possible,' he told the English ambassadors shortly after his release, 'I shall take off my mask' and disown a treaty signed under duress.[20]

19. Jacqueton, op. cit., p. 323. Wolsey repeated this claim in 1527 (*L.P.*, iv, 3105). Cf. Giberti's judgement that he was urgent for peace with France, made in June 1525 (*L.P.*, iv, 1474).

20. *L.P.*, iv, 2079.

Wolsey had already guessed as much and, as soon as he had
heard of that treaty, written, 'I cannot persuade to myself
that the French king is determined ... to perform the
same'.[21] A little later, the king and the 'lords of the secret
council' had arrived at the convenient judgement that the
treaty was impossible for Francis to discharge and would
make Charles 'monarch, not only of Italy, but also all Christendom' and allow him 'to give laws to all the world'.[22] The
new situation was fraught with danger. Unless Charles
abated his demands a new European war could not be
avoided. Charles must give back the French princes; Burgundy – handed over to Charles in the treaty – must stay
French; Milan might be committed to English trusteeship or
restored as an independent state. Only thus could a recrudescence of war be averted. But how was the emperor to be persuaded to all or some of this? How could he be brought to
relax what were not only hereditary claims but now rights
based also on a treaty signed and sealed? The only way was
by threatening him with force unless he yielded. Since the
previous summer (1525) English diplomacy had been helping to piece together a confederation of Italian powers. In
May 1526, after months of burrowing and cajoling, a league
was formed at Cognac, composed of France, the Papacy,
Venice, Milan and Florence, and aimed openly at the
emperor.[23]

England had a large share in the creation of this league
but, to the surprise, then the dismay and finally the anger of
its members, refused to become a participant. Her position
was as clear as it was unpalatable. She wanted to force
Charles to terms which Francis could accept, and which
would thus make peace possible. She hoped that the league as
it now stood would be sufficient to do this and that mean-

21. *L.P.*, iv, 1963. This was before the remark of Francis I, quoted
above.

22. B.M. Calig. D, ix, fols 199v f. (*L.P.*, iv, 2148).

23. Since the pope had come to terms with Charles in January
1526, Wolsey had pushed the former very hard to get him into this
league. For a while Anglo-Papal relations were very strained (cf.
L.P., iv, 1956, 1967).

while she could stand by as an observer ready to step in as 'honest broker' as soon as Charles started talking. For the moment it was for others to do the fighting (which promptly broke out in northern Italy) – and to pay for it. But should the present league prove inadequate to bring Charles to reasonable terms then she would throw more and more weight on its side. Her open adhesion to the league would be the last sanction, however. Before then she hoped to have tipped the scales so manifestly against the emperor and created such an imbalance of power that the latter would have accepted her plans for a new treaty of universal peace to be concluded at London, under the presidency of king and cardinal. Writing to Henry with that high-flown, almost megalomaniac optimism which rarely deserted him, Wolsey sketched a future in which the emperor would have 'come unto reasonable conditions in such wise as Your Highness, God willing, shall have in your hands the conducing of universal peace of Christendom, to your great merit, high laud and perpetual renown; the success whereof I shall signify to Your Grace from day to day, as the case shall require'.[24] Doubtless the plan ignored the dangers of using force to secure amity; it exaggerated Wolsey's influence wildly; it overlooked the possibility of another Pavia. But it did offer the chance of peace and, however much overlaid with vanity and power-lust, it was probably sincerely meant. That this was another attempt to rebuild European peace – on the same principles as before – was stated by Wolsey so often, in public and private, to all manner of persons (from the king downwards)[25] that it must be extravagant cynicism to dismiss it as trumpery and nothing but trumpery. What is more, those about him, like foreign ambassadors, took him seriously.[26] Like Charles they may have resented the manner and noted the vainglory; but they allowed the end.

Throughout the summer of 1526 a chorus of entreaties

24. *St.P.*, i, 168, (*L.P.*, iv, 2325).
25. E.g. *L.P.*, iv, 1902, 1926, 2148, 2325, 2388, 2556, 2573.
26. *Ven. Cal.*, iii, 1305, 1349, 1351, 1374, 1377, 1435, 1450; iv, 49.

went up from the confederates that England should throw
in her lot with them, or that Henry should at least accept
the title of protector of the league, or send some money.
But she remained unmoved. Wolsey, said the Venetian ambassador, would give 'nothing but words'.[27] On 1 August he
emerged from a stormy session with the papal, French and
Venetian envoys and wrote to Henry 'I have not seen any
men in my life more vehement. . . . Howbeit Sire, they have
not been so hot, but I have been as cold, and have made as
many reasons, dissuading your short entry into the said
league and contribution thereto, as they have made for
acceleration and advancement thereof'.[28] A little later, lest
England's aloofness should damage the morale of the confederates, he had to play with them – 'to begin to commune
with them' as he explained to More – and without going
to any 'express refusal' would so dilly-dally that it would
be too late to do anything this year.[29] He would not jeopar-
dize his potential position of mediator. To a pope angered
by the legate's disregard, he wrote blandly that he regretted
that circumstances prevented him serving the Holy See as
zealously as he would like.[30]

By October, however, he could hold out no longer without damaging the very weapon to which he looked for
success. The league was desperate for cash and asked for
35,000 ducats. Eventually he offered 30,000 on condition that
England was exempted from any further activity. He was
confident that next year would bring victory and wrote to
Henry promising that 'your grace shall have high and
notable thanks of the Pope's holiness, the French king, the
Venetians, and all the league; you shall not be driven to
expose any treasure more than this exile sum; your grace
shall conserve your amity with the emperor, acquiring, with
God's grace, great thanks of him for concluding the peace;
and finally the glory and honour thereof, and of all the
good successes, shall principally be ascribed unto your

27. *Ven. Cal.*, iii, 1401.   28. *St.P.*, i, 171 (*L.P.*, iv, 2388).
29. *St.P.*, i, 174.   30. *L.P.*, iv, 2454.

highness by whose counsel this league has been begun and, God willing, shall take this virtuous and honourable end'.[31]

By the winter of 1526, Wolsey's conspiracy seemed to be making ground. A few months before, in August 1526, the Turks had won a crushing victory at Mohacz in Hungary and exposed eastern Habsburg territories to the full weight of Suleyman the Magnificent's cavalry. Perhaps under this impetus Charles expressed a readiness to commute his demand for Burgundy into cash and eventually granted a commission to his ambassador in England to take part in an international peace conference under Wolsey's direction; and a few days before Venice did likewise.[32] A thaw was beginning. But stiffness or truculence in Francis could still impede it; so too the collapse of the league, the lever of peace; so too Charles's stubbornness. All this must be provided against – especially the latter. But here was the rub. Had a sufficient sanction against the emperor yet been found and would he, in the end, submit to English arbitration?

A new Imperial ambassador, Mendoza, had at last arrived in England in December 1526. Charles had taken months to choose him and weeks to draft his instructions. He had been arrested in France on his way to England and when he arrived, six months after setting out, his instructions sent by sea and at one time said to be lost were out of date. Months would pass before new powers arrived.[33] More pressure had therefore to be applied on Charles. At the end of April, a new Anglo-French treaty was signed. It was celebrated at Greenwich with feasts, jousts and disguisings, Henry, wearing a black velvet slipper over a foot damaged

31. *St.P.*, i, 179 f. (*L.P.*, iv, 2556).

32. Heartened by this news, Wolsey went to Greenwich a couple of days after Christmas to tell the king that peace was in sight. *Sp. Cal.*, iii, ii, 18. By February 1527 English cash had persuaded the pope to promise similar powers for the nuncio in England. *L.P.*, iv, 2875.

33. *Sp. Cal.*, iii, ii, 29, 32, 37, 55, 66. Wolsey was in a frenzy of impatience.

at tennis, having to sit out the dances.[34] The new treaty was
a grave step. It went hand in hand with a marriage treaty
between Mary and the French royal house; it was to be
ratified by another personal meeting of Henry and Francis,
a second Field of Cloth of Gold. But the die was not cast.
If Charles wanted war he could have it – and Mary would
marry Francis himself. If he wanted peace, he could have
that, too, in which case Mary was to marry Francis's second
son, and Francis a sister of Charles. After Henry's meeting
with Francis, Wolsey would go on to another destination to
negotiate a general peace. It was hoped, undoubtedly, that
this new treaty would finally persuade Charles to accept
terms. A few days after it was concluded, an Anglo-French
embassy set off for Spain with their final offer.

There had been fighting in Italy since last summer. On
6 May 1527, the day on which rain was spoiling Anglo-
French jousting at Greenwich, the large Imperial army
which Bourbon had brought down from Lombardy burst
through the walls of Rome and set about sacking the city.
Hungry, unpaid, mutinous and tinged with Lutheranism,
the troops ran through Rome to smash and plunder, pillaging palaces and basilicas, shops and homes in a fearful
orgy which lacerated the city and sent the pope fleeing along
the tunnel which led from the Vatican to the Castel Sant'
Angelo. Two years ago Charles had had the French king
a prisoner. Now he had the pope. Without his knowledge,
the troops of the Most Catholic king and the deacon of
Christendom had desecrated the Eternal City and driven
the vicar of Christ to flight.

Would this sacrilege shock Charles into peace or greater
stubbornness? What would it do to Francis? What would
happen to the pope, around whom the league had been
formed? Would he succumb and perhaps even be taken off
to Spain, or would he be the more resolute? A few days after
the news of the Sack of Rome reached England, and as he
had recently promised, Wolsey set off for France once more

34. *Ven. Cal.*, iv, 105.

to meet Francis and prepare the way for a second interview
with Henry which, if necessary, was to lead to an offensive
alliance against Charles.[35] Like his visit to Calais in 1521,
this was a desperate peace errand. On 2 July he and a train
of nearly a thousand horse arrived at Boulogne. By 4 August
he was at Amiens where Francis had come to meet him.
As he made his way to the king, through the triumphal
arches and pageants and endless speeches, his plans took
shape. They were nothing if not capacious. The future demanded the immediate release of the pope. Only peace
would secure this. Francis must therefore reduce his demands and Wolsey would go to Spain, if necessary, to
persuade Charles to lower his. Meanwhile England must
stay neutral. However, if this plan proved impossible and
the pope remained captive, then Wolsey would go from
Amiens to Avignon (whither the cardinals had already
been summoned by letters from Henry) to preside over a
caretaker government of the Church, that is an assembly
of cardinals exercising, under Wolsey, the *plenitudo
potestatis* during the pope's imprisonment. At Avignon,
once more the centre of the Christian world, Wolsey would
administer the Church as the vicar's vicar and there too
negotiate a European peace.[36] The necessary commission for
himself was being drafted and would be taken secretly to
the pope in hiding for him to sign. Such was his majestic
programme – audacious almost beyond belief and with few
rivals, if any, in English history. Certainly it had peace as
its objective. It is impossible to believe that this was mere
strutting and completely dishonest, for the effort it demanded of its author and which he had already begun to
make was, surely, too great, too elaborate for this. But no
less certainly it was designed to guarantee for Wolsey
security of jurisdiction in another matter, one that must
have seemed a minor, peripheral affair to a man who would
take the cares of Christendom into his hands, a distraction

35. *St.P.*, i, 191 ff. (*L.P.*, iv, 3186).
36. *St.P.*, i, 205, 225 ff,. (*L.P.*, iv, 3243, 3310, 3311).

of the kind that Henry often threw across his steps – the
matter, that is, of the king's divorce.

Henry's marriage to Catherine had long since grown cold.
Though his wife remained, and would remain, loyal and
devoted, Henry was in very different case. The raptures of
the early days had faded and the consequent demands upon
him for self-discipline and generosity had found him wanting. Catherine was five years his senior. In 1527 he was still
in his prime, in his mid-thirties, she over forty. As king
he could satisfy desire all too easily, for who would refuse
a king easily, especially a king such as he? Fidelity was
rare among monarchs and the temptation besetting him,
in particular, strong.

At first Henry had been a gallant husband. Catherine
had accompanied him to every feast and triumph, he had
worn her initials on his sleeve in the jousts and called himself 'Sir Loyal Heart'. He had shown her off to visitors, confided in her, run to her with news. Though there had been
talk of a lady to whom he showed favour while campaigning
in France, he had slipped home ahead of his army and
galloped to Catherine at Richmond in order to lay the keys
of the two cities he had captured at her feet.[37]

We cannot know when he first succumbed to the temptation of adultery, but it must have been within five years
of his marriage, when there appeared on the scene one
Elizabeth Blount, a lady-in-waiting of Queen Catherine
and a cousin of Lord Mountjoy – and she may not have
been the first.[38] She caught the king's eye during the New
Year festivities in 1514, that is, shortly after he had returned
from the first campaign in France. Bessie Blount eventually bore him a son, in 1519. Subsequently she married into

37. *Hall*, 567. For the Belgian lady, see *L.P.*, i, 1349.
38. Perhaps *Sp. Cal. S.*, p. 36, indicates a row in 1514 between
Henry and Catherine over the former's regard for the duke of Buckingham's sister. It is not possible to date the source of the contre-
temps, or to be precise about Catherine's complaint.

a gentle family, the Talboys of Lancashire, with a dower of lands in that county and Yorkshire assigned by act of Parliament.[39] Hers, then, was a fate less than death; and her son, the duke of Richmond, was occasionally to acquire considerable political and diplomatic significance. Next there was Mary Boleyn, since 1521 wife of William Carey, daughter of a royal councillor and diplomat, and sister of Anne. That Mary was at one time Henry's mistress, and this presumably after her marriage, is beyond doubt.[40] Years later there was a strong rumour that she too had borne Henry a son,[41] but we cannot be sure. Anyway we may guess that the liaison was over by 1526, and when her younger sister climbed on to the English throne, with perhaps pardonable pique, she dismissed Mary from the court. The latter was to do well enough, with her family at the centre of affairs during the reign of her niece, Elizabeth I – which was more than could be said of Bessie Blount. And finally there was Anne, Thomas Boleyn's younger daughter.

Following in the wake of her sister, who had been in the entourage that accompanied Mary Tudor to France in 1514, Anne had crossed the Channel about 1519 to enter the household of Queen Claude, wife of Francis I, an amiable lady who had several young girls in her care and supervised their education. The newcomer to the royal school must have been about twelve years old. She stayed in France until the outbreak of war in 1522 and then came home, by which time she was on the way to becoming an accomplished and mature girl. She does not seem to have been remarkably beautiful, but she had wonderful dark hair in abundance and fine eyes, the legacy of Irish ancestors, together with a firm mouth and a head well set

39. Mattingly, *Catherine of Aragon*, 123.
40. Friedmann, *Anne Boleyn* (1884), app. B – which destroys Froude's attempt to exculpate Henry of this adultery.
41. In 1535 John Hale, vicar of Isleworth, said that a Brigettine of Sion once showed him 'young master Carey', saying he was Henry's bastard. *L.P.*, viii, 567.

on a long neck that gave her authority and grace. On her return, if not before, her future had apparently been settled, ironically by Henry and Wolsey. She would marry Sir James Butler, an Irish chieftain and claimant to the earldom of Ormond, to which the Boleyns, rivals of the Butlers, had long aspired. Anne was therefore to mend the feud by uniting families and claims. Had this familiar kind of device been executed, and had this been the sum total of her experience of how marriage and politics could interweave, things might have been very different for England, if not for Ireland. But Butler's price was too high and Anne remained in England.[42]

Her father, aided perhaps by her grandfather, the second duke of Norfolk, had meanwhile brought her to Court, as he had her sister before her. There she eventually attracted attention, first from Sir Thomas Wyatt, the poet, a cousin of hers; then from Henry Percy, son of the earl of Northumberland and one of the large number of young men of quality resident in Wolsey's household. Alas, Percy was already betrothed. At the king's behest, Wolsey refused to allow him to break his engagement and, summoning him to his presence, rated him for falling for a foolish girl at Court. When words failed, the cardinal told the father to remove his son and knock some sense into him. Percy was carried off forthwith – and thus began that antipathy for Wolsey that Anne never lost.[43] But it may well be that, when Henry ordered Wolsey to stamp on Percy's suit, it was because he was already an interested party himself and a rival for the girl's affection of perhaps several gay courtiers, including Thomas Wyatt. The latter's grandson later told a story of how Wyatt, while flirting once with Anne, snatched a locket hanging from her pocket which he refused to return. At the same time, Henry had been paying her attention and taken a ring from her which he thereafter wore on his little finger. A few days later, Henry

42. See Friedmann, op. cit., 42 f.
43. *Cavendish*, 29 ff.

was playing bowls with the duke of Suffolk, Francis Bryan and Wyatt, when a dispute arose about who had won the last throw. Pointing with the finger which bore the pilfered ring, Henry cried out that it was his point, saying to Wyatt with a smile, 'I tell thee it is mine.' Wyatt saw the ring and understood the king's meaning. But he could return the point. 'And if it may like your majesty,' he replied, 'to give me leave that I may measure it, I hope it will be mine.' Whereupon he took out the locket which hung about his neck and started measuring the distance between the bowls and the jack. Henry recognized the trophy and, muttering something about being deceived, strode away.[44]

But the chronology of Anne's rise is impossible to discover exactly. All that can be said is that by 1525-6 what had probably hitherto been light dalliance with an eighteen- or nineteen-year-old girl had begun to grow into something deeper and more dangerous. In the normal course of events, Anne would have mattered only to Henry's conscience, not to the history of England. She would have been used and discarded – along with those others whom Henry may have taken and who are now forgotten. But, either because of virtue or ambition, Anne refused to become his mistress and thus follow the conventional, inconspicuous path of her sister; and the more she resisted, the more, apparently, did Henry prize her.

Had Catherine's position been more secure she would doubtless have ridden this threat. Indeed, had it been so, Anne might never have dared to raise it. But Catherine had still produced no heir to the throne. The royal marriage had failed in its first duty, namely, to secure the succession. Instead, it had yielded several miscarriages, three infants who were either still-born or died immediately after birth (two of them males), two infants who had died within a few weeks of birth (one of them a boy) and one girl, Princess Mary, now some ten years old. His failure to produce a son was a disappointment to Henry, and as the years went by

44. Thomson, *Sir Thomas Wyatt and His Background* (1964), 28.

and no heir appeared, ambassadors and foreign princes began to remark the fact, and English diplomacy eventually to accommodate it, provisionally at least, in its reckoning.[45] Had Henry been able to glimpse into the second half of the century he would have had to change his mind on queens regnant, for his two daughters were to show quality that equalled or outmeasured their father's; and even during his reign, across the Channel, there were two women who rendered the Habsburgs admirable service as regents of the Netherlands. Indeed, the sixteenth century would perhaps produce more remarkable women in Church and State than any predecessor – more than enough to account for John Knox's celebrated anti-feminism and more than enough to make Henry's patriarchal convictions look misplaced. But English experience of the queen regnant was remote and unhappy, and Henry's conventional mind, which no doubt accorded with his subjects', demanded a son as a political necessity. When his only surviving legitimate child, Mary, was born in February 1516, Henry declared buoyantly to the Venetian ambassador, 'We are both young; if it was a daughter this time, by the grace of God the sons will follow.'[46] But they did not. Catherine seems to have miscarried in the autumn of 1517 and in the November of the following year was delivered of another stillborn. This was her last pregnancy, despite the efforts of physicians brought from Spain; and by 1525 she was almost past child-bearing age. There was, therefore, a real fear of a dynastic failure, of another bout of civil war, perhaps, or, if Mary were paired off as the treaty of 1525 provided, of England's union with a continental power.

Catherine, for the blame was always attached to her and not to Henry, was a dynastic misfortune. She was also a diplomatic one. Charles's blunt refusal to exploit the aston-

45. Cf. Wernham, *Before the Armada, etc.* (1966), 98 ff., which argues that, since 1521, the need to provide for the succession by marrying Mary to Charles V had dominated English foreign policy.
46. *Ven. Cal.*, ii, 691.

ishing opportunity provided by his victory at Pavia and to leap into the saddle to invade and partition France had been an inexplicable disappointment. Of course, had Henry really been cast in the heroic mould he would have invaded single-handed. But established strategy required a continental ally. Eleven years before, in 1514, Ferdinand of Spain had treated him with contempt and Henry had cast around for means of revenge, and there had been a rumour then that he wanted to get rid of his Spanish wife and marry a French princess.[47] Whether Henry really contemplated a divorce then has been the subject of controversy, which surely went in favour of the contention that he did not – especially when a document listed in an eighteenth-century catalogue of the Vatican Archives, and thought to relate to the dissolution of the king's marriage – a document which has since disappeared – was convincingly pushed aside with the suggestion that it was concerned with Mary Tudor's matrimonial affairs, not Henry's.[48] Undoubtedly, this must dispose of the matter even more decisively than does the objection that, in the summer of 1514, Catherine was pregnant.[49] In 1525, however, the situation was different. Charles had rebuffed Henry's military plans and, by rejecting Mary's hand, had thrown plans for the succession into disarray. For a moment the king evidently thought of advancing his illegitimate son – who, in June 1525, was created duke of Richmond. But this solution was to be overtaken by another which Henry may have been contemplating for some time, namely, to disown his Spanish wife. Catherine, therefore, was soon in an extremely embarrassing position. Tyndale asserted, on first-hand evidence, that Wolsey had placed informants in her entourage and told of one 'that departed the Court for no other reason than that she would no longer betray her mistress'.[50] When

47. *Ven. Cal.*, ii, 479.
48. Behrens, 'A note on Henry VIII's divorce project of 1514', *B.I.H.R.*, xi (1934), 163 f.
49. Mattingly, op. cit., p. 127.
50. *Practice of Prelates, Works*, i, 454.

Mendoza arrived in England in December 1526, he was prevented for months from seeing the queen and, when he did, had to endure the presence of Wolsey who made it virtually impossible to communicate with her. It was the ambassador's opinion that 'the principal cause of [her] misfortune is that she identifies herself entirely with the emperor's interests'; an exaggeration, but only an exaggeration.[51]

The king, then, had tired of his wife and fallen in love with one who would give herself entirely to him only if he would give himself entirely to her; his wife had not borne the heir for which he and the nation longed, and it was now getting too late to hope; he had been disappointed by Catherine's nephew, Charles V, and now sought vengeance in a diplomatic revolution which would make the position of a Spanish queen awkward to say the least. Any one of these facts would not have seriously endangered the marriage, but their coincidence was fatal. If Henry's relations with Catherine momentarily improved in the autumn of 1525 so that they read a book together and appeared to be very friendly,[52] soon after, probably, Henry never slept with her again.

The divorce, which came into the open in early 1527,[53] was therefore due to more than a man's lust for a woman. It was diplomatically expedient and, so some judged, dynastically urgent. As well as this, it was soon to be publicly asserted, it was theologically necessary, for two famous texts from the book of Leviticus apparently forbade the very marriage that Henry had entered.[54] His marriage, therefore, was not and never had been, lawful. The mis-

51. *Sp. Cal.*, iii, ii, 37, 69.
52. Mattingly, op. cit., 173.
53. In September 1526 John Clerk wrote to Wolsey from Paris and referred to '*istud benedictum divortium*' – which has been taken by some to refer to Henry's divorce. It almost certainly referred to that between Margaret of Scotland and the earl of Angus. Henry's divorce, i.e. nullity suit, did not formally begin until the spring of 1527.
54. Leviticus xviii, 16; xx, 21. For these texts see below, p. 218.

carriages, the still-births, the denial of a son were clearly divine punishment for, and proof of, transgression of divine law. Henry had married Catherine by virtue of a papal dispensation of the impediment of affinity which her former marriage to Arthur had set up between them. But Leviticus proclaimed such a marriage to be against divine law – which no pope can dispense. So he will begin to say. And thus what will become a complicated argument took shape. Henry had laid his hand on a crucial weapon – the only weapon, it seemed, with which he could have hoped to achieve legitimately what he now desired above all else. How sincere he was is impossible to determine. More than most, he found it difficult to distinguish between what was right and what he desired. Certainly, before long he had talked, thought and read himself into a faith in the justice of his cause so firm that it would tolerate no counter-argument and no opposition, and convinced himself that it was not only his right to throw aside his alleged wife, but also his duty – to himself, to Catherine, to his people, to God.

At the time, and later, others would be accused of planting the great scruple, the levitical scruple, in Henry's mind. Tyndale, Polydore Vergil and Nicholas Harpsfield (in his life of Sir Thomas More) charged Wolsey with having used John Longland, bishop of Lincoln and royal confessor, to perform the deed.[55] But this was contradicted by Henry, Longland and Wolsey. In 1529, when the divorce case was being heard before the legatine court at Blackfriars, Wolsey publicly asked Henry to declare before the court 'whether I have been the chief inventor or first mover of this matter unto your Majesty; for I am greatly suspected of all men herein'; to which Henry replied, 'My lord cardinal, I can well

55. Tyndale, op. cit., *Works*, i, 463. Polydore Vergil, *Anglica Historia*, 324. Harpsfield, *Life of More*, p. 41. Catherine also thought Wolsey guilty of being prime mover of the divorce. See *Sp. Cal.*, iii, ii, 69. But it was easy for her, at this stage, to have misunderstood the situation.

excuse you herein. Marry, you have been rather against me
in attempting or setting forth thereof'[56] – an explicit statement for which no obvious motive for misrepresentation can
be found and which is corroborated by later suggestions that
Wolsey had been sluggish in pushing the divorce forwards.
Longland too spoke on the subject, saying that it was the
king who first broached the subject to him 'and never left
urging him until he had won him to give his consent'.[57]

On another occasion Henry put out a different story:
that his conscience had been first 'pricked upon divers
words that were spoken at a certain time by the bishop of
Tarbes, the French king's ambassador, who had been here
long upon the debating for the conclusion of the marriage
between the princess our daughter, Mary, and the duke of
Orleans, the French king's second son'.[58] It is incredible that
an ambassador would have dared to trespass upon so delicate a subject as a monarch's marriage, least of all when
he had come to negotiate a treaty with that monarch. Nor
was it likely that he should have suggested that Mary was
illegitimate when her hand would have been very useful
to French diplomacy. Besides, the bishop of Tarbes only
arrived in England in April 1527, that is, a few weeks before Henry's marriage was being tried by a secret court at
Westminster. The bishop could not have precipitated events
as swiftly as that. No less significantly, another account of
the beginnings of the story, given by Henry in 1528, says
that doubts about Mary's legitimacy were first put by the
French to English ambassadors in France – not by the
bishop of Tarbes to his English hosts.[59] He and his com-
patriots may have been told about the scruple or deliberately encouraged by someone to allude to it in the course

56. Stow, *Annals*, 543.

57. As Harpsfield recalled, quoting Longland's chaplain, loc. cit.

58. *Cavendish*, 83. Thus Henry spoke before the legatine court in
1529.

59. See below, pp. 285 f. It is interesting that, meanwhile, English
ambassadors had been told to drop the story of the bishop of Tarbes.
St.P., vi, 595.

of negotiations, but did not invent it; nor, probably, did
Anne Boleyn – as Pole asserted.[60]

It is very likely that Henry himself was the author
of his doubts. After all, he would not have needed telling
about Leviticus. Though he might not have read them, the
two texts would probably have been familiar to him if he
had ever explored the reasons for the papal dispensation
for his marriage, and he was enough of a theologian to be
able to turn to them now, to brood over them and erect
upon them at least the beginnings of the argument that
they forbade absolutely the marriage which he had entered. Wolsey said later that Henry's doubts had sprung
partly from his own study and partly from discussion with
'many theologians';[61] but since it is difficult to imagine that
anyone would have dared to question the validity of the
royal marriage without being prompted by the king, this
must mean that the latter's own 'assiduous study and erudition' first gave birth to the 'great scruple' and that subsequent conference with others encouraged it. Moreover,
Henry may have begun to entertain serious doubts about
his marriage as early as 1522 or 1523, and have broached
his ideas to Longland then – for, in 1532, the latter was said
to have heard the first mutterings of the divorce 'nine or
ten years ago'.[62] By the time that Anne Boleyn captured the
king, therefore, the scruple may already have acquired
firm roots, though probably not until early 1527 was it mentioned to Wolsey who, so he said, when he heard about it,
knelt before the king 'in his Privy Chamber ... the space
of an hour or two, to persuade him from his will and
appetite; but I could never bring to pass to dissuade him
therefrom'.[63] What had begun as a perhaps hesitant doubt
had by now matured into aggressive conviction.

60. In his *De Unitate, etc.,* in Roccaberti, *Bibliotheca Max. Pont.*
(Rome, 1698), xviii, lxxvi.
61. *L.P.,* iv, 3641.
62. ibid., v, 1114.
63. *Cavendish,* 179.

But if the royal marriage were to be declared null and
void then this must be done by due process of law and by
the sentence of unimpeachable authority. Accordingly, in
May 1527, an extraordinary tribunal was called into being
to test the validity of the king's union to Catherine. Acting
by virtue of his legatine powers, and with Warham as
assessor, Wolsey set up a secret court in his residence at
Westminster and cited Henry thither to answer a charge
of having for eighteen years unlawfully cohabited with the
wife of his deceased brother Arthur. The court began on
17 May. Conscious perhaps of the gravity, not to say
enormity, of the proceedings, Wolsey started by begging
the king's consent to this citation. Henry consented. Then
Wolsey put to the king the facts of his marriage – how he
married Catherine by virtue of the papal dispensation, how
he now had grave doubts about the validity of that dispensation and wished the matter to be put to the legate's
judgement, etc. The king replied briefly that this was so
and that full evidence would be brought forward later. He
then named his proctor and promoter (i.e. counsel) and retired, leaving it to them to bring to a swift conclusion what
– since no one outside, not even Catherine, knew about it –
was little short of a conspiracy. Further sessions were held
on 20, 23, 31 May, during which time the king's counsel,
Richard Wolman, built up Henry's case against Julius's
bull.[64]

Then something went wrong. Wolsey – or was it Henry?
– lost his nerve. The matter was so serious and complex
that it was decided that the court must call up the help
of notable theologians and canonists, the bishops of
Rochester, Lincoln and London among them. Then there
was another problem. Three weeks before the Imperial
troops had sacked Rome and made the pope their prisoner.
Were Catherine to appeal against the sentence of this court
– as she surely would – it would be to a pope wholly in her
nephew's power that that appeal would come. Clement

64. P.R.O. S.P. 2/C i. (L.P., iv, 3140).

would inevitably quash Wolsey's judgement. News of the sack reached England on 1 June[65] and Wolsey was not slow to assess its significance for international diplomacy and for the divorce. The collusive suit at Westminster was brought to a precipitate close. In a few weeks, Wolsey would be off to France, as we have seen, evolving as he went a majestic plan to meet a group of cardinals at Avignon, take over administration of the Church while the pope was incapacitated and include in the business of the interregnum not only the negotiation of a European peace but also a definitive sentence on the king's marriage. As efficient as ever, Wolsey would soon draw up the commission by which Clement would delegate his whole authority to him. The draft, written in the pope's name for him to sign, went on to bestow upon Wolsey absolute power 'even to relax, limit or moderate divine law', proclaimed that he should be taken as the very voice and mind of the pope in all that he said or did and promised on release to ratify all that he had done.[66] With this *carte blanche* Wolsey could have done wonders indeed. Suitable judges to try Henry's case would have been quickly appointed[67] and, by the time Clement was free, their work would have been completed and ratified irrevocably by the papal viceregent. The collusive suit had been a false start but, with luck, lost time would now easily be made good.

On 22 July Wolsey crossed the Channel as the king's plenipotentiary and lieutenant to carry out the vast agenda of which, it will be recalled, the divorce was but one and, as he may still have thought, a minor item. But if the divorce were of less moment than his constant concern, peace, there was a danger that it was also incompatible with it. As he anxiously perceived,[68] Charles was not likely to be more responsive to English diplomacy when he heard of Henry's intention to renounce his aunt. It was desperately important, therefore, that news of Henry's intentions

65. *St.P.*, i, 189 (*L.P.*, iv, 3147).   66. *Pocock*, i, 19 ff.
67. *St.P.*, i, 271 (*L.P.*, iv, 3400).   68. ibid., vi, 595 (*L.P.*, iv, 3327).

should be suppressed. But it had already slipped out. Someone told Catherine and someone (probably Catherine) told
the Imperial ambassador, who promptly passed the report
on to his master.[69] Rumours were buzzing about London.
Within a few days of the opening of the collusive suit, John
Fisher's brother had picked up the story and carried it to
Rochester. On his way to France, Wolsey had stopped at
Rochester and tried to sound Fisher's views on Henry's
problem, though he pretended that the inquiry was merely
to quieten some doubts that the French ambassador had
raised. But Fisher already knew what was afoot. Catherine
had sent him an oral message saying that she desired his
counsel on 'certain matters' between the king and her, and
he had decided that the subject must be 'a divorce to be
had between [his] highness and the queen' because of what
his brother had told him.[70] What an error that abortive
trial had been. It was already too late to convince the emperor with the lies that had been used with Fisher, and
doubtless others, though the ambassadors in Spain were
to try to do so.

Meanwhile Henry had run ahead of his chancellor. On
22 June he had confronted Catherine with the news that
he and she had been living in sin for eighteen years and
that he must separate from her. Catherine burst into tears
at this terrible sentence and temporarily unsteadied Henry,
but he persisted, even though he was not to separate from
her completely for some time to come.[71] Then Catherine
began to strike back. Determined to make a direct appeal
for help to her nephew, and through him to Rome, she
devised an elaborate plot whereby a sewer of her household, one Felipez, came to Henry begging permission to
visit his sick mother in Spain and saying that Catherine
had refused to let him go. Henry saw through all this, but
'knowing great collusion and dissimulation, did also dis-
simulate' and granted the licence, even pleading with

69. *Sp. Cal.*, iii, ii, 69.   70. *St.P.*, i, 198 (*L.P.*, iv, 3231).
71. *Pocock*, op. cit., i, 11.

Catherine to let the man go and offering to ransom him should he fall into enemy hands on the way. But Henry's real purpose, as was explained to Wolsey, was that, despite a safe conduct, Felipez 'may be let, impeached and detained in some quarter of France so that it should not be known that the said let, arrest or deprehension should come by the king, by your grace, or any of the king's subjects'.[72] Felipez, therefore, was to be spirited away *en route* and Henry left not only innocent but aggrieved.

But Felipez defeated him. Travelling at speed and perhaps by boat instead of across France, he had reached the emperor at Valladolid at the end of July, and there poured out the story of what was planned against the English queen. Charles reacted swiftly. He wrote to Catherine promising full support, to Henry begging him to halt, to the pope that he should likewise protest, revoke Wolsey's legacy and recall the case to Rome immediately – whither he dispatched the general of the Franciscans to plead Catherine's case.[73] Though the emperor was not to sustain this first vigour, which was largely begotten of shock at the insult aimed at his family, it remains true that Felipez's dash to Spain was a turning-point in the story of the divorce. Henry's domestic affair had now become a public international issue and his path to Rome snared.

In the meantime Wolsey continued on his way across France, magnificent and confident. On 9 August he met Francis at Amiens and found him so pliant that it would not be necessary to go to Spain, as had been suggested earlier, on a last-minute peace errand. The ratification of the Anglo-French treaty could go ahead, peace between Francis and the emperor was at hand, the pope might soon be at liberty and, once all this was accomplished, a new treaty of universal peace could be negotiated. Lest these plans failed, Wolsey had set in motion his alternative pro-

72. For all this, see the very confidential letter from Knight to Wolsey, dated 14 July 1527. *St.P.*, i, 215 f. (*L.P.*, iv, 3265).

73. This story is well told by Mattingly, op. cit., 185 f.

gramme. Letters had been sent to the cardinals inviting
them to Avignon and, with the letters, safe-conducts and
offers of cash to cover travelling expenses. Meanwhile
agents had set out for Rome to persuade Clement to sign
the commission conferring all power on Wolsey during his
captivity.[74]

The cardinal had now reached the very pinnacle of his
rampant self-confidence. Henceforth a swift series of setbacks was to tear this riot of hyperbole to pieces. First, the
peace of Europe slipped from his grasp because neither
Francis nor Charles was as amenable as he had supposed.
Then the cardinals would not be drawn to Avignon. There
were four of them with him now (three Frenchmen and
Sadoleto, papal nuncio in France), but the rest would not
'by any means be induced or persuaded, leaving Italy, to
come to Avignon'. Sensing danger, Clement had forestalled
any move to undercut his authority and forbidden any
cardinal to move.[75] The chances of an Englishman taking
on the role of emergency vicar of the pope thus quickly
evaporated. But the worst was yet to come. Wolsey was
separated by two hundred miles and the Channel from the
source of his being, the king – a king subject now to all
manner of pressures and influence both hostile to the
legate and outside his control. While he was in France,
caught in his own vast machinations, others would profit
from his absence, like Anne, the duke of Norfolk, her
father or the duke of Suffolk, while Wolsey could only
watch and fret. He sensed trouble as soon as he reached
France and anxiously bade Sir William Fitzwilliam,
treasurer of the Household, to tell him what the king was
doing and who was with him. The reply came, 'He daily
passeth the time in hunting ... he suppeth in his Privy
Chamber ... there suppeth with him the dukes of Norfolk
and Suffolk, the marquis of Exeter and the lord of Roch-

74. *St.P.*, i, 235 ff. (*L.P.*, iv, 3337), 254 f. and 270 (*L.P.*, iv, 3340, 3400).

75. ibid., i, 267 ff. (*L.P.*, iv, 3400).

ford'[67] – ominous words, for Rochford was Anne's father. On 24 August John Clerk, now in his entourage, was sent home clearly to explain and justify what Wolsey was about.[77] Probably at this time Wolsey wrote an extraordinary letter to Henry, couched in terms of extreme subservience, protesting the success of the king's 'secret matter' to be his 'most inward desire', that every day separated from him felt like a year, and signing his letter 'with a rude and shaking hand of your most humble subject, servant and chaplain'.[78] Something was wrong. Then, a little later, startling news reached him that Henry was about to make a direct appeal to Clement for a solution of his marriage problem without reference to Wolsey and behind his back, while he, the man who had hitherto done everything for the king, was away in France. The king had decided to send his secretary, William Knight, to Rome to gain access to Clement and present for signature and sealing a document presumably of Henry's own devising and of a kind which the pope had probably never seen before and was not likely to see again, namely, a dispensation for him to marry again even if his first marriage had not been annulled; that is, a dispensation for bigamy.[79] Knight set out ahead of his documents, which were to follow him post-haste, with orders to travel via Wolsey at Compiègne, but to reveal nothing of his errand to the cardinal. Rather, he was to pretend that he was going to Rome to aid Wolsey's plans for setting up a caretaker government of the Church. However, an unnamed third party, of whom Henry said later, 'I know [him] well enough',[80] had divulged the plan to the cardinal. Stunned to discover that the king had acted without his

76. P.R.O. S.P. 1/42, fol. 255 (*L.P.*, iv, 3318). Cf. *St.P.*, i, 261 (*L.P.*, iv, 3361).

77. *St.P.*, i, 264 (*L.P.*, iv, 3381).

78. ibid., i, 267 (*L.P.*, iv, 3400).

79. The text of the dispensation is not extant and its contents can only be guessed from a letter of Knight to Henry (*St.P.*, vii, 3).

80. Henry to Knight, no date. Printed by Gairdner in 'New Lights on the Divorce of Henry VIII', *E.H.R.*, xi (1896), 685 f.

knowledge and convinced that Knight's mission must fail,
Wolsey immediately prepared to halt it. But Henry soon
knew that he knew what was afoot. 'The secret bull I sent
you for is at this hour known perfectly to my lord cardinal',
he wrote to Knight, presumably on the report of an informant placed in Wolsey's entourage. Knight, therefore,
was not to go ahead with the first plan, lest Wolsey 'suspect
that you were sent (as ye be indeed) for things that I would
not he should know'. The shocking draft bull had been set
aside and Knight was frankly to admit the truth about it.
He was to reassure Wolsey that the royal initiative had
been abandoned and that he himself was now to go to
Rome solely to serve the cardinal's interests there. However, the real reason why Knight was still required at Rome
was because Henry had devised a second plan, again unbeknown to Wolsey, for dealing with his problem.[81]

When Knight arrived at Compiègne he found Wolsey
confident that he had scotched Henry's scheme for direct
and manifestly ill-judged action, and that a message would
soon arrive recalling Knight. He therefore forbade the
latter to proceed with his journey. But the next day a letter
came from Henry, as Knight secretly knew it would, commanding him to make for Rome immediately. Wolsey was
no doubt mystified, but had to yield. There had been a
letter for him also, a deceitful piece in Henry's own hand,
full of phrases that now have a hollow ring, praising his
diligence and promising that this would never be forgotten
by a master who, anyway, was not given to ingratitude,
especially to him; and to which Wolsey replied with
another extravagant outpouring, saying that this last letter
from Henry was a token which 'I shall reserve and keep
for a perpetual monument and treasure', and professing
'ardent and reverent love' for its author.[82]

Knight was to go on because, as he had already been

81. Gairdner, art. cit., 685 f.
82. Gairdner, loc. cit., *St.P.*, 1, 177 ff. (*L.P.*, iv, 3423) for Wolsey's
reply.

told, there was still something for him to do. The first bull
had been abandoned, but only because Henry had a second;
and this was one 'which no man doth know but they which
I am sure will never disclose it to no man living for any
craft the cardinal or any other can find' – a blunt revelation of his attitude to the chief minister, written at the same
moment as that letter to Wolsey, just mentioned, whose
warmth had apparently put all anxieties to rest. The second
draft bull provided for the following: if Henry's first
marriage should be declared null and void, and he absolved
from the sin and excommunication which he had incurred
by living with Catherine, then he should be free to marry
any woman, even one related to him in the first degree of
affinity, even one whose affinity sprang from illicit intercourse and even one with whom he himself had had intercourse already.[83] Knight was to present this document to
the pope, hustle him into approval and let its contents be
divulged to no one.

Understandably this document has provoked much comment. It is, in the first place, a remarkable acknowledge-
ment by Henry of the scope of papal authority. It is the
first document which affirms (implicitly) Henry's intention
to marry Anne, a fact which hitherto was not obvious to
observers (including Wolsey), for, since her sister had been
Henry's mistress, she was related to him in the first degree
of affinity. And in asking that an affinity derived from lawful and unlawful union be dispensed, Henry conceded his
adultery, or rather, since he claimed not to be a married
man, his fornication with Anne's sister.

It is a cardinal point that, since Mary Boleyn had been
his mistress and since affinity sprang from illicit as well as
licit *coitus,* Henry was related to Anne Boleyn in the same
degree of affinity as he was related to Catherine by virtue of
her first marriage. Thus, if divine or natural law forbade
him Catherine, the same law forbade him Anne. He could

83. *Pocock,* i, 22 ff. The last phrase is not so much proof that Anne
had yielded as optimistic provision for the future.

not have it both ways – and that he tried to has been used
as evidence of patent insincerity. But Henry's mind was
subtle. So far he had staked his case on the text from
Leviticus which forbade marriage of a man and his
brother's wife. The bull which Knight was to proffer to
Clement allowed Henry to marry any woman provided
that she was not a brother's relict, i.e. provided that she
did not come under the explicit ban of Holy Writ. And
Anne did not. She was a mistress's sister, not a brother's
wife. The affinity was the same, but Leviticus, literally interpreted, would not apply to her. The distinction was not,
perhaps, an impressive one, but it would have been enough
to settle Henry's malleable conscience.

As far as it went, this second draft bull seemed promising. But it did not go far enough. Henry's first marriage to
Catherine had still to be found invalid before it could
serve him. In his letter to Knight, as the latter neared
Compiègne, Henry wrote of a third bull which might be
sent on to him. Perhaps that was to meet this other, preliminary problem.[84] Perhaps Henry still hoped that Wolsey
might procure a papal commission which would solve
everything. Whichever was his aim, the dispensation to
acquire a second wife was clearly valueless until he had
shed the first.

Knight's errand was a grievous blow for Wolsey. All the
plans he had been making seemed to have been knocked
out of his hands. Henry had acted without him, in a sense
in defiance of him, and sent to Rome a secretary who 'hath
no colour or acquaintance' with what he was about and
who, if he bungled, would tip the king's secret into the laps
of the ambassadors of Europe.[85] True, the first document
had been scotched, but only at the price of uncovering a
conspiracy which could have made Wolsey's efforts on the

84. But there is no sign of this third bull later on. See below, pp.
270 f., for how the second bull (a dispensation for Henry to marry
Anne may have been intended to smuggle past Clement a statement
that Henry's union to Catherine was invalid.

85. *St.P.*, i, 270 ff. (*L.P.*, iv, 3400).

king's behalf redundant. Never before had Wolsey tasted the king's duplicity thus. And now Knight was on his way to Rome after all. Why? Wolsey did not know, but he was entitled to suspect that it was to work apart from, not with, him. As commanded by the king, Knight had not shown him the second bull because he would have clearly adduced from it that it was Henry's intention to marry Anne Boleyn once he was free. Wolsey had gone to France in the belief that Catherine would be replaced, not by such as Anne, but with a diplomatically creditable spouse, like Renée, the sister-in-law of Francis I, and though he had not yet broached the king's 'great matter' to Francis, he had begun to explore the way to this union. Only when he returned home would he discover Henry's real intentions and how actively people were working behind his back; but already there were rumours of poisoning talk in Henry's presence that he was not giving his full energy to the divorce and that he was seeking the commission of viceregency out of vanity and power-lust.

God I take to be my judge [he wrote to Henry when he heard this] that whatsoever opinion ... your grace hath or might conceive, I never intended to set forth the expedition of the said commission for any authority, ambition, commodity, private profit or lucre, but only for the advancement of your grace's secret affair. . . . Assuring your highness that I shall never be found but as your most humble, loyal and faithful, obedient servant ... enduring the travails and pains which I daily and hourly sustain without any regard to the continuance of my life or health, which is only preserved by the assured trust of your gracious love and favour.[86]

Wolsey's world had been thrown into disarray and he must return to England to rescue something more precious even than his plan for international peace. By 21 September, eight days after writing the letter just quoted, he was back at Boulogne hurrying homewards – to find Henry closeted with Anne and willing to summon him for audience only with her approval.[87]

86. *St.P.*, i, 278 (*L.P.*, iv, 3644).   87. *Sp. Cal.*, iii, ii, p. 277.

7

The Canon Law of the Divorce

HENRY assaulted the validity of his marriage to Catherine with two distinct arguments: the first that the union of a man and the wife of a brother was contrary to the law of God and that therefore any papal dispensation pretending to allow it was worthless; the second that the particular dispensation granted by Julius II, by virtue of which he had married Catherine, was invalid.

The first rested on two texts of Leviticus: 'Thou shalt not uncover the nakedness of thy brother's wife: it is thy brother's nakedness', and again, 'If a man shall take his brother's wife, it is an impurity: he hath uncovered his brother's nakedness; they shall be childless'.[1] These were the texts which Henry and his supporters quoted again and again. But to serve the royal purpose they had to be glossed to prove what, in themselves, they did not necessarily prove, namely, that it was absolutely forbidden to take a brother's wife in all circumstances, whether or not the wife had previously been put away and, more important, whether or not that brother was dead. Furthermore, those texts had to prove that what they forbade was forbidden *per se*, by divine or natural law, and was hence beyond the reach of papal dispensation.

But against these texts from Leviticus stood the words of Deuteronomy: 'When brethren dwell together, and one of them dieth without children, the wife of the deceased shall not marry to another; but his brother shall take her, and raise up seed for his brother.'[2] Here, at first sight in open conflict with Leviticus, was a mandatory text imposing the duty of marrying an elder brother's relict in order to secure the direct descent of the family line and inheri-

1. Leviticus, xviii, 16; xx, 21.   2. Deuteronomy, xxv, 5.

tance – the duty of the so-called levirate (from 'levir', brother-in-law), an institution with deep roots in human history and practised not only by the Jews but peoples in every continent.[3] If Henry were to succeed, therefore, Deuteronomy must be explained away, or it would ruin the case which Leviticus seemed to uphold. For Leviticus, a rigorous, almost fundamentalist interpretation was required; for Deuteronomy, abolition.

A galaxy of Greek and Hebrew scholars, Christian and Jew, of theologians and canonists, of religious houses and universities, first in England and then on the Continent, were to be called upon to provide evidence for the king. Soon English agents were abroad, in France and Italy especially, quizzing and cajoling, ransacking libraries, interrogating university faculties, drawing up lists of signatories in this or that friary, urging canonists and Scripture scholars to take up the pen. By the end they had assembled a weighty corpus of *libelli*, tracts, opinions and *obiter dicta* from scores of scholars and institutions. Meanwhile, of course, the other side had been no less energetic. Men great and small rallied to defend Queen Catherine, meeting tract with tract, opinion with opinion. By 1529–30 the king's divorce had occasioned an international debate as violent and swift-moving, though on a much smaller scale, as the contemporary conflict between Catholic and Protestant polemicists. It was the sort of competition in scriptural exegesis which the printing press and the recent renewal of Greek and Hebrew studies made easy and, to some, highly congenial; and after dipping into that prolific pamphlet warfare one can only come away marvelling at the learning of so many of the contestants; at their ease with the Fathers, with the remoter Councils, with minor scholastics; at their dialectical acumen; at their energy.

In the matter of Leviticus there were available to the 'king's friends' a long line of decrees of provincial Councils from the fourth to the ninth centuries, which apparently

3. *Dictionnaire de la Bible*, s.v. 'Levirat'.

supported Henry's cause in strong terms – some fifteen
Councils, though only a handful were discovered at the
time.[4] In the course of the long debate, many Fathers will
be brought forward on Henry's side, led by four of the
greatest, who seemed to give particular support, Basil, Tertullian, Augustine and Gregory the Great. These will be
joined by about twenty scholastics (Bonaventure, Aquinas,
Scotus, Anthony of Florence among them) and nearly a
dozen popes – a harvest gathered mainly from continental
libraries.

Deuteronomy had to be glossed away. It was attacked
along several lines. That a man should take his brother's
relict was, some argued, but a ceremonial or 'respective'
precept of the law, allowed to the Jews but, like circum-
cision, abrogated by the coming of Christ. To re-introduce
it now would be to judaicize and to transgress that absolute
law of Leviticus which only God can dispense. Others
argued that the levirate as prescribed in Deuteronomy was
permissible only under certain rare conditions, none of
them present in Henry's case, particularly that the second
brother's children should carry the first's name; or that the
examples of the levirate found in the Old Testament (and
these were a considerable source of embarrassment) were
illusory since there was no evidence that the first marriage
had been consummated. Some followed a line of argument
prompted by Origen, St Ambrose and St Augustine, among
others, and interpreted the text figuratively: the dead
brother is Christ, the living brother every preacher of the
Church, sent to raise up Christ's seed and bring forth sons
to bear his name. Much play was made with this allegorical
exegesis. Others produced an argument of a different kind,
a true fruit of humanist ingenuity: the word 'frater', used
indifferently in the Vulgate, must be distinguished. In
Leviticus it means *'frater germanus'*, brother in the strict
sense, in Deuteronomy *'cognatus'*, relative. One might not

4. Viz. those of Neocaesarea, Agde, Tribur, Toledo. For the full
list, see *Dictionnaire du Droit Canonique, s.v.* 'Levirat'.

marry a true brother's wife; but one might marry the relict of a brother in the wider sense. The conflict between the two books of Holy Writ was, therefore, merely linguistic – the work of St Jerome, not the inspired author. Thus, with Deuteronomy's text set aside, Leviticus stood unchallenged as an absolute, indispensable prohibition of marriage with a brother's wife, whatever the circumstances.[5]

Such, very briefly, were the main lines of Henry's argument. In one form or another they recurred again and again. If progress was made during the long debate it consisted in refining these arguments, bringing forth additional authorities, answering objection and counter-objection, rather than in finding new paths of attack.

What was the value of these arguments? Certainly Henry had a case – at least in a sense that his supporters could gather material enough to fill sizeable tracts. But when his opponents had finished with it, and when it was set alongside theirs, it looked little better than makeshift.

But before descending into the details of the controversy, two things must be noted which made Henry's position worse than it might have been. In the first place, it was his misfortune to have against him some of the most distinguished men in Europe. There was Vives, the author of

5. In these two paragraphs I have gathered in synopsis the main arguments of the literature produced on behalf of the divorce which I have been able to read, viz. Previdelli, *Concilium pro Invictissimo Rege Angliae, etc.* (1531); the tracts in P.R.O. S.P. 1/59, fols 196 ff.; B.M. Otho, CX, fols 179 ff.; *Harleian* 417, fols 11 ff.; ibid., fols 33 ff., the anonymous tract attached to *The Determinacions of the moste famous and mooste excellent universities of Italy and France* (1531); *A Glasse of the Truthe*; two works in Strype, *Ecclesiastical Memorials*, App. 38, 39; three libelli in P.R.O. S.P. 1/63, fols 265 ff., 304 ff., 359 ff.; the succession of short tracts in P.R.O. S.P. 1/64; Cranmer's *Articuli Duodecim, etc.*, in *Pocock*, i, 334 ff. These pieces sometimes contain materials supporting *both* of Henry's arguments, viz. that based on Leviticus and the strictly canonical argument against the particular bull of Julius II. The latter will be summarized later in this chapter (pp. 240 ff. below).

a long-winded but competent book on Catherine's behalf;[6] there was John Fisher, a mere bishop of Rochester but already of international repute by virtue of his enormous output against Luther, Oecolampadius and others; there was Thomas de Vio, Cardinal Cajetan, apart from Bellarmine probably the most considerable Catholic theologian of the century, who, some years before the divorce arose had written a commentary on the *Summa Theologiae* of St Thomas Aquinas and quoted Henry's marriage to show how the dispensation on which it stood fitted into the master's and current thinking on the question of affinity[7] and now, a decade or so later, when Henry challenged that dispensation, delivered himself of a quick retort that is a model of well-mannered, economical destructiveness.[8] Later on, when Rome had at last spoken against Henry, the Spanish Dominican Vittoria surveyed the celebrated story of the divorce and developed Cajetan's line of thought, adding his authoritative voice to the chorus of opposition to Henry.[9] Finally, much later, Robert Bellarmine closed the debate with a magisterial survey of the whole area of discussion.[10] Vittoria and Bellarmine, of course, must be set aside now, for they entered the story as undertakers, not combatants. But even without them Catherine's defence was a formidable thing. And what could Henry produce against it? There were such as Edward Lee, competent enough but, as yet, a nonentity; or one Previdelli, willing but insignificant; the author of *A Glasse of the Truthe*, who remained anonymous; and Cranmer, so far scarcely known.

Vives, Fisher and Cajetan stood out from among those others who wrote on Catherine's behalf, and often wrote

6. *Apologia sive Confutatio, etc.* (1531).
7. *Commentaria super Summam Theologicam, etc.*, iia, iiae, qu. clix, art. ix.
8. *De Coniugio regis Angliae cum relicta fratris sui* (Rome, 1530).
9. *Relecciones Teologicas. De Matrimonio*, pars iia, ii, art. 4 ff.
10. Bellarmine, *De Controversiis, etc. De Matrimonio*, in *Opera Omnia* (Naples, 1872), ii, 844 ff.

very well, like Thomas Abel, or Fernando de Loazes, bishop of Segovia and servant of Charles V, or Bartolomeo de Spina.[11] Of them all, it was Fisher who earned the palm. He wrote at least seven books on Catherine's behalf,[12] and their clarity and range of learning are remarkable. He had an eagle eye for the essential and the decisive, his command of sources was staggering. Several times he exposed crucial misquotation and misrepresentation, as we shall see, and showed himself as much at home in Hebrew textual exegesis as in the intricacies of the Canon Law of affinity. Having declared himself an opponent of Henry at the very beginning, in 1527, he sustained his opposition for eight years, flailing the king with his pen, devastating new works of the latter's party as they came out, providing the backbone of Catherine's defence in court and eventually, when he had no more to write, carrying on the campaign from the pulpit. That Henry should have had this indefatigable bishop fulminating on his doorstep (and, in this, Fisher was very different from the silent More) must have been an insult so provocative that one can only marvel that ultimate retribution was delayed until 1535. There could have been no other solution to the problem of this man than death.

11. Abel, *Invicta Veritas* (Luneberg, 1532); Loazes (Cardinal d'Osma), *In Causa Matrimonii Serenissimorum Dominorum Henrici et Catherinae, etc.* (Barcelona, 1531); de Spina, *Tractatus de Potestate papae super coniugio, etc.* in *Tractatuum ex variis Iuris Interpretibus, etc.* (Lyons, 1549), xvi. The first two works are of a high order. Others which I have read are: Petropandus Caporella, *Questio de Matrimonio Serenissimae Reginae Angliae, etc.* (Naples, 1531); Ludovico Nozarola, *Super Divortio Caterinae ... Disputatio* (? 1530); Cochlaeus, *De Matrimonio Serenissimi regis Angliae, etc.* (Leipzig, 1535); Harpsfiled, *The Pretended Divorce between Henry VIII and Catherine of Aragon*, ed. Pocock, Camden Society (1878), pp. 12 ff.; a tract by one Montoya in B.M. Add., 28,582, fols 219 ff.

12. So he said when he was interrogated in the Tower in 1535. B.M. Cleo. E, vi, fols 174 ff. (*L.P.*, viii, 859). I have been able to read only his *De Causa Matrimonii serenissimi Regis Angliae, etc.* (Alcala, 1530) and his short tract in P.R.O. S.P. 1/42, fols 165 f. (*L.P.*, iv, 3232).

Nor was it merely the quality of the opposition which oppressed Henry. It is easy to gain the impression that his divorce opened up what had hitherto been, canonically speaking, virtually *terra ignota*. This is far from the truth. The problem of reconciling Leviticus and Deuteronomy had often been discussed long before Henry's case occurred. Almost every theologian of note had treated of marriage and the impediment of affinity – which is our concern here – and several had thrashed out the very question which Henry was to raise. There was little that Henry could throw up which had not been the subject, long since, of learned and often conclusive debate. The marriage law contained in Holy Writ had been extended and refined by the *Corpus Iuris Canonici*, and around this had grown up a vast body of commentary, not just on the *Decretum* and *Decretals* in general, but on the law of marriage in particular. And, of course, the Roman Curia, guided by and guiding canonical theory, had reduced that law virtually to an exact science for the purposes of dealing with nullity suits and above all granting dispensations from the complex of impediments which, if it had not discovered, the law had at least defined and graded. Certainly there were divergent opinions among the authorities on almost every point. It was of the very nature of medieval theology, which proceeded dialectically, by concordance of discordants, that this should be so. And it was this that gave Henry the makings of a case. He had a chance not because his problem was a novelty but because it was a chestnut. But though he could pick up friends here and there from the generations of lawyers and theologians who had discussed these matters, there can be little doubt that the broad flow of opinion was against him.

How was the apparent conflict between Leviticus and Deuteronomy to be resolved, as resolved it must be unless one would have Holy Writ forbid and command the same thing at the same time? There were, as St Augustine had pointed out (and as the Henricians who used him had to forget), three possible ways.[13] It could be argued that Leviticus only forbade intercourse with a brother's wife when the latter was still alive – that is, it imposed a particularly severe penalty on what would be incestuous adultery – while leaving complete freedom for a younger brother to obey Deuteronomy's command to take the wife of an elder brother who had died without issue. Alternatively, Leviticus forbade a second brother to marry, while the first brother was still alive, one whom the first had put away, say, for adultery. It did not forbid marriage with a *dead* brother's wife and therefore did not impinge on Deuteronomy. Thirdly, Leviticus could be interpreted maximally to forbid one brother taking another's wife, whether that wife were a widow or not, *except* in the very case which Deuteronomy described, that is, when the elder brother had died without issue. Then Leviticus no longer operated, for this was an area outside its scope and from which the barrier of affinity was held off by the duty of the younger brother to take this woman and raise up his brother's seed. Or, as the more sophisticated argument presented by Cajetan and developed by Vittoria and Bellarmine will run,[14] the good which should come out of the second marriage will outweigh the inescapable baseness of a union of brother and sister-in-law; the base being made 'honest' by the good which ensues.

Of the three possible interpretations set forth by Augustine, the first, though it had distinguished support (including that of Alexander of Hales and Albert the Great) had the defect that it tended to make Leviticus otiose. It merely condemned adultery, and adultery was condemned already. The second never had much of a following and would seem to have limited the text too narrowly. The third, that Leviticus forbade any marriage with a brother's wife unless the brother had died without issue, proved the most accept-

13. Questionum S. Augustini in Heptateuchum, in *Migne, P.L.*, 34, col. 705. I owe this text to Fisher.

14. In their works cited above.

able. It allowed the fullest play to Leviticus while bringing
it into peaceful coexistence with Deuteronomy; further, it
fitted the examples of the levirate (and comments upon it)
to be found in Scripture.[15]

After all, Juda, son of Jacob, had ordered no less than
three of his sons in succession to marry Thamar, the second
after the first had died childless, the third after the second
had refused to obey his father.[16] This was as convincing an
example as could be wished of the imposition of levirate
in exact obedience to Deuteronomy (as Fisher and others
observed). Again, did not Jacob and Heli, twin brothers,
marry the same woman in turn (of whom St Joseph was
born)? St Augustine, in an unguarded moment, had said
that they were not brothers. Henry's men seized upon this
for welcome relief – only to be humiliated by Fisher, an
ardent Augustinian and here, as elsewhere, as vigilant as a
hawk, who threw back a chapter of the *Retractations* in
which Augustine withdrew this opinion and now not only
allowed that the two were twins but also explained that St
Joseph was called the son of both, though in fact the son
of Jacob, precisely because the latter had obeyed Deuteronomy and raised a brother's seed in the brother's name:
a bad defeat for Henry.[17] Again, did not Ruth perform the
elaborate ceremonies laid down in Deuteronomy against
a brother-in-law who refused to relieve her widowhood and
eventually marry another member of her dead husband's
family?[18] In short, there could be little doubt that, under
the old law, the levirate was a living custom ordained, not
forbidden, by God and to claim (as was now claimed) that

15. I quote Fisher here, in his *De Causa Matrimonii, etc.*, 17 ff.
Whenever I have checked any of his references I have found them
correct. It is from him that I have taken the names of supporting
authorities.

16. Genesis xxxviii.

17. *Retractations* ii, cap, vii, in *Migne, P.L.*, 32, col. 633. Fisher, op.
cit., 11. As Augustine noted here, it was this levirate which accounts
for the different genealogies of Christ given by Luke and Matthew.

18. Ruth, iv, 1–3.

in these cases the first marriage had not been consummated was to assume something *prima facie* improbable and empirically unverifiable.

Nor was it a convincing escape to quote allegorical interpretation of Deuteronomy. The allegorical does not exclude the literal; both were members of that famous quartet of Nicholas of Lyra by which the full wealth of Scripture might be quarried, and St Augustine used both when treating of Deuteronomy. All the texts produced to defend this kind of exegesis were necessarily indecisive. So it was that the argument based on the different meanings of the word 'brother' was brought into play. It was not a successful venture. Neither Fisher nor Cajetan had much difficulty in showing that the Hebrew for 'levir' in Deuteronomy indisputably meant carnal brother of the dead husband and that there was no difference in terminology between this text and Leviticus.[19] Besides, as Fisher observed (and this was a shrewd blow), the Fathers, and even writers later than those whom the other side was quoting, clearly assumed an identity of terms. 'Brother' in Deuteronomy and Leviticus not only meant the same to Juda, Ruth and the rest, but also to Augustine, Hilary, Chrysostom, Ambrose, Bonaventure, Aquinas and so on – not to mention the three Evangelists, Matthew, Mark and Luke. Fisher had thus pitched his opponents onto a sharp dilemma: either they must cling to traditional exegesis and lose their point, or else they must push forward a new one which lacked the respectability which only hallowed authority could bestow. The argument was therefore dropped. Short of adopting the strikingly simple solution later proposed by Melanchthon and Beza that those who practised the levirate in the Old Testament committed sin thereby[20] – and none of Henry's supporters was bold enough for this –

19. Fisher, op. cit., 4v. He says here that he dealt with this in his third book, which I have not been able to see. Cajetan, op. cit., 194 f.; cf. Bellarmine, loc. cit., 847 f.
20. Quoted by Bellarmine, loc. cit.

there were now only two ways out of the impasse: to argue
that Deuteronomy was a concession to the Jews only and
abrogated by the new law; to argue that the levirate had
been and could be allowed only by special divine dispensation. Ideally the two arguments would run together for, if
the first were advanced alone, it would implicitly concede
the principle that the levirate was not contrary to divine
law. Such a deduction could only be avoided if it were
claimed that the levirate was on each occasion commanded
to certain particular persons of the Old Testament by God
Himself.

The first argument was plausible in that the levirate was
obviously not a Christian custom. Nonetheless, to sustain
it completely, two incidents in the New Testament had
to be carefully glossed. John the Baptist, it will be recalled,
solemnly rebuked Herod for marrying the wife of his
brother, Philip. Now, did this not suit Henry's case exactly?
Did not this harbinger of the new law thereby condemn a
survival from the old, the levirate? So Henry's supporters
asserted. But there was a flaw in their argument. As most
commentators had assumed,[21] and as Abel conclusively
demonstrated by internal evidence from the New Testament,[22] Philip was still alive when Herod took his wife.
John, therefore, condemned what all parties agreed was
forbidden by Leviticus, namely, incestuous adultery, and in
no way impugned the levirate of Deuteronomy. Again,
what of the case which the Sadducees, to trip Christ, put to
him of the woman who married seven brothers in succession and, when she came to heaven, might be exercised to
know which was her true husband?[23] It was no good
Henry's apologists pushing the incident aside on the ground
that it was 'fantasy' – as doubtless it was – for, in the first
place, it showed that the levirate was still a living custom
in Christ's time and, in the second, Christ's reply was

21. E.g. Peter of Blois, *Epistola* cxv; *Migne, P.L.*, 207, cols 343 ff.
22. *Invicta Veritas* (no pagination).
23. Matthew, xxii, 23–7; and elsewhere.

simply that the beatific vision would transcend marital
affection and the problem would not arise, *not* that the
parties concerned had violated divine law.[24] This was indeed a point to Catherine.

Accordingly, there was left intact only the last argument we have noted – that the levirate had always required special divine intervention. But what evidence was
there for this? Did not the mandatory tone of Deuteronomy argue against this assumption? Did not the examples of the levirate in the Old Testament suggest that
it was an established custom which needed no special *fiat*
from God? The argument's strength was that no positive
evidence could be brought against it; its weakness that
none could be brought for it, except as we shall see, a
little support from a few late scholastics. But it was the best
that could be done. The final argument therefore ran thus;
God alone can dispense from the impediment of affinity
of the first degree collateral, because such an impediment
rests on God's law. The proof that it did so rest (and this
is the critical point) is that God alone has dispensed from
it. *Ergo* Henry's marriage, for which God granted no express permission, is invalid.

All this had brought Henry to an extreme and, in the
canonical sense of the word, improbable notion of the
nature of affinity, to appreciate which we must move away
from this point and come to it again by another path.

Medieval theologians and canonists had given much
thought to the question of affinity – to the question, that is,
of the relationship set up by the sexual union of A and B,
between A and the relatives of B, and B and the relatives
of A (a relationship to be distinguished, of course, from
consangunity, which exists between A and his own relatives, and between B and hers). They had repeatedly discussed the question upon which the whole of Henry's debate turned, namely, whether the impediment of affinity
was founded on divine or natural law, or merely the posi-

24. As Fisher pointed out.

tive law of the Church. Several answers had been given. Duns Scotus had asserted that affinity impeded marriage by the law of the Church only and would have denied that marriage even within the first degree of affinity in the direct line (e.g. between son-in-law and mother-in-law), let alone in the collateral (e.g. between sister-in-law and brother-in-law), was forbidden by natural law.[25] Others took a less radical view. As regards the direct line, ascending and descending, one school (of which Johannes Andreae was a leading member),[26] held that affinity impeded by natural law in all degrees; another, including Peter of Palude, for instance,[27] that it did so only in the first degree in either direction. When they came to collateral or transverse affinity, that is affinity between persons of the same generation (which is our concern here), a few would say that none impeded in natural law.[28] Thus St Thomas, while agreeing that a mother and son could never be joined together, would not allow that natural law forbade the union of brother and sister – for Abraham married his sister, and so must every son of Adam have done. If Thomas exempted the first degree collateral of consanguinity he must do the same for affinity. Cajetan followed suit, and this view was to gain ground until, by the eighteenth century, it held the field. But by the early sixteenth century this was still a minority opinion. Most argued that the first degree collateral of affinity did indeed impede by divine or natural law.

And was this not exactly what Henry said? No. Most of the authorities, having said this, then qualified their opinion. The first degree collateral of affinity impedes in natural law *except* in the case of marriage with the widow of a brother who has died without offspring. This special case, because of Deuteronomy, stands apart, stands apart exactly

25. *Questiones super quattuor libros Sententiarum*, iv, dist. xli.
26. See the tree in his *De Arbore Consanguinitatis et Affinitatis*.
27. *Quartum Sententiarum, etc.*, dist. xli, qu. i, art. 5.
28. E.g. Richard of Middleton, in *Quartum Sententiarum, etc.*, iv, dist. xli, art. ii.

as Augustine had suggested (as we saw above). So wrote Peter of Blois and Bonaventure; so too St Thomas when, in another place, he seems to have changed his mind and admitted collateral affinity as an impediment in natural law after all; so too canonists like de Butrio, Anthony de Rosellis and the great John Torquemada, uncle of a man known for reasons other than literary.[29] The list could be extended further, but there is no need. The point is clear enough that scholastics and canonists who asserted that an impediment of the first degree collateral of affinity was rooted in natural or divine law, and therefore could not be dispensed, usually explicitly exempted from this class one case, *which was Henry's very case.* And if a few did not make this exception explicitly they certainly did not deny it, so that for Henry to claim them as friends was perilous.

Faced with this poverty of support, Henry's proponents were driven to a number of expedients. They talked at length of the differences between natural and positive, moral and judicial laws – which proved little. They quoted texts which established that forbidden degrees existed – which was not in dispute – without touching the question, the real question, of whether they were dispensable. They quoted texts that marriages forbidden by the laws of God and nature were no marriages – again an issue not in dispute – which did not show that Henry's was in this category. They quoted authorities who, since they did not deal with what was indisputably the special case of the affinity between a man and his brother's widow, provided inconclusive testimony.[30] Worse still, they occasionally misquoted.

29. Peter of Blois, *Epistola* cxv; Bonaventure on the *Sentences* iv, dist. xxxix, art. ii, qu. iv; St Thomas, *Summa Theologiae*, 1a, 2ae, qu. cv, art. iv; De Butrio, *Lectura super Quarto Decretalium* in *c.* Deus qui Ecclesiam; Anthony de Rosellis, *Monarchia, etc.* (edn Venice, 1497), 89; Torquemada, *Commentaria super Decreto*, ii, causa xxxv, qu. 1 and 2.

30. Thus Origen on Leviticus *c.* 20, Chrysostom's Homily no. 77, Ambrose's *Epistolae* li, 8, no. 66, and other texts, were not relevant because they dealt with cases specifically different from Henry's.

Previdelli[31] claimed Anthony of Butrio as an ally but, as
has been said, he was not. Bonaventure was misused more
than once, and so too St Thomas.[32] These may have been
slips born of haste. The same cannot be said of the mal-
treatment of Torquemada. In his commentary on the
Decretum, the cardinal spent a long time on impediments
of the first degree of affinity. He had served in the Curia
as a canonist and was able to cite two interesting cases, one
in which Louis XI supplicated Eugenius IV for permission
to marry his dead wife's sister and the other in which a
count of Armagnac asked Pius II to allow him to marry
no less than a natural sister. In both cases, Torquemada says,
he argued against the supplicants; and in both cases they
were refused. Much play was made with this by Previdelli,
and Torquemada was cited by him several times as Henry's
ally. In reality, as Fisher observed, he undid Henry. Both
before and after telling these stories he stated explicitly
that the wife of a brother who had died without issue was
the one person within the first degree of affinity who was
not forbidden to a man by divine law; in allowing her to
take her dead husband's brother, he goes on to say, the
pope does not exactly dispense, rather, he consents to or
commands the second marriage in fulfilment of Deuteronomy's precept – a novel opinion. Torquemada argued
against King Louis because the latter wanted to marry a
dead wife's sister, which was not what Deuteronomy had
prescribed. But a dead brother's wife was different. She was
in no way forbidden by divine law; quite the contrary.[33] It
would be difficult to find any writer who discussed the
issues involved in the divorce more fully than did Torquemada, or anyone who had dismissed (in advance) Henry's
argument so firmly. To claim him now as one of Henry's

31. In his *Concilium, etc.*, noted above.
32. In the tracts in P.R.O. S.P. 1/59, fol. 234v; B.M. Harl., 417, fol.
42v.

33. *Commentaria super Decreto*, ii, causa xxxv, art. iii, art. 3; and
qu. 2.

friends was a misappropriation so glaring that it can scarcely
have been honest.

Four Fathers in particular were brought forward as witnesses to the justice of Henry's argument about affinity –
Jerome, Basil, Tertullian and Gregory the Great. Jerome
and Tertullian were misquoted. Both had discussed the
Baptist's rebuke to Herod for marrying his brother's wife,
but the first believed that the brother (Philip) was still
alive and the second that he had died leaving a daughter.
Neither, therefore, thought that Herod had been condemned for obeying Deuteronomy, as Henry would have
liked to argue, and hence neither passed sentence against
Henry's marriage. Tertullian, indeed, implied that he
would have approved it.[34] Basil's evidence was valueless. He
had only declared that marriage to the sister of a dead
wife was impermissible – and this shed no light on what
he would have thought of Henry's case.[35] Of the four
Fathers, Gregory the Great came nearest to aiding Henry.
In a letter to Augustine of Canterbury (in reply to the
latter's query) he had certainly said that a man was forbidden a brother's wife by the law of God and pointed to the
Baptist's words and martyrdom as witness.[36] But even this
was of questionable worth for there was no proof that he
was writing of *dead* brothers' wives and of brothers who
had died without issue. Patristic exegesis had taught that
John rebuked Herod because his brother was still alive or
because he had left offspring. No other Father seems to

34. Jerome, *Commentaria in Evangelium S. Matthaei*, in *Migne,
P.L.*, 26, col. 97. Tertullian, *Adversus Marcionem*, in *Migne, P.L.*, 2,
col. 443.

35. *Epistola* clx, in *Migne, P.L.*, 77, cols 1189 f. In early 1530
English agents found another letter of Basil's in Venice (after long
search) in which he wrote that anyone who took a brother's wife
must put her away. Though stronger evidence, it still does not dispose of Deuteronomy (*L.P.*, iv, 6229, *Migne, P.L.*, 77, col. 723). Moreover, like all the patristic evidence, it threw light on liceity, not
dispensability. It left untouched the question of whether the pope
could dispense what all were agreed *was* an impediment.

36. *Migne, P.L.*, 77, cols 1189 ff.

have argued that Herod had performed the levirate and
that John condemned him for it. No other Father had said
that John abrogated Deuteronomy. Was it likely, as was
now alleged, that Gregory thought he had? At least it could
not be proved that he had thought thus and, as long as
this was so, Gregory's words must remain indecisive. The
gravity of Henry's case required rigour; and rigour required
that Gregory's name be struck off Henry's list.

Nothing less than explicit statement that to marry the
relict of a brother deceased without issue was against
divine or natural law could be of any real service to Henry;
and this was a stringent requirement. By the time that
scrutiny had winnowed the Fathers and scholastics whom
Henry's supporters had gathered, removing those who did
not say what they were said to say, removing what was
irrelevant and what, according to the criterion just noted,
was inconclusive, a previously impressive yield had been
much reduced.

There were only five persons, it seems, who gave Henry
incontrovertible support: one a lone figure from the twelfth
century; four of them Dominicans who make up a minor
'school' stretching from the early fourteenth to the early
sixteenth centuries.

The first was the poet and bishop (later archbishop),
Hildebert of Tours. In a letter to an inquirer, and it is a
tribute to the fineness of their search that Henry's men
should have spotted it, he stated categorically that a girl
could not marry the brother of a deceased to whom she had
previously been betrothed.[37] *A fortiori*, it was argued,
Hildebert would not allow a second union if the first had
been consummated. Though his opinion apparently won no
following it certainly seemed to favour Henry and could
not be disposed of by the latter's opponents. Two centuries
later, one Peter de la Palu, or Palude (Petrus Paludanus),
an early fourteenth-century Dominican, eventually patri-

37. Migne, P.L., 171, cols 207 f. 'Desponsatam tamen fratri, frater
habere non potest,' he wrote.

arch of Jerusalem and a man much involved in ecclesiastical events of his day, wrote a commentary on the *Sentences*
of Peter Lombard (while a master at Paris) in the course of
which he declared that marriage with a brother's relict, even
if that brother had left no issue, was forbidden by divine
law and that the levirate as practised in the Old Testament
had been allowed only by special divine dispensation, in
God's gift, not the pope's.[38] A near-contemporary of his, one
James of Lausanne, also a Dominican, subscribed to this
view.[39] More than a hundred years later, no less a person
than St Anthony of Florence repeated it, quoting Paludanus
almost verbatim.[40] The levirate was at times permitted by
God, like bigamy, but the pope can dispense for neither.
Then, in the early sixteenth century, Silvester Prierias,
sometime papal master of ceremonies and one of the several
who confronted Luther in disputation, repeated almost
exactly what Paludanus and St Anthony had written.[41]

Thus we have returned, by a different path, to the point
we were at previously: the initiative in employing Deuteronomy's precept to the limit, or exemption from Leviticus's
prohibition, lies with God alone. Out of the often conflicting hotch-potch of argument put forward on Henry's side
this was the only one which has real strength. It showed
respect for the letter of Deuteronomy and accommodated
the overwhelming evidence that Fathers and scholastics had
taken that text literally; it had no need of the double-edged
weapon of Hebrew philology; it gave full credence to the

38. In *Quartum Sententiarum*, dist. xli, qu. i.
39. In his *Super Quartum Sententiarum*, qu. cxvi, concl. 2a. Henry
had much trouble in finding a copy of this work. When at last a
copy, presumably borrowed from afar, came into his hands he had
an attested transcript of the relevant passage made. I have not been
able to find James's work and have therefore used this text, for which
see *Rymer*, xiv, 390 f. That Henry should personally have supervised
this transcription shows how actively he was involved in the minutiae
of the campaign.
40. In his *Summa Theologica*, iii, tita, io., ca. ii.
41. See his *Summa Summarum*, s.v. 'papa', qu. 17.

examples of the levirate to be found in Holy Writ; it had
the support of two distinguished theologians and one recent
canonist.

Yet the argument was weak. In the first place, it rested
on the gratuitous assumption that whenever Deuteronomy
was obeyed God had specially allowed or commanded the
persons concerned. Secondly, against the five who gave
Henry unimpeachable support stood Scotists,[42] Thomists
(in the main), Bonaventure, Torquemada and others. These
five represented but one thread in the thick weave of
medieval thought; and even if those who did not discuss
Henry's precise case were taken as neutral, and probably
they would have come out against him,[43] what, one may
ask, were these against so many? Moreover, they were not
merely a minority. Their opinion was in conflict with important facts.

The dispensation which Julius II had granted Henry
was not a commonplace; but no more was it a glaring
novelty. Martin V had been ready to allow a man to marry
a sister-in-law and said that many doctors of theology and
law, and a majority of those present at the Council of Constance, had repeatedly told him that he could dispense within the Levitical degrees. Alexander VI had allowed a king
of Portugal, Emmanuel II (whose son was now alive), to
marry in turn two daughters of Ferdinand and Isabella –
i.e. sisters of Catherine of Aragon – even though he had had
a son by the first. The same pope had dispensed the king of
Naples to marry his aunt, and in more recent times, that
is, since Henry's dispensation was granted, Leo X had given
a faculty to members of the Augustinian order to dispense
impediments of the first degree of affinity; and Clement VII
had allowed at least two noblemen to marry the sister of a

42. For an example of a later Scotist who declared all impediments
of affinity to be based on positive law, see Steinbach, *Gabrielis Biel
Supplementum*, etc., dist. xli, qu. i, art. 2.

43. In view of *Deus qui Ecclesiam*, for which see below.

previous wife.[44] All the impediments dispensed in these cases were more serious than the one which had stood between Henry and Catherine, because they were not backed by Deuteronomy. If Martin V, albeit after some heart-searching, had dispensed in the first degree collateral of affinity, and if Alexander VI had done the same – both without any support from Deuteronomy – how much more confidently could Julius have obliged Henry, whose case had fitted Deuteronomy exactly? And if Julius's dispensation had seemed secure enough when it was granted, how much more secure must it be now, twenty-five years later, in the light of these subsequent dispensations?

Julius had acted within the area of established papal competence. He stood, in fact, on ground which no less a person than Innocent III had staked out. More than three hundred years before Henry challenged Julius's dispensing power, Innocent had given a ruling to the hierarchy of Livonia that pagans who, in obedience to the law of Moses, had married the widows of brothers deceased *sine prole* were not to be separated from their wives on reception into the Church. Their marriages were to be declared valid.[45] This was explicit approval of the levirate and the law of Deuteronomy. Moreover, this letter, from one of the most authoritative of the canonist-popes of the Middle Ages, had passed into Canon Law[46] and become the *locus classicus* for subsequent judgements by canonists and theologians that first degree affinity, if it impeded by divine law, did so in all cases save one; that the levirate, though not a Christian custom, was not defunct; that for sufficient cause the pope could dispense a man to marry his brother's widow provided the latter was childless.

44. These cases were noted by Fisher. The latter made the common error of believing that Martin V dispensed a man to marry his own sister. On the history of this misconception and on Martin's bull, see Joyce, *Christian Marriage, etc.* (1948), 528 n.
45. For full text, see *Migne, P.L.*, 216, cols 1183 f.
46. Lib. iv, tit. xix, c. ix.

Innocent was a catastrophe for Henry. The only defence
was attack. In the *Corpus*, of course, only the core of a
document is quoted, not the whole text. In the hope that
the complete letter might contain a loophole, the king's
agents in Rome were ordered to search the papal registers
and send back a full transcript of the original. This they
did, but it made no difference. The *Corpus* had not misrepresented the pope. But Innocent had used the word
'*concedimus*' – 'we concede' – to these neophytes the privilege of continuing in their marriages. This, it was then
argued, was not as sufficient as '*dispensamus*', 'we dispense';
which was a dubious objection.[47] True enough, the concession was made because the supplicants were neophytes;
true enough, Innocent forbade anyone to contract such marriages thereafter. Nonetheless, the bull remained a definitive
statement that the impediment between a man and his
brother's widow did not stand on divine or natural law.
There was an impediment of some kind, of course, but of
positive, ecclesiastical law. To dispense from it, Innocent
had to show sufficient cause and, because the impediment
was there, he took pains to make sure that his dispensation
should not be taken as an open licence for the future.

Fisher was right when he said that this bull, *Deus qui
Ecclesiam*, was decisive.[48] No amount of royal ingenuity
could finally dispose of it. As we have seen, the king's men
quoted decrees of early provincial Councils.[49] But even for a
radical conciliarist these could scarcely compete with a
papal pronouncement; and anyway they were ambiguous,
for it was not obvious that they vetoed marriage with the
wife of a deceased and childless brother and arguable that
they named what was *illicit*, not what was indispensable (an
important distinction).

47. This is argued in B.M. Harl., 417, fols 18 f.
48. Fisher, op. cit., 1.
49. Esp. Neocaesarea, c. 2. We must also note the sentence of Convocation, confirmed by the Council of Constance which condemned
Wyclif's teaching that the Levitical bans were judicial only – which,
despite what Henry said, was *not* to say that they were based on
natural or divine law.

Had Julius's dispensation been unique it would still have had strength from the fact that it was the fruit of a plenitude of power which was the master, not the servant, of academic opinion. To a thorough papalist the proof that the pope could dispense this impediment was the fact that he had done so. But though Julius was apparently the first pope since Innocent to grant this dispensation, time did not run against a pope any more than it did against the king. Besides, *Deus qui Ecclesiam* had not been lost meanwhile. It had been kept alive in the *Corpus,* noted repeatedly by commentators and incorporated into their thinking. Julius, therefore, did not dig up a fossil. He applied a living law.

The five who were friendly to Henry, Hildebert, Paludanus, James of Lausanne, St Anthony and Prierias, ignored Innocent's bull – for reasons which cannot be given. But because they did so they must be judged as not only a small minority but also a peripheral school in conflict with the mainstream of canonists and with the Curia. Furthermore, in so far as they all followed Paludanus almost verbatim, their opinion can be described as the work of one man. In his later years, however, Paludanus wrote a commentary on Scripture in which, when he came to discuss Leviticus xviii, he *withdrew* the views contained in his youthful commentary on the *Sentences* and now asserted that the impediment of first degree collateral affinity was grounded in positive law after all. It was Thomas Abel who uncovered Palulanus's recantation and flung it in Henry's face.[50] Whether it reduced the value of what the other four wrote is difficult to say. But certainly it did not help Henry.

Hence, of the main arguments which Henry advanced, none showed great strength, though they were repeated again and again. What they did to Deuteronomy and Leviti-

50. I have not found a copy of this work by Paludanus and therefore rely on the man who found it and quoted it against Henry, namely, Abel, in his *Invicta Veritas.* Abel has proved accurate whenever I have checked him. Abel got his text probably with the help of the Imperialists at Rome who petitioned for a copy of this rare work to be sent from Paris. *Sp. Cal.,* iii, ii, 667.

cus was either so extreme or novel as to be insupportable, or else, on any strict assessment, gratuitous. None had the explicit, unquestionable allegiance of a single Father; only one could call up the support of later authorities and this support was cracked at the base. Though there were a number of scholastics who did not speak explicitly against Henry it is likely that, had they considered his case, they would have been guided by *Deus qui Ecclesiam* – as were many of their fellows – and passed sentence against it. Henry's dispensation was a comparative rarity but not novel. Much that was presented on his side proved, on inspection, to be indecisive, irrelevant or worse. Against him stood the sacred text of Deuteronomy and the undeniable fact that Old Testament Jewry had practised the levirate in obedience to it. Against him, at many points, too many points, stood one Father after another. Against him stood many scholastics and canonists and, above them all, Innocent III. Against him stood the fact that Julius II had granted him a dispensation which, we are entitled to assume, Martin V and Alexander VI before him, and Leo X and Clement VII after him, would not have withheld. Against him, armed with all this, stood Fisher, Cajetan, Abel and the rest.

To claim that Julius's dispensation had been *ultra vires* was, of course, to begin to challenge papal authority itself and thus to embark on dangerous waters. This was one reason, but probably not the only one, why a second campaign was launched – not against all dispensations of the kind that Julius had granted, but against this particular one.

The Canon Law of dispensations was exact and exacting. In the first place, sufficient cause (*causa*) had to be shown why the grant should be made. The circumstances and motives of the supplicants and the exact nature and degree of the impediment were to be stated, and were normally briefly rehearsed in the preamble of the dispensation. If any of the facts alleged proved wrong, or should material facts have been withheld, then the bull would be judged either obreptitious or subreptitious, and hence invalid, and the supplicants would have to begin again. All this was necessary caution, and it gave Henry a new opportunity to burrow against his marriage.[51]

It was the *causa* of Julius's dispensation that he attacked first. Quoting the supplication, the pope had given as his motive for granting the request his hope that peace between England and Spain would be strengthened thereby.[52] Two objections were raised against this: the first that such a *causa* was insufficient, indeed frivolous; the second that, if it were canonically sound it was not so historically, for, at the time of this petition, England and Spain were established allies and Henry's union to Catherine could not have been intended to produce peace so much as to bear witness to it. Thus Julius founded his bull on a misunderstanding.

Much energy was to be expended in urging these points. Some were to add the refinement that, since the dispensation was granted to preserve peace between Henry VII and Ferdinand and Isabella, and since, when Henry VIII married Catherine, his father was dead, the dispensation had lost its validity when the time came to use it.

But the first objection was absurd. There was no better *causa* known to Canon Law than the furtherance of good relations between states.[53] Secondly, Julius had not said that the marriage would create Anglo-Spanish peace, but that it would strengthen it; and at its best, peace can always be better. The words put into his mouth (by the English, it should be noted), 'that the existing peace may endure the longer', expressed a genuine motive accurately. Moreover, a dispensation dispensed from the moment it was issued,

51. For what follows I have digested arguments contained in several 'royalist' tracts, viz. B.M. Add., 4,622, fols 104 ff.; *Harleian* 417, fols 11 ff. (by Edward Lee); *A Glasse of the Truthe*. For the counter-arguments I have relied mainly on Loazes, who deals very fully with the whole subject.

52. '*Ut hujusmodi vinculum pacis et amicitiae . . . diutius permanet*'.

53. See Dauvillier, op. cit., 235 ff.

immediately and permanently. To argue that it only became
effective when it was put to use would be to open the way
to massive difficulties. If Henry VII's death invalidated the
bull, then, if his son had married Catherine in 1504, would
the marriage have become invalid in 1509, when the father
died? Obviously not. If the bull had referred to Henry VII
as though he were alive when he was in fact dead, then
things would have been different; but it had not done this.

Contrived though it was, this argument threw up much
dust and proved a vexatious, elusive thing to repel once and
for all. It was because of this that the discovery in Spain, in
1528, of a second dispensation, a brief this time, was so
important. The brief, of the same date as the bull and
supplementary to it, differed in certain significant details.[54]
Where the bull had said of the first marriage that it had *perhaps* been consummated, the brief showed no such hesitation and stated simply that it had been. Where the bull
said that the dispensation was granted in order to foster
peace between the two nations, the brief said it was for this
and other reasons (unspecified). By adding these words the
main argument against the bull was wrecked. Insufficiency
of cause could no longer be alleged in the face of these
'other reasons' which, for all men knew, might have been
far more weighty than the betterment of Anglo-Spanish
relations. But even without the brief – which will be discussed again later[55] – it is difficult to see that Henry had
yet made any headway in his argument.

This being so he had to look elsewhere. In the spring of
1505, it will be recalled,[56] the future king made a protest
against his contract of marriage to Catherine and publicly
stated his determination not to take her to wife. It was now
to be argued that, in doing this, he publicly and permanently renounced the dispensation which he had been given
and, having renounced it, could not subsequently revive it.
But this was plainly a specious argument. Henry could not

54. For text, see *Burnet*, iv, 610 f.   55. Below, pp. 287 ff.
56. Above, p. 24.

annul the dispensation because he had not given it; and he could no more replace the impediment afterwards than he could remove it before. A papal bull is no more subject to a prince's protest than is an impediment to affinity.

It was true that the petition for the dispensation had been drawn up in Henry's name and the bull addressed to him as prince. At the time, Henry was twelve years old. It was now to be claimed that he was too young either to desire Catherine or to express the reasons given for the marriage. But he was not below the canonical age for *contracting* marriage, which was seven, and if he were of sufficient age to contract marriage then he was old enough to be the subject of a dispensation for it. That diplomacy was as yet beyond his reach did not make the diplomatic facts contained in the supplication untrue, and it was only untruth which could make the bull subreptitious. Besides, the bull, as was common form, stated that the petition had been presented to Rome '*pro parte vestra*' – 'on your behalf' – which was not to say that Henry was its very author. Indeed, it was careful to avoid saying so.

The arguments, therefore, ran in two directions: Julius's bull was invalid from the start because subreptitious, or because Henry was too young at the time, and so on; or the bull had become invalid by the time it was used – because Henry had renounced it in his protest or because his father was dead. In no form, it seems, would these arguments have survived in a court of law for much longer than the time it took to state them and in any form they were exposed to two embarrassing retorts – the first: why is it that all this has just been discovered?; the second: if the bull is as transparently defective as is claimed, those who either asked for it or acted upon it have been fools or knaves, which is incredible.

All the arguments presented against Henry's marriage, therefore, were inadequate. None the less, it is arguable that the marriage was *not* valid. Henry had a case in con-

temporary Canon Law, a better case than the ones he
actually presented. But he did not grasp it.

One of the two main arguments against Julius's bull has
been concerned with affinity, that is, with the relationship
established between one person and another's relatives by
the sexual union of those two persons. This relationship
springs solely from physical union and derives from illicit
and licit coition, from fornication and adultery as well as
from marriage. It can coexist with consanguinity, if A has
a blood-tie with B and, say, has fornicated with B's sister.
Like consanguinity, affinity sets up a so-called diriment
impediment, that is, an impediment which, if not previously
removed, invalidates a marriage contracted in defiance of
it – as distinct from a prohibitory or impeding impediment
which it would be an offence to ignore but which could not
invalidate the sacrament. Thus, if a man disregarded the
impeding impediment of simple vows of religion (a matter
of positive ecclesiastical law only) and married a nun, he
and she would be guilty of disobedience at least, but they
would be man and wife nonetheless. However, if the nun
were either the man's second cousin or his sister-in-law, and
if the consequent diriment impediment of consanguinity or
affinity had not been dispensed, then the marriage would
have been null and void from the start. There are two kinds
of diriment impediment, one dispensable (like many of the
degrees of affinity and consanguinity); the other indispensable (like error, force, absolute impotence, etc.). No pope
could allow a marriage in which one party was to be taken
violently to the altar or deceived about the identity of the
other when he got there; but he could make it possible for
a man to marry his second cousin.[57]

So far we have discussed two kinds of dispensable, diriment

57. Henry's first argument, of course, has been that the impediment of the first degree collateral of affinity existing between a man
and his brother's relict is an indispensable diriment impediment; the
crux of the reply was that it was a dispensable one.

impediments, affinity and consanguinity. But these were not the only ones; there were some half-dozen more, of which only one matters here.

Affinity springs *ex coitu*, that is, normally from a consummated marriage. But formal betrothal and non-consummated marriage, i.e. marriage *per verba de futuro* (espousals) and marriage *per verba de presenti* (the marriage contract), these two, the marriage ceremonies as distinct from the marriage act, also set up an impediment to subsequent marriage between either of the parties and the other's relatives – to which the title of 'the impediment of the justice of public honesty', or simply 'the impediment of public honesty' was given. Public honesty or, as we might prefer, public decency and propriety, required that where a *proximitas animorum* as close as that created by betrothal or marriage at the altar had occurred, there an impediment similar to, but distinct from, affinity had arisen. Like much of marriage law, the impediment of public honesty had its origin in the Old Testament and civil law; by 1500 it had long since passed into canonical thinking, having been listed by Gratian, shaped further by decretists and decretalists, given new precision by Boniface VIII and thus provided with an established place on the list of dispensable diriment impediments. Thus if A is solemnly and validly betrothed to B and then B dies, A is prevented by this impediment from marrying any relative to the fourth degree of B. If B did not die until the marriage contract was ratified (but not consummated), the same would be true. And what happens if a marriage is both ratified and consummated? From the consummation affinity arises; from the previous ratification public honesty has arisen, and remains. Much later, thanks largely to a ruling of Benedict XV, it will be argued that by consummation the second, a *qua si* affinity, is absorbed into the first. But this was not how a late medieval canonist thought. For him every valid and consummated marriage produced a double impediment between A and the relatives of B, and *vice versa*, affinity joining public honesty as soon as the marriage contract was consummated.

Thus the impediment of public honesty – in any degree a dispensable diriment impediment – could stand alone when A and B were but solemnly espoused or their marriage not yet consummated. Likewise affinity could stand alone if A and B have, for example, committed fornication. Often, however, they coexisted and, of course, might be joined by consanguinity, not to mention other impediments, both diriment and prohibitory, which we can leave aside.[58]

Let us now turn to the matter of dispensations. Assume that a marriage has been contracted and consummated between A and B, that B dies and A wants to marry a kinswoman of B, whom we will call C. Between A and C stand the two impediments of affinity and public honesty. When A seeks dispensation from Rome, must he ask explicitly for both impediments to be removed? One would expect the answer to be in the affirmative, for the law concerning dispensation is rigorous. Faced with this question, the early fourteenth-century canonist, Johannes Andreae, a leading authority on marriage law, had said 'yes'.[59] But by the fifteenth century this rigorous ruling had been softened. Answering the same question, Panormitanus, one of the century's most considerable canonists, had made an acute distinction. The two impediments are indeed separate. One is not absorbed by the other, as will later be argued. Never-

58. See, for all this, Brillaud, *Traité Pratique des Empêchements et des Dispenses de Mariage* (Paris, 1884); Freisen, *Geschichte des Canonischen Eherechts* (Tübingen, 1888); Esmein, *Le Mariage en Droit Canonique* (Paris, 1891); *Dictionnaire du Droit Canonique*, s.vv. Empêchement and Honnêté Publique; Mansella, *De Impedimentis Matrimonium Dirimentibus, etc.* (Rome, 1881). The reader must be warned that we have been discussing the Canon Law of marriage before the coming of the Code in 1918, which altered the *Corpus* as radically in this field as it did in most others. Today affinity springs from licit union only and the impediment of public honesty, by a remarkable metamorphosis, from concubinage.

59. *Solemnis Tractatus de Arbore Consanguinitatis et Affinitatis* (edn Lyons, 1549), 55.

theless, where an impediment of affinity necessarily implies that of public honesty, it is enough to dispense the first for the second to be *ipso facto* removed.[60] So it is in our hypothetical case. Because A confesses an affinity with C set up by consummated marriage with B he necessarily implies the impediment of public honesty between himself and C. A bull of dispensation of affinity must at the same time dissolve the other impediment even though it does not mention it specifically. But had he not stated that he was *married* to B, then, because the affinity might have arisen from illicit intercourse with her, he would not necessarily have implied that an impediment of public honesty existed between himself and C and therefore the dispensation for the first would not have carried with it, annexed to it, a dispensation for the second.

When Panormitanus wrote in the early fifteenth century, the question to which his answer has just been rehearsed had, he said, been hotly debated in the Roman Curia and was still under discussion. As the century wore on his views won the day. Not only were they accepted by subsequent canonists[61] but, which is more important, they carried curial practice. As the fifteenth-century *Calendars of Papal Registers* show,[62] when the affinity alleged sprang from valid, consummated marriage and therefore public honesty was necessarily attendant by virtue of the previous marriage contract, it was enough for the bull of dispensation to deal explicitly with the first only. The impediment of public honesty was usually mentioned only in circumstances which

60. *Commentarius in Libros Decretalium, etc.* (edn Venice, 1588), vii, 56.

61. E.g. Stephen Costa, *Tractatus de Affinitate* in *Tractatuum ex variis iuris Interpretibus Collectorium* (Lyons, 1549), xvi, 52; Angelus de Clavasio, *Summa Angelica de Casibus Conscientiae* (edn 1513), fol. lxvii; Nicholas Milis de Verona, *Repertorium, etc., s.v.* Dispensatio. All three wrote in the fifteenth century. Perusal of sixteenth-century writers shows that this opinion became universal.

62. *Cal. Papal Reg.*, viii, 508; ix, 32, 179; x, 130, 608 f.; xi, 242; xii, 424, 442; xiii, 219.

Panormitanus and the others apparently did not foresee, which indeed they would not have thought it necessary to foresee. A might be related by legitimate affinity to C by reason of his previous marriage to B (and therefore also come under the sanction of public honesty), and as well as this C might at some time have been betrothed to D, a relative of A – in which case a second impediment of public honesty would stand between him and C. The first would be automatically removed with the affinity, but the second would require separate, explicit dispensation.

This last complexity is beside the point. All we need cling to is this fact: that by the early sixteenth century canonical opinion and curial practice were firmly agreed that where an impediment of public honesty arising out of a valid contract of marriage coexisted with an impediment of affinity resulting from the *consummation* of that marriage, it was enough if the bull of dispensation mentioned only the affinity. The other was necessarily presumed because necessarily present; and if necessarily present, no less necessarily dispensed. The impediment of public honesty in such a case received what we may call 'implicit dispensation'.

But suppose A had *contracted* marriage with B, that B had died before the marriage was *consummated* and that now A wanted to marry C, a relative of B. Since the marriage was ratified but not consummated there was no impediment of affinity, only one of public honesty. If A applied to Rome for permission to marry C, clearly he could not employ the principle of implicit dispensation because there was no affinity from which the other could be deduced, to which it was annexed, by which it was necessarily implied. No canonist can be quoted to this effect for the very good reason, surely, that the matter was so obvious that it merited no comment. In such a case the supplicant must ask explicitly for a dispensation of the impediment of public honesty, no more and no less, omitting the irrelevance of affinity.

We have come to the end of the canonical excursus. Let us turn back to the case of Henry VIII.

The bull of Julius II which was sought in order that Henry might marry the widowed Catherine of Aragon was a strange document. In the preamble it talked of Catherine's first marriage to Arthur and said, hesitantly, that it was '*perhaps* consummated', '*forsan consummatum*'. It then went on to dispense Henry and Catherine from an impediment of affinity that stood between them and which could only have arisen if there had been *coitus*.[63] In effect the bull says 'if the marriage was consummated, we dispense the consequent affinity'; and, thanks to the principle of implicit dispensation, it also removed the impediment of public honesty between Catherine and Arthur's relatives set up by her contract with him and necessarily implied by the declaration of affinity.

If Catherine's marriage to Arthur was consummated, then the bull was valid. If, however, it was not, then there was no question of affinity, but equally certainly there was still the question of public honesty. In this case, moreover, as has been said, the principle of implicit dispensation cannot be invoked. It cannot be argued that the impediment of public honesty, undoubtedly present, is implicitly dispensed at the same time as the affinity which necessarily contains it, because the affinity is non-existent. If that marriage had not been consummated then Henry required a straightforward dispensation from the impediment of public honesty, with no mention of affinity; a common enough thing, several examples of which are to be found in the *Calendars of Papal Registers*.[64] In other words, having dealt with affinity derived from consumation, the bull – if its author had followed to their conclusion the implications of the 'perhaps' – should have turned to the consequence of non-consummation, namely an impediment of public honesty, which now required separate and specific treatment. But it did not. The 'perhaps' ('*forsan*') was an unpondered safeguard.

How are we to account for this omission? A possible answer will be suggested later. For the moment let us dis-

63. For the text, see *Burnet*, iv, 15 f.
64. E.g. *Cal. Papal Reg.*, viii, 27, 365, 602, 626; ix, 559; x, 259 f.

pose of what may be a source of confusion, but is irrelevant. In the *brief* of dispensation, discovered in Spain in 1528, there is no *'forsan'*. No doubt is expressed about the consummation of Catherine's first marriage. Though the brief was to be of significance in the debate on the king's 'great matter', since it obviously did nothing to make good the bull's failure to provide for the consequences of non-consummation it is not of interest here.

To return, therefore, to the point. The conclusion is that, if the marriage between Catherine and Arthur was *not* consummated then probably the subsequent marriage between Catherine and Henry was rendered invalid by the diriment impediment of public honesty set up by Catherine's contract with Arthur and, by error or misjudgement, apparently not dispensed by the bull.

We move, therefore, to the question: was that first marriage consummated? The answer must be 'no'. Catherine herself consistently denied that Arthur had known her. Immediately after his death she wrote to her father that the marriage had not been consummated – this in defiance of English wishes and at the risk of complicating things yet further for herself. Her only credible motive for writing this is that it was true; and her statement was forcefully echoed by Doña Elvira, her chief attendant, who descended like an avenging angel upon an idle-tongued chaplain who, guided by supposition merely, had expressed an opposite opinion.[65] What is more, Henry himself had said that Catherine came to him a virgin.[66] True, in 1527–8 a rag-bag of gossip was collected from those who had been in attendance on the prince and princess during their brief marriage twenty-five years before purporting to prove that it had been consummated – half-remembered kitchen talk and snippets

65. Mattingly, *Catherine of Aragon*, 49.
66. In April 1533, he admitted this to Chapuys, but claimed that he had said it in jest (*L.P.*, vi, 351). But in October 1529 Catherine said that Henry had more than once admitted that she came to him a virgin (*Sp. Cal.*, iii, ii, p. 352), and in June 1531 she claimed that there were people alive who had heard him assert this. So *L.P.*, v, 308.

of coarse bravado overheard from Arthur's lips; but the evidence, as distinct from the abundant surmise, would scarcely suffice to hang a dog.[67] All who were in a position to know and to speak affirmed unhesitatingly that Catherine was married only in name to her first husband.

It therefore seems possible to conclude that, since Catherine's first marriage was not consummated, and since a diriment impediment had been set up between her and Henry and not dispensed by the bull of 1503, her second marriage may well have been invalid in the eyes of the Church.

There are, however, several difficulties in the way of this thesis.

In the first place, if it is granted, as it must be, that the non-consummation of Catherine's first marriage is a moral certainty, one may well ask if it could ever have been a legal one. Could the fact ever have been established at law twenty-five years after the event? Canon law knew well enough a procedure for establishing *present* virginity but clearly it could not have acted retrospectively. The presumption of the law, a strong current, would have run hard against the claim that a married couple who had been placed in the marriage bed and cohabited for several months had not consummated their marriage. To argue against it would not have been easy, certainly; but neither would it have been impossible. After all, there was the *forsan*. There had been doubt in Julius's mind. Then there was Catherine's solemn word. Had the king, the *Defensor Fidei*, added his testimony to hers, might not this have tipped the scales? It had been enough for King Louis XII of France merely to affirm, on the word of a monarch, that his first marriage had been forced upon him and not consummated for Rome to grant him a decree of nullity.

This first difficulty is one presented, or threatened, by the

---

67. At least not in the face of Catherine's solemn statement in writing to the pope of the non-consummation of her first marriage (*L.P.*, iv, 5762) and her solemn oath to the same effect in November 1528, for which see *Pocock*, ii, 431 ff.

canon lawyer. The second is the work of a theologian – alas, none other than St Thomas himself. Hitherto affinity has been defined as deriving solely from the sexual act, and public honesty as the consequence not only of espousals *de futuro* but the marriage contract itself, marriage *per verba de presenti*. This was a common view, but it was not the only one. In his commentary on Peter Lombard's *Sentences* (and taking his lead from the *Magister Sententiarum*), as well as at the end of the *Summa Theologiae*, St Thomas had put forward a subtler thesis that affinity sprang not just *ex copula carnis* but also from what, following on the heels of Aristotle, he termed *societas conjugalis*. It was merely by living together in conjugal partnership, as well as by physical union, that affinity was established. Marriage *per verba de futuro* begets public honesty, he argued; marriage *per verba de presenti*, that is ratified marriage, begets something more, namely, affinity; the subsequent consummation only confirms it.[68]

Clearly St Thomas's teaching cuts the ground from under the argument presented above. By his reckoning Catherine's marriage to Arthur, whether consummated or not, would have set up affinity – and the bull of dispensation been sufficient. But Thomism was never more than one of several schools of thought. The view which St Thomas expressed on the matter of affinity was not accepted by many other theologians and never won much ground among canonists – who clung to the simpler definition. True, by the late fifteenth century and through the sixteenth, Dominican and then Jesuit theologians gave Thomism its first taste of pre-eminence, and from then onwards we can see Thomas's views on affinity winning support. At least one fifteenth-century canonist accepted them.[69] In the early sixteenth

68. *Commentary on the Sentences*, iv, dist. xli, qu. i, art. i. *Summa Theologiae Suppl.* quest. 55, arts 3 and 4.
69. Namely one Alexander de Nevo – according to the Jesuit Sanchez, who wrote in the early seventeenth century. I have not been able to find the work of de Nevo to which Sanchez refers.

century Silvester Prierias, one of Henry's supporters, could argue that affinity is contracted *ex sponsalia de presenti principiative*.[70] It is there in principle or, as Sanchez, an early seventeenth-century Jesuit, describing this middle position wrote, *'initiative et large'*. By then (viz. the early seventeenth century) St Thomas's view was to acquire impressive supporters, Peter de Soto and, tentatively, Bellarmine among them.[71] But in the early sixteenth century, theirs was very much a minority view. A hundred years later, when Sanchez wrote, he could list a dozen authorities who held with St Thomas; some five who took a middle position like Prierias, and over twenty-five who rejected the Thomist definition, preferring to cling to the old dictum, *affinitas ex copula proveniens*.[72] St Thomas would have provided Catherine, or rather those whom she would presumably have called to her

70. *Summa Summarum. Matrimonium*, viii, nu. 14.

71. Peter de Soto, *Commentaria in Quartum Sententiarum, etc.*, iv, dist. 41, qu. i, art. 2. Bellarmine, *De Controversiis, etc. De Matrimonio*, in *Opera Omnia* (Naples, 1872), iiii, 839, 857. De Soto observes that the question whether a *matrimonium ratum* sets up affinity or public honesty is a matter of words only (since a diriment impediment occurs in either case). This is an opinion which one meets elsewhere, e.g. Ludovicus Lopez, *Instructorium Conscientiae* (Salamanca, 1594), ii, 1146. But having made this point, de Soto goes on to say *'nihilominus D. Thomas videtur ad rem vicinius loqui'*.

72. Sanchez, *Disputationum de Sancti Matrimonii Sacramento*, vii, dist. lxiv, n. 24, 25. Sanchez himself rejected St Thomas's views. In fact the number supporting St Thomas should be reduced by one, for Sanchez includes Peter de Ledesma twice: once in the list of Thomists and again among those who, like Prierias, take the middle position. He certainly belongs to the second group. In reply to the question whether a non-consummated marriage begets public honesty or affinity, he gave it as 'probable' *'que por el matrimonio rato non consumado se contrahe afinidad no perfecta, y consumada sino como initiative'*. So his *Summa* (edn Saragossa, 1611), 78. Though a Dominican, Ledesma is not a thorough-going Thomist on this matter. It may also be observed that Sanchez seems to go too far in numbering Bellarmine among the true Thomists. The latter speaks of *'alia quaedam affinitas'* arising out of non-consummated marriage – a hesitation which, surely, places him nearer Prierias than St Thomas himself. See *Opera Omnia*, iii, 839.

aid, with a weapon with which to fight but not to win, for the majority stood against Thomas. His concept of the nature of affinity was certainly as yet far from the status of '*tutior*' or '*probabilior*' and, which is decisive, shows no sign of having impinged on curial thinking.[73]

If it is right to argue the inadequacy of Julius's bull, then one may well ask how it ever came to be written and why the defect was not noticed at the time – exactly the same objection as that brought against Henry's indictment of the bull. No really satisfying answer to this can be offered.

When, after Arthur's death, a second marriage for Catherine into the Tudor house was mooted, Henry VII and his councillors discussed the question of the dispensation which it would require and also, we know, raised the question of whether the first marriage had been consummated.[74] According to Catherine's father, the 'wretched' English, in order to remove all doubt about the succession, decided to tell Rome that consummation had occurred even though, so he said (with little evidence, no doubt), it was well known in England that this was not true. Presumably because they feared that someone might find it incredible that there had not been consummation and therefore might be moved to impugn the validity of the second marriage and the legitimacy of its offspring, Henry VII and the council decided to play safe, to assume consummation and therefore seek a dispensation of the larger impediment, affinity. What they failed to do was to play doubly safe by asking for a dispensation of the impediment of public honesty which non-

73. Clarifying a decree of Trent, Pius V ruled that, whereas an impediment of public honesty arising out of marriage *per verba de futuro* extended no further than the first degree, '*impedimentum hoc proventum ex matrimonio rato et non consummato durat in omnibus illis casibus ubi de iure veteri ante concilium Tridentinum erat*' – i.e. to the fourth degree. Pius V therefore was no Thomist. See Esmein, op. cit., ii, 265 n. As Friesen observes (op. cit., 505), St Thomas's views on affinity won no following, though the judgement is accurate for the later Middle Ages only.

74. *Pocock*, ii, 426 ff.

consummation created. Perhaps they were ignorant of the need for it (which is scarcely credible); perhaps they were distracted by what was in this case the irrelevant principle of 'implicit dispensation' (which is possible); perhaps they were so occupied with suppressing doubt, with blocking one possible threat to the succession – *prima facie* the more likely one – that they overlooked the second (which is the most probable explanation). Rome was told that the marriage had been completed. As soon as she heard of this, Catherine protested and wrote to her father begging him to write in turn to the pope that she was yet a virgin and that the English had maligned her.[75] This he did; and it was in response to his letter, perhaps, that Rome placed the word *forsan* in the bull, thus admitting that very doubt which the English had been at pains to prevent. Why then did the bull fail to pursue the implication of the *'forsan'* and deal with the separate impediment caused by non-consummation? Perhaps it was because the English supplication had been so firm on the point that the Curia was, as it were, carried by it, or regarded it as inopportune to talk about what was, by English design, not there.

The supplication was sent to Rome in the summer of 1503, but the death of Alexander VI in August, the short pontificate of Pius III (he ruled less than a month) and the election of Julius II delayed response until the end of December. Then, however, a strange thing happened. The dispensation was granted, but the bull not dispatched. Henry VII wrote repeatedly for it, but Julius II, for reasons unknown, withheld it. Eventually in late 1504 he was persuaded to send a copy to Spain to console Catherine's mother Isabella, on her death-bed. From Spain a copy made its way to England, arriving about Christmas 1504. To Henry's evident irritation and Julius's chagrin, the text of the bull first came to England by this roundabout way. Not until March 1505 was the original dispatched from Rome directly to England, some twenty months after the suppli-

75. *Pocock*, i, 5 f.; ii, 429 f.

cation had been drawn up.[76] But by then times had changed.
The projected marriage between Henry prince of Wales and
Catherine was off. Henry was about to make his protest
against his betrothal to Catherine, who was now set aside.
Whether or not her first marriage had been consummated,
the implications of the '*forsan*' – these were now dead issues.
The much-sought bull had therefore suddenly become a
museum-piece. Four years later it was to matter once more
when Catherine was called from unhappy obscurity to her
second wedding and the throne of England. But by then
memories must have grown dim. Catherine herself, as later
events proved, did not appreciate the canonical position and
assumed that the bull was sufficient. If anyone had earlier
perceived the implications of her plea of virginity he may
well have forgotten it or disappeared from the scene. Confident, apparently, that only an impediment of affinity had
stood in the way, the realm rejoiced in the new alliance.

The argument is, therefore, that somebody blundered;
that in 1503 when the decision was taken to apply for a
dispensation for Henry to marry Catherine, somebody failed
to think out to the full the canonical significance of the
affair. After all, this was just a routine matter. Who could
have guessed the future of this projected union between
Catherine and Henry? The English error was far less implausible and embarrassing than the gross incompetence
alleged by Henry in his arguments against the validity of
the bull. But an error it was. Rome did not repair it. Subsequent events contrived to mask it.

There remains the gravest objection of all to the thesis.
If it is right to contend that Julius's bull was insufficient,
why was this fact not quickly pounced upon in 1527, and
thereafter, when the king's 'great matter' was afoot? Why
did not the scores of nimble doctors, the international team
of theologians and canonists whom Henry called up to cut
his Gordian knot leap upon this point? How could Henry
himself as, like a captive panther, he paced the cage of his

76. *Pocock*, i, 7, f.; *Sp. Cal.*, i, 426.

wedlock, thrusting at every bar, fail to notice the open door?
In short, if the argument is sound, why did no one advance
it when it was worth not just a horse, but, indeed, a kingdom?

The answer is that at least one person did. Wolsey saw
the point, and saw it with that swift precision which was
the hallmark of his intelligence. When, in June 1527,
Catherine was first informed officially of Henry's scruples
about the legitimacy of his marriage to her she had shown
herself 'very stiff and obstinate' and, thinking thus to silence
all doubt once and for all, had flung back the reply that
Arthur had in fact never known her and that Henry's
scruple was therefore groundless.[77] Wolsey pondered the
point. A few days later he was writing to Henry that, if
Arthur had never known Catherine, 'there was no affinity
contracted; yet in that she was married *in facie ecclesiae*,
and contracted *per verba de presenti*, there did arise *impedimentum publicae honestatis*, which is no less *impedimentum
ad dirimendum matrimonium* than affinity; whereof [*sc.*
public honesty] the bull making no express mention'.[78] The
point has been put exactly. Lacking full grasp of canon law,
Catherine has unwittingly exposed herself to a terrible
threat. If there had been no *copula carnis*, as she asserted,
there had been no affinity; but there had been the diriment
impediment of public honesty, with which the bull does
not seem to have dealt. And not only did the cardinal
grasp the point now; he held on to it. Some months later
he rehearsed the argument to Stephen Gardiner, then in
Rome, asking him to put the point to learned men, including Stafileo, former dean of the Rota.[79] A few weeks before,
Richard Fox, bishop of Winchester and one of the few who
took part in the events of 1503 and was still alive, was
closely interrogated. Among the questions put to him (and
we may assume that Wolsey gave at least broad shape to
the interrogatories) was one asking whether Julius had

77. *St.P.*, i, 195.   78. ibid.
79. *Pocock*, i, 150 f. (*L.P.*, iv, 4251).

been supplicated to remove an impediment of affinity or
of public honesty; to which Fox replied that he believed
it was the former.[80] Wolsey's mind was working very acutely.
He was clearly wondering whether the '*forsan*' could be
stretched to prove that the bull had, by implication, dealt
with public honesty derived from non-consummation, and
had seen that the supplication was of relevance.

But though Wolsey himself made the leap, at the time
no one else of consequence seems to have followed. Why?
The answer, perhaps, is this. Outside promptings may have
helped him onwards, but the true initiative for the divorce
had come from Henry himself. What is more, it was he who
determined the weapon with which the campaign was to
be fought – namely Leviticus. Leviticus was, so to speak, his
discovery and he committed himself to it from the start.
But the claim that Holy Writ forbade absolutely marriage
with a dead brother's wife depended on the consummation
of the first, the dead brother's, marriage. At least, so Henry
reasoned; and, though there is room for discussion on this
point today, then it was probably right, and certainly safer,
so to do. Wolsey's argument, therefore, was brushed aside
because, by the time it was presented to the king, Henry
was already affirming that Catherine had been known by
Arthur and was therefore forbidden to him by Scripture.
There were two other factors at work also. First, because it
was his own argument, because it was apparently so simple
and sweeping, because there was already a feeling that he
was being guided by the finger of God's right hand, Henry
would have been reluctant anyway to listen to an alternative.
Secondly, Wolsey was already suspect. Hyper-sensitive, perhaps paronoiacally sensitive, to sluggishness in this matter,
the king had smelt disaffection and begun to work behind
Wolsey's back as early as the summer of 1527. Henry was
already beginning to assume that any advice from Wolsey
was bad advice. Indeed, when Wolsey first suggested orally
to Henry that, if he accepted Catherine's statement that her

80. P.R.O. S.P. 1/54, fols 362v–363 (*L.P.*, iv, 5791).

first marriage had not been consummated he had at hand a weapon with which to split his union with her, his remark was taken by a petulant master as evidence of disloyalty, presumably because it took the queen's word for truth. The letter quoted above, setting out the argument again, was written to show that there was 'no doubt in me' that he had only meant to help. A few days later Wolsey was off to France, still suspiciously regarded, and for several weeks was out of close contact with the king. By the time he was back, the king's design had finally hardened and Wolsey no longer had the full confidence of the king. At the very moment when Henry needed him most, when (perhaps) he had most to offer Henry, the latter, by a supreme irony, turned away. Rarely has pig-headedness, or suspicion, been more harshly rewarded.

Once launched, the Levitical argument was an absorbing one. Its novelty, the speed with which it unrolled, its many ramifications, philological and canonical, its many side issues, like the problem of Christ's genealogy, the date of Philip the Tetrarch's death or the distinction between 'concede' and 'dispense', its appeal to scholars of many disciplines and many nations – all these made it difficult to step out of the hurly-burly to excogitate an argument that was not only radically different in kind but took for its premise what the other had brushed aside as nonsense from the start, namely, the non-consummation of the first marriage. Henry and his men had set off in a splendid, headlong quest, but in the wrong direction. Once they were off, it was difficult to turn back; and they could turn back only at the price of publicly abandoning what had been stated as a certainty.

It was not the wrong end of the stick that Henry grasped, therefore, but the wrong stick. It cannot be said that if he had followed Wolsey's line of reasoning he would certainly have won his case, for there would still have been obstacles in his way. Catherine would have had to swear non-consummation of the first marriage, and would she

have given this testimony now, at the price of destroying
herself? Surely it would not have been beyond the wit of
Henry and Wolsey to wring an oath from this honest, upright woman. Catherine would have turned to St Thomas
and to the '*forsan*' for aid. But they could not have protected
her for long. At least it is arguable that public honesty
offered Henry a better chance of success than the arguments
he in fact chose, and this not just because a far more impressive canonical case could have been built on it. A grave
weakness in the Levitical argument was that it required
that Rome should admit she had misused her jurisdiction
and challenged the *plenitudo potestatis* itself. The second
argument required Rome to admit that she had been
wrong about facts, which was far less serious but only palat-
able if it could now be shown that those facts were manifestly wrong. Wolsey's argument put the blame on no one
save the English. The error lay in the supplication. Julius
had merely done what he had been asked to do. If Clement
now declared Henry's marriage null and void because Julius
had been asked to do the wrong thing, he would cast no
reflections on his predecessor and disown no jurisdiction.
However, though Henry spoke fleetingly about it to
Catherine herself in 1529,[81] the argument based on the impediment of public honesty was not presented to Rome
until five years after the long tussle over the divorce had
begun, and then only *en passant*, in a letter from Henry

81. On 8 October, Chapuys reported that, a short while ago, Henry
had been disputing with Catherine after dinner and had said, 'You
wish to help yourself and defend the validity of your dispensation by
saying that your former husband, Prince Arthur, my brother, never
consummated marriage. Well and good, but no less was our marriage
illegal, for the bull does not dispense *super impedimento publicae
honestatis* and, therefore, I intend disputing and maintaining against
all people that a dispensation thus conceived is insufficient.' *Sp. Cal.*,
iii, ii, 275. But Henry did not thereafter publicize this argument,
despite his bold words. However, it appears from what Chapuys said
that the king had momentarily begun to assert that Catherine's first
marriage had not, after all, been consummated.

to his agents there.[82] Whether they ever put it to the pope,
or how it was received, we are not told. But it was not for
Rome to ferret out details of a now remote past to discover
that argument for Henry. It was not for the judge to do
the plaintiff's work and, anyway, Henry had always categorically stated that Arthur had known Catherine. Of
course Clement's subservience to Charles V, such as it was,
presented an obstacle to Henry and would still have been
one. But Clement's difficulty was not just that Charles was
Catherine's nephew, but that Charles was Catherine's
nephew and Henry's case a feeble one. True enough, the
Curia was not always too exacting in the matter of matrimonial (or any other) dispensations; but it was not as lax
as has, on occasion, been suggested.[83] True enough, in late
1530 Clement proposed what Henry himself proposed more
than once, namely, that the king should be allowed to commit bigamy. But the pope's apparently shocking suggestion,
as one who heard it quickly guessed, was in reality a ruse.
If Henry allowed Rome authority to license bigamy, he implicitly allowed it authority to dispense from the less serious
impediment of affinity of the first degree collateral. Besides
– and this was the more likely motive for it – this proposal
would surely waste a great deal of time, by the end of
which the whole affair might have blown over.[84] No,
Clement had some regard for the law; and he could not
flout both the emperor and the law at once. Had either

82. In 1532. See below, pp. 373 f.
83. See Hardy, 'Papal Dispensation for Polygamy', *Dublin Review*,
cliii (1913), 266 ff. for criticism of Pollard's contention that Henry IV
of Castile had received papal authority to commit bigamy and that
this was a precedent (albeit unknown) for Henry VIII. No such
licence was granted to the Castilian king.
84. So Benet to Henry, 27 October 1530. *L.P.*, iv, 6705. Two other
letters from Rome reported the same proposal, viz. Casale to Henry,
a letter dated 18 September (ibid., 6627), and Ghinucci to Henry, an
undated letter of probably about the same time (ibid., App. 261). In
his dispatch, Benet said that Clement had made the suggestion
'doubtfully'. He also quoted the pope as saying that a great doctor
had told him he might grant this licence, to avoid greater scandal,

horn of his dilemma been less sharp he might have moved.
Had Henry's case been better, had justice been evidently
with him rather than evidently against him, things would
have been much easier.

but he would advise further with his Council. Lately, however, Benet
went on, 'he has said plainly he cannot do it'. Likewise Ghinucci said
that the pope had 'found several difficulties, saying the emperor
would never consent to it'.

The Struggle for the Divorce

By the end of 1527 England faced a dilemma of her own making. She wanted the war then being fought in Italy between Charles and the League of Cognac (of which France was the leading spirit) to end, but at the same time the most obvious way to persuade Clement to grant Henry the divorce was probably to keep the war alive, join the League and help avenge the wrongs done to the pope by the emperor.

It is often remarked that the Sack of Rome by the Imperial troops and Clement's captivity made Henry's case hopeless. There is obvious truth in this. But it is also true that it alone made the divorce feasible. Had emperor and pope been good friends Henry could not have begun to hope, for Clement would never have struck at Charles in cold blood. But Charles played into Henry's hands and made an enemy of the pope just when Henry most wanted him to. True, there were frightening moments while Clement was trapped in the Castel Sant' Angelo, when anything could have happened. To escape from his prison in the ravaged city he might have agreed to strip Wolsey of his legatine powers, quash the divorce there and then, and perhaps be shipped to Spain. But Charles had no intention of exploiting his unwelcome victory and, instead of wringing Clement, released him in early December. Rome was still in uproar, so the pope took himself, with a handful of cardinals, to Orvieto. There, in a tumble-down, half-furnished palace of the local bishop, the pope, bearded, whimpering and swollen-footed, set down the wreckage of his Curia.[1] He may have been in forlorn circumstances but he was now free and, perhaps as never before, susceptible to Henry. He needed protection, friends, money; and so too

1. *Pastor*, x, 1 ff.

did the cardinals with him, for they had lost much of their
worldly goods in the Sack, and curial business had meanwhile been reduced to a trickle. An urgent client ready to
reward services generously was therefore well placed. It was
true that Clement was frightened lest Charles should send
his terrible lanzknechts again. This ran against Henry. But
he was no longer physically subject to Charles and, more
important, there was bitterness in his heart. Just when
Henry was asking Clement to affront an emperor, an
emperor for the first time in generations had inflicted on a
pope an affront which cried out for vengeance. So tense was
the situation that even Wolsey's talk about deposing Charles
did not seem wholly absurd;[2] and Henry was asking the pope
to depose only the emperor's aunt. From one point of view
Henry could not have been provided with a more promising
situation. And is it not reasonable to suggest that, if he had
succeeded, historians would have had no more difficulty
in finding a political explanation for his success than they
have had in finding one for his failure?

  Wolsey had hoped that the League would force Charles
to come to terms. Once more, he hoped that his policy of
getting others to do the fighting would bring peace and that
England would never need to be more than a potential com-
batant. But Charles had not succumbed. An Anglo-French
embassy sent to Spain in mid 1527 with final terms was
repulsed. Accordingly on 21 January 1528 the English
herald delivered a declaration of war to the emperor at
Burgos. Henry and Wolsey later said that the English
ambassadors had acted precipitately and rebuked them for
it.[3] This may or may not be true; but certainly there was
no intention of active campaigning. Henry and the cardinal had foreseen the damage to trade with the Netherlands
which open warfare would cause and quickly concluded a
commercial truce with Margaret;[4] but they must have fore-

----

2. *L.P.*, iv, 3757, 3783.   3. ibid., 3827, 4564.
4. ibid., 3879, 4147, 4426, etc. It was reported that, after initial upset, English merchants had a bumper season at Antwerp, ibid., 5171.

seen also that an English army on the Continent, denied the hoys, horses, carriages and so on regularly supplied by the Low Countries, would have found the going very hard. No, the fighting would take place south of the Alps. England would supply money and encouragement, particularly to a pope who wanted to stay neutral. But she would not fight. Wolsey's economical mind would not allow her to edge forward any further than was necessary, according to his finely-calibrated diplomacy, to tip the balance.

By March 1528 he thought success was in sight. 'I see well there is right good light and appearance', he wrote to Henry, 'that means may be studied and devised to conduce peace between the French king, your highness, and the said emperor.'[5] A few days later news came that Charles was softening. Accordingly, at the end of March, John Clerk was sent to France with a new and detailed plan for the return of the French king's sons, the withdrawal of armies, and a truce – which Clerk was to present to Francis and implore him to accept. Francis must 'leave the extremities' and yield a little for the sake of peace.[6] At the same time Wolsey arranged with Margaret that she and he should send emissaries to France in Clerk's wake and that, as soon as Francis accepted the proposals, both should go to Spain and present them to the emperor. For this purpose, Silvester Darius, the papal collector in England and a neutral, was dispatched. 'Hitherto', said Wolsey to the French ambassador in England at the end of a long discussion, 'I have had little hope of peace.... Now I regard it as certain.'[7] Wolsey said that these proposals had been carefully debated by the king and Council, but it is clear that they were his own.[8] He believed that, exactly as he had planned,

5. *St.P.*, i, 187 (*L.P.*, iv, 4002); *Sp. Cal.*, iii, ii, 367, 386.
6. *L.P.*, iv, 4155.
7. P.R.O. 31/3/3, fols 237 f. These transcripts from Paris contain several valuable letters not in *L.P.*
8. *L.P.*, iv, 4206.

Charles was cracking and that his complex programme
would satisfy all sides. His purpose was to bring the combatants to a truce and thence to a new European peace –
perhaps a renewal of the treaty of 1518. Campeggio was in
England in that year; he was to return in late 1528 as papal
legate to deal with the divorce. Wolsey was prepared to
have him as a colleague in these peace negotiations as he
had nominally been before, and badgered Rome for a
suitable commission. He was preparing himself for another
major diplomatic display.[9]

Darius, the man sent to placate Charles, left France in
late May and was in Madrid probably by the end of June.
He waited there six weeks for the emperor, and when he
at last met him found him at best non-committal. Time
brought no improvement, and by the end of September
Darius was in despair. What had seemed a compelling
plan at Hampton Court made no mark on Madrid. By
early November he was on his way home, empty-handed.[10]
The situation was now swinging dangerously against England. The German soldiers had left Rome and the Papal
States, in June Clement moved to Viterbo, and four months
later he was back in Rome, which he found 'a pitiable and
mangled corpse'.[11] Desolate though his world was, he was
beginning to recover his grasp and, in particular, was ready
for a *rapprochement* to Charles. There were several reasons
for this – but not the least was his alarm at the rumours of
an Anglo-Imperial *détente* caused by Darius's mission.
Wolsey's dispatch of the latter had made him thoroughly
nervous and, in part, accounted for his friendly moves
towards the emperor. But if these succeeded, if he
and Charles came together, Henry would have lost his
case.

At last Henry saw the point. Four new agents – Knight,
Francis Bryan, Peter Vannes and William Benet – were

9. *L.P.*, iv, 4915, 4956.
10. For this mission, see ibid., 4269, 4637, 4802, 4909–11.
11. *Pastor*, x, 29.

swiftly dispatched to Rome to recover the situation. Their first task was to poison Clement's mind against Charles with tales of his perfidy, his evident ambition to overrun Italy, and so on. Then they were to offer the pope an Anglo-French bodyguard of 2,000 picked men to protect Rome against another assault. Henry, it was said, had already persuaded Francis to agree to this. But this was not true, and so two of the four now dispatched were to halt in France to clinch the plan with Francis while the others went on to Rome. Next, the pope was to declare a truce and propose a peace conference at Nice or Avignon over which he himself would preside and at which Wolsey would represent Henry. Once peace was signed Francis's children were to be handed back to their father and Charles at last crowned emperor by the pope – all at Avignon.[12]

This magnificent vista was, it seems, largely of Henry's creation. It was full of blatant, and probably inept, guile. Its first objective was to keep Charles and Clement apart until the expiry of a lengthy truce and thus gain several months in which to procure the divorce. The contingent of troops, the 'presidy', as it will be called, was a startling device. Its purpose was allegedly to enable Clement to proceed freely with Henry's affairs; but the real aim was different. 'As you know,' said Wolsey to the agents, 'and as was declared to you in Council, one of the things noted to be much to the advancement of the king's cause was that the pope's holiness, taking the presidy, should thereby be brought to have as much fear and respect towards the king's highness as he now has towards the emperor, and consequently be the gladder to grant and condescend unto the king's desire.'[13] Henry had pondered the story of Charles's lanzknechts and was preparing to send a contingent of his own to Rome under the pretence of offering protection, but in reality to turn the pope into his own prisoner. Two thousand men would scarcely protect Rome, but they might

12. *L.P.*, iv, 5028, 5050, 5053.
13. ibid., 5179.

hold the Curia in fee.[14] Such, almost incredibly, was apparently the king's purpose.

By the time the peace conference had assembled at Avignon the divorce, it was hoped, would be a fact. Then Charles could befriend Clement as much as he liked. Lest the pope had meanwhile proved obstinate and defied even the presidy, a further weapon was in Henry's hands. Without English adherence, the spectacular peace conference at Avignon, over which the pope should preside and at which so much was to be accomplished, would fail. If Clement were reluctant to yield on the divorce, Henry could say, as he and Wolsey often did say,[15] that Wolsey would not go to Avignon. Wolsey's quest for peace has not been abandoned, therefore, though the pope, not he, is now to be its president. Peace and the divorce have been reconciled by the submission of the first to the second. The resolution of the dilemma was, it seemed, largely of Henry's devising. It was to be accomplished by as ruthless, as circuitous and, in a sense, as improbable a plan as Henry had ever concocted.

It was in the late summer of 1527 that Henry had suddenly taken the initiative and sent William Knight to Rome to ask Clement to cut the Gordian knot at one stroke – at the very time when Wolsey was in France busy with a plan to take over the administration of the Church during the pope's captivity. Wolsey had already dispatched three people to Rome to procure the necessary commission for himself, namely, Ghinucci, bishop of Worcester and now English representative in Spain, Gambara, papal nuncio in England, and Gregory Casale, a member of an Italian family which rendered continual service to Henry and was well versed in the ways of Rome. Better than most, Gregory would be able to squeeze into Castel Sant' Angelo, persuade the pope to sign the commission and slip out again

14. The English ambassadors were also to play with the possibility of Charles's summoning a General Council.

15. *L.P.*, iv, 5314, 5428, 5480, 5572.

through the mêlée of refugees and rampaging soldiers. It was Wolsey's intention that Clement should be told nothing about Henry's problem, but rather, having granted a commission of viceregency and committed himself to automatic confirmation of all that was done in his name, should find on his release that the divorce had meanwhile been quietly settled and have no option but to confirm the sentence.[16] Henry, however, wanted to approach the pope directly and to have him solve the matrimonial problem. The king's will prevailed. Knight went on to Rome, while Wolsey, conscious that his affairs were going adrift, hastened homewards, calling out to Henry as he came that 'there was never lover more desirous of the sight of his lady, than I am of your most noble and royal person'.[17]

Having survived a nearly lethal attack twelve miles outside Rome, Knight arrived in the city in early December (1527). He made contact with Clement by letter and received what was apparently a most encouraging reply from the pope, who, there can be little doubt, was pleased with this prospect of making a friend.[18] Two or three days later he escaped from his prison and rode to Orvieto; and with that escape, Wolsey's plans for acting as his deputy collapsed. Henry's judgement had been surer. The only realistic course was to approach Clement openly and receive from his hands a complete, unimpeachable solution. All the king's efforts must, therefore, concentrate upon persuading this timid man to give his *fiat* to perhaps no more than a couple of documents; and for nearly three years one embassy after another was to be sent from England to accomplish this apparently simple thing. One after the other they were to be brought to a near standstill by the remarkable mixture of hesitancy, furtiveness, intelligence and inscrutable obstinacy that was Clement, and were to be sent home not exactly empty-handed but without the

16. *St.P.*, i, 271 f. (*L.P.*, iv, 3400).
17. ibid., 278 f. (*L.P.*, iv, 3423).
18. *St.P.*, vii, 16 (*L.P.*, iv, 3638).

document which really mattered. Then, when this relay of missions had failed, Henry would take to sterner tactics, openly bullying the Church in England and the Holy See.

Had Knight's mission been more skilfully planned and had he reached Rome at the beginning of Clement's imprisonment instead of at the end, he might have succeeded. While a prisoner in Sant' Angelo, Clement had let Knight understand that he would grant Henry what he desired. When Knight followed the pope to Orvieto he found a calmer man. He presented the documents he had brought with him for papal signature, but Clement refused to assent to them before experts had scrutinized them, and handed them over to the Grand Penitentiary, Lorenzo Pucci, Cardinal Sst Quatuor. The draft which Knight presented was primarily a dispensation for Henry to marry Anne. But in the preamble it stated as a fact that the present marriage was invalid, indeed sinful. Maybe Henry had thought it would be more difficult to procure the dispensation to marry Anne than the decree of nullity, and had therefore not bothered too closely about the latter; or he may have hoped to smuggle the declaration of nullity into this dispensation without Clement noticing. Whatever the facts, Pucci saw that this clumsy document seemed to be trying to do two things at once. '*Expungatur*,' he wrote indignantly against the preamble: '*alienissima est*' and unworthy of the king; and the rest must be modified thus and thus.[19]

By 1 January 1528 Knight had emerged from the papal palace with a bull for Henry signed and sealed. He wrote jubilantly to his master, sent the bull on ahead and himself set off for home.[20] But what he had acquired was merely a dispensation for Henry to marry Anne *if* his first marriage was proved unlawful. In itself, therefore, the document was worthless. A dispensation of the impediment of first degree collateral (illicit) affinity, a larger concession, be it

19. *Pocock*, i, 22 ff. (*L.P.*, iv, 3686).
20. *Ehses*, pp. 14 ff. for the text of the bull.

noted, than Julius's to Henry (because unsupported by Deuteronomy), had not proved so difficult to procure; but, thanks to Pucci, the real problem, that of getting rid of Catherine, remained unsolved.

Shortly after he returned home, if not before, and certainly weeks before the text of Knight's bull was in his hands, Wolsey had perceived that the expedition to Rome had been badly handled. Gregory Casale was by now on his way to the pope to procure Wolsey's commission of viceregency and it was decided that, instead he should rescue Knight and his inept bull. Casale's earlier instructions were therefore cancelled. In early December 1527, just as Knight was making first contact with Clement, Wolsey sent off a thick wad of instructions to Casale, who received them when he reached Orvieto just before Christmas, telling him to take over the whole business from Knight and virtually begin again.

Heavily disguised, he was to smuggle himself into the pope's presence and deliver to Clement a mixture of threats and blandishments. Then, turning to fundamentals, he was to demonstrate to the pope the evident invalidity of Henry's marriage to Catherine. It was not the Levitical argument with its dangerous innuendo against papal jurisdiction which he was to present, nor the argument from public honesty, but the humbler one that the particular bull of Julius II on which the marriage rested was defective. Once persuaded of this, the pope was to agree to set up a court in England to settle Henry's case and to issue a decretal, as distinct from a general, commission to the judges-delegate, that is, a commission in which the law was stated definitively and the judges empowered merely to examine the facts of the case and then apply that law. This decretal commission would have declared that any one of the defects alleged in Julius's bull would have been sufficient to invalidate it. It would have commanded the recipient to examine the charges made and, if any was verified, declare the marriage null and separate the parties. Against

this decision there could, in theory, be no appeal save on
grounds of suspicion of the judges-delegate.

Casale was supplied by Wolsey with the necessary document. It needed only seal and signature. Lest the pope, or
indeed the world, should think Wolsey suspect, he was to
be asked to send a legate from Rome to try the case alone
– Campeggio, for instance, or Farnese (later Paul III), or
anyone who was not an Imperialist. So Wolsey wrote in a
second letter to Casale. That he himself might stand down
was, he said, Henry's suggestion. It was a revealing one, and
must have stung him. Of course, once the commission was
granted, Henry would need a dispensation to marry Anne
of the kind which Knight was about to procure. Presumably for fear that Knight had bungled or the Curia thrown
his hybrid bull aside, a new draft of this was sent to be
signed. Casale was to be content with nothing less than all
this and to set to work immediately, sparing nothing. To
help his labour ten thousand ducats were being credited to
bankers at Venice and would be sent on to him by his
brother.[21]

The scene was therefore set: a papal commission was to
declare the first marriage void; a papal dispensation to
allow the second. The problem had now been correctly set
out. With these letters to Casale, dated 5 and 27 December
1527, the campaign for the divorce really began. Knight's
mission had been but an amateurish rehearsal.

Wolsey was sure that Casale would do the deed in a few
days, all the more so when the news came of the pope's
release – which would allow free access to the latter for the
English agents. Casale, working with Knight, did indeed
procure a commission with remarkable speed. But once
again Cardinal Pucci had cut to ribbons the draft presented
to him, despite the offer, which he declined, of two thousand ducats. What was sent off to England was exactly what
Wolsey did not want – not a decretal, but a general com-

21. *Burnet*, iv, 19 ff.; *Pocock*, i, 23 ff. (*L.P.*, iv, 3641); *St.P.*, vii, 29 ff.
(*L.P.*, iv, 3693).

mission to examine the case without the right of definitive sentence. No statement of law was given and no promise to confirm without appeal.[22] Clearly Rome had not begun to yield. Indeed, Rome was evidently surprised and irritated by the fuss surrounding this comparatively trivial affair of Henry's. The obvious procedure, so it seemed to Clement's closest advisers, was for Wolsey to use his existing legatine authority, or this commission, to try the case in England. Let Henry marry again if Wolsey found for him and only if that second marriage were challenged need the matter be taken to Rome.[23] Why ask for so much to be settled in advance when so little might ever be in dispute? Why ask for such heavy weapons as decretals and legates when the cardinal of York was, to Roman minds, already adequately equipped? Perhaps there was wisdom in this. If so, it eluded the English. Henry had not the courage to take matters into his own hands and risk a solution which might well have worked, and, instead, insisted on absolute certainty – which was prudent enough, but may have been an error of judgement none the less.

The sudden dispatch to Orvieto of a couple of agents with complicated and, for all he knew, dubious proposals to make concerning Henry's wife and, presumably, mistress was not the best means of presenting what looked like a storm in a tea-cup to a pope preoccupied with his own massive misfortunes. Now, indeed, Wolsey would pay the penalty for his neglect of the Curia in times past. Unlike some other powers, England had no established party in the Sacred College and her diplomatic representation at the Holy See was feeble. In the immediate past she had even abandoned the practice of keeping permanent English proctors at the court, that is, professionals who knew their way around, could handle big business and had staffs and status and, instead, had relied on cameral merchants or two Italian clerics, resident at the Curia, who could be called upon from time to time to serve English interests in return

22. *Pastor*, x, 253 f.; *L.P.*, iv, 3751, 3756.   23. *L.P.*, iv, 3802.

for a West Country bishopric – Ghinucci, absentee bishop
of Worcester, and Campeggio, absentee bishop of Salisbury.
But since these men could scarcely cope with so consequential a matter as the divorce Henry was now forced to
rely on a succession of *ad hoc* missions. Happily for the
latter, Gregory Casale would be available for much of the
time to receive newcomers and initiate them into the ways
of the Curia. But the royal cause needed something much
larger, more permanent and more professional than this
largely hand-to-mouth arrangement.

By early February 1528 Wolsey had cast aside the dispensation and commission which Clement had granted to
Casale,[24] and announced a new embassy consisting of
Stephen Gardiner, his secretary, and Edward Fox, the
king's almoner. This embassy was to be rather different
from its predecessor. It was sent off amidst a fanfare of
commendatory letters to pope and cardinals; under Wolsey's direction it was given minute and wide-ranging instructions. The new envoys were to start working again for
a decretal commission for Wolsey and another cardinal to
settle the matter in England; or for one legate only; or for
Wolsey and Warham or some other English bishop. They
were to impress on Clement the gravity of their mission,
protest Henry's devotion to the Holy See, his many services
to it and Anne's excelling qualities. They were to explain
that Wolsey's fate was in Clement's hands and that, if
justice was denied, the king might be compelled by the
dictates of natural and divine law to cast off an allegiance
which in the past he had given so generously to the Holy
See[25] – words which they may only have been intended to
play and to bully with, but which give us a glimpse of how
brittle things were and how easily the divorce could get
out of hand.

24. The commission has disappeared. But we may be sure that it
did not contain the necessary clauses forbidding appeal to Rome,
etc. Pucci had cut this out of the draft. See *L.P.*, iv, 4120.

25. *L.P.*, iv, 3913.

After a terrifying crossing from Dover which took them forty hours and then a long wait at Genoa for a boat to take them southwards, Gardiner and Fox arrived at Orvieto, sodden with rain, on 21 March and made their entry into the palace where, amidst fallen ceilings and a handful of servants, the sovereign pontiff resided. There, day after day, the two would wrestle with Clement. Sometimes they would see him alone, sometimes Sst Quatuor and several other cardinals, and Simonetta, the dean of the Rota, would be there. Sometimes an audience would begin at seven in the morning, sometimes not end till one o'clock in the night. Soon the English were joined by Gambara and a little later by Stafileo, a former dean of the Rota, then nuncio in France, and one whom, because of his support for the divorce and his authority as a canonist, Wolsey had persuaded Francis to send to Rome to give weight to the campaign. The debate turned on one point: would Clement grant a decretal commission and thus commit himself in advance to confirming the legates' sentence, or would he concede only a general commission which would leave principles undeclared and give Henry no certainty that what was loosed in England would be loosed also in Rome? A decretal commission could provide a swift, and probably final, decision; the other was only a beginning, slow and dangerously public – a device for postponing ultimate judgement. For this very reason Clement preferred the latter. 'The pope's holiness,' the Englishman wrote back in near-despair, 'although he perceiveth better and sooner all that is spoken than any other, yet to give an answer yea or nay, *numquam vidi tam tardum*.'[26] By Palm Sunday, that is, after about a fortnight's wrangling, the two envoys were convinced that, try as they might, a decretal commission was out of the question. Despite Gardiner's

26. *Pocock*, i, 128 (L.P., iv, 4167). For details of Gardiner and Fox with Clement, see their frequent dispatches in this section of *L.P.* But Gardiner exaggerated his mastery of the situation. See *Ehses*, 23 ff.

effrontery, despite his quoting by heart from the *Decretals*
the text of the canon *Veniens* which set out the form of a
decretal commission exactly as Henry required, Clement
refused to move, saying all the while that such a document
was alien to curial usage and could never pass the Chancery. Gardiner and Fox therefore reluctantly fell back on
the alternative – a general commission accompanied by
some kind of promise to confirm the commissioners' judgement. Clement produced a draft bull for this purpose.
Gardiner complained first about its contents, then its style.
He was told to produce his own draft, which he did. It was
handed over to some cardinals who fell upon it 'as though
there were a scorpion under every word'. At last on 13 April
this commission was sealed. Clement was warned that it
would not satisfy the king. He replied wearily that even
this document was a declaration against the emperor and
that he feared punishment for what he had done.

Bullied and at some moments apparently broken, yet in
reality never mastered, Clement had been pulled hither
and thither by his need for Henry, his fear of Charles and
a certain residual sense of justice which would not permit
him entirely to ignore Catherine's cause. Such was the skill
of the man that it was difficult to know exactly how much
he had now conceded. Three bulls had been sealed: the
first a new dispensation for Henry to marry Anne; the
second a general commission to Wolsey, with Warham or
any other English bishop as assistant;[27] the third, sealed but
not dispatched for some time, a general commission to
Wolsey and another legate from Rome, empowering them
summarily to investigate the validity of Henry's marriage
to Catherine and pass sentence upon it.[28] Should they judge
it void, Henry and Catherine were to be separated and
might contract marriage anew. What was more, no appeal
would be allowed against the legates' sentence. This was
seemingly a decisive document, but, in truth, there were

27. For the text, see *Rymer*, xiv, 237 f., dated 13 April 1528.
28. For the text, of the same date, see *Ehses*, 28 ff.

fatal loopholes in it. Rome had not given that statement of law which would make Wolsey's work simple and sure, the vital matter of papal confirmation had not been established and the commissioners' broad powers and immunity to challenge did not protect them against appeal on the ground of partiality. However, in conversation with Fox and Gardiner, Clement had said that he might yet agree to confirm the delegates' sentence and promise not to revoke or inhibit their progress.[29] All this was certainly much more than Knight and Casale had got; but was it enough?

It had already been agreed that the second commission, to Wolsey and another cardinal legate, would be used and that Campeggio would be that other. Gardiner was therefore to go to Rome, where Campeggio was in temporary charge of administration and, when he was ready, accompany the cardinal to England. Fox had left Orvieto immediately, carrying his dubious trophy homewards as fast as horse and sail would take him. By early May he was at Greenwich kneeling before his king. Henry fell on him eagerly and, by the time he had heard and read all, was convinced that his prayers, if there ever were any, had been answered. He called Anne to hear the good news and poured happy questions on the ambassador about his errand. Late that evening Fox was at Durham House to deliver the documents to Wolsey, then in bed. By the next afternoon the latter had pondered them and had also decided that victory had been won. Two days later, in the morning, he was still, apparently, of the same mind. But by afternoon he had changed it. The commission, after all, would not do. It was a half-empty packet that had come from Rome. Mature reflection, it seems, had brought him back to where he started: that nothing less than a decretal commission would suffice. Perhaps it was an exaggerated caution or unreasonable appetite for the best which discovered so many flaws in what had been brought to him. Perhaps he should have been content with what he had

29. *Pocock*, i, 141 ff. (*L.P.*, iv, 4251).

acquired and, as the Roman advice had run, have taken a
risk. Instead, he demanded all; and Henry, who had apparently (and inexplicably) shed all the doubts about the
cardinal's reliability which he had so evidently entertained
not long ago and was now as dependent as ever on his
judgement, also changed his mind and concurred.[30]

So the king must turn to Gardiner again, Gardiner must
return to Orvieto and try once more; must argue, plead,
grapple once more, while Henry and Wolsey endured
another agonizing delay. Clement had granted one commission. This was all that the world need know about. Let
him concede, in utter secrecy, a decretal commission which
only Henry and Wolsey would see and which Wolsey
would have by his side not to use, but for his reassurance
and protection (though whether he intended to abide by
this arrangement was another matter). Such were the new
instructions to Gardiner, sent off in mid May 1528.[31]

However, by late June there was still no news in England
of the decretal and no sign of Campeggio. The latter should
have set out – so as to be in his place as soon as the commission arrived. But the cardinal was suffering terribly
from gout and lay immobile in Rome while Wolsey and
Gardiner implored him to make haste. Frustration frayed
tempers, and before long Gardiner and Casale were being
lashed with charges of slackness and incompetence. Henry
was heard to say – so Fox reported to Gardiner – that 'in
case [Campeggio] never come, you [are] never to return'.
But try as he might, Gardiner could report nothing but
'great difficulties ... contrived delays ... great uncertainties'.[32] Then, while Henry waited in an agony of impatience,
the latest letter from his agent, perhaps *the* letter, was lost
en route. A package had arrived in England which, as references in some of the other contents clearly indicated, should
have contained a letter from Orvieto. But it did not. The
very letter that had been 'longed longest for' was missing,

30. *Pocock*, i, 141.   31. ibid.
32. *L.P.*, iv. 4289, 4355.

intercepted, it was feared, somewhere in France.[33] It was never recovered, though a man was sent off to look for it. Probably it contained only news of further shilly-shallying, but its loss was maddening.

Soon afterwards sweating sickness broke out in London – a fierce, swift outbreak which, as the French ambassador said, brought more business to the priests than the doctors. In a short while thousands had been struck and the epidemic was spreading into the provinces. Wolsey promptly halted the legal term. Most business stopped – except for notaries, who did a roaring trade in wills. The epidemic hit the court almost immediately, carrying off several leading figures. Among those taken ill was Anne Boleyn (and what might have happened if the sickness had overcome her?),[34] and as soon as he heard of her infection, Henry cast gallantry to the winds and fled from her side, keeping on the move for several weeks, dosing himself with numerous medicaments, hearing three Masses and confessing daily, it was said, and communicating frequently.[35] True, he wrote lovingly to Anne lamenting his separation from her and comforting her with the information that the sweat seemed to spare women; but the effect was spoiled by a two-edged *envoi* which begged her not to come back too soon. 'Whoever strives against fortune is often the further from his end,' he wrote philosophically from Hunsdon.[36] By the time he had arrived at his new resting-place there, though still spending hours with his physicians and supping apart in a tower, he had begun to relax. None of his suite had fallen sick since they came to Hunsdon, and Anne had passed danger-point. Though now troubled with his bladder, Henry had begun to take a fitful interest in international affairs and to listen to letters from Wolsey read to him by Brian Tuke – at least the shorter ones. In one of these Wolsey

33. The phrase was Brian Tuke's, who, as master of the Posts, was much involved in the affair. *L.P.*, iv, 4358, 4359, 4361, 4390.

34. *L.P.*, iv, 4391, 4398, 4440.

35. ibid., 4542.   36. ibid., 4403.

happened to express his concern to Tuke for a painful
affliction which had hit the latter. Henry, pricking up his
ears at the mention of illness, but misinformed about Tuke's
complaint, promptly prescribed a cure *'pro tumore testicu-
lorum'*. This, however, was not the trouble. Tuke said so;
whereupon Henry, unabashed, produced a remedy for the
actual complaint 'as any most cunning physician in England
could do'. Then he spoke knowledgeably about the sweat,
how it behaved, how to treat it and who had succumbed to
it, and sent Wolsey a message to eat and drink lightly, avoid
wine and take 'Rasis' pills once a week. Wolsey was to cast
away fear and be merry, the advice ran on, 'commit all to
God' and put his spiritual life in order as he, Henry, had
done.[37] Shortly afterwards the king asked for the prescription
used in Wolsey's household and suggested nation-wide processions for good weather and abatement of the plague. His
mind was full of sickness and cures. The marchioness of
Exeter was ill, at her home. Henry told the marquis and all
who had been in his company to depart from Court and, to
be doubly sure, himself moved from Tittenhanger to Ampthill, where he was delighted with the clearness of the air.[38]
A few days later he was complaining, as he often did, of
pains in his head and took off to Grafton, where the pains
disappeared. Meanwhile Wolsey had retreated from London
to Hampton Court with an entourage riddled with disease.
Perhaps he himself was at one time stricken – for in early
July, he wrote a strange letter to Henry which reads like a
valedictory message of a servant who felt death near him.[39]
But he survived, and during those harsh summer months
remained at the centre of things in minute control of the
king's business, sifting the rush of requests for dead men's
lands and offices precipitated by the ravages of the epidemic.

37. *St.P.*, i, 296 ff. (*L.P.*, iv, 4409). 'Rasis' comes from 'Rhazis', an
Arab physician.
38. ibid., 305, 312 (*L.P.*, iv, 4449, 4468); *L.P.*, iv, 4486, 4507.
39. *St.P.*, i, 309 f. (*L.P.*, iv, 4468). Or it was the letter of a man
anxious to protect himself against slander.

All this had temporarily damped down the tempo of the divorce. By August it was quickening again. Campeggio had at last bestirred himself and had embarked from Tarquinia, some fifty miles north-west of Rome, to sail for Provence. One month later he had reached Lyons, by which time the sweating sickness was beginning to relax and Anne had been reunited with her lover. Stephen Gardiner was not with Campeggio as planned. Instead, the cardinal travelled alone to Paris where John Clerk was to meet him and accompany him to England in style. But his progress was painfully slow and he had reached no further than Paris by 14 September, seven weeks or so after taking ship. He would have done better to go the whole way by sea, for his gout was so bad that to ride a mule was agony, and for most of the time he was carried in a horse litter. The journey from Paris to Calais took another fortnight, and it was only on 29 September that, for the second time in his life, he set foot on English soil, at Dover. From there he came to Canterbury and Dartford and arrived in London on 9 October, where the great of the realm had assembled to receive him. Henry too, having closed in gradually on the capital by way of Sutton Park, near Guildford, and Woking, was there. His reunion with Anne had been brief. Thinking it ill-judged to have Campeggio find her at his side he sent her away and resumed passionate letter-writing, confident now that the long wait would soon be over.[40] But Campeggio was too ill to take part in the reception prepared for him – indeed, there was rumour that he was dead – and not until a fortnight after his arrival was he fit enough to be taken by barge to meet the king at Bridewell. From the river's edge he was carried in torrential rain to the palace, with Wolsey beside him on a mule, to be solemnly received by the king. The end was now surely in sight.

For Campeggio had the precious document with him. *Mirabile dictu*, Gardiner and Casale had more or less won the day, as Wolsey had instructed them. Tortured with doubt and fear, Clement had yielded the desired decretal

40. *Sp. Cal.*, iii, ii, 541.

commission – a document which was to be in the sole care of
Campeggio, to be shown to no one but the king and Wolsey,
and not to be used in court. It was a gesture only, to bolster
Wolsey.[41] Moreover, it left undecided whether the two
legates could give *final* sentence on Henry's marriage.
Clement had promised in writing never to revoke this commission,[42] but this was not quite all that was required; and,
besides, there was a long delay before this promise, the so-
called 'pollicitation', arrived in England. However, there
indisputably *was* a decretal commission in Henry's favour
available to the legates. Wolsey, therefore, now possessed
a public general commission which was thoroughly inadequate, but hoped to profit from a second and sufficient, or
nearly sufficient, commission which in theory must remain
secret; while Clement had undertaken to honour a document which, in his heart, he intended should never be used.
This was a near-ludicrous situation which promised the
worst of all worlds to all parties.

Campeggio found Henry buoyant and urgent for swift
action. He was so utterly convinced that his marriage to
Catherine was contrary to God's law that, said Campeggio,
an angel from heaven could not dissuade him; and he was
remarkably informed about his case – better, in fact, than
many theologians and canonists – and highly skilful in
argument.[43] From Wolsey came, day after day, the arguments *ad hominem*: that the divorce was a political necessity; that unless Campeggio was prepared to act he, Wolsey,
was finished; that if the divorce were refused England would
throw off her allegiance to Rome.[44] This last he repeated
again and again. Taken aback by this intensity of feeling
and so tormented with gout that he would sometimes conduct long, wrangling sessions with Wolsey from his bed,

41. *Pocock*, i, 172 (*L.P.*, iv, 4380); *St.P.*, vii, 104 (*L.P.*, iv, 4897). The
commission is not extant, but it was probably close to the draft presented by Gardiner, for the text of which see B.M. Vit. B, xii, fol. 133.
42. *Ehses*, 30 f. for the text of the promises.
43. ibid., 48 ff., 54.   44. ibid.

Campeggio had to fight hard to obey the instructions which Clement had undoubtedly issued to do whatever he could to delay and discover some way of solving Henry's problem that was simpler and less incriminating than a full-scale, public court case.

For a while he hoped to solve all by persuading Catherine to enter religion. This was an entirely new proposal and one which he had brought back with him. Theologically dubious but with a trace of pedigree,[45] such a solution had much to commend it. It could solve in a twinkling and spare all parties the pain of a trial. It would exculpate Clement. It could not offend Charles as repudiation of Catherine must offend him and it would allow her honourable retirement. The day after his visit to Bridewell, Campeggio received Henry at Bath House, where he was staying. Henry came to demand an immediate start to proceedings – in a voice that so often became loud and excited that an eavesdropper could recall all that passed between him and the cardinal.[46] It was in the course of this interview that Campeggio put his new plan to the king.[47] Henry approved it enthusiastically. Next day Campeggio and Wolsey went to Catherine, and formally put the proposition to her, calling upon her to abdicate her marriage and, like Jeanne de Valois, sometime wife of Louis XII, retreat to a nunnery. Catherine listened gravely and made no reply. On the following day, attacking now from the flank, Campeggio saw Fisher, and he believed, impressed him with his proposal.[48] Then Henry joined in, with typical violence, to tell Catherine that all the world now agreed that her marriage to him was unjust and that unless she took the veil of her own volition she would be forced to do

45. The argument was that, if one spouse entered religion, he or she thus underwent a 'spiritual death' and left the other free to re-marry. It derived originally from Bonaventure and received intermittent approval from later scholastics, including Scotus. The majority of theologians, however, would not have accepted it. For all this, see Dauvillier, *Le Mariage dans le Droit Classique de l'Église* (Paris, 1933).

46. *Sp. Cal.*, iii, ii, 841 f.   47. *Ehses*, 54.   48. ibid., 56 ff.

so. Again Catherine listened quietly.[49] Like Fisher, she was of a world which Campeggio and Henry probably neither knew nor understood. At last, with Henry's permission, she came to Campeggio to give her answer. She asked him to hear her confession, which he agreed to do; whereupon she told him about her marriage to Arthur, how he had never known her and how she had come to Henry a virgin, and then announced that she would never accede to his suggestion for, come what may, she would live and die in that vocation to matrimony to which God had called her. Humbly, but absolutely, she cast the cardinal's proposal aside, at the same time giving him permission to break the seal of the confessional and tell the world what she had told him.[50] Next day the two cardinals visited her again. Wolsey fell on his knees and begged her to yield. A little later a deputation of English prelates came to her on the same errand. And each time she solemnly refused their entreaties.

Campeggio had offered the solution of the man of the world, and the formula for smothering noise and dispatching business expeditiously and cheaply. But he had encountered an integrity which had no time for his accomplished discretion. Unmoved by bullying, Catherine was already preparing for a public ordeal. With Henry's permission she had appointed a council for her defence, consisting of Warham, Fisher, Clerk, Tunstal, Vives and George Athequa, her Spanish confessor and bishop of Llandaff, among others; and with these behind her she would face the legates' court.

In theory, Wolsey and Campeggio were almost ready to set about this business, for the general commission which empowered them to try the case had arrived long ago and, hounded by the audacious skill of Gardiner and Casale, Clement had since given Campeggio the precious decretal commission containing the necessary statement of law concerning obreptitious dispensations and requiring the judge

49. *Sp. Cal.*, iii, ii, 842.
50. *Ehses*, 58 f. Cf. Catherine's public protest of her original virginity in *Pocock*, ii, 431 – dated 7 November.

merely to discover the facts of the case. But, as has been said, having made this concession, he half withdrew it by commanding that it should not be used in a court of law, nor go out of Campeggio's hands; and scarcely had he granted this much than he was bitterly regretting what he had done, saying, later on, that he would give the fingers of his hand to undo it. Wolsey would probably have given more to have had him do it better.

This was the famous document which had cost Henry so much and about which much dispute had taken place. Henry saw it. He demanded to see it as soon as Campeggio arrived.[51] Then it disappeared. Campeggio destroyed it before the trial began, probably on Clement's orders. Moreover, the commission was not watertight until the 'pollicitation', the promise never to hinder or revoke the commission at anyone's request, or '*mero motu*', had been added.[52] Though Clement had drafted such a document in his own hand in the summer of 1528 it did not arrive in England until the next spring and then was found to be 'so couched and qualified' that it left the pope free to revoke virtually at will.[53] In view of this incredible, maddening setback it was not yet safe for Henry's cause to come on trial.

Indeed, it was probably not even possible for it to do so, because Campeggio was himself very reluctant to act. Clement had ordered him to dilly-dally and this he was increasingly ready to do, for he plainly found the whole business distasteful.[54] News from the Continent told of continual Spanish successes and, as Henry's allies fell to Charles one after another, Clement repeated his instructions to Campeggio not to proceed to any sentence without express orders.[55] Moreover, at the same time the emperor was told that Campeggio would do no harm to his aunt and that the case would eventually be revoked to Rome.[56]

Ever since he arrived, the legate had manufactured delays,

51. *St.P.*, vii, 104 (*L.P.*, iv, 4897).
52. *Ehses*, 30 f.; Gardiner in *E.H.R.*, xii (1897), 8.
53. *Burnet*, iv, 98 (*L.P.*, iv, 5523).   54. *L.P.*, iv, 5604; *Ehses*, 107.
55. *L.P.*, iv, 4721, 4736–7.   56. ibid., 4857.

refusing to take any decisive action until he had made every attempt to reconcile the parties or before he had sent full reports to Rome. All this could take months. His loitering, abetted by Clement, could drive his hosts to dementia. Reluctantly, therefore, the latter decided that another assault had to be made on the Curia, another heave to carry Clement and galvanize his legate. On 1 November 1528, therefore, Wolsey wrote to Casale a letter in which he poured out his disappointment, his terrible fears, his master's frustration. Henry, he said, had been inhumanly treated. Unless Clement responded as a loving father and true vicar of Christ, the cost might be more than any man could reckon – ignominy and ruin of the Church, the destruction of papal authority in England. 'I close my eyes before such horror. ... I throw myself at the Holy Father's feet. ... I beg him to look on his royal majesty's holy and unchangeable desire ... his most just, most holy, most upright desire ...' So the letter ran on, through pages of hyperbolic pleas and bullying, the purpose of which was to batter Clement, yet again, into granting a plenary and unequivocal decretal commission, and giving Campeggio the signal to go about his business.[57]

On top of all this uncertainty there were other problems for Henry to face. Catherine was without doubt so popular a queen that the growing rumour, which Campeggio's arrival fortified, of the king's intention to cast her aside inevitably aroused consternation.[58] One day when she and Henry were passing through a gallery joining Bridewell Palace to Blackfriars so large a crowd cheered her that Henry gave orders that the public should no longer be allowed to gather outside.[59] Sensing growing hostility, Henry then summoned a concourse of notables to Bridewell one Sunday afternoon to explain to them how the great scruple first began, a different account from that which had been given before, and how Campeggio had come to pass judgement on the mar-

57. *St.P.*, vii, 102 ff. (*L.P.*, iv, 4897).
58. *Hall*, 754.   59. *Sp. Cal.*, iii, ii, 845.

riage. Should he find no fault in it, said Henry with unblushing dishonesty, then 'there was never thing more pleasant
nor more acceptable to me in my life', for Catherine's
qualities of mind and body were so manifest that 'if I were
to marry again [and] if the marriage might be good, I would
surely choose her above all women'. But should Campeggio
find the union to be contrary to God's law, then he must
leave her, lamentable though it would be both to part from
'so good a lady and loving [a] companion', and to acknowledge that for nearly twenty years he had lived in sin, 'to
God's great displeasure'. It was, therefore, as one anxious
to discharge his conscience, as a hapless victim, conscientious
father of the nation and son of the Church that Henry delivered his oration. 'These be the sores that vex my mind,
these be the pangs that trouble my conscience and for these
griefs I seek a remedy,' he ended.[60] The speech, we are told,
impressed some of his hearers. But affection for the queen
was still widespread and would require him to tread warily.

Then the brief, the second dispensation for Henry to
marry Catherine, appeared on the scene. English envoys in
Spain first picked up rumours of its existence in early 1528,
but they did not discover its contents. A copy was in
Catherine's hands probably by April of that year, having
been delivered to her by the Spanish ambassador, Mendoza.[61]
She discreetly kept it to herself until, six months later, provoked by the hostility around her, she showed it to Campeggio; and in so doing nearly ruined her husband.

The decretal commission for which Henry had laboured
so long had been concerned only with Julius's bull of dispensation. It may have recited its text and would certainly
have referred to it. But here was a new document which had
not been seen before, which the decretal commission did
not touch and which would require separate treatment.
Further, as we have seen, the brief made good, or avoided,

60. *Hall*, 754 f. These words were not Henry's *verbatim*, however,
but only what Hall, who was present, 'could bear away' with him.
61. *L.P.*, iv, 3844; *Sp. Cal.*, iii, ii, 845.

some of the major flaws alleged in the bull. In other words,
it threatened not only to halt much that Henry had so
painfully prepared but also to destroy his argument.[62] If the
brief stood, the whole complex business of the divorce could
come to a standstill and he would have to begin, and think,
again. Henry, like Wolsey, was stunned by what Catherine
had so quietly, so unexpectedly done. How had she known
about the brief? When did she procure it? Who had brought
it to her? What else did she know? And what was to be
done now?

Understandably, the first reaction was to denounce the
brief as a forgery. Its appearance was so sudden, its contents
so convenient that it was easy to be suspicious and furthermore, the text now in Henry's hands contained a technical
error of dating of exactly the kind which a forger might be
expected to commit. But a mere copy of the brief would
never suffice to disprove its genuineness. Nothing definitive
could be done until the original was in England – and
Charles, obviously, would not be quick to part with it.
Alternatively, if the brief could not be exploded it must be
ignored. There must be a new campaign to force Catherine
to take the veil and thus side-step all the paraphernalia of
briefs, bulls, legates, commissions, etc. In a short while,
therefore, Catherine was visited by Warham and Tunstal,
two of her council, bringing a message from the king which
was clearly intended to break her. It warned her that there
were certain ill-disposed persons abroad who might make an
attempt on Henry's person or the legate's and that Catherine
would inevitably be blamed for it. It complained that she
was flippant and showed herself too much to the people,
rejoicing in their acclaim, nodding, smiling and waving to
them. It complained that she tortured the king in the matter
of the brief and accused her of hating Henry. It announced
to her that the Privy Council no longer deemed it safe for
her to share his bed and board, and that he would not suffer
the Princess Mary to come into her company. The cruelty

62. See above, p. 242.

of this document is obvious. It was designed to force her into a nunnery or at least to be a party to a plot to filch the brief out of Spain.[63] But it did not move her.

At first Henry had a plan to send the treasurer of his household, Sir William Fitzwilliam, to Spain to persuade Charles to part with the brief.[64] But this scheme was dropped, for reasons not given, and replaced a few weeks later by another device. A letter went to Charles, written by Catherine in her own hand, imploring her nephew to send the original brief to England on the ground that it alone could stand in a court of law and protect her interests and those of her child. Pressure had been applied to her a few weeks before. By early December 1528 she had been sent away from Greenwich to Hampton Court and Anne Boleyn had moved into her rooms next to Henry's.[65] More pressure had then been exerted via her council and by late December the letter had been forced out of her. However, the messenger who was to take it across France to Spain broke his shoulder – so that a second letter had to be dispatched, this time in the care of no less a person than Thomas Abel, the one who would soon write an excellent book in Catherine's defence and eventually suffer long imprisonment and death for her sake and Rome's. Why Henry should have entrusted him with this mission is a matter for marvel, for Abel was to ruin the effect of Catherine's letter by promptly telling Charles to ignore it, to cling to the brief and put every pressure on Rome to halt the divorce proceedings. Once again a plan to trick Charles had been sabotaged by the queen. Several more attempts to procure the brief were made, but Charles, if he did not know before, now understood exactly what was afoot. He would provide an attested transcript, certainly; he would allow the document to be read to the

63. *Sp. Cal.*, iii, ii, pp. 844 f. In *L.P.*, iv, 4981 is an undated draft of an address to Catherine by persons unnamed. I have assumed that it was used on this visit.

64. *Sp. Cal.*, iii, ii, 592.

65. *L.P.*, iv, 5016.

English ambassadors; he would allow them to read it themselves; but he would never part with it.[66]

The king's cause was therefore in disarray. The whole
campaign had to be reappraised and a new initiative
launched. Such were the circumstances of the dispatch early
in December 1528, even before Catherine had written to
Charles, of that new, quadruple embassy to Rome, led by
Knight and Bryan. Its instructions show that the situation
was so desperate that foreign policy was now to be wholly
subordinated to the divorce, that Clement's hand was to be
forced by means of what was none other than an elaborate
plot, and that Henry was prepared to use physical force
against the sovereign pontiff, or at least to have it in readiness.

The four envoys had a host of instructions. First, they
were to deal with the brief by denouncing it as a forgery,
for reasons set out in a 'book' supplied to them. To prove
their case, with the help of a scribe or clerk of the Curia
they were to search registers for the original, collect speci-
mens of the writing of one Sigismund, the clerk whose signature appeared on the brief, study examples of Julius II's
fisherman's seal, the seal used on briefs. They must proceed
in utter secrecy, else the 'forgers' would amend their work
as flaws were found in it – all of which, of course, was in
anticipation of the brief now in Spain being handed over.
Once they had gathered sufficient evidence they were to
present their case to Clement and require that Charles be
commanded to send the original to England. Then Clement
must grant a decretal commission – another one! – to the
legates so that they might pass final sentence on the document. If this proved impossible, then Clement must decide
the matter himself. The two legates would hand over to him
the problem of the brief, provided that he gave a written
promise beforehand to find against it. All the necessary
documents were provided herewith, which Clement had only
to sign. Next, the pope was to remove the nullifying restric-

66. *L.P.*, iv, 5375, 5423, 5471; *Sp. Cal.*, iii, ii, 662.

tions on the decretal commission, the one which Campeggio
had brought, so that, as soon as the brief was dealt with, the
divorce case could go forward at speed. But alongside this
and as a security against failure to explode the brief, the
envoys were to investigate thoroughly the proposal for
Catherine to enter some 'lax' religious house. The best advo-
cates in Rome were to be hired to give their opinion on this
theologically questionable solution to the problem in order
that the Englishmen might face Clement armed to the hilt.
They were to work on the cardinals, particularly that rigorist,
Sst Quatuor. But even if Clement of his absolute, as
distinct from his ordinary, power agreed to allow Henry
to remarry if Catherine entered a convent, the problem
would remain of how to persuade the queen to cooperate.
If she cunningly said that she would enter religion and take
a vow of chastity only if Henry did the same, and if, to be
rid of her, he did so, would the pope then dispense him
from his vows so that he could resume the quest? There
must be diligent inquiry about this. It would be a hideous
irony if this plan miscarried and Henry were trapped half-
way, hooded and cloistered, for the rest of his life. But if,
for one reason or another, this plan failed, 'yet to the more
cautel, and to show that nothing shall be pretermitted on
the king's behalf which man's wit can excogitate or devise',
the agents were to inquire into the possibility of Clement
allowing Henry to have two wives at once. Such a solution,
it was conceded, might strike the pope as eccentric ('right
rare, new and strange'), but Henry took courage from the
examples of 'plurality of wives' found in the Old Testament.
Yet another decretal commission, the third, would be required for this, the preamble of which, setting forth all the
Biblical support for his request, particularly the achieve-
ments of certain patriarchs, was supplied herewith. In all
things the agents were to act with the utmost dispatch and
discretion, dwelling long on the urgency of the situation,
on Henry's incomparable services to the Holy See, on
Clement's many debts to him, so far unpaid. Let Rome

open her heart abundantly to him and not be 'distrained or minced with the quiddities and discrepant opinions of the laws'.[67]

Henry now had a triple policy, therefore: to carry through what had been begun, provided that a thorough commission was granted and provided that the brief was somehow strangled first; to bustle his wife into religion and canonical oblivion; or to let her be, but to duplicate her. The first would have declared that his first marriage was null and void and make him a bachelor; the second that it was valid but terminated by death – a spiritual death – and make him a widower;[68] the third that it was still valid but not unique, and make him a bigamist. Any one of these solutions would be acceptable, but it would be better if Clement would agree to any two, best if to all three.

Add to all this their complicated diplomatic instructions concerning a universal peace treaty and an Imperial coronation at Avignon, and it will be allowed that the programme set out for these men at least had size, if nothing else. They were sent off in two pairs, Bryan and Vannes first, Knight and Benet later. The first was in Rome by late January 1529. The second, having been instructed to halt in France to explain the new policies to Francis and enlist his support, remained there as their assignment proved more difficult than had been expected. Accordingly, it was decided to let these two stay in France and keep talking, while Stephen Gardiner set out from England once more for Rome to join the others in their place.

The new plans made the pope more the centre of Henry's world than ever. He was to establish the truce, summon and preside over the peace conference, crown an emperor – and, of course, the vast intricacy of the divorce plans turned wholly on him. It was stunning news, therefore, that reached England in early February 1529 that Clement had died. This could ruin everything. If there succeeded a

67. *L.P.*, iv, 4977–9, 5181, 5441–3. Cf. ibid., 4980.
68. See above, p. 283 n. 45.

thorough Imperialist like, say, Quiñones (whom Charles had sent to halt the divorce in the first instance), then Henry would be finally defeated. But what if Wolsey were to be elected? If Clement's death meant a halt to everything, Wolsey's accession would more than recompense the delay. Accordingly, as never before, Henry now mobilized his resources to carry his candidate through the conclave; and now, as never before, Wolsey joined the hunt with desperate seriousness, for he knew that, this time, his life was probably at stake. Suddenly, therefore, the newly-arrived English ambassadors were told to lay aside their previous instructions and throw all they had into procuring Wolsey's election – arguments, threats, money.

A few days later came another blast of news to strike Henry down anew. Clement was not dead after all. He was stricken with a serious, intermittent fever which baffled his physicians and which, rather than carrying him off swiftly, might merely keep him out of action for months. For Henry this was perhaps the cruellest setback yet. Rome was in uproar. The jockeying of factions had begun in anticipation of a conclave and for the moment the English could do nothing. Clement, like himself even on his sickbed, hovered between life and death and then drew upon unexpected resilience to recover.[69] By the end of March, though still weak and subject to bouts of fever, he was able to receive the English emissaries, who now took up where they had left off two precious months before. Meanwhile Henry and Wolsey, teased almost beyond endurance by the delay, kept up a flow of letters to Rome full of new ideas.[70] During Clement's sickness Casale and Vannes had been able to organize a search among the registers for a trace of the brief, but had found nothing – a fact which fortified the suspicion that the document in Spain was spurious.[71] Encouraged by this, Gardiner used his first interview with Clement to plunge straight into the question of the brief and to demand

69. For all this, see *L.P.*, iv, 5368–73, 5314, 5325, 5375.
70. ibid., 5427–9.   71. B.M. Vit. B, xi, fol. 22 (*L.P.*, iv, 5179).

that it be denounced, at source, as a forgery. Clement parried, saying that he would hand the matter over to the cardinal Sst Quatuor.[72] A month later the English had made no progress. Clement refused to condemn the brief and turned down the demand that Charles should be ordered to send the original to Rome. Gardiner hounded the ailing pope mercilessly, at one point repeating a threat which Henry suggested when talking to him in a gallery at Hampton Court shortly before his departure, namely, that a disappointed king might befriend the cause of the Lutheran princes of Germany; and a little later Henry had instructed Gardiner to tell the pope that he, Henry, was ready to appeal from his holiness to the true vicar of Christ (whatever that meant).[73] But it was of no avail. Clement was irritated rather than moved by Gardiner's bombast. On 6 March a secret letter arrived from Catherine asking the pope to take the case away from England and have it tried in Rome. At long last she had done what had been urged upon her for months; and at the end of April 1529 Charles's agents in Rome formally protested against what had been prepared so far and petitioned Clement to revoke the cause to the Curia.[74]

The diplomatic situation was now running hard against Henry. Pope and emperor were fast coming together and in a few weeks Clement would confess to a confidant, 'I have quite made up my mind to become an imperialist and live and die as such.'[75] Though the pope would hesitate yet, in the face of all this Henry was not likely to make much headway with a programme which, in even the most propitious circumstances, would have been a thorny one to handle. One of the envoys warned him that things were going badly. Despite all effort, 'the pope will do nothing for your grace.

72. *St.P.*, vii, 154 (*L.P.*, iv, 5401).

73. *L.P.*, iv, 5476. Cf. *Sp. Cal.*, iii, ii, 661; *St.P.*, vii, 184 (*L.P.*, iv, 5650).

74. *Sp. Cal.*, iii, ii, 652, 676–7.

75. ibid., 652 and 974.

... There is not one of us but that hath assayed him both by fair means and foul, but nothing will serve,' he wrote frankly. Clement had given 'fair words and fair writings ... but as for deed, I never believe to see, and especially at this time'. Since there was no point in remaining in Rome the envoys asked to be recalled. Francis Bryan, a cousin of Anne, had written to that lady recently, but, he said to Henry, 'I dare not write to her the truth of this', and left it to the king to break the news of the impasse at Rome.[76] A fortnight later Gardiner reported to Henry that, not only had the pope conceded nothing, but there was now talk of revoking the commission to the legates. The embassy had met, and confessed, defeat.[77] By the time that Bryan's letter, dated 21 April, reached England, Henry had decided to wait no longer. The two legates were to proceed with the case, acting on the commission they had received months ago. If Rome were to make a last-minute concession and amplify the grant, so much the better; but Henry would go forward with what had already been won. Gardiner and Bryan were to come home after telling Clement of the grief he had caused and having made one more attempt to procure an unambiguous 'pollicitation', or promise by Clement not to interfere in the legates' work. Such a document, it will be recalled, had been drafted in the previous July. Wolsey told Campeggio he had it. But it had been left behind in Rome and only arrived in England now. When Wolsey discovered how insufficient it was he ordered Gardiner to trick another version out of the pope. He was to go to Clement and, announcing that the original had been damaged by rain and travel, sit down then and there and pretend to re-write it from memory though, in reality, producing a very different text. Presumably the pope was to sign it immediately, innocently believing it to be identical with its predecessor.[78] But these

76. *St.P.*, vii, 166 f. (*L.P.*, iv, 5481).

77. *Burnet*, vi, 23 (*L.P.*, iv, 5518).

78. *Burnet*, iv, 99 (*L.P.*, iv, 5523). See ibid., vi, 26 for the text which Gardiner prepared.

were acts of despair. The campaign at Rome was, for the moment, over.

By late May Henry was at Windsor. He summoned Campeggio's secretary thither to fulminate against his tribulations, especially the news that Charles had formally petitioned the revocation of his cause to Rome.[79] Little did he know that Campeggio, sickened by the whole business, had himself asked Clement to do this and thus spare him the ordeal of action. Henry was urgent for the court to begin work. On 29 May licence was issued under the great seal for the two legates to proceed. But at that very moment a letter was on its way from Rome bidding Campeggio exploit every tactic of delay until Clement should have the courage to revoke the cause.[80] Next day the legates appeared in the Parliament Chamber at Blackfriars and appointed apparitors to summon Henry and Catherine to appear before them on Friday, 18 June.[81]

On 11 June Henry came back by boat to Greenwich. Catherine, now beleaguered and deeply distressed, travelled ahead by road and called on Campeggio *en route* to ask if Rome had responded to her appeal and to seek comfort. Campeggio tried to console her, but gout and the cold and damp of an English summer were upon him, he was short of cash and harried by deputations from Henry, who came to him armed with piles of books and lectured him as he lay in bed. The English demanded action; Rome bade him dawdle. 'God help me,' he wrote.[82]

The extraordinary legatine court charged with the task of passing sentence on Henry's marriage opened on 18 June at Blackfriars. Henry appeared by proxy, but, to the surprise of all, Catherine came in person, attended by four bishops, to protest boldly against the judges and announce her appeal to Rome. Three days later the court met again

79. *Ehses*, 89 ff.   80. *L.P.*, iv, 5604.
81. ibid., 5602, 5611, 5613.
82. ibid., 5636, 5681; *Ehses*, 109. At this interview, Campeggio made a last effort to persuade Catherine to take the veil.

for the session vividly portrayed by Shakespeare. Henry and
Catherine were both there. First the judges announced that
they had overruled Catherine's protest; then Henry, seated
beneath a canopy of cloth of gold, spoke to the court about
his great scruple, his desire only for justice and deliverance
from doubt. When he had finished, Catherine suddenly rose
to her feet and, moving round the court-room, came to Henry
to kneel before him and deliver a long plea to him not to
cast her aside, not to dishonour her and her daughter. Only
Rome, she said, could settle this matter and hence to Rome
she had appealed. Having said this, she withdrew. Three
times the crier called her back, but she paid no heed. She
would never return. The court would declare her contumacious, but she no longer acknowledged its jurisdiction,
and it was left to her council, particularly Fisher, to conduct
her defence henceforth, though, because of her withdrawal,
he and his colleagues could now speak only in their own
names.

Fisher fought like a lion. Two sessions later, on 28 June,
he unleashed a thundering speech affirming the validity of
the marriage and proclaiming his readiness to lay down his
life, as John the Baptist, for the cause of matrimony – a
stinging equation, this, of Henry to Herod, which drew
upon his head a virulent reply, probably composed and
delivered by Gardiner in the king's name, in which Fisher
was accused of arrogance, temerity, disloyalty and similar
shortcomings. After Fisher, Bishop Standish and one Robert
Ridley, another of Catherine's council, spoke. Catherine
had not been abandoned. Fisher would have at least one
more violent passage with Henry, which ended with him
virtually accusing the other side of forging his seal and
signature.[83] Meanwhile the sessions of the court followed
in rapid sequence. Sentence was expected soon. The court
had examined Julius's bull and heard about Catherine's
first marriage, including all the tittle-tattle which such as

83. See *The Earliest English Life of St John Fisher*, ed. Hughes,
90 f., for an account of the trial and Fisher's part therein.

the dowager duchess of Norfolk brought as evidence that
the marriage had been consummated.[84]

When he took courage into both hands and decided to
act, Henry had evidently hoped to be able to present
Clement with a *fait accompli* and stampede him into ratify-
ing all that happened. The legates, therefore, had gone
about their business as swiftly and quietly as possible, while
Benet, the latest English envoy in Rome, tried to throw dust
in Roman eyes. He swore that the trial had not begun
and would not begin. When news from England refuted
him, he swore 'a hundred times' that no sentence would be
passed.[85] But even as he (and Casale) were perjuring themselves, letters from Campeggio and his chaplain were arriving in Rome giving full accounts of all that was afoot.
Clement was in near-despair and Spanish anger mounted.
Weeping, he said he prayed for death. Would that he had
never granted that commission. Whichever way he turned
he saw scandal, discord, ruin.[86] Henry wrote disarmingly
to him, and Benet succeeded in intercepting Campeggio's
latest letters.[87] But as soon as Rome heard that Catherine
had publicly and formally appealed against the legatine
court and been declared contumacious by the legates the
king's cause was virtually lost.

The queen's friends worked very quickly. Her protest
against the legates and her appeal to Rome, together with
powers of attorney for the Imperial ambassador there, were
rushed via Brussels to Rome and passed immediately on
arrival (on 5 July) to the Segnatura.[88] Though Benet and
Casale still hoped that they might be able to stave off
Nemesis long enough to allow the legates to complete their
business, their letters home warned that the sands of time
were running out. They were right. Each day brought more

84. *L.P.*, iv, 5774, 5778.   85. ibid., 5725.
86. ibid., 5725, 5762.   87. ibid., 5769.
88. *Sp. Cal.*, iv, 83, 97. The documents were probably those drawn
up by Charles in April and sent to Catherine for her use. See *Sp. Cal.*,
iii, ii, 674.

news from England which gave extra force to Imperial pressure. On 13 July Clement succumbed and agreed to halt the legatine court. After a further forty-eight hours of hesitation the document of revocation was drawn up and next day, while ill in bed, Clement allowed it to be promulgated in a Congregation, that is, a meeting of Consistory at which the pope is not present. The most for which Benet could now hope was either that its dispatch might be delayed or that only a single copy would be sent (and sent quietly) to England, where Wolsey might intercept it.[89] But on 23 July one copy of the revocation was published in Rome, two went to Flanders and several others were handed to the emperor's agent, one Miguel Mai, to be sent to Catherine, and he dispatched them, for safety's sake, by six different ways. All proceedings in England were thus quashed and the very thing that Henry had most wanted to prevent, the thing he had fought with so many threats, embassies and blandishments, brought to pass.[90]

Meanwhile, at Blackfriars, the king's case had been going badly, for reasons that are not clear. Perhaps it was Campeggio himself, or Fisher, or the intrinsic weakness of Henry's case, or all three, which caused the trouble. Anyway, on 27 July Wolsey reported that proceedings were in a quagmire of minute, technical disputes. Benet urged him to hurry. Would that he could, he said. What was more, he warned, the legal term ended in a week, whereupon the court would be prorogued for two months – and Rome's revocation would surely come before it had reassembled. All that he could hope was that Clement would suspend the court *sine die*, without going so far as citing Henry to Rome. Let Clement understand that if he called Henry either in person or in proxy to Rome his summons would be resisted 'unto the death', and if he had already ordered

89. *L.P.*, iv, 5780. Some attempt was made to intercept this revocation in Italy (*Sp. Cal.*, iv, 100), and Campeggio is said to have warned of measures to stop it reaching England. So ibid., 134.

90. *Sp. Cal.*, iv, 97, 121.

the revocation this itself must be revoked.[91] But these desperate words would be of no avail. Grateful perhaps to be
able to extricate himself from noisome business, Campeggio
had announced that, on the last day of the month, the legatine court would follow the Roman calendar and adjourn
for the summer vacation. Stunned by this subterfuge, Henry
sent the dukes of Norfolk and Suffolk to the next session
to demand that the court should continue and give sentence.
But Campeggio was adamant. On 31 July he declared an
adjournment until October – whereupon Suffolk 'gave a great
clap on the table and said "by the Mass, now I see that the
old saw is true, that there was never legate nor cardinal that
did good in England" '.[92] With that, he and the rest withdrew, leaving Campeggio and Wolsey looking pensively at
one another.

Thus on this almost farcical note the events at Blackfriars
ended. Long before the court could resume, the papal
letters of inhibition staying it for ever, together with the
citation of Henry to Rome, had arrived. The king's attempt
to rush the citadel had failed. To succeed, it had required
flawless management and great good fortune. It had received neither. The court had not moved with either
enough speed or enough stealth to prevent both Clement
and the Imperialists knowing more about the process even
than Benet, and the latter's clumsy bluffing had been no
antidote to the regular news which Campeggio was sending
to the papal secretary. Catherine's strength of character,
Spanish competence, Charles's determination made matters
worse. So too did Fisher. But a really ruthless efficiency on
the part of the organizers would never have let him, or them,
upset proceedings.

By failing, Henry had predictably brought upon himself

91. *St.P.*, vii, 193 ff. (*L.P.*, iv, 5797).
92. *Hall*, 758; *L.P.*, iv, 5791 says the court ended on 23 July. This
is wrong. It must be that on that day Campeggio announced the
forthcoming adjournment – which accounts for Wolsey's statement
on 27 July that it was imminent – and a week later executed it.

the humiliation of being cited to Rome, like any other suppliant, to put his case before the Rota. This was not only an indignity, but also a grave risk; for Henry knew well enough that in Rome he would probably be denied the justice which it had certainly been his wish to deny Catherine in England. The tables had been turned against him. One thing was clear in the dark weeks of the summer of 1529, namely, that every weapon was to be used to stop the revocation taking effect, and to keep the case out of the hands of the Rota.[93] The appellant, the queen and her council must understand that there could be penalties for pressing the appeal and perhaps be frightened into calling off the hunt. Then there was Campeggio. Perhaps Henry could bully the pope through him.[94] In fact it was months before Clement made up his mind to allow the appeal to be heard and during those months English agents in Rome worked prodigiously to try to force him into handing back the case to its native land. Henry's determination and energy were remarkable. But the fact remained that he had suffered a heavy, public defeat. And since he was a man unused to accepting blame for anything he looked around for another recipient. Inevitably, as Catherine had foretold,[95] his choice fell on Wolsey.

Henry had been a taxing man to serve – now glad to release all into his minister's hands, now irrupting suddenly and decisively into affairs both big and small, now in enthusiastic partnership with his servant, now, equally unpredictably, lapsing into lazy indifference to public business. Now he was hot, now he was cold. Now he was masterful, now docile; now wax, now steel, now honey. He was neither *roi fainéant* nor working monarch, but each in turn, erratically.

It always had been a weak link in Wolsey's dependence that he and Henry saw one another comparatively in-

93. *L.P.*, iv, 5854, 5877, 5909.   94. ibid., 5820, 5864–8.
95. *Sp. Cal.*, iv, 83.

frequently and were often miles apart. While the king was
on his long summer progresses, for example, Wolsey would
stay at Westminster or Hampton Court presiding over the
effective centre of national government, his household, and
communicating with the king by letter and messenger.
During the legal term, if Henry was near by, it was the
cardinal's habit to go to Court on Sundays to dine with the
king and perhaps attend a Council meeting. But at other
times the two might not be together for weeks on end.
Their separation has left behind for the historian vivid
letters to him from a series of royal amanuenses – More,
Knight, Tuke and so on,[96] but for Wolsey it meant that a
volatile, impressionable king was constantly exposed to other
influences, that the king was never his sure captive.

There can be no doubt that for long an aristocratic party,
led by the dukes of Norfolk and Suffolk, had been hoping
to 'catch him in a brake' and dispossess him, and that they
looked to Anne Boleyn as their weapon.[97] Popular hostility
to Wolsey there may have been, but it was an aristocratic
faction that led the way – and had led the way some years
ago when John Skelton, a client of the Norfolks, had unleashed his outburst against the cardinal, savaging him for
allegedly ousting the aristocracy from their rightful place in
the realm. This was the heart of their charge against him:
that he had puffed himself up with splendid pomp, lived too
gorgeously, thrust them from the king's table, ridden rough-
shod over them, made them and the whole kingdom his
footstool, 'accroaching' the royal authority (to use a medieval
verb) and usurping the place which belonged to the king's
'natural' councillors.[98] It is the charge which we have heard
several times before in past reigns. That he was an ecclesi-

96. They have often been used in this study. It may be observed
that they make it easier, in some ways, to discover the springs of
policy during this part of the reign than during Cromwell's period of
power.

97. *Cavendish*, 43 f.

98. See the charges brought by Darcy and Palsgrave in *L.P.*, iv,
5749–50.

astic made matters worse; that he was so competent made them worse yet.

Wolsey, then, was under attack from 'below'; he was the victim of an aristocratic *putsch* – and this was not the last time that the great aristocracy dragged down an overmighty and base-born minister. But having exploited his failure in the divorce to the full and inherited his problem, they too found it insoluble. Three years after ridding themselves of him they were to be elbowed out by one as base as he, and a former member of his household, Thomas Cromwell.

As we have seen, Wolsey's position had seemed to be crumbling fast in the summer of 1527.[99] However, despite the fact that he had returned from France empty-handed and anxious, he apparently soon dispersed his opponents and so completely cast his spell over his master once more that he was able to resume direction of the divorce proceedings forthwith and to enjoy Henry's warm solicitude during the outbreak of plague in the summer of 1528. But his recovery was short-lived.

Trouble began again soon after the death, in late April 1528, of the abbess of the large Benedictine nunnery at Wilton in Wiltshire. The election of her successor was compromitted (that is, handed over) to Wolsey and he eventually chose the prioress, who seems to have been a good enough choice. Alas, Henry had meanwhile given his support to another candidate, the sister of William Carey, Anne Boleyn's brother-in-law, a ne'er-do-well who was guilty of fornication with at least three men, two of them priests. When Henry heard of her misdemeanours he withdrew his support, but instead of now accepting Wolsey's nominee he produced a third, partly out of pig-headedness and partly to spare himself having to confess to Anne that he had dropped her nominee only to pick Wolsey's. He wrote three times to Wolsey insisting on his choice. But the cardinal rashly went ahead with his nomination, which the convent accepted. At length Henry took up the pen and wrote in his

99. See above, pp. 212 ff.

own hand a stout, patriarchal letter of the kind that the
cardinal was more accustomed to send than to receive.
'*Quem diligo castigo*', it began. It was the duty of a trusted
servant to serve, not to act against, his master. What was
Wolsey about? Had not Henry's mind been absolutely clear?
What was the meaning of Wolsey's disregard for Henry's
bidding and his subsequent attempt to pretend he had
been ignorant of his master's wishes? It was a double offence
to do ill 'and colour it' also. Therefore he was not to practise
this now, for there was no man living who hated it more
than Henry. Wolsey was to understand that there were
ugly rumours about how he had acquired materials for his
buildings at Ipswich and Oxford – which Henry now reported for the good of 'your soul and mine, as a loving
sovereign, lord and friend'. It was a pompous, swingeing
homily.[1] Of course there had been altercations between the
two before, and they had blown over. But nothing so petty
as this had ever generated such irritation – nor had the king
ever been party to such sinister innuendoes against his
minister. Wolsey's enemies were clearly making headway.

Moreover, he became more vulnerable daily. Though the
cold war with Charles had done minimal damage to the flow
to Antwerp of unfinished cloth, there was acute fear that
this main artery of English trade would be cut. The people,
Wolsey confessed, began to cry 'Murder' and those who
hated him rejoiced, hoping that other things would go
wrong and they could cry 'see what the Legate has done'.
His rivals, therefore, were preparing to name him an enemy
of the people.[2]

And was he not also an enemy of the king? Did the
divorce matter to him with the same overwhelming abso-
luteness that it had for Henry? We know that he had tried
to discourage it and that he and Anne were not friends. In
May 1527, when he had set about dealing with Henry's

1. *Fiddes*, 174 ff. (*L.P.*, iv, 4507). On all this, see Knowles, ' "The
Matter of Wilton" in 1528', *B.I.H.R.*, xxxi (1958), 92 ff.
2. *L.P.*, iv, 3951.

case in a court presided over by himself and Warham, he had apparently lost his nerve and decided to turn to Rome for further powers. This, perhaps, was a revealing hesitation. We know that he had never cared for the Levitical argument with its awful implied challenge to papal authority.[3] He would not play with such fire and instead staked Henry's case on the inadequacies of the particular bull of Julius II. Again Wolsey lost his nerve. But was it merely prudence or a portent when, in December 1527, Casale was bidden, on Henry's instructions, to ask for a commission for Wolsey *and* another, or simply another?[4]

In August 1528 Henry lost his temper with Wolsey and swore at him because he seemed cool about the divorce.[5] Our informant, the French ambassador du Bellay, believed that the latter was not on the inside of affairs – as he certainly had not been in the beginning, when he had planned that Henry should marry a French princess once he had cast off Catherine, little realizing that Mistress Anne was to be raised from the status of plaything to that of queen. Small wonder that, shortly afterwards, Wolsey was writing urgently to Rome for permission to show the decretal commission to some of the king's Council in order to prove that he had omitted nothing for the king's cause – a favour which Casale was to ask for on his knees.[6]

Then, as could happen so easily in relations with Henry, all suddenly seemed to mend once more. He and the cardinal hunted together.[7] Wolsey's candidature for the papacy was eagerly taken up when news of Clement's death arrived – and so on. But this was no more than a brief glimpse of sun in the winter of Henry's discontents. The king had already blamed Wolsey behind his back for the endless delays in Rome and for Campeggio's maddening dilatoriness;[8] and if Clement's supposed death suddenly heightened Wolsey's value, his recovery could only hasten

3. *Ehses*, 69; *L.P.*, iv, 4942.   4. See above, p. 272.
5. *L.P.*, iv, 4649.   6. *Pocock*, i, 174 (*L.P.*, iv, 4812).
7. *L.P.*, iv, 4773.   8. ibid., 5177.

its depreciation. It is clear that, by the time the legatine court
opened at Blackfriars, the vultures were hovering about the
falling man. Norfolk and his fellows were confident that
success was at hand and were saying openly that the cardinal had dragged his feet over the divorce.[9] In early June
1529, Suffolk wrote Henry a letter full of blunt hints about
those whom he trusted and who deceived him – Suffolk,
the man who owed so much to Wolsey.[10]

Had the legatine court passed sentence as Henry required, Wolsey might yet have been entirely rehabilitated.
Instead, of course, it brought disaster; and by then foreign
affairs also had gone appallingly wrong. The vast plans for
an international peace conference and a new universal
treaty, defeated because neither Charles nor England's
allies would behave as the complicated agenda required,
had fallen to bits. By early 1529, moreover, there were
rumours of a separate Franco-Imperial understanding that
would isolate England completely; and talks had already
begun at Cambrai.

Henry refused to believe that this conference, which
threatened to exclude him and, worse, finally bring pope
and emperor together, could ever succeed. But to make
sure, an embassy was dispatched to France, headed (significantly) by the duke of Suffolk, to pull the ally out of
the peace talks and keep the war going.[11] Henry and Wolsey
were entirely committed to their own grandiose plans for
the so-called papal presidy, the coalition against Charles,
the peace conference at Avignon (provided the divorce was
granted) and the rest, and resolutely refused to take seriously the talks soon in full spate at Cambrai.[12] Moreover,
the French fooled them by stating categorically that those
talks were of no import – which soothing words were confirmed by a special embassy to England that seems to have

9. *L.P.*, iv, 5210, 5581.
10. ibid., 5635. Wolsey had protected Suffolk from Henry's wrath
when he married the king's sister Mary, rather hurriedly, in 1515.
11. *L.P.*, iv, 5571, 5599.   12. ibid., 5571.

convinced Wolsey entirely.[13] Then the legatine court opened. Wolsey had little time for the disquieting news from Cambrai and, if he had, consoled himself with the belief that nothing could be accomplished without him and that, if necessary, he would travel thither after the divorce was settled and majestically take over what others had doubtless imperfectly begun.[14] So also Henry reckoned. By late July 1529 the full size of their miscalculation was apparent. The peace talks at Cambrai had made extraordinary progress while Henry had been at a standstill at Blackfriars. If they were successfully concluded, all of England's advantage would be lost. The union of pope and emperor would mean that dispensations and commissions wrung from Clement would be revoked, the divorce halted, Wolsey's plans ignominiously put aside for ever and England isolated. Henry and his cardinal were stunned at finding themselves mocked by their ally and trapped in a desperate situation. The only possible counter-action was to send an embassy to Cambrai post-haste before the last document was signed, to save a little face and perhaps rescue something from the wreck. Wolsey could not go because he was still caught in the slow-moving wheels of Blackfriars, so Tunstal, More and Hacket were dispatched in his stead.[15]

On 24 June Wolsey had heard of Clement's final refusal to yield any further on the matter of divorce, and one month later came the disastrous finale of the legatine court. On 5 August the treaty of Cambrai was signed and the so-called 'Ladies' Peace' accomplished, England having been accommodated at the last moment. For a few more weeks Wolsey remained at the centre of affairs carrying the weight of daily decision on his shoulders, while the king hunted with the dukes of Norfolk and Suffolk. At the end of August the new Imperial ambassador, Eustace Chapuys, reported that Wolsey was sinking. Foreign ambassadors were denied access to him by the king; state

13. *L.P.*, iv, 5583, 5599, 5601.
14. ibid., 5636, 5713.   15. ibid., 5710, 5744.

affairs were being handled by Norfolk, Suffolk and Anne's
father, Rochford; a request from Wolsey for a personal
interview with the king was answered by Gardiner, the new
secretary, with a rebuff.[16]

But Wolsey was not yet beaten. If he could only see
Henry he might still redeem his power. Campeggio was
about to leave England and would take formal leave of the
king. With great difficulty he wrung permission to bring
his brother-legate with him to Court – which then lay at
Grafton – on condition that they came without pomp. It was
unfortunate that Wolsey should have had to make his
entrée in the company of Campeggio, scarcely *persona
grata*, but he had no alternative; and before the cardinals
arrived the Court buzzed with speculation, indeed, laid
bets, on how the audience would go.

They rode into Court on Sunday 19 September. When
Campeggio was led immediately to his lodgings within the
house, Wolsey followed, thinking that he would go to his
accustomed place, only to be told that there was no room
for him; so a friend lent him a chamber in which to take off
his riding clothes. Then came the summons to attend the
chamber of presence. The cardinals found the room full of
councillors and others who had come to watch what would
happen when king and minister met. Henry entered;
Wolsey knelt – whereupon a smiling Henry raised him up
and, to the astonishment of all, led him by the hand to a
'great window' and fell into long discussion with him. But
it was evidently a tense discussion. Henry at one point
pulled a letter or writing from his bosom and was overheard saying, 'How can that be? Is this not your own
hand?' What this document was we do not know, but perhaps it showed slackness or double-dealing in the matter
of the divorce. Then Wolsey was sent away to dine while
Henry retired to eat with Anne in her sumptuous apartment
and, it is said, to be chided by her for entertaining a man

16. *Sp. Cal.*, iv, 189, 195; *St.P.*, i, 343 ff. (*L.P.*, iv, 5936). Wolsey was
an exile, said Chapuys, forbidden to come to Court unless summoned.

who had done so much ill to him and the realm. After
eating, Henry returned to Wolsey and led him off to his
privy chamber for more long discussion, all of which
'blanked his enemies very sore and made them stir the
coals'. Since there was still no accommodation for him at
court, Cavendish, his gentleman usher and the man who
told this story, rode off to find him lodgings some three
miles away at Easton, whither Wolsey rode by torchlight
after supper.[17]

It may be true, as Cavendish says, that with Wolsey's fate
now apparently nicely balanced, it was Anne who struck
the decisive blow. Next day 'by her special labour', either
of her own or others' devising, she persuaded Henry to go
riding with her to see the site of a new park, or hunting
ground, near by. When Wolsey arrived from Easton to resume yesterday's conversation, Henry was about to set off.
Hastily, but kindly, he told the two cardinals that there was
no time for conversation and bade them take their leave.
Anne had thoughtfully provided a [picnic?] lunch so the
king was not back until late, by which time Wolsey and
Campeggio had left – the latter to set off to Rome; the
former, finally separated from the king over whom he might
yet have re-cast his spell, to brood at The More.[18]

Two days later came the command to hand over the great
seal. It was delivered by the two dukes. After an argument
which sent his visitors back to the king for written commands, Wolsey surrendered his seal of office and came down
to the river's edge to set out for Putney, enduring as he went
some jeers and ribaldry from merciless onlookers. The next
part of his journey, from Putney to Esher (whither he had
been commanded to retire), would be by mule. Shortly after
he had begun this stage, as he started up Putney Hill, a
strange incident occurred. A messenger from Windsor suddenly appeared from the top of the hill with a message
from the king to be of good cheer and to trust a master

17. For all this, see *Cavendish*, 92 ff.
18. ibid., 100 ff.

who had cast him down only to satisfy certain hostile
spirits, but still held him in favour. As a token of his true
love Henry sent him that ring which was always 'the privy
token' between them 'when the king would have any
special matter dispatched'. Wolsey was overcome by the
astounding news, leapt off the mule and fell on his knees in
the mud in joyous thanksgiving. While the messenger, Sir
Henry Norris, the same man who had lent him a room at
Grafton a few days before, knelt beside him, he tried to uncover his head; but a knot defied him, so he tore his bonnet
off. Eventually he and Norris rode to the top of the hill and
parted. Full of radiant joy he gave Norris his most precious
possession, a small gold cross about his neck containing an
alleged relic of the true Cross, and sent to Henry a jester
he had in his entourage. Then he rode to Esher to await,
as he now presumed, his rehabilitation.[19]

What had happened? Was this a trick or had Henry
really decided to rescue him? Was it that he could not
bring himself finally to strike down a servant who had
given him so much? Was Henry really being pushed by
others whom he was too weak to resist openly? Was this
incident an impulse of mercy or a piece of ruthless dangling? The truth seems to be that it was not Henry who was
Wolsey's fiercest enemy and not he who wanted his complete, bloody destruction. Henry was unable to forget either
his failures or how remarkable a servant he had been and
might be. But Wolsey was not to be restored. If Henry had
momentarily faltered, Wolsey's enemies were quick to push
the king onwards. On 8 October he paid a lightning visit
to London, clearly to settle the ex-chancellor's fate. Next
day the legal term opened and a *praemunire* charge was
brought against Wolsey. He was found guilty: whereupon
the king hesitated again and pardoned him. Final action
had been postponed and the cardinal left in an uneasy
limbo between retirement and disgrace.

Henry 'much consulted with his Council' before deciding

19. *Cavendish*, 101 ff.

who should replace Wolsey as chancellor.[20] Warham's return was suggested, but he was too old; and besides, the
king was determined not to give the chancellorship to a
cleric. Suffolk was mentioned as a candidate for the office,
but, we are told, Norfolk had no mind to see 'such high
hands' receive the seal. Eventually the choice fell upon Sir
Thomas More, a man who had been close to both Wolsey
and the king for a dozen years or so, for whom the latter
had real affection and respect, who was sufficient for the
post and yet not too big.

More's training as a lawyer and in royal service, his international prestige as the most accomplished humanist in
England and his rare qualities of mind and life made him
obviously suitable for what was still the greatest office in
the realm (though it would rarely again enjoy the influence
which Wolsey had wielded through it); but he accepted it
with a heavy heart. Indeed, at first he refused it and only
accepted when the king angrily bade him do so. More was
as zealous a critic of the contemporary world and as
anxious to see reform in Church and state as any Erasmian.
But, as his violent exchanges with Luther and (more recently) the English protestant William Tyndale had shown,
he was steadfast in the old faith. By 1529, however, Henry
was almost certainly no longer the bastion of orthodoxy
that he had once been. Worse – far worse – More had so
far refused his support for the divorce; that is, he had refused to speak either for or against it. Henry may have believed that he could yet overcome the new chancellor's
scruples or that they would not obstruct him, and, for the
moment, promised that his 'great matter' would be handled
only by those 'whose consciences could well enough agree
therein'. He would use More 'otherwise', he said, and 'never
with that matter molest his conscience'. Rather, More
'should look first unto God, and after God unto him'. This is
what More did. In May 1532, after two and a half inconspicuous and probably unhappy years in office, he resigned

20. *Hall*, 761.

the chancellorship and retired from public life. Two years
later, in April 1534, he went to the Tower. Though More
remained resolutely silent about the divorce, Henry's
promise not to 'molest' him had been broken.

Eight days after taking his oath of office, More was making a speech at the opening of Parliament. There had been
rumours for some time that the legislature would be summoned again after some six years' pause. The election writs
had been enrolled on 9 August and were sent out, after an
intriguing delay, in early October. On 3 November the so-
called Reformation Parliament assembled.

Twelve more months of life remained to Wolsey, months
of torment, penury, humiliation and penitence, of constant
scheming to recover lost power, of frequent moments of
exultation when it seemed that his enemies would be
scattered and he himself restored to that favour which, he
said, he was ready to spend the rest of his life in a hermi-
tage to recover.[21]
For the first three or four weeks of his banishment to
Esher, and until he could borrow stuff from friends, this
prince of the Church and his household were without 'beds,
sheets, table cloths, cups and dishes'; and Wolsey was so
short of cash that he had to beg money from his chaplains
in order to pay his servants their wages.[22] The bishopric of
Winchester and the abbacy of St Albans were taken from
him, his school at Ipswich soon suppressed and his college
at Oxford in danger of destruction. Hampton Court had
already gone to the king (in exchange for the royal house
at Richmond) and even as the cardinal lay forlornly at
Esher a new gallery which he had recently erected there
was taken down, before his very eyes, and carried off to
Westminster for the king's use – a depredation suggested to
Henry by the Council 'only to torment him'.[23] Nor was this
all. Shortly before, Chief Justice Shelley had come to Esher
to announce that it was the king's pleasure to have the

21. *L.P.*, iv, 6011.   22. *Cavendish*, 104 ff.   23. ibid., 123.

cardinal's house at Westminster, called York Place, the property not of Wolsey but of the archbishops of York. Henry had consulted the judges and the Council learned, and been told that, if Wolsey 'should recognize before a judge the right thereof to be in the king and his successors', it could be his. Shelley had therefore come to receive the necessary declaration. For all his desolation, Wolsey was not so cowed that he would acquiesce in this naked robbery without indignant protest. Tell the 'fathers of the law and learned men of his Council,' he said, 'to put no more into his [*sc.* the king's] head than ... may stand with good conscience'. 'When ye tell him "this is the law", it were well done ye should tell him also that, although this is the law, this is conscience, for law without conscience is not good to be given unto a king in Council.' Conscience, he reminded his visitor, was the rule of Chancery, and Chancery had 'jurisdiction to command the high ministers of the Common Law to spare execution and judgement when conscience had most effect'. And how could he, Wolsey asked, give away a palace 'which is none of mine'? 'If every bishop may do the like then might every prelate give away the patrimony of their church which is none of theirs.' But Shelley was adamant and when Wolsey had read the judge's commission he yielded. 'Report to the king's highness that I am his obedient and faithful chaplain and beadsman whose royal commandment and request I will in no wise disobey,' he said. But, he added, 'show his majesty from me that I most humbly desire his highness to call to his most gracious remembrance that there is both heaven and hell'.[24] 'Both heaven and hell.' Henry had never before been spoken to thus by a subject. Wolsey had never before dared thus to speak to him. But despite this rebuke the king took York Place.

Thereafter, and presumably because he was now sated, Henry relented. He sent the cardinal another ring as a token of favour. He sent him four of his own physicians

24. *Cavendish*, 117 ff. See below, p. 647.

when Wolsey fell seriously ill at Christmas time, and was reported as saying, 'I would not lose him for £20,000' – a valuation which may or may not have been a consolation to the sufferer. Soon yet another, the third, ring was on its way, one which Wolsey had given him and which was engraved with the king's likeness. Moreover, Anne Boleyn was pressed by the king into parting with 'her tablet of gold hanging at her girdle'; and these two gifts were delivered with 'the most comfortablest words'. At Candlemas Henry sent three or four cartloads of furnishings to Esher and soon afterwards gave permission (unbeknown to the Council) for the exile to move thence to Richmond.[25]

Encouraged by all this, Wolsey daily hoped for rehabilitation, and for months had been seeking the help of Francis I and the French queen mother, his old ally, as well as that of the emperor and Rome. If Henry had not been subject to such as Norfolk and the Boleyns, all might have come right for the fallen chancellor. But the latter's enemies, fearful lest he might yet recapture the king and alarmed both by his move nearer to London and Henry's lingering regard for him, resumed the pursuit and persuaded the king to dispatch him northwards to his metropolitical see of York. Since the beginning of Lent (1530) Wolsey had been lodging by the Carthusian house at Richmond, in rooms built by John Colet, and used to spend much time 'with the ancient fathers of that house in his cell, who ... persuaded him from the vainglory of this world and gave him divers shirts of hair to wear, the which he often wore afterwards (as I am certain)'.[26] Though he still yearned for lost favour and power, Wolsey was becoming a new man. For a moment he tried to resist being sent to the North, but the king (or was it Norfolk?) forced the issue, and on 5 April he set out thither – though not before Henry had given him £1,000 towards his expenses and sent him a message to be of good cheer.[27] He spent Holy Week at Peterborough Abbey, washing the feet of fifty-nine poor men on Maundy

25. *Cavendis*h, 120 f.   26. ibid., 130.   27. ibid., 132.

Thursday and singing High Mass on Easter Sunday. By the end of the month he had come to Southwell and, for the first time, set foot in his province.

Presumably Henry intended the cardinal to eke out the remainder of his days, as another ex-chancellor (Warham) had done and was still doing, in honourable retirement in his archdiocese. Maybe he had not yet abandoned all idea of recalling him some time to the centre of things. But Wolsey had not given up the struggle and nor could his enemies relax. He continued to look for sustenance from abroad, including Rome; and having recovered something of his old energy and buoyancy had decided, among other things, to summon Northern Convocation on his own initiative to meet at York on 7 November next, when he himself would be solemnly enthroned in his cathedral. Then, as if in response to his appeals, a papal nuncio arrived in England in early September 1530. A little later Wolsey's chaplain was arrested on his way to the continent, and shortly after this letters from his physician, one Agostini, were intercepted, containing passages in cipher. There had been rumours that Wolsey intended to flee and rumours that he had ridden to York with eight hundred horse; and not long before Henry had instructed his agents in Rome to search for any evidence of secret dealings by the cardinal with the Curia.[28] As we shall see, in the late summer of 1530, royal policy as a whole acquired a new direction and aggressiveness – and it may be this that finally brought Wolsey to his doom. On 1 November a groom of the king's Chamber set out from Greenwich for York carrying a warrant for his arrest.

The cardinal, Henry would declare, had 'intrigued ... both in and out of the kingdom', and had entered into 'presumptuous sinister practices made to the court of Rome for reducing him to his former estates and dignity'.[29] He

28. *L.P.*, iv, 3024; *Hall*, 773.
29. *L.P.*, iv, 6720; *St.P.*, vii, 212. The story of Wolsey's last months is, of course, fully told by Pollard in his *Wolsey* (chapter vii).

was therefore guilty of treason. On 4 November he was arrested while at dinner. Sick and humbled, he set out under escort for London to face trial and, doubtless, execution. But on the morning of 29 November, as he lay at Leicester Abbey a hundred miles from his destination, the Tower, he died a quiet, natural death and thereby cheated his master of the final reckoning.

For all his faults, there had been something lofty and great about him – as a judge, as a patron of education, as a builder, as an international figure. For all his faults, he had deserved more generous treatment from his king, and has, perhaps, deserved more generous treatment from some historians. Furthermore, though it is true that he failed to use his large legatine authority for any but rather desultory and tentative ecclesiastical reform, and was himself seriously ill-equipped to promote the renewal which the Church in England so manifestly required, it is not just to accuse him (as he has been accused) of having left that Church brow-beaten and dispirited — easy prey, in other words, to the king – and, to compound his guilt, of having clearly pointed the way to the Royal Supremacy by his own union of high spiritual and temporal authority. Wolsey as 'author of the schism' is scarcely more convincing than Wolsey as 'author of the divorce'. As will be suggested later, English churchmen showed little sign of having been broken by the legate and, in the months that followed the latter's fall, met the king's advances firmly. When he set out on his new course, Henry showed no sign of having learnt a lesson from Wolsey's example; and it is difficult to see precisely what lesson there was to be learnt. If anything, one might remark how little, rather than how much, the cardinal taught his master.

The Campaign against the Church

THIS is not the place to attempt an account of how the medieval Church in England came to an end, how an ecclesiastical and theological revolution was carried out, how England threw off Rome, pulled down her monasteries and so on; in short, how a people accomplished what was, by any standards, a radical breach with its past and a remarkable act of national amnesia. All that is required is a quick sketch of a backcloth against which Henry can stand.

Though today few people would sustain the thesis of an autonomous pre-Reformation English Church, it is still easy to assume that the breach with Rome was never truly revolutionary because the Roman primacy had, *de facto*, never meant very much to England and perhaps at best had been seen, as for years Thomas More saw it, as merely a human institution and little more than an administrative convenience. But the truth is that England was a thoroughly papalist country, perhaps the most so in western Europe, and that the two provinces of the Church in England were unthinkable and inexplicable without Rome. Despite the celebrated statutes of provisors and *praemunire* (which must be handled with caution), despite the indisputable fact that ecclesiastical life was enmeshed in the secular, the *Ecclesia Anglicana* could not have been what it was without Rome and took its dependence so much for granted that, like many large facts, that dependence is very difficult to prove quickly. Although on one level the Church in England manifestly depended from the king, served him and was subject to his law, on another (the more important, the spiritual) it manifestly lived a life separate from the secular order, as a member of the Universal Church in which

Rome's place at the centre of Christendom and the over-lordship of her bishop were as much part of the universe as the sun and the moon. Informed Englishmen knew what they were doing when they repudiated Rome. They, including the king, made a conscious, explicit choice. Henry did not proceed by stealth or sleight of hand, but with loud oaths and statutes. He asked the politically aware nation – however large that was – to make a considered, public repudiation of a foreign bishop whose identity was as well known as was his place in English life. Unless this is seen, the full size of the event will be hidden and it will be difficult to explain the many statutes passed against Rome's jurisdiction and the intense propaganda campaign against it subsequently – sermons, plays, pageants, books, pamphlets. Only deep roots have to be dug out thus.

But once this is said, and the task of understanding thereby made more difficult, it must be quickly added that, though papal authority was understood and accepted, it was probably not often an object of personal commitment; faith in the divine institution of the see of Rome was not a 'lively', loving faith – and small wonder, for Rome was, humanly speaking, unlovable. The act of believing is as complicated as man himself and we can carry something well within the threshold of certainty without ever bringing it into the full light and warmth of the centre of our being. Rome's primacy was a cold, juridical fact, obvious and necessary enough in the institutional life of the Christian Church, not a central, compelling, gratifying truth in the experience of the individual Christian. Only the rarest spirit could have set aside the repugnance he must have felt for Rome, on the human level, and laid down his life for it. Fisher and More had to die with their hearts cold, and despite the warmth they felt for Henry and their country. They may be thought misguided, but they cannot be denied staggering clarity of mind and courage. Most of their fellows preferred the warmth.

Despite what has sometimes been said or implied, it is

probable that the English Church was in no worse condition, spiritually speaking, in 1529 than it had been fifty, a hundred, or a hundred and fifty years before. The picture of slow, steady decline unto Nemesis is suspect. Not only is it factually questionable (for it is arguable that on the eve of the Reformation the English Church, though still largely wretched, was in some ways in better case than it had been for decades); worse, it misguides. For the really significant thing that had happened was not so much any change within the Church as a rise in standards of society, lay society, without it. What had been tolerated before and patiently accepted as part of the given order, though often bitterly mocked, would be tolerated no longer. This was a drastic, avenging society which believed that change could and must come, that it was no longer enough to deride, that the world could no longer muddle along with this ramshackle Church on its back. Why standards should have risen, why society should have been undergoing a 'revolution in expectation' and would no longer endure what previous generations had borne, is another matter. But it is clear that this had come about and that sentence had been passed against a Church which, though not yet derelict, was seriously in need of deep renewal.

It is customary to label the growing opposition to the Church as anticlericalism. This is unexceptionable, provided it is recognized that the anticlericalism concerned was a many-headed hydra, an amalgam of what were often opposites or, at any rate, incompatibles. We may distinguish several strands. The first was a negative, destructive anticlericalism which could range from hostility to the local parson and resentment of tithes, of the workings of the ecclesiastical courts and of frivolous excommunications, etc., to a programme of wholesale dispossession of 'abbey-lubbers' and lordly bishops – a policy often innocent of much philosophical or theological implication. Though this may have been the most widespread and, in a sense, the most successful, it was not the only force pressing for action.

Alongside this appetitive and basically selfish creed stood
two of a higher order. For there indisputably was a positive
and idealistic, though secular, anticlericalism (personified
perhaps by a Thomas Cromwell) which argued that the
Church needed radical purging, that society could no
longer carry this uneconomic burden, this vast institution
which absorbed so much manpower, sterilized so much
wealth, took so much and gave back so little; that its energy
and wealth should be turned to more positive ends, social
and educational; that the English Church's dependence on
a foreign power, the privileges and franchises of this great
estate, and especially the autonomy of the Courts Christian,
were an obstacle to political progress, a threat to jurisdictional wholeness; and that the flow of English money to
Rome, so offensive to prevailing bullionist theory, damaged
her economy. By such reckoning, therefore, the clerical
estate must be both clipped and re-ordered – for the sake
of the 'Commonwealth'. But there was also a positive, idealistic, and religious anticlericalism, itself a thing of many
shades, which would argue that, for the sake of Christian
life in England, radical change must come. For some this
may not have gone much further than a desire for traditional reforms; for others (like, say, a More or even a Fisher)
it may have sought drastic attention to monasticism and
the secular clergy, and some rehabilitation of the layman;
for yet others it may have meant the full Erasmian programme – a simple, Biblical, strongly lay pietism.

Of course this picture is too easy. There may have been
many who would not fit into any of these categories and
some who moved from one to another or chose elements
from all of them. It was certainly complicated further by
the fact that these three main forms were accompanied by
a fourth which shaded imperceptibly into, and yet could
easily be at cross-purposes with, all of them – namely the
anticlericalism of heresy. It is beyond doubt that Lollardy,
itself a very varied phenomenon, had survived intermittent
repression, indeed had recently gained ground, and would

now come to the surface to lend the voice of its strongly
anti-sacerdotal, anti-sacramental creed to the clamour.[1]
And to this indigenous heresy, which was to provide a
seed-bed for it, was soon to be added the potent new life of
the continental Reformation. Lutheranism had won con-
verts in the English universities very quickly; Lutheran
literature was in London and elsewhere in sufficient
quantities to worry the authorities by the early 1520s and,
when added to the writings of Zwingli, Oecolampadius and
other Protestants, would give to the layman and the anti-
clerical cleric a last weapon against a clericalism which had
so long oppressed and drained them.

Such, in heavily schematized simplicity, were the basic
forces of change building up against the established
Church. How strong they were is impossible to gauge. But
it is clear that, if the activists were a small minority, hostility to churchmen was widespread and often bitter, and
the conviction that something must be done intense. There
had been talk of reform for generations and nothing had
come of it; but each time it was discussed and promised it
was brought nearer because made more familiar. It had
come to a crescendo with the humanists and, when uttered
by an Erasmus or More, finally made respectable, indeed
authoritative, for they spoke from the inside and the top.
Nor was there merely talk. Not only were there germs of
great things within the Catholic Church but, of course, the
rebellion was well under way in Germany. There the *ancien
régime* was crumbling like rotten wood and the massive
success of the rebels could only serve as a stimulus, object
lesson and warning elsewhere.

In the autumn of 1529 a momentous thing happened.
Henry VIII threw in his lot with this anticlericalism, which
could never have made full progress without him. He sig-

1. See Thomson, *The Later Lollards 1414–1520* (Oxford Historical
Series, 1965); Dickens, *Lollards and Protestants in the Diocese of
York 1509–1558* (Oxford, 1958) and *Heresy and the Origins of English
Protestantism* (Inaugural lecture, 1962).

nalled his alliance with three actions: first, he dismissed
Wolsey, the supreme clericalist, though less insensitive to
the world of Erasmus than has been often supposed;
secondly, Henry replaced him in a post hitherto regularly
occupied by a cleric, but which he had determined should
not so be occupied now, by a layman – and no ordinary layman either, but a semi-Erasmian radical and author of the
most shocking book yet written in the English language,
namely, *Utopia*; thirdly, he summoned Parliament, the
organ through which, as nowhere else, anticlericalism could
find expression, a parliament which, with his blessing, would
immediately set about the chastisement of the clerical
estate and end by ripping a large section of it to pieces.

Anticlericalism needed Henry if it were to succeed and
Henry now needed it. The two have come together in a
powerful partnership which was to produce what was both
an act of state and (to fabricate an antithesis) an act of the
community. But if Henry had made his new liaison clear
he had left an important question unanswered: with which
form of anticlericalism had he allied? It could not be with
all of them, at least not permanently, because they were in
reality pulling in several different directions. His upbringing, his papal title and so on might suggest that he would
choose More's way, especially now that More was his chancellor. But his recent bullying of Clement had suggested
other tendencies. The Boleyns had Lutheran connections
and Cranmer was not far away from the Court. Nor, for
that matter, was Thomas Cromwell. Perhaps Henry had
not made up his mind. Perhaps he did not want to, preferring to enjoy maximum support for as long as possible.
Perhaps he had not yet perceived the necessity of choice –
for, after all, he was a newcomer to the scene and its complexity may not yet have been evident. Perhaps he was not
aware of what he had done. Wolsey had not been dismissed
because he was the arch-priest of clericalism, but because
he had failed the king; More did not replace him because
he was a radical, but because Henry wanted him. There is

no sign that Henry had a prepared plan of campaign when Parliament assembled. Presumably he intended it to mark the end of a regime and perhaps deal with its author; to provide money; to be a stick with which to beat Clement for the sake of the divorce. But was that all?

Now, and during the next year or so, we see Henry more clearly than ever before. Wolsey's great bulk, which has so often obscured him, is gone. We can now see the whole of the king, look steadily into his mind and watch his influence on policy, hitherto muted and erratic, become dominant. As he himself said, alluding to Wolsey's period of power, in the past 'those who had the reins of government in their hands deceived me; many things were done without my knowledge, but such proceedings will be stopped in future'.[2]

After dinner on Sunday 28 October 1529 Henry had a long conversation with the new Imperial ambassador, Eustace Chapuys, in which he poured out interesting thoughts. Would to God, he said, the pope and cardinals could set aside vain pomp and ceremony, and live according to the precepts of the Gospel and the Fathers. Had they done so in the past, what discord, scandal, and heresy would we have been spared! When Luther attacked the vices and corruption of the clergy, he was right. Had he stopped there and not gone on to destroy the sacraments and the rest, Henry would willingly have taken up the pen in his defence instead of launching out against him. Though there was a good deal of heresy in Luther's books, this should not obscure the many truths they had brought to light. The need for reform in the Church was manifest. It was the duty of the emperor to promote it. It was Henry's duty to do likewise in his own domains. He intended to make his small contribution to this cause and take up arms against scandal. Then he ended with a startling remark. The only power, he said, which the clergy had over laymen

2. *Sp. Cal.*, iv, 250. Cf. *Ven. Cal.*, iv, 601.

was absolution from sin. Even papal power was severely
restricted.[3]

We should dwell on these remarks. Henry's appraisal of
Luther sounds platitudinous today, but it was not so then.
His words were a long way from the reaction of Catholic
officialdom, a long way from that of English churchmen
who condemned the new creed as heresy *simpliciter* and
would have no further dealings with it, and a long way
from Henry's own uncompromising repudiation of Luther
in his book eight years before. He had spoken now like a
moderate and, perhaps, like an Erasmian. Again, it was
common form to call upon an emperor to look to the needs
of Christendom – especially an emperor like Charles V –
but there was now an interesting extension of that duty
to the king of England. Neither was this exactly new; but
it was new when applied to Henry, by Henry. The contemporary Church had often been judged against the Gospel
and the Fathers, but it is interesting that Henry should
have appealed to them now. In the context of 1529, these
words, when set alongside his trenchant remarks about the
jurisdiction of the clerical estate, read like a lay manifesto:
wild words, maybe, but omens. A few months before, Campeggio had protested to Henry about the literature abroad
at Court which, among other things, called upon the king
to strip the clergy and return to the ideals of the primitive
Church. Henry was apparently unmoved by the protest and
rebutted the cardinal's defence of the present regime (an
appeal to decrees of Councils) by replying sardonically that
these decrees were the work of an interested party, the
clergy themselves – an equally hostile and revealing remark.[4]

Henry's mind was on the move. But who was moving it?
What had he been reading recently? To whom had he been
talking? We know that there now stood by him men like
Norfolk and Suffolk who openly proclaimed their intention to follow up their destruction of Wolsey with an assault

3. *Sp. Cal.*, iv, 349 f.   4. ibid., 228.

on the whole clerical estate;[5] and we may assume that they were encouraging the king forwards. We know also of another person who had particularly influenced him – William Tyndale. The latter's *Obedience of the Christian Man*, the first thorough-going apologia of Caesaropapism, argued on the evidence of the Old Testament and early Christian history – and brought to him by Anne Boleyn – made a mark. 'This is a book for me and for all kings to read,' he said when he had finished it.[6] Tyndale's sweeping assertion of the rights and duties of princes and their claim to the undivided allegiance, body and soul, of their subjects, may well have opened up a new world for Henry even if he did not yet intend to realize the new order of kingship in England. Simon Fish's *A Supplication for the Beggars* – a bitter harangue against greedy, over-fed clerics – was addressed to the king and distributed over London in 1529, and was certainly soon in Henry's hands. There are two stories of how it came there: the first that Anne Boleyn gave it to him and that Henry was subsequently most gracious to Fish's wife; the other that it was brought to him by two merchants, one of whom read it to him then and there in his privy closet and that, when it was finished, Henry said, 'If a man should pull down an old stone wall, and begin at the lower part, the upper part thereof might chance to fall upon his head' – meaning that Rome must be dealt with first before he could turn to the English clergy. Henry thereupon took the book and forbade the two to tell anyone he had it.[7] Whichever story is true (if either), it seems certain that Henry knew this diatribe and had been impressed by it. Perhaps it helped to shape his mind and prod him onwards. Further, it was not only anti-clericals who could be encouraged by events on the continent. The Diet of Speier of 1526 had affirmed the rights of the

5. So the French ambassador, du Bellay, in October 1529. *L.P.*, iv, 6011.

6. Strype, *Ecclesiastical Memorials*, I, i, 172.

7. ibid., iv, 657 f.

godly prince, and Luther soon after had elaborated his ideas
on the special kind of stewardship which was his. There
may be no hard evidence that, say, Frederick the Wise of
Saxony served as his model, but, as one prince after another
joined the Reform, it is scarcely credible that Henry would
not have been moved by them. More than once, as we have
noticed, he had warned Clement that he might follow
their example if the pope did not let him have his way in
the divorce.

Of course the latter was of paramount importance.
Henry's failure to get rid of Catherine drove him onwards
to attack Clement and his Church in England. But this was
not the whole explanation of his actions. There were two
ideas present in his mind: that he must procure a divorce;
that kingship conferred on him a position in the Christian
community that was not actually his, which had been
usurped by others, which he must recover. The first was
already a conviction; the second was beginning to break
the surface. They were indivisible and fed one another. The
Royal Supremacy, Henrician Caesaropapism, call it what
you will, grew with the divorce campaign, but was distinct
from it. Had there been no divorce, or had Clement yielded,
there would probably still have been a clash between the
clerical estate and a prince who, in the name of reform, was
beginning to claim new spiritual jurisdiction. The divorce
did not directly beget Henricianism though it affected its
growth profoundly. It may have carried incipient caesaropapism to the breach with Rome when otherwise the latter
might have halted at a stringent concordat; conversely,
Henry's discovery of the true nature of Christian kingship
gave a new thrust to the divorce campaign. But the divorce
and the Royal Supremacy were not related exactly as cause
to effect. Strictly speaking they were autonomous, though
in complicated interplay – now accelerating, now hamper-
ing one another.

Probably Henry was never a Catholic in any but a conventional way. His allegiance to the old faith would seem

to have been a formal, habitual thing, devoid of much interiority and never urgent enough to invade deeply into a sturdy egoism. Maybe he did hear several Masses a day, but this does not prove that he was a good Christian. Maybe he did go to Walsingham and perform all the accepted acts of piety, but one still looks in vain for signs of a supernatural life of virtue. Certainly he had a taste for theology, but there is no evidence that he loved the real object of his study. His Catholicism smacks strongly of the notional and the superstitious and seems to have been of the very kind which a Luther or a Loyola deplored and fought most – external, mechanical, static; something inherited and undemanding. Doubtless he was no better and no worse than countless others were, had been, and would be; doubtless he was as much the victim of his environment as many have been. But the fact remains that his apparent piety, grasp of the Faith and, hitherto, allegiance to Rome were probably not deeply rooted.

In 1515, at the end of a fracas concerning relations between lay and clerical jurisdiction Henry had declared, before an assembly containing judges and bishops, 'we are, by the sufferance of God, king of England, and the kings of England in time past never had any superior but God', and spoken boldly of the rights of the crown.[8] It is difficult to know what to make of this; but it cannot, surely, have been a pre-echo of the Royal Supremacy, a hint of Henricianism which lay dormant for about fifteen years thereafter. Rather, it was a flamboyant assertion of regal overlordship which no more denied the essential immunity of the Church of England than Henry's formal reluctance to admit a papal legate in 1518, or to allow publication before scrutiny of the bull excommunicating Luther[9] – both of them traditional displays of a certain local autonomy – conflicted with his evident obedience to the see of Rome.

Henry's was a conventional Catholicism which would not

8. Keilway, *Reports* (1602), 180.
9. *L.P.*, ii, 4073. Ellis, 2nd ser., i, 286 (*L.P.*, iii, 1233).

bear any great weight in time of crisis or ever cost its owner much. Recently it had threatened to cost him a good deal. His allegiance to the old Church had brought him the delays and humiliations of the divorce campaign; it would stand in the way of recovery of rights (so he would discover more and more) which he considered were his birthright and had been filched from him. He would need the anti-clericalism of Parliament as a weapon with which to bully his opponents, and would use it with some skill, on the one hand allowing Parliament to attack Clement and his Church directly, and feeding its attack; on the other pointing to himself as one who deserved the most tender treatment from Rome, for he alone stood between Parliament and the object of its militancy.

Thus the forces of change now had a chance to move forward fast and looked to the king for leadership or at least approval. As Hall observed, when the Reformation Parliament forgathered it dared immediately to take up arms against the clergy, saying things which 'before this time might in nowise be touched nor yet talked of by no man except he would be made an heretic or lose all that he had, for the bishops ... had all the rule about the king'. But now things were different because 'God had illumined the eyes of the king'.[10]

Parliament began on 3 November. Henry came by water to Bridewell, robed there and thence passed to Blackfriars to assist at solemn high Mass. Then he went to the lords to hear the speech of the new chancellor, More, and, three days later, to receive the new speaker of the commons, Thomas Audley. The commons forthwith fell upon the clerical estate. They sent a petition to the king asking him to command the spiritual lords of Parliament to declare to his majesty whether 'by the laws of God and Holy Church'

10. *Hall*, 765 ff. More had said in his speech at the opening of Parliament that the king intended to turn at once to the urgent need for clerical reform.

spiritual men might buy and sell for gain, take in farm any
temporal possession, hold secular office, possess more than
one benefice with cure of souls and indulge in non-residence
– an aggressive document the exact purpose of which is
unclear, but which was presumably addressed to a king
because the authors knew that he would be responsive.[11]
About the same time as they completed this petition, the
commons may have aired some of the grievances against
the Church courts which eventually found their way into
the Supplication against the Ordinaries of 1532;[12] and they
are said to have talked also about the need to prune English
monasticism.[13] This upsurge of anticlericalism, long pent
up, was immediate and spontaneous. Henry did not create
it. He had no need to. He merely actively allowed it.

The commons had asked him to command the spiritual
lords publicly to justify the misdemeanours of their estate.
This he apparently did not do. Instead, the petition was
turned (wholly or partly – we cannot tell) into commons'
bills forbidding the things of which the petition had complained. Whether these bills were genuine products of the
lower house or disguised government legislation we cannot
know, but the passage from a petition asking the king to
expose clerical misdemeanours to a collection of bills which
illegalized them was clearly accomplished by royal *fiat*.[14]

When the first of these bills reached the lords, the
spiritual peers, now thoroughly alarmed, 'frowned and

11. B.M. Cleo. F, ii, fol. 249 (*L.P.*, iv, 6401).

12. Elton, 'The Commons' Supplication of 1532; Parliamentary
Manoeuvres in the reign of Henry VIII', *E.H.R.*, lxvi (1951).

13. *The Earliest English Life of St John Fisher*, ed. Hughes (1935),
109 ff. According to this it was proposed to dissolve smaller monasteries in order to recompense the king for the expenses of the
divorce – but Fisher's stout opposition quashed the measure.

14. Chapuys quoted Henry as saying, on 5 December, that he had
issued orders for the reform of the clergy and was concerned with
clerical fees, pluralism and, so Chapuys said, annates, *Sp. Cal.*, iv, i,
353. The report must refer to the anti-clerical legislation of this first
session of the Reformation Parliament.

grunted'. For them, clerical reform was a clerical monopoly, and aggression from below, by the lay lower house, must be strenuously resisted. John Fisher launched the counter-attack against those who cried 'down with the Church' and, having pointed to Bohemia, the land of heresy, talked ominously of the 'lack of faith' of certain persons. His words stung the commons who, taking them to be an imputation of heresy, sent a deputation to Henry to complain. Henry listened to them sympathetically and sent for Fisher, the archbishop of Canterbury, and six other bishops. Fisher explained that he had spoken of the lack of faith of the Bohemians, not of the commons house – and his fellow-bishops corroborated this.[15] Henry could only dismiss the bishops and report Fisher's reply to the commons, whom this 'blind excuse' pleased not at all. One wonders how Henry felt at finding the man who had stood in his way so much now at odds with the house of commons as well. The incident passed – but it had a moral: it showed the impetus of the attack; it showed once more that the attackers looked to Henry for aid; and, since Henry did not rebuke the commons' deputation for taking so much into their hands (and it must have been this as much as their actual intentions which riled Fisher), it showed him implicitly abetting them.

Two of the commons' bills he caused to be re-drafted and presumably toned down. As a result, they passed the lords, with the spiritual peers reluctantly assenting. The commons then produced a third bill, dealing with pluralism, non-residence, clerical economic ventures – in short, very obviously usurping Convocation's responsibility for clerical manners. The bill was 'sore debated' in the lords and the spiritual peers 'would in no wise consent'. Henry intervened, summoning eight members from each house to 'intercommune', that is, confer, in the Star Chamber – a common enough procedure, but not usually prompted by royal initiative. There the bill was fiercely argued, until the spiritual peers gave way.[16] Again Henry had effectively

15. *Hall*, 766.   16. ibid., 767.

acted against them. The three acts provided that offenders
– clerics guilty of non-residence, pluralism, holding land in
farm, engaging in commerce – should be brought before
the Exchequer and that the informant, as was common
practice, should receive his moiety of the fine. Even without this incentive these acts provided an alluring chance to
settle old scores and soon dozens of clerics, 'mere' clergy
(parish priests and the like), were being pursued for misdemeanours most of which would in the past have come
within the compass of Canon Law and ecclesiastical courts.[17]
Under the king's aegis, an important inroad had been made
by the lay estate into the clerical franchise. Moreover, the
last of the three acts had laid it down that no papal dispensation for pluralism should avail against it, and that anyone who procured such a dispensation from Rome after 30
April next would be fined £20; a notable early thrust, this,
against the authority of Rome.[18]

Then, in May 1530, Henry called a conference of the two
archbishops, several bishops and representatives of both
universities which met in St Edward's Chapel on the east
side of the Parliament Chamber at Westminster. He presented to the company copies of English theological works
printed abroad 'to hear their advice and judgement of
them'. The assembly were to read the books and discover
what heresy they contained. This was done; whereupon,
convinced of their 'detestable errors', Henry determined
that the books (seven of them) 'were utterly to be expelled,
rejected and put away out of the hands of his people' –
together with all translations of the Scriptures, including
Tyndale's. He also ordered that preachers should go forth
bidding all who possessed copies of the forbidden works to

17. See King's Remembrancer memoranda rolls, P.R.O. E. 159/
309 ff., *communia* sections, for these actions.
18. 21 Hen. VIII, *c.* 13, paragraph ix. But a proclamation of 12
September 1530 threatened imprisonment for anyone who 'put in
execution' or published 'anything' bought in Rome which was contrary to this and the other acts. *Hughes and Larkin*, 130. This proclamation greeted a new papal nuncio on his arrival in England.

cast them aside and hand them to the authorities.[19] It was
Henry who summoned this gathering, who presided over
its meetings and now sent the preachers abroad. Indeed,
he had come to London especially to attend.[20]

The sermon in which the clergy were to warn the people
of the evil fruit being offered to them was drawn up by
the conference. It asserted that, in having these books condemned and their errors listed, the king was 'most chiefly
regarding the wealth of their [i.e. his subjects'] souls', an
interesting statement of royal responsibility,[21] and went on
to claim, on the authority of St Paul, that it was a king's
duty to punish those who refused to surrender the forbidden books. Furthermore, at the same gathering Henry had
asked whether, as some said, it was his lawful duty to provide his people with translations of the Scriptures. Those
present advised against it and, Henry said, he allowed his
conscience for the moment to be guided by their judgement. But he added that he would cause the New Testament 'to be by learned men faithfully and purely translated into the English tongue to the intent that he might
have it in his hands ready to be given to his people as he
might see their manners and behaviour meet, apt and
convenient to receive the same'; that is, if his subjects
would put away polluted books he would in return deliver
to them the clear waters of truth. The preachers were to
announce this news – and a proclamation issued at the end
of the next month (June 1530) repeated the promise.[22]

Of course the prince had always had concern for the
spiritual welfare of his people, but had a prince ever been
quite so confident and active? No English king had ever
claimed the duty to give the Word of God to his people;
indeed, for Henry to have suggested such a thing to a clergy

19. *Wilkins*, iii, 727 ff.   20. *L.P.*, iv, 6376; *Sp. Cal.*, iv, 302.
21. But, it must be noted, the same thing had been said in the
proclamation of early 1529, which banned a long list of heretical
books. *Hughes and Larkin*, 122.
22. *Wilkins*, loc. cit. *Hughes and Larkin*, 129.

which had so long set its face against translation of Holy
Writ into the vernacular was as startling a novelty as his
suggestion that he should withhold it until his people
showed themselves worthy to receive it. It is possible that
Henry came to this conference in order to launch, or to
prepare to launch, the translation at least of the New
Testament and that he was overcome by shocked clerical
opposition.[23] Just before the conference got under way, the
ultra-conservative bishop of Norwich, Richard Nix, reported angrily of how the avant-garde in his diocese boasted
that their opinions had royal support and that they had
heard that the king intended to put forth the New Testament in English.[24] Even if they were optimistic and even if
it is too much to suppose that Henry had already seriously
intended to take so momentous a step now, it is still true
that he had shown a *cura religionis* of a new brand; that
if some of what had just taken place was not absolutely
new, most was new for Henry. Was he not doing exactly
what, in conversation with Chapuys a few months before,
he said he ought to do, namely, assume a wider responsibility for the spiritual affairs of his kingdom? It has been
suggested that 1529 saw the beginning of a new stage of
an Erasmian reform movement in England;[25] wittingly or
otherwise, Henry, the friend of moderate clerical reform
and the benevolent prince who had now promised to put

23. Hall reports another conference between the king, Council and
some prelates which took place the day after this one ended, in the
Star Chamber. It too discussed translations of the New Testament
and ended with the king commanding the bishops to commission a
translation by a team from the universities – a plan which, Hall
says, the bishops quashed by inaction (*Hall*, 771). Perhaps Hall was
in fact talking about the conference in the Parliament Chamber,
which he mis-dated and misplaced. But if he was right, if the first
conference was followed immediately by further discussion in Star
Chamber, this would tend to support the idea that Henry was pushing his project hard against clerical opposition.

24. *L.P.*, iv, 6385.

25. McConica, *English Humanists and Reformation Politics*
(Oxford, 1965), 106 ff.

the New Testament in the ploughboy's hand as Erasmus
wished, was preparing to become its patron.

Probably some months later, perhaps as late as the end of
1531, Henry would give further evidence of the extent to
which royal competence had expanded. Even as the Parliament of 1529 was legislating against them – and perhaps
to parry the blow – the clergy themselves had begun to discuss reform in Convocation. Eventually a large and impressive corpus of reform decrees, dealing with a host of
clerical matters, was drawn up by Southern Convocation.
But before it was promulgated (in early 1532), the king
scrutinized it. We have a preliminary draft of the decrees
with corrections in the king's hand – alas all too few corrections, for Henry seems to have got no further than the
first three pages before he tired – but enough to yield
precious evidence of his mind. Thus, where the archbishop
and bishops have referred to the lower clergy as their 'subjects', Henry has objected. He has struck out the word and
written 'inferiors'. Why? Because subjects belong to kings,
not bishops, presumably. Then he has tightened up two of
the decrees. Where their authors have declared that a clerk
should not be able to purge himself easily or quickly, the
king has written that he should not be able to do so at all
'except for the most urgent reason'. Where they piously required all to obey the canons and constitutions of the
Church, Henry has added 'which have been lawfully received and approved by the use and customs of the kingdom'.[26] Royal censorship of the work of Convocation is
remarkable for having occurred, let alone for pointing thus
to the future.

By early 1530 the project for collecting opinions on the

26. P.R.O. S.P. 1/57, fols 112 ff. It is impossible to date this document exactly, but it must have been drafted before February 1532
and may have been drawn up as early as 1530. All Henry's corrections were incorporated in the final version of the decrees, for which
see *Wilkins*, iii, 717 ff.

divorce from those most solemn authorities, the universities, was in full swing. According to Foxe's celebrated story, it was Thomas Cranmer, then but a youngish don eking out a living as tutor to two boys at Waltham, who first made the suggestion when, in the late summer of 1529, Henry and his Court came to the abbey near by and Edward Fox and Stephen Gardiner found themselves billeted in the house where Cranmer was staying. When Henry heard this suggestion he declared that its author had 'the sow by the right ear' and summoned him to Court; and thus began Cranmer's public career.[27] There seems no reason to doubt the substantial truth of this story. It rings true; it is confirmed by Morice (Cranmer's contemporary biographer); criticisms of it are, perhaps, unconvincing.[28]

Early in the following year, royal emissaries rode into Oxford and Cambridge to demand and, with some difficulty, secure, categorical judgements on the king's behalf. Meanwhile nearly a dozen agents began touring the universities of France and northern Italy – and, indeed, more than universities. Reginald Pole, John Stokesley (newly-made bishop of London), Richard Croke and Cranmer himself, to name but the leaders, not only visited faculties of law and theology to procure support for the king's cause but scoured libraries and bookshops of all sorts and sizes in search of anything that might be of aid; Scripture, manuscripts, patristic writings, conciliar decrees, scholastic commentaries and the like which were not available in England. They sent home copies of valuable texts in Latin,

27. *Foxe*, vii, 6 ff.
28. Thus it has sometimes been asserted (e.g. by Ridley in his *Thomas Cranmer*, Oxford, 1962, 27) on the strength of a letter from the scholar Richard Wakefield to Henry, written probably some time in 1527 (*L.P.*, iv, 3234), that the idea of consulting the universities was mooted then. But what Wakefield said was that he was willing to defend the king's cause in all the universities of Christendom – which is not at all the same as seeking their approbation of his cause. Mr Ridley's other criticisms of the story are not altogether convincing. Ridley, 25 ff.

Greek and Hebrew. They wooed influential individuals, bishops like Giberti and Caraffa, professors and provincials of religious orders, in the hope that they would carry others with them or even take up the pen themselves, as some did. They argued with Scripture scholars, Hebrew scholars, canonists, doctors of medicine, rabbis, friars, laymen. They held formal sessions at universities, and, where successful, dispatched homewards the so-called 'determinations' thereof. They gathered lists of signatories, collected copies of rare letters of Fathers and rabbinical writings. They even sent home from Venice two Hebrew scholars ready to support Henry's case – one of them, Marco Raphael, a recent convert from Jewry and, among other things, famous for his invention of a new invisible ink.[29] Their campaign was a quite remarkable affair. Rarely has learning been more hungrily interrogated, or earned more money with so little exertion. It was also occasionally uproarious and violent. There was fighting at Cambridge and great obstinacy at Oxford. At the latter place, in the course of weeks of effort, two of the royal visitors (including John Longland) were stoned by sturdy Oxford women and another similarly treated when he was caught immobilized as he relieved himself against a town wall.[30] At Paris, after a promising beginning, an Imperial counter-attack reduced a certain majority to a bare pass.[31] Meanwhile Croke and Ghinucci, accompanied but, as Croke maintained, not aided by several members of the Casale family, were hard at work in northern Italy, proceeding by stealth at first and pretending to be moved by a merely academic interest in the problems of Leviticus and Deuteronomy (which their large purses made implausible), until Gregory Casale absent-mindedly let the cat out of the bag – or so Croke, who had used the pseudonym of John of Flanders, said.[32] But Croke

29. *L.P.*, iv, pt. iii, *passim*. On the appeal to Jewish authorities see esp. Kaufmann, 'Jacob Mantino', *Rev. des Études Juives*, xxvii (1893), 49 ff.

30. *Sp. Cal.*, iv, 270.   31. ibid., 315, 396.   32. *L.P.*, iv, 6193, 6229.

was a whining, tiresome man, who seems to have been able to quarrel with anybody. Thereafter things went badly awry. The Venetian authorities took fright at anything which might annoy Charles or upset a Portuguese king whose father had married Catherine of Aragon's two sisters in succession, and bade the English desist.[33] Try as he might, Croke could not shake the Signory, and then Perugia and Bologna, both papal cities, were warned by Rome not to meddle in the affair.[34] Catherine's friends hindered the king's agents at every turn. A Franciscan provincial took fright and came to Croke wanting to give back all the money he had received;[35] at Vincenza a friar in Croke's employ had just procured a list of subscribers to the cause when the papal nuncio there snatched up the document and threw it into a fire – and not even a personal letter from Henry would persuade the Signory to let the disappointed friar try again;[36] and on 21 March, yielding at last to Imperial pressure, Clement issued a bull forbidding individuals to write or speak against the royal marriage.[37] Charles's agents had more prestige and bigger purses than Henry's, and this was beginning to tell. As well as this, the former were blessed by two valuable windfalls. First, one Raphael Coma, a canon of Padua who had just written a book in support of Henry, suddenly produced a complete recantation which, he said, expressed his true mind on the matter. His volte-face and the subsequent publication of his two works in a single volume brought Croke to a near-halt, and left relations between him and Casale (whom he blamed for this, of course) even worse.[38] Then came a second blow. Though rabbinical opinion was moving steadily against Henry's contention that Leviticus's prohibition of his marriage was absolute,

---

33. *Ven. Cal.*, iv, 589, 595, 597; *Sp. Cal.*, iv, i, 310, 312.
34. *L.P.*, iv, 6634, 6581, 6609, 6611.
35. *Sp. Cal.*, iv, 317, 563; *L.P.*, iv, 6642.
36. *L.P.*, iv, 6407; *Ven. Cal.*, iv, 597.
37. *L.P.*, iv, 6279.   38. ibid., 6592, 6672, 6689, 6702, etc.

it had nonetheless publicly maintained that no union with
a brother's relict had been known since the fall of Jerusalem or could *de facto* occur. It was a lamentable mishap,
therefore, that, at this very moment, two levirate marriages
between a Jew and his dead brother's wife should have
taken place, publicly and noisily, under the Englishmen's
very noses, one in Bologna, the other in Rome. Between
them they discredited the royal case more effectively than
could a score of learned treatises and university determinations.[39]

However, by mid 1530 Stokesley, Pole, Croke and the
others had procured judgements in Henry's favour from
eight universities, including Paris and Bologna,[40] and a
corpus of texts and signatures garnered from libraries, religious houses and the like. In a sense, these represented a
considerable success. But what, precisely, was Henry to do
with these new-found weapons?

The appalling débâcle of the legates' court at Blackfriars,
followed by Catherine's appeal and the 'advocation' of the
cause to Rome, undoubtedly stupefied Henry and left royal
policy in confusion for some months. Initially there was the
idea of simply ignoring the revocation, pretending that it
had not happened, as it were, or preventing its promulga-
tion;[41] but clearly this could not halt the machinery which
Catherine, Charles and Campeggio had set in motion. A
more positive counter-attack was required to force Clement
to admit the intrinsic justice of Henry's case and give
judgement in his favour. Such would be the use of all

39. *L.P.*, iv, 6229; *Sp. Cal.*, iv, 446.
40. But the university of Angers had spoken *against* Henry – a
fact which was overlooked later when the determinations were
flaunted before the world. *L.P.*, iv, 6370; *Rymer*, xiv, 391.
41. Though in September 1529, in the course of Chapuy's first
audience with him, Henry had said that the case must be heard in
England, that he and Catherine could not suffer the indignity of
being cited to Rome, etc. – which was as he would argue when the
real trial of strength began in the late summer of 1530. See *Sp. Cal.*,
iv, i, 160.

those 'determinations' and writings which his agents had
gathered on the continent and such would be the purpose
of all his own efforts in the first months of 1530. But – and
this is the essential point – until the late summer of that
year, when he announced a new principle with which to
fight, he had resigned himself to his case being tried in
Rome and was preoccupied with battering Rome into giving the right verdict. He had not yet said that the case did
not belong to Rome at all.

In early 1530 a historic meeting took place between pope
and emperor at Bologna, where, at long last, Charles would
be crowned. Henry sent a large embassy to salute and con-
gratulate the emperor, and to plead with him and Clement
about the divorce, an embassy led by no less a person than
Anne Boleyn's brother, Lord Rochford (at least at first
sight a choice of dubious taste). His purpose was to persuade
these two, emperor and pope, to agree to give judgement in
Rome for Henry.[42] He had little chance of success. Charles,
crowned and at peace with the pope, was less disposed than
ever to yield and Clement was now the emperor's good
friend. England had finally lost the diplomatic advantage
which had been hers nearly three years before when emperor and pope were at daggers drawn. Hence Boleyn's
mission failed. Henry could no more win a favour by exploiting an hour of gladness and triumph than he could
by bullying Clement in the shambles of the bishop's palace
at Orvieto. Accordingly, he tried a new tack.

On 12 June 1530 great men of the realm, ecclesiastic and
lay (but only those known to be friendly to Henry's cause),
were assembled at court to subscribe to a remarkable letter
to the pope demanding a quick solution to the marriage
problem. They had been summoned some weeks beforehand and told to bring their seals with them. But, when
they arrived and saw the letter which they were to subscribe,
some were so unhappy about it and, in particular probably,
its belligerent language that the matter was postponed for

42. *Sp. Cal.*, iv, i, 373.

a few days. Then the letter was apparently redrafted at
court and carried round from house to house for signatories to sign and fix their seals thereto.[43] The finished
document[44] is, physically, perhaps the most impressive piece
uttered by Tudor England – a large, finely-executed sheet,
from which hangs centipede-like a thicket of seals of two
archbishops, four bishops, twenty-five abbots, two dukes,
forty other lay peers and a dozen lesser folk – and is a bold
manifesto, full of menacing hints about turning to other,
harsher remedies. But throughout it openly concedes that the
case rightfully belongs to Clement. It begs him, Christ's
vicar on earth, or, rather, who calls himself such, to open a
paternal heart to his loving subjects in England, to bow
down before and confirm the massed weight of learned
opinion that has found for Henry. It is for him to pass final
judgement on this cause. Let him do so without further
delay: 'let your holiness declare by your authority, what
so many learned men proclaim . . . as you not only can but,
out of fatherly devotion, ought to do.' When the intended
signatories to this document had gathered at court on 12
June, they had been asked if the king could take the law
into his own hands and, if necessary, go ahead without
papal consent. But few would agree to this radical proposal,
and one, it was said, implored Henry on his knees to hold
back on account of popular discontent with the divorce.[45]
The subsequent letter, by calling upon Clement to give swift
judgement, showed that Henry would not yet dare to challenge papal jurisdiction. Indeed, his case had formally begun in the Rota in early June and he had already sent to
Rome, William Benet (accompanied by one Edward Carne
and Thomas Cranmer), against the opening of proceedings
there – though with instructions to prevent by whatsoever
means available 'any innovation of process'.[46]

43. *Sp. Cal.*, iv, i, 354, 366. The original text had probably contained the threat of an appeal to a General Council.

44. In the Vatican Archives. For text, see Herbert, op. cit., 331 ff.

45. *Sp. Cal.*, iv, 354.

46. *L.P.*, iv, 6462. B.M. Add., 48,044, fol. 27.

In the light of this last it was churlish of Henry to complain about delay. As Clement pointed out in his reply to
the letter just discussed, had Henry sent proctors to answer
the appeal his case would have started much sooner.
Catherine's proctors were already there; but where were
his?[47] Furthermore, as soon as the trial began, Ghinucci
halted it with a quibble and then embarked on a filibuster
until the summer vacation had overtaken proceedings and
suspended them until October. Henry would now play the
card that Campeggio had used against him a year before.
In the past Clement had dawdled, Heaven knows; but now
it was Henry who did so – and this so successfully that, as a
special favour to the king, Clement eventually agreed to an
elaborate plot whereby he would leave Rome just before the
new legal year began in October, ostensibly for only a couple
of days, go to Ostia and then move on to Civitavecchia,
tarry there a fortnight or so and effectively hold up the Rota
until November.[48]

By the early summer of 1530, therefore, however unwillingly, Henry had been forced to face public trial in Rome,
having delayed process long enough to assemble an overwhelming weight of international learned opinion in his
favour with which to carry the Rota. But by August 1530 a
decisive change occurred. Henry now became something
more than an importunate subject knocking aggressively at
the door of the Curia; he began to deny that he was even a
subject. The Levitical argument, which held the field almost
exclusively now and upon which the universities were being
asked to give judgement, had always contained a latent
threat to papal jurisdiction. Now, however, Henry not only
challenged the pope's authority but threatened withdrawal
from it; and, to do so, began to advance a new authority of
his own over and against the papal. This explicit assertion
may have been an obvious conclusion to a previous, implicit
denial. It was none the less momentous. Hitherto he had
questioned the theology upon which a papal dispensation

47. *L.P.*, iv, 6638.
48. *Sp. Cal.*, iv, i, 358. B.M. Add., 48,044, fol. 47v.

rested; now he enunciated a new theory of English monarchy. He had both a grudge and a claim; two claims, in fact.

The first asserted that neither he nor any fellow-countryman could be summoned to a Roman court because, by
ancient custom and the privileges of the realm, so he declared, Englishmen could not be cited out of their homeland – 'ne extra Angliam litigare cogantur' – to submit to
a foreign jurisdiction.[49] These were not casual words that
tumbled out accidentally in the course of heated debate;
the statement was advanced as a principle upon which
Henry was more than entitled to act and which he himself
had brought to light.[50] We can find no trace of it before
August 1530 when the English ambassadors at Rome were
instructed to place it before the pope.[51] In early September
Henry bombarded a newly-arrived papal nuncio with a long
harangue in which the rights of Englishmen, confirmed, he
said, by several popes, were set forth – the first of several
diatribes to which the nuncio would be subjected[52] – and
shortly afterwards, Benet and Carne were told once more
to announce the new doctrine to the pope. At the beginning
of October Henry summoned a gathering of lawyers and
clerics to consider whether, in view of the privileges of the
kingdom, the papal inhibition against taking any action in
the divorce while the appeal was pending at Rome could
be ignored and the cause committed willy-nilly to the archbishop of Canterbury. His audience was clearly as much
taken aback by his novel words as were the agents in Rome

49. *St.P.*, vii, 261 (*L.P.*, iv, 6667). Henry to Benet, Ghinucci and
Casale, 7 October 1530.

50. ibid., 262.

51. In the letter just quoted, Henry refers to a reply from his
agents, dated 17 September, in which they confess that they have
not yet spoken to the pope about this matter. They must therefore
have been instructed to do so in a letter of late August. That letter,
like their reply of 17 September, is not extant. We have, therefore,
to work back two steps from the one letter of Henry's, dated 7
October.

52. *Sp. Cal.*, iv, 429, 433, 460.

and Clement himself. They answered 'no'.[53] Undeterred by
this setback, he dispatched a truculent letter to Clement in
early December setting out his claim once more and presenting it as an inviolable, unquestionable fact.[54]

As a result the royal programme now had a new character.
The agents in Rome had already been instructed to demand
that the case be handed back either to three English bishops
(Canterbury, London and Lincoln), or to the whole clergy
of the southern province; or that the pope should allow
Henry to proceed *de facto* and take the law into his own
hands, without waiting for any formal halt to the appeal –
the thing which on 12 June and again in early October he
asked his fellow-countrymen if he could do and was told
that he could not. Benet and the others had been badgering
the pope to agree to one of these three courses for weeks.
The newly-discovered birthright of an Englishman to answer
no court but an English one was added later, perhaps a week
or so later, to give force to these demands, or 'degrees', as
they were called. Henry's conviction was robust. Should
Clement fail to acknowledge this ancient prerogative to
which he now appealed, then let the ambassadors ask him
whence were derived the prerogatives of Rome. Both sprang
from history and to doubt one was to doubt the other. And
what were the prerogatives of Rome? As the university of
Padua has said, to treat of man-made laws only, not to
touch the things of God, not to usurp the rights of his kingdom, not to set aside the settled laws of England. Let
Clement understand that neither he nor his people would
suffer the national inheritance to be infringed. If the pope
resisted justice then the ambassadors were formally to appeal
to a General Council; they were to remind Clement of his
illegitimate birth; to inquire whether his election was not
simonaical and, if enough cardinals would swear that it was,
whether he might be deposed.[55] Thus was the new policy
launched.

53. *Sp. Cal.*, iv, 460.   54. *Burnet*, vi, 41 (*L.P.*, iv, 6759).
55. ibid.

But the ambassadors did not keep up with their master. As late as December they were still trying merely to delay and obstruct the Rota without denying that the king was answerable to it – which was the policy of the early summer. Henry was now far bolder. 'We would,' he wrote, 'be loath to use such means ... lest we should, by them, enter into further inconvenience and, by our own act, acknowledge and grant so much of the pope's jurisdiction, power, authority and laws as we should thereby preclude ourself from such remedies as we may attain here at home ... By none act, appearance or allegiance to be made there ... tacit or express, oblique or direct, implicit or explicit' were the ambassadors to 'consent, allow or approve the pope's jurisdiction, but that we may hereafter depart from the same without contrariety in our own acts.'[56] This was December 1530 – not 1532 or 1533. And lest we have not felt the full force of this letter let us dwell on its final point – a distinction which Henry drew between 'entire Englishmen' and 'Englishmen papisticate'. Here indeed was the beginning of a new trail. Meanwhile, Henry had harangued the nuncio again, telling him that the pope had no more jurisdiction than had Moses (whatever that might mean), that the rest was usurpation and that he was minded to take up the pen against the papacy.[57] We may not yet have reached the idea of Royal Supremacy; but we have certainly parted company with those days when Henry begged Rome to invest him with the kingdom of France or adorn his style with a new title.

Not only was Henry ahead of his ambassadors, he also shocked them. They knew that appeals to a General Council against the pope had been forbidden time and again, and before Henry's awful command they quailed. They could not obey instructions and face Clement with the royal threat and, instead, sent back to Henry copies of bulls of Pius II and Julius II which would have drawn down anathemas upon them and the king. Nor dared they call

56. *St.P.*, vii, 269 (*L.P.*, iv, 6760).   57. *Sp. Cal.*, iv, 460.

Clement a bastard or, in the name of one who had been prepared to buy for Wolsey the throne which Clement had won, charge him with the sin of Simon Magus; and again they sent home a bull, also of Julius II, which they dared not trespass. And then there was the matter of the new-found customs and privileges of England, which they must announce to the pope. How were they to substantiate them? Clearly, the English agents were taken aback by what was required of them and cautiously consulted experts in their employ, who were unimpressed by Henry's words. They knew nothing of the alleged privileges of England. Once more the ambassadors' nerve broke and they had to confess to Henry that his command had not been executed.[58] That this should have happened is remarkable – and, as well as remarkable, eloquent proof that Henry was entering new and frightening territory in which some did not feel at ease.

The royal reaction to this disobedience was angry renewal of the command. At last the English agents plucked up courage and went to the pope to say what Henry had bidden. They announced to Clement the news of English immunity, to which the pope made the obvious and decisive reply: prove it. They did not know how to and, much ruffled, withdrew. A few days later they returned to the point, attaching to it (as they had been bidden) remarks implying that the English prerogative was no less authentic than the papal and that the two stood or fell together; all of which Clement angrily swept aside, saying that he could prove his jurisdiction better than Henry could his custom and adding 'in a great fume' that he would give the English no further audience.[59] As both he and the cardinal of Ancona vigorously pointed out, Henry had had his full measure of sympathetic treatment when Campeggio was sent from Rome to try the case, with Wolsey, in England. Rome was bound to listen to Catherine's appeal against the legates'

58. For all this see P.R.O. S.P. 1/59, fol. 189v (*L.P.*, iv, App. 262).
59. B.M. Add., 25,114, fols 44 f. (*L.P.*, iv, 6705).

sentence of contumacy and she was protected by the principle of canon law that the accused (in this case Catherine)
should not be tried in the accuser's domain. Henry disputed
Catherine's plea that any English judge would be suspect,
but it was not for him to do so – and anyway, the letter
recently sent from England signed by some eighty worthies
lent substance to her statement. Henry spoke of English
privileges and customs, but how did he explain the decretals
in the *Corpus Iuris Canonici* in which popes dealt with two
English matrimonial causes, one of them involving no less
a person than King Henry II?[60]

And what were those privileges which Henry brandished
so confidently and which took his fellow-countrymen (not
to mention Clement and his advisers) by surprise? Whenever
he spoke about them himself the king was somewhat vague.
The basis of Henry's claim was provided by those stern
injunctions of the Constitutions of Clarendon and Northampton which attributed to the king close surveillance of
the Courts Christian, empowered him to command that
causes should be determined in the archbishop's court, forbade appeal beyond this without royal assent, condemned
the bishops of London and Norwich for having promulgated
a papal excommunication without royal licence, and so on;[61]
and the privilege which Henry claimed was that famous
national right, allegedly granted by the Holy See itself and
to which Henry III and Edward I had appealed, that no
Englishman could be cited out of England by papal letters.
This was classic *privilegium Angliae* which, three centuries
ago, had been worked hard. But it had never had much
substance, even if the statutes of Provisors and Praemunire
had seemed partly to buttress it, and had even less when it
was resurrected now.

60. As previous reference. For the cardinal of Ancona's references,
see *Decretals* iv, tit. I, cc. vii and xi.
61. See the very interesting collection of texts, ending with the
relevant passages from the Constitutions of Clarendon and Northampton, in P.R.O. S.P. 1/236, fols 204 f. (*L.P., Addenda*, 673).

Henry suddenly started talking about this special national privilege in the autumn of 1530, and he talked about it time after time in the following months, indeed years. It was an indisputable fact, embedded in the laws of England, confirmed by several popes, including Innocent III. But presumably because it was rather frail, it was commonly accompanied, and eventually overshadowed, by another argument which pointed in the same direction, but which was not wholly in line with it, namely, that the fundamental laws of the Church forbade any ecclesiastical cause ever to pass out of the province of its origin, wherever that might be. By this reckoning, it was not just a national privilege conferred on Englishmen that was at stake but the far larger cause of the right-ordering of the whole structure of Christendom. So Henry was to begin to argue and what he said was to be expanded and repeated again and again in that spate of highly skilful, vigorous propaganda with which he and his Council tried to present the repudiation of the Roman 'usurpation' as a righteous, long-overdue restoration of the true Christian polity. As he now asserted, and as was later argued by such tracts as *A Glasse of the Truthe* of mid 1532, the *Articles devised by the holle consent of the King's Council* of late 1533, the deliciously named *A Little Treatise against the Mutterings of some Papists in Corners*, and their companions, the Council of Nicea had firmly decreed that all causes should be settled by the metropolitan of the province of their origin, and subsequent Councils of Constantinople, Chalcedon, Carthage VII, Milevum and Antioch had explicitly or implicitly confirmed this ruling. Innocent I had bidden bishops of any province to decide all causes arising therein. Chalcedon and Antioch had called for twice-yearly provincial Councils for this end; and in a letter to Celestine I (which came as manna from Heaven to Henry and his friends) the African bishops had argued that an appeal of a layman, cleric or even a bishop should go to the metropolitan or, in major cases, to a provincial Council, not to the pope – and this on the ground that an individual must needs discern truth less clearly than a Council.[62]

Doubtless some of the materials required to support this new argument were found in England. But before long the search had extended to the Continent and required those who had hitherto been involved in hunting down rare books and manuscripts and touting the universities for the sake of the divorce – men like Stokesley, Croke and Casale – to move on to this new cause. They were now to search out any patristic material or collections of conciliar decrees not available in England which would give strength to Henry's appeal to the Early Church against that of his own day.

Within this general commission lay two particular assignments. For some reason or other Henry (or those about him) were convinced that Pope Innocent III, the same pope who had done so much damage to his Levitical argument, would give special support to this one. How Innocent in particular should have become the object of such intense concern is not clear, but he did. Presumably his numerous contributions to the *Corpus* first attracted attention to him. But the difficulty was that no complete set of his letters was available in England with which to check and amplify the extracts in the *Decretals*. If the pope's letters were not to be found here then they must be found in Italy. There were five bulls that Henry was interested in, three of them of particular concern, namely, *Cum olim*, *Inter divinas* and *Gaudemus in Domino*. Croke, then at Venice, was bidden find copies of them there; but he searched in vain. Then he heard that a collection of the pope's letters was in Bologna and set out thither, only to learn that a quick-fingered friend of Catherine, the prior of the Servites there, had removed it to a destination unknown.[63] This was the sort of obstruction

62. Some of these texts are also contained in the document cited in the previous note – apparently an early collection, probably drawn up in late 1530.

63. *L.P.*, iv, 6595, 6607.

that he had met time and again. Accordingly, when he heard
of Croke's failure, Henry ordered Benet and Carne to make
their way into the Vatican Library (an obvious but rather
inaccessible place) and look for the bulls there, which they
did – successfully.[64]

One of Innocent's bulls was not especially relevant; two
of them, *Cum olim* and *Gaudemus in Domino*, did indeed
show ecclesiastical causes being committed to local judgement – and *Cum olim* handed an English matrimonial case
to three English judges – but these were, of course, commissions to judges-delegate which in no way disowned papal
jurisdiction, ran counter to the notion of local autonomy and
said nothing about English privileges.[65] On the contrary,
Cum olim showed England knitted into a universal jurisdiction and subject to its centre. Innocent's decretals fortified
the English demand that Henry's case should be heard by
papal commissioners in England (though it is difficult to
know why it should have been necessary to have searched
out justification for this when the institution of papal judges-
delegate was well established and cared for by a whole title
of the *Corpus Iuris Canonici*);[66] but Innocent would never
have had any truck with ecclesiastical particularism.

Meanwhile, the king's agents had been set a larger task
than hunting out papal decretals. They were to return to
those universities which they had visited some months ago
and wring from them a second set of 'determinations'.
Those who had previously declared that a marriage to a dead
brother's wife was unlawful and impermissible were now to
declare that Henry could not be cited out of his realm, that
his case belonged to England and not Rome. This second
tour of the universities is an obscure and badly-documented
affair. It seems to have been launched in Italy by mid
September 1530 and must have come to France soon after.[67]

64. Their transumpts are in B.M. Add., 48,044, fols 123 ff. Cf. *L.P.*,
iv, 6602, 6605.
65. For texts, see *Migne, P.L.*,ccxv, cols 534 ff.
66. Viz. *Decretals* i, tit. xxix.   67. *L.P.*, iv, 6633.

It succeeded in the latter country only. In June 1531 the universities of Paris and Orleans determined that Henry could not be compelled to appear before the Rota, that his so-called excusator should be admitted to plead his excuse and the case handed back to England.[68] This was not a very substantial victory. Only two academies had been found to speak for the king and what they said was that Henry's case ought to be heard in England by papal judges-delegate – which, again, fortified part of the English case, but not the whole of it (as will be suggested later).[69]

Although the argument concerning England's immunity became a mainstay of Henricianism, it was not the only line of attack. The claim to a national privilege and some kind of national autonomy was accompanied by a claim that the king was possessed of a *personal* dignity and immunity – which is a different thesis, to be distinguished from the one which we have just considered, even though it frequently ran alongside it. It was the duke of Suffolk and Anne Boleyn's brother, then just back from Italy, whom we first hear announce this, when speaking to the nuncio in late September 1530. England cared nothing for popes, they said, not even if St Peter himself should come to life again; for 'the king is absolute emperor and pope in his kingdom'.[70] This was the fateful word: emperor – an old enough one, with a new meaning now and a long history in front of it, signifying a personal jurisdiction which knew no superior on earth, be it the temporal overlordship of the German emperor, or (so it will finally be argued) the spiritual author- ity of the pope. A few days later Henry spoke – a little more discreetly. Tell the pope, he bade Benet and the others, that he was 'not only prince and king, but set on such a pinnacle of dignity that we know no superior on earth'; that he was supreme in his kingdom and, therefore, much offended at having his cause advoked out of his realm, to Rome; that because he was supreme master of his kingdom,

68. *Rymer*, xiv, 416 (*L.P.*, v, 306).
69. See below pp. 376 ff.   70. *Sp. Cal.*, iv, 445.

it was given to him to forbid and take away from inferiors the right and remedy of appeal.[71] Henry had not used the word 'emperor', nor denied the papal primacy, but his words went far towards both. He would allow to the pope, he said, jurisdiction over only those things which can rightfully be subject to *human* authority. He himself claimed to be more than mere prince and king – and what could that be, save emperor? He had given a definition of that 'pinnacle of dignity' which he occupied, claiming that he who was supreme could not be appealed and was at no one's suit because there was no authority on earth above him and that the pope had greatly insulted him by advoking his cause to Rome.

Probably a few days before this, that is, in early September 1530, Henry wrote to Benet and Carne perhaps the most extraordinary letter of his reign. It will be recalled that these two agents were already groaning under the load imposed upon them, having been required to announce the news of England's birthright to Clement, prepare an appeal to a General Council, threaten deposition of the pope – and meanwhile set to find and copy some letters of Innocent III in the Vatican Library. On top of all this there now came a new and staggering commission. Henry had decided that he would send to Rome itself to find proof of the imperial authority to which he was now laying claim; he would dose Rome with her own medicine, hoist her with her own bulls. He no longer required transumpts of two or three decretals of one pope, therefore. Rather, Benet and Carne were to go through *all* the registers of *all* the popes and gather evidence on the following four topics. First, they were to search for anything which proved the 'authority imperial' which Henry had within his realm. Next, they were to discover from the registers whether Henry, 'having authority imperial, be under the pope in any other matter than heresy', and whether jurisdiction in matrimonial cases belonged to the pope from the earliest times or was a recent acquisition.

71. *St.P.*, vii, 262 (*L.P.*, iv, 6667).

Finally, from the same source, they were to learn 'after what sort the popes used emperors in causes of matrimony and chiefly in the realm of England'.[72] In these four questions we may glimpse Henry's aspirations exactly. Add to them his words (just quoted) to Benet and the others, and the contents of the royal mind stand revealed as never before.

The task which he had set his agents was truly immense. To have consulted but a small fraction of 'the infinite number of registers here' (as Benet said) would have consumed hours of labour, and to have covered the whole collection quickly would have needed an army of searchers. There were other difficulties besides the volume of the task. It required 'all policy and diligence ... and ... experiment by divers means privily to come into the pope's library where the said registers were' and, once inside, Benet and Carne were not allowed to copy anything – though by pretending to take brief notes they were able 'at sundry and divers times and by piecemeal' to compile transcripts. The invasion of the library by these two Englishmen could scarcely fail to arouse suspicion, and Alexander, the librarian, who was known to be hostile to Henry's cause, concluded that they were up to mischief and acted accordingly. Registers were said to have been lost in the Sack of Rome, left at Avignon or shut up in the Castel Sant' Angelo. Every move that the Englishmen made was reported to Clement and any register in which they showed interest carried off afterwards for careful scrutiny.

Their labours – which must have been extremely cursory – yielded worse than nothing. They had to report that they had found no evidence in support of the king's imperial authority, though, they added hastily, 'it is not to be doubted of'. Contrary to royal hopes, they had indeed found

72. B.M. Add., 40,844, fols 31–31v, 36v. These are two letters from Benet and Carne to Henry dated 18 October 1530 (and not in _L.P._). Henry's preceding letter is not extant but can be reconstructed from them. Cf. Scarisbrick, 'Henry VIII and the Vatican Library', _Bibl. d'Humanisme et Renaissance_, xxiv (1962), 212 ff.

'divers processes which had been made by popes against divers emperors and kings not only in cause of heresy but also in causes [of] perjury, adultery, *dotis, restitutionis bonorum et contempus censurarum ecclesiasticarum,* etc.' Thirdly, they had been unable to discover when jurisdiction over causes matrimonial had first been exercised by Rome, but local experts had told them that it had existed 'since the first creation of the dignity papal'. Finally, they reported that they had gathered all they could find which illustrated papal dealings with the matrimonial affairs of emperors – and especially English 'emperors' – and had found nothing which could challenge Clement's dealings with Henry.[73] The king's four articles were not just unconfirmed but largely refuted. The sad news must have reached England by about mid November. A short while later we find Henry writing of 'our dignity and prerogative *royal*'[74] – a rather tame *coda* to the previous *bravura* passage.

But it marked the end of a movement only. If Henry had been repulsed in his attempt to establish his title with bulls brought from Rome, this did not mean that the quest had to be abandoned. That his monarchy was endowed with imperial status was an idea that had long lurked in the half-light on the edge of his consciousness. In 1513 and 1514 ships had been named *Henry Imperial* and *Mary Imperial*;[75] in 1521 Henry resisted More's protest that, in his book against Luther, the pope's authority was too 'highly advanced and with strong arguments mightily defended' with the retort, 'Nay, we are so bounden unto the see of Rome that we cannot do too much honour unto it. . . . For we received from that see our crown imperial'[76] – a most perplexing statement which, if it is to be taken seriously, suggests that Henry

73. B.M. Add., 40,844, fols 31–31v, 36v.
74. *St.P.*, vii, 269 (*L.P.*, iv, 6760).
75. *L.P.*, i, 1661, 1663, 2305, 2686, etc. See Koebner, 'The Imperial Crown of this Realm: Henry VIII, Constantine the Great and Polydore Vergil', *B.I.H.R.*, xxvi (1953), p. 30.
76. Roper, *Life of Sir Thomas More*, 68.

then subscribed to an extreme hierocratic, papalist view of
the cosmos, whereby all authority on earth, secular and
spiritual, descended from that universal monarch who was
the vicar on earth of Christ the Priest and King. In late 1525
a great seal was ordered which would show on one face
Henry sitting in majesty wearing, not the flat crown of a
king, but the domed crown imperial – as he would eventually be shown on a new seal cut in September 1532, when
Audley became lord keeper.[77] Yet, some vague, innocent
delusions of imperial status seem to have been part of his
flamboyant dream-world. They may even have been fed –
in a very circuitous manner – by Maximilian's dangling of
the crown of the Holy Roman Empire before his young
eyes years before and have helped to prompt his own attempt
in the Imperial election of 1519.

But if Henry, as his remark to More suggests, hitherto
derived his imperial dignity from an ultra-papalist theory of
sovereignty which required him to accept not only the
principle that Rome was the mediator of all authority on
earth but also the historicity of the Donation of Constantine (and thus made him yet more subject to the overlord
of Christendom from whom all legitimate authority, spiritual
and temporal, was derived), at the same time he could find
an alternative source for that dignity in the legends concerning early British history which the sixteenth century had
inherited from Nennius, Geoffrey of Monmouth and *The
Brut*. According to these, ancient Britain had been conquered by Brutus, grandson of Aeneas of Troy and founder
of a dynasty of British kings (culminating in King Arthur)
who, under the symbol of the red dragon, had conquered
all Britain, Scandinavia and Gaul and defeated a Roman
army in battle. Arthur's line had come to an end in Cadwalader, but not before Merlin had prophesied the eventual triumph of the British over the Saxons, of the red
dragon over the white. Moreover, by virtue of the fact that
he had had a British mother, the Emperor Constantine had

77. *L.P.*, iv, 1859; v, 1295.

united British kingship with Roman emperorship, and imparted a special status to Arthur and his line. Thus early Britain had sired an heroic dynasty upon which the first Christian emperor had bestowed a peculiar halo and from which would one day spring a conqueror who would reclaim the British heritage.

Despite what some enthusiasts have asserted,[78] early Tudor England did not produce a sudden renewal of Arthurianism nor a very energetic official campaign to parade the Tudors as direct heirs of Brutus and Cadwalader, come out of Wales to recover their British inheritance in fulfilment of ancient prophecy. The early years of Henry VII saw a few attempts to provide the new king with a British lineage, but there had been as many, or more, on behalf of Edward IV. The *British History* had been the stock-in-trade of much fifteenth-century political propaganda, and when Henry VII called his first son Arthur there was little suggestion that this implied a direct descent from the British hero. Moreover, as the sixteenth century wore on, Geoffrey of Monmouth's patriotic fantasies received increasingly short shrift from reputable historians, and it was only antiquarians like Leland who clung to the so-called historical primitivism which appealed to a legendary past to support the notion of a Tudor 'mission'. A statue of King Arthur holding a round table appeared on the palace built for the reception of Charles V at Calais in 1520 and again, wearing an imperial crown, in a pageant at Cornhill on the occasion of Charles V's entry into London in 1522. On the same visit, Charles would be shown the Round Table at Winchester. Arthur and Arthurianism were not forgotten, therefore. But no attempt was made to make political capital out of them. Arthur was paraded as but one of many heroes of old – not as a direct ancestor of the Tudor dynasty whose mantle the latter must carry; and it was the union rose rather than the

78. E.g. Millican, *Spenser and the Table Round* (Cambridge, Mass., 1932), esp. 15 ff.; and Greenlaw, *Studies in Spenser's Historical Allegory* (Baltimore, 1932). Cf. Koebner, art. cit.

red dragon which had pride of place in political pageants and royal architecture.[79]

Yet, though the saga of early British history had hitherto been neglected (not least by Henry himself) and cast aside by the more critical writings of such as Polydore Vergil and John Rastell, it momentarily burst back into living politics now, when Henry was advancing his new imperial claims against Rome. In January 1531, the duke of Norfolk treated Chapuys to a harangue about the king's imperial status and plunged deep into British antiquity in support of the argument. He told how Brennus, a legendary British king, had conquered Rome; how Constantine had reigned here, how he had had a British mother – all of which was presumably meant to prove (though Chapuys does not say explicitly that the duke so used it) that kings of England were not to be intimidated by Rome, that they were heirs to Constantine's imperial status. And then the duke went on to say how he had lately shown the French ambassadors the seal of King Arthur which bore the legend, 'Arthur, *Emperor* of Britain, Gaul, Germany and Denmark' – which was presumably meant to prove (though, again, Chapuys does not say explicitly that the duke so used it) that, in claiming imperial status himself, Henry was merely recovering an inheritance from his ancestor.[80] This is an obscure episode. It would scarcely be worth dwelling on – and certainly could not sustain the thesis that the farrago of myth and patriotic legend about Constantine and Arthur did, after all, matter in the story of how English monarchy achieved the greatest victory in its history – were it not for the fact that, having suddenly appeared now on the lips of the duke of Norfolk and then disappeared, it should equally suddenly have re-emerged in the opening of the preamble to the act of Appeals of 1533, an act which has regularly been taken as

79. See the sobering article by Anglo – 'The *British History* in Early Tudor Propaganda', *Bull. John Rylands Library*, xliv (1961), 17 ff.

80. *Sp. Cal.*, iv, i, 598.

the foundation stone of the new order. For, when that statute proclaimed that 'by divers sundry old authentic histories and chronicles it is manifestly declared and expressed that this realm of England is an empire' it was clearly referring to Geoffrey of Monmouth and the rest of them. True enough, the allusion is cryptic. It had to be, if the statute were to remain respectable. But there is no doubt about the allusion.

Thus what had previously been innocent, indeed ultra-papalist, imperial pretensions of the king had been turned by pressure of circumstances into an overt claim to autonomy which effectively annihilated Rome's overlordship. We have seen two attempts to sustain this claim: the first in Rome itself, with that remarkable foray into the Vatican library where the truth of Henry's imperial dignity was, it was hoped, to be vindicated; the second by appeal to British history. The first was unsuccessful, the second somewhat unconvincing. Henry was unlucky that neither his father nor he himself had pushed Arthurianism vigorously in recent years and that the statute of Appeals should have come at a time when the 'higher criticism' of Renaissance historiography inevitably made Geoffrey of Monmouth, *The Brut* and their fellows unpalatable. It was not surprising, therefore, that when the time came for providing a solid, comprehensive rationale of the Royal Supremacy, apologists should largely have turned to a third source, namely the sacral kingship of the Old Testament and the caesaropapism of the early Christian emperors. This was another form of historical primitivism, but it provided sturdier material than King Arthur and the British inheritance of Tudor kingship. It invoked the name of Constantine once more, but now the appeal was to Constantine as Christian emperor and source and exemplar of all true Christian monarchy, not as one who had mysteriously imparted imperial status to the leaders of his mother's people.[81]

The late summer of 1530, then, was probably the crucial

81. See below, pp. 499 f.

moment in the story of Henry's jurisdictional struggle with universal papalism – indeed, perhaps the crucial moment of his reign. It saw him launch the claim to a national immunity against Rome's sovereignty; it saw him announce a personal claim to imperial status which could neither acknowledge nor allow any superior on earth. It also saw the first attempt to manhandle the clerical estate within his realm.

In Michaelmas 1530, fifteen clerics were cited to the King's Bench on *praemunire* charges, charges, that is, of lesser treason, punishable with loss of goods and imprisonment. Of the fifteen, eight were bishops (including John Fisher and John Clerk), three abbots and the rest lesser folk. The charges against them were that they had all entered into some compact with Wolsey whereby they should retain their jurisdiction in return for a cash settlement and that they had thereby implicated themselves in his guilt.[82] The indictments clearly exude government malice, and it is immediately noticeable that several of Catherine's best friends were among the victims. The motive for the attack was, presumably, to reward them for their loyalty to the queen, to encourage the others, to frighten Clement and to announce to the English clergy the new caesaropapism to which English monarchy was beginning to aspire. But the attack, which seems to have been hastily launched, was called off before the sides were joined. 'The prelates shall not appear in the *praemunire*', wrote Cromwell to Wolsey on 21 October. 'There is another way devised.'[83] The 'other way' was far more drastic: a *praemunire* charge against the whole clergy of England, on the ground (eventually) of nothing less than having exercised the jurisdiction of the Courts Christian within the realm. The destruction of the papal legate and the attempt to implicate others who had abetted him were

82. P.R.O. K.B. 29/162, ro. 12. See Scarisbrick, 'The Pardon of the Clergy, 1531', *C.H.J.*, xii (1956), 25 ff.

83. Merriman, *Life and Letters of Thomas Cromwell* (Oxford, 1902), i, 334 (*L.P.*, iv, 6699).

themselves striking displays of confident aggressiveness by the secular power. But this was something more: a thrust at the heart of the clerical estate and the freedom of the Church in England. If the ecclesiastical courts, so long established and so much a part of daily life, both lay and clerical, were not legal, then what was? One would like to know the thinking behind this charge. On what grounds could the courts of the Church be declared illegal, except because they functioned apart from the system of royal justice, applied their own law and had Rome for their summit? And if this were so, then could they have acquired legality only by disowning Rome and being anglicized? This *praemunire* indictment was perhaps the logical concomitant of the claims to national and personal autonomy which were being presented to Rome at the same time. It was clearly another step towards Henricianism. Had Henry therefore suddenly decided to fling himself against the clerical estate and break it? Was this action intended to bring to a climax his bold talk about his imperial status and to lead directly to the Royal Supremacy?

These are unanswerable questions. But it seems that this assault, like so much of royal policy in these years, was full of uncertainty. Though it had been decided upon in October 1530, it was not delivered until next January, when Parliament and Convocation met again after a series of prorogations; and it was probably only at the last minute that it was decided to charge the clergy with illegal exercise of the Courts Christian rather than, as was probably originally intended, with being collectively implicated in Wolsey's guilt – which would have been a considerably less fundamental challenge. Moreover, scarcely had this precipitate violence been launched than it was called off. Faced with this extraordinary *praemunire* charge, the clergy apparently succumbed and sued pardon. How and why they were able to do so we do not know; but they did. On 24 January 1531 Southern Convocation formally submitted to Henry, as the northern body would do soon after, and received royal pardon – at the price of £100,000.[84] But though the clergy had admitted a guilty past, they were not forced to compromise their future. The act of Parliament which contained their pardon apparently restored all that had been theirs hitherto, leaving the structure of the Courts Christian intact and imposing no theoretical or practical concession on the clerical estate. Thus what had just been declared illegal had been inexplicably restored unchanged. True enough, the clergy were £100,000 the poorer; but as a clerical subsidy was now due they would have paid the king a handsome sum anyway. Henry, surely, had lost his nerve and retreated from the field. By 24 January, the day on which the text of the grant which bought pardon was drawn up in Convocation, peace had been made and Henry's extraordinary manoeuvre had finally petered out.

Then suddenly the king was on the attack again. First, he demanded that, if necessary, he should have the money just voted to him by the Convocations more quickly than the clergy had provided. Then, when the latter sent him a petition to confirm their privileges, define the compass of *praemunire*, give positive protection to ecclesiastical courts and lighten the burden of the anticlerical legislation of 1529, he refused.[85] Finally, the archbishop of Canterbury was summoned to a conference with a group of royal councillors to be told that the text of the clerical grant (voted on 24 January) was unacceptable. Warham was to have five additions inserted forthwith. In the first place, Henry was to be styled not just king and Defender of the Faith, but 'protector and only supreme head of the English Church'; secondly, the clergy were to speak of a 'cure of souls' having been committed to him; then the privileges and liberties which, in the course of their grant, they had asked him to defend, were to be defined as those which 'do not detract from his power and the laws of the realm'; next, they were to ask for pardon more humbly; finally, they were to point out that the laity, too, had been implicated in their guilt,

84. *Wilkins*, iii, 725 f.   85. Scarisbrick, art. cit., 31 ff.

for they too had sued and been sued in ecclesiastical
courts.

Henry had resumed the pursuit, but from a different angle,
demanding a new title of supreme head of the Church and
a categorical statement of the royal cure of souls. All this
was caesaropapism more overt than anything yet heard from
the king. Faced with it, the clergy rallied. To the new title
which Henry demanded Convocation attached the famous
saving clause – that Henry was supreme head of the Church
'as far as the law of Christ allowed'; an unhappy formula,
perhaps, but intended to repulse the king. Then, by alter-
ing a case-ending and shuffling the word-order of the second
article, the clergy obliterated the royal claim to a cure of
souls and, instead, accorded the king a platitudinous care
for subjects whose souls were committed to their, the clergy's
charge. As for the rest of the articles, these were either made
innocuous or omitted.[86] There can be no doubt that in this,
their first straight encounter with the prince, the English
clergy had held much of their ground. Moreover, after the
hue and cry were over, Henry received three protests from
clerical sources stoutly affirming opposition to his incipient
caesaropapism, which showed how shocking his action had
been – to some, at least – and how little they intended to
yield.

One came from Cuthbert Tunstal, bishop of Durham,
shortly after Northern Convocation had voted the new,
qualified title. Despite careful preparation, things had not
gone smoothly for the king in the North, so much so that
Tunstal had had a formal protest against the new royal
style entered into the register of Convocation and then, in
May 1531, written directly to Henry a long letter in which
he set out traditional theory that the king possessed a temporal overlordship which the Church readily acknowledged,
but that this could not and did not extend to spiritual
matters; that the new title was to be understood as merely a
temporal attribute; that the law of Christ allowed it to be

86. Scarisbrick, art. cit., 34 f.; *Wilkins*, iii, 742.

no other, else the visible unity of Christendom would be broken to pieces.[87]

The other two protests came from humbler sources than the bishop of Durham and were the work of more than one person. We know about them only thanks to Chapuys. On 22 May the latter wrote home that four days previously the clergy of York and Durham, and those of the province of Canterbury, had also protested to the king against his recent attempt to assert his sovereignty over them.[88] When the ambassador spoke of a document from the northern clergy he may, of course, have been confusing it with Tunstal's letter. Probably, however, he was not. Probably there was a formal statement uttered by the lower clergy of York and Durham, and possibly a rather mysterious document in the Public Record Office is a stray draft of it – a document without heading or signatures or any means of identification. It does no more than quote the king's new title and then, briefly and bluntly, declares that that title is not, and was not, intended to infringe in any way the primacy of the supreme pontiff or the authority of Rome.[89] What else it said, how many signed it and who they were we cannot know, for the completed protest sent to Henry has disappeared. Nor should this fact surprise us. The letter which Tunstal sent to Henry is no more – and offending passages in the copy of it entered into his episcopal register were torn out by an unknown hand. Moreover, had it not been for the alertness of Chapuys, a copy of the third protest – from Southern Convocation – would not be available today. The original has likewise vanished.

87. *Wilkins*, iii, 745, for Tunstal's protest. His letter to Henry is not extant and must be reconstructed from Henry's reply – for which see below.
88. *L.P.*, v, 251. Cf. the confirmatory report in *Mil. Cal.*, i, 869.
89. *L.P.*, v, App. 4. But it must be emphasized that it is only a guess that this fragment was somehow produced in the course of compiling this protest. It is just possible that it was a draft of the protest sent by the lower house of Southern Convocation (which is discussed shortly in the text above) and that no protest at all came from the northern body.

When he heard what was afoot, Chapuys procured a transcript of this last document, which he sent across the water
to the Low Countries. It is now in Vienna.[90] It is a trenchant
declaration, signed by seventeen members of the lower
house, of the true meaning of the new title which had
recently been granted by them to the king. What they had
conceded, they stated, was not intended to weaken the laws
of the Church, or to impeach her liberty, the unity of
Christendom, or the authority of the Holy See. They had
conceded nothing new. They remained loyal to the old
order and intended no disobedience to it. They there and
then denounced and disowned as schismatic and heretical
anything which *in the future* they might do or say in derogation of sacred canons, the integrity of the Church, the
primacy of Rome – for this would not be their true mind
but the work of the Devil or of their own weakness. Here
indeed was a fanfare, the last blast of the trumpet for the
regiment of Rome and the old ecclesiastical order. Henry
responded directly. Shortly after the dispatch of this protest four of its signatories were put on various *praemunire*
charges. Of the four, one Peter Ligham, a friend of Fisher's,
fought back; the rest pleaded guilty.[91] And when the final
crash came all who survived made peace with the new order
which, in 1531, they had so trenchantly damned in advance.

These outspoken clerics, then, were quickly chastised.
Tunstal's protest, however, drew a long and temperate reply,
written in the king's name and, if not composed by him, at

90. In the Haus-, Hof- und Staatsarchiv, reference: England, Ber.,
Fasz 5, Varia 2. The document is in two halves. The first is written in
the name of Peter Ligham, on behalf of the clergy of Canterbury and
Menevia (whose proctor he was) and is subscribed by seven others.
The second half, a shorter and even more trenchant piece, is subscribed by nine clerics, six in the name of the clergy they represented,
viz. of Bath and Wells, Worcester, London, Coventry and Lichfield,
and Rochester (for whom there were two signatories). Apparently,
therefore, nearly one third of the English dioceses produced a 'protestant' who signed on behalf of his clergy.

91. For their cases see P.R.O. K.B. 29/164 and K.B. 27/1080. They
were all eventually pardoned – Ligham in July 1531, the others in the
previous November. *L.P.*, v, 559 (22) and (35); 1139 (10).

least expressing his mind. It is an absorbing discourse, full of apparent benevolence and yet shot through with ominous undertones, learned and yet undeniably specious, clearly revolutionary and yet seemingly so innocent that the lengthy and, as it turns out, largely irrelevant display of semantics with which it begins can easily carry the reader across non-consequence and make the grief expressed at the bishop's obstructiveness sound both entirely reasonable and moderate.[92]

Be not misled by human perversity into forcing false construction upon innocent words, the letter begins. Understand first the sense in which terms are used before judging the statement; distinguish contexts; distinguish metaphorical from literal; guided by good sense read the true meaning, rather than pervert with 'subtle wit'. We are not the head of the Church if by the Church you mean the whole Mystical Body. Certainly not. It were blasphemous to suggest so, for Christ is its only head. We have never meant this, as you perversely suggest. Rather, we must distinguish. Just as St Paul spoke both of the Church and the church of Corinth, so we must speak of the Church as a whole, whose head is Christ, and of the Church of England of which we are head; and when we say we are head of this Church we mean head of the clergy of England. In what does this headship consist (which is the critical question)? You will allow us what you call a temporal overlordship. But the texts which you quote do not show that things spiritual are excluded from a king's care. On the contrary, it is clear that 'all spiritual things, by reason whereof may arise bodily trouble and inquietation, be necessarily included in a prince's power': and the only possible consequence of this is that the clerical estate, 'its persons, acts and deeds' should be 'under the power of the prince by God assigned, whom they should acknowledge as their head'. Since the Church is our mother, the clergy's duty is to minister to us, to preach, to administer the sacraments. In respect of these

92. *Wilkins*, iii, 762 ff.

functions, emperors and princes are subject to them; but, for the rest, they are subject to princes. Princes are therefore sons of the Church in one sense, but supreme heads in another, 'after whose ordinance ... they [the clergy] be ordered and governed'.

In short, though Henry allows a radical distinction between the Church and Caesar, between what Tunstal had called by their traditional names of spiritual and temporal, he gives to these terms quite different meanings. 'Spirituals' have hitherto meant, and meant to Tunstal, the teaching, sacraments, jurisdiction and government of the Church; now it is to mean the ministry of the word and sacraments only – the *potestas ordinis* – instituted by Christ to be brought by the clergy to the Christian man. 'This is not as the common speech abuseth it,' Henry openly concedes, 'but as it [*sc.* the term 'spirituals'] signifieth indeed.' All the rest, the whole external ordering of the Church, belongs to the prince's charge. It may indeed, says Henry, be described as *temporalia* – though, strictly speaking, the word is superfluous (by which he means likely to imply too little and, therefore, unwelcome). It is better simply to speak of those things which belong to the prince as *supremum caput*.

And in what exactly does this princely authority consist? Henry lists three things: as prince he licenses and assents to elections of bishops and abbots – for 'is any bishop made but he submitteth himself to us and acknowledgeth himself as bishop to be our subject?' (which had a truth in it, but avoided, surely wilfully, the crucial question of what was meant by a man acknowledging himself to be his subject *'as bishop'*); secondly, all clerical goods are subject to a prince's 'occasion and order'; thirdly, the Courts Christian operate 'by our sufferance' and receive a delegated jurisdiction – and 'there is no doubt but as well might we punish adultery and insolence in priests as emperors have done, and other princes at this day do, which ye know well enough'.

The point of Henry's letter is to show that 'we and all

other princes be at this day chief and heads of the spiritual men', that his title acknowledges facts rather than presages any radical novelty. But the novelty is there all the same, even if Henry has either not yet thought out the full implications of his Byzantinism or has deliberately, and at times somewhat disingenuously, tried to disarm his correspondent with moderation. A Christendom made up of a collection of national communities under the supreme headship of princes would have little room for the papacy and not much visible unity; and, if the papacy were virtually excluded, then it would presumably be the princes who conferred jurisdiction on those bishops whose elections they licensed and approved. Implicitly, therefore, Henry has laid his hand on the *potestas iurisdictionis*. It is from this source that he who has recently impeached the clerical estate for their exercise of the Courts Christian and restored them by act of Parliament confers on these courts a delegated jurisdiction; and it is because of this that the clergy are merely 'ministers' of religion. The boundary between temporal and spiritual has been shifted deep into what had previously been the latter's territory. This is precisely what Tunstal and the 'protestants' from the lower house of Convocation had foreseen. When they granted that Henry was head of the Church as far as the law of Christ allows they meant that this was not very far at all – no further than the king, as temporal lord, patron, protector of the Church and *de facto* nominator of bishops had long been allowed. Henry, however, believed that the law of Christ allowed, indeed commanded, what was objectively the beginnings of an ecclesiological revolution. Both sides may have been satisfied with the new title, but only because they gave it diverse interpretation. For the clergy it was not even the thin end of the wedge; for Henry it was only the thick.

But perhaps this will be thought too categorical. Perhaps Henry had not yet crossed the Rubicon. Had Clement suddenly yielded and granted Henry what he wanted, would the king not have forgotten all those bold theories, would not England have settled back into her old ways? In short, was not this all bluff and bluster? Henry himself on occasions seemed to suggest that this might be so. Talking to the papal nuncio in February 1531 he declared, with unusual amiability, 'I can assure you that there never was a question of any measure that could affect his holiness. I have always upheld the authority of the Church in this my kingdom and fully intend to do so in the future.' A little later he would deny that a *'nouvelle papalité'* had been set up in England and could promise that nothing would ever be done against papal authority, 'provided his holiness had for him the regard he was entitled to'.[93] Henry, therefore, was apparently threatening, not intending, violence. Other facts seem to sustain this thesis. In 1531 two new episcopal appointments were made to fill the gaps left by Wolsey – Stephen Gardiner to Winchester, Edward Lee to York. Both received papal provision at royal request, as would Cranmer a little later. Had Henry really believed in his own authority would he have sought papal provision for these two servants? Ought we not, after all, to argue that during 1530 and 1531, and perhaps during much of 1532, Henry's only purpose was to bully Clement into granting the divorce and that, if he had had his way, he would have let bygones be bygones, quietly consigned the talk about imperial dignity, national privileges, supreme headship of the Church and so on to the weapon-cupboard and become once more a dutiful son of Rome?

The answer to this question should probably be 'no' – though with some qualification. But before attempting to justify this assertion, we must resume the story of how Henry managed his divorce suit at Rome.

Primary responsibility for the conduct of Henry's affairs at the Curia lay with two English envoys, William Benet and Edward Carne, able and stout-hearted men, but of

93. *Sp. Cal.*, iv, 641.

small status – and, in the case of Benet, at least, secretly
friendly to Catherine.[94]

These two, supported by Ghinucci, Gregory Casale and
expensive, but not always helpful, counsel hired in Rome,
by occasional French intervention and frequent, but not
always judicious, irruptions by Henry, were required to
hold back the Imperialists, master the Curia and bring
to successful issue a case now so complicated that one can
only marvel that it did not wholly daunt them – a mere
archdeacon of Dorset and an unknown layman whose only
title was an Oxford doctorate in canon law.

They had a single purpose: to prevent the case being
heard in Rome and recover it for English judgement. 'We
would in any wise that all ways and means were used to
put over the process, as long as ye may, and until Michaelmas at the least',[95] Henry wrote in April 1531, and these
words were repeated in one form or another time and again.
Whatever happened, the case must not go forward. Carne,
the excusator, that is, the one who was to prove Henry ex-
cused from responding to Catherine's appeal, must convince
the Curia that the king could not come to Rome to answer
the citation. Shortly after the Rota began to move (in the
first months of 1531), Carne had opened his campaign with
an elaborate argument that Henry was prevented from coming to Rome by a 'necessary, probable, temporary impediment';[96] that not only could he not attend himself but that
the case was so grave that he could not be represented by

94. Chapuys said Benet eventually wrote to Catherine begging
pardon for what he had been required by duty to do against her
(*L.P.*, v, 696), and Clement said he confided in him his sorrow for
Henry's waywardness (ibid., 834).

95. *St.P.*, vii, 297 (*L.P.*, v, 206).

96. The impediment alleged was that the safety of the realm and
of Henry's person at this critical time prevented his attendance. The
argument, buttressed by a vast array of canonistic and civil learning,
was exactly chosen. The impediment was necessary, as distinct from
voluntary, because beyond Henry's control. Because it was not permanent, and contingent on circumstances (probable), Henry could
not be required to send a proxy.

a proctor; that Rome was suspect; that the case belonged to England and nowhere else.[97] However, because he had no powers to act as a proctor, or rather, because he said that he had none (whereas he had them only for use 'in extremity'[98]) Carne was not admitted by the Rota to present Henry's 'excuse' – which served him well enough because, if there were no respondent, the appeal could not be heard.[99] But it could also be dangerous – for the other side would now have a chance to demand judgement *per contradictas*, that is, to ask that, in view of the contumacy of the respondent, the appeal should be heard without him.[1] To block this dangerous counter-move, Carne promptly appealed against the Rota's refusal to admit him *sine mandato* (without proctorial powers), whereupon the Imperialists replied by asking for *apostoli refutatorii*, that is, letters of the court disallowing that appeal.[2] Thus, exactly as he wished, Henry's case quickly became bogged down in preliminaries, as the contestants argued about the validity of Carne's appeal against the Rota's decision not to admit him to present Henry's reasons for refusing to answer Catherine's appeal – all of which was nearly as fatal a quagmire as the arguments supporting Henry's claim (which the court had not yet begun to consider) that he was impeded from answering by a necessary, probable, temporary impediment. Moreover – and to make matters even more confused – before the *apostoli refutatorii* were obtained, the case had been taken to Consistory, where, in early 1531, Carne would spend many weeks and much energy trying to prove that he should be admitted to the Rota and setting out the arguments concerning Henry's impediment, his exemption from sending a proctor, the necessity of restor-

97. See *Acta Curiae Romanae in Causa Matrimoniale cum Catherina Regina* (1531) – an account of Carne's pleading in Consistory in February and March 1531.
98. *St.P.*, vii, 281 ff., 297 (*L.P.*, v, 93, 206).
99. *St.P.*, vii, 281 ff. (*L.P.*, v, 93); *L.P.*, v, 102; *Sp. Cal.*, iv, 630.
1. *L.P.*, v, 256; *Sp. Cal.*, iv, 659.   2. ibid., 654, 657; *L.P.*, v, 147.

ing the case to England, and so on; though in the meantime, before and after the long summer vacation, the case
was also being discussed in the Rota. Eventually, in
November 1531, that court gave final judgement that
Carne should not be admitted.[3] Here was crisis-point, for,
if this decision were ratified by Consistory, as it must and
probably would be, then there was a serious risk that Henry
would be declared contumacious for his failure to send a
proctor with full powers to answer in his name, and lose the
case *per contradictas*. Benet dashed home for further instructions while his colleagues in Rome made a blistering
counter-attack, declaring the Rota's decision invalid and
demanding that it be publicly disputed in Consistory by
experts hired by both sides.[4]

The English pinned their hopes on Consistory primarily
because, unlike the auditors of the Rota, many of the cardinals were not canonists and were men of the world susceptible to political pressure and cash.[5] Though they lacked
the support of an English cardinal or two, this, they judged,
was the weak point in their opponents' assault works and
here they should counter-attack. Hence, after intense
lobbying, they elbowed Clement into agreeing that the
question of Carne's admittance should be debated anew in
Consistory – despite the fact that the issues to be raised had
already been settled in the Rota. Of course it would take
time to gather materials and experts for the disputation
which they had demanded. The English asked for six
months; they were eventually granted two. Then the Imperialists tried to stop them hiring counsel in Bologna,
Padua and elsewhere; whereupon Carne was able to delay
matters further by appealing to Clement to intervene
against this obstruction. Clement refused to act on his own
initiative and referred the matter to Consistory, where
there began a new debate to decide whether experts could
be summoned thither by papal licence to discuss the decision that Carne should not be admitted to the Rota[6] – all

3. *L.P.*, v, 553.   4. ibid., 565, 586, 594.
5. ibid., v, 908.   6. *St.P.*, vii, 332 (*L.P.*, v, 731).

of which took so long that it was not until the end of February 1532 that the disputation itself could begin. Carne opened the latter by presenting twenty-five 'conclusions' concerning Henry's impediment, why he was not bound to send a proctor, why Rome was not safe, why the excusator was therefore to be admitted and so on, which were to be debated one by one at weekly Consistories.[7] Such an arrangement could have dragged out the disputation for months. The Imperialists demanded that the whole matter be settled at one session, *'precipitanter'*, Carne that the points should be heard *'singulariter'* – and so the argument went on until Clement intervened and declared that they should be taken three at a time.[8] Even so it was not until May 1532 that the end was reached, by which time, according to one cardinal, Consistory had long since been brought to screaming-point ('all the Consistory crieth out,' he said) by the intricacy of the case, the deviousness of the English and the loquacity with which, like many lawyers, they were endowed.[9] Not until June was final sentence given to the effect that the case was to be heard in the Rota (though the vacation was now at hand and nothing could be done until next term) and that an excusator who lacked proctorial powers could not be admitted. Henry was given until October to provide a mandated proctor and if he defaulted he must face the penalty of contumacy.[10] Carne had lost the round. But he had already held up the case for nearly eighteen months and now postponed its commencement a further four; he had inflicted a gruelling ordeal on his opponents and, if the case really began in October (1532), he could still pull the secret powers out of his pocket, step into the Rota and there begin another round of masterly obstruction. Clement told a Spanish cardinal that if Henry

7. *L.P.*, v, 835. For the 'conclusions' (i.e. articles), see *Ven. Cal.*, iv, 743.

8. *L.P.*, v, 895; *Sp. Cal.*, iv, 913.

9. *L.P.*, v, 895. See P.R.O. S.P. 1/69, fols 163 ff., 180 ff. (*L.P.*, v, 852, 867, for details of arguments produced by the English at the Consistories of 6 and 18 March).

10. *L.P.*, v, 1157, 1159.

had not come to heel by October then, without fail, the axe would fall;[11] but he was optimistic.

The campaign which Carne and the others conducted so skilfully was exactly what Henry required, and it was something at which he himself was adept. Henry knew as well as anyone how to blow hot and cold, how to dangle and exploit others, how to give in order to take, how to keep wheels turning without letting them go anywhere. In the hope of breaking the impasse, Clement had begun to talk of committing the cause to a place which both sides would accept as indifferent. This was not what Henry wanted (for he wanted somewhere 'safe' for himself) but, to use later words of his, 'the more dulcely to handle' the pope,[12] he told Benet to give the impression 'that we may hap to condescend' to the plan.[13] Perhaps encouraged by this pliancy, Clement then suggested Cambrai, an Imperial town but near England, as a suitable site. Henry did not explicitly reject what was an unacceptable proposal, but waited for Charles and Catherine, who were determined to have the case tried in Rome and nowhere else, to do that for him, as they did;[14] and just when the Imperialists were proving the more intransigent, Henry, who had hitherto demanded that the case be tried by the archbishop of Canterbury (alone or with the help of two or three fellow-bishops or abbots) or by the upper house of Convocation, now suggested that it might be entrusted to four judges sitting at Calais or Guines, one named by himself, one by Catherine or the emperor, one by Francis and one by the pope.[15] At first sight this looks like a major concession. Henry seems to have yielded to papal jurisdiction after all and to have yielded also in the matter of locale. But the proposed sites

11. *L.P.*, v, 1194.

12. *St.P.*, vii, 305 (*L.P.*, v, 327). Henry to Benet in July 1531.

13. *St.P.*, vii, 298 (*L.P.*, v, 206). Henry to Benet in April 1531.

14. *L.P.*, v, 352, 355. Cf. a report in early 1533 that Henry would agree to come to Cambrai (*L.P.*, vi, 23) – which was also another device for delay.

15. *St.P.*, vii, 305 ff. (*L.P.*, v, 327).

were, of course, both in English possession and, what was more, the pope's nominee was determined in advance. He was to be none other than Henry's subject, the archbishop of Canterbury! Such an arrangement would have cost Henry no real constitutional surrender and would have guaranteed him three voices out of four. Moreover, and this was probably the real motive for the proposal anyway, it would have consumed months of debate before Rome and Charles agreed to it.

By the summer of 1531, Henry was preparing new weapons. Twice, at his instance, deputations of councillors went to Catherine to persuade her to abandon her appeal and herself ask Rome to hand back the case. On both occasions she refused. She would not be used thus by her husband and stoutly repulsed her visitors.[16] At the same time the king softened his approach to Clement. Speak to the pope, he instructed his agents in Rome, in a way that implied that his wound was not too deep for time to heal; say that he trusted Clement still, that he would yet forgive him, that he blamed his evil counsellors, not him personally, and so on.[17] But Henry had not changed his heart, only his manner of speaking.

Early next year (1532), when he made what was in effect his last direct appeal to Rome, it was one concocted after the old manner. Carne was to demand once more, and yet more boldly, that he be admitted and to warn the Romans that, if they persisted in their course, they would do such damage as they would 'never be able afterwards to redub'. The pope knew that 'by God's law, the laws of nature and natural reason, the laws of emperors, the decrees of holy Councils, the constitutions of the canons and finally the whole consent of holy and well-learned men', his action stood condemned. If he persisted in flouting equity, universal justice, the law, the judgement of the world then, said Henry, descending rather quickly from the global to

16. *L.P.*, v, 287, 478.
17. ibid., 326; *St.P.*, vii, 305 ff. (*L.P.*, v, 327).

the particular, he was to be told that the citation which was delivered hither was invalid because issued *per edictas*, that is, as a public document, rather than delivered personally. If Henry had not been lawfully cited he could not be declared contumacious. Let the pope know that he would come to Rome in person – given sufficient warning – if Clement could prove three things: that the citation was valid, that the excusator ought not to be admitted, that Rome was safe.

This might seem a momentous change in royal policy, a signal of impending surrender. But it was said only to unsteady Clement and, as he himself conceded, thereby to cause the 'empeachment or at least the delay' of sentence. Having said that he would come to Rome if Clement could prove these three things, he declared in advance that the only proof which he would accept was the unanimous verdict of what he called 'indifferent universities'; and this verdict, he was confident, was unobtainable. Clement had to do what, as he said, 'we know is impossible for him to do'. If all this failed to halt the process, then tell Clement, Henry went on, to pass sentence of contumacy against him. It would be of no avail – for Henry would retort with an appeal to a General Council (and a draft of such an appeal was enclosed).[18]

It was at the end of this belligerent list of instructions that, at long last, there came from Henry's lips the real argument, the only argument (so it may be thought) against the validity of his marriage. If Clement were still unmoved, Carne was to tell him that in the fundamental matter of the marriage – which had long been buried under the argument concerning the excusator and questions of jurisdiction and procedures – justice was on Henry's side. If Catherine's first marriage was unconsummated there had never been an impediment of affinity between her and Henry; therefore the pope 'dispensed upon nothing, and so his bull was nothing worth; and consequently, for lack of

18. *St.P.*, vii, 352 ff. (*L.P.*, v, 836).

sufficient dispensation the marriage was not good, the impediment of justice of public honesty letting the same'. At
the trial before the legatine court (as records showed)
Catherine's counsel deliberately asserted that her first marriage *had* been consummated in order, Henry now said, to
protect her against this argument. Their assertion was perjured. Catherine's case must fall to the ground.[19]

Such was Henry's fourth and final salvo. At last, five
years too late, he had put to Rome what was probably the
only viable argument. Why he had not done so earlier is
difficult to say. So too is why he suddenly invoked it now
and why he failed, as he did, to use the argument to greater
advantage. Tentative answers to some of these questions
have been offered earlier.[20] We cannot answer the others.
We can only repeat that this is what he did.

To return to the question: how far had Henry broken
with his past, how deeply was he already committed to
carrying out an ecclesiastical revolution? Were the three
years, 1530 to 1532, years without a policy, years of aimless
bombast and bullying, of makeshift and fumbling?

It has been argued above that the struggle for the divorce
and the advance towards Henricianism – though obviously
intimately connected – are to be distinguished, even to the
extent of allowing that the latter could have occurred without the former, that even if there had been no divorce
Henry might yet have taken issue with the Church. But
Henricianism, the assertion of the true nature of Christian
monarchy, must in turn be dissected. The fully-grown
Royal Supremacy rested on, and proclaimed three principles: that the king had a direct, God-given cure of souls
of his subjects; that he was overlord of the clergy of the
national Church; that he owed no obedience to the bishop

19. *St.P.*, vii, 360. This passage (curiously) was repeated verbatim in
a letter sent to the English ambassador with the emperor in July (?)
1533. *Pocock*, ii, 495 (*L.P.*, vi, 775).

20. See above, pp. 258 ff.

of Rome. Clearly, these three were closely interconnected.
To assert any one explicitly was to assert the others implicitly; all three were aimed against the single monster,
clericalism; all three would bring to an end a usurpation
and restore a right order.

We have seen Henry advance the first claim, his pastoral
ambitions, since late 1529 – and seen it come to a climax
in early 1531 when the clergy were required, and refused,
openly to acknowledge the king's cure of souls. We have
seen the beginnings of the second, Henrician Erastianism
(which, like its predecessor, had little or nothing to do with
the divorce) during the first session of the Reformation
Parliament, in the attack on the Courts Christian in 1531,
in Henry's reply to Tunstal shortly afterwards, in his edit-
ing of Convocation's reform decrees; and it was to grow
steadily. We have seen the beginnings of anti-papalism –
from the late summer of 1530 – with the enunciation of
the claim to national autonomy on the one hand and the
imperial rights of the king on the other. The three ran
together, though sometimes only the third has received
much attention.

It is true that the road which led to the repudiation of
Rome and the proclamation of the Royal Supremacy was
a devious one. In the first place, it was not clear exactly
how the national immunity, the *privilegium Angliae*, was
related to the personal imperial claims of the king. Though
the two were invoked at about the same time, there was perhaps the germ of an important conflict here.[21] Secondly,
when Henry launched his campaign to recover his case
from Rome for English judgement, that is, when he sent
Carne and Benet to the Curia to resist Catherine's appeal
and force Clement to allow the suit to be heard in its
country of origin, his intentions were apparently ambiguous. On the one hand he was soon arguing that he could
not go to his Canossa, that for him to respond to Catherine's
appeal was conduct prejudicial to his imperial status, that

21. See below, pp. 508 ff.

the case belonged wholly to English judgement, that – as
the decrees of early councils and the rest proved – each
province of the Church was autonomous: in short, he
argued that his cause was no concern of Rome's whatsoever.
On the other hand he also advanced the much less stringent argument that the case should be returned to England
to be judged there by papal judges-delegate – which was
a very different proposition. Moreover, he could argue both
these things at the same time. On two occasions at least it
was proposed *in the same letter* that either Henry would
go ahead and settle his affair independently in his own
realm or Clement should be persuaded to commission, say,
the archbishop of Canterbury, or the upper house of Convocation, to handle it.[22] Had the latter course been agreed,
then Henry would have submitted his case to a tribunal
which was constitutionally no different from the legatine
court which had met at Blackfriars in 1529. As we have seen,
Henry's concern with the decretals of Innocent III sprang
from his desire to prove his right to having his case passed
back to England, to be tried there by papal commissioners;
and when the universities of Paris and Orleans declared
that Catherine's appeal was invalid, they added that
Henry's case ought to be heard *in partibus* (that is, in
England) by judges-delegate in accordance with common
practice – which clearly meant that the case would remain
within Rome's jurisdiction.[23] Though Henry allowed this to
be obscured, these university determinations in no way
supported any anti-papal particularism.

Thus at one moment Henry uttered the direct claims to
autonomy, while at the next, by demanding commissions
for his case to be heard in England, he implicitly acknowledged his complete dependence upon Rome's universal
jurisdiction. Which of these two, then, did he really want?

Probably as early as the autumn of 1530 he was already
largely committed to securing the first. England's autonomy,
his imperial dignity which admitted of no superior on earth

22. *L.P.*, iv, 6705; *L.P.*, v, 327.   23. *Rymer*, xiv, 416.

and could answer no tribunal on earth, the papal usurpation – these were the ideas which had pride of place, which
he shouted most loudly, for which he seemed to work most
strenuously.[24] Beneath the bluster and bluff there was
already a hard kernel of conviction which, despite hesitations and setbacks, would grow steadily until it achieved its
fullness in the breach with Rome and the act of Supremacy
in 1534. Over three years before this there had taken
root in Henry's mind and begun to grow into irrefutable
articles of faith the belief that the Early Church had been
innocent of a papacy as it now was, that local causes should
be settled locally by the clergy of the province, that the
Christian community had been set by God under the rule
of emperors and their successors. History and the fundamental law of Christendom, the 'laws of nature and natural
reason, the laws of emperors',[25] the canons of Nicea and
the other Councils, the judgement of the learned world
(that is of two universities – whom he certainly misrepresented) have swept all else aside. One should not ask how
he could have such faith in the righteousness of his cause;
it is enough to say that he knew it to be just and knew it
with the burning sincerity of an egoist who, having identi-
fied his own purposes with the divine will, now saw himself
not as one seeking personal advantage, but as the chosen
instrument of God commissioned to restore a right order
on earth and, as he said, to assert 'the immunities and
princely liberties of our realm and crown' which it was his
sacred duty, sealed before God by solemn oath at his
coronation, to uphold.[26]

What he really thought about Rome and the papal
primacy was stark enough. Let the pope do what he will,

24. For further examples of Henry talking (or being quoted as
talking) about his imperial authority and the privileges of the kingdom see *L.P.*, v, 206, 208, 327, 472, 478, 697, 836; *L.P.*, vi, 102, 194;
Sp. Cal., iv, i, 699, 853. These eleven occasions cover the period from
April 1531 to February 1533.

25. *St.P.*, vii, 354 (*L.P.*, v, 836), quoted above, p. 373.

26. *Burnet*, vi, 72 f. (*L.P.*, vi, 102). Henry in January 1533.

he shouted at the nuncio one day in June 1531, 'I shall never consent to his being judge in that affair [*sc.* the divorce]. Even if his holiness should do his worst by excommunicating me and so forth, I shall not mind it, for I care not a fig for all his excommunications. Let him follow his own at Rome, I will do here what I think best.'[27] The first deputation sent to Catherine (about the same time) explained to her that the king was now supreme in matters spiritual and temporal, as Parliament and the clergy had lately attested – a false account, this, of recent events.[28] A few weeks before, Henry had heard about a cleric who had been accused of heresy and, seeing that one of the articles objected against him was a denial of the papal primacy, had, it was reported, declared that this was no heresy and secured the man's release.[29] Maybe this was just bravado. But certainly Henry was acquiring a picture of the structure of Christendom that left little room for the papacy.

Probably from late 1530 or early 1531 he was beginning to see the Christian world, as he believed it had been in the first centuries, as a federation of autonomous churches whose government was committed by God to princes, beyond whom lay no appeal, from whom the local church depended; and this was how the Church in England should be organized. He must restore what had been usurped, rehabilitate what had been trampled down.

Of course he occasionally appeared to weaken. Sometimes it seemed that his violent words were mere bullying by a wilful man bent on snapping Clement's intransigence. But his retreats were tactical only. We have seen him play with the papal suggestions that the case should be heard at Cambrai, or suggest that it be tried before four judges, one of whom was to be named by the pope, or offer to come to Rome if Clement could prove those three things which, he said in advance, it was 'impossible for him to do'.[30] But all

27. *Sp. Cal.*, iv, 739. Henry will say several times that he does not fear excommunication (ibid., 853; *L.P.*, v, 148, 738).

28. *Sp. Cal.*, iv, 739.   29. *L.P.*, v, 148.   30. See above, pp. 373 f.

these devices to confuse the issue and gain time were part
and parcel of the intricate campaign of obstruction which
Benet and Carne had been conducting adeptly for months.
Similarly, in December 1531, Henry let it be known that his
case might be heard at, say, Avignon. He did not agree to
submit to judgement there – he merely said that this compromise solution (probably proposed by Rome) would be
thought by some less objectionable than being cited to the
Curia itself:[31] a very guarded move, doubtless designed to
gain more time and prompted by a brief from Clement
(brought home by Benet) warning the king that he could
wait no longer and must finally settle Catherine's appeal.
Though Henry may now have been less forthright than he
had been in late 1530, his ambitions had not abated and he
had disowned nothing. Nor should we be impressed by his
occasional displays of friendliness, even remorse, towards
Rome – as when he denied to the nuncio all intention of
setting up a *'nouvelle papalité'* in England or when, as he
did, he made a friendly reply to Clement's announcement
of a forthcoming General Council and promised his support.[32] He had every motive for occasionally putting on an
amiable front.

Throughout these months, Henry was determined to stop
any action against him by Rome. At all costs he must prevent the catastrophe of a decision for Catherine by the Rota
and he must hold off Clement from uttering any censures
against him – for either of these would encourage the queen
and her party, and probably cause him international embarrassment. But this still leaves unexplained his ultimate
purpose. Why did he want to gain time? Not because he

31. *Pocock*, ii, 148 (*L.P.*, v, 610); *L.P.*, v, 611. I do not feel the force
of the argument, therefore, that this suggestion represents Henry's
final failure to cope with his divorce problem, as Dr Elton argues in
'King or Minister? The Man behiind the Henrician Reformation',
History, xxxix (1954), 228 f.

32. *St.P.*, vii, 284 f. (*L.P.*, v, 97).

had no solution to his problem, but more probably because he did not yet dare to implement it.

Where did Henry acquire all that talk about the customs and privilege of England? Whence his claims to imperial status? Who told him about Innocent III, Nicea, Cyprian and Bernard? Who suggested the search in the papal registers? Who was feeding him with these ideas? Who was behind him at that critical time in the summer of 1530 when so much seems first to have taken root? We cannot know. Some may feel that several of these new ideas were brash enough to have been Henry's own – and no better explanation can be given here. But perhaps the question of genesis is more intriguing than important. What really matters is the certainty that, whatever their source, Henry soon made them his own. It is clear that, as never before, Henry was now in control – and that he was the effective pace-maker. We have seen Benet and Carne taken aback by the violence of royal instructions to them (which, if not dictated verbatim by the king, must have represented his mind). Chapuys and the nuncio so often found him full of invective against the pope and the clergy, so full of threats, so bent on having his way, that it is difficult not to believe that his was the main thrust behind policy.[33] On at least three occasions, after Henry had lashed the nuncio with wild words, the duke of Norfolk intervened to soothe the baron. Once, after del Burgo had been particularly set upon, the duke swore that Henry would not carry out a threat just uttered; once he begged him to discount the king's violent words, promising to take good care that they would be forgotten by their author; once, having made excuses for Henry, he begged the nuncio not to report to Rome what the king had said.[34] Was this part of an act, or did it mean that Henry was driving at least one of his ministers at a frightening pace? Henry was so much in evidence now,

33. See, for example, reports by the papal nuncio and Chapuys, in *Sp. Cal.*, iv, 429, 433, 460, 739, 853.

34. ibid., 433, 492, 522.

was so often to be heard shouting and threatening, the
fierce letters to Rome so clearly bore his mark, that it must
be reasonable to propose him as the effective author (which
is not to call him the absolute initiator) of policy during
these years.

That policy yielded no fruit. In the first place it was
apparently too shocking and novel for most of his subjects.
Twice in 1530, first in June and then in October, Henry
called a gathering of notables to court to ask them
whether they would agree that he should disregard Rome
and have the divorce settled once and for all in England,
by the English clergy; and on both occasions he met refusal.
He was running ahead of at least some of his subjects (not
of all of them, by any means) and, although angered by
the rebuff, dared not force the issue.[35] He had met, and
would meet again, keen opposition in Convocation and, to
make matters yet worse, had failed to find any convincing
evidence of his imperial dignity. A rasher man might have
struck out for truth regardless of these setbacks, but Henry
bided his time, waiting for the impasse to dissolve. If, to
stave off a fatal counter-move, he occasionally tempered the
wind of revolution and allowed it to be thought that he
would yet submit to papal jurisdiction, this was probably
above all due to the lack of solid support for the revolution

35. Cf. the interesting episode which Chapuys recorded in early
February 1532 – much later. A number of notables was assembled at
Norfolk's London residence and told by the duke that Rome had no
jurisdiction over the king's case not only on account of the 'privileges
of England', but also because, as certain doctors declared, matrimonial causes belonged to the temporal, not the spiritual, jurisdiction. The duke also spoke of Henry's imperial authority. When he
asked for the approval of those present, Lord Darcy (a prime mover
of the Pilgrimage of Grace) replied that he thought that matters
matrimonial evidently pertained to the spiritual – and most, said
Chapuys, agreed with him. Maybe if other sorts of people had been
interrogated on this and the previous occasions they would have
given different replies. Maybe the judges and bishops and nobles
who spoke then were untypical and (as it was to prove) comparatively
uninfluential conservatives; but their conservatism was nonetheless
real. For this meeting in February 1532, see *L.P.*, v, 805.

at home. If he followed ancient procedure and procured appointment of new bishops to English sees, this was because there was as yet no alternative course of action. Not until early 1532 did he begin to claim the right to appoint bishops on his own authority. But, behind the screen of apparent pliancy and uncertainty, his anti-papalism and anticlericalism stood firm. From late 1530 until early 1532 (and, of course, beyond) he continued to talk confidently about the national privilege and his own imperial dignity.[36] In November 1530 he told the Imperial ambassador that the right of convoking a General Council lay with the secular princes, not the pope, and that the latter was no more above a Council than he was above princes; that it would be doing God's service to take away the clergy's temporal possessions; that he had no need of a Council for, like any prince, he could redress the evils of his own country without intervention from without.[37] In April 1531 he interrupted a preacher who, in his presence, said that Constantine had refused to judge a dispute between two bishops – saying loudly that this was a lie. And when the preacher stood his ground, Henry walked out.[38] A little later, in July 1531, he refused entry into England to the abbot of Chalais who had been sent by the general chapter of the Cistercians to visit houses of that order in England, saying that none could meddle in the affairs of his kingdom, that he was king and emperor and had full spiritual jurisdiction in his land. Though the abbot was allowed to pass through England to visit Scottish Cistercian houses, in April 1532 five English abbots were commissioned, under the great seal, that is on royal authority, to visit all the Cistercian houses in the king's domains – on the ground that it would be inconvenient to allow a foreigner to perform this task.[39]

36. See above, p. 378 n. 24.
37. *Sp. Cal.*, iv, 492. He also said that Charles should grant the Lutheran request to have the clergy stripped of their temporalities.
38. *L.P.*, v, 216.
39. ibid., 361, 494 (2), 978 (6). English monasticism was, therefore, being 'nationalized'. This process was completed by the act of Dispensations of 1534. See below, p. 422 n. 63.

Certainly the Royal Supremacy was not born fully-fledged. It took three or four years to grow to full maturity and become a comprehensive doctrine. But by the end of 1530 Henry was already largely committed to it. He knew what he wanted – in broad terms. From the talk in 1530 about the prerogatives of the realm and of Henry's imperial rights it is not a large step to the statement of 1533 that 'this realm of England is an empire'; the proclamation of the Royal Supremacy in 1534 was no more than the fulfilment of Henry's assertion of his cure of souls, of a prince's right to reform his clergy and summon a General Council, of the clerical estate's dependence upon his authority – all of which he had claimed (and more than claimed) since 1529 and 1530. As early as September 1530, Henry showed that he understood the procedure by which his claims must finally be vindicated. Speaking to Chapuys, he said that he would never allow his case to be brought before any papal judge and that, if Clement refused to allow it to be tried by English judges, 'having fulfilled my duty to God and my conscience . . . I will appeal to Parliament for a decision which that body cannot fail to give'.[40] At the assembly of clerics and lawyers which he summoned in the following month he had asked whether Parliament could authorize the English clergy to flout Rome and settle his cause on their own authority. He would not have to be shown, later on, how to use the legislature to give legal force to his claims. He had perceived this long before. He had the will and he understood the constitutional, legislative implications – that Parliament would finally declare and make enforceable the new order. All that was lacking, probably, was something in between: the nerve to act, the *pièce justificative*, the support. He had not yet been able to find *proof* of what he asserted and what he claimed – proof that would carry his subjects and convince the world.

These, then, were not years without a policy, but years without a successful one. When success came in 1533 and

40. *Sp. Cal.*, iv, i, 433.

1534 there was still no very solid proof offered. Indeed, the opening of the act of Appeals, referring to 'divers sundry old authentic histories and chronicles', is almost laughably vague. What is new is not so much the sandcastle itself as the indifference to its being made of sand. Many more months of waiting, frustration and pressure, of reiteration of what was then a novelty and fast became normal, and finally the decisive event of Anne's pregnancy made his subjects less exacting and Henry less sensitive either to them or the demands of historicity.[41]

But Henry's dispute with Rome concerned jurisdiction. He might still have allowed Rome a primacy of honour and a very limited, strictly spiritual authority (according to the definition of 'spiritual' which he gave to Tunstal). As the duke of Norfolk explained to Chapuys in January 1531, the pope had no jurisdiction save in matters of heresy; all the rest was usurped (and Henry's letter to Tunstal a few weeks later would accommodate this thesis).[42] A year later, in early 1532, Henry stated himself clearly to the same effect. True enough, he said, the pope was 'in the whole congregation of Christian men ... a chief and a principal member', but he 'hath attained and forged himself such a throne and power as soundeth greatly to the blasphemy of Christ and his very Church'.[43] Henry would allow the pope, then, but not the papacy. He rejected papal authority 'as it is now used'.[44] He might yet have settled for a radical concordat with Rome which would virtually have annihilated papal authority in England but avoided outright schism. He was preaching an English Gallicanism, of a thorough kind; an ecclesiology with which, in part, William of Ockham would have felt sympathy – as too some orthodox Christians, and some modern non-Catholics – which would leave Rome little more than an honorific, charismatic role

41. *Sp. Cal.*, iv, i, 460.   42. *L.P.*, v, 45.
43. *St.P.*, vii, 358 f. (*L.P.*, v, 836).
44. To quote a phrase of his from early 1533. *Burnet*, vi, 73 (*L.P.*, vi, 102).

at the centre of the communion of virtually autonomous
national churches and a Christendom possessed of a largely invisible unity; though with this difference – that what
Rome shed the king himself would put on.

The Henrician Reformation was a movement of inexplicable halts and starts, sudden hesitation and zig-zagging.
At almost every point of the story there are unanswerable
questions – why exactly the Reformation Parliament was
summoned, how exactly its first legislation came into being,
why Parliament did not meet during 1530, what the purpose was of the *praemunire* indictment of the whole clergy,
how and why it was decided to attack the Courts Christian
at that moment, why the clergy were so easily pardoned
and then suddenly attacked once more, why no further
move was made in 1531. And the questions come equally
thick and fast thereafter – in 1532 and 1533, and beyond.
But this is not to deny the overall purposiveness of these
years. They were as was Henry himself – belligerent and
outwardly confident, yet nervous and uncertain; and they
were thus precisely because he dominated them.
Even if Rome, say in 1531, had surrendered to him and
declared his marriage null and void, or handed back his
case to English judgement, there could have been no going
back to the old ways, no refilling of Pandora's box. Matters
had gone too far. Henry had passed beyond the immediate
problem of his marriage, important though this still was,
into larger and yet graver issues. He had begun to discover
truths about Christian kingship which had hitherto been
hidden from him and which he could not now revoke. If
Rome came to her senses and surrendered before the manifest justice of his case then he might have allowed her to
salvage something from the debris. It is quite possible that
this is what he expected would happen. As, during 1530,
1531 and 1532, Henry and his dogged agents at Rome
twisted and shilly-shallied, and drove the Curia to near
dementia with their endless dialectic, Henry may well have

been (in part) gaining time in the hope that, sooner or later, sooner rather than later, Clement would put aside what he diagnosed as purblind obstinacy and pusillanimity, and accede to justice. But if Rome did not concede him a blood-less victory, then he might easily destroy yet more than, in 1531 or early 1532, he intended.

Though he had reached an impasse in the campaign for the divorce and though his attempt to establish his imperial dignity had stalled, this did not halt the onward march of his Erastianism against the clerical estate in England. On 8 February 1532 the attorney general laid in the King's Bench *quo warranto* indictments against six laymen and sixteen clerics – who included the archbishop of Canterbury, the bishop of Bangor, seven heads of religious houses and three principals of colleges – charging them to answer 'by what warrant' they enjoyed such private jurisdiction as the right to hold assizes of bread and ale, to seize treasure trove, to return writs, to appoint coroners, etc.[45] The privileges and franchises concerned were trivial – the common appurtenances of lords of manors and private hundreds, lay and clerical – and, in themselves, of no great moment. But that so large a number of illustrious clerics should suddenly be attacked with the ancient weapon of *quo warranto* at this moment strongly suggests official malice. Possibly, despite the presence of the six laymen among the indicted, this assault was to prepare the way for legislation which would clean away perhaps all such petty, local jurisdiction of territorial lordship enjoyed by clerics,[46] and, like the *praemunire* campaign preceding

45. P.R.O. K.B. 9/518, fols 1 ff. for the indictments. The religious houses concerned were the abbeys of Bruton, Eynsham, Walden, Glastonbury and St Alban's, and the priories of Tynemouth and St Helen's Bishopsgate (a nunnery); the colleges concerned were All Souls, Oxford; Queens', Cambridge; St Mary's, Winchester. The remaining four clerics were Richard Pace, dean, and three prebends of St Paul's.

46. A document dating from early 1533 lists bills left over from the previous parliamentary session, including one dealing with 'the re-

the Pardon of the clergy twelve months or so before, act as
a softening-up bombardment before a new frontal attack
on their ecclesiastical jurisdiction. The bill to abolish their
secular franchises never materialized; but the royal assault
on their spiritual liberties did.

The weapons which Henry used – the famous *Supplication against the Ordinaries*, a long list of complaints against
the workings of the ecclesiastical courts, clerical fees, frivolous excommunication and tithes – had a complex history.
It may have begun its life in the first session of the Reformation Parliament in 1529 and been intended as a companion
piece to the petition presented to the king complaining of
clerical misdemeanours which resulted in the anticlerical
acts of that year;[47] or it may have started its life when the
commons reassembled for the second session in early 1531
– but without coming to fruition.[48] When Parliament resumed in 1532, however, the commons spontaneously returned to bitter discussion of their complaints against

sumption of the liberties etc. of the prelates'. P.R.O. S.P. 1/74, fol.
146 (*L.P.*, vi, 120). This must refer to the franchises which had recently
been challenged in the King's Bench, and may well have been a comprehensive clearing away of all local territorial rights enjoyed by the
clergy rather than those of only the actual victims of the *quo
warranto* attack (which, incidentally, petered out rather inconclusively. For the subsequent history of these cases, see P.R.O. K.B.
27/1083 ff.; K.B. 29/164 ff.)
  47. As Dr Elton argues in 'The Commons' Supplication of 1532.
Parliamentary Manoeuvres in the reign of Henry VIII', 515 ff.
  48. There is no *explicit* evidence that the Supplication, or rather,
the grievances contained therein, was discussed in 1529. But Chapuys
reported on 8 March 1531 that Parliament was occupying its time
with, among other things, hearing complaints against the clergy –
which could fit the future Supplication very well. When he wrote a
week before that Henry had been down to the lords for one and a
half hours on the previous evening and urged them to discuss the
privileges and immunities of the Church which sheltered malefactors
and which he was determined to put down, the ambassador was
alluding to the discussion of sanctuaries. But the commons might
easily have been encouraged to air their 'griefs' about ecclesiastical
courts. See *Sp. Cal.*, iv, i, 646, 648.

Church courts and the rest. On 18 March the final draft of
the *Supplication* which Cromwell had seen through its
several preliminary stages[49] – and then handed back to the
commons – was presented to the king. Probably it was not
yet clear what precise use was to be made of this document.
The commons wanted a reformation of their 'griefs' and
doubtless expected that the *Supplication* would produce
legislation in the same way as had their petition of 1529;
but – and this was an incongruity which Henry remarked
somewhat tartly – at the same time they requested that
Parliament should adjourn for Easter, before they had
passed a government bill concerning wards and primer
seisin.[50] However, on 12 April (by which time Parliament
had resumed), the *Supplication* was laid before Convocation, having been passed thither by the king. About a fortnight later the clergy's reply to the long list of complaints,
a strong unyielding document, came back to Henry who,
on 30 April, handed it on to the speaker with the words 'we
think their answer will smally please you, or it seemeth to
us very slender'.[51] Then, after the commons had agreed
with Henry and found the reply of the ordinaries 'sophisti-
cal', and the latter had been asked for a fuller answer to the
first article of the *Supplication*, the story took a new and
decisive turn. On 10 May Convocation received a royal
demand to subscribe to the following articles: that all
future clerical legislation should receive the king's assent;
that all obnoxious constitutions from the past should be
annulled by a royal committee of thirty-two persons; that
all which were approved by it should henceforth stand by
virtue of royal assent.[52] By a process still not clear, these
three demands were drawn out of the long list of popular

49. Elton, 'The Commons' Supplication of 1532, etc.'.
50. *Hall*, 784; Cooper, 'The Supplication against the Ordinaries Reconsidered', *E.H.R.*, lxxii (1957), 616 ff., which criticizes Dr Elton's
argument. I have followed Mr Cooper on several points.
51. *Hall*, 788. For the *Answer* of the ordinaries, see Gee and Hardy,
Documents Illustrative of English Church History (1896), 154 ff.
52. *Wilkins*, iii, 749.

complaints and effectively set them aside. The Commons'
Supplication had been replaced by a royal ultimatum –
precisely how, when and by whom cannot be told.

There followed now five days of hectic manoeuvring.
Warham, the archbishop of Canterbury, had already
crossed swords with Henry – when he denounced the king's
policies some weeks before, and then drove at the heretical
royal protégé, Latimer, and tried to destroy him – in defiance of repeated counter-action by Stokesley and Gardiner
(acting presumably for the king) – and shortly the archbishop would be faced with a patently trumped-up *praemunire* charge.[53] Amidst an atmosphere of mounting
tension and incipient violence, Convocation first fought
back hard against Henry's latest thrust and refused the
king's three demands; whereupon, Henry summoned a delegation from Parliament and, holding a copy of the oath
to the pope which all bishops took, spoke the following:
'well-beloved subjects, we thought that the clergy of our
realm had been our subjects wholly, but now we have well
perceived that they be but half our subjects, yea, and scarce
our subjects'. The king thereupon handed the deputation
a copy of the oath (and of the oath which bishops took to
the king) for them to peruse, and sent them away 'to invent some order, that we be not thus deluded of our
spiritual subjects'[54] – by which he apparently meant them to
attend to the passage of an act of Parliament abolishing
clerical legislative independence (an act which was drafted,
but, in the event, never passed).[55] Never before had Henry
so imperiously thrust himself forward as an enemy of the
clergy as now, 11 May 1532, when he stood before the
speaker and his companions, fingering the bishops' oath to

53. Kelly, 'The Submission of the Clergy', *T.R.H.S.*, 5th ser., xv
(1965), 103 ff. See below, p. 430, for Warham's *praemunire* charge.
54. *Hall*, 788.
55. P.R.O. S.P. 2/L, fols 78 ff. and S.P. 2/P, fols 17 ff. (*L.P.*, v, 721
(i); vii, 57 (2) – misplaced) for drafts thereof. Very probably the bill
came before Parliament, since, on 13 May, Chapuys reported that that

the see of Peter and insinuating treason. Two days later a
new draft of the demands was sent to Convocation, and
met firm reply; further drafts followed on the morning of
15 May and in the afternoon. Parliament had been adjourned hastily on the previous day and Convocation was
similarly threatened. Norfolk, the two Boleyns and three
other lay peers came to the clergy to hustle them into final
submission.[56]

During these few days the bishops were fighting for their
lives. A week before, on 8 May (probably), they presented a
'book' to the king setting out the Scriptural basis of their
claim to legislative immunity, and their first reply to the
royal ultimatum, though making the near-fatal concession
to the king that all future ecclesiastical laws directly affect-
ing the laity, i.e. not those touching faith and morals and the
correction of sin (an obscure distinction), should be submitted to his scrutiny, resolutely refused the rest of his demands and even referred him to what he himself had written
about clerical immunity in his *Assertio*, which 'we reckon
that of your honour you cannot, nor of your goodness you
will not, revoke'.[57] Up to the last moment, therefore, the
bishops, or at least many of them, consistently opposed
Henry's advance. Henry won no easy victory over the
Church – and it is small wonder that, during the previous
eighteen months, he had found it prudent, indeed necessary,
to hold much of his fire and proceed with cautious hesitancy
as he set out to achieve his complex revolution.

Late on 15 May, however, after days of pummelling, the

body was about to reduce churchmen to a status lower 'than that of
shoemakers' (*L.P.*, v, 1013) – which would have been a way, and a
typical one, for him to describe it. If it did come before Parliament
it must have been dropped within a few days – further evidence of
official uncertainty and hesitation. For more remarks on this draft
bill see below, p. 513.

56. Kelly, art. cit., 113 ff.

57. *Wilkins*, iii, 753 f. In this reply, the bishops refer to the book
(which has disappeared) of which mention has been made. Cf. *Hall*,
788.

upper house of Southern Convocation surrendered. Henceforth, they promised, no Convocation would be assembled
except by royal writ and no new canons enacted without
royal assent; and all existing canons were to be submitted
for scrutiny by a royal committee of thirty-two persons, half
of them lay, half clerical. Henry had bludgeoned his way
to victory over the spiritualty. But Convocation's surrender
was not approved by its lower house; of the upper, eight
bishops were absent (including Fisher, then ill at Rochester),
three consented with reservations (including Longland of
Lincoln and Stokesley of London) and Clerk of Bath and
Wells refused outright. Only three bishops, therefore, gave
unequivocal assent – Warham and the bishops of Exeter
and Ely. It was a battered minority, a 'Rump' Convocation,[58] which on 15 May yielded to the king the clergy's
precious freedom of legislation. Next day, Thomas More
resigned the chancellorship which he could no longer, in
conscience, retain.

The Submission of the Clergy was not used, and was
probably never intended, to serve the cause of the divorce
by intimidating Clement because, as has been said more
than once, the royal programme was considerably larger
than merely a quest for the solution of a matrimonial
problem.[59] The latter still mattered, of course, and still
shaped policy. In late February of this year, a bill threatening to halt the payment of annates to Rome (i.e. fees paid
by bishops when provided by Rome to their sees) and to
allow bishops to be appointed to English sees without
Rome's provision had come before Parliament. Henry later

58. The phrase, and the remarkable facts (just cited) which justify
it, are Dr Kelly's (art. cit., 116 f.).

59. The surprise which some have expressed at the fact that the
Submission was not so employed is needless. It springs from an
exaggerated concern with the divorce – that is, from the conviction
that, somehow, everything that Henry did between 1527 and, say,
1533, was primarily directed towards breaking his matrimonial knot.
But Henry never had, and certainly had not now, a one-track mind.
The *idée fixe* was not his.

claimed that the act was popular in origin.[60] Certainly there
may have been much support for a plan to halt the flow of
English cash to foreign parts, for this had long been found
objectionable. But no less certainly the bill, however much
it sprang from, and exploited, popular feeling, was essentially a 'government' production. In its final form it provided that henceforth only five per cent of the first year's
income should be paid by any new bishop by way of
annates, that any nominee to a see who was denied his
bulls from Rome because he refused full payment of his
taxes should nonetheless be consecrated by his metropolitan
and that no riposte by Rome in the shape of excommunication or interdict should take effect in the kingdom. However, the act was not to come into force for a year and even
then it would be for the king to determine whether it
should become law. If Rome acceded to Henry's wishes,
therefore, its supply of revenue from England would not be
interrupted; if Rome refused to yield, the king would cast
off his friendly ways and strike her hard.

It met strong opposition in the House of Lords, where all
the bishops and two abbots, supported by but a single lay
peer, opposed it, and passed only after Henry had been
down to Parliament three times. It met trouble in the lower
house, too, where the proviso that, even if the act came into
force, the pope should still receive five per cent of his previous income, was added; and it only passed there after
the first recorded division of the house.[61]

Shortly after it became law, Henry sent a copy to his
agents in Rome to show the pope and cardinals – together
with a menacing letter in which the latter were invited to

60. *L.P.*, v, 832; *St.P.*, vii, 362 (*L.P.*, v, 886). In a sense he was right.
The bill sprang from a (perhaps) genuine petition (for text, see
Wilkins, iii, 755) – but the petition did not envisage the use of the
halting of annates as a means of bullying Clement into compliance.
61. *L.P.*, v, 832, 898. All the spiritual lords (apparently) opposed
the act of Citations when it passed the upper house – an act restrict-
ing the power of archbishops to summon laymen out of their diocese
except on certain specific matters (appeal, heresy, probate); *ibid.*, 879.

see that it was for them either to ward off the act, or, by
their own wantonness, to bring it down on their heads. He
had only done what justice and public clamour against an
old grievance required. Truth and justice came first, he said,
friendship second. It was for the pope and cardinals to
show whether they wanted to keep his friendship, by themselves acting towards him according to truth and justice.[62]

Thus a new technique had been found for cajoling Rome.
Three days before this letter was written, Henry had received the commons' *Supplication against the Ordinaries*
and thereby set out to grapple a second time with Convocation. By this time also, Thomas Cromwell, the minister
who would bring the royal campaign to final victory, had
moved into the centre of policy-making.

He was born in Putney about 1485. Of his early life little
is known, except that he received some legal training,
travelled in Italy and the Netherlands, and sat in the House
of Commons in 1523. Some time thereabouts, like so many
others who served the king in church and state in the 1530s
and 40s, he entered Wolsey's household – for about fifteen
years the true seat of royal government – and (among other
things) was particularly concerned with the suppression of
the twenty-nine religious houses which supplied the cardinal's school at Ipswich and college at Oxford. Wolsey's fall
brought him anxious moments; but on the day before
the Reformation Parliament met he was hurriedly elected
burgess for Taunton and thus began a new stage of his
career. Probably in late January 1530 he entered royal service – though exactly how and when he became the object of the king's favour is not clear – and was employed as
a link between the court and his former master. By the end
of 1530 he was sworn of the king's Council; by the end of
the next year he was moving from the position of a lesser
royal servant to that of a leading councillor. By early 1533
he was the king's chief minister. He had been made
master of the king's jewels and keeper of the Hanaper of

62. *St.P.*, vii, 360 ff. (*L.P.*, v, 886).

Chancery in April and July 1532; in April 1533 he became chancellor of the Exchequer (at that time a second-rank official). About twelve months later he received the office of principal secretary – one which he would do much to invest with major political significance – and, in the following October, that of master of the Rolls. Finally (for the moment), he was appointed lord privy seal in July 1536.

In riding to high place, he overtook Stephen Gardiner, bishop of Winchester and another of Wolsey's protégés, and one who had seemed well set for pre-eminence, as well as brushing aside the duke of Norfolk, who, with Gardiner and the duke of Suffolk, took first place about the king during the months following Wolsey's fall. Far from being the ruthless Machiavellian of legend, Cromwell was a man possessed of a high concept of the 'state' and national sovereignty, and a deep concern for Parliament and the law; an administrative genius; one who may have lacked profound religious sense (though instinctively favourable to some kind of Erasmian Protestantism), but something of an idealist nonetheless. That the 1530s were a decisive decade in English history was due largely to his energy and vision. He was immediately responsible for the vast legislative programme of the later sessions of the Reformation Parliament – a programme not rivalled in volume and moment until the nineteenth or even twentieth centuries. He oversaw the breach with Rome and the establishment of the Royal Supremacy. He effected a new political integration of the kingdom and imposed upon it a new political discipline by making war on local franchises and the entrenched bastard feudalism of the northern and western marches, handling the final incorporation of Wales into English political life and giving Ireland a foretaste of determined English overlordship. He directed the immense operation of the dissolution of the monasteries. He was either the direct or posthumous founder of the two Courts (we would say ministries) of Augmentations and First Fruits, which handled the new income from the dissolved

religious houses and the secular Church, and the two courts
of Wards and Surveyors, which were designed to exploit
more efficiently the crown's feudal rights and lands. Indeed,
he left a deep mark on much of the machinery of central
and local government. Finally, he was the first royal servant fully to perceive the power of that young giant, the
printing-press, and, when the time came to launch a large-
scale propaganda campaign on behalf of the new order,
supervised the first effort by an English government to
shape public opinion.[63]

He won primacy of place by virtue of his outstanding
qualities and he served his prince with tireless zeal. His
relations with Henry are impossible to establish with final
certainty, and any verdict thereon must be somewhat tentative. Henry remained what he had always been – often
helpless without his servants about him, erratic in signing
or reading important correspondence, uninterested in day-
to-day administration. But the impression remains that a
king who had so evidently been absorbed in the conduct
of his affairs during the years between Wolsey's fall and
Cromwell's final ascent did not allow the latter, or any
subsequent minister, the freedom which the cardinal had
once enjoyed. The testimony of ambassadors and the admittedly patchy evidence of the state papers suggest that
Henry never sank back into that carefree unconcern which
had marked the sunny days of the first years of his reign;
and though Cromwell's care of his master's business was
all-embracing and immediate, this does not mean that he
had ultimate responsibility for all policy. At least as far
as the central event of the 1530s is concerned, namely, the
establishment of the Royal Supremacy, he was the execu-

63. The *locus classicus* for Cromwell's career as an administrator
is Elton, *The Tudor Revolution in Government*. On other aspects
which Dr Elton has written about, see Bibliography. But see also the
criticisms put forward by Harriss and Williams in 'A Revolution in
Tudor History?', *Past and Present*, 25 (1963). An excellent short survey of Cromwell's whole career is to be found in Dickens, *Thomas
Cromwell and the English Reformation* (1959).

tant of the king's designs. In executing them he doubtless left his own imprint on them. It was for him to convert them into statutory form, to give them precision and draw out their full meaning. He may have determined timing and sequence, shown what was possible and what was not, what was necessary and what was not, and intervened with decisive suggestions. But he neither worked alone nor was the true initiator of these royal undertakings.

[10]

The Royal Supremacy

HENRY did two imprudent things to Wolsey. The first was to ignore him when he perceived a possible truth about the invalidity of the royal marriage; the second, to destroy him. Without Wolsey, as the stalemate of 1530–32 showed, Henry was ill-equipped to manipulate the Curia and, more precisely, the sovereign body of Consistory. He had thrown away the only man who might have redeemed the situation – and, try as he might, he could not make good his powerlessness. He tried desperately hard (as he and Wolsey had been trying since 1528) to secure a red hat for Ghinucci, the absentee bishop of Worcester and an auditor of the *Camera Apostolica*, but the Imperialist party saw the point and blocked him. He tried to gain a red hat for his good friend Gregory Casale, but the Casale family rallied to oppose this; he tried to do the same for Gianbattista Casale, for Giberti (bishop of Verona), for Stephen Gardiner – always without success.[1] Cardinals were more easily unmade than made. Henry's inability to build up a dependable, influential party in Consistory showed how little leverage he had, how little bargaining power other than bald threats, which a sophisticated pope was not likely to find impressive.

In his frustration he turned to Francis I for aid. By a happy coincidence, in 1530 France acquired two new cardinals: one no less a person than Gabriel de Grammont, bishop of Tarbes, the man who was alleged to have raised the first doubts about the validity of Henry's marriage three years before; the other the great ecclesiastic, François de Tournon. Henry would therefore look to his brother king and these two cardinals to lead his campaign against the Curia in his

1. See *L.P.*, iv, 5025, 5427, 6322, 6735; v, 1036, 1522. *Ven. Cal.*, iii, 635. *Ehses*, 80. B.M. Add., 48,044, fol. 28v.

name and be his instruments – and who could act for Henry more appropriately than Grammont? Nor was this to be mere casual support given by a casual third party. By the summer of 1531, four or five months after Henry had formally asked for French aid, the English envoys in France had suggested that the two kings should meet in person once more to re-enact the scenes of the Field of Cloth of Gold and thus commit Francis to public espousal of the cause. Though he later tried to disguise the fact, the initiative for this meeting certainly came from Henry. It was not favourably received at first. Indeed, it was met by rumours of a meeting between Francis and Charles that would have left Henry finally isolated and, for the moment, brought him near to a paroxysm of anxiety.[2] But he pressed on – with flattery, threats and pleas – hoping against hope that somehow the diplomatic situation would shift and allow his plan to be achieved.

By the spring of 1532 it was beginning to do so; by the summer the royal meeting was agreed and the elaborate preparations for shipping food and furnishing, including (once more) Henry's bed, across the Channel were in hand. On 20 October the two monarchs were embracing one another about half-way between Calais and Boulogne.

Henry had spent the summer, as was his wont, on progress. On Sunday 1 September, he came to Windsor to confer on Anne her first public mark of favour, the title of marquis of Pembroke (not marchioness, because she held the title in her own right) and lands to the value of £1,000 per annum to support her estate. She came in procession to the king, knelt before him and heard the bishop of Winchester read the patent of creation.[3] Then Henry invested her with her mantle and coronet and, having thus bestowed a remarkable honour upon a woman whose exact status it was not easy to define, rode off to Mass. From Windsor he moved to celebrations at Greenwich, and from Greenwich came to

2. See e.g. B.M. Add., 48,044, fols 10 f., 57 ff. Cf. *L.P.*, v, 791.
3. *L.P.*, v, 1274. *Hall*, p. 790.

Canterbury, en route for Dover. By 10 October the royal party and an entourage of over 2,000 persons were ready to embark, despite the plague and despite the anxiety of some at the prospect of the king facing the Channel crossing so near winter-time. Early next day Henry boarded the *Swallow*, and four hours later, for the third time in his life, stepped ashore at Calais with Anne and most of the pride of England at his side.[4] Catherine meanwhile languished at Bugden, having been constrained to surrender much of her jewellery for the adornment of the new marquis, who now lived like a queen and accompanied Henry everywhere.[5]

By 19 October Francis I had come to Boulogne. Next day, both monarchs set out for their carefully planned rendez-vous. As with the encounter twelve years before, there was much anxiety on both sides lest one should outdo the other, and every episode, every move, was hedged about by elaborate, calculated protocol. At last the two kings met at the appointed spot with flamboyant cordiality and rode in triumph to Boulogne. Henry spent five days there (lodged in the abbey) as Francis's guest and then rode back with the French king and his train to Calais, to entertain them on English territory for five days more. On 30 October the meeting came to an end when the royal pair rode to the edge of the English pale, embraced and then parted. Twelve days later, after sudden storms and fog had kept him captive at Calais, Henry crossed back to Dover and came thence to a solemn entry into London and thanksgiving in St Paul's.[6]

The meeting had been dressed in all the panoply of buoyant monarchy: trumpets, cloth of gold, jousts and revels, twenty-four-course banquets and the rest – all set in perfect weather. It had also been outrageously expensive. Henry had

4. *Hall*, ibid. For a full account of this visit, see Hamy, *Entrevue de François premier avec Henry VIII à Boulogne-sur-Mer en 1532* (Paris, 1898).

5. There was persistent rumour to the effect that Henry and Anne would marry while at Calais. *Ven. Cal.*, iv, 802, 803, 824.

6. Hamy, op. cit., *L.P.*, v, 1485–6; *Ven. Cal.*, iv, 822–4.

spared nothing on food (including £284 worth of fish, for example) or on his wardrobe; he had thrown away money in gambling, losing £157 at tennis in one day; he had showered horses, jewels and cash on the French so generously that, when it was Francis's turn to emulate his gallant friend, he had to borrow money. But the meeting had also had hard political purpose. First, it had shown the world, and especially Clement and Charles, what was apparently the very perfection of brotherhood between two monarchs. Secondly, it had been agreed that the two new French cardinals, Grammont and Tournon, should be sent (once more) to Rome – to announce the new Anglo-French *entente* and, it was hoped, finally sweep away all opposition to Henry's designs. Then it was agreed that these two should conclude a marriage alliance between Francis's second son and the pope's niece, Catherine de Medici; and finally, as a climax to all this, they were to carry an invitation to Clement to come to a meeting with Francis at, say, Nice – at which Henry himself might be present.[7]

It might have seemed that Henry's fortunes had thus received dexterous advancement. Two illustrious cardinals had finally been acquired, by adoption, to press his cause at Rome. Armed with a draft (from England) of a diatribe against Henry's enemies, they were to supervise the campaign now being fought by Carne and Benet, and lead the assault in Consistory, warning Clement and their fellow-cardinals as they did so that, by virtue of the new empathy between the two monarchs, whatever was done to Henry would be done also to Francis.[8] Further, Henry had manipulated others' purposes to his own ends. The idea of a marriage between Francis's son and Clement's niece had

7. Much of this is pieced together from subsequent material, e.g. *L.P.*, v, 1541; vi, 254, 1404, 1426, 1572.

8. *L.P.*, v, 1541; vi, 424; B.M. Add., 48,044, fols 17 ff. – a document headed 'What the two cardinals shall say to the pope'. It is not certain, however, that this belligerent document was even sent to the cardinals or, if it were, that it was delivered to Clement. Grammont had aided the English in 1530. *L.P.*, iv, 6705.

been mooted for over a year (and had threatened to carry
Francis further away from Henry into the pope's sway).
But at Calais – so Henry afterwards said – Francis promised
that he would never consent to this marriage *unless* Clement
first decided the divorce in his favour.[9] For the first time for
months, therefore, Henry had some real bargaining power.[10]
Likewise a meeting between Francis and the pope had been
in prospect for some months, primarily to offset a projected
meeting between the pope and Charles (which was to take
place in December 1532), and rumours of this had frightened
Henry badly. But now Francis would go to that interview as
Henry's sworn friend and perhaps with Henry, having
promised to do all in his power for Henry's marriage.[11]
Such, apparently, was the fruit of this royal encounter at
Boulogne. But Henry knew in his heart, and the knowledge
gnawed at him,[12] that Francis would easily betray him; and
he might praise Grammont's bold spirit, good learning and
courage, but the cardinal was Francis's subject first and, like
Tournon, went to Clement to promote a marriage rather
than dissolve one. Neither of them was a wonder-worker as
Wolsey might have been. Nonetheless, here was an opportunity for Henry to conscript foreign aid for that campaign
which we have seen mounted in 1530: the campaign, that
is, to force Clement to admit the rights of the English king
and kingdom, to confess the papal usurpation, disallow
Catherine's appeal and hand back Henry's case forever to
where, in equity and law, Henry said it belonged.

Henry might even yet have won some ground. Things did
begin to go his way. The meeting between Francis and the
pope did take place – at Marseilles in October 1533. Francis
was prepared to exert himself for Henry, and did so;[13] and

9. *L.P.*, vi, 1404, 1479. Cf. ibid., 230.
10. True, by virtue of the act in Conditional Restraint of Annates,
Henry had a fiscal 'purchase' on Rome; but this was a clumsy, im-
personal weapon, less effective perhaps than a marriage treaty.
11. *L.P.*, vi, 444, 846, 1288.
12. ibid., 230, 614.   13. ibid., 424, 1163.

perhaps Clement, worn down by Henry's wrangling, did prove malleable. Probably it was never seriously intended that Henry should attend this meeting himself; but he did send none other than the duke of Norfolk, until recently his leading servant, to represent him.

But Norfolk never reached Marseilles and Francis never had a chance to test Clement's mind. Events overtook plans. The meeting at Marseilles was a year, perhaps only some months, too late. For, a few weeks after Henry came back from Calais, that is some time in the middle of December 1532, Anne conceived her child by him. Perhaps what has often been surmised is true: that even until now she had refused his final demand.[14] Perhaps she had surrendered when she was made marquis of Pembroke. We cannot know, and it does not matter that we cannot. The decisive thing was that she was now pregnant and that the discovery of this fact inevitably broke the impasse. Come what may, the longed-for heir must be legitimate. Henry could wait no longer on Rome but must take the law into his own hands. Anne's pregnancy must have been discovered about the middle of January 1533. On the 25th of that month she was secretly married to the king; and once this happened Henry broke irrevocably with his past.

In mid March 1533, Henry was walking up and down the garden at Greenwich with the Imperial ambassador, fulminating against vainglorious papalism which made princes grovel before it, dared depose emperors and, as he had just read in a book 'forged' (he said) in Rome, claimed kings as feudatories. He promised to put an end to all this and re-

14. Why did she yield now? Perhaps Warham's death in August 1532, which opened the way to a thoroughly amenable successor, helped to decide the matter (but it is to be noted that Canterbury was left vacant a long time, five months, before Cranmer was named. Until that time was Henry debating whom he should choose, e.g. Gardiner, Lee, Stokesley or Edward Fox, who, at first sight, were more obvious candidates?). Perhaps Henry came back from Boulogne so convinced of invincible French support that he felt it safe to force the issue.

quite the insult to Henry II and John, who had been tricked
into offering this realm as a tributary to the Holy See.[15]
Those furious ideas about regal rights and papal usurpation
which had been in his mind for some three years, had now
come to maturity and must at last be translated into action.[16]
Even as he spoke to Chapuys, Parliament was busy with one
of the most famous statutes of its career – the act in Restraint
of Appeals – which proclaimed England's jurisdictional self-
sufficiency and finally declared that causes – including
Henry's marriage, of course – were to be heard and settled
within the sovereign national state without appeal to any
higher earthly authority, because none existed. Thus did
England throw off Rome, though not before Henry had
wrung from Rome one last, vital concession.

In mid January 1533 Cranmer, just returned from an
embassy to the emperor and as yet a mere archdeacon, was
nominated to the see of Canterbury which had been vacant
since Warham's death in the previous August. Doubtless
encouraged by the Boleyns, Henry had seen in him all that
he could want of a primate. But Cranmer must, of course,
be provided (i.e. appointed) by Rome. The English agents
there were bidden press for his provision at once; despite
the act in Conditional Restraint of Annates, all taxes
were to be paid, with Henry advancing money out of
his own pocket.[17] On 21 February Cranmer's appointment
was 'proposed' in Consistory by Campeggio, cardinal-
protector of England, and promptly agreed. Ignoring warnings that the candidate was no fit person to be elevated to
Canterbury and showing a carelessness and extraordinary
readiness to placate Henry wherever possible that were
conspicuous traits of the man, Clement had now undone
Rome's cause in England. About a month later the necessary

15. *L.P.*, vi, 235. I cannot identify the book to which Chapuys referred with any confidence, but it may have been an edition of Valla's
famous work on the Donation of Constantine.
16. See *L.P.*, vi, 194, 230 for other anti-papal outbursts by Henry.
17. ibid., 89.

bulls had been brought to England and Cranmer consecrated archbishop. Twelve days later, even before the temporalities of the see had been restored by the king, Cranmer
was writing to Henry begging permission to hear and determine Henry's great matter. The request had to be delicately
poised, for Henry's argument had not only been (and still
was) that the English clergy were competent to decide his
case, but also that he himself was under none save God and
answerable to no earthly tribunal. How then could he be
cited by one who was his subject, as cited he must be if he
would preserve the posture of one who was, alas, required
to answer a charge of living in sin? Henry's reply to the
archbishop's request solved this dilemma and showed how
his mind had completed the evolution begun in 1529 or
thereabouts. Though he was without superior on earth, he
wrote, and though Cranmer was his subject, ordained archbishop and primate by God and the king (to no other is
credit given for his promotion; and no mention made of the
pope from whom, as Cranmer's very recent bulls and pallium
testify, his ordinary and metropolitical jurisdiction were
sprung), though the archbishop enjoyed jurisdiction over
spiritual causes within the realm only 'by the sufferance of
us and our progenitors', 'yet because ye be, under us, by
God's calling and ours, the most principal minister of our
spiritual jurisdiction within this our realm', Henry granted
permission to him to examine and determine the royal
cause.[18]

During March and April 1533, as Henry and Cromwell
braced themselves for the final resolution of the problem of
the royal marriage, there had clearly been doubt and heart-
searching as to how it should be done. Probably the first
intention was to commit the case to the judgement of Convocation and to ratify its decision in Parliament.[19] Such was
the purpose of two draft parliamentary bills, the first of

18. *St.P.*, i, 392 f. (*L.P.*, vi, 332). Cranmer's letter is ibid., 390 f.
(*L.P.*, vi, 327).

19. Thus was the Cleves marriage annulled seven years later.

which authorized the clerical assembly (or at least a large
portion of the upper house of Convocation) to give final sentence on Henry's marriage and forbade appeal against its
findings; while the second, having declared the marriage
definitely, clearly, and absolutely' invalid, went on to announce that Henry was free to marry anyone and to settle
the problem of Catherine's future style – that of dowager
princess – as well as to determine the succession.[20] These two
bills would have cut deeper and wider than did the legislation which eventually, after much drafting and re-drafting,[21]
took their place, namely, the act of Appeals. For reasons
unknown they were set aside. But though they were discarded, the plan for securing a judgement from Convocation,
presumably to act as a buttress for Cranmer's court, survived.

On 5 April, after days of debate, Southern Convocation
broke the silence imposed by Rome on all parties *lite pen-
dente* and, with only some twenty-five dissentients (of whom
John Fisher was the most eminent), gave its verdict that a
marriage like that of Henry to Catherine was impeded by
divine law which no pope could dispense and thus retrospectively cleared the way for the union which the king had
already entered.[22] For months Henry had been arguing that
the English clergy alone were competent to decide his case
and that it should be handed over to them. The act of
Appeals had restated this; now at last, after much hustling

20. P.R.O. S.P. 2/N, fols 155 ff., fol. 163v (*L.P.*, vi, 311 (4), (5)).
They belong together, though the first was intended to precede Convocation's judgement, the second to follow it. They suffer from over-
lapping which, doubtless, subsequent drafting would have rubbed
out.

21. Elton, 'Evolution of a Reformation Statute', *E.H.R.*, lxiv (1959),
174 ff. The first of the two drafts listed in the previous note is treated
in this article, but not the second.

22. *Wilkins*, iii, 756 ff.; *Pocock*, ii, 442 ff. Fisher was arrested on
the following day and held in custody until after Anne's coronation.
Ven. Cal., iv, 870. The Northern Convocation, despite very careful
preparation, gave its assent only after much argument. Four members, including Tunstal, probably, refused. *Wilkins*, iii, 767; *L.P.*, vi,
451, 487, 653.

by the king,[23] the clergy had dared to act on these words. The spiritual men had spoken for Henry, Parliament had declared the archbishop's tribunal both competent and supreme, and the new archbishop, his credentials and his loyalty beyond reproach, had just received licence from the king to pass definitive sentence. Hence, on the afternoon of 10 May, in the priory of St Peter in Dunstable and attended by two bishops and a handful of officials, Cranmer opened the court which was to settle all. It was important that its work should be quickly and quietly done. Dunstable had been chosen because it was away from the capital but near enough for Catherine (now at Ampthill) to pass to and fro without causing commotion. As it happened, she made matters easy by refusing to appear either in person or by proxy, and was therefore declared contumacious (once more) and excluded from the court whose jurisdiction she would never have acknowledged anyway.[24] The king's men had apparently not expected so rapid a victory and were caught without all the witnesses and evidences ready. But the court was quickly in its stride and concluded its work after only four sessions – before most knew that it had begun. This was the sort of dispatch which Henry had wanted of Campeggio nearly four years before. On 23 May 1533, fortified by the 'determinations' of the universities and Convocation's recent findings, Cranmer declared Henry's marriage to Catherine null and void.[25] Thus, as far as Henry was concerned, the last scene of the great drama, previously sited in London, Rome, Bologna, and so on, had ended – and ended rather improbably in a meagre Augustinian house in Dunstable. And thus at a touch the bonds of that first marriage fell from the king.

Even before Cranmer had given his judgement, Anne had

23. *Sp. Cal.*, iv, 1057, a letter dated 31 March, in which Chapuys says that the king has pressed the prelates so hard that they have hardly had time to eat.

24. ibid., 1072.

25. *L.P.*, vi, 461, 495–6, 525, 529, 661.

been confidently calling herself queen. Henry, brazen yet
nervous, had watched people's faces as she did so, and had
called the great of the realm to pay her court.[26] When he
heard how most of a London congregation had walked out
of the church when the preacher called for prayers for the
new queen he summoned the mayor before him and angrily
told him not to let such a thing happen again (though what
a mayor of London could do about popular sentiment was
not very evident).[27] Now that her marriage had been annulled, Catherine must surrender the title of queen and
suffer her household to be cut down to that of a mere dowager princess, that is, widow of Henry's elder brother, which
was all she was; while workmen went about stripping her
arms off walls, off Westminster Hall, off the royal barge.[28]

Six days after Cranmer had given judgement, Anne came
from Greenwich to the Tower for her coronation. She came
by river, accompanied by a fleet of over three hundred resplendent barges and smaller boats, hung with banners and
flags, and ringing with music. On Saturday 31 May she rode
in triumph through the City to Westminster, carried on a
litter under a canopy of gold, with her marvellous black
hair pouring down on to her shoulders. Next day, Whit
Sunday, she was anointed and crowned with the crown of
St Edward at the hands of Thomas Cranmer.[29]

The most important thing that happened in 1533 was
Henry's discovery that he had begotten a child by Anne.
All else was consequent upon this – Convocation's sentence,
the act of Appeals, the judgement at Dunstable. It was now,
too, that Cromwell finally moved into the front as the king's
leading minister. But it is difficult to see how his arrival
could have given any more urgency to the situation than it

26. *Sp. Cal.*, iv, 1061.

27. ibid., 1062.

28. ibid., 1073, 1091, etc.

29. *Hall*, 798 ff.; *Ven. Cal.*, iv, 912; *L.P.*, vi, 584. But it may be that
Anne was not well received by the populace all the way. See *L.P.*,
vi, 585, an obviously hostile account, but which may have some truth
in it.

already possessed. Cromwell's coming and the new decisiveness of royal policy were perhaps nōt so much related as cause and effect as, both of them, effects of the same cause. Again, granted that the statute of Appeals was Cromwell's work and that it was a major event in the story of the Reformation, then it may be added that what the statute said, namely that England possessed jurisdictional self-sufficiency and contained within herself all that was needed to settle spiritual as well as temporal causes within the kingdom, was what, in one way or another, Henry had been proclaiming for nearly three years. Time and again Henry had said that he was of imperial status and answerable to no one, that this realm of England was, by ancient privilege and custom, subject to no earthly authority, that, since spiritual causes (and not just his own marriage) should by law be determined in the province of their origin, his marriage suit should be remitted to English judgement.

Certainly the words 'this realm of England is an empire' – the celebrated opening fanfare of the preamble of that act – had not been used before, but the 'imperial' argument that no appeal lay beyond England to a foreign court was by now an old one. Cromwell's famous preamble brought three years of argument to a climax and canonized it. It did not invent the argument. Hitherto Henry had resisted Rome on a multiplicity of grounds: that he was an emperor, that the fundamental laws of the realm exempted Englishmen from foreign jurisdiction, that (as 'determinations' of universities confirmed) decrees of Councils and popes forbade his citation to Rome, and so on. His argument had grown rather confused. Cromwell's preamble cut out this knotted pleading and not only pushed the case on to rather different ground,[30] but set England's autonomy on one foundation only, that of secular national history. We hear only of 'divers sundry old authentic histories and chronicles' which have 'manifestly declared and expressed that this realm of England is an empire'. It was to the world of Arthur and Constantine and

30. Below, p. 510.

Geoffrey of Monmouth, therefore, that, rather hesitantly and cryptically, appeal was made. All else had gone. But whether this was pure gain, whether this rather flimsy substructure could support so consequential a claim, is another matter.

Nor, as things turned out, was the act remarkably efficacious. Its immediate purpose, apart from authorizing Cranmer's court, was to prevent Catherine appealing to Rome against its sentence or calling for retaliation.[31] Though doubtless prudence required that the queen should be thus circumvented, since she never acknowledged the court and certainly would not have done so, act or no act, there was never any question of her appealing against it; and she studiously avoided any action which could have exposed her to its penalties. But she had already appealed to Rome in mid 1529 (which was a further reason why she was unlikely to appeal now). Hence the question immediately arose: did this act cover that appeal? It was doubtful whether it did, or could. Though the act dealt with 'causes already commenced' in the realm, it prohibited only *future* appeals; and Catherine's appeal was nearly four years old. Was the act a broken reed, then? According to Hall, this very question was quickly discussed in Parliament and Convocation immediately after the statute in Restraint of Appeals had been passed – where it was eventually decided that the decrees of the Councils of Carthage and Toledo and the rest, not, after all, Parliament's recent act, damned Catherine's appeal.[32] Hence scarcely had a law been made than it was necessary to go behind it and use old material, apparently discarded, with which to plug an unforeseen loophole. It was not the chronicles and histories of England which refuted Catherine, but the decrees of some early Church

31. Section ix of the act provided that appeal could be made to the upper house of Convocation. Catherine was therefore to be heard by an assembly which, on 5 April, immediately after the act was passed but before the court at Dunstable opened, had declared against her.

32. *Hall,* 795 f.

Councils. Furthermore, though the act was a massive piece of political engineering, in some not insignificant respects it was less comprehensive than the two draft bills which it almost certainly replaced. It left unsettled the matter of Catherine's future and the vital matter of the succession – both of which had to wait for separate statutory treatment, the second for nearly a year. Again, though it forbade appeal to Rome in a wide span of causes, not just Henry's case (as did the draft bills), it did *not* halt appeal in cases of heresy. Earlier drafts of the act had done so. They had included the prohibition of appeal in cases concerning 'correction of sins'. But this was deliberately excluded from the final text.[33] In 1530, Henry had bidden Benet and Carne search the papal registers to see whether, by virtue of his 'authority imperial', he was 'under the pope *in any other matter than heresy*'.[34] He had not then dared to renounce the see of Peter utterly. Was there not the same hesitation at the last minute now? Had so much progress been made in three years after all? Was it prudence that held Cromwell back, or were conviction and nerve lacking? Was the statute of Appeals perhaps a *pis-aller* rather than an assured *coup de main*?

Two further things remain to be said about this statute. First, the word 'empire' which made its appearance here and which has been seen as so consequential an addition to English political vocabulary, made its début only to disappear almost completely. We hear, time after time, of 'the imperial crown', of course. But this is rather different. 'Empire' is henceforth virtually lost.[35] Secondly, the statute

33. Elton, art. cit., p. 185.
34. See above, p. 351. Cf. the duke of Norfolk's remark in January 1531 that the pope had no jurisdiction save in matters of heresy (above, p. 385).
35. I have not been able to find it in any subsequent official government document. But it recurs, for example, in Francis Bigod's *Treatise concerning Impropriations of Benefices* (c. 1535), A iii (quoted Dickens, *Lollards and Protestants, etc.*, 70 n.) and in Richard Morrison's dedication to Henry of his translation, in 1539, of a work on warfare by Sextus Julius Frontinus. McConica, op. cit., 181.

made very little immediate difference to English policy towards Rome.

Francis I was due to meet the pope in the summer of 1533, and the duke of Norfolk was to represent Henry at the interview. So the latter had agreed with Francis at Boulogne in the previous October. The duke left England with a large suite just before Anne's coronation (and had therefore to hand the duties of earl marshal at the ceremony to his brother), made his way to near Lyons, where the French court lay and whence he was to move, with Francis, to the rendezvous with Clement. The instructions which the duke received for his mission are interesting.[36] They show Henry eaten up with anxiety lest Francis and Clement should, between them, stab him in the back. He smelt treachery in their every move and now wished that the meeting would fall through. News had just come that the pope did not want it to take place until September. Norfolk was to press Francis to take advantage of this postponement and call the whole thing off, warning him constantly against those who made it their pastime to 'play and dally with kings and princes', and begging him beware being 'so handled with the pope so much to our dishonour and to the pope's and emperor's advancement'.[37] If the interview did take place Norfolk was to attend, but to exercise the greatest vigilance. Whatever happened, and especially if Francis met the pope, the French king must throw his whole weight on Henry's side – either in person or via the cardinals Tournon and Grammont. The excusator must be admitted. Clement must be made to understand that by refusing to admit Carne, by refusing to reject Catherine's appeal and surrender the case to England, he threatened the 'greatest dishonour that ever might be imagined or compassed towards the dishonour and liberties of princes'. Let Francis 'conceive in his stomach'

36. For text, see *St.P.*, vii, 473 ff. (*L.P.*, vi, 641). These are a second set of instructions sent to Norfolk after he had set out. The first is not extant.

37. ibid., 474, 475.

the peril to monarchs, nay, 'the utter violation and subversion of the authority and pre-eminence of all princes' which is at hand; let him have it continually sounded and blowen' in Clement's ears that the pope would bring about the ruin of the papacy unless he undid the 'apert injury' which he had inflicted upon Henry and, through Henry, on all princes,[38] and so on.

Despite what has happened – the act of Parliament, the decision of Convocation, the judgement of Cranmer's court – Henry still demanded what he had been demanding incessantly for years, namely, that the excusator should be admitted by the Rota to announce that Henry could not come to Rome in person or by proxy to answer Catherine's appeal. The pope's authority in England had not yet been finally annihilated. Much of his jurisdiction had been destroyed. In July of this year 1533 the act in Conditional Restraint of Annates was brought into effect by royal letters patent, and thus the flow of taxes to Rome reduced to a trickle. But Clement was still, in some minimal way, the head of the Church in England. Not till the following year would Convocation declare that he had no more authority in England than any other foreign bishop, and Parliament declare Henry head of the English Church. The schism, then, was not complete. Henry would not undo what he had done, but he still wanted Clement publicly to confess that he had been wrong and to concede him a bloodless victory. Doubtless there were many diplomatic reasons for this tactic, but that is not precisely the point. Henry was not prepared to stake all on the sovereignty of statute and say '*causa finita*'. The act of Appeals had proclaimed the English clergy's sufficiency, but the excusator remained at Rome, fighting the old battle with the old weapons.[39]

38. *St.P.*, vii, 477.
39. That this letter to Norfolk was a mere lapse, or that Henry wrote thus because he had not yet 'caught up' with the recent statute, is disproved by his continued talk about the need to secure the admission of the excusator. See Francis I's allusion to this in *L.P.*, vi,

It was perhaps Rome rather than Parliament that really forced the issue. News of what had been happening recently in England reached there quickly and, of course, caused consternation. Henry's open disregard of the papal inhibitions and the decisions of the English clergy and Cranmer galvanized the Curia and left Clement powerless to resist the Imperialists any longer.[40] In Consistory, on 11 July, Clement solemnly condemned Henry's separation from Catherine and his marriage to Anne, and gave him until September to take back his former wife – under pain of excommunication.[41] Clement had been driven to this by the king and, in the circumstances, had treated him lightly. The papal sentence was not on the principal cause, as it was called, but *'super attentatis'*, that is, it had not judged the fundamental question of the validity of Henry's marriage to Catherine but only what had been 'attempted' against it. A decision on the other was still some months off. Only a lesser die was cast, therefore. If he had to thank Catherine's counsel in Rome for this (for, incredibly, they had not yet put her case in sufficient order to ask for judgement on the principal), Henry could also be grateful to Clement for deliberately heading off the enemy towards this lesser success.[42] Furthermore, Henry had been given until September, by which time Clement would have met Francis and the whole situation might have changed radically. Nevertheless, the pope's action was a shock. However much it had been overworked, excommunication was still a fearful sanction, and it was the first time for generations that it had been raised against an

---

1288. In early 1534, Paget was sent on a mission to German princes to justify Henry's actions and win their support. He was to explain that the privileges of the realm, the decrees of Councils, the determinations of universities, etc., had condemned Clement's action, that Henry should never have been cited, that he was impeded by a just impediment, that the excusator should be admitted, and so on. These, again, are the old arguments. The statute of Appeals has not replaced them. See *L.P.*, vii, 148. Cf. ibid., 21.

40. *L.P.*, vi, 725; *Ven. Cal.*, iv, 936. Cf. *L.P.*, vi, 663.

41. *L.P.*, vi, 807 and App. 3.   42. *Sp. Cal.*, iv, 1095, 1104.

English king. Though stern action by Rome had been imminent for months (more than once Clement had come to the brink and then halted) Henry was stunned by the news and, without pausing either to see the loopholes or thank Heaven for what he had been spared, made the disaster complete by retaliation.

It was the duke of Norfolk who first heard about the excommunication. He was then at Lyons, waiting in the summer heat to accompany Francis to his meeting with the pope. When he received the fateful news, it is said, he nearly fainted. There was only one thing to do: he must leave for home immediately. But the French soothed him and eventually he decided to send his companion, Rochford (Anne's brother), back to England post-haste for instructions.[43] Henry was probably at Guildford, whither he had retreated after his physician fell ill with sweating sickness, when the news from Rome reached him. How he reacted we do not know, but we do know that, on his return, Rochford was instructed to tell Norfolk to come back home at once with the rest of his embassy. Henry decided to boycott the interview, if he could not do better and stop it happening altogether,[44] and at the same time wrote to his agents in Rome terminating their commissions.[45] He would never yield to Clement's censure and met public rebuke by breaking communications. More was to come.

The interview which Henry had once expected so much from and now feared deeply took place despite his protests. On 13 October Francis met Clement at Marseilles. The encounter was an amiable affair. Clement was friendly, the French king happy to do all reverence to him and the marriage of the pope's niece to the king's son quickly

43. *L.P.*, vi, 1572.

44. Efforts to dissuade Francis from attending now increased. See *L.P.*, vi, 1038.

45. *Ven. Cal.*, 967. Benet, Carne and Bonner were to come home, Casale and Ghinucci to stay but do nothing. However, Benet died shortly afterwards – thereby prematurely ending a career which might have reached high ecclesiastical preferment.

agreed. There was only one untoward episode at the meeting, supplied by the English.

Months before, in late June, Henry had taken the precaution of drawing up an appeal to a future General Council against any papal excommunication that might be uttered against him.[46] The document, an explosive thing repeatedly forbidden by papal decree, had been prepared as an ultimate weapon against the Curia. It would be employed now. Stephen Gardiner had been English ambassador in France recently and was with the French king at Marseilles (for he had not been included in Norfolk's recall), and he was soon joined there by Edmund Bonner, whom a royal courier had intercepted at Lyons while he was on his way back to England from Italy. These two, Gardiner and Bonner, would now have a final interview with Clement in Henry's name at Marseilles. On 7 November Bonner made his way with some difficulty into the pope's chamber and, as Clement stood at a window winding and unwinding his handkerchief as he did when he was 'tickled to the very heart with a great choler', began to deliver Henry's message. Alas for Bonner, the dramatic intensity of the moment was spoiled by the unexpected arrival of the French king for an audience of the pope before he had finished his piece, and it was not until an hour later, when Francis had concluded a hearty conversation with Clement, that he could complete his errand.[47] When it was done, both sides knew how deep the rupture was. Henry had refused Clement's call to submit. Clement, of course, had refused the king's appeal to a General Council.

News of the meeting at Marseilles, of how Francis had kissed Clement's foot and grovelled before him, of how he had settled his son's marriage and so on, drove Henry to dismay – so much so that he crumpled up a dispatch from Marseilles and threw it on the floor, saying that he had been betrayed, spurned and humiliated. Again and again

46. *L.P.*, vi, 721. This was drawn up a fortnight before the pope's sentence.

47. See Bonner's vivid account in *Burnet*, vi, 56 ff. (*L.P.*, vi, 1425).

he would say Francis was traitor to all princes, the pope's
gull, an ingrate and a fickle villain.[48] But he was wrong. It
was largely thanks to Francis that the sentence of excommunication, due to fall in September, had been suspended
for two more months and even then was not promulgated.[49]
The French cardinals had exerted themselves on Henry's
behalf at Rome and there was reason to suppose that, at the
interview, Clement could even yet have been brought to
make concessions.[50] As Francis retorted to Henry's rebukes,
if anyone was guilty of ineptitude it was Henry, not he.
After first wanting to come to the interview himself, Henry
had suddenly changed his mind and sent Norfolk, only to
withdraw him at the last minute and instead send Gardiner,
who had inexplicably arrived without any powers to negotiate. Since the meeting at Boulogne, Henry had provoked
Rome with one outrage after another, but Francis had
battled on for his sake. Now, on the very evening when (so
he could conveniently say) he came to Clement expecting to
bring days of delicate negotiation to a successful conclusion
and secure great advantage for Henry, he found Bonner
delivering a belligerent broadside against the pope.[51] With
this final folly, insulting to his guest and shaming to him,
Henry had not only undone all his work but made it impossible for him to ask for a larger dowry for his son's wife.
'As fast as I study to win the pope,' he said to Gardiner,
'ye study to lose him.' 'Ye,' he said with splendid contempt,
'ye have clearly marred all.'[52]

48. *L.P.*, vi, 1479. Henry said all this, and more (and often), to the
French ambassador.

49. ibid., 1163; *Sp. Cal.*, iv, 1147.

50. It was later authoritatively stated that at Marseilles Clement
acknowledged that Henry's marriage was null (on what grounds is
not stated) and promised that if the king would send a proxy, i.e.
withdraw his excusator and answer Catherine's appeal, he would give
sentence for him. See *L.P.*, vii, 695 and 1348. This report should be
treated with caution, but at least it is likely that Clement had become
more amenable.

51. *L.P.*, vi, 1426.

52. ibid., 1427.

Clement's sentence and the awful consequences which
theoretically it could bring – deposition, civil war, invasion
– stirred up a good deal of alarm. Parliament had been due
to meet in the autumn of this year, and probably in the late
summer, perhaps just after the news of the excommunication
arrived, someone drew up an agenda for it. There were
some astounding entries: that if the pope vexed the kingdom
on account of Henry's marriage, all annates should cease
immediately and be paid to the king for defence of the
realm; that anyone supporting the pope would be guilty of
high treason; that an ecclesiastic guilty of treason would
forfeit the lands held by any corporation of which he was
head; that the king should have for his defence half the
lands of the Church.[53]

About this time, too, occurred the case of Elizabeth
Barton, the 'holy maid of Kent' – a celebrated, and rather
mysterious, affair.[54] Eight years before, Elizabeth had won
fame by uttering prophecies, seeing visions and being
publicly cured of a disease which had afflicted her. Thereafter she retired quietly to a convent in Canterbury – only
to re-emerge into the limelight about 1527, when she began
to speak out vigorously against the royal divorce. Henry
himself summoned her to him and was roundly warned of
what would befall him if he persisted in his plans. She
threatened the pope with divine punishment if he yielded
to the king, and was said to have had sufficient sway over
both Warham and Wolsey to unnerve both of them. So far
she had probably been acting on her own initiative only.
But there can be little doubt that she was eventually
exploited by a group of clergy centred on Canterbury –
especially one Dr Edward Bocking, her spiritual director and
a monk at Christ Church – who were opposed to the divorce
and saw in her a useful weapon with which to harass the

53. B.M. Titus B, i, fol. 150 (*L.P.*, vi, 1381 (3)).
54. For an account of it see Cheney, 'The Holy Maid of Kent',
T.R.H.S., n.s. xviii (1904), 107 ff., and also Knowles, *Religious Orders
in England*, iii, 182 ff.

king. The nun now prophesied that Henry would cease to be king one month after marrying Anne Boleyn, that he would not be king in God's eyes one hour after doing so and that he would die a villain's death. As authentication of her supernatural gifts, it was claimed, she had received a letter written by Mary Magdalen in Heaven in the nun's name, in gold lettering. Elizabeth was a woman whose remarkable and irreproachable life had hitherto won her a wide reputation as a probable saint and visionary, and she was associated with illustrious folk like Fisher and More, the Friars Observant and the London Carthusians – the leading opponents of the divorce. As well as this, if Bocking and the others had had their way, she might have been used to stir the commons and fire serious unrest of the kind that England had seen at the time of the Peasants' Revolt of 1381 or Jack Cade's rebellion in 1450. Times were tense and the king could not have ignored these dangerous rumblings. In mid July (1533) he ordered Cromwell and Cranmer to strike. The nun was arrested, closely and repeatedly interrogated, and taken to the Tower. Meanwhile, all copies of the account of her early life, of writings about her by her admirers (several of them, perhaps, printed works) and all seven hundred copies of a probably highly inflammatory work called *The Nun's Book* which had just been printed were seized and have since vanished – a novel, and highly efficient, display of governmental concern with the printing-press.[55] On or before 20 November a large gathering of privy councillors, judges and many nobles summoned from every part of the land debated the dangerous affair of the nun for three days. Some cried 'To the stake with her'; and Henry would have had her and her associates condemned as heretics and traitors.[56] Instead, on 23 November, Elizabeth and her leading adherents were brought to a scaffold at St Paul's Cross and subjected to public ridicule and humiliation while one

55. On all this, see Devereux, 'Elizabeth Barton and Tudor Censorship', *Bull. John Rylands Library*, 49 (1966), 91 ff.

56. *Sp. Cal.*, iv, 1153.

John Salcot (*alias* Capon), abbot of Hyde and soon to be promoted to a bishopric, spoke a long sermon denouncing the nun as a fraud, a harlot and a victim of her own vanity and the monkish guile of such as Bocking.[57] Shortly afterwards she, Bocking and five others were attainted for high treason; while six more, including Fisher and Thomas Abel, were convicted of misprision of (i.e. lesser) treason. There is evidence that Henry thrust the attack onwards[58] and it may well have been he who turned an assault on the nun into a purge of more illustrious opponents. Fisher had had cautious dealings with her and was easy to ensnare. For a while Thomas More was implicated and, had he not disowned Elizabeth as a 'lewd nun' and 'wicked woman', would also have been attainted. So, too, might Catherine – had she not prudently refused ever to be visited by the nun or to be associated with her.

The attack on Fisher and the others was temporarily called off. Elizabeth, Bocking and four others were hanged at Tyburn in April of the following year. Thus the affair ended. The sturdiest scepticism has, perhaps, not yet succeeded in dismissing the nun as a mere hysteric or fraud, nor the most favourable pleading lifted her above all suspicion; but whatever else she may or may not have been, she was indisputably a powerful, courageous and dangerous woman whom the wracking anxiety of the late summer and autumn of 1533 required should be destroyed.

The excommunication of the king also gave rise to that vivid piece of Henrician political writing, the *Articles devised by the holle consent of the King's Council, etc.*, which appeared in late 1533 and was designed to provide a short, simple justification of royal policy. It briefly rehearsed the

57. The text of this sermon is printed by Whatmore in *E.H.R.*, lviii (1943), 463 ff.
58. It was he who apparently launched the attack, as *L.P.*, vi, 887 shows. Chapuys (in *Sp. Cal.*, iv, 1153) was quite sure of Henry's role. Cf. Cromwell's remembrance in *L.P.*, vii, 52: 'To know what the king will have done with the nun and her accomplices'.

evidence drawn from the Councils of Nicea, Milevum, etc., that Henry's case belonged to English judgement, it asserted that the bishop of Rome (such was his new style) was subject to a General Council and justified Henry's appeal to one, it called upon the nation to ignore any Roman counter-blast, it lashed at the 'pomp, pride, ambition' of the bishop of Rome and declared that he had no more authority outside his province than any other bishop – the formula that Convocation would solemnly canonize in the following May. Finally, it denounced Clement as bastard, simoniac and heretic, and proposed to the nation, as evidence of divine approval of all that had recently been accomplished, such evidence as Anne's speedy delivery of a child, the 'fair weather with great plenty of corn and cattle', the 'peace and amity lately sought by divers princes', the 'pureness of air without any pestilential or contagious disease'.[59] Nor was it surprising that, having thus flouted Rome and the emperor and fallen out with Francis, Henry should now make an effort to win support in Germany. In early 1534 a mission was sent thither to woo the alliance of princes for the struggle against the tyranny of Rome.[60]

While all this was afoot Anne had come to her time of delivery. By early September 1533 she and Henry were back at Greenwich awaiting the birth. Doctors and astrologers had assured him that he would have a son – to be called Edward or Henry. He had had a fine bed, a duke's ransom, it was said, brought out for Anne and prepared splendid celebrations for the event.[61] On the afternoon of 7 September Anne was delivered of a girl : probably the most unwelcome royal daughter and most celebrated woman in English history. Elizabeth was christened and confirmed three days later in the chapel of the Observant Franciscans at Greenwich, with Cranmer, appropriately, as her godfather. The christening was, of course, a magnificent occasion, even if it were marred by the irony of the child's sex. But one person

59. *Pocock*, ii, 523 ff.
60. See esp. *L.P.*, vii, 21, 148.   61. *L.P.*, vi, 1069.

does not seem to have been present, namely, Henry himself.[62]
Was he too disappointed to attend?

To the act in Restraint of Appeals must be added five
more major statutes which completed the breach with
Rome: the act of Dispensations, which provided that henceforth ecclesiastical dispensations, licences, faculties and so
on be supplied in England and not from Rome;[63] the act of
Succession which settled the dynasty's future and imposed
an oath to be administered throughout the kingdom acknowledging the king's new marriage and its offspring; the
act in Absolute Restraint of Annates, which finally halted
all payments to Rome for benefices and provided for the
appointment of bishops by the king alone; the act for the
Submission of the Clergy, which consecrated in statutory
form Convocation's surrender of May 1532; and the Heresy
act which declared that it was no longer heresy to deny the
papal primacy. These were the work of the first session of
1534. Later that year, in a second session, they were brought
to their climax by the act of Supremacy which explicitly
and unconditionally declared Henry head on earth of the
English Church.[64] Thus the umbilical cord uniting English
Catholicism to Rome was cut.

62. At least he is not mentioned in Hall's full account of the
christening (*Hall*, p. 806). Henry was present in the palace, certainly.
After the procession, following the christening from the chapel to the
palace, he sent the duke of Norfolk to thank the mayor and aldermen of London for attending. This is the only mention which Hall
makes of him.

63. The act also forbade visitation of exempt English monasteries,
i.e. houses which were part of an international system, by foreign
visitors and members of English houses from being used as visitors
or attending chapters, congregations, etc. abroad. The act therefore
effectively 'nationalized' English monasticism – a fact which has not
often been noticed.

64. We may add, for its symbolism, a sixth act which deprived
the absentee Italians, Ghinucci and Campeggio, of their sees, Worcester and Salisbury, which they had received years before in payment for services to Henry, past and future, at the Curia.

Within five years – a short time – a momentous revolution had been accomplished. Of course it is right to call this revolution primarily a jurisdictional one, but wrong to think that it was not, therefore, a theological one. England had indisputably been subject to Rome hitherto, and to confer full spiritual authority on the prince was indisputably a radical innovation. Hitherto there had been no such thing as the English Church, but, rather, two provinces of Western Christendom in visible communion with the other provinces and subject to the see of Rome. The Royal Supremacy not only ended an old allegiance; it also created a new, single, autocephalous Church *of* England. However much spiritual and temporal had intermingled in medieval society and however much *de facto* influence in ecclesiastical affairs the prince of late medieval Europe had enjoyed, the authority which Henry now acquired was something quite other than anything that England had seen hitherto.

Doubtless many ordinary folk did not understand the great revolution that was being accomplished, did not want to understand or did not notice it. So much of the old religion remained unchanged – especially the Mass and at least the outward form of the sacraments – that the profound inward change could easily have escaped notice. Some acquiesced passively, confident that the breach was a conflict between pope and king of the kind that had often occurred. For many, permanent schism may have been inconceivable. Few would have thought Clement and the English clergy worth dying for; some may have been or were becoming strongly conciliarist, or at least had been shaken by recent scholarship in their belief in ultramontane papalist and clerical claims. Others, as we know from them later, subscribed out of fear and, like Friar Forrest, denied Rome 'by an oath given by his outward man, but not with the inward man'.[65] Many must have been carried by their sincere loyalty to the king, by national pride and a deep concern for the nation's future, which demanded unity and an heir to the

65. *L.P.*, xiii, i, 1043.

throne. Some may have rejoiced for base reasons to see Rome
disowned, the clergy humbled, the monks routed; others
because these things were God's will. It is perhaps banal to
remark that this was a time of intense intellectual ferment
when so much that had hitherto seemed secure was being
prised out of position by criticism and discovery. But without doubt this was a world living in the thick of change and
re-appraisal, in which new ideas and new prophets undermined and liberated, above all by discovering the often
startling truths about the early Church against which to
judge the present. We should not underestimate the sense of
crusade which animated the best of the English Reformation. Henry proclaimed himself, and was sincerely proclaimed, as a Moses delivering a chosen people from the
bondage and darkness of papal thraldom. He promised the
restoration of the kingdom, renewal, rebuilding of the right
order; and the promise, to some, rang true.

He frankly admitted that his conversion was a radical
breach with his past. In December 1533 Cuthbert Tunstal, a
friend of More and Fisher, and one who nearly followed
these two to the Tower until, at the last moment, he chose
for his king, was still pleading with his master to hold back
and dared to remind him that he had once made war on
Louis XII of France precisely because that king 'assisted and
nourished a schism', just as Henry was now doing himself.
'Then', wrote Henry in reply, 'we were but young and having
but little experience in the feats of the world.'[66] 'We gave
them [*sc.* popes] a primacy,' said the *Protestation* of 1537,
speaking in the name of Henry and the Council, 'we gave it
to you indeed.... If we, being deceived by false pretence of
evil-alleged Scripture, gave to you that which ought to have
been refused, why may we not, our error now perceived, your

66. P.R.O. S.P. 6/9, no. 18 (*L.P.*, vi, 820). Tunstal's letter has not
survived. This is Henry's reply thereto, from which the contents of
the bishop's letter can be reconstructed. On the dating of this document and the reasons for believing it was addressed to Tunstal, see
Sturge, *Cuthbert Tunstall* (1938), 195 and App. xiii.

deceit espied, take it again? We princes wrote ourselves to
be inferiors to popes; as long as we thought so we obeyed
them as our superiors. Now we write not as we did.'[67] The
king had seen the light, as the Greeks long since and the
German and Scandinavian princes recently had seen it.[68] Of
course, the *Assertio Septem Sacramentorum* was an embarrassment – which Henry now disowned, telling the world
that he wrote it not of his free will but at the behest of
Wolsey and other bishops.[69] As he had explained to the papal
nuncio in 1533, when the latter had quoted the *Assertio*
against its author, since writing that work he had read and
studied more, and found the truth very different from what
he had then innocently written.[70] His conversion may have
been the act of an opportunist, undisciplined in honesty, in-
capable of distinguishing truth from advantage or of hearing
what he did not want to know, but it was lived with a feverish conviction which swept along the hesitant. Henry's
majestic, awesome confidence would have been sufficient
authority for many less assured than he, the nation's hero
and Defender of the Faith.

Furthermore, though he had proceeded briskly, he had
proceeded piecemeal. It had not been easy to find a point
at which to stand and fight. The divorce had been extraordinarily complex; the legislation of 1529, the events of
1531, the clergy's surrender of 1532 (which we can now see
was decisive), even the act of Appeals could have been interpreted as reasonable and not necessarily a total assault on
the prevailing theology of the Church. The line between
fatal compromise and judicious accommodation is a fine one.
The meaning of Henry's intentions was not fully evident till
the end of 1534 (and perhaps for some not until he attacked

67. *A Protestation made for the most mighty and redoubtable King
of England etc.* (1538), C4-v.
68. So Henry said to Chapuys in January 1536. *L.P.*, x, 141.
69. *Sp. Cal.*, v, i, 9.
70. *Sp. Cal.*, iv, 1057. The bishops of Southern Convocation had
likewise reminded Henry of his past writings during the crisis of
May 1532. See above, p. 391.

monasticism and turned openly to Protestantism); and then
it was too late. What distinguished men like Fisher and
More was their courage and foresight, and when, in later
years, John Stokesley, bishop of London, was reported to
have exclaimed that he wished he had followed their
example, he may have spoken for many who awoke too late.[71]
Moreover, Henricianism was not simply a call to England to
disown Rome's jurisdiction but, in its largest terms, a promise
of radical and necessary renewal of the whole commonwealth. Some may have regarded abandoning an incorrigible
Rome as a small price to pay for being able to clean the
Augean stables of the Church in England or securing
England's political future, or both, even if they felt no more
enthusiasm for the Royal Supremacy itself than they had
for Rome. Some may have faced a terrible dilemma in having to choose, on the one hand, between the admittedly lawful but deadening authority of Rome and the racket-ridden,
ponderous ecclesiastical system which Rome supported, and,
on the other, a king whose claims were certainly extravagant
but who might at last cut back the clerical estate and re-
vivify Christian life. They disowned Rome, perhaps temporarily, because this was the lesser evil, because it would
otherwise be impossible to tackle the urgent problems of
their society. There may only have been a few of these, but
they deserve a mention as much as do those who were more
or less committed to some form of Erasmianism or of Protestantism and for whom the Royal Supremacy, *per se*
acceptable, or a thing 'indifferent', or (as, say, a Francis

71. 'Oh! that I had holden still with my brother Fisher, and not
left him, when time was!' he exclaimed, according to the author of
The Earliest English Life of St John Fisher, p. 160. Cf. the confession
of the abbot of Woburn, in early 1538, that he wished he had followed
Fisher and More. The abbot had kept copies of his abbey's papal
bulls against the day when they might be used once more and had
rebuked one who erased the pope's name from Mass-books, saying 'it
will come again one day'. *L.P.*, xiii, i, 981. Cf. Bonner's famous statement later on: 'Fear compelled us to bear with the times, for otherwise there had been no way but one.' *Foxe*, viii, 110.

Bigod will discover) repugnant, was subordinate to the larger problem of true reform – a means and not an end.

Finally, it may be observed that those who consciously disowned Rome might plausibly have argued that Rome disowned them first. Throughout the crisis she had been almost completely silent, allowing a cardinal legate to be struck down without protest, uttering no warning to Henry as he attacked her flock in England, neither guiding nor encouraging those who remained loyal to her. Preoccupied with local and family affairs and the catastrophic events in continental Europe, fearful of making yet another enemy, convinced of Henry's fundamental loyalty and uninformed about what was really happening, Clement was objectively guilty of fatal negligence. It was typical of him that he should have had as nuncio in England so apparently ineffectual a man as Baron del Burgo; that in 1532, when the battle had just reached full heat, he should have seen fit, and had nothing better to do, than to write to Henry asking permission for a servant to tour ecclesiastical libraries in England looking for items which were lacking in the papal collection.[72] Not until early 1535, when the new pope, Paul III, gave a red hat to Fisher (then in prison) did Rome show any real sign that she cared for her beleaguered English sons; and Paul's gesture was not only overdue but provoked Henry into final action against the cardinal – or at least was used as an excuse for it.[73]

The Henrician Reformation had large support, sprung from all manner of motives, high and low. Though essentially an act of state, it was carried by a multiplicity of forces in a sense greater than it, which pre-existed it, which it finally released and canalized. But if there was widespread and often bitter anticlericalism, it was probably only a minority who gave enthusiastic support to Henry's breach with the past. There may have been approval of Henry's

72. Scarisbrick, 'Henry VIII and the Vatican Library', *Bibl. d'Humanisme et Renaissance*, xxiv (1962), 215 f.

73. *Sp. Cal.*, v, i, 174, 178.

desire for an heir, for this was still urgent; but Catherine
was an honoured queen and her rough treatment was not
popular. As the passage of the act of Annates suggests, antipathy to Rome's taxes was one thing, the use to which Henry
put this antipathy another.[74] We hear of some overt opposition in the House of Commons – now anxiety about the
effects of the king's action on foreign trade; now a plea to
remit the divorce to Rome and an offer of £200,000 if he
would do so; now a plea from one Temse to take Catherine
back.[75] We know how Henry urged the commons onwards
in 1531 and 1532, and how he went to Parliament allegedly
to hasten the passage of the act of Appeals.[76] On the surface
king and Parliament seem to have cooperated easily; but,
throughout this story, there is a strong impression of a
largely unenthusiastic, conservative nation being man-
oeuvred into radical action which was neither foreseen nor
quickly accepted.

In the early stages of the revolution Henry had met stout
opposition from many of the clergy.[77] Maybe that opposition
had sprung from all manner of motives and maybe it was
only such as Fisher and Tunstal who were able to rally an
often timorous group of bishops, but much of the clerical
estate had fought as a united body until May 1532. Shortly

74. See above, p. 393, n. 60.

75. *Hall*, p. 788; *L.P.*, v, 989; vi, 324. *Sp. Cal.*, iv, 1057–8, 1069, 1073;
v, i, 8.

76. On 28 February 1531 he went to Parliament to bid members
'consider certain liberties of the Church by which malefactors had
had full immunity' (*L.P.*, v, 120); he was said to have been there
three times to urge the passage of the Annates act of 1532 (ibid., 879);
for his visit to Parliament to hasten the act of Appeals see *Sp. Cal.*,
iv, pp. 661, 663. Fisher, Tunstal, Lord Darcy and others were bidden
not to attend the lords for the first session of 1534, when the act of
Succession (the first) was passed. *Sp. Cal.*, v, 8.

77. The conservative bishops had, as we have seen, unitedly rejected the first attacks which ended in their Submission in May 1532.
As has been noted above (p 393) all the bishops present, two abbots
and a lay peer (Arundel) opposed the act in Conditional Restraint of
Annates in the house of lords. *L.P.*, v, 879.

before this, Archbishop Warham had stood up in the house
of lords and denounced the king's tactics in the divorce and
then drew up at Lambeth a public instrument condemning
all that Henry had done against the liberty of the Church
and his own see, and the authority of Rome.[78] Yet on 15 May
he was one of the three members of the upper house of Convocation who accepted without reservation the royal demand
to surrender and had carried the document recording the
clergy's submission to the king. Had the old archbishop
broken – or had he drawn up that protest at Lambeth
three months before in anticipation of later events and, like
the clergy of the lower house who had subscribed a protest
in 1531 which repudiated any future submission, intended
thereby to salve his conscience and disown in advance the
public action which he feared he could never escape? We
will never know. Natural death was to carry off this sturdy
octogenarian in August 1532 before he had been required
finally to declare himself. But his sudden disavowal of the
king some months before must have been alarming. He had
fought to defend the clerical estate. So too had John Clerk,
bishop of Bath and Wells, and Cuthbert Tunstal, bishop of
Durham. So too had John Fisher – the life and soul of the
resistance. Besides this there had been remarkable signs of
loyalty to the old regime and to Catherine (who had friends
among all ranks of the clergy) in the lower house of Convocation, especially in 1531 and 1532;[79] and after the public
submission of the clergy in May 1532 (a suspect victory for
the king), individual bishops continued to hold out – Tunstal
of Durham, Nix of Norwich, perhaps Standish of St Asaph's
and, above all, John Fisher. Each year death removed members of the old guard and made way for Henricians – at Winchester, York, Canterbury, Coventry and Lichfield, and Ely;
and each year saw one bishop after another who was for-

---

78. *Ven. Cal.*, iv, 754; *Wilkins*, iii, 746, for Warham's protest against
all measures in derogation of Rome and his own see – dated 24
February 1532.

79. See above, p. 362 f., 392.

merly an opponent come to terms with Henry. Death – above
all Warham's death in mid 1532 – served Henry well; and
he had served himself well with judicious bullying. Each
major assault on the clerical estate had been preceded by a
preliminary bombardment. *Praemunire* indictments had
prepared the way for the first round in 1531; and *quo warranto* indictments against sixteen clerics had begun the complicated war of nerves conducted partly from above (that is,
the king and the Council) and partly from below (that is,
the Commons), which ended in the Submission of 1532. Likewise individual recalcitrance was quickly rewarded. Four of
the clerics of the lower house of Convocation who signed
the protest of 1531 were quickly put on *praemunire* charges;
when, in early 1532, the ancient Warham suddenly spoke
out against Henry and publicly condemned all that he was
doing, the latter had the archbishop put on a *praemunire*
charge – for having consecrated the bishop of St Asaph's
without royal permission *fourteen years before*.[80] A little
later, Richard Nix of Norwich, now old and blind but still
a firebrand, found himself facing a *praemunire* charge and
a fine of £10,000, allegedly for having violated the liberties
of Thetford by citing the mayor thereof to his diocesan
court, an offence for which the customary penalty was a
fine of 6s. 8d. The mayor had appealed to Cromwell, who
used the case, it seems, to bring the old bishop to heel –
which it did.[81] Cuthbert Tunstal, one of Catherine's best
friends, had protested against the first signs of caesaropapism
in 1531 and had apparently persisted in his opposition ever
since, until, in late 1533, he wrote a remarkable letter to
Henry begging him to halt and return to the path of
righteousness before it was too late. He and Henry were

80. We know about this affair primarily by virtue of the draft of a
thundering speech of defence which he had prepared but presumably
never delivered because of his death. P.R.O. S.P. 1/70, fols 236 ff.
(*L.P.*, v, 1247).

81. P.R.O. K.B. 29/166, ro. 42; K.B. 27/1091, ro. 13, for the case.
Also *L.P.*, vii, 158, 171, 262 (18), 270, 296.

friends and the king answered him good-naturedly. But by the beginning of 1534 there was no room left for hesitation or deviation. Tunstal was suddenly called to London to declare himself and, as he came southwards, royal agents sped to Durham to ransack his palaces and seize all evidence against him. Arrived in London, Tunstal came face to face with the king and was probably told to choose between him and the Tower.[82] Under this pressure, the bishop snapped. He would live to undergo prison in the next reign and confinement in Elizabeth's, but not in this one. For the rest of Henry's time Tunstal would be a king's man, serving a Royal Supremacy which he had at one time so obstinately repudiated.

So it was that, out of a hierarchy that had started well, only one stood firm until the end. Fisher had been a relentless opponent of Henry since 1527, standing across every path the king tried to follow, unmoved by threats, undaunted by his growing loneliness, busy in Convocation and Parliament, tireless in his support of Catherine, and, after he had said all he had to say in so many books on the divorce that he could not later remember exactly how many he had written, speaking out from the pulpit. Before his final imprisonment he had endured one confinement, two attempts on his life, several verbal warnings, two charges of treason. Unlike Thomas More, Fisher became increasingly bold and blunt the further Henry advanced, and in 1533 had taken the supreme step of appealing secretly to the emperor to use force against the king, a most remarkable, desperate action.[83] The appeal met no response, and in April 1534 Fisher was called to Lambeth to take the oath of Succession, which he refused, and thus joined More, the Carthusians, John Haile (a secular priest) and Richard Reynolds (a Brigettine) in the Tower.

82. Sturge, op. cit., 190 ff. *L.P.*, v, 986–7 (misplaced, in 1532); ix, ii, 750. He was said eventually to have sworn the oath of Succession with reservations. *L.P.*, vii, 690.

83. *L.P.*, vi, 1164, 1249. On other details of Fisher's life, see Reynolds, *St John Fisher*.

This group and the Observants who remained loyal to the old order, together with a handful of men and women in the household of Catherine and her daughter who stood by these two and suffered later,[84] were the stalwarts of the opposition. In all there were about forty-five who were indisputably martyrs for the old cause in Henry's reign. But this was not the whole of the opposition by any means. Some fled abroad – including relatives of More and Fisher and, later, Richard Pate, nephew of the bishop of Lincoln, who absconded to Rome while on an embassy in Germany and would return to England in Mary's reign as bishop of Worcester. Others, lay and clerical, stayed at home and grumbled; and there was a good deal to grumble, or at least to be anxious, about. The treatment meted out to Catherine and her daughter, now officially a bastard, caused consternation. Since the act of Succession named Elizabeth as Henry's successor, in default of male heirs, and since Henry was no longer young, it seemed possible that England was either, after all, to see a queen on the throne (and perhaps a disputed succession if Mary's supporters proved numerous), or else face the prospect of a long minority. After years of effort, therefore, the one thing that Henry had not succeeded in doing was to secure the succession. Then the execution of Fisher and More and the others, but especially these two, was alarming. Undoubtedly Henry broke faith with More, whose conscience he had promised to leave alone when he took Wolsey's place in 1529; and, besides this, he pursued him and Fisher vindictively. By refusing the oath of Succession, these two had incurred the penalties of misprision of treason which included, but did not extend beyond, imprisonment during the king's pleasure. Henry had already brushed aside an attempt by Cranmer to allow them to swear only to the new succession, as they were prepared to do, without going on to disown Rome,[85] for he had been bent on bringing them

84. See Paul, _Catherine of Aragon and her Friends_ (1966) for a study of this group.
85. _L.P._, vii, 499.

to the Tower. There they could have stayed, out of harm's
way and perhaps forgotten, had not the second parliamentary session of 1534 produced a new Treason act which
made 'malicious' denial of the king's title punishable by
death. It is likely that Henry was behind this act which, with
the help of perjured evidence, alone enabled him to bring
them to the block. Those who were not explicitly for him
were against him, and he could not rest until they had been
destroyed.

The execution of Fisher and More, and of Reynolds and
the Carthusians shocked much of the outside world, won
the victims immortality and cast a large blood-stain on the
new regime. A year before, Rome had at last given its verdict on Henry's marriage to Catherine. Seven inordinately
protracted years ended with final sentence on the principal
cause (i.e. on the case itself, as distinct from judgement
'*super attentatis*'). After six hours of debate, concluding yet
another review of the whole case, Consistory finally found
for Catherine.[86] However, despite this and despite Henry's
persistent disobedience, Rome took no immediate action
against him. Henry had been talking recently of another
meeting with Francis,[87] and Clement, incredibly, persuaded
himself that, if a papal envoy were to attend that meeting, a
settlement with the English could still be patched up.[88]
Henry (and many since have done the same) complained
bitterly of how Clement had maltreated him; but could he
have had a less aggressive opponent?

In September 1534 Clement's unhappy pontificate came to
an end at last – and, equally incredibly perhaps, it was
Henry's turn to be sanguine. The much-travelled Casale was
sent to Rome to assist the French cardinals in securing an
amenable successor to Clement. The conclave chose Cardi-

---

86. *L.P.*, vii, 363, 368, 370. Even now, French influence delayed this
sentence (ibid., 311). It was given on 23 March 1534 – but only after
the whole case had been reviewed for a fourth time. *Sp. Cal.*, v, 29.
87. ibid., 662, 783, 784, etc. Talk of a meeting continued in 1535.
88. ibid., 851.

nal Farnese, now Paul III, which suited Henry well; for he
had declared himself anxious to please him beforehand and
within a week or so of becoming pope had sent to Casale for
advice on how he could satisfy his dear son, Henry, and recover English allegiance.[89] Casale spoke honeyed words,
assuring the pope that Henry might well return to obedience, that Henry only asked him to be generous and reasonable.[90] But none of this meant that the king was weakening
or that he was prepared to undo the Royal Supremacy. He
would not bargain with Rome. It was for the new pope to
surrender entirely to him – to withdraw his predecessor's
judgement on the divorce, abandon the threatened excommunication, approve the Royal Supremacy.[91] And by
early 1535 Henry was beginning to think that at least some
of this might be possible, 'since', in the matter of his marriage, 'we do perceive by letters thence [i.e. from Rome] both
the opinion of the learned men about the pope there to be
of that opinion that we be of and also a somewhat dis-
position to that purpose in the bishop of Rome's self'.[92] By
June 1535 Casale could report that Paul had received favourably a suggestion from Cromwell that Henry's case might be
reopened and heard by a new commission – not of auditors
of the Rota, like the stiff-necked Simonetta (no friend of
Henry), but of more acceptable folk.[93] With Francis ap-

89. *L.P.*, vii, 1255, 1262, 1298. Paul was not the only optimist. In
Imperial circles it was still supposed that Henry would come to terms,
accept a General Council and let the whole thing blow over. Just as
Philip II would later shield Elizabeth, so now they argued that no
excommunication should be passed against Henry. *Sp. Cal.*, v, i, 173.

90. ibid., 1397.

91. ibid., 1483; viii, 176.

92. *St.P.*, vii, 588 f. (*L.P.*, viii, 341). This passage (in a letter to the
admiral of France) was written by Henry himself. Cf. *L.P.*, viii, 399,
for a report of Henry speaking hopefully of the new pope.

93. *L.P.*, viii, 806–7. That Cromwell wanted Rome to reconsider
Henry's case is beyond doubt. Presumably this was for diplomatic
reasons only – and with English connivance, not her public approval.
He was not preparing to undo the national autarchy proclaimed in
the preamble to the act of Appeals.

parently sympathetic and Charles anxious to keep England
in his orbit while he was on an expedition to Tunis, Henry
seemed to be about to disperse the storm clouds which had
hung over him since late 1533. Rome might not concede
the Royal Supremacy, but if it at last gave approval to the
divorce this would help to justify him to the world and to
his subjects without costing him anything.

Then came the news of the executions. Today we remember More's first, perhaps; but at the time, it was the killing of
Fisher, a prince of the Holy Roman Church, which rang out
louder. News of what had happened reached Rome quickly.
Once again Henry had driven the pope to extreme action
and on 30 August a second excommunication was drawn
up.[94] But once again the document was not fully expedited.
Paul was not prepared to proclaim Henry's deprivation and
discharge his subjects of their allegiance unless he could
call upon the secular powers to enforce his sentence. But,
since June 1535, Charles had been occupied in Tunisia and
Francis was not prepared to lose a friend. Then, in January
1536, Catherine of Aragon died.[95] Years of insults and deprivation – above all of the company of her beloved daughter,
whom, at Henry's behest, she had not been able to see for
the last five years of her life – and, recently, the threat of
following Fisher and More to the scaffold had broken neither

94. *L.P.*, ix, 207. But the bull of deprivation was not finally approved in Consistory until January 1536. *L.P.*, x, 82.
95. The chandler who embalmed Queen Catherine, 'found all the
internal organs as healthy and normal as possible, with the exception of the heart, which was quite black and hideous to look at. He
washed it, but it did not change colour; then he cut it open, and the
inside was the same. Moreover, a black round body stuck to the outside of the heart.' Inevitably it had been rumoured that Catherine
was the victim of poisoning, but the embalmer's report is conclusive
evidence that she died of cancer. His description of the 'black round
body' and her blackened heart exactly fits that of a secondary
melanotic sarcoma. He apparently did not notice the primary growth.
For a full discussion of this, see MacNalty, 'The Death of
Queen Catherine of Aragon', *Nursing Mirror*, 27 December 1962,
257 ff.

her courage[96] nor her serenity, and she died with that same
humble confidence that had marked her life. When the
news of her death at Kimbolton reached London, Henry –
dressed from head to toe in exultant yellow – celebrated the
event with Mass, a banquet, dancing and jousting.[97] He
would mock her even in death and, no less cruelly, try to
make capital out of her departure. In April 1536 Charles
passed through Italy on his way back from North Africa.
Thither went an embassy to ask that, since Catherine was
now dead, the old Anglo-Imperial amity should be restored.
Charles, as ever keen for friends, was agreeable, and before
long serious negotiations were afoot.[98] A few weeks later, in
May 1536, Anne Boleyn was executed and thus not only was
the woman no more for whom Charles had been bound to
fight by dynastic loyalty, but the usurper whom none of the
Catholic world could accept had also been removed. Charles
was now confident that the storm was over and that Henry
could be brought back into the fold, perhaps by remitting
his differences with the pope to a General Council.[99] So too
was the pope. Apparently ready to forget that it was only a
few months since Fisher was beheaded and Henry's excommunication decreed in Consistory, he hailed recent
events as providential and called upon Henry to grasp this
divine opportunity for reconciliation, promising that if he
would make obeisance to the sovereign pontiff he could
then enjoy the same authority in his realm as the emperor
and the French king enjoyed in theirs. The smallest gesture

96. See, for example, her letter to Paul III, written three months
before her death, in which she says that she does not know whom to
blame the more – her husband or the pope (*Sp. Cal.*, v, i, 211). As
this astonishing rebuke shows, Catherine was far from the somewhat
resigned, forlorn person that has sometimes been portrayed. She had
the fire of a Teresa of Avila.

97. *L.P.*, x, 141 (p. 51).

98. ibid., 575, 670, 688, 699, 926.

99. E.g. ibid., 888, 1161, 1227. Charles hoped that Henry, now indisputably a free man, might marry a Portuguese princess or his
own niece, the dowager duchess of Milan.

could have opened all the doors to forgiveness and reconciliation for the prodigal son.[1] And a week or so after the
pope had said this, old Lorenzo Campeggio, that sure
weather-cock of papal intentions, was once again making
ready to visit England – in the hope of recovering his lost
bishopric of Salisbury (of which Parliament had deprived
him) and the cardinal-protectorship of England, and also,
quite certainly, to negotiate terms for Henry's return to the
fold.[2] Rome assumed that the root-cause of the trouble had
now been removed and that the English schism would
therefore soon be brought to an end once certain techni-
calities were settled, with which Campeggio, despite his unfortunate experiences in England on two previous occasions,
would deal.[3]

These plans and the optimism which, ever springing
from the Curia, had promoted them, of course came to
nothing. Henry wanted only two things: to have the excommunication lifted or at least to shield himself against it;
to sabotage the General Council which, in June 1536, Paul
III summoned to meet at Mantua in the following year –
the Council for which Christendom had called for decades,
which was not in fact to meet until 1545, to which Henry had
appealed in 1533, which, in the wrong hands, might cause
him grievous harm and must, therefore, be prevented at all

1. So Paul to Casale on 27 May 1535 – by which time he had just
heard of Anne's fall, not her execution. *L.P.*, x, 977.
2. ibid., 1077. The letter is from Campeggio to his brother – who
is to go forthwith to England to procure the cardinal a safe-conduct
and begin negotiations. A few days later, the pope wrote to James
V exhorting him to receive the nuncio now on his way to treat with
Henry, ibid., 1183. As early as January 1536 Chapuys reported Cromwell as saying that a legate might now come to confirm 'all their
business', ibid., 141. What this meant is not explained, but presumably the nuncio was expected to bring Rome's acceptance of at least
some of what had been done in England against the Church.
3. The subsequent story of Campeggio's errand is not given. Probably he never set out from Rome. His embassy was overtaken by the
Pilgrimage of Grace, which brought about a radical change in papal
policy.

costs. Finding himself now suddenly wooed from all sides,
he was prepared to use his advantage to secure these ends
and these ends only. He would be even better placed if war
should break out between the emperor and Francis, for this
would increase his value to both, smother the excommunication and postpone the Council. A renewal of the Habsburg–Valois contest would serve him admirably. By the
summer his wish had been granted. By resuming their
conflict, Charles and Francis enabled Henry to turn the
tables on acute danger and become the most sought-after
personage in Europe, thereby winning for himself, as it was
to prove, two more years' breathing space.

Nonetheless, though Henry would remain sheltered from
external danger until this latest Franco-Imperial war came
to an end in June 1538, England was still in an anxious state.
The excommunication had been scotched, not killed. The
executions, Catherine's fate and her daughter's plight were
not quickly forgotten and inevitably rumours started that
Catherine had been poisoned.[4] Then the fall of Anne
Boleyn brought new uncertainty about the future and
seemed to make the prospect of an heir to the throne even
more remote. 1536 had seen negotiations begin for a union
between Henry and the Lutheran princes of Germany which
promised to commit England to the Confession of Augsburg
and bestow on Henry the title of 'Defender of the
Evangelical League'. It had seen, too, the appearance of the
Ten Articles, the first formulary of faith produced by the
Supreme Head and a blatantly heterodox document which
treated of only three sacraments (implying that the missing
four, as the Reformers preached, were to be discarded) and
derived much of what it said, about justification, for
example, almost verbatim from Lutheran theology.[5] It was
plausible to assume that England was about to do what, to
the Protestant, was the logical conclusion to the repudiation
of Rome and embrace the continental Reformation in its

4. *L.P.*, x, 670.
5. For further discussion of this, see below, pp. 517, 520, 531.

entirety. The Royal Supremacy, then, was after all to be the door by which England would enter the Protestant world.

Added to this, 1536 saw the first stage of the dissolution of English monasticism. That vast enterprise, the *Valor Ecclesiasticus*, a survey of the wealth of the English Church, had been drawn up in 1535; next year the first act of Dissolution of monasteries of less than £200 annual value was passed. Tudor England was about to embark on its most massive single enterprise. We need not trace the story of this piece of redistribution of monastic wealth. Suffice it to say that English monasticism was a huge and urgent problem; that radical action, though of precisely what kind was another matter, was both necessary and inevitable, and that a purge of the religious orders was probably regarded as the most obvious task of the new regime – as the first function of a Supreme Head empowered by statute 'to visit, extirp and redress'.[6] The real question was not whether the monks should be hammered but whether the purging of monasticism should not be included in a much larger programme which tackled the problem of redisposing the wealth of the entire Church, secular as well as regular, bishoprics, chapters and parish churches, etc., at the same time as religious houses. In March 1533 Henry had told Chapuys that he was determined 'to reunite to the crown the goods which Churchmen held of it, which his predecessors could not alienate to his prejudice, and that he was required to do this by the oath he had taken at his coronation'.[7] Whatever Henry may have meant by this, it is clear that he saw the problem of clerical wealth as one which involved the whole Church, not just a segment of it. Further, the *Valor Ecclesiasticus* had been a survey of ecclesiastical wealth as a whole and not simply monastic income. In 1534 a start had been made towards stripping the secular clergy when the act of First Fruits and Tenths

6. As the act of Supremacy empowered the new head of the Church.

7. *L.P.*, vi, 235.

bestowed on the crown the whole of one year's income from every newly-acquired benefice and a tenth of the annual income thereafter; and at the same time there had been official plans for endowing bishoprics with a fixed, and reduced, income of 1,000 marks per annum (except Canterbury and York, which were to receive 2,000 marks and £1,000) and for seizing half the income of collegiate churches and cathedrals, and the whole of that of archdeaconries.[8] Throughout 1534 Chapuys reported that Henry was being pressed by councillors to set about the wealth of the Church, secular and regular, and it was with some surprise that he found that nothing had happened by the end of the year.[9] Perhaps such an operation was too vast to be undertaken; perhaps official plans were as yet unformed; perhaps the institution of the new and burdensome levy of first fruits and tenths was thought sufficient. Clearly there was some hesitation. The first commissions for Cromwell and his assistants to visit religious houses were drawn up probably in December 1534, only to be set aside while the commissioners appointed to compile the *Valor* did their work, and not till 1536 did the suppression of English monasticism begin. By the autumn of that year, thanks to the prodigious efficiency of the visitors, monasteries were being dismantled fast. But just when this was under way, the storm broke – in the form of a massive rebellion against the new order, the so-called Pilgrimage of Grace.

Those who were enthusiastically behind the Henrician Reformation were probably a small minority. The majority, probably, were made up of that body of the largely indifferent already described, who, for one reason or another, faced the regime with anything from passive reluctance to lukewarm, or qualified, approval. There undoubtedly emerged another kind, perhaps also a minority but maybe a larger one than the first, men of all sorts and conditions,

8. B.M. Cleo. E, iv, fol. 174 (*L.P.*, vii, 1355). *L.P.*, vii, 1356 proposes lower rates.

9. *Sp. Cal.*, v, i, 7, 37, 87, 112, 115.

who actively feared or disliked what was happening, even though they had not so far laid down their lives to defeat it and might never actively have shown their opposition had not others presented them with the opportunity to do so. To describe the Henrician Reformation as popular *tout court* is inadequate. In the first place, it anachronistically ignores the sociological fact that the lower orders, the 'many-headed monster', were expected to follow (and often did follow) the political and religious opinions of their social betters. The principle *cuius regio eius religio* worked at more than one level of society and would soon be working in different directions, on behalf of different religious allegiances, within any one society. In the second, it ignores the evidence that the mass of the population was not actively behind it, that there was by now a growing ground-swell of opposition. We can see the tenseness and near-incredulity of the enthusiasts like, say, Cromwell, that the revolution which has been accomplished in law is being successfully carried by proclamation, preaching, pamphlet and pageant into the daily life of a society at once conservative and volatile. Cromwell himself had no doubt about the magnitude of the task, and the historian who fails to see how uncertain and complicated the situation was will fail to do him justice. In the last half of the 1530s all was unsettled and hazardous.

The Reformation did not bring a new unity to England; on the contrary, it created a new and long-lived disunity, inside a new sense of nationhood. We can see that new disunity happening – in the growing amount of angry and treasonous talk reported to Cromwell (not by spies in the technical sense but, often, by ordinary folk, anxious enthusiasts like him) and the mounting tide of wild rumours which were abroad. What is recorded in the state papers from the lips of a parson here or a yeoman there can only have been a small fraction of the whole. Rarely, one imagines, had more sedition been spoken by so many, so suddenly. In 1534 and through 1535 Chapuys reported the makings of a rebellion under the leadership of Lords Sandys and Darcy, and others, which

was ready to enlist the emperor's and Scottish support.[10] By
the summer of 1536, a time when Henry was riotously happy
celebrating his third marriage amidst incessant music,
pageants and warm days on the river, there was grumbling
unrest in the Midlands and North. In October it burst into
rebellion. First in Lincolnshire, then in Yorkshire and the
neighbouring counties, then in the North-West, there broke
out a series of rebellions collectively given the name the
Pilgrimage of Grace – a title more properly confined to the
outbreak in Yorkshire which began about 8 October and had
Robert Aske as its leader.

The risings were so complex, were sprung of so many
different motives in any one area and varied in structure and
character from one region to another so widely as almost to
defeat generalization. In part they were the fruit of a neo-
feudal conspiracy which northern Marcher lords like
Thomas Darcy, John Hussey and Thomas Dacre – actively
abetted by the Imperial ambassador – had been planning for
about three years.[11] In the North-West, in particular,
economic and social grievances were predominant. Elsewhere landlordism, fiscalism and local politics played their
part. Many of the commons who formed Aske's force, the
tenantry of such as Darcy or Lumley, may have been carried
into rebellion by more or less blind obedience to their noble
or gentry landlords, or have been moved by motives very
different from those of the captains. In Sir Francis Bigod –
a very remarkable young man – the Pilgrims had an ally
(and later the leader of a separate rising) who was an
advanced Protestant in rebellion primarily against the
Erastianism of the Royal Supremacy and wholly out of step
with Aske.[12] But when all this has been said and full allowance made for the way in which the risings were inevitably
caught up in local and secular issues, exploited by adven-
turers who smelt easy loot, by victims of enclosure or rapa-

10. *L.P.*, vii, 1206; *Sp. Cal.*, v, i, 8, 127, 138, 139, 165, 157.
11. Mattingly, *Catherine of Aragon*, pp. 285 ff., deals with this.
12. Dickens, *Lollards and Protestants in the Diocese of York*, 53 ff.

cious landlords and so on, it may still be argued that the Lincolnshire rebellion and the Pilgrimage proper were first and foremost protests on behalf of the old order against the recent religious changes. Not that there was unanimity of religious aim. The Lincolnshire men were on the whole ready to accept the Royal Supremacy, while Aske, after some debate, called for England's return to obedience to Rome. But all (including Bigod) were against the further suppression of the monasteries and the continued spoliation of the Church by the levy of first fruits and tenths. Both in Lincolnshire and Yorkshire the rebels demanded that the advance of heresy should be halted, that the heretical or heterodox bishops should be cast out (especially Cranmer), that Cromwell and Rich and other base-born councillors should be supplanted by men of decent birth, that Leigh and Layton, the leading figures in the suppression of the religious houses, should be punished for their inquisitorial methods, their spoliations, their calumnies. In short, it is difficult to rebut Aske's repeated assertion that even if other factors had not intervened, religious grievances (in the widest sense of that adjective) would have sufficed to generate rebellion. It was these grievances which gave the Pilgrimage the little shape and direction that it had; that they were not alone, that they mingled with a multiplicity of secular motives does not in itself impugn the essentially religious character of the core of the movement.[13]

In their articles drawn up at Pontefract in early December, the Pilgrims set out their protest against religious changes and a full list of demands, great and small – that Mary be legitimized, that the act empowering Henry to devise the crown by will, the statute of uses, the statute of treason by words be repealed; that the law and parliamentary elections be remodelled; that remedy be provided against corrupt

13. I therefore support the contention of Professor Knowles (*Religious Orders in England*, Cambridge, 1959, iii, 322) that the Pilgrimage was primarily a religious event, which, of course, is a long way from saying it was exclusively this.

escheators; that enclosure be halted and old holidays restored, etc.[14] But these last, lesser requests should not obscure
the issue. The Pilgrims at Pontefract implicitly condemned
the divorce, they explicitly condemned the breach with
Rome and the dissolution of the monasteries; they condemned Henry's innovations and incipient autocracy; they
condemned his leading servants. Before and during the
rebellion the country was thick with prophecies and political
ballads, unflattering stroies about Henry and, above all,
violent rumours to the effect that all Church plate and
jewels were to be seized and tin crosses and censers exchanged for silver, that only one parish church per five miles
would be allowed to stand, that there would be a tax on
white bread, pigs, geese and capons, a tax on weddings,
burials and christenings.[15] That such things could be said
and, apparently, believed, suggests a collapse of confidence
in royal government such as England had not known perhaps since as long ago as the 1450s. Certainly Tudor England had not seen its like before, nor would it again. The
Pilgrimage must stand as a large-scale, spontaneous, authentic indictment of all that Henry most obviously stood for;
and it passed judgement against him as surely and com-
prehensively as *Magna Carta* condemned King John or the
Grand Remonstrance the government of Charles I.

Moreover, the rebellion might well have been an even
larger convulsion than it was. It could have openly enlisted
latent Yorkist sentiment and thus acquired dynastic over-
tones; its fire might have spread to other parts of England;[16]

14. *L.P.*, xi, 1246.   15. E.g. ibid., 972, 973, 975; xii, i, 70.
16. There was mention later of a Cornish painter having been
asked to paint a banner of the Five Wounds – the Pilgrim's standard
(*L.P.*, xii, ii, 56). There was much discontent in East Anglia and
rumblings of rebellion there (see Oxley, *The Reformation in Essex*
(Manchester, 1965), 116 f. Cf. reports of unrest in Norfolk in *L.P.*,
xii, i, 1065). If East Anglia had joined, the whole movement would
have had a much stronger socio-economic flavour – but, as a contemporary priest reckoned, joined with the North 'they had been able to
go through the realm'. *L.P.*, xii, ii, 21.

there could have been Scottish intervention; there were moves towards calling for help from the emperor. Finally, Rome was ready to intervene. As soon as news arrived there that the North was up, Reginald Pole was made a cardinal and sent to Flanders, nominally to call upon Henry to repent and submit, but also to muster support for the Pilgrims and, maybe, to come to England at the head of a military force. The crown was scarcely in greater peril in 1588 or 1642. And yet, presumably because it fought for the wrong side and because it failed, the Pilgrimage has often been treated by historians as a minor, peripheral upset wrought by a few provincial conservatives, a somewhat pathetic rising which could never have succeeded against Henry's solid regime.

But the truth is that, if it had wanted, it might have swamped him. The king was saved not so much by the loyalty of his friends as by the loyalty of the rebels. Time and again Aske refused to take advantage of his opponents' weakness and held back the hotheads who wanted to march boldly southwards and conquer, as they might have done, insisting that he and his followers were pilgrims, not rebels, come to plead with the king, not to bury him. Aske was Henry's most loyal, as well as his most critical, subject, and it was his integrity, his simple confidence that Henry would hear their petition, his faith that the king would not break his word nor wreak bloody revenge which really defeated the Pilgrimage.

At first, understandably, Henry failed to grasp the size of the rebellion and was confident that it could be quickly suppressed and avenged.[17] After Norfolk and Suffolk, the leading royal commanders in the field, had convinced him that this was a large-scale revolt he remained confident, if not truculent, offering what was certainly shrewd advice on occasions,[18] but showing no sympathy for the difficulties

17. See, e.g., *L.P.*, xi, 752, 771, 984.
18. E.g. *St.P.*, i, 491 ff. (*L.P.*, xi, 884) – a letter heavily corrected by Henry.

facing his outnumbered, hesitant armies. Instead, he sent northwards a stream of belligerence which at one point, in December, broke into a tirade of rebukes and accusations of timidity, panic and incompetence.[19] Nor, of course, did he begin to show any sympathy for those subjects of his who were now firmly but humbly presenting their complaints to his lieutenant. As far as he was concerned they were 'false traitors and rebels', full of 'wretched and devilish intents', who must be punished for the 'detestable and unnatural' sins of rebellion against their natural sovereign, their contempt for the solemn decrees of Parliament and ingratitude for his tireless solicitude for their welfare.[20] He knew only his own rights, his own virtues, his own complaints – none of theirs. He did not begin to doubt his own righteousness or to investigate the Pilgrims' petitions. They were to be brought to unconditional surrender by any methods, as soon as possible, punished and forgotten. They could not have anything to say to which he should listen, there was nothing to be said for them. Throughout these critical weeks, Henry was full of vigour, drafting replies to the rebels, supervising the campaign and speaking violence all the time. He told the men of Lincolnshire that they hailed from 'one of the most brute and beastly shires of the whole realm' and promised 'the utter destruction of them, their wives and children'.[21] Whatever he might be forced to say in public for tactical reasons, his intention was always bloody revenge; and when the risings were put down, he had it. Some seventy peasants of Cumberland, for instance, were to be hanged in their villages, on trees in their gardens.[22] The chief monks of Sawley, one of the religious houses which the Pilgrims had reopened, were to be 'hanged on long pieces of timber or otherwise out of the steeple' – while about 150 other

19. *L.P.*, xi, 1227, 1270.
20. See Henry's reply to the Lincolnshire rebels in *St.P.*, i, 463 ff., and to the Yorkshire rebels in *St.P.*, i, 506 ff.
21. ibid., 463. *Hughes and Larkin*, 245.
22. *L.P.*, xii, i, 479.

victims, including one woman who was burned to death, would be executed in London and various places in the north for their part in the rebellion.

Few contemporaries would have expected Henry to deal humanely or magnanimously with the rebels and fewer still, probably, would have applauded him if he had done so. A prince who lacked a standing army and a police force, a society which had known so much civil commotion in the previous century, inevitably tended to look upon rebellion as heinous sin crying out to God for condign punishment – indeed, as the sin of sins, for, as the Homily on Obedience of 1547 explained, 'where there is no right order there reigneth all abuse, carnal liberty, enormity, sin and Babylonical disorder'. Ironically, in so far as the Pilgrimage was a feudal protest against the central authority and an attack on upstarts like Cromwell who had dispossessed the king's 'natural councillors', these rebels were not so much threatening to overturn the social order as trying to restore it. But the great northern Marcher lords like the Percies and Nevilles were still so untamed and had caused so much trouble in bygone days that no king could afford to look lightly upon this apparently sinister recrudescence of ancient ambition and lawlessness. As was pointed out in the official tracts which quickly followed the rebellion, such as Thomas Starkey's *An Exhortation to Christian Unity* and Richard Morison's *A Remedy for Sedition*, in raising their hand against the Lord's Anointed and Supreme Head the rebels not only committed a capital offence against God and man, and threatened the whole commonwealth with uproar, but had sought to assert antique, feudal pretensions against the sovereignty of 'imperial' kingship.

After he had discovered the full size and enormity of the rebellion Henry's first policy was to play for time and allow the many tensions among its participants to do their disruptive work.[23] To this tactic he soon added more or less open deceit. He sent a message to the Pilgrims' council at York

23. See, e.g., *L.P.*, xi, 1174.

(via the two envoys who had come down to him after the first parley with Norfolk on Doncaster bridge) which was designed to mislead them and send them home thinking that all would be well.[24] But the Pilgrims guessed what was afoot and would not disperse. Instead they drew up their final, comprehensive petition, discussed above, which was to be presented to Norfolk at the second Doncaster conference on 6 December when their representatives met the duke and presented their request for a free general pardon and a promise that a Parliament should be called soon, in the North, to set right their grievances. In preparation for this meeting, Henry had given way to the advice of his Council and explicitly empowered Norfolk to agree to both these requests, for a pardon and for a Parliament, as a last resort. He was to reply initially that his commission did not empower him thus far but that he would make suit to Henry on their behalf, and after some days' delay, to produce (as though it had just arrived) a pardon which Sir John Russell was already bringing to him. If the rebels demanded yet more than this, Norfolk was to secure a longer truce to allow massive royal forces secretly to be gathered to smash the rebellion once and for all.[25] What precisely happened when Norfolk met the thirty Pilgrims in Doncaster priory is not clear. But he certainly told them of the king's pardon and his promise of a Parliament, exactly as he had been empowered, by the king, in the king's name, to do. Taking his words at their face value, the Pilgrims believed that their gracious king had met their desires just as they had always known he would and that the Pilgrimage had achieved its purpose. When the promised pardon was read later, Aske took off his Pilgrim's badge, the five wounds of Christ, saying, 'We will wear no badge or sign but the badge of our sovereign lord', and on his orders the Pilgrims now finally dispersed,

24. *L.P.*, xi, 1061. It gave them 'instructions of comfort' to the effect that Norfolk would bring a sympathetic reply to their petition – which Henry probably did not intend.

25. Thus *St.P.*, i, 511 ff., esp. 514 ff. Cf. ibid., 521 f.

confident that their bloodless and entirely loyal demonstration, like Ket's rebellion later in the century, essentially an appeal by loving subjects to a loving ruler against the misdeeds of others, had won the day and that a Parliament would soon meet to set all aright. Shortly afterwards, Aske – whom, with Darcy, Henry had earlier planned to detach from his rank-and-file with a secret offer of pardon for himself alone[26] – was persuaded to come south to make final peace with his prince.[27]

But though Henry never repudiated what Norfolk had promised (indeed, he implicitly confirmed it), he never carried it out. The pardon which the herald read out was a *promise* of pardon and no more. The Parliament to which he had agreed never met, and was probably never intended to. Now that their leader had sent the rebels home and himself come to court for safe-keeping, it would have seemed that Norfolk and the others could set about reducing the North to obedience. What exactly Henry planned is not clear, for events overtook any plans he may have had. Yorkshire soon saw a new wave of unrest, including a rising led by Bigod, prompted by the insufficiency of the previous 'pardon' and a realistic conviction that Henry would now launch a counter-attack; and in mid February stricken peasants of Cumberland and Westmorland laid siege to Carlisle. This second surge of rebellion gave Henry the opportunity he wanted to strike with bloody finality. Lincoln, York, Durham, Newcastle and Hull, and the towns and villages of Cumberland would now witness awful punishment – while London saw most of the leaders brought to death. Aske, like Darcy and the others, had not been party to these later uprisings – indeed, he had opposed them. But Tudor government, though often extraordinarily scrupulous in its regard for the law, especially when the defendants were small fry and their alleged treason of no great moment, was less in-

26. *St.P.*, i, 519.
27. *L.P.*, xii, i, 43–6. But see ibid., 67, in which Aske warns Henry of the dangers of duplicity and further taxation.

hibited when the king was bent on blood and the victims
important figures. Then, as Thomas More, John Fisher and
Anne Boleyn – not to mention Cromwell himself – were to
find, a servile judiciary would not give fair trial. In mid May
1537 seventeen of the chief participants in the risings were
condemned in London and then, most of them, dispatched
homewards for execution, Sir Robert Constable to Hull,
Hussey to Lincoln, Aske to York.

Shortly after the first rising in Lincolnshire, Henry announced that he himself would soon set out northwards to
deal with the troubles, and this promise was repeated or
discussed many times afterwards in letters to his harassed
lieutenants and the Pilgrims.[28] It was, in many ways, a
sensible plan. What could better assuage the north, where,
it must be remembered, Henry had never been seen, than a
royal visit, or what be better evidence to Aske and the others
of his sincere and much-vaunted concern for his subjects? If
Norfolk and his colleagues were as inadequate as, at one
time, Henry suggested, was it not his duty to take over from
them? Was it not perhaps his duty to do so anyway? One
might have thought so. But Henry never came. Instead he
stayed in or around his capital and had the Tower re-
inforced. Then, when the rebellions were quelled, he promised a royal summer progress in the north, to York, even to
Carlisle.[29] But again he never came. Why was this? Norfolk
was told that Henry's leg was bad, but the king went on a
lengthy progress in the south soon afterwards. It is difficult not to conclude that he shirked his visit to the north out
of cowardice.

By the end of June 1537 England was apparently tranquil
again. Not only were the rebels finally put down but the
threat from without (such as it was) had evaporated. As has
been said, when Rome saw the possibilities of the northern
rising, Pole had been commissioned legate *a latere* to go

28. *L.P.*, xi, 716, 765, 799, 874, 885, 907–8.
29. *L.P.*, xii, i, 918, 973, 1118; ii, 77 – in which Henry announced
that he had put off his journey until the next year, i.e. 1538.

towards England and collect support for the rebels. Thus
would Henry's excommunication, still not fully expedited,
be put into force. But as so often happened where Pole was
concerned, things moved both slowly and inconclusively.
Having been empowered to call upon Henry – when he came
near to England – to return to the fold and, if he refused,
to work for his destruction by force of arms, Pole did not
set out until mid February 1537.[30] Rome already knew that
the rebellion which had excited high hopes had been put
down, but evidently thought that Pole's presence near by
could resuscitate it and mobilize outside aid. But it was a
forlorn expedition. Pole was too late, had too little money to
raise mercenaries and was not likely to impress either Francis
or Charles, both of whom were intent on gaining English
support in their war against the other (indeed, Charles was
trying to win Henry with an offer of the Portuguese infante
for Princess Mary).[31]

To Henry, Pole was an arrant traitor who must be brought
to justice. He was to be seized, 'trussed up and conveyed to
Calais', whence he would be taken to England to face trial.[32]
As soon as his mission was known the English ambassadors
in France and the Low Countries were ordered to have him
arrested and extradited, or, if this were impossible, kidnapped or murdered. There is no doubt that Henry went to
considerable lengths to get him and that Pole was in serious
danger. As it happened, he escaped his pursuants, but Henry
succeeded in persuading Francis to agree to expel him from
France and was able to hinder him further when he moved
on to Cambrai and Liège.[33] Pole's embassy was something of
a fiasco and ended, on the last day of June, with his recall

30. *L.P.*, xii, i, 779.
31. *Sp. Cal.*, v, ii, 140 for Charles's realistic assessment of Pole's
embassy. But Charles was also considering helping Mary secretly to
escape from England if Henry wanted to force her into another
match.
32. *L.P.*, xii, i, 865, 923, 939, 993, 1032, etc. See ibid., 1242, for
Pole's account.
33. ibid. 865, 923, 993, 1032.

to Rome.[34] Frustrated at every turn by English agents, Pole
had waited at Liège for weeks in the vain hope that a new
rebellion would break out and allow him to accomplish his
extremely improbable mission. Convinced that if the schism
were not nipped in the bud and if the present generation of
his fellow-countrymen 'shall transmit their ideas to their
children, England will be lost for ever',[35] and like Aske, heedless of his personal safety, Pole (again like Aske) never had a
realistic grasp of the nature of his mission. As in 1570, papal
action came too long after rebellion to be effective. Nonetheless, the crisis of the Pilgrimage of Grace, Paul's bull and
Pole's expedition was far graver than that of the Northern
Rising of 1569 and Pius V's famous excommunication of
Elizabeth. Henry was extremely lucky that Pole took so long
to arrive, that Charles and Francis were keener to preserve
than to destroy him and that Aske was one of the most trust-
ing and upright subjects in the kingdom. Had things been
only slightly different, his Reformation might have been
wholly or largely undone, Cromwell, Cranmer and the rest
expelled, he himself destroyed and Mary brought to the
throne, either with a Portuguese husband or even married
to Pole himself (who was not yet ordained priest), sixteen
years ahead of her time.

Months before the Lincolnshire rising broke out and
threatened this terrifying train of events, two important
things had happened in Henry's private life. On 21 January
1536 he fell badly from his horse and was knocked unconscious for two hours. He was now forty-four and getting
stout, and a fall like this could have done serious damage.[36]
According to Anne, it certainly harmed her. She was pregnant at the time and was so shocked by the news of Henry's
mishap (which Norfolk brought to her) that, so she explained, she miscarried. On 27 January, the day on which

34. *L.P.*, xii, ii, 174.
35. ibid., i, 1242.
36. See below, p. 624.

Catherine was buried, she was delivered of a three and a half-month-old child (probably a boy).

Her position had already become insecure. Perhaps as early as mid 1534 Henry had started flirting seriously with Jane Seymour.[37] Now tasting the sort of bitterness which Catherine had endured at her hands for years, but without her resources to endure it, Anne raged and fumed – but the amour continued. Her miscarriage – when Henry was confident that she was about to produce the son which, of course, was still urgently desired – was a disaster that he was not likely to forgive.[38] He spoke to her little now and at Shrovetide left her at Greenwich to enjoy himself elsewhere.[39] By April (1536) there were clear signs that the Boleyn family was coming to the end of its years of prosperity and yielding to the Seymours. Incredibly, a second divorce was afoot. Henry's servants were being asked to deliver him from the marriage which had cost so much to effect. Bishop Stokesley of London, who had won promotion for his efforts in the first divorce, was conscripted to perform again;[40] Cromwell examined a possible ground for divorce (i.e. nullity, of course) in Anne's alleged pre-contract with the earl of Northumberland's son years before – the engagement which Wolsey had intercepted and thereby incurred her anger – but received categorical refutation.[41] But Anne had to go; and if there were nothing wrong in the marriage itself then there must be something wrong in her living of it. On 24 April Henry set up a commission headed by Cromwell and Norfolk to find a damning fault in her. Within a few days it had brought against her a charge of adultery with several courtiers – including her brother – and, by a wide construction, alleged that this constituted treason. On May Day 1536 jousts were held at Greenwich during which Anne is said to have revealed her infidelity by dropping a handkerchief to a

37. Henry's interest in Jane Seymour was noted in September 1534. *Sp. Cal.*, v, i, 90.
38. *L.P.*, x, 282, 495.   39. ibid., 351.
40. ibid., 752.   41. ibid., 864.

lover and thus sent the king stalking off in a rage, or, as an
alternative story goes, fired him to pounce on several courtiers with the news that they were suspected of adultery with
the queen. One suspect, Henry Norris, an old favourite of the
king and a courtier *par excellence*, went to the Tower immediately. Next day, 2 May, Anne followed him in near-
hysteria. Norris and three others were tried on 12 May;
Anne and her brother three days later. On 19 May she was
beheaded by the headsman specially brought over from
Calais – after having said of Henry as she approached her
death 'a gentler nor a more merciful prince was there never;
and to me he was ever a good, a gentle and sovereign lord'.
Meanwhile a new attempt had been made to prove the nullity of her marriage to Henry. Two days before she died a
court presided over by Cranmer at Lambeth reached the
astounding conclusion that Henry's adultery with her sister
had rendered the marriage void from the start. On the day
that she died Cranmer issued a dispensation from affinity in
the third degree between Henry and Jane Seymour.[42]

Anne had lived in a libidinous court. Inevitably she had
been the stimulant to, and priestess of, that elaborate cult of
courtly love by which high society sought to turn eroticism
into gallant posturing. Before Henry won her, she had been
the object of Sir Thomas Wyatt's affection and may have
allowed him to advance further than, for long, the king
could go – until Henry stepped in and Wyatt was dismissed
from court. Thereafter she remained the centre of attraction
and revelled in it. 'Pastime in the queen's chamber', love-
lyrics and music, dancing, tokens, sighs – these were the
very stuff of a young, and probably flirtatious, queen's daily
round.[43] Certainly she had been indiscreet with Mark
Smeaton, the Court musician, with Norris and perhaps one
Francis Weston, seeing too much of them, dancing too
familiarly with them, sharing too many romantic secrets

42. *L.P.*, x, 915.
43. See Thomson, *Sir Thomas Wyatt and His Background*, 28 ff., for
an excellent discussion of this, and of Anne's fall.

with them. But it is difficult to believe that she was ever
guilty of adultery with them, or of incest with her brother.
Would she have been so extravagantly indiscreet as her
accusers alleged? Is it credible that, as has been suggested,
adultery was the last throw of a woman who despaired of
conceiving a son by her husband and took to this extreme in
order to disguise her failure (which was probably not hers
anyway)? Would she have conspired to kill the king and
been guilty of 'often saying to her lovers that she would
marry one of them as soon as the king was dead'? All the
accused denied their misconduct to the end – except Mark
Smeaton; and his confession was procured by Cromwell
under threat of torture. Henry, of course, believed in her infidelity. Indeed, he talked of her having committed adultery
with a hundred men.[44] He exulted in her fall, saying he had
long foreseen it. He had even written a 'tragedy' on the subject in his own hand, which he displayed proudly. Clearly
he was bent on undoing her by any means. And why did he
require a decree of nullity as well as her execution? To open
the way to the duke of Richmond? To debase his second, and
unwanted, daughter? To complete the obliteration of an
incestuous union which he now (conveniently) found ab-
horrent? Did the charge against Anne of incest with her
brother and Henry's especial concern with Norris, who was
attached to one Margaret Shelton (in whom the king himself
had recently been interested), likewise show psychosexual
motivation?[45] Would anything less have enabled him to confess that he had entered a forbidden union yet a second
time?

As soon as Henry heard that Anne's execution was accomplished, he entered his barge and visited Jane. Next day
he was betrothed to her. On 30 May he was married quietly
at York Place, in the Queen's Closet.[46] Thus, with great
rapidity, he acquired his third wife. She had been a maid
of both Catherine and Anne, was an admirer of the former

44. *L.P.*, x, 908.   45. Flügel, art. cit., 138 ff.
46. *L.P.*, x, 926, 1000.

and far less of a termagant than the latter. Since the succession still lay with the offspring of the previous marriage,
as the Succession act of 1534 had authorized, Parliament had
to be reassembled to deal with the new situation. A second
Succession act was passed which, taking account of the possibility of Henry now having no further issue and thus
leaving no legitimate heir or heiress, conferred on him the
remarkable power to appoint any successor at any time by
letters patent or by will.[47] If the act was not constitutionally
extraordinary (for it was from Parliament that Henry received authority to do personally what was normally done
by statute) it was certainly so politically. With both his
previous marriages declared invalid, if Henry were to die
suddenly before he had named a successor, England would
find herself in exactly that crisis which the whole of his
policy in recent years had been advertised as preventing.
The first act of Succession had made things anxious enough.
But now Henry was older and another fall might kill him.
Even if he did name a male successor, how would the latter
fare in the face of those two illegitimate daughters, each at
one time an heiress to the throne and the elder with undoubtedly a widespread following, as the Pilgrimage was
to show? Perhaps Henry intended to name his illegitimate
son, the duke of Richmond, as his successor. But a few
weeks after the act was passed allowing him to do so, Richmond died. Presumably to save face and avoid further
anxiety among the populace which was certainly concerned
for the dynasty's future, Henry ordered Richmond's body
to be wrapped in lead, instead of a splendid royal coffin,
hidden in a wagon under straw and taken to Thetford,
where the duke of Norfolk would have him quietly buried.[48]
Richmond's death, so ironically timed, made it yet more

47. 28 *Henry VIII c.* 3.
48. *L.P.*, xi, 221, 233. Afterwards Henry complained that his son
had not been honourably buried. But the royal instructions were
clear. Norfolk now heard a rumour that he was destined for the
Tower. So ibid., 233. Cf. ibid., 236.

clear that, unless Jane produced a son there could be no security – and even then, that security would be undermined by the fact that the heir's right had been put in the gift of an unpredictable father. The words of Richard Rich, speaker in the Parliament of 1536, were a little fulsome when he described Henry as a benevolent sun drying up all harmful vapours and ripening all things good and necessary.

Meanwhile Princess Mary – her mother dead, her mother's rival beheaded – had made peace at last with her father: a total surrender, in which she acknowledged the Royal Supremacy, renounced Rome and admitted her own illegitimacy. Though Henry had not been especially vindictive towards her (he had even sent his physician to her when she fell ill),[49] Mary's life during the past years had been gruelling. She had been forced to give precedence to Elizabeth, humiliated and sometimes mishandled by the latter's household, prevented from going out to Mass lest local folk salute her, moved around from palace to palace and, above all, forbidden access not only to her father but also to her mother, despite Catherine's urgent entreaties. One can see how embarrassing, indeed dangerous, these two strong women were to Henry; but if one can understand the impatience with which he put down any appeal on Mary's behalf, it is impossible to forgive his refusal of Catherine's last and only request – that she should have her daughter with her. Mary, whether Henry liked it or not, was a popular figure who was warmly greeted wherever she went. Moreover, she was an international one. Charles's ambassador kept in touch with her and Catherine; it was through him that Mary smuggled out letters to the pope and the emperor, through him that Charles tried to rescue her by arranging a marriage for her to the dauphin, the king of Scotland, Reginald Pole or the Portuguese infante – only to be told by Henry, in effect, to mind his own business. The king was convinced that the daughter whom he had left stranded and yet regarded with an erratic pride, would come to heel and serve his purposes.[50]

49. *L.P.*, vii, 1129.   50. ibid., 1209.

But Mary, like her mother, refused to surrender and placed herself in increasing danger.

So evident was that danger that, by early 1535, the emperor was ready to consider plans to smuggle the princess out of England – by ship from Greenwich to the Low Countries. But Henry smelt the plot and promptly had her moved. Then she fell ill. After her mother died in January 1536 she was desperate to escape, but nothing came of her plans.[51] At last, hoping that the kindly Jane Seymour might soften her father's heart, she turned to Henry and begged for restoration. Reasonable and generous as he often was, Cromwell acted as go-between. But Henry made no reply to her letters[52] and instead sent commissioners to her at Hunsdon to demand that she take the oath and make a complete submission to him, including an admission of her illegitimacy. This she refused to do, despite threats. When Henry heard of her obstinacy, he fumed. Her friend, Lady Hussey, went to the Tower, even Cromwell feared for himself, two were excluded from the Privy Council for alleged sympathy with the recalcitrant girl and there was talk of legal action against her. Browbeaten, unwell and alone, counselled even by Chapuys to submit, Mary at last gave in and signed a document which acknowledged Henry as Supreme Head, renounced the pope and declared the marriage between Henry and her mother to have been 'incestuous and unlawful'.[53] Chapuys suggested to her that she should make a protestation 'apart', i.e. secretly forswear her submission. Instead she signed the document without reading it and then asked the ambassador secretly to procure papal absolution for what she had done.[54]

Had Mary not surrendered, she might have been put to death. But now that she had in theory done so, and now that Richmond was dead, it would presumably be she that Henry must name as his successor, as the recent act empowered him. Though still illegitimate and unable to see her father,

51. *Sp. Cal.*, v, ii, 21.   52. *L.P.*, x, 1108, 1133, 1136, 1186.
53. ibid., 1137.   54. *L.P.*, xi, 7.

she was climbing back into favour and might even recover
the title of princess.[55] Henry had lost an illegitimate son, but
he was gaining an illegitimate daughter.

Then came the great rebellions in the North from which,
as we have seen, Henry emerged the victor. A few months
afterwards came a third, crowning success. At Hampton
Court, on 12 October 1537, Queen Jane was delivered by
Caesarean section of a son, christened Edward shortly afterwards – just ten years since Henry first publicly set out on
the task of getting rid of Catherine in order to save his
dynasty. Henry was not with his wife at this moment. Plague
had driven him to Esher and kept Jane in isolation. But he
hurried back to her as soon as he heard the good news and
launched a splendid round of triumphs and banquets. There
remained still one last menace to be combated, namely, the
papal Council, still not met; but constant diplomacy might
well prevent that from harrying him.[56] For the rest Henry
was marvellously assured, so assured that Jane's death
twelve days after the birth of her son could pass off largely
unnoticed. According to Cromwell, the queen had been the
victim of those about her 'who suffered her to take great
cold and to eat things that her fantasy called for'.[57] Probably the poor creature was the victim of that terrifying thing,
Tudor medicine.

Ebullient and secure Henry may have felt and seemed,
but in reality there was something irreparably wrong with
the state of England. His matrimonial affairs, the breach
with Rome, the attack on monasticism and the steady spoliation of the Church, the fate of the two princesses, the
insecure succession, the executions, the rebellions and their
suppression had left behind discontent and anxiety. The age
of enchantment was over, at least for some of his subjects.
There were rumours of imminent heavy taxation – fortified
by the injunction of 1538 requiring every parish to register

55. So Cromwell suggested, *L.P.*, xi, 219.
56. *L.P.*, xii, ii, 911, 923.
57. *St.P.*, viii, i (*L.P.*, xii, ii, 1004).

births, deaths and marriages – rumours that all unmarked
cattle would be seized[58] and, above all, inflammatory
rumours that Henry was dead.[59] There were hostile things
being said about Henry himself. When a Sussex man reported Henry's fall he added, 'it were better he had broken
his neck'.[60] He was called 'a mole who should be put down',
'a tyrant more cruel than Nero', 'a beast and worse than a
beast'.[61] It was said that 'Cardinal Wolsey had been an honest
man if he had had an honest master',[62] that Henry was 'a
fool and my lord privy seal another'.[63] 'Our king', said one
malcontent, 'wants only an apple and a fair wench to dally
with,' while another told indignantly how Henry had
spotted his woman while out riding near Eltham, grabbed
her and taken her to his bed.[64] Things like this would never
have been said fifteen, ten or even five years ago – about
Wolsey, yes; about Henry, never. Perhaps there was some
truth in what a Kentish man said a little later, that, if
Henry knew his subjects' true feeling, 'it would make his
heart quake'.[65]

58. *L.P.*, xii, ii, 353, 357. Cf. *L.P.*, xii, ii, 57, 413, 1171 for evidence
of the persistence of these reports.
59. ibid., 1185; xii, i, 57, 76.
60. *L.P.*, xiii, ii, 307.
61. *L.P.*, xii, i, 1212; ii, 908; xiii, ii, 986.
62. *L.P.*, xii, ii, 979 – a remark said to have been made by Lord
Montague in April 1536.
63. *L.P.*, xiii, i, 95.
64. *L.P.*, xii, i, 1301; ii, 764.
65. *L.P.*, xiv, i, 1239. The remark was reported in July 1539.

11

England and Europe, 1537 to 1540

JANE SEYMOUR died on 24 October 1537, and was buried at Windsor on 12 November. Within a week of her death the search for her successor began. Jane herself had replaced Anne Boleyn swiftly enough by any standards, but circumstances then had been exceptional and Anne had been on the wane for months. To begin to look so quickly for a replacement for Jane was extreme haste even for an age which did not associate marriage, and especially royal marriage, with romantic love – and it was perhaps a sign of embarrassment that Cromwell, having reported that Henry had been bereaved but a few days before, should quickly have added that he was in no way disposed to marry again and had only overcome his feelings when faced with the argument of his Council that it was his duty to set out once more on the 'extreme adventure' of matrimony.[1] The truth may well have been that Henry's evidently short-lived reluctance was not much to the fore and that what the Council (and especially Cromwell) did was to persuade him to look for a wife abroad. A foreign princess was less likely than the daughter of an English noble house to be the agent and pawn of festering hostility to the secretary.

Within a few hours of Jane's death, therefore, the English ambassadors in France and the Low Countries were instructed to begin inquiries about possible consorts for the king. Thus began two years of intense marriage-mongering, in the course of which at least nine women were seriously considered, several more glanced at and five of them required to sit for portraits by Hans Holbein the younger. Before long English ambitions were to gallop ahead to produce plans for a quadruple alliance – involving Henry and his three child-

1. *St.P.*, viii, 1 (*L.P.*, xii, ii, 1004).

ren and (mainly) various members of the Habsburg
dynasty. Negotiations produced a plethora of embassies
hither and thither, reminiscent of those which the divorce
ten years before had occasioned (and even brought out
Edward Carne again). They saw Henry beaten to the post,
inevitably made the object of ribald badinage and yet wondrously persistent. They ended in a disastrous choice.

The value of a foreign marriage was not just that it would
spare Cromwell unease. If France and the Empire ended
hostilities, as they seemed likely to do, England would be
isolated; worse, continental peace would allow the papal
Council to meet and perhaps turn Catholic Europe against
Henry. England must provide against this chain of events.
Whether or not the offer of a marriage alliance would give
her effective leverage in Europe was an open question, for,
if Francis and Charles were to come together, neither would
have particular need of Henry or much incentive to accept
the price which he, as ever a demanding suppliant, would
ask for his hand. But it was worth a try. At least matrimonial
diplomacy might confuse the scene and cut across the
Franco–Imperial *rapprochement*.

Though in theory an Imperialist wife would have done as
well as a French one, it was to France that Henry first turned.
Two possibilities were mentioned immediately:[2] Francis's
daughter, Margaret, and Marie, daughter of the duc de
Guise. The latter, already a widow, was the favourite. Henry
had heard her praises sung loudly by his ambassador,
Wallop; she was a mature woman and, as he explained later,
'he was big in person and had need of a big wife';[3] no less
agreeably, there was talk of her marrying the Scottish king
and it would be pleasing if Henry could swoop in, carry off
the lady and thus damage the Auld Alliance. But Henry was
to receive a rebuff. In December 1537, Peter Mewtas, one of
the Privy Chamber, was sent secretly to sound her and

2. In Cromwell's letter of late October, quoted above.
3. So he explained to Castillon, the French ambassador. *L.P.*, xii,
ii, 1285.

apparently came home convinced that she was free to accept Henry's offer. Accordingly, in February 1538, he returned to France to fetch a picture of her, leaving Henry both ardent and confident.[4] But before Mewtas's second visit, formal articles of her marriage to James had been drawn up and in early May she married him. Scottish diplomacy had been too swift for the English and left Henry empty-handed.

Happily, the king had meanwhile become enamoured elsewhere. In the previous December, in response to the command to scour the neighbourhood, the English ambassador at Brussels had sent back a fulsome report on a girl who had just arrived at the Regent's court, one Christina, second daughter of the deposed Christian II of Denmark and niece of the emperor, who had married the duke of Milan at the age of thirteen, been widowed within a year and was now sixteen.[5] There had been talk of her marrying the duke of Cleves, but this plan had fallen through and she was now on the market. By January 1538 Henry was enthusiastic about her and instructed Sir Thomas Wyatt, then ambassador with the emperor, to suggest her as his bride – though Wyatt was to pretend that the suggestion was his own and then stir Charles into offering her to Henry.[6] Only thus could the latter demand a *quid pro quo* and exploit his widowerhood to diplomatic advantage. But there was a difficulty. Henry was determined never to be saddled with a wife not to his taste. Since it was impossible to have this girl (known throughout this story as the duchess of Milan) brought, say, to Calais for his inspection, he must have a reliable picture of her. Hutton was told to procure one, but before he could do so another member of the Privy Chamber, Philip Hoby, was secretly dispatched to interview her. With Hoby went the younger Hans Holbein, who had been in royal employ for about three years. They left London in early March. On the 12th Holbein spent three hours with

4. *L.P.*, xiii, i, 56, 203.
5. *St.P.*, viii, 5, 6 f. (*L.P.*, xii, ii, 1172, 1187).
6. *L.P.*, xiii, i, 123.

the girl. He was back in six days – breakneck speed – with a
drawing that is said to have delighted Henry and from
which the splendid portrait of the lady, now in the National
Gallery, was produced.[7] Henry was soon a merry man and
full of talk of music and pageants (sure signs of amorous-
ness), and boasting, quite wrongly, that he was being wooed
from all sides.[8] Furthermore, there were now plans for a
double marriage: between Henry and the duchess, and
Mary and the brother of the Portuguese king.[9] Indeed, this
was only a beginning. At the same time Henry was discussing four marriages with the French ambassador: of himself
to Marie de Guise (who was not yet known to be out of the
running), of Mary to the Portuguese prince, Edward to the
emperor's daughter and Elizabeth to the king of Hungary's
son.[10]

Whatever Henry might say to the French, his first choice
for himself was the duchess of Milan, and negotiations for
her, with Mary added as an extra boon, now began. But
there were several serious difficulties in Henry's way. In the
first place, as a price for the two matches Henry required
Charles not only to include him in any future peace treaty
with France, and thus deliver England from isolation, but
also to refuse to support the coming papal General Council.
And why should Charles compromise himself thus? Why
should he ever think of taking up the Protestant cry – as
Henry suggested – for a free Christian Council, summoned
by princes and held in a neutral place?[11] This was an impossible demand. Next, there were the usual arguments
about dowries and rights of inheritance – but complicated
in this instance by the fact that the princess whom Henry
was offering to Charles's family was, in English law, illegitimate and, it was insisted, could not be restored. Then there

7. *L.P.*, xiii, i, 380; *St.P.*, viii, 17 ff. (*L.P.*, xiii, i, 507). Holbein and
Hoby also brought back a portrait which Hutton had meanwhile
acquired – said to have been inferior.

8. *L.P.*, xiii, i, 583.   9. ibid., 241.   10. ibid., 271.
11. ibid., 387, 695, 1132–3, etc.

were two particular problems which gave the whole affair a last, ironical twist. The duchess of Milan was Charles's niece and therefore Catherine of Aragon's great-niece. Hence an affinity existed between her and Henry, a double affinity indeed, by virtue of Catherine's marriage to Arthur and her union (licit or illicit, depending on which way one looked at it) with Henry. If the latter was to marry the duchess, the impediment had to be removed. But by whom? The Imperialists, of course, named the pope. But to Henry this was obviously out of the question. The English offered the services of the Supreme Head of the Church of England; and to the Imperialists this was no less obviously unacceptable.[12] Finally, there was the duchess herself to consider. According to a credible report, she was far from comfortable at the prospect of becoming the king's fourth wife, 'for her Council suspecteth that her great aunt was poisoned, that the second was put to death and the third lost for lack of keeping her child-bed'.[13] It was not surprising that, before succeeding these three women, the spirited duchess should have been anxious for guarantees of the safety of her person. Henry's suit could not bring unalloyed pleasure to anyone with a normal instinct of self-preservation.

While Henry was engaged in these fruitless negotiations with the Habsburgs, the French (in May 1538) cut in with two proposals which shifted his main attention back to France and helped him into a better bargaining position: that Mary should take Francis's younger son and Henry marry a sister of that Marie de Guise whom the Scots had filched from him.[14] The offer met quick response. The day after it was made Sir John Russell went to the French ambassador in London to make inquiries about the new nominee for the king's hand, Louise de Guise, and to ask for a

12. *L.P.*, xiii, i, 1126; xiv, i, 299, 405.
13. *L.P.*, xiv, ii, 400. The report came from the reformer George Constantine. His words probably helped to earn him a charge of treason.
14. *L.P.*, xiii, i, 915, 917, 994.

picture of her.[15] Once more Henry was all enthusiasm for
the French and showered gifts of stag, deer and great arti-
chokes from his gardens on the ambassador;[16] and once more,
when there was delay in the dispatch of a portrait of the
lady from her home country, Henry impatiently sent Hoby
and Holbein to fetch one directly. They found Louise at Le
Havre in early June and came home with two drawings of
her.[17]

Scarcely were they back than Henry heard of yet another
possible candidate, a third de Guise girl, yet more beautiful
than her sisters – Renée by name – who was destined for
religion but, happily, had not yet been professed.[18] She
sounded exquisitely attractive; but again, Henry could not
be sure until he had seen with his own eyes; and again Holbein must let him see her through his. In August 1538,
therefore, Hoby and Holbein were back in France, at Joinville, in search of a picture of Renée which could be set in a
double, hinged frame alongside that of her sister, Louise, for
Henry to ponder.[19] But events were now moving more swiftly
than ever because Henry had recently heard about no less
than three other French women, namely, Marie of Vendôme, Anne of Lorraine (Francis's cousins) and Francis's
sister. Holbein was therefore to go on from Joinville to
Nancy to draw Anne of Lorraine, while the French ambassador would produce portraits of the others who were not
yet in Henry's collection. As it happened, Renée de Guise
eluded Holbein. But he found Anne at Nancy.[20]

By midsummer, the situation was approximately thus:
while his suit for the duchess of Milan dragged on in London, Brussels and an itinerant emperor's court, and while a
match for Mary to Charles de Valois was debated in London
and an itinerant French king's court, Henry was bidding for

15. *L.P.*, xiii, i, 994.   16. ibid., 1101. Cf. 1320.
17. ibid., 1135.   18. ibid., 1217.
19. ibid., 380. For this visit by Holbein (and his previous errands)
see Chamberlain, *Hans Holbein the Younger* (1913), 138 ff.
20. Chamberlain, op. cit., 149 ff.

any one of five French girls (having lost one, Marie de Guise, previously); Holbein had provided pictures of two of these five, Louise de Guise and Anne of Lorraine, and the French had meanwhile produced a portrait of their own of Louise and probably also one of Marie de Vendôme.[21] Even so, Henry was not satisfied. From the start he had wanted candidates for his hand to come to him in person for inspection. Now that he was dealing in bulk, so to speak, he proposed that a bevy of the ladies from France should be gathered at Calais for him to make his choice.[22] As with Charles, so with the French, Henry had already demanded a high price for the proposed unions – that Francis, too, should include him as principal in any treaty, obstruct the papal Council, or at least prevent it from taking any measures against him, and so on. As the French observed, Henry's idea of a bargain was somewhat lop-sided.[23] When he added to all this the request that a carriage-load of royal ladies be escorted to Calais by the French queen he laid impudence upon importunity. Why could he not send someone to inspect the ladies and make the choice on his behalf, he was asked? 'By God,' Henry replied, 'the thing touches me too near. I wish to see them and know them some time before deciding.' Would the knights of the Round Table have treated their womenfolk like this? the French ambassador asked – at which Henry blushed.[24] It was not the French custom, Francis observed, to send damsels of good house to be passed in review like horses for sale. He would have any *one* of the girls sent to Calais, and that was all.[25]

So the bartering ran on well into the autumn of 1538, with Henry appearing to move now towards France, now towards the emperor, now back to France. Crude and bumptious though Henry may seem in the marriage market when one recalls the feline deviousness of his daughter Elizabeth later

21. *L.P.*, xiii, i, 1356, 1451–2.
22. ibid., 1355. These would perhaps be joined by the Habsburg candidates and thus make a large-scale beauty-parade.
23. ibid., 909, 1003. 24. *L.P.*, xiii, ii, 77. 25. *L.P.*, xiii, ii, 277.

on, he played his part to full diplomatic advantage. It was particularly acute to exploit the potential rights of the duchess of Milan, the leading Imperial candidate. She was not only the second daughter of the deposed king of Denmark and Sweden, but also the widow of Francisco Sforza of Milan (and hence might bring her duchy with her). Before long Henry was suggesting a most complicated arrangement – that if the duchess were given first claim to her father's Scandinavian inheritance when she came to England, the emperor should confer Milan on the Habsburg candidate for Mary.[26] Milan was constantly to the fore throughout the marriage talks. And this was shrewd dealing by the English, for that duchy was a neuralgic spot of Europe without equal, the place that mattered most to Francis and more than a little to Charles. To Henry it could be made a fertile seed of discord between the leading monarchs of the west and at least two people saw his purpose.[27]

All this – the lurching to and fro between Francis and Charles, the plans for multiple marriages,[28] the desire to make trouble – had the single objective of providing against the threat which was building up on the Continent. It was of no avail. In June 1538 Charles and Francis met at Nice under the pope's aegis and signed a ten-year truce. Shortly afterwards the two monarchs met again at Aigues Mortes. During the past few years it had been the greatest comfort to Henry that continental politics, and then Charles's campaigns in North Africa, had shielded him from a Catholic crusade against him and denied domestic opposition any effective support from outside the kingdom. But this situation had now ended. Charles and Francis had concluded a treaty

26. *L.P.*, xiii, ii, 679, 756, 1133.

27. Namely Chapuys and Francis I. *L.P.*, xiii, ii, 232, 277.

28. By October 1538 Henry had even thought of offering to Charles, as make-weights, Elizabeth, Lady Margaret Douglas and even Mary Howard, to be married to such princes as Charles should decide. B.M. Vesp. C, vii, fol. 71 (*L.P.*, xiii, ii, 622). This document and its companion (Vit. B xxi, fol. 168) are heavily corrected by Henry and show his intense interest in this matrimonial diplomacy.

which, to his intense chagrin, ignored him.[29] Despite his recent efforts, he had been mocked by his brother monarchs and now faced the threat not only of a papal General Council but also of assault by Catholic Europe. Rome too saw the potentialities of the new situation. On 17 December 1538 the pope at last prepared to promulgate the bull of excommunication which had been drawn up over three years previously but since suspended, deposing Henry and absolving his subjects from obedience.[30] The continuing destruction of English monasticism, the open negotiations between Henry and the Lutherans and the spoliation of shrines (particularly, of course, that of Becket) had finally convinced Paul that Henry must be overthrown. Two days after Christmas, Reginald Pole set out secretly from Rome to rally the Catholic powers against 'the most cruel and abominable tyrant', the king of England.[31] Meanwhile David Beaton was made a cardinal and sent home to rouse James V to the crusade.[32] Officially Pole's purpose was to call upon Charles and Francis to withdraw ambassadors from England and impose a commercial embargo, but there can be no doubt that he thought in terms of military action and had set out for Spain and France to preside, as he hoped, over an invasion of his motherland. Moreover, on 12 January 1539, Francis and Charles concluded a pact at Toledo in which each promised not to enter into any agreement with England without the other's consent[33] – a familiar preliminary, this, to offensive action. Soon afterwards there was talk that the French and Imperial ambassadors in London would be recalled.[34] It seemed that the crusade was about to begin.

29. *L.P.*, xiii, i, 1347, 1451.
30. *Wilkins*, iii, 840 (*L.P.*, xiii, ii, 1087). But even this time the bull was not fully promulgated. Paul waited until Catholic Europe was ready to act before releasing it. See *L.P.*, xiv, i, 1011; ii, 99.
31. *Sp. Cal.*, vi, 33. *L.P.*, xiv, i, 36.
32. *L.P.*, xiii, ii, 1108–9, 1114–16, 1135–6.   33. *L.P.*, xiv, i, 62.
34. ibid., 345, 365. The French ambassador left with no successor in the offing, but it was eventually agreed not to withdraw Chapuys until his replacement had arrived.

In the early months of 1539 many at home thought that
the supreme moment of testing had come. This was a time of
acute crisis – more acute perhaps than the months of rebellion in 1536 – when England apparently faced triple attack,
from Scotland, the Low Countries and Spain, and, as
Wriothesley wrote, must be 'but a morsel amongst these
choppers'.[35] The country was seized with war-panic. Counties
were mustered, defence-works at Calais and Guines and on
the Scottish borders stiffened, stone from dissolved monasteries hauled to the coast to build blockhouses, beacons got
ready. Ragusan ships in the Thames and Venetian at Southampton were stayed on the strength of a proclamation forbidding any ship, English or foreign, to depart from English
shores without royal licence under pain of death. South-east
England was in a frenzy of preparation as ditches were dug,
barricades, ramparts and palisades set up, munitions collected. Meanwhile, there was alarming news from the Continent – of fleets gathering at Antwerp and Boulogne, of an
army in the Low Countries.[36] Henry himself toured coastal
defences, supervised the building of bulwarks and visited his
ships at Portsmouth. On 8 May he was back in London for a
march-past of troops who had mustered between White-
chapel and Mile End and thence passed through the City
and Westminster to St James's, where the king reviewed
them.[37] At the same time as these preparations went forward,
Edmund Bonner and Thomas Wyatt, English ambassadors
with Francis and Charles, were bidden to do all in their
power to put asunder these two monarchs whom ill-fate had
recently joined together, to protest against the fleet gathered
in Antwerp and to checkmate Pole – who had now arrived
in Spain on the first leg of his ambitious embassy.

These were months of alarm, and understandably so. In

35. *L.P.*, xiv, i, 433. Cf. 115, 580, 670 for evidence of expectation of
invasion – including that of Cromwell (in ibid., 580).

36. ibid., 652–4, 670–1, 682, 711–12, 802–3, etc. *Hughes and Larkin*,
no. 190.

37. *L.P.*, xiv, i, 940–1.

theory, at least, Henry was in peril. It only needed a re-crudescence of rebellion at home to complete the crisis – and this was not out of the question. There were rumours abroad of new royal taxes, reminiscent of those which had helped to precipitate the outbursts of 1536, which could have roused an already anxious populace.[38] If, this time, Pole had arrived on the other side of the Channel before, instead of after, rebellion broke out at home, and if he had had troops and ships at his command, Henry might have been hard put to it to survive.

However, the tide soon began to turn in England's favour. Though Pole pretended to the French that he had found Charles sympathetic to his mission,[39] the emperor was quite unwilling to take any action against Henry. The Turks and the Lutherans were more than sufficient evils for his day and he had no desire to acquire new burdens.[40] So dispirited was Pole by his meeting with Charles that he postponed his journey to Francis and withdrew to the papal city of Car-pentras to await further instructions from Rome; though he sent on ahead to Francis, to prepare the way, two com-panions (including one Robert Brancestor, a man of many parts, who may have been the first Englishman to go round the Cape of Good Hope, a feat which he accomplished in a Portuguese ship some seven or eight years previously).[41] At first Francis seemed favourable to the idea of an 'enterprise' against England, but it was quickly apparent that his interest had shallow roots. He was willing, he said, to do his duty, but only when the emperor was ready to act; he thought it inadvisable for Pole to come to France in person, lest this caused suspicion and gave Henry time to prepare himself, and so on.[42] In early March, quite unexpectedly, he sent an ambassador to England. A month later he wrote to Henry assuring him that French war preparations were aimed at

38. *L.P.*, xiv, i, 87, 507, 553, 815.   39. ibid., 536.   40. ibid., 603.
41. Scarisbrick, 'The First Englishman round the Cape of Good Hope?', *B.I.H.R.*, xxxiv (1961), 165 ff.
42. *L.P.*, xiv, i, 723, 724, 1110, 1237.

Charles, not him; a letter which mightily relieved Henry.[43] In short, Francis had no more intention of responding to the papal trumpet than had Charles. By August the pope had virtually abandoned his project and suggested that Pole – still marooned at Carpentras, somewhat bewildered and fearful of assassination – had best come back to Rome.[44] The cardinal's second mission had petered out scarcely less wretchedly than his first. Though Henry remained fearful of Charles and the pope, lest they might yet rally France against him, by July the immediate crisis had sufficiently abated to allow the hasty preparations against invasion to be called off.[45]

But that crisis had had important repercussions upon Henry and his kingdom. In the first place, it brought to a conclusion the virtual annihilation of the legitimate Plantagenet line in England, the nobles of the White Rose – the Courtenays, the Nevilles, the Poles – who had long been objects of suspicion. Courtenay's wife, the marchioness of Exeter, and Lady Margaret Pole had been especially close to Catherine of Aragon and her daughter, and were implicated in the affair of the Nun of Kent. It was said in Cornwall that Courtenay was true heir to the throne and that some time he would 'wear the garland' and bring better days;[46] while his cousins, the Poles, though they had dissociated themselves from the overt treason of the cardinal, were taken as evident malcontents, tarred with the same brush as the infamous Reginald. It may well have been the grave international situation which prompted Henry to strike in the late summer of 1538 and, as he had once confessed his intention to be, make an end of the White Rose.[47] Geoffrey Pole (the cardinal's younger brother) was suddenly taken to the Tower and, on the strength of his confessions,

43. *L.P.*, xiv, i, 907–8.

44. *L.P.*, xiv, ii, 52. But Pole did not leave until late September and then made his way to Verona.

45. *L.P.*, xiv, i, 1260; ii, 35.

46. *L.P.*, xiii, ii, 802, 961.

47. ibid., 753.

his eldest brother Henry, together with Courtenay and Sir Edward Neville, were brought to trial, found guilty on the flimsiest evidence and beheaded on 9 December 1538. Henry Pole's small son and heir disappeared in the Tower, Courtenay's young son remained in prison there until Mary's accession to the throne in 1553. Early next year, when Reginald Pole's new mission got under way, the king's avenging hand stretched out to the latter's old mother, Lady Margaret Pole, countess of Salisbury. After several fierce interrogations and some months of custody at Cowdray in Sussex, she was eventually attainted by act of Parliament in June 1539 and taken to the Tower. There she remained for nearly two years until the discovery, in April 1541, of a conspiracy in Yorkshire involving a member of a lesser branch of the Neville family (and sprung of the same neo-feudalism which had been behind the Pilgrimage of Grace) brought her to her death on Tower Green.[48] Thus ended a very remarkable woman and a life remorselessly pursued by tragedy. Her father, the duke of Clarence, had been murdered in the Tower; her brother, Edward earl of Warwick, had been executed in 1499; her eldest son had been judicially murdered in 1538; her youngest son Geoffrey, pardoned after bearing witness against his brother and Courtenay, now roamed Europe half-crazed with remorse; her only other surviving son, Reginald, had been declared a traitor and knew that he faced assassination. And thus, too, more blood fell across Henry's reign.

A new Parliament met in April 1539. A good deal of its business was prompted by the threatening external situation – the attainders of the countess of Salisbury, Pole himself and fellow-exiles in his entourage (including Robert Brancestor),[49] and the celebrated act of Six Articles, which

48. For the destruction of the Poles and the others, see Dodds, *The Pilgrimage of Grace, 1536–7, and the Exeter Conspiracy, 1538* (Cambridge, 1915), ii, 277 ff.; Paul, *Catherine of Aragon and her Friends*, 232 ff.

49. *L.P.*, xiv, i, 867.

seemed to halt the progress towards Protestantism of the Henrician Church. It it difficult to explain this act fully, but certainly it was partly prompted by two motives: to assuage a largely conservative nation at a moment when it was supremely necessary to avoid all domestic unrest; to take the sting out of the foreign crusade against a heretical king then being mooted.[50] The act was probably above all else a panic-measure, therefore, a sudden display of orthodoxy to disarm enemies at home and abroad.

Indeed, the crisis of early 1539 had an altogether extra-ordinary effect on English religious policy – or, at any rate, the confusions of that policy in the early months of 1539 can only be made intelligible in the light of that crisis. As has been said, in May of that year the notorious act of Six Articles was passed, which seemingly damned the future of the Gospel in England and caused cries of disappointment to rise from the friends of true religion everywhere.[51] Yet, at the same time, Henry was involved in perhaps the largest diplomatic advances towards the continental Lutherans which he had yet essayed. In January 1539 Christopher Mont was sent to the duke of Saxony and the landgrave of Hesse to promise Henry's allegiance to the Protestant league of Schmalkalden, to warn them of the danger of being tricked by the emperor at the Diet about to meet at Frankfort and to ask (once more) that a delegation of front-rank Lutheran divines be sent to England to draw up a common confession of faith.[52] Apparently Henry was urgent to enter the Evangelical league of Protestant powers which would have him as its leader and provide mutual aid for its participants. Soon afterwards, Robert Barnes was despatched in Mont's wake to travel to Saxony and thence to the king of Denmark and the city of Wismar, carrying with him an offer of an English alliance against the papists.[53] Whether Henry was now pre-

50. Such was the judgement of Marillac and Bucer at the time. *L.P.*, xiv, i, 1260; ii, 186.
51. See below, pp. 543 f.
52. *L.P.*, xiv, i, 103, 580.   53. ibid., 441–3, 955.

pared to succumb to the demands which he had hitherto
refused and to accept a full Lutheran doctrinal settlement
may be doubted. But certainly he was so desperate for friends
that he was at least ready to pretend that he would pay the
price for admission to their league which the Lutherans had
always demanded – just as he was ready (once more) to go
cap in hand to a king of Denmark with whom he had been
seriously at odds, or to put out feelers to the duke of
Urbino, whose duchy the pope had just seized, and offer
him, and any other prince who threw off the yoke of Rome,
aid against papal attack.[54]

Not surprisingly, Henry found the Lutherans very cool.
Christian of Denmark replied hesitantly to Henry's offer
of an alliance, regretting that at the moment he could not
send ambassadors to England, though he would be ready to
join Saxony and Hesse in negotiations with England some
time in the future;[55] and Mont found the Germans equally
reluctant to put out a helping hand to a king in distress.
As Henry bitterly complained of the Germans, they had
given no warning of the dangers which had come upon him,
offered him no aid, kept Mont waiting for answers and
parried the urgent request for a league of mutual defence;
and to complete his disappointment they then refused to
send a new embassy to England on the ground that it had no
more chance of success than its predecessors and there was
no point in opening old wounds.[56] Eventually they changed
their minds and sent a small, undistinguished delegation,
headed by the vice-chancellor of Saxony, Francis Burckhardt. It arrived in England on 23 April.

Doubtless – as the Lutheran princes suspected – Henry
had never intended finally to accept their comprehensive
confession of faith; perhaps it was their rebuff which decided

54. *L.P.*, xiv, i, 104, 114, 144, 188, etc. Perhaps the proclamation of
26 February 1539 providing that for seven years foreign merchants
should pay the same customs duties as natives was also designed to
win friends abroad. *Hughes and Larkin*, no. 189.

55. *L.P.*, xiv, i, 981.   56. ibid., 580.

the matter. Anyway, Parliament met five days after the
arrival of the German emissaries. Membership of the House
of Commons had been closely scrutinized by Cromwell[57]
(though to what end is not yet clear), but it was quickly
ablaze with furious theological argument, especially concerning the sacrament of the Altar. On 2 June, after much
furore, the act of Six Articles passed the Commons. Meanwhile, Henry had heard how the Lutheran princes at the
Diet of Frankfort had betrayed him exactly as he had feared
they might, and come to terms with the emperor; whereupon
he bluntly told Burckhardt and his colleagues to go home.[58]
What had begun as an apparently decisive final swing into
the Protestant camp – largely for diplomatic reasons –
ended in bitter mutual recrimination, after both sides
(especially Henry) had decided, for reasons of policy, to
play safe.

It was wise to draw back. But the act of Six Articles was
limited in extent and effect, and seemed more significant to
outsiders than it really was. It represented no fundamental
retreat and certainly in no way implied that the mainstay
of Henricianism was buckling.[59] Shortly after its passage
the aggressive, confident anti-papalism of the regime was
vividly demonstrated by a rumbustious pageant on the
Thames, played before the king and a throng of Londoners.
Two barges put out in the middle of the river, one manned
by a crew representing the king and his Council; the other
by some stalwarts dressed up as pope and cardinals. The two
boats met in combat and grappled – until the 'papal' barge
was worsted and its contents pitched ignominiously into the
river.[60] Popular propaganda of this kind, the necessary concomitant of the outpouring of anti-papal statutes, proclamations, learned treatises and sermons, had been employed

57. Pollard, 'Thomas Cromwell's Parliamentary Lists', *B.I.H.R.*,
xi (1931–2), 31 ff.
58. But they did not. They lingered in England until the end of
the summer.
59. See below, pp. 543 ff.   60. *L.P.*, xiv, i, 1137.

for years in an effort to heave a sluggish nation out of its past. Cranmer and Cromwell had patronized companies of players who performed heavily-loaded plays and interludes (like those of John Bale) on village commons and at market squares; and probably many a village feast and game was given an anti-papal twist.[61] The spectacle on the Thames in June 1539 was only a more elaborate and more entertaining example of a now widespread genre of political propaganda; and it doubtless owed something to the present fear of the machinations of the pope, the emperor and the 'brainsick Pole'.[62]

Finally, so too did Henry's tangled matrimonial negotiations, which had limped on during the early months of 1539.[63]

Since it was now clear that neither the king's pursuit of the Imperialist duchess of Milan nor that of the numerous French ladies would split Charles and Francis apart and win him a new friend, indeed, had done nothing to hold off the coalition against him, it was obviously urgent to try elsewhere. As early as June 1538 a double marriage had been proposed into the house of Cleves – of Mary to a son of the duke thereof and Henry to a kinswoman.[64] But the suggestion was buried under the pile of other proposals. It was resuscitated in January of the following year. When Christopher Mont was sent to meet the duke of Saxony and the landgrave of Hesse his instructions were not only to press for a politico-religious liaison with the Schmalkaldic league, but also to sound the two princes about these marriage proposals, to make inquiries about the duke of Cleves's elder daughter, and to give the elector and the landgrave 'a

61. See Harris, *John Bale*, Illinois Studies in Language and Literature, xxv (1939); Reed, *Early Tudor Drama* (1926), esp. 22 ff., Baumer, op. cit. and Zeeveld, *Foundations of Tudor Policy* (1948) discuss the literary campaign.

62. As Cromwell called him.

63. *L.P.*, xiv, i, 92, 194, 299, 245, etc.

64. *L.P.*, xiii, i, 1198. But in 1530 the old duke of Cleves had suggested a marriage with England. *L.P.*, iv, 6364.

prick to offer her' to Henry. As was now common form,
Mont was instructed to procure a picture of the lady –
though he was also to explain that royal *amour-propre*
prevented Henry from sending in return a picture of his
daughter.[65] Some six weeks later a three-man embassy,
including Edward Carne, one who had already spent a good
deal of energy on Henry's marriage affairs and now re-
emerged to conclude, rather than undo, an alliance, was
sent to the duke of Cleves. Neither the latter, nor his father
(whom he succeeded in February of that year) were
Lutherans. Nor, on the other hand, were they of the 'old
popish opinion'. They stood betwixt and between the new
and the old, strongly under the influence of Erasmus, rather
as did Henry himself. Further, the present duke had
inherited Gelderland in July 1538 and was soon at logger-
heads with the emperor as a result. In short he was an
admirable ally – theologically respectable without being
either demanding or provocative, no less under the shadow
of Charles than was Henry himself, possessed of two un-
married sisters, linked to the growing 'third world' of
Lutheranism by the marriage of another sister to the elector
of Saxony and able to supply some much-needed mercenaries. Carne was therefore to suggest a strict alliance with
Cleves, to discuss the double marriage for Henry and Mary,
bring back a picture of sister Anne and one hundred
seasoned cannoneers.[66]

By the middle of March encouraging news had reached
England from Mont. He had found the duke of Saxony
ready to encourage Henry's marriage into the house of
Cleves and heard ecstatic praise of Princess Anne's person
– that 'as well for the face as for the whole body' she was
incomparable and that she excelled the duchess of Milan
'as the golden sun excelleth the silver moon'.[67] But the duke,
her brother, would not yield either swiftly or easily. He
wanted Henry to come to him publicly and on bended knee
with his request for a league and his sister's hand. The

65. *L.P.*, xiv, i, 103.   66. ibid., 489–90.
67. *St.P.*, i, 605 (*L.P.*, xiv, i, 552).

English were told that Anne was promised to the duke of Lorraine and could get no firm undertaking to send ambassadors to England to conclude the treaties. The only local painter suitable for Henry's commission, namely, Lucas Cranach the elder, was ill and the king would have to be content with portraits of the two sisters, Anne and Amelia (for Henry was now interested in both of them) painted six months ago but not at the moment available. When the English asked to inspect the two girls in order later to be able to check the portraits against the originals, the duke's chancellor was evasive. The ambassadors had already caught sight of them, but under such a 'monstrous habit and apparel', they said, that this 'was no sight neither of their faces nor of their persons'. 'Why,' replied the chancellor, 'would you see them naked?' 'The further we go, the more delays,' the English complained, 'appear in this matter.'[68]

In early July another envoy, William Petre, was ordered to Cleves to hasten the negotiations, inspect the two sisters and check the two portraits, which had still not been produced.[69] Shortly afterwards one of the original embassy returned, perhaps with the pictures, but probably not. He was promptly sent back to Cleves, accompanied by Hans Holbein – who thus returned to the story of the quest for Henry's fourth wife. By 11 August Holbein had painted Anne and Amelia; by the end of the month he was back in England and had brought the paintings to Henry, then at Grafton on his summer progress.[70] On 4 September Duke William at last commissioned an embassy to England to conclude the marriage treaty between Henry and Anne. It arrived on 24 September.[71] The problem of Anne's pre-contract to another had apparently been overcome, and it was to be she, not her younger sister, who was to bring Henry's two years of widowerhood to an end.

Negotiations concerning the marriage settlement and Anne's journey to England moved on quickly – though

68. *L.P.*, xiv, i, 920.
69. ibid., 1193.
70. *L.P.*, xiv, ii, 33, 117.
71. ibid., 127, 222.

complicated by an unsuccessful last-minute attempt by her
brother-in-law to push the duchess of Milan back into the
picture.[72] On 6 October 1539 the marriage treaty between
Henry and Anne was concluded.[73] Lavish preparations for
her arrival were in hand, and by 11 December she was at
Calais waiting for a favourable wind to carry her across to
England.[74] It had been agreed that she should travel thus
by land, from Düsseldorf via Antwerp and Gravelines to
Calais, for the winter sea was dangerous and, besides, might
spoil her complexion.[75] As she waited over a fortnight at
Calais (being taught how to play cards), Henry waited at
Greenwich.

She crossed the Channel on 27 December. From Deal she
came to Dover and Canterbury, and thence, on New Year's
Day 1540, to Rochester.[76] Understandably impatient, Henry
dashed down to Rochester in disguise to have a quick
glimpse of his new bride, in order, as he told Cromwell, 'to
nourish love'. Two days later she was solemnly received on
Shooter's Hill and taken by the king to the riverside palace
in a triumphal procession. On 6 January she and Henry were
married.[77]

Henry was bitterly disappointed the moment he set eyes
on her at Rochester. 'I am ashamed that men have so praised
her as they have done, and I like her not,' was his verdict.
He had rushed to meet her, armed with New Year gifts.
But he did not give them to her. Instead, he sent them by a
companion next morning, with a cold message of greetings.
When he returned to Greenwich he told Cromwell that he
liked Anne 'nothing so well as she was spoken of' and added
that, if he had known the truth about her, she would never
have come to England. Next day she was at Greenwich. The
marriage had been intended to take place within twenty-

72. *L.P.*, xiv, ii, 169, 222, 328. The brother-in-law was the count
Palatine. The duchess was the daughter of the deposed king of Denmark and sister of the count's wife. He was pushing his wife's claims
to Denmark and wanted to involve Henry in the conflict.

73. ibid., 286.   74. ibid., 732.   75. ibid., 258.

76. *L.P.*, xv, 14.   77. *Hall*, pp. 833 ff.; *L.P.*, xv, 823.

four hours, but was postponed for two days while Henry
tried to find an escape from union with 'the Flanders mare';
and meanwhile reports went abroad of how disappointing the
girl was. But there was no way out. The foreign situation
forbade it. Charles V had arrived in Paris on his way from
Spain to Germany and was being fêted by the French king.
England was as evidently isolated as ever and could not
afford to alienate what thin friendship she had produced
for herself in Germany. Had Henry been a really bold man
and risked making 'a ruffle in the world', or had Charles not
been in Paris at that moment, Anne might have been sent
home at first sight, without more ado. Instead the king
reluctantly agreed that he had no other course but to 'put
my neck in the yoke'; and as he prepared to go to his nuptials
– in a quiet ceremony in the palace – he said plaintively to
Cromwell, 'My lord, if it were not to satisfy the world and
my realm, I would not do that I must do this day for none
earthly thing.'[78]

The marriage was never consummated. After his first
night with her, Henry spoke frankly of how his distaste had
grown, how he had been 'struck to the heart' by physical
repugnance and 'left her as good a maid as he found
her'; and though he lay by her regularly thereafter, he
never touched her.[79] Shortly after Easter, by which time
Charles's entertainment in France had ended, a new 'great
scruple' had taken root in Henry's heart – that this, his
fourth, marriage was as invalid as the first.

Two grounds for the divorce (i.e. nullity) were alleged:
Henry's lack of consent thereto, proved by his failure to
consummate it; Anne's incompetence to consent thereto, by
virtue of her pre-contract to the son of the duke of Lorraine,
undertaken years ago. The first was certainly sufficient,
difficult to prove, but true; the second would have been
equally sufficient and easier to prove, but was probably untrue.

The English had known for months that, many years
before, Anne had been promised to the duke of Lorraine's

78. *L.P.*, xv, 822–3, 850; ibid., 23.   79. ibid., 823, 825.

son. Henry's ambassadors had heard this in May 1539, but had been assured by the chancellor of Cleves that the agreement had been entered into only by the parents of the children, that Lorraine had taken no steps to redeem the promise in a dozen years and had recently given his son to the French king's daughter.[80] It is also certain that, in 1535, the pre-contract was formally renounced by an ambassador of the duke of Gelders acting on behalf of Lorraine. However, the English agents at Cleves were instructed to pursue the documents relating to the pre-contract and establish beyond doubt that Anne was free, but apparently never succeeded in doing so. Instead their hosts promised that the documents would be delivered to Henry by the ambassadors sent from Cleves to England to negotiate.[81] They were not so delivered. Nor did they come with Anne herself. Probably there was nothing sinister in this. It is quite likely that Anne's espousal to Lorraine's son was now so remote an event that the documents had been mislaid. But Henry had apparently worried about the matter all along and now, after Anne had arrived in England and as he searched for a way out of his impending marriage, tried to take refuge behind Anne's previous engagement. Thereupon the ambassadors from Cleves were called before the Council and told about this difficulty. Much astonished, they replied that the pre-contract had certainly been revoked and promised to remain as prisoners in England until they received a copy of the revocation from home. When Cromwell told Henry of this, he was evidently disappointed, and muttered, 'I am not well handled.' To make matters doubly sure, Cromwell then and there had Anne herself formally renounce the pre-contract.[82] Even if the document of 1535 were non-existent, this – so Cranmer and Tunstal stated at the Council table next day – would have served as sufficient discharge.[83] Henry's last-minute attempt to break free was stifled. Cromwell had resolutely 'travailed on him to pass the matter

80. _L.P._, xiv, i, 920. 81. _L.P._, xv, 1193; ii, 33; ibid., 850.
82. ibid., 822–3, 861 (2), i. 83. ibid., 824.

over'.[84] Doubtless he assumed that, once Henry had taken the plunge, all would be well and the pre-contract quickly forgotten.

But the king's bitter disappointment in Anne kept his convenient scruple alive. Furthermore, when the documents relating to the queen's past and a copy of the renunciation of 1535 at last arrived from Cleves, in February 1540, they opened up a new source of doubt. It had been assumed hitherto that Anne had entered a pre-contract, a marriage *per verba de futuro*, with Lorraine's son. But it now appeared (or apparently could be argued) that perhaps she had been given in marriage *per verba de presenti*, a binding contract which renunciation could not undo.[85] It seems doubtful whether this was so, but it was a Heaven-sent convenience to be able to hint that it was. The matter had now taken on sufficient complexity and confusion for the ingenious to weave a plausible argument against the validity of Anne's marriage to Henry.

The divorce case began in early July, with an allegedly spontaneous petition to the king from Parliament listing the causes impeaching the marriage and begging him to inquire into them – which, of course, it was said he was bound to do. Next day (7 July) Convocation was commissioned under the great seal to open proceedings. Two days later their decision was signed and sealed. The marriage was declared null and void. And what Convocation found, Parliament quickly confirmed.[86]

A fortnight before the case opened, Henry had sent Anne out of the way to Richmond, 'purposing it to be more for her health, open air and pleasure'.[87] To his evident surprise she proved utterly docile. She agreed to the divorce proceedings when, shortly after they began, the chancellor led a deputation to her to secure her consent. She promised to hand over any letters from her brother, her mother and any others – for the English were fearful of how her relatives

84. *L.P.*, xv, ii, 850 (4).   85. ibid., 850 (4).
86. *Wilkins*, iii, 851; *L.P.*, xv, 908, 930.   87. *Hall*, 840.

might take her sudden dismissal. She confirmed that her
marriage had not been consummated and in that letter
obediently addressed the king as 'brother' and signed herself 'sister'.[88] Though her true brother, the duke of Cleves,
was upset by events and anxious that Anne should return
home,[89] she herself settled down, apparently without much
demur, to enjoy Henry's gift to her of two houses, a sufficient
household and an income of £500 *per annum* – the reward
for six months of loveless marriage and humble submission.
But one cannot help wondering what would have happened
if, as originally planned, she had married Lorraine's son,
the nephew of the famous cardinal, and if, after all, Henry,
not Lorraine's son, had married a sister of Francis I; or if
Henry had married Lorraine's daughter Anne – both of
whom had been in the running before the Cleves match
came to the fore.

It was not Holbein's picture which had misled Henry, as
Burnet and others have suggested.[90] The idea of the king
being brought to matrimonial disaster by a great portrait
painter who allowed art to eke out nature rather too fluently
makes a good story, but does injustice to the painter.
Wotton, one of the envoys to Cleves and in a position to
know, described Holbein's portrait as 'a very lively [i.e. life-
like] image',[91] and it was of ambassadors' words, not
Holbein's brushwork, that Henry later complained. It was
they, he said, which had misled him. But even this is not
just. One ambassador had written of her, 'I hear no great
praise neither of her personage nor beauty' – though, true
enough, he had written this to Cromwell in 1537 when the
search for a new wife had just begun and before Anne had
begun to be considered as a candidate.[92] But in May 1539
Wotton had been very frank and reported that she spent
most of her time sewing, was not highly educated and could

88. *L.P.*, xv, 925, 908, 930.   89. ibid., 970.
90. Chamberlain, op. cit., 178 ff.   91. *L.P.*, xiv, ii, 33.
92. So Hutton to Cromwell. *St.P.*, viii, 5 (*L.P.*, xii, ii, 1172).

not sing or play any instrument, 'for they take it here in Germany for a rebuke and an occasion of lightness that great ladies should be learned or have any knowledge of music'. His sketch of the princess ended with the words, 'I could never hear that she is inclined to the good cheer of this country and marvel it were if she could, seeing that her brother, to whom yet it were somewhat more tolerable, doth so well abstain from it.'[93] Wotton uttered a warning, but it was not heeded.

Whether or not Cromwell prevented these words from reaching Henry we cannot know. Certainly he reported to his master the fulsome reports about Anne (only reports) which Mont sent from Frankfurt. But the suggestion that Cromwell all along pushed Henry into this marriage, without the latter either fully knowing about it or wanting it, is incredible. It is clear from the letters which passed between king and minister at this time that Henry was fully informed of all that was afoot – the attempts to draw the Lutheran princes into a closer alliance, the marriage negotiations at Cleves – and that Cromwell was, as ever, Henry's utter servant, keeping him fully informed of news as it came in, receiving and executing royal reactions thereto; while a letter from Cromwell to Mont recording Henry's response to the latest news from Frankfort makes it clear that the king was anxious to force the pace.[94] In the summer of 1538 Henry had stamped on the suggestion that he should send someone to inspect for him the French candidates for his hand with the words 'By God, I trust on no one but myself. The thing touches me too near.'[95] If this were so, would Cromwell ever have dared to foist a bride on him? Would Henry ever have allowed him to?

Henry may not have been the absolute initiator of the match and he was certainly persuaded into it by Cromwell (and others) at the very last minute, when, having seen Anne, he wanted to bolt. But he had been fully party to the

93. *L.P.*, xiv, ii, 33.
94. See *L.P.*, xiv, i, 552, 580, 781, 834.   95. *L.P.*, xiii, ii, 77.

plan to bring her to England and to the concurrent negotiations at Frankfort. It was convenient to blame, or to be
encouraged by others to blame, someone else for the disaster;
but it was not just.

In truth, if one may judge from Holbein's portrait of her
in the Louvre (which is not the portrait done in Cleves and
which Henry saw, but a painting based on it),[96] Anne had a
rather charming face and was certainly as agreeable to look
at as several of Henry's other wives; and surely she was a
good deal better endowed than Jane Seymour, her immediate predecessor – which, in all conscience, is not to say
a great deal. Perhaps her real shortcoming was not so much
in her physiognomy as her personality. Wotton, whom we
heard a short while ago, had warned that she was neither
accomplished nor gay, and portrayed a rather dull, shy girl.
What he wrote, Holbein painted. The latter's portrait of her
shows a melancholic, pale-faced creature, unused to the
world and strangely unhappy in her gorgeous coronation
robes. One can imagine how lost she must have been to find
herself carried off one winter from her home to England, to
be offered to Henry's noisy bed and board, and how disappointed the king – whose next choice, it is illuminating to
recall, would be the sensual Catherine Howard – must have
been when he first saw his timid, unexciting bride-to-be. She
was neither a high-spirited minx like Catherine Howard,
nor a comfortable matron like Catherine Parr, but something disastrously different – an unawakened girl, lacking
both charm and fire. It was perhaps indicative of Anne's flat
personality that, after a brief moment of fame, she should
have accepted dismissal so easily and settled down to eighteen years of complete and apparently contented obscurity
as an exile in a land which openly disdained her.

At 3 p.m. on Saturday 10 June 1540, a month before Convocation's declaration of the nullity of her marriage was con-

96. Chamberlain, op. cit. 181; Ganz, 'Holbein and Henry VIII',
Burlington Magazine, lxxiii (1943), 271.

veyed to Anne and accepted by her, the captain of the guard had arrested Thomas Cromwell at the Council table – as he sat there, amidst his enemies, about the royal business. When he learnt that his relentless opponents had at last undone him, he threw down his bonnet in appalled anger, while Norfolk and Southampton stripped him of his decorations. He was taken out of the Council room through a postern to a waiting boat and thence to the Tower.

Cromwell's fall and judicial murder are full of mystery.[97] Probably we will never know exactly how and why he was toppled, nor fully uncover the intrigue of those who hounded him to his death. But some things are clear. First, Henry's disavowal of him was sudden. If the Six Articles act of 1539 represented a defeat for him (which is not certain), he showed no sign thereafter of having lost royal confidence. Though Norfolk, his arch-enemy, was soon more in evidence and in February 1540 returned to major diplomacy for the first time since 1532 to head an embassy to France, he had at least been posted out of the country, away from the king – which may well be taken as a measure of Cromwell's continuing control of affairs. In April 1540 Cromwell was clearly in charge of parliamentary business, when he announced in the Lords that two committees would be set up apparently to prepare a yet more advanced statement of doctrine and a book of ceremonies.[98] On 18 April he was at last given the peerage which one would have expected to have been his some time before and made lord great chamberlain of the Household. It is impossible to believe that these promotions were not signs of royal goodwill.

Secondly, there is little evidence of a major divergence of policy between king and minister. That Henry either discovered how Cromwell had planned (and more than planned) to lead the country astray, or that for months they

97. For his last days see Elton, 'Thomas Cromwell's Decline and Fall,' *C.H.J.*, x (1951), 150 ff.; L. B. Smith, *A Tudor Tragedy: the Life and Times of Catherine Howard* (1961), 115 ff.

98. *Lords Journals*, i, 128 ff.

had been pulling in opposite directions and that now the
king struck down a minister whose policies, in his heart, he
had always deplored – this can scarcely be supported by the
evidence. As has been said, Henry himself thrust forward
the negotiations with Cleves and the Lutheran princes.
Despite the fiasco of the marriage, he continued to seek a
treaty with Saxony and Hesse, albeit a political league first,
but one which, he said, would lead to a religious understanding later; and this was his policy.[99] In mid May, as the
last great debates concerning religion raged in Parliament
and among the bishops, Henry was in the thick of the controversy. The plans for further religious change (if such they
were) were not pushed forward behind his back – for he himself saw and annotated the bishops' replies to a preliminary
questionnaire designed to elucidate episcopal opinion on the
points at issue.[1] Rarely did Henry look less like a victim of
an overpowering minister than now. Possibly, as he himself
confessed to Marillac shortly before his fall. Cromwell had in
the past favoured the Imperialist cause more than did others.
But apparently the Council was now in accord.[2] There is no
evidence that differences concerning foreign policy had
caused deep tensions in the Council, or that Cromwell was at
cross-purposes with his king; and if Cromwell were really
anxious to patch up relations with the emperor, then he was
not the ardent Protestant sometimes presented to us. Moreover, though his fall marked the end of religious change, it
did not affect foreign policy significantly. England continued
to watch and woo Francis and Charles, while an embassy was
sent to Cleves to assure the duke of English friendship
despite the divorce of his daughter; and there is no evidence
that policy would have been different if Cromwell had not
been dispatched. Finally, the charges eventually drawn up
against Cromwell for his attainder – which we may presume
listed the most damaging things which could be said against
him – accused him of many things, but not of having

99. *L.P.*, xv, 310, 509.
1. See below, pp. 533 f., 537 ff.   2. *L.P.*, xv, 652.

deceived or misled his master on matters of major policy. He was not held responsible for the Cleves marriage and, though he was accused of favouring heretics at home, he was not charged with having conspired, against Henry, to lead England into alliance with the Lutheran princes abroad.[3]

Cromwell had long had enemies – rivals like Stephen Gardiner, whom he had worsted in the competition for power in 1534 and continually struggled to keep away from Court ever since; some of Gardiner's fellow-bishops, conservatives like Sampson, Stokesley and Tunstal, who rightly saw him and Cranmer as the men who were encouraging Henry into doctrinal radicalism; above all, aristocrats like Norfolk and Suffolk, who had been thrust from influence by this upstart and, except for a brief period when they had emerged to quell the Pilgrimage of Grace, had been kept at home, fretting at their distance from the centre and resentful of Cromwell's omnicompetence.[4] Norfolk had been badly set back when Anne Boleyn fell from grace; and he and his fellows had been denied a chance of recovery in late 1537 when Henry was persuaded to seek a foreign wife rather than take the daughter of a noble house and thus rehabilitate aristocratic influence at Court.

The final jostling between Cromwell and his opponents may have begun in the spring of 1539. In June of that year Cromwell and the duke had a furious argument at Cranmer's house – started by Norfolk, but about what we do not know.[5] For some months Cromwell was apparently secure, especially when Norfolk was sent to France in February 1540. But by then the duke and his friends had begun to rally and were about to strike a fatal blow. Norfolk was away for only about three weeks, and the failure of the Cleves marriage exposed Henry once more at his most vulnerable point. Catherine Howard, Norfolk's niece, had been placed before a ready king, and the bait worked quickly. Cromwell was about to be

3. For the attainder, see *Burnet*, iv, 415 ff.
4. Elton, art. cit., 154 ff.   5. *Burnet*, i, 425.

trapped. As Henry became increasingly infatuated with
Catherine so his demand for a divorce from Anne grew. But
if Cromwell secured the king that divorce his enemies would
have captured the citadel.

In the few weeks before Cromwell's fall there were clear
signs that he was fighting for his life. The sudden imprisonment of Bishop Sampson (Gardiner's ally), of the courtier
Sir Nicholas Carew and of Lord Lisle suggests the swirl of
faction-struggle.[6] On 1 June Marillac reported that there
were five other bishops whom Cromwell wanted to suppress,
and that he had nearly been unhorsed by them only a short
while ago.[7] We cannot follow the details of the bitter fight
as it must have been played out during May and early June
1540. We can only pick up odd pieces of the story – of arrests
and rumours of arrest, until suddenly, on 10 June, Cromwell was finally vanquished.

His fall was very like Wolsey's. He was hustled out from
below, the victim of a conspiracy waged by the same Norfolk,
aided by Gardiner and his fellows, who used Catherine
Howard, as Anne Boleyn had been used before, as their
pawn. Working no doubt with Catherine in the van of the
attack, the conspirators may well have convinced a disappointed king that it was Cromwell who had been responsible
for the débâcle of his recent marriage and the fruitless
negotiations at Frankfort, as well as feeding him with the
charges which would later appear in the act of Attainder –
that Cromwell had set at liberty persons guilty or suspected
of treason, sold export licences, granted passports and drawn
up commissions without royal knowledge, that he, a man of
base birth, had usurped royal power and lorded it over the
realm, and so on. But the decisive charge, the one which
seems to have moved Henry most and which formed the

6. Elton, art. cit., 175. But the arrest of Lisle, an illegitimate
Plantagenet, was probably part and parcel of the assault on the
White Rose – and occasioned by an alleged plot to hand over Calais
to the king's enemies.

7. *L.P.*, xv, 736–7.

bulk of the attainder, was that he was a detestable heretic who had spread heretical literature, licensed heretics to preach, released them from prison, rebuked and refused to listen to their accusers; that in March 1539 he had said in London that the English Lutheran Robert Barnes and others taught truth, that even if the king turned from this truth, 'yet I would not turn, and if the king did turn, and all his people, I would fight in this field in mine own person, with my sword in my hand against him and all other'.[8]

Thus was he charged with treason and heresy. Certainly the attainder was 'a tissue of half-truths and lies', cleverly given a spuriously convincing tone by mixing 'the vague and the particular'.[9] But the extent of the conspiracy wrought by Norfolk and his colleagues was, perhaps, yet greater than has been supposed. Immediately after the arrest, Marillac reported that the charge against Cromwell was that, *as a Lutheran*, he had favoured heretics. Shortly afterwards he told how, on the following day, incriminating letters were found which he had exchanged with Lutherans – letters which so appalled the king that he vowed that his name should be abolished for ever.[10] But either his adversaries later shifted their ground, or (which is more likely) Marillac was somehow misled. The heresy alleged against him was not that of the Lutheran but of the extreme religious radical, the sacramentary. In a plaintive letter to Henry from the Tower – the second which he wrote – in which he protested his innocence and cried out for mercy, he once more rebutted the incredible charge of treason against him who 'was, is and ever hath been' Henry's loyal subject, and then went on to refute the charge of heresy. The letter is badly mutilated, but enough remains to make it clear that the writer is crying out to God that he was neither a traitor nor a *sacramentary*, that he was a faithful Christian man and so would he die.[11] Indeed, the attainder itself suggests

8. *Burnet*, iv, 415 ff.   9. Elton, art. cit., 181.   10. *L.P.*, xv, 766, 804.   11. B.M. Otho. C, x, fol. 247 (*L.P.*, xv, 824). The relevant part of the text reads, '... oche grevyd me that I sholde be notyd ... e I hadde

that his heresy was that of the extreme radical, when it
accuses him of having said that it was lawful for every
Christian to be a minister of the sacrament and of having
caused books to be translated into English expressly against
the sacrament of the Altar. Cromwell certainly favoured
the Reformation. He was as much a Lutheran as the *Bishops'
Book*, the official formulary of faith, required all Englishmen
to be. There is no evidence that he had accepted those items
of Lutheran belief which had been refused so far by Henry,
namely, such things as Communion under both kinds and
consubstantiation, or that he wanted to abolish clerical
celibacy and even the Mass. Moreover, he was not now
accused of this. Instead, his accusers ran howling to the king
that his minister was a member of that rabid sect, denounced
as violently by Lutherans as by Catholics, which denied the
Real Presence in the Eucharist and preached anarchy – and
to give colour to their charges subsequently told him about
those letters which had been found in Cromwell's chamber
(letters which Henry was probably only told about and
never shown). Small wonder that, in his speech from the
scaffold, Cromwell should have declared that he died 'not
doubting in any article of my faith, no, nor doubting in any
sacrament of the Church', adding, 'many have slandered me,
and reported that I have been a bearer of such as have maintained evil opinions; which is untrue'.[12]

To have traduced Cromwell thus was shrewd, for Henry
had shown himself violently opposed to such as he was now
alleged to be; and it was not long ago that the king had
presided over the trial of John Lambert in the banqueting
hall at Westminster and sent him to his death for denying

your lawse in my brest and . . . ementarye god he knowythe the . . .
he ton and the other gyltles'. I would reconstruct this passage, in
modern spelling, thus: 'it much grieved me that I should be noted a
traitor when always I had your laws in my breast; and that I should
be a sacramentary, God he knoweth the truth and that I am of the
one and the other guiltless'.

12. *Foxe*, v, 402.

the Real Presence.[13] Moreover, it seems that, to give substance and credibility to their charge against Cromwell, the latter's pursuants were prepared to traduce others as well and to hound them to death. Two days after Cromwell was executed, three well-known reformers, Robert Barnes, William Jerome and Thomas Garret were burned as heretics at Smithfield. All three were innocent of the heresies attributed to them.

Barnes was a Lutheran, nothing more or less. He had proved himself (after a hectic early life) in his ambassadorial services to the king and had himself once been on a commission to 'extirpate sacramentaries' and Anabaptists. He was a rash, voluble man, who in Lent 1540 rather foolishly provoked Stephen Gardiner by making a personal attack on him in the course of a sermon delivered at Paul's Cross. He, and then his supporters, Jerome and Garret, were eventually brought before the king and recanted some over-enthusiastic statements concerning the worthlessness of good works; whereupon they were required to prove their orthodoxy publicly in sermons at St Mary Spital in Easter week. After they had done so, Gardiner – though he later denied this – somehow contrived to have the three quickly transported to the Tower. The affair is obscure, but it seems that Gardiner (or someone), 'by his privy complaining to the king, and his secret whisperings in his friends' ears', bustled Henry into putting these three men into custody.[14] It is not obvious now, and probably was not obvious then, why exactly they had been imprisoned. But Barnes was closely associated with Cromwell and Jerome was vicar of Stepney, where Cromwell lived. Clearly their arrest was part of the manoeuvring which preceded the assault on the minister. How could the wild accusations against him and the need for a swift purge be made more credible than by seeming to uncover a dangerous network of heretical conspirators?

These three men were burned at Smithfield on 30 July, two days after Cromwell's execution. Like Cromwell, they

13. *Foxe*, v, 229 ff.   14. ibid., 430 ff.

were not brought to trial in an open court, where the
fraudulence of their indictment might too easily have been
perceived, but were dispatched with the swifter instrument
of act of Attainder, in which they were briefly stated to be
guilty of the grossest heresies, 'the number whereof were
too long here to be rehearsed'.[15] At the stake, however, Barnes
made a protestation which tipped into the open the truth
about how he had been handled. In his last speech to the
crowd he protested that he had never preached sedition and
disobedience, nor said that 'our Lady was but a saffronbag',
as some had slanderously alleged; that he had never been an
Anabaptist, but that all his study and diligence had been
'utterly to confound and confute all men of that doctrine'
(which was true). He had been accused of the wildest heresy
and utterly denied his guilt. He was no heretic. He was condemned to die, 'but wherefore I cannot tell' – though, since
he and his companions were to burn, he presumed that
their crime must be heresy. Had the sheriff, who stood by,
'any articles against me for the which I am condemned?'
he asked. The sheriff answered 'no'. He then asked the
crowd if anyone knew 'wherefore I die, or that by my
preaching hath taken error', and none spoke. From what
followed, it is clear that Barnes half suspected that Gardiner
had something to do with his impending execution and that
others of the Council had acted against him either 'through
malice or ignorance'; but, for the rest, he was as baffled by
what had overtaken him as were, apparently, the onlookers
at the execution. Extreme heresies had been imputed to
him, which he had certainly never held and for which there
was no evidence, and he who had been swept mysteriously to
the Tower was now about to be swept mysteriously to a
terrible death.[16]

15. House of Lords, Original Acts, 32 Hen. VIII, *c.* 60. In this same
attainder four men from Calais were condemned to death for
treasonous dealings with Pole; an Irishman for supporting the rebel
Fitzgerald; and Charles Carew of Surrey for robbery.

16. *Foxe*, v, 434 ff.

Apparently it was the same with the others. As they prepared to die, they professed 'in like manner their belief, reciting all the articles of the Christian faith, briefly declaring their minds upon every article, as the time would suffer; whereby the people might understand that there was no cause nor error in their faith, wherefore justly they ought to be condemned: protesting moreover that they denied nothing that was either in the Old or New Testament set forth by their sovereign lord the king'.[17] Presumably, like Barnes, they had been accused of being Anabaptists and now faced the flames no less bewildered than he to find what charges of heresy had been planted on them.

The victims themselves were baffled by their fate; so too was an alert, informed contemporary. In his chronicle, Edward Hall confessed that he had never been able to understand why these men 'that professed the Gospel of Jesus Christ and were preachers thereof' (i.e. were no heretics by his reckoning) had been so cruelly executed – 'although I have searched to know the truth'. He had taken the pains to inspect their attainder and noted its highly suspicious vagueness; he knew how, at Smithfield, Barnes had asked the attendant sheriff if he could explain the condemnation and received no answer.[18] For Hall, these executions clearly reeked of murder. Likewise Luther could write in the preface to an account of Barnes's faith, quickly produced by the Lutheran world as a memorial to a great son, 'the cause why Barnes was martyred is still hidden, because Henry must be ashamed of it'.[19] But he was only half right. Henry was not the author of his death and probably never knew exactly how it came about.

Nor is this the end of the matter. On the day that Barnes

17. *Foxe*, v, 436 f. But Foxe gives only a small portion of their speeches verbatim and it is therefore impossible to state categorically that they were snared as Barnes certainly was.

18. *Hall*, 840.

19. *L.P.*, xvi, 106. Cf. the statement by Richard Hilles to Bullinger that he too had been unable to discover why Barnes and the others died. *L.P.*, xvi, 578.

and his two companions died, three defendants of the old
Faith were also put to death, namely, Edward Powell,
Richard Fetherston and the illustrious Thomas Abel.[20] This
double persecution of three for Protestant heresy, three for
popish treason, has often been remarked as evidence of
Henry's fine sense of equilibrium and his firm intention to
steer exactly between Rome and Wittenberg. But maybe the
blood of neither trio is to be laid at his door. Maybe the
martyrdom of the three Catholic priests was also, somehow,
part of the plot against Cromwell – an attempt to confuse
the issue, to placate, to intimidate. And certainly those who
destroyed Barnes and his fellows did not thereby, wittingly
or unwittingly, place England on a judicious *via media*; for
Barnes (for certain) and the others (probably) were burnt as
Anabaptists, not Lutherans, and thus were dealt with in a
manner which Luther himself approved for members of
those sects which so confused and hindered his own preaching.

About eight months after Cromwell's death, Marillac reported that Henry was gloomy and malevolent; that he suspected that his very ministers had brought about Cromwell's
destruction by false accusations 'and on light pretexts'; that
he had said so to their faces; that he now knew that Cromwell had been the most faithful servant he had ever had.[21]
At the time, probably, Henry had never fully understood
how and why Cromwell was suddenly swept away. The king
had been stampeded by a faction bent on a *coup d'état* and
swept along by it, like the suggestible man that he was. It
is no contradiction to say this so soon after asserting his
complete absorption in, and command of, the policies which
some have said Cromwell was furtively trying to foist on
him. For Henry was often this: a vulnerable and volatile
thing, just at the moment when he seemed most assured
and thrustful. When the furore was over and it was too late

20. These three have at last received worthy treatment – in Paul,
Catherine of Aragon and her Friends.
21. *L.P.*, xvi, 589–90.

to repair the damage, he began to see the dark truth about how he had been captured and exploited; and he began to regret. He had lost for ever a genius, perhaps the most accomplished servant any English monarch has enjoyed, a royal minister who cut a deeper mark on the history of England than have many of her monarchs.

The Royal Supremacy and Theology

THE Royal Supremacy made Henry the spiritual father of his people and master of that new institution, the national Church of England. In the words of the act of Appeals, the spiritualty and temporalty were but two 'sorts and degrees of people' who made up the single body politic of which Henry was the 'one supreme head and king'; or, as Stephen Gardiner argued in his *De Vera Obedientia* (and his argument became a commonplace), because the inhabitants of the realm were also members of the all-inclusive national Church, he who was head of the first must be head of the second.[1] Henry consistently maintained – in a letter to Cranmer in 1533, for instance, and in his own revision of the royal coronation oath – that the spiritual men were ministers of the crown, *his* clergy, exercising an authority delegated by him.[2] As Cranmer wrote in 1540, just as his highness had under him a descending scale of civil ministers, from the lord chancellor down to sheriffs and mayors and the like, so he had another set of ministers, running down from bishops to the humblest parochial clergy, whose authority was likewise derived from the royal plenitude of power.[3] Hitherto the bull and pallium from the universal ordinary of Rome

1. See Janelle, *Obedience in Church and State* (Cambridge, 1930), 93 ff.

2. *L.P.*, vi, 332. There is a facsimile of the text of the oath, with Henry's corrections, in the frontispiece of Ellis, 2nd ser., i. For the transcription thereof see *Ellis*, 176 ff.

3. *Miscellaneous Writings and Letters of Thomas Cranmer*, ed. Cox, Parker Society (1846), p. 116. Cf. Whitgift's analysis of the queen's double cure, spiritual and temporal – 'as she doth exercise the one by the lord chancellor, so doth she the other by the archbishops'. Whitgift, *Works*, ii, 246.

had bestowed the *potestas iurisdictionis* on the recipient; now it flowed from the king in London. Thus the acts in Restraint of Annates had provided and, as evidence of the new order, the bishops of England were required to exchange their bulls of appointment for royal letters patent and bring to the king all papal privileges and indults addressed either to them or their churches, 'to be confirmed or cancelled at your majesty's pleasure'.[4]

The English Church was the king's Church. Its clergy were his ministers, his vicars, his servants;[5] and if official statements never allowed it to be said that the *potestas ordinis*, the spiritual powers as distinct from the jurisdiction of the clergy, flowed from the Supreme Head (though both Cranmer and perhaps Henry came near to doing so),[6] they were careful to state that the actual manner of election and appointment of clergy was a matter of local usage allowed by princes, and the offices of patriarch, primate, metropolitan, archdeacon, dean and the like due either to 'the consent and authority or else at least ... the permission and sufferance of the princes and civil powers'.[7] Parishes, sees, cathedrals, monasteries – these were for the king to 'visit, repress, redress, reform, order, correct, restrain and amend',[8] either in his own person, or through his ministers, the clergy, or through Cromwell, his vice-gerent in spirituals, and vicar-general (an ecclesiastical title, significantly enough, of a bishop's deputy), or through anyone, lay or cleric, commissioned by the king under the great seal. Convocation would

4. So the text of the new oath to be taken by bishops and archbishops on their appointment, in P.R.O. S.P. 6/3 fol. 64v.

5. These terms were used, for example, by Bishop Sampson in a sermon on the Supremacy (Strype, *Ecclesiastical Memorials* I, ii, 166), in a treatise on the Courts Christian in P.R.O. S.P. 6/5, fol. 25v, and repeatedly in the *Bishops' Book* of 1537.

6. See below, pp. 536–7.

7. So the *Bishops' Book*. See Lloyd, *Formularies of Faith put forth by authority during the Reign of Henry VIII*, Oxford, 1856, 118. The *King's Book* repeated these ideas – which became common form.

8. So the act of Supremacy.

be assembled only by the king's writ and have a layman as its president, namely the king's vicar-general or his deputy. If it was still for the clergy 'to command, to reform, to reward, to punish' their flock, this was only in virtue of a derivative authority and according to canons which, in theory, had either been approved by the royal committee of thirty-two persons – which never completed its work during this reign – or which had received royal assent. The Courts Christian, hitherto a separate legal system lying alongside the royal courts but piped to Rome, ran now to the *Curia Regis*. Henceforth, final appeal in ecclesiastical causes was to lie with the king's majesty in the court of Chancery.[9] The Dispensations act halted the flow of supplications for licences, faculties, indults, dispensations, etc. which previously went to Rome and empowered the archbishop of Canterbury to stand in Rome's stead. But all the more important grants were either to be issued by the king and Council or to be confirmed under the king's great seal and recorded in Chancery; and fees for the same were to be shared between Church and State. It was for the king to 'order and redress' all indulgences granted by Rome – 'as shall seem good, wholesome and reasonable for the honour of God and weal of his people'[10] – and, finally, for him to declare doctrine, to tell Englishmen what was true and what was false, what they must assert and what they must deny. The act of Supremacy had spoken only of the crown's negative protection of doctrine against heresy, but before long Henry would be setting before his people comprehensive statements of the Faith, composed by his clergy, set forth as truth on his authority and by his licence; just as the same authority would issue injunctions determining the number of holy days, instructing the clergy about their sermons, veneration of saints and relics, decrying pilgrimages, requiring every parish to purchase an English Bible, and so on. The king was the vicar of God, and, as Henry said of

9. 25 Henry VIII, *c*. xix.
10. So section xxi of this act.

himself, his 'high minister here', the 'soul of the whole kingdom', who, having overthrown the blasphemous thraldom of the self-styled vicar of Christ, must 'animate, rule and save' his people.[11]

We who, today, know a very faded Royal Supremacy have to struggle hard to recapture that apotheosis of monarchy in its full colours – by pondering, perhaps, Stephen Gardiner's attempt, albeit one which sprang out of hostility to the archbishop, to prove that Cranmer's title of 'primate of all England' derogated from the king's spiritual overlordship;[12] by recalling how, decades later, such as Prynne would curse divine-right episcopacy of Laud and his fellow Arminians on the ground that it set bishops directly under God, instead of under the king, and thereby established 'a Papall and Episcopall exploded usurped Jurisdiction, Independent on, and underived from the Imperiall Crowne'.[13] The near-idolatry which a man like Cranmer, followed by so many of his contemporaries, bestowed on the Supreme Head, was based on the conviction that true Christian kingship had at last been discovered after centuries of desolation and darkness. A powerful new national epic, indeed, theology of History, had been born – of which Foxe will later be the most fulsome exponent – telling how for generations England had groaned under the tyranny of the bishops of Rome; how that tyranny had been made possible by the servility of princes and people, and the fraud and forgery of vainglorious popes; how these last had steadily thrust themselves above their fellow bishops and usurped the authority of those to whom all obedience is due, God's vicars on earth – Roman emperors and their successors, the princes of Christendom – how the hour had come to throw off this usurpation, strike down this ravenous pride and greed, and restore the pristine right order. Now at last princes were beginning to see 'what way

11. *Foxe*, v, 535; 'Treatise on Royal Power', in P.R.O. S.P. 1/238, fol. 245.

12. *L.P.*, viii, 704.

13. Lamont, *Marginal Prynne 1600–1669* (1963), 17.

this wily wat [i.e. the pope] had walked all this long while'.[14] Rome's pre-eminence had been the work of ambitious, megalomaniac popes, exploiting accidental advantage of history and geography, the disorders of past times, the weaknesses of others. The Apostles, it was argued, had been given a 'universal' power not attached or restricted to any geographical area. Peter had never been at Rome anyway; or, if he had been, had never enjoyed any primacy himself; or, if he did, his primacy was a personal attribute, not to be passed to his successors; or, if it was, it was the primacy of honour and of 'the ring-leader in virtue', not 'an extreme and fleshly power, such a one as Christ never exercised, nor committed it at any time to any man to exercise'.[15] The early Church knew nothing of later Roman claims to universal primacy, it was argued. Manifestly the first Councils were not 'papal' councils and accorded to Rome no greater authority or honour than they did to the other patriarchates. Neither the Fathers nor 'the common consent of the whole Catholic Church' acknowledged a papacy as it now claimed to be; indeed, one of the bishops of Rome wrote to the emperor at Constantinople confessing 'his primacy to extend only to bishops of the west and north parts' – and so on. Official attitudes to the papacy varied – from extreme vilification to the moderation of, say, a Stephen Gardiner, who thought in terms of a Christendom which kings ruled but over which the pope still exercised some primacy of service as teacher and leader, as in the early Church, when bishops

14. Thus spoke *A Little Treatise against the Mutterings of some Papists in Corners* of 1534 (*Pocock*, ii, 539 ff.). In what precedes and follows this quotation I have summarized the main contents of a number of tracts – viz. *A Glasse of the Truthe*, *A Little Treatise* etc., *Articles devised by the holle consent of the Council* etc., a tract by the archbishop of York for the guidance of preachers in P.R.O. S.P. 6/3, fols 75 ff. (*L.P.*, viii, 292), a discourse on the Royal Supremacy in P.R.O. S.P. 6/6, fols 44 ff. and 84 f. (*L.P.*, viii, 294–5), and two *opuscula* on the same subject in P.R.O. S.P. 1/238, fols 238 ff. and 240 (*L.P.*, Addenda 912–13); as well as Gardiner's *De Vera Obedientia* and the relevant passages in the *Bishops' Book*.

15. See Janelle, op. cit., 153.

of Rome were 'valiant in preaching Christ and defending the Faith'.[16] All, however, agreed that the English Church was not subject to the direct government and jurisdiction of this foreign bishop, but should stand under the prince alone.

Christian kingship must take as its model the kingship of Israel and Judah – from David, Jehoshaphat, Hezekiah and Josiah, anointed, sacred kings, whom God set over His flock, to whom priests and people were subject, who appointed priests and levites, and punished them with death, who led their nation in battle and the service of God. Comparatively little appeal, it seems, was made to more recent apologists of the Christian prince – the publicists who had fought papalism on behalf of medieval emperors or a Philip IV of France. Ockham was quoted now and again, and so too Gerson; in 1535 a specially trimmed translation (to suit English conditions) was produced of that major textbook of anti-papalism and Erastianism, Marsiglio of Padua's *Defensor Pacis*. But in the main, the Henrician propagandists went back to the sources, to the Old Testament, to those texts in the Gospels in which Christ allegedly submitted himself and his Church to the emperor in bidding Peter and the Apostles to render unto Caesar the things that were Caesar's or denied that He sought a kingdom on this earth, and to those famous texts in the Acts of the Apostles and the Epistles in which Paul appealed to Caesar and urged obedience to earthly superiors, and Peter commanded Christians to honour the king. In short, they brought out once more that collection of taxes which had already been used time and again in the great debates about Christian obedience. But above all they appealed to the example of early Christian emperors – and especially to the alleged caesaropapism

16. Janelle, op. cit., 149. Gardiner went on to pray for Paul III with the words 'God send him good life, and well to fare in the Lord'. Cf. the similar moderation of Bekinson, who accepted Peter's primacy but likewise denounces the power-mania of his successors and the iniquities they had caused. So his *De supremo et absoluto regis imperio* (1547), 51 ff.

of Byzantium. Did not Constantine preside over the first great Council at Nicea and manifestly hold the spiritual and temporal swords in his hand? Where was the papacy then? Did not Justinian take the determination of disputes about the Holy Trinity in his imperial sweep, impose laws on bishops and hunt down heresy? Where was the papacy then? And had not Fathers like Tertullian said that princes were next to God and applauded emperors' care for Holy Church?

The Royal Supremacy is 'annexed and united to the imperial crown of this realm', the statutes were continually to say. It springs from the *imperium merum*, the 'whole and entire monarchy' which rightfully belongs to the Christian prince, which unwary princes have in the past suffered to be usurped by popes, which is now to be restored. English monarchy is imperial monarchy. So, as we have seen, Henry has long been arguing. Now this truth was to become the very spine of his kingship – as it will be for his successors. What he had begun to assert in 1530 has become a solemn political fact. The imperial ambition has been realized. Henry is not an emperor *tout court*, but a king possessed of the 'imperial crown of the realm' because his kingship has been restored to its full inheritance and endowed with the authority of the early Christian emperors. It is not exactly clear how this has come about, for the writers are a little ambiguous. For most of the time it seems that restored monarchy simply takes the emperors of old as its model; but at least one statement seems to argue a direct descent from the old to the new. What had previously been a single headship of the Church vested in the Byzantine emperor has subsequently been distributed among all the princes of Christendom, conferring on them 'absolute power in their realms'.[17] This was the authentic *translatio imperii*, therefore. For a long time the Roman bishops have intercepted an inheritance destined for princes and have foisted on the world the fable of Constantine's Donation to them; but now the rightful heirs of

17. See the opinion of some bishops on the subject of General Councils in *St.P.*, i, 543.

Constantine and Justinian were coming forward to claim their own.

Early sixteenth-century Scriptural scholarship may have been elementary, and knowledge of early Christian history flimsier still, but they were sufficient to convince men of integrity that kings had been called by God to be His vicars on earth and endowed by Him with the sacred duty of nursing the spiritual as well as the temporal lives of their subjects. It was not only expediency, or anger, or hope of gain which caused Englishmen to abandon their allegiance to the old order. Though the doctrine of the Royal Supremacy seems remote and uncongenial now, and evidence which supported it suspect, we must remember that, to such as Cranmer and doubtless many others, it was real and compelling – both a revelation and a liberation – and that for them the king's headship was a holy thing which demanded obedience as to a father in God. One of the Henrician pamphleteers tried to argue that effectively there was nothing new in the Royal Supremacy, since the bishops of Rome had never been allowed any authority in England, and English kings had always steadfastly resisted the Roman usurpation.[18] But this argument – a precursor of the long-lived legend that, to quote an admirable epigram, would have English Christianity Protestant before the Reformation and Catholic after it – could not have been approved by many of his fellows, whatever their persuasion. The Royal Supremacy may have been a restoration of a long-lost right order, and of the true polity; but it was also a startling, violent breach with several centuries of the immediate past. And if it is wrong to argue that it effected no real change in the structure of the English Church, it is equally misplaced to assert that it reduced the latter to a mere department of state. Certainly it produced a Church utterly subject to the prince; but only because the prince himself had been elevated to the portals of Heaven.

18. So *A Treatise proving by the King's laws that the bishops of Rome had never right to any supremitie within this realm* (1534).

The Church of England, then, is a 'particular' church, *a* catholic church. Henry himself will write of it as 'but a part of the whole Catholic Church', or, rather unfortunately, as a 'known private church'[19] – which is a difficult piece of ecclesiology. The essential unity of Christendom was not denied. As the *Bishops' Book* of 1537 said, all the particular churches, including that of Rome, are 'compacted and united together to make and constitute but one Catholic Church or body'[20] – that is, if those princes elsewhere who were yet unawakened would only rise to their true status and the bishop of Rome descend to his. Over and above the particular, local churches there should still stand the General Council, the supreme (and unique) visible mark of the unity of Christendom. General Councils, as has been noticed, caused Henry some difficulty. In 1533 he had appealed to a future Council against the pope. But when Paul III prepared to summon the very Council to which Henry had appealed, the latter had to side-step this threat by taking up the Protestant cry for a 'free, Christian Council', by which he meant one truly representative of the Christian people and directed by princes, not the pope. Henrician propaganda quickly took up the argument that the *ius concilium convocandi* belonged to princes alone as their imperial right. Henry could affirm his intense desire for a Council, echoing the plea of generations of fellow-Christians – 'we crave nothing so oft of God as that we may have one', the *Protestation* of 1538 asserted – but only a Council summoned by

19. In his corrections to the *King's Book* of 1543. B.M. Cleo. E, v, fol. 34, and again on fol. 35v.

20. Lloyd, op. cit., p. 55. Cf. Henry's affirmation, reported by Chapuys in 1538, 'I never wished to make a God of my own and separate from the whole corps of Christendom, which besides being a scandal, would bring great harm on me.' *Sp. Cal.*, v, ii, 223. Some may distinguish intention from reality, but they cannot deny the intention. Henry claimed to have overthrown a *false* unity and, if what he put in its place was both in theory and practice a minimal thing, like the Protestants, he believed that the essential oneness of Christendom had been preserved.

the authority of the emperor, kings and princes, as were the early Councils.[21] And even this carried difficulties within it, for, if a legitimate Council were ever to meet, what precisely would its authority be? Would it stand above those vicars of God, the Christian princes? Could it bind and coerce them or would it be merely 'charismatic' and leave the princes free to enforce its decrees as they saw fit? As it happened, this was an academic point, but it was one which irritated the Henrician world almost as much as it did the Protestant. The Henricians at first insisted that the voice of a Council must be authoritative and binding.[22] But some wavered and left the Supreme Head unfettered in his headship. A draft of the last official formulary of faith of Henry's reign, the *King's Book* of 1543, echoing its predecessor of 1537, affirmed that 'we must all humbly submit to the judgement of the whole Church', i.e. to a General Council. And then Henry intervened. He corrected this pious statement to read 'we ought to think and esteem that the whole Church assembled as it ought to be, which is by the whole assent of the princes and *potestates* of the Christian world, is deeper of judgement and ought to be more universally to be obeyed than the opinion of any one private church [he repeats the term] touching the Catholic ordering of the same'[23] – which was something less than the original statement that 'we must all humbly submit'. But neither the latter nor Henry's correction appeared in the final version. The problem was shelved.

21. *A Protestation made for the most mighty and most redoubted King of England etc.* (1538) no pagination – a tract against the papal council just summoned to meet at Vincenza in the following November. Cf. another work setting forth royal conciliar theory in the same terms, *An Epistle ... to the Emperor's Majesty, to all Christian Princes etc.* (1538); and the tract in *St.P.*, i, 543 f.

22. On all this see Sawada, 'The Abortive Council of Mantua and Henry VIII's *Sententia de Concilio*, 1537', *Academia* (Nagoya, Japan), xxvii (1960), 1 ff., and 'Two Anonymous Tudor Treatises on the General Council', *Journal Eccl. Hist.*, xii (1961), 197 ff.; F. van le Baumer, *The Early Tudor Theory of Kingship* (New Haven, 1940), esp. 51 ff.

23. B.M. Cleo. E, v, fol. 34v.

This was a subsidiary issue. The essential, central fact was
the overthrow of the tyranny of the bishop of Rome and the
recovery by the king of England, the new Constantine, of an
imperial spiritual supremacy which had so long been
usurped. Once the Royal Supremacy had been announced, a
massive programme was launched to carry the news of
England's liberation into the highways and byways of the
land. All of consequence were to swear oaths acknowledging Henry as Supreme Head and renouncing Rome; the
pope's name was to be erased from the twenty-five places
where it occurred in the Liturgy; and in every parish church
sermons were to be preached four times a year telling simple
folk of their timely deliverance from the bishop of Rome's
engine of darkness. A stream of books, pamphlets and tracts,
some official statements issued by the king and Council,
others the work of a group of writers gathered round Cromwell and employed by him, rehearsed again and again the
arguments from Scripture and early Church history to support the Royal Supremacy and do down Rome's pretensions;
while popular plays and pageants brought the same message
in simpler terms to the common folk. A nation was to be
re-educated. To achieve this end, the government, directed
by Cromwell, would undertake a propaganda campaign
without precedent and the printing press be given its first
opportunity in England to demonstrate its full potentialities.

At the core of the Royal Supremacy there lay a constitutional problem. The act of Supremacy merely declared that
Henry was the head of the English Church. It did not make
him so, because it could not. Only God could – and had
done. Thus by the terms of this act, and as is stated or implied by many of the apologies of the new order, Henry's
Supremacy was absolute and personal, a gift directly received from Heaven and held *Dei gratia.* But elsewhere it is
implied that the Supremacy was vested in king in Parliament. The acts which have been mentioned above –
concerning Appeals, Annates, the Submission of the Clergy,

Dispensations – were not merely declaratory. They did not simply declare aspects of the new order and prescribe punishments for those who resisted what had been declared; they authorized them. Step by step, they authorized intrinsic, necessary functions of the Royal Supremacy – the king's right to appoint bishops without Rome, the subordination of ecclesiastical courts and Convocation to royal control, the provision of a domestic supply of all ecclesiastical faculties and dispensations; and what they did was by authority of king, lords and commons. If the essential ingredients of the Royal Supremacy (for such they were) were legalized by the parliamentary trinity, then clearly sovereignty in spiritual matters would seem to be vested in that trinity and not in any one member of it.

On the one hand, therefore, we hear a theory of 'descending' power,[24] by which sovereignty in spiritual matters was conferred on the king by direct divine grant; on the other an 'ascending' or 'immanentist' theory of autarchy which placed spiritual sovereignty in the supreme legislature, Parliament. Of course, until the act of Supremacy was passed and the former theory proclaimed, there was no alternative to the latter. Until he dared to claim authority directly from Heaven, Henry could receive the attributes of his spiritual overlordship only from Parliament. The new arrangements concerning annates, appeals and the rest could have no authority save that of king, lords, and commons. In late 1534 the 'descending' theory was proclaimed and thereafter Henry's personal Supremacy was preserved intact. Henceforth the Supreme Head issued injunctions and put out statements of faith on his own authority – and subsequent acts of Parliament touching religious matters either authorized what was consequent upon Henry's Supremacy, such as the new measure of 1536 for 'extinguishing the authority of the bishop of Rome',[25] or laid down punish-

24. I borrow this term, and its antithesis, from Ullman, *Principles of Government and Politics in the Middle Ages* (1961).
25. 28 Hen. VIII c. x.

ments for disobeying what had already been determined,
as did the act of Six Articles of 1539 (though, in truth, this
is almost a borderline case since the statute stated that the
articles which it now made enforceable at law had previously
been shown to both houses of Parliament for them to discuss
and approve).[26] But, despite the fact that it rested on a different principle, the act of Supremacy did not sweep away the
earlier acts – of Annates, Appeals and so on. On the contrary, it rested upon and capped them.

From the start, therefore, there was some confusion as to
whether the king enjoyed his Supremacy as a direct, personal
divine grant, or whether it was held by king of Parliament.
There was statutory evidence for both ideas. There was
ideological ambiguity in the core of Henricianism. Ever since
Henry had appealed both to the prerogatives of the realm
and to his own imperial rights as a king, he had brought together ideas which at least overlapped even if they were not,
in the last resort, irreconcilable. Furthermore, the act of
Appeals had, perhaps, consecrated this ambiguity. Its
famous preamble proclaimed the 'empire' and hence a Marsilian autarchy of the sovereign state – and this relied on an
'ascending' or 'immanentist' theory of power. But it spoke
thus only once. Immediately afterwards it told of the imperial crown of the realm, endowed by God with 'plenary,
whole and entire power, pre-eminence, authority, prerogative and jurisdiction', to whom all are bound in obedience –
which suggests a strongly 'monarchical' view of things.
Although the statute thereafter swings back towards
Marsilianism, its preamble appears to stand between the
parliamentary Supremacy of the foundation statutes of Henricianism and the personal Supremacy of the act of that
name.

This complexity was matched by a similar complexity in

26. So its preamble recited. *Statutes of the Realm*, iii, 739. What
may have been sound political tactics, therefore, brought Henry very
near a dangerous concession. What had presumably been allowed as
an act of grace could easily be claimed as a right.

the nature of secular sovereignty. English kings were kings *Dei gratia*, by gift from above, as coronation showed, and by descent; but at the same time, the idea of contract, of responsibility, of 'ascending' power was deeply embedded in English thinking. English monarchy was limited by the Aristotelian principle that political power was vested in and sprang from the whole political community, and by the constitutional fact that the highest form of law-making was the statute – which required the consent of the whole nation represented in Parliament.[27] English monarchy was, so to speak, amphibious; a creature of man and God; '*politicum et regale*', a *via media* which held in unity the opposed principles of Divine Right and the populist doctrines of thorough-going Aristotelians like Marsilius and Ockham.[28] To sustain this polarity and to answer the demands of what was at once an 'ascending' and a 'descending' theory of power was the crux of English politics. Provided that *both* demands were reasonably well met, no one was anxious to resolve by force what may often have seemed a contradiction inherent in the system. Simplicity and clarity were difficult to acquire and dangerous when acquired. It was better to leave the constitution wrapped up in time-honoured complexity than attempt to 'unravel' it.

Hence the duality of a Royal Supremacy which was not only a personal attribute of the imperial crown but also a function of 'empire', that is, of the whole body politic, would seem to match the duality of a secular sovereignty which was at once vested by Divine Right in an anointed, legitimate king and was yet resident in the whole political community.

27. Neither Henry nor Cromwell 'discovered' Parliament, therefore. They merely used it; and they had no alternative to it. What was new in the 1530s was the claim that the self-sufficient body politic – the empire – could do anything. The new autarchy affirmed the omnicompetence of statute, not the established fact that it was the highest form of law in the land.

28. See Wilks, *The Problem of Sovereignty in the Later Middle Ages* (Cambridge, 1963), esp. 118 ff., for an analysis of the *Via Media*, as the author terms it.

This last had happened to grow thus over the centuries, whereas the Royal Supremacy was the conscious work of man over a few years; and one cannot but wonder if the ambiguity of the Royal Supremacy was fortuitous.

Despite what has just been said about the act of Appeals, it seems that Cromwell was a constitutionalist of the Marsilian school. His political creed rested on the omnicompetence of statute and the sovereignty of Parliament. Furthermore, as is shown by the preamble of the Dispensations act, with its remarkable testimony to the legal supremacy of Parliament over ecclesiastical affairs, this was true for him of spiritual and temporal matters. The body politic possessed of itself both spiritual and temporal autonomy and exercised it through the sovereign legislature.[29] If this was his mind, then it may be observed *en passant* that what he thought about secular sovereignty was simpler than reality, for his tidy system ignored the dualism which we have just noted.

But Henry seems to have been of different persuasion. If, in former years, he shook the stick of the liberties and immunities of England, he probably never saw these as conflicting with his personal, imperial prerogatives. He thought of the Supremacy in simple terms, seeing ecclesiastical authority descending from God to himself and thence onwards and downwards into the body spiritual. As has been said, this is how he regularly spoke and acted. Moreover, this is how the act of Appeals might have spoken. One of the drafts of that act contained the statement that civil and canon law both derived directly from the king – and we know that Henry added that statement himself.[30] It was deleted from the final version. Why? Not necessarily because it had been abandoned by its author. Because it was too provocative and difficult to substantiate? Perhaps. Because it conflicted with another political theory, the 'empire'

29. On all this, see Elton, 'The Political Creed of Thomas Cromwell', *T.R.H.S.*, 5th ser., vi (1956), 69 ff.

30. B.M. Cleo. E., vi, fol. 185. On this and other drafts, see Elton, 'The Evolution of a Reformation Statute', *E.H.R.*, lxiv (1949), 174 ff.

theory, and was overruled by it? Perhaps. In the previous year (1532), as the attack which ended in the Submission of the clergy was under way, a statute was drafted in preparation for the moment when Convocation would surrender. It provided that no past or future ecclesiastical canons, ordinances and constitutions should henceforth be published or put in execution unless they had been confirmed by act of Parliament. The 'authority and jurisdiction royal ... united and knit by the high providence of God to the imperial crown of the realm' would be thus protected against clerical usurpation – by Parliament.[31] However, the bill never became law. Instead, the clergy agreed to submit past canons to inspection by a committee of thirty-two persons appointed by the king, and not to promulgate new legislation until this had received royal assent (*not* until confirmation by act of Parliament). Thus the plan for a parliamentary control of Convocation's activities was replaced by a 'royal' one. Why? Because the former was cumbersome? Perhaps. Because it conflicted with another political theory and, this time, was defeated by it? Perhaps. And why was the Submission of the clergy confirmed by act of Parliament some two years later, in 1534? Because it would thereby acquire the full sanctions of law, or because a political theory which required the functions of the Royal Supremacy to be authorized by Parliament had reasserted itself? It is true that this act also modified and clarified the procedure of appeals in ecclesiastical causes as it had been laid down in the act of 1533. But this can scarcely have been the whole reason for it. Details concerning the course of appeals could have been dealt with in a separate statute, instead of being inserted, rather incongruously, into this one. Clearly we must find additional motive for it – in either of the reasons, or both, which have just been suggested.

The argument, therefore, is that there was a confusion in the statutes of the Henrician Reformation concerning the

31. See two drafts of this bill, one heavily corrected, the other a fair copy, in P.R.O. S.P. 2/L, fols 78 ff. and S.P. 2/P, fols. 17 ff. (*L.P.*, v, 721 (i) and vii, 57 (2)).

source and location of the Royal Supremacy. On statutory
evidence it could be argued either that it was a personal
attribute of the king derived directly from God, or that it
was sprung of the whole body politic, and exercised by king
in Parliament. It would be agreeable to be able to state that
these two theories belonged to Henry and Cromwell respectively, that the confusion and evident see-sawing resulted
from a tussle between the two theories, and that the act of
Supremacy of 1534, which affirmed personal headship of the
king, marked the final victory of Henry's ideas over his minister's. The evidence, however, will not allow so categorical a
statement. But it is possible that this was so.

However, it can be said that two things made this confusion or tension more acute than it might have been. First,
it was present also in the pamphleteers who wrote on behalf
of the new regime. To a Stephen Gardiner, the Royal
Supremacy was vested in the king alone; but other writers,
especially the lawyer Christopher St Germain and the anonymous author of the *Treatise proving by the king's laws etc.*,
attributed ecclesiastical authority to king in Parliament.[32]
The dualism was not confined to the statutes, therefore.
Secondly, though Protestantism seemed to raise the prince
aloft and to preach the most extravagant things about his
sacred function, it had within it a quite opposite tendency.
Henry's Supremacy was far more stringent than anything
the Lutheran princes had won and was looked at askance by
the Reformers. It so shocked the English Protestant, Francis
Bigod, that he could join the Pilgrimage of Grace partly in
protest against its radical Erastianism – and thus be temporarily united to conservatives who opposed it for quite different reasons.[33] Authentic Protestantism looked for a prince
who would serve true religion, not one who would take upon

32. See Baumer, *The Early Tudor Theory of Kingship*, 56 ff.
33. On Bigod's interesting career, see Dickens, *Lollards and
Protestants in the Diocese of York*. Cf. Luther's remark that he and
Barnes used often to discuss how Henry could have taken the 'hor-
rible title' of Defender of the Faith and Supreme Head. *L.P.*, xvi, 106.

himself the role of autocratic *summus episcopus*; above all, it uncovered the precious idea of the Christian community which 'called' its minister, disciplined itself and, if it had any superstructure, derived it from below. Essentially, its polity was an 'ascending' one; and, much as it might praise the prince, it could never easily live with hierarchy sprung from above and a 'descending' theory of Royal Supremacy. The conflict between these two ideas would come out into the open in Elizabeth's reign and after. But it may have been present, though smothered, now.[34]

It was not with the act of Uniformity of 1549, therefore, in which the new Prayer Book was authorized by king, lords and commons, that the personal Supremacy of the king was first crossed by the conflicting idea of a 'parliamentary' Supremacy, for an amalgam of the two principles had been present since the early 1530s; and when Elizabeth's first Parliament of 1559 passed at one and the same time a declaratory act of [personal] Supremacy and an act of Uniformity authorizing the third Prayer Book, an ambiguity created in her father's reign was reproduced. Further, when Elizabeth tried to repulse parliamentary attacks on her religious settlement with the argument that religion was a matter of state and the exclusive concern of her prerogative in which no Parliament might meddle, she was standing on questionable ground. The parliamentary Puritans who battered at the

34. One might add that the Henrician appeal to a General Council also tended to run counter to a 'descending' theory of power, because, as some of the Henrician conciliar literature conceded, the Council represented the whole Church in which the *plenitudo potestatis* resided and through which it was diffused. See Baumer, op. cit., pp. 54 f. Thus, ironically, the Henrician personal supremacy was threatened by the same notions of the Church as *universitas* and *congregatio fidelium* possessed of authority in both head and members which had made medieval Conciliarism so clear a threat to the papal primacy (see Tierney, *Foundations of Conciliar Theory* Cambridge, 1957). Henry thus inherited both the power and the problems of the papacy. And like the popes', as Tierney has shown, Henry's position was threatened by his own apologists, the successors to the canonists who had first produced a conciliar theory.

Elizabethan Church and tried to storm its Supreme Governor have been accused of knowing no history. But was the
ignorance all theirs?

Unless Henry were to be 'like one that would throw down
a man headlong from the top of a high tower and bid him
stay when he was half way down',[35] for a significant, and
growing, number of contemporaries the overthrow of papal
authority in England and the declaration of the Royal
Supremacy was to be the beginning, not the conclusion, of
the story. To them it was incredible that, having been delivered of the tyranny of Rome, England should not then
turn to the far larger task of reform and renewal of her
Christian life.

In part, the years following the breach with Rome saw the
implementation of what may be loosely described as an
Erasmian reform programme – the attack on 'superstitions'
like relics, shrines, pilgrimages, as well as on monasticism;
the printing of the Bible and primers in English; the outpouring of Erasmian writings, many of them translations
of Erasmus's own works, others original pieces of lay pietism,
devotional literature and prayer manuals, alongside the innumerable treatises on education, social and economic justice, service to the prince and the commonwealth, medicine,
etc. produced by the humanist circles which formed first
around Thomas Cromwell and then around Queen Catherine
Parr.[36] But these years indisputably also saw England being
caught up in the great European movement of the Reformation. For some, Erasmianism may have been an end in itself;
but for others the assault on popish shrines and images, the
dissolution of the monasteries, the printing of the Bible
were stepping-stones towards continental Protestantism. Between 1525 and 1547, it has been reckoned, some eight hun-

35. Harpsfield, *The Pretended Divorce between Henry VIII and
Catherine of Aragon*, 297.
36. On all of which see McConica, *English Humanists and Reformation Politics etc.*

dred separate editions of religious works were printed in English and a large proportion of these were of strongly Protestant hue – by such as Barnes, Coverdale, Richard Tracy, Becon, Taverner and Joye, as well as by the Reformers themselves, Luther, Melanchthon and Calvin.[37] The first official statement of faith, the *Ten Articles* of 1536, followed the classical exposés of Lutheran theology, the *Augsburg Confession* and the subsequent *Apology*, almost verbatim for much of the way; and these two works were translated and printed in England in the same year by Taverner at Cromwell's behest and dedicated to him.[38] The second formulary, the so-called *Bishops' Book* of 1537, again owed much to the *Apology* as well as to Luther's *Catechisms*; and its successor, the *King's Book* of 1543, though it retreated from the tempered Protestantism of the former works, still bore marked traces of the Reformation. That Henricianism was merely 'Catholicism without the pope' will not do. Though the repeated negotiations with continental Protestantism were, on the whole, unhappy, and though Luther was eventually disappointed to find that, despite her early promise, England had not moved as fast or as far as he at one time expected, there can be no doubt that the Henrician Church took long strides towards the Reformers and that the English Protestantism which came to full flower in the next reign had many roots in this one. During Henry's reign, the English Church shifted a good way from the old orthodoxy. It moved erratically, now lurching towards Wittenberg, now pulling back – as diplomacy, the varying fortunes of jostling factions among the hierarchy, the king's own instincts and doubtless several other factors dictated. And over this strange evolution Henry himself presided. He

37. Knox, *The Doctrine of Faith in the reign of Henry VIII* (1961), ix.

38. These are, of course, but a few of the numerous overtly Protestant publications of these years, for which see Knox, op. cit. In 1535, Melanchthon dedicated his *Loci Communes* to Henry himself and received two hundred crowns in reward.

was never a Lutheran; indeed, in some matters he was intransigently conservative. But that febrile, wayward mechanism, Henry's mind, was in ferment – exploring, questioning, seizing on novelties, often pushing far away from its theological past, juxtaposing new and old in a curious medley. The picture sometimes presented of Henry having halted after lifting the yoke of Rome off his realm and himself, of him either not feeling or resisting the demand for further theological advance, is inadequate. The king who had once written against Luther, who had once held his own in a disputation on the esoteric subject of whether vocal as well as mental prayer was required of a layman,[39] who evidently delighted in presiding over a heresy trial and, so we are told, in confounding the heretic in public, whose quick mind throve on theology and had grasped enough to be effective but not enough to cease to be dangerous, plunged as an active contestant into the great doctrinal debates which marked the last third of his reign, and especially the years 1536 to 1540.

In 1531 direct communication between Henry and Wittenberg, broken after the bitter exchanges of the 1520s, was restored when the king sent Robert Barnes to Luther to secure his approval of the divorce. Doubtless any support from any source was desirable at this juncture, but that Henry should have taken this initiative is significant. To a zealot of orthodoxy the opinion of a notorious heretic, let alone one so recently denounced in public, would have been immaterial and his support more an embarrassment than a boon. That Henry should even have wanted to consult the heresiarch indicates how far he had already shifted from his past – even if it cannot be used as evidence of a sympathy for Protestant doctrine.

But Luther was a disappointment. In the previous year the English Lutheran, William Tyndale, had published his

39. So Erasmus tells us. See H. M. and P. S. Allen, *Opus Epistolarum Des. Erasmi*, iii, 582, and v, 127.

Practice of Prelates at Marburg, in which he trounced the king's levitical argument, insisting that Leviticus's ban referred to the wife of a living brother and was restricted thereto by Deuteronomy. And this was how both Luther and Melanchthon argued – though both went on to suggest that Henry could solve the problem of the succession by bigamy, after the manner of Abraham, David and the others, a solution which, curiously, Clement VII had made shortly before to the English agents in Rome in an hour of bleak exasperation.[40] Luther's opposition to the royal divorce was absolute. The dispensation under which the king and Catherine married should never have been granted, he argued, not because the Mosaic law was still binding but because such a union was contrary to human, secular law; but since that marriage had been consummated it would be grave sin to dissolve it. Catherine was 'the true and legitimate queen of England, made so by God himself', and the divorce a 'crime in God's sight'. Other reformers – Oecolampadius, Zwingli and Calvin, but not Bucer – gave judgement for Henry. But with one exception the Lutheran world rebuffed him: and the exception was Osiander, reformer and pastor of Nuremberg, who even wrote a work on Henry's behalf, but who, since his wife's niece had secretly married Thomas Cranmer, may have had a special interest in the cause.[41]

Wittenberg's verdict, a certain amount of which ran remarkably, and ironically close to that of Fisher, Abel, their Spanish companions, and the rest of Catherine's supporters, was delivered to Henry by Barnes at Christmas-time 1531. Though it was a setback, it did not prevent the first of a series of exploratory embassies to the Lutherans eighteen months later – which would eventually mature into negotiations for a doctrinal and political union.

We cannot trace here in detail the complex story of the many embassies and their intricate theological negotiations,

40. See above, p. 261.
41. On all this see Doernberg, op. cit., 85 ff.; Tjernagel, *Henry VIII and the Lutherans* (St Louis, 1965), 73 ff.

nor analyse the contents of the official statements of faith, especially the *Ten Articles* of 1536 and the *Bishops' Book* of the next year which owed so much to England's advances to the Lutherans. This has been done several times elsewhere[42] – and our concern is, rather, with the evolution of Henry's own mind. It is enough to recall that, between 1532 and 1534, embassies passed between England and the Hanseatic towns of Lübeck and Hamburg, which came to a climax with the arrival in the summer of 1534 of a highpowered delegation from both towns, carrying with them not only the offer of their confession of faith and a league against the pope, but also, from Lübeck, an appeal to Henry to attempt to acquire for himself the recently vacated throne of Denmark – a proposal which sufficiently excited the king for him to gather ships for an expedition and dispatch Bishop Bonner and Cavendish to the Baltic, laden with cash, apparently to prepare the way for an expedition to conquer Denmark.[43] How seriously the plan was entertained we shall never know, for another aspirant to the Danish throne, the duke of Holstein, soon snatched the trophy away and brought this extraordinary and little-known episode to an end. But it may well be that, for a while, Henry toyed with the idea with some enthusiasm.

Meanwhile, following an approach by the German Lutheran princes in 1531, Robert Barnes had passed several times between England and the Schmalkaldic League, until, in late 1535, he, Edward Fox and Nicholas Heath arrived at Wittenberg to propose an *entente* with the princes and to open major negotiations with Luther himself and Melanchthon. To the conditions immediately put forward by the duke of Saxony for the *entente* – the first of which stipulated

42. E.g. by Jacobs, *The Lutheran Movement in England during the reigns of Henry VIII and Edward VI* (1892); Prueser, *England und die Schmalkaldener* (Leipzig, 1929); Hughes, *The Reformation in England*, ii, 22 ff.; Tjernagel, op. cit., 120 ff.

43. This story is investigated in Alexander, 'The life and career of Edmund Bonner, bishop of London, etc.' (unpublished Ph.D. thesis, University of London, 1960).

that England must accept the *Confession of Augsburg* and Melanchthon's *Apology* – Henry appeared to give a qualified assent, despite Stephen Gardiner's protest, and after weeks of discussion Fox and his companions agreed to the so-called *Wittenberg Articles*, a statement of faith drawn up largely by Melanchthon and intended to serve as the basis of a final doctrinal concord to be agreed by a Lutheran embassy to England headed, doubtless, by Melanchthon, whose dispatch thither Henry repeatedly requested. But though these articles were a main source of the royal *Ten Articles*, produced a few weeks later, the Lutheran embassy did not come to England for two years. Between 1536 and 1538 Anglo-Lutheran relations virtually expired, until Christopher Mont's expedition to Saxony in early 1538 brought forth the long overdue delegation and a new set of proposals, the *Thirteen Articles*, no less Protestant than their predecessor, the *Wittenberg Articles* of 1536. The Germans arrived in May and left at the end of September 1538, with nothing accomplished. Next April a second embassy arrived in London, at royal invitation. It stayed for months, rather forlornly, achieved nothing and returned home in the summer of 1540. The act of Six Articles and Cromwell's fall brought these uncertain and erratic exchanges temporarily to an end. Three years later appeared the last doctrinal utterances of the reign, the *King's Book* of 1543 – a partial retreat from the formulary of 1537. Finally, in 1545 – as we shall see elsewhere[44] – a new bout of negotiations with the German Protestants began.

Such, in perhaps bewildering compression, are the broad outlines of the story. We may now turn to watch the doctrinal movements of Henry's mind against this background.

The Supreme Head, after his own fashion, had been intimately involved in the events rehearsed above. Doubtless with the encouragement of Cromwell and Cranmer, and doubtless with motives both profane and otherwise, he had followed closely the course of the innumerable embassies to

44. See below, pp. 584, 595 ff.

and from the Continent, and perhaps occasionally thrust them onwards. He worked over at least some of the documents connected with the embassy which came from Wittenberg in 1538, scribbling in marginal corrections.[45] He may have looked at Convocation's *Ten Articles* of 1536 and made a few, albeit very minor, corrections.[46] He certainly studied its successor, the so-called *Bishops' Book*, very closely. Shortly after its publication in September 1537 he sent a long list of comments and criticisms to Cranmer – to which Cranmer made detailed reply. His annotations and Cranmer's counter-objections have survived and make intriguing reading.[47] Nor were the remarks he addressed to the archbishop the sum total of his objections to the book. There survive two further documents containing his corrections to what had been written about the sacrament of Confirmation and prayers for the dead.[48] Indeed, for one who was not addicted to writing and who, according to Cranmer, handed long works of theology to his courtiers for them to read for him, the hundred-odd often lengthy corrections and additions he made to the text of this sizeable work must stand as a monument to his theological enthusiasm. Next, in a long reply to Tunstal in 1539 he set out his views on auricular confession and peppered the bishop's letter addressed to him with shrewd, hostile *marginalia* – as he had done to a paper by Latimer on Purgatory.[49] He drew up the final text of the Six Articles of 1539. In 1540 he worked over a couple of the surviving replies of the bishops to searching questions concerning the sacraments, adding terse remarks beside their

45. P.R.O. S.P. 1/135, fols 151 ff. and 179 ff. – articles on Communion under both kinds and on private Masses. Henry made the arguments against the first more scathing and wrote 'bene' and 'nota bene', etc. against the arguments in support of the latter.
46. *Burnet*, iv, 272 n. for these. It is not certain, however, that Henry made them.
47. They are to be found in *Miscellaneous Writings and Letters of Thomas Cranmer*, ed. Cox, Parker Society (1846), 83 ff.
48. P.R.O. S.P. 6/3, fols 9 ff. and S.P. 6/8, fols 95 ff.
49. B.M. Cleo. E. iv, fols 131 ff.; Cleo. E, v, fols 140 f.

answers.[50] Finally, there survive two documents containing about fifty of his corrections to the text of the *King's Book* of 1543.[51] In short, when all these royal writings, most of them jottings and annotations, are put together, they amount to a considerable, if necessarily scrappy, corpus; and as their centrepiece stands Henry's most considerable effort, his corrections to the *Bishops' Book*.

Of course he remained himself even amidst theology. The Supreme Head could not always sustain his appetite for the sacred sciences against counter-attraction. On at least one occasion he had not gone very far with his work before he tired and his pen dropped from his hand,[52] just as it had done years before when he was correcting Convocation's reform decrees; and on at least one occasion, when he was required to approve the *Bishops' Book* for publication, he did not even start to work. That book, which had been commissioned by the king, was finished in mid July 1537. On the 20th of that month Edward Fox, who had been closely involved in its compilation under Cromwell's aegis, wrote that it was ready except for a few notes on the Creed and asked to know the king's pleasure about its printing, and, in particular, whether it was to go out in his name or that of the bishops.[53] He repeated this question four days later when he sent the last pages of the work to Cromwell.[54] Despite his letters and despite an appeal from Latimer that the king should purge the book of any 'old leaven' before it was put forth,[55] Henry did not read it. The book was printed with a grovelling episcopal petition as preface, begging the king to grant his approval, 'without the which ... we knowledge and confess that we have none authority either to assemble

50. B.M. Cleo. E, v, fol. 39v; Cleo. E, vi, fols 41 ff.
51. B.M. Cleo. E, v, fols 8 ff. and 327 ff.
52. I.e. with his corrections of the section of the *Bishops' Book* contained in P.R.O. S.P. 6/8 fols 95 ff. His corrections cease at the bottom of fol. 95v.
53. *St.P.*, i, 555 (*L.P.*, xii, ii, 289).
54. *L.P.*, xii, ii, 330.
55. *St.P.*, i, 563 (*L.P.*, xii, ii, 295).

ourselves together for any pretence or purpose or to publish any thing that might be by us agreed on and compiled', and asking Henry to make any correction which he saw fit, 'whereunto we shall ... conform ourselves, as to our most bounden duty to God and to your highness appertaineth';[56] but their wish was not granted. Attached to this preface was the royal reply announcing that the king had not had enough time to 'overlook' the book but, being 'otherwise occupied', had but 'taken as it were a taste' of it.[57] It therefore went out after Henry had done no more than flip over a few of its pages and without full royal approval. This strange episode has often been remarked, but never explained. Perhaps the explanation was that, at the time when he was required to work through the bishops' offering, Henry was absorbed in Jane Seymour and the approaching birth of her child, and the last thing which a love-sick expectant father wanted on his hands was a weighty theological treatise. Edward's birth and Jane's death left him with time to kill and a stomach for theology. It was then (about December 1537) that he read the book – some months after it had been published – and found, after all, much that displeased him.

What emerges from the corpus of 'writings' which have been listed above? At times Henry was alarming. He took it upon himself to re-write the First Commandment so that it read 'Thou shalt not have, nor repute any other God, or gods, but me Jesu Christ' – a proposal which not only sent a shudder through Cranmer's obeisance to this vicar of God, his king, but clearly brought him as near an expletive as he had ever been.[58] Henry corrected the *Bishops' Book* to imply that saints are mediators between man and Christ, and suggested that the Christian can pray only to Christ, not to God the Father.[59] At times he was somewhat inept as, for

56. Lloyd, op. cit., 26 f.
57. *Miscellaneous Writings etc. of Thomas Cranmer*, 469.
58. ibid., 100. Henry also wanted the Lord's Prayer to end 'and suffer us not to be led into temptation', ibid., 106.
59. ibid., 106, 93.

example, when he persistently wrote of 'consecrating' sacraments, or crossed out a long section of notes after the passage on the Ten Commandments.[60] Many of his corrections to the *Bishops' Book* and the *King's Book* were minor ones, the work of a rather enthusiastic pedant – and several times (as Cranmer vigorously protested) they obscured the sense of the passage, broke the flow of the argument or introduced irrelevance and redundancy.

Others of them are wondrously revealing of the royal view of all that is in Heaven and on Earth. Where the *Bishops' Book* stated that all men, rich and poor, 'the free and the bond' are equal in God's eyes, Henry cut down this egalitarianism with the proviso that the equality existed 'touching the soul' only. Where the book called upon the rich to succour the poor, he added the warning 'that there be many folk which had liever live by the graft of begging slothfully' and that these 'should be compelled by one means or other to serve the world with their bodily labour'. The bishops denounced such superstitions as believing in 'lucky' days or thinking it unlucky to meet 'in a morning with certain kind of beasts, or with men of certain professions' and so on – and their words were crossed out by the king. They went on to denounce astrology, divination, palm-reading and the rest of the apparently ineradicable paganism of their fellow-men; but the king, who himself kept an astrologer at Court, promptly pruned the bishops' list of forbidden crafts and exempted astrology and 'physiognomy' from their prohibition – much to Cranmer's dismay. Where they prayed that we should impute adversity which befalls us to the will of God, not to the Devil or evil men, Henry altered the text to read, 'Make us when any adversity chanceth unto us that we may attribute it unto our desert' – a view of the human condition which drew from Cranmer a shocked lecture on God's inscrutable dealings with man. Where the bishops spoke sternly against 'uncleanly and wanton words, tales, songs, sights, touchings, gay and wanton apparel and lasci-

60. ibid., 97, 102.

vious decking', Henry reduced the censure to cover only
'uncleanly sights and wanton words'; and where they denounced 'surfeiting, sloth, idleness, immoderate sleep', he
deleted all but the third[61] – all of which was doubtless an
honest antipathy to rigour. He crossed out the perhaps embarrassing allegation that a prince's duties towards his people
include 'to provide and care for them, that all things necessary may be plenteous', and, perhaps even more significantly,
where the book stated that princes might kill and coerce
their subjects 'but by and according to the just order of their
laws', he so altered the passage that it read that 'inferior
rulers', as he called them, i.e. ministers of the crown, not
princes, were limited by 'the just order of their laws'.[62]

Throughout the annotations to the *Bishops' Book* Henry
revealed what, to a Protestant at least, must look like strongly
Pelagian tendencies. To put the same thing another way, he
continually refuted the uncompromising statement of justification by faith alone which the book sustained and, indeed,
upon which it was based, and he did so in a manner which
was occasionally dubious even by Catholic standards. Faith
for him was mere assent to revealed truth – *fides non formata*, as the scholastics called it; 'story faith', or 'faith in the
mouth' as Tyndale and Cranmer called it (somewhat un-
fairly?) – not the 'lively', 'feeling' faith of the Reformers,
which establishes a new, personal relationship between man
and God and must, of its very nature, bring forth the fruit
of good works, of steadfastness, obedience and joy (which is
really what the Scholastics meant by *fides formata*). Time
and again, therefore, Henry fell upon passages in the
Bishops' Book where it affirmed the all-sufficiency of 'right
Christian faith' and made corrections which Cranmer judged
as unnecessary, misleading or downright erroneous. Where,
for example, the book proclaimed that the Christian was the
'inheritor of his [i.e. God's] kingdom', Henry added 'as long

61. *Miscellaneous Writings etc. of Thomas Cranmer*, 106, 108, 100,
105.
62. ibid., 104, 105.

as I persevere in his precepts and laws'; where it promised that we shall rise again, Henry added in parenthesis, after 'we', the words 'continuing a Christian life'.[63] Man is by 'grace first called, and then by faith', he wrote; my faith will save me, 'I doing my duty'.[64] One long passage on the meaning of faith he deleted and re-wrote;[65] another he completely destroyed by the insertion of two words – the two words in italics in this quotation of the passage: 'The penitent must conceive certain hope and faith that God will forgive him his sins and repute him justified ... not *only* for the worthiness of any merit or work done by the penitent but *chiefly* for the only merits of the blood and passion of our saviour Christ.'[66] 'Only' and 'chiefly', with remarkable economy, turned upside down this statement of justification by faith alone. As has been said, Cranmer's comments on the royal corrigenda have also survived. To many of Henry's corrections Cranmer replied with a trenchant, even tart, directness which we hardly associate with the archbishop when addressing his king. Whenever he saw what he took to be the popish theology of works riding off Henry's pen, he unhesitatingly struck it down. He had already treated the king to a splendid discourse on the glory of the unfeigned faith of the Christian, a piece which deserves to be placed among the most prized of his remains;[67] when he discovered what the king had done with his two additions, 'only' and 'chiefly', he hit back with the injunction, 'These two words may not be put in this place in anywise.'[68]

It was the same with the *King's Book* six years later. Once more Henry struck at the root of Protestantism. Once more, when that book said that faith makes us members of the Mystical Body, he added 'as long as we so continue' in faith[69] – and so on. It was not that he had not grasped

63. ibid., 84, 90.   64. ibid., 87, 89.   65. ibid., 92.
66. ibid., 95.   67. ibid., 84 ff.   68. ibid., 95.
69. B.M. Cleo. E, v, fol. 19. Again he writes that we will rise again 'if we continue in living well' and insists that we become Christians by '*right* faith' and baptism.

what Cranmer was trying to tell him, but that he did not
accept it. In a short paper by Latimer on Purgatory, which
Henry read and annotated, the author at one point quoted
St Augustine saying that a man goes to Heaven '*pro meritis
bonis*'; and Henry has written in the margin, 'this text to
[*sic*, for 'doth'] make against you in another of your
opinions'.[70] He clearly saw at least something of what was at
issue, therefore, in the debate concerning faith and good
works. But, to Cranmer's mind, he had not taken hold of the
all-sufficiency of Calvary nor of man's total dependence on
grace and of its efficacy. We have to be 'willing to return to
God', he said, to 'conform our wills in this world to his
precepts' and to 'join our wills to his godly motions' in a
life of struggle and effort.[71] Henry did not explicitly deny the
role of grace, but it certainly seems that he instinctively
thought of an order of *human*, unaided good works which,
because they are naturally good, merit grace. We have to
'join our wills' to God's 'motions' – and this may easily become a doctrine of human works which share the labour of
sanctification with divine grace as an equal partner. Christ
is our 'sole redeemer and justifier', but he is also the 'chief
and first mean whereby sinners attain the same justification'[72]
– the 'chief and first', not, therefore, the only mean. To
Cranmer, at least, Henry looked like a creature of his time,
seemingly afflicted with a merit-theology which is no more
truly Catholic than it is Protestant, but is, at root, a semi-
Pelagianism which could threaten the whole redeeming
mission of Christ.

The king's conservatism is no less evident than his perhaps
impoverished understanding of the Redemption and of
grace. In his hostile comments on Latimer's paper he showed
how he clung to the doctrine of Purgatory; and his additions
to the draft of the Six Articles of 1539 were all designed to
secure greater rigidity. Though the original text of the first
article had affirmed both the Real Presence and transubstan-

70. B.M. Cleo. E, v, fol. 144.
71. *Miscellaneous Writings etc. of Thomas Cranmer*, 87, 92, 93.
72. ibid., 112.

tiation, the king made doubly sure of the latter by adding
that, after consecration, there remained not only no substance of bread and wine, but also 'none other substance but
the substance of his [Christ's] foresaid natural body'. He
expanded the fifth article upholding 'private' masses to make
it more explicit and binding. Where the second article had
stated that communion under both kinds was not necessary
'by the law of God', he slipped in the addition that it was
not necessary *ad salutem* by the law of God' – which may
not have added much, but gave the article a new precision.
Vows of chastity, the fourth article had decreed, were to be
observed 'by the law of God'; vows of chastity 'or widowhood', wrote the Supreme Head with that zeal for others'
righteousness which rarely deserted him. Finally, as he
worked over this draft, the king was no less vigilant in safe-
guarding his own station in life. In the preamble of the text
he had been described rather laconically as 'Supreme Head
... of this Church of England'; after he had finished with
it his style ran 'by God's law Supreme Head ... of this whole
Church and congregation of England'.[73]

But alongside stubborn conservatism lay an often startling
radicalism. The king who stuck so fervently to transubstantiation, clerical celibacy and Purgatory, who took part in the
procession of the Blessed Sacrament to the Altar of
Repose on Maundy Thursday, received holy bread and holy
water every Sunday, and daily used 'other laudable ceremonies',[74] who hanged a man for eating meat in Lent and,
had not his physician, Dr Butts, pleaded with him while he
was with his barber, would have had the curate of Chartham
in Kent whipped out of the country merely because the
latter's congregation had publicly celebrated his acquittal of
a charge of heresy,[75] this king could also utter views which
were as far removed from his Catholic past as some of the
residue of that past was from the 'true religion' put out in
the *Bishops' Book*. In the bitter wrangles which preceded the

73. B. M. Cleo. E, v, fols 330, 327. All of Henry's corrections were
incorporated into the final text of the Articles.
74. *L.P.*, xiv, i, 967.   75. Ridley, *Thomas Cranmer*, 243 ff.

enactment of the Six Articles, the conservative bishops, led
by Tunstal and Gardiner, fought Cranmer, Latimer and
their fellows with tooth and nail. Several times Henry came
down to the Lords to preside over the debates and 'confound'
(so we are told) the radicals with his learning.[76] At one point,
however, when auricular confession was under discussion,
the conservatives were apparently worsted, and after the
debate Tunstal did what we have seen him to do on two
previous occasions – he wrote a long letter to Henry lamenting what had happened, setting out once more his argument
that auricular confession, that is, confession to a priest, was
necessary by the law of God, was *de iure divino*. When he
received this missive, the king scribbled hostile comments
in the margin such as 'false', 'this is an example, not a precept', 'all these authorities recommend, not command'. He
then wrote a stinging riposte. Tunstal and Gardiner, it
began, had been so fully answered the other day in the
house of lords that it was surprising to receive this letter
setting out the same argument and same texts again. Unless
Tunstal was blinded by his own fancy, why did he now provoke the king, unskilled as he was, to make answer to him?
He quoted St Chrysostom, but 'your author in this place
furthereth you but little in your fallax argument … small
reason is the ground of your fallax argument … you gather
a wrong sense upon his words'. The other authorities did
not prove the bishop's point – rather they proved Henry's,
that auricular confession is not required either by reason or
God's law – and 'I marvel you be not ashamed eftsoons to put
them in writing'. 'I think that I have more cause to think
you obstinate than you me', for Tunstal quoted Origen
when the latter plainly meant that we must confess to God
and said nothing about confessing to a priest; he quoted
Cyprian, and his words do not command us to confess, and
so on.[77]

76. *L.P.*, xiv, i, 1003, 1015, 1040.
77. B.M. Cleo. E. iv, fol. 131 for Henry's reply; ibid., fols 134 ff.
for the letter from Tunstal which provoked it.

Tunstal's attempt to swing the debate by this direct appeal to the king received rough handling and he lost his point. The sixth of the Six Articles reads 'auricular confession is expedient and necessary to be retained and continued, used and frequented in the Church of God'. The important thing is the omission. This time the words 'by the law of God' do not occur. Auricular confession is 'expedient' and hence its necessity is pragmatic only. Although it had not been dismissed as some may have wanted it to be, Henry had had his way and refused it the necessity of divine sanction which Tunstal and Gardiner argued for it. The point may seem trivial now, but it was significant then. What this article said about auricular confession was as hesitant as the words of that notoriously 'advanced' document, the *Ten Articles* of 1536.[78] In 1539, therefore, the Protestant party salvaged something from the wreck.

In 1536 the official statement of faith spoke of three sacraments only. Next year, in the *Bishops' Book*, the missing sacraments were 'found again' – but with this proviso: that the sacraments of Baptism, Penance and the Altar had a higher 'dignity and necessity', by virtue of their manifest institution by Christ, than the other four. Thus were the factions among the clergy reconciled. But Henry dissented from their compromise. To the three 'first-class' sacraments, and at their head, he added Matrimony.[79] The sacrament in which he was personally so extensively involved was to have primacy of place. The conservative counter-attack had already won one victory by 'finding' the four sacraments which had been ignored in the previous year and now Henry would have that advance consolidated by lifting one of them to pre-eminence. But having thus given his

78. Which said of auricular confession that the people 'ought to repute the same as a very expedient and necessary mean whereby they may require and ask this absolution at the priest's hands'. In 1539, Cranmer had wanted the formula 'very requisite and convenient' to be used. *L.P.*, xiv, i, 1065.

79. *Miscellaneous Writings etc. of Thomas Cranmer*, 99.

support to the 'Catholic' party, he quickly went on to undo
it by inflicting severe damage on the remaining three 'lesser'
sacraments.

It is notorious to the historian of theology that the sacrament of Confirmation has been, and still is, the subject of
considerable debate. Several questions have continually
exercised the minds of theologians, medieval and modern,
Roman Catholic and non-Catholic (and especially modern
Anglicans among the latter), such as the evidence of its
dominical institution, the necessity for its reception and the
age at which it should be received. But the most vexatious
matter of all has probably been to determine the exact relation between it and Baptism. In the main, medieval theologians, despite minor divergence of view, were agreed that
Confirmation completed and perfected Christian initiation,
that it brought an *augmentum ad gratian*, not in the sense
of merely intensifying the baptismal gifts, but also of 'sealing' and arming the adult Christian with the full presence
of the Holy Spirit, that it did indeed carry Christian initiation to a stage beyond that of Baptism.[80] This was how St
Thomas, for example, had written; and this was how Henry,
too, wrote in 1521. The *Assertio* had spoken in the boldest
terms of Confirmation bringing 'perfect strength' to those
regenerated in Baptism and of the 'sealing' and the full
coming of the Holy Ghost.[81] Sixteen years later Henry's mind
was different. In his corrections to the *Bishops' Book*, which
had spoken in an orthodox, though limited, manner to the
effect that the sacrament causes us to be not only 'corroborated and established' in the graces of Baptism, but also
to 'attain increase and abundance of the other virtues and
graces of the Holy Ghost', the king consistently reduced
Confirmation to the status of a sacrament which, in essence,

80. Leeming, *Principles of Sacramental Theology* (1956), Appendix,
for a summary of these matters; and Dix, *The Theology of Confirmation in relation to Baptism* (1946) – which Leeming, loc. cit.,
criticizes and corrects.

81. *Assertio Septem Sacramentorum*, ed. O'Donovan, 358 ff.

restored the gifts of the sacraments already received –
Baptism, Penance, the Eucharist and, presumably (since,
curiously, he speaks of *four* sacraments) Matrimony. Though
Confirmation bestows 'other graces of the Holy Ghost, as
speaking of languages, prophesying and such others',
primarily it merely confirms graces already bestowed. It is
'a restoration and new illumination of the graces given by
the others [sic] iiii sacraments; a new restitution and restoration of graces granted by Christ to the iiii sacraments
instituted by him', by which Christians are to be 'the better
restored to their pristine state and established in the religion
of a Christian man which they had before professed'.[82] In
1540 the bishops were required to answer seventeen questions
about the sacraments. One set of answers affirmed that the
imposition of hands in Confirmation 'is grounded in Scripture' – against which opinion Henry scribbled the comment
'laying of hands being an old ceremony of the Jews is but
a small proof of Confirmation'; and where it had been
answered that the 'thing' of Confirmation, though not the
name, is found in Scripture and the use of chrism something
that 'hath been in high veneration and observed since the
beginning', Henry had written, 'This answer is not direct
and yet it proveth neither of the two points to be grounded
in Scripture.'[83] Three years later, when he came to correct
the text of the *King's Book*, not only did the curious ideas
about the effect of this sacrament which he had put forward
in 1537 make a brief reappearance, but chrism was denied
its adjective 'holy'.[84] Clearly the king was sceptical about
Confirmation and would allow it only a subsidiary place in
the sacramental economy, and a position which, though not
Protestant, was vulnerable to the assertion of, say, Wyclif
and the Puritans, that this sacrament was 'superfluous'.

82. P.R.O. S.P. 6/3, fols 12v, 13, 15. But (inexplicably) these corrections do not recur among the amendments which Henry sent to
Cranmer. Nor is it possible to date them.
83. B.M. Cleo. E, v, fol. 39v.
84. P.R.O. S.P. 1/178, fol. 109.

However, none of what he wrote in 1537 came out in the book of 1543; and the latter spoke of '*holy* chrism', despite his correction. The theory of the Royal Supremacy was one thing; its practice another.

Henry was harsh also to the sacrament of Extreme Unction. He crossed out a long passage in the *Bishops' Book* which gave the traditional explanation, to be found also in the *Assertio*,[85] of how the anointing was 'a visible sign of an invisible grace', conferred *ex opere operato*, just as, to Cranmer's dismay, he deleted the strongly Protestant statement that the anointing was 'an assured promise' that the sick man should be restored and his sins forgiven.[86] And in 1540, when that same set of answers to the questionnaire on the sacraments asserted that 'Unction of the sick with prayer is grounded in Scripture', Henry wrote in the margin sharply 'then show where'.[87] There is the same doubt, the same probing scepticism that we have met before – perhaps of a more thorough kind. Three years later, when the *King's Book* came to treat of this sacrament, what Henry had deleted in its predecessor was not restored. This time the king had his way.

But of all the sacraments, it was that of Holy Orders which suffered most.

What the *Bishops' Book* had to say about this sacrament was startling enough. In the first place it made no mention of the Mass among the functions of a minister and spoke only of his power 'to consecrate the blessed body of Christ in the sacrament of the altar'[88] – by Catholic standards, a very inadequate statement. The word 'Mass' is used only twice in the book, and then *en passant*, in the course of a short disquisition on Purgatory and on the fourth Commandment (to keep the Sabbath holy), where it survived

85. *Assertio Septem Sacramentorum*, ed. O'Donovan, 442 ff.
86. *Miscellaneous Writings etc. of Thomas Cranmer*, 99. The account of this sacrament was anyway a far cry from Catholic orthodoxy. See Hughes, op. cit., ii, 39.
87. B.M. Cleo. E, v, fol. 39v.   88. Lloyd, op. cit., 101.

probably more by chance than intention.[89] Secondly, the book omitted all mention of the sacrament conferring an indelible 'character' on the recipient – a cardinal idea of Catholic theology, which the Reformers strenuously opposed. Thirdly, it consistently spoke of bishops and priests as though they were not specifically different. In the New Testament, it stated, 'there is no mention made of any degrees or distinctions in orders, but only of deacons or ministers, and of priests and bishops'; and the words 'priest' and 'bishop' were used indifferently throughout. 'Unto priests or bishops belongeth by the authority of the gospel to approve and confirm' candidates for benefices 'elected and presented unto them' (and notice 'elected'); the ministry set up by Christ and his apostles was given 'unto certain persons only, that is to say, unto priests *or* bishops whom they did elect, call and admit thereunto'; 'the said bishops *or* priests be but only his [*sc.* God's] instruments or officers'; 'for surely the office of preaching is the chief and most principal office, whereunto priests *or* bishops be called'[90] and so on, repeatedly. Not only is the ministry defined in a strongly Protestant way, with preaching taking first place and ministration of the sacraments (and no more than this) second, but the specific distinction of order between priest and bishop is clearly denied, exactly as Protestant theology denied it. Moreover, at one point the book defined bishops and archbishops as 'superintendents or overseers' whose office was to 'oversee, to watch, and to look diligently upon their flock';[91] and, if those two terms were but direct translation of 'episcopus', they were also telling borrowings from the Lutheran vocabulary.

Henry went over this chapter of the book with the closest

89. Lloyd, op. cit., 146, 211.

90. ibid., 104 ff. Cf. Croke's letter to Cromwell of March 1537, in which he says that he has preached sixty sermons asserting, *inter alia*, that in the early Church bishops and priests 'were all but one'. *L.P.*, xii, i, 757.

91. Lloyd, op. cit., 109.

attention, making more corrections here than anywhere else. It is impossible that he did not perceive its strongly Lutheran drift. But he made no attempt to reverse it. He re-wrote the definition of the functions of the ministry, starting with 'authority to preach and teach the word of God', and spoke only of the clergy's power 'to consecrate sacraments' – an inappropriate verb which Cranmer quickly corrected.[92] He inserted no reference to the Mass.[93] He allowed the words 'superintendent' and 'overseer' to stand and introduced no specific differentiation of order between priest and bishop; and he who, years ago, had been the author of a work which condemned Luther for denying the indelibility of the 'character' of orders now made no effort to restate what, apparently, he had once proclaimed so earnestly.[94] Further, he took pains to alter the text in more explicit favour of the Royal Supremacy. Where it had described how Christ set over the Church militant the governance of kings and princes and 'certain other ministers and officers' with spiritual duties to perform, Henry deleted 'other', so that the clergy no longer stood in seeming equality with their betters; and where the book instructed the clergy to preach to the people 'committed to their spiritual charge' about the iniquities of the bishop of Rome, Henry amended the text to read 'committed to our and their spiritual charge'.[95] Where the book affirmed that 'it belongeth unto the jurisdiction of priests or bishops' to make rules concerning holy days, ceremonies and rites, Henry wrote instead that 'it is

92. *Miscellaneous Writings etc. of Thomas Cranmer*, 96 f.

93. Except at one point (ibid., 103) where he tempered the bishops' assurance that a Christian would not break the Sabbath by saving corn or cattle that was in danger, by adding the words 'so that we neglect not Mass and Evensong' – not a very substantial reparation of the omission of the Mass hitherto, especially as, soon afterwards, he let go by the text that on Sunday the Christian was required to 'hear the word of God, to give thanks for the same, to pray and exercise such other holy works as be appointed for the same'.

94. *Assertio Septem Sacramentorum*, ed. O'Donovan, 409 f.

95. *Miscellaneous Writings etc. of Thomas Cranmer*, 96.

therefore thought requisite and right necessary' that the clergy should do these things.[96] Where the book explained that the Fifth Commandment enjoined obedience not only to the spiritual father, 'by whom we be spiritually regenerated and nourished in Christ', but also to 'all other governors and rulers, under whom we be nourished and brought up, or ordered and guided', Henry removed the bouquet to the clergy and left the passage so that it urged obedience to natural parents 'and all other governors and rulers' only.[97] Where the bishops recalled that Christ empowered the Apostles to 'elect, call and admit' their successors, 'that is to say, ... bishops or priests', the Supreme Head put in the margin 'Note, that there were no kings Christian under whom they did dwell'.[98] Most alarmingly of all, he put his pen through a passage exactly similar to one he deleted from the chapter on Extreme Unction – i.e. that in which it was said that the sacrament of Orders is rightly so called because it was instituted by Christ and consists of two parts, 'a spiritual and inward grace, and also an outward and a visible sign'. Once more this piece of traditional sacramental theology was removed. All that remained was the somewhat vague sentence that the sacrament 'was institute to the intent that the church of Christ should never be destitute' of ministers. 'It was institute' (Henry's formula) replaced the explicit statement of the sacrament's nature and dominical authority.[99] Finally, wherever the words 'Holy Orders' appeared, he removed the adjective. Orders were to be no more 'holy' than was chrism.

Three years later (in 1540) came the questionnaires to the bishops on the sacraments. The questions themselves are of the greatest interest: they asked, for example, what the word 'sacrament' meant in Scripture and to the Fathers, whether it should be confined only to the seven sacraments, and what Scriptural authority there was for auricular Confession, Confirmation, Extreme Unction. Six of the seventeen ques-

96. ibid., 98.   97. ibid., 103.
98. ibid., 97.   99. ibid., 97.

tions concerned Orders. One asked whether the apostles 'in not having a Christian king among them, made bishops by that necessity, or by authority of God'; another whether bishops or priests were first and whether they 'were not two things, but both one office in the beginning of Christ's religion'; another whether bishops alone might make priests; another whether, on the evidence of the New Testament, both appointment and consecration were necessary, or whether a bishop was made solely by his appointment; another whether 'a prince Christian learned', who conquered infidels and had no clergy with him, could preach and teach the word of God; and the last whether, if all the clergy of a region died, the king thereof 'should make bishops and priests to supply the same'.

Some of these questions reopened disputes which had been present for some years. Some opened up matters with which we have already seen Henry deal. Some, particularly the last few quoted above, pushed inquiry into new territory.

The replies to these questions show that the feuds and disagreements between the factions had not abated. A number of the bishops reiterated the time-honoured formulae learned in the Schools. Others have evidently moved on. Cranmer, in particular, showed how far he had advanced. 'I know no cause why this word "sacrament" should be attributed to the seven only,' he said. The ceremonies of 'the committing of the ecclesiastical office' have 'no more promise of God' than those 'in the committing of civil office'; 'bishops and priests were ... both one office in the beginning of Christ's religion'; a Christian king finding himself alone among infidels would be bound to preach the gospel and 'it is not forbidden by God's law' that he should 'make bishops and priests'.[1]

Henry commented on two of these sets of replies. Some of his remarks we have already quoted when discussing his views on Confirmation and Extreme Unction. We must

1. See his replies, *Miscellaneous Writings etc. of Thomas Cranmer*, 115 ff.

return to them now because they also throw light on his attitude to the sacrament of Orders. One of the bishops' replies says that the making of a bishop is in two parts – appointment, which in the Apostles' time was by election (and is now performed by princes), and ordering. To this the king made a swift retort. 'Where is this distinction found? Now, since you confess that the Apostles did occupate the one part which now you confess belongeth to princes, how can you prove that ordering is only committed to you bishops?'[2] In his replies, Cranmer came very near to bestowing the *potestas ordinis* upon the king. Civil and ecclesiastical ministers are equally sprung of royal appointment, he asserted; the prince who found himself alone among infidels would not be prohibited by God's law from ordaining a clergy.[3] Henry seems to have been pushing to the same conclusion. If the Apostles performed one function in the making of a bishop [i.e. his election] which is known to belong now to princes, why should not the second part, consecration, belong to princes also? How can the bishops prove that their monopoly of ordering is not 'wrongly committed' to them? And when the same document says that the Apostles, when they ordained, followed rules taught by the Holy Spirit and ordered 'by imposition of hands with prayer and fasting', Henry wrote *'Ubi hic?'* – 'where do you find this?'[4] He was still as sceptical about this sacrament as he had been in 1537.

It would be unjust to place too much upon these marginal comments and jottings – particularly those which have just been quoted – and argue therefrom that Henry had arrived at a coherent, carefully considered radicalism. Maybe he was not prepared to push all his ideas to their conclusion. He never made overt claim to the *potestas ordinis*; the *King's Book* did not contain all the corrections which he had made to the previous statement of faith. Nonetheless, it is clear

2. B.M. Cleo. E, vi, fol. 42.
3. *Miscellaneous Writings etc. of Thomas Cranmer*, 116 f.
4. B.M. Cleo. E, vi, fol. 42v.

that his mind was on the move, that he was toying with violent novelty, questioning and doubting much more of the Faith of his forefathers than merely the Roman primacy. The result was a highly personal admixture of new and old. Henry was his own theologian. Much of what he believed may have been uncompromisingly 'Catholic', but alongside a firm allegiance to transubstantiation, clerical celibacy, and the rest there was much of a very different colour. His ideas on Confirmation and Extreme Unction were not those of the Council of Trent, just as his ideas on Matrimony were not those of Luther. If he never accepted justification by faith alone, he certainly allowed, and himself put forward, the most heterodox views on the priesthood. Indeed, if there is any single thread to his theological evolution it is his anticlericalism. He who had persistently called the clergy his ministers and mere 'doctors' of the soul, and had thrust forward – against the clergy – the prince's claim to a cure of souls, now allowed the strongly Protestant description of the ministry in the *Bishops' Book* to stand, stripped the sacrament of Orders of its essential theology and its title of 'holy', and by 1540 was stabbing into it yet deeper. Furthermore, the deletions which he made in 1537 were not undone in 1543. The *King's Book* did not give back 'holy' to the sacrament of Orders, nor restore to it the exposition of its operation as a visible sign of an invisible grace, instituted by Christ. In that book the sacrament appeared as merely a gift 'given of God to Christian men ... conferred and given to the apostles as appeareth in the Epistle of St Paul to Timothy';[5] and no more than the *Bishops' Book* did this one make a specific distinction between priest and bishop.

A belligerent anticlericalism which, wittingly or otherwise, had a strongly Protestant flavour went hand in hand with an unremitting, but strongly un-Protestant, insistence on clerical celibacy, from which Henry would not shift. He asserted it by proclamation, allowed it to do much to wreck the Anglo-Lutheran negotiations of 1538, reaffirmed it and,

5. *The King's Book etc.*, ed. Lacey (1932), 65 f.

as we have seen, widened its compass in the Six Articles of 1539. Indeed, the latter lifted the prohibition of clerical marriage to a new level by declaring that what most would have judged to be a matter of ecclesiastical discipline only was forbidden 'by the law of God' – an addition which Henry himself made in the preamble of that act, where its authors had omitted it.[6] In the previous year, the Protestant Bullinger sent to him a presentation copy of his latest work – on the authority of Scripture – which touched on many topics, including the *cause célèbre* of vows of chastity. Though Henry was said to have expressed the wish to have it translated into English,[7] he does not seem to have waded very thoroughly through its pages. But he at least flipped through it and on page 94 spotted Bullinger's attempt to deliver the clerical estate from the Romish yoke of celibacy. In the margin is a crisp verdict that the author's argument is irrelevant.[8] The rest of the book is clean of annotation. A little later, perhaps in 1539, Henry jotted down some random notes on the priesthood, for what purpose is not stated, but perhaps in preparation for some conference or disputation. In the course of the royal ruminations occurs the following syllogism: matrimony is a '*negotium seculare*'; but no priest ought to involve himself in '*negotia secularia*'; ergo ...[9] Thus spoke the king. Some may judge that the enthusiasm to impose on others a discipline which he himself would not have carried lightly sprang from Freudian, rather than theological, motives; but Henry, besides seeking to uphold the will of a God to whom he always seemed to have easy access, also presented severely practical reasons for his rigidity. In a particularly vigorous outburst against the clergy, which he made in April 1541 to two foreign ambassadors, he argued that, unless celibacy were enforced, clerics

6. B.M. Cleo. E, v, fol. 327v.

7. So Nicholas Elyot wrote to the author. Elyot had brought the book to Cranmer for him to give to the king. *L.P.*, xiii, ii, 373.

8. The presentation copy is in the B.M. (reference: 1010, *c.* 3).

9. Strype, *Ecclesiastical Memorials*, I, ii, no. 100.

would build up menacing strength through family clientage, make benefices hereditary and thereby become an even greater threat to the authority of princes.[10] His intuition was perhaps sound. If the clerical profession had proved itself so assiduous at nepotism (in its exact sense) when it was celibate, how much more so would it be when there were sons and grandsons, as well as nephews, to provide for?

What did Henry think about the Mass? To this fundamental question, alas, no definitive answer can be given. In the collection of notes concerning the priesthood to which reference was made a short while ago, Henry scribbled the definition of a priest as one 'dedicated to offering sacrifice'[11] – which at least contains the essential ingredient, that of sacrifice, in the theology of the Mass. But his version of the fifth of the Six Articles concerning private Masses merely stated that from them 'good Christian people receive both godly and goodly benefits';[12] which, if it amplifies the very terse original formula 'that private Masses be agreeable to the laws of God', is still cryptic and avoids the assertion, perhaps intentionally, that the 'private' Mass avails, as a sacrifice, for the benefit of the souls of the dead – which, after all, is how the 'private' Mass began and what it was mainly used for. Yet the king who was addicted to hearing several Masses a day, who himself served the truncated Mass (virtually a communion service only) in the old Easter liturgy on Good Friday 1539 – 'his own person kneeling on his grace's knees', as our informant tells us[13] – and who ordered several thousand Masses for the repose of Jane Seymour's soul, in that same year, 1537, allowed the almost complete silence of the *Bishops' Book* about the central event in the spiritual

10. *L.P.*, xvi, 733, 737. Henry had just heard about the agreement reached at the Colloquy of Ratisbon concerning clerical celibacy, communion under both kinds, etc.

11. Strype, *Ecclesiastical Memorials*, loc. cit.

12. B.M. Cleo. E, v, fol. 330.

13. So John Worth wrote to Lord Lisle in May 1539 (*L.P.*, xiv, i, 967) – his wonderment at the display of royal humility doubtless giving birth to this exquisite anatomical tautology.

life of a Catholic and a major topic of dispute between the Reformation and the old Church to pass unrepaired. True enough, the *King's Book* partly made good the omission. It defined a minister's duties as including the 'consecrating and *offering* the blessed body and blood of Christ in the sacrament of the altar' – though this was second to preaching the Word of God and was only stated once.[14] It was not an impressive performance. Three years later, at a famous scene at Hampton Court, Henry would discuss with the French ambassador a plan for abolishing the Mass in both England and France.[15] Whether or not this was a serious proposal is a matter of debate. But at this point we may note two considerations: first, the suggestion could scarcely have been made by a man for whom the Mass was sacrosanct; secondly, the large discrepancies between the theological opinions which he expressed in the 1530s and what he had written years before in the *Assertio* are such clear evidence that his mind was on the move, discarding much of its past and venturing, however tentatively, into novelty, that his proposal of 1546 concerning the Mass could well have been the climax of a slow withering away of an ancient belief.

The act of Six Articles, as has been said elsewhere, came as a serious disappointment to the Lutheran world which, despite all the previous hesitations and setbacks, yet hoped that England might be won to the cause. Anne Boleyn's death had been shocking enough, but this act stamped hard on those very points which had been most in debate between the English and the Lutheran delegation of 1538. It seemed a public and final rejection of the Reformation. To Luther, Melanchthon and their friends, it was final proof of Henry's hypocrisy and his cynical unconcern for the things of God; and even Barnes, Luther said, had written, 'our king holds religion and the Gospel in no regard'.[16] Though some comforted themselves with the belief that the 'impious statute'

14. Lacey, op. cit., 66. My italics.
15. See below, pp. 609 ff.   16. *L.P.*, xiv, i, 967.

was the work of the 'wicked and impudent Winchester' and
his fellow papistical bishops, the act marked the end of the
current Anglo-Lutheran negotiations, which Cromwell's fall
only confirmed.[17]

But we must be careful not to overstate the meaning of
these events nor to exaggerate the extent of the subsequent
reaction. The act of Six Articles did not put an end to the
theological ferment of the Henrician regime. It was *after*
the act, in May 1540, that the questionnaires concerning the
sacraments which we have been quoting above were drawn
up in preparation for a new formulary of faith which might
have been more advanced and far-reaching than anything
which had yet appeared. At least this is what reports of
what was afoot suggest[18] and certainly the contents of the
questionnaire imply that a major statement was planned.
It was never made. Cromwell's fall and trial, together with
the divorce of Anne of Cleves, swamped it. By the time
these great events were accomplished Parliament and Convocation had apparently spent their energies and dispersed
– to escape a fierce summer and an outbreak of disease in
London.

The picture of the 'Catholic' party swinging England away
from Protestantism has been fortified by misrepresenting
the attack on Cromwell and on Barnes and his fellows. As
has been said in the previous chapter,[19] these four were
charged with being sacramentaries and Anabaptists, not
Lutherans. Though it is true that conservatives like
Gardiner and Norfolk were now in power and, without
Cromwell, such as Cranmer severely hemmed in, not until
1543 did England retreat from the progress she had made
towards Wittenberg in the 1530s – and even this was far

17. *L.P.*, xiv, i, 1092, 1224; ii, 186, 379.
18. *L.P.*, xv, 697, 766. The writer (Marillac) reported that Henry
was in tight control, examining all the arguments and deciding
matters for himself – a judgement which the royal annotations of the
bishops' replies support.
19. See above, pp. 493 ff.

from a complete withdrawal. The act of Six Articles and the events of the next year did not *undo* the first planting of Lutheranism in England. Rather, they halted its further growth. After the passage of the act, Melanchthon could lament that in England truth was oppressed and the enemies of the Gospel had triumphed.[20] But shortly after its passage Bucer reported a message from Henry to the effect that, though he disagreed with the Reformers in some matters, he continued to be their friend.[21] Furthermore, though the act imposed savage penalties on dissidence, only six persons suffered death under it. Five hundred people who had been quickly rounded up were released by a general pardon in which the king forgave his subjects 'all heresies, treasons, felonies, with many other offences committed before the first of July 1540'.[22] Over two hundred were charged in the diocese of London – Bishop Bonner's diocese – but only three were imprisoned.[23] Though the English Protestant party was now in disarray, with Latimer and Shaxton removed from their sees and men like Coverdale and Joye abroad, the Six Articles were not the savage catastrophe which many expected them to be. Once the international crisis of 1539 was weathered, the attack was called off; and if no more major religious changes were undertaken during the rest of the reign, this did not mean that the slow erosion of the old order was halted. A royal proclamation of July 1541

20. *L.P.*, xii, i, 1224. He also wrote to Henry appealing to him to reconsider the act and stating his belief that it must have been the work of the bishops, especially Gardiner; a remark which, in view of the king's many corrections to the text of the Articles, must have incensed Henry. ibid., 4444.

21. ibid., xiv, ii, 413. Henry's motive for this was probably secular, of course. But in February 1540 the English Protestant, John Butler, could write to Bullinger (from Basle) that the Gospel was prospering in England. There was no persecution, he said, the word of God was freely preached, godly books were being sold, etc. (*L.P.*, xv, 259). He had no tale of gloom to tell, then. Cf. the similar report of Nicholas Partridge to Bullinger at the same time. ibid., 269.

22. Tjernagel, op. cit., 230. Cf. *L.P.*, xvi, 271.

23. *Foxe*, vi, 440 ff.

abolished the 'many superstitious and childish observations'
which marked the feast days of St Nicholas, the Holy Inno-
cents, etc., when children dressed up and disported themselves in streets and churches; three months later the
Supreme Head reiterated his command that all shrines
were to be dismantled and ordered that lighted candles were
to be placed before the Blessed Sacrament only;[24] and, had
not a sudden shift in international diplomacy made this
inopportune, he would have abolished the custom of ringing
bells on All Hallows E'en, of covering statues in Lent and
'creeping to the Cross on Good Friday' – a ceremony to
which he himself had at one time been addicted.[25] Above all,
despite the triumph of Gardiner and the rest of the conservatives, despite their desperate attempt to destroy him in
1543, Cranmer stood firm. Henry never abandoned him.
Indeed, in February 1543 the king gave him his assent to
a project mooted, and perhaps first essayed, some years
before to amend the Breviary, the Missal 'and other books',
and thus to set about the task of major liturgical reforms
which came to its fruition in the next reign.[26] In May 1544
an English translation of the Litany was published which
virtually suppressed all prayer to saints, commemorating
them along with patriarchs and prophets, but replacing
invocation to the traditional fifty-eight *beati* with bidding
prayers for the Church. Exactly twelve months later,
Richard Grafton printed the first official English Primer,
that is, a simple prayer-book in the vernacular for layfolk,
an event which, in some ways, marked a climax of Erasmian
lay Evangelism; and, unlike Cromwell's production of 1539,
the Hilsey Primer, this version contained virtually no com-
memoration of saints in its Calendar.

24. *Hughes and Larkin*, no. 203; *L.P.*, xvi, 1262.
25. See below, p. 609, for further discussion of this incident. Henry
took part in the veneration of the Cross on Good Friday 1539, 'creeping' on his knees from the door of the Chapel Royal to the altar.
L.P., xiv, i, 967.
26. Butterworth, *The English Primers, 1529–1545 etc.* (Philadelphia,
1953), 247 ff. Ridley, *Thomas Cranmer*, 247.

Nonetheless, England's *doctrinal* evolution was largely halted in 1540. Several factors may account for this, but not the least, probably, was the change in the king's own interests. In the first place, he was soon to be swept once more into the arms of matrimony and, if he had passed some of the last days of his alliance with Anne of Cleves working over the bishops' replies to the questionnaire on the sacraments, before long he would carry off Catherine Howard and thus, perhaps, leave theology behind. Secondly, and this is a more substantial reason, Henry would soon return to his other love, war-making. After an interlude of a decade, in which he had been largely absorbed in the great ecclesiastical and doctrinal furore, he would end the reign as he began it, by hurling his nation into massive war on two fronts.

[13]

The Return to War

To A. F. Pollard, the last dozen years of Henry's reign saw
a now fully matured and confident king unfold a magnificent, coherent policy of unification of his inheritance. *Rex
et Imperator*, purposeful and far-sighted, the king who had
struck down that great obstacle to national unity, the medieval Church, went on to incorporate Wales finally into the
English political system and to throw the full weight of
English authority upon recalcitrant Ireland (a policy which
was crowned in 1541 when he was proclaimed king of that
land) and then turned with clear logic to realize his
suzerainty over Scotland. If, on top of all this, he strove
once more to assert his rights in France, this was primarily
to hold off French support for the Scots as he set about
the latter's kingdom and was, therefore, a necessary concomitant to an aggressive imperialism which ultimately
looked to the unity of the British Isles and the Henrician
'Empire'.[1]

But it is doubtful if Henry was ever either capable or
guilty of such high statesmanship. The full incorporation of
Wales into her neighbour's political life in the mid 1530s
and the serious attempt to tackle the problem of Ireland
which began at the same time were probably more the fruit
of Cromwell's rather than Henry's, zeal for unity and efficiency; and the acquisition of the title 'king of Ireland',
in place of mere 'lord', can scarcely be interpreted as the
product of lofty imperial vision. The improvement of the
royal style had been urged on the king by his servants in
Ireland for some four years, and this for the severely prac-

1. Pollard, *Henry VIII* (edn 1951), 290 ff. Pollard's ideas have been
partly restated, in sophisticated form, in Wernham, *Before the
Armada: the Growth of English Foreign Policy, 1485–1588*, 149 ff.

tical reason that Henry's headship of the Church of Ireland, which the Irish Parliament had set up in 1536, could never be complete as long as the English king remained mere 'lord', a title which implied that he was no more than viceroy of the true sovereign of the land, namely, the pope. When, in June 1541, the new style was declared by an act of the Parliament of Ireland, the successor of Henry II concluded his repudiation of the authority of the successor of Adrian IV, the pope who, in the bull *Laudabiliter*, had first bestowed the island on English monarchy. Henry himself had insisted that the act should declare the title to be his by right of inheritance and conquest, and not something which the Irish gave 'unto his highness by a common consent of themselves'.[2] To make doubly sure, he then repudiated the Irish act and proclaimed himself king of Ireland.

The new style, therefore, is to be seen as the culmination of old purposes rather than the inauguration of new and as something demanded by a policy of 'Thorough' which began with the appointment of a new lord deputy in 1536 and the assertion of the Royal Supremacy in both kingdoms. As well as this, it was yet another addition to his collection of trophies by a man always greedy for new titles. Furthermore, we may be equally sceptical about the farsightedness

2. *St.P.*, i, 659 (*L.P.*, xvi, 1019). For other documents relating to this affair, see ibid., ii, 480; iii, 30, 278 – in the last of which Henry is urged to assume the new title and thus disabuse the Irish of 'a foolish opinion amongst them, that the bishop of Rome should be king' of their land (The lord deputy and Council to Henry, 30 December 1540). Cf. Bagwell, *Ireland under the Tudors* (1885), i, 258 ff. It is interesting to note that in March 1527 there was talk of Henry's wish to name the duke of Richmond as king of Ireland. The idea probably sprang from a desire to enhance the value of this royal bastard in the international marriage-market and especially to command him as suitor for the hand of one of Charles V's nieces. The Spanish ambassador reported that the proposal was most unpopular among some people who feared that Richmond's elevation would be 'tantamount to having a second king of Scotland', and that Catherine was much opposed to the idea (as one would expect), though she was told little about it. *Sp. Cal.*, iii, ii, 37, 39, 209, etc.

of royal dealings with England's northern neighbour. It is very arguable that concern for Scotland during the last years of his reign was secondary to his preoccupation with France and that, as in 1513, he looked to the North only because he was about to plunge into the Continent. The chances are that it was unnecessary for him to do so, for the Scots were not anxious to risk another Flodden, and that he needlessly pulled on to himself a huge, bloody problem. Thanks to the sudden and wholly unforeseeable death of James V, what had been planned as a quick action to secure the rear exploded into a major involvement. Thereafter Scotland seemed at times to have eclipsed all else, as Henry laid claim to the kingdom, floundered amidst the factions to which James's death allowed full play and which he tried to master with a mixture of blandishments and violence. But in reality his sovereign concern remained what it had been at the beginning, namely, some 'notable enterprise' against France. The assault on Scotland, far from springing from any long-term design for the British Isles, was a concomitant of a new upsurge of ancient belligerence and ancient dynastic ambition against the king of France. Henry failed in Scotland not least because he hesitated so often, because he allowed himself to be hoodwinked by the 'fair words' of Scots whom he erroneously believed to be at his beck and call, because he would never expend the necessary troops and money to conquer and occupy, rather than merely to raid the country. He did all this probably because Scotland was a comparatively remote and secondary theatre of war.

Cromwell had no successor. No one minister would ever again monopolize the conduct of affairs in Henry's reign. Though pride of place belonged to such as Gardiner, Norfolk, Wriothesley and Paget, Cromwell's fall allowed the Privy Council finally to emerge into the full light of day as an omnicompetent entity. For the first time since the beginning of the reign it supervised the whole of royal affairs, issuing letters in its name and insisting that dispatches be directed to it as a collectivity and not to any individual member thereof, exchanging correspondence between its two halves when it broke up into the Council attendant upon the king (when the latter went on progress) and the Council in London.[3] There had undoubtedly been such a body throughout Henry's reign. It had temporarily sprung back into prominence after Wolsey's great weight had been lifted from it in 1530 and, later, Cromwell had given some attention to its structure.[4] But never before had it enjoyed such clear and continuous life as a corporate executive, even if it had never before been so ridden with increasingly bitter faction-struggle.

Furthermore, after Cromwell's departure Henry can be seen – as he could be seen in 1530 and 1531 – as the dominant policy-maker. The Council suggests, discusses, pleads; problems are tossed between it and the king; ambassadors are sent to and fro between them. But the policy which it executes is essentially the king's.

It was probably in the spring of 1541 that Henry decided to resume his military career. A little while before, around Shrovetide, he had fallen into deep depression and shut himself inside Hampton Court, away from his wife Catherine Howard, courtiers and music. His ulcerated leg had swollen badly and given terrible pain, and as he fought his melancholia he muttered dark things about his Council and his perverse subjects. It was now that, brooding over recent events, he began to smell the truth about Cromwell's fall and growled at those whom he suspected had dragged the minister down. However, by Easter-time the darkness had apparently lifted and he was ready to spring back into boisterous life; and it may well be that the intention to take up some grand military escapade was born as his huge body and spirits began to rally. At least from about then a straight

3. See, for example, *L.P.*, xvi, 24, 43, 122, 157, 347. A perusal of the remaining volumes of *L.P.* will show that the Privy Council is now regularly acting as a body.

4. Elton *The Tudor Revolution in Government*, 347 ff.

line can be drawn which runs directly to his return to the battlefield in 1544.

In April 1541 he announced his intention of carrying out an unprecedented progress to the North of England, an area which he had never visited, despite his many promises at the time of the Pilgrimage of Grace, and which he had subsequently treated harshly. Yorkshire had recently been roused once more by the conspiracy led by Sir John Neville, and it was probably in order to settle domestic upsets before embarking on military adventure that Henry decided to visit this disturbed county at last and bring his healing hand to its sores. It was certainly a desire to fasten a back-door before leaving for foreign parts that explains why this journey acquired an additional purpose, namely, a meeting with James V of Scotland at York. Henry had begun to woo his Scottish brother with especial care some months ago, when, in February 1540, he had sent Ralph Sadler on embassy to Scotland carrying instructions which were both highly cynical and paternal in tone on how James should set about the profitable business of suppressing such religious houses in his kingdom 'as might be spared' and promising his nephew 'our best advice and counsel ... aid and help ... to bring his good determination to a perfect end and conclusion'.[5] Over a year later he wrote an equally revealing piece, this time directly to James, scolding the latter for his evident victimization by bold churchmen and recommending that he should destroy the pretensions of the clerical estate, else the clergy would set up a kingdom of their own in his realm.[6] Sadler's embassy, like this letter, clearly revealed Henry's hope that the Scottish king would follow his example, declare for 'true religion', break with Catholic Europe and remain neutral (at least) should England take to war with France. No doubt the meeting now planned with James at York would encourage this and consolidate the new liaison.

Henry set out on his journey on the last day of June, with a train that resembled an army of occupation more

5. *L.P.*, xv, 136.   6. *L.P.*, xvi, 766.

than the suite of a royal progress.[7] Five thousand horses, a thousand soldiers and artillery were gathered to strike a decent fear, as well as love, in the hearts of the querulous northerners. Henry himself travelled in huge pomp, with archers in front and councillors and courtiers, ablaze with cloth of gold, aft. Alas, the weather was so foul that the procession took nearly three weeks to reach Grafton. But by 9 August the king had come to Lincoln and made triumphant entry amidst flags and pennants and ringing bells. From Lincoln he came to Stamford and Scrooby. By 24 August he was at Pontefract – where the Pilgrims had presented their Articles nearly five years ago and where Neville had recently planned to base his rising. On hearing of that conspiracy, Henry had graciously remarked that he had an evil people to rule and promised that he would make them so poor that they would never be able to rebel again[8] – a promise, which, as it turned out, he did his best to fulfil once he resumed foreign war. But it was a jovial, benevolent sovereign who had made his way north on this progress. Everywhere he went he met fulsome hospitality and dispensed regal warmth, promising all who 'grieved for lack of justice' free access to present their complaints to him and bringing desolation only to the hundreds of stags, deer and swans who fell to the lavish royal hunts which punctuated the progress and which must have swept clean of much of its wild life a wide track from London to Yorkshire. When he entered that county he was met by five or six thousand men on horse and showed himself full of graciousness. Those whose loyalty had failed them five years ago were brought before him. One of them made a speech on behalf of them all, confessing their guilt (set out in lengthy written submissions) and begging pardon. Henry gave a benign reply, whereupon the pardoned men rose and accompanied the king to his apartments.[9] Meanwhile, as Henry closed slowly on to his destination, breaking the journey with more hunt-

---

7. As Marillac observed. *L.P.*, xvi, 868.
8. ibid., 903.   9. ibid., 1011, 1130–1.

ing expeditions, the old abbey of St Mary at York was being furbished to receive him and his visitor from Scotland. Hundreds of men had been at work, day and night, building and painting and putting up tents against the coming influx.[10] Henry arrived in York on 18 September. He waited there nine days. James never came. On 29 September Henry left York and made quickly for home, having been publicly mocked by his sister's son, the king of Scots. When he returned home he found his own four-year-old son Edward ill of a quartan fever.[11] On 2 November Cranmer brought him written proofs of the misconduct, in bygone days, of his queen, Catherine Howard. And as if all that were not enough, even as he bitterly lamented the failings of one whom he had loved, a letter came from Cleves suggesting that he might now take back their daughter Anne.[12]

Catherine Howard made the decisive step from the obscurity of the Norfolk household to the dazzle of the royal court at the end of 1539, when she was appointed a maid of honour to Anne of Cleves, then about to arrive in England. How exactly she arrived in this post and the circumstances in which she first came to the king's quick notice are obscure, but we do know that, as soon as Henry saw her, he 'did cast a fancy' to her.[13] She was about nineteen, a short, rather plump, vivacious and experienced girl; he an aggressive forty-nine, stirred rather than abashed by the distance between their ages and doubtless already bent on escaping somehow from that union with Anne which still encompassed him. By April 1540 royal gifts and favours were beginning to flow towards Catherine; her relatives, who on the whole were remarkable for the vigour with which they

10. *L.P.*, xvi, 1183.   11. ibid., 1297.
12. *St.P.*, i, 716 (*L.P.*, xvi, 1449).
13. L. B. Smith, *A Tudor Tragedy. The Life and Times of Catherine Howard*, 103. For much of what follows on the career of Queen Catherine Howard I have relied very much upon Prof. Smith's dazzling biography – as will be apparent to all who have read it.

disliked one another, busily praised Catherine 'for her pure
and honest condition', while her aunt advised her on 'how to
behave' and 'in what sort to entertain the king's highness
and how often'. Stephen Gardiner received her and Henry
at his London house, the Norfolks at theirs; and as the
bishop and the duke, like the procurers they virtually were,
dangled the willing girl before the willing (but married)
king, so did she stride towards the throne of England, they
edge back into political power and Cromwell feel himself
being throttled. By June Londoners' tongues were wagging
about the king's innumerable assignations, day and night,
on the south bank of the Thames where Gardiner and the
Norfolks resided. By 10 July the Cleves marriage had been
declared null and void, and Gardiner and Norfolk, with the
rest of the Council, came to the king to beg him 'to frame
his most noble heart to love' in order to secure 'some more
store of fruit and succession', to the comfort of his realm.[14]
On 28 July Henry and Catherine married quietly; on the
same day Thomas Cromwell was beheaded – and thus were
accomplished a divorce, a fifth royal marriage and a *coup
d'état*.

The raptures of love not only blinded Henry to the scuf-
flings which had been taking place in the political bear-
garden, but put new life into the ailing, middle-aged king
and temporarily cured him of theology. He was a transformed man, rising daily between five and six in the morning, hunting until about ten, moving frequently from place
to place about the countryside, pouring affection and gifts on
his young captivating bride. Catherine received, among
other donations, the lands of the late Thomas Cromwell, a
lavish household and enough jewellery to deck a Sultan. At
least for a few months, all was rapturous abandon, as
Catherine danced and banqueted with her doting husband
and revelled in her new-found opulence. For a while she
even befriended Henry's 'beloved sister', Anne of Cleves,
brought her to court, danced with her and had Henry

14. ibid., 121 f.

join them for what must have been an incongruous dinner *à trois*, but which apparently pleased the participants.

Despite appearances and despite all that has often been either hinted or asserted, Henry was probably neither a remarkably accomplished nor endearing lover. He may have been a sensual man who never denied himself, or was never denied, what he desired; he had certainly taken up and discarded women easily in the past. But he was no spectacular profligate, no Don Juan, no sophisticated student of the *Ars Amoris*; and compared with Francis I or Charles V, or many English kings before and after him, he was almost modesty itself. Behind his troubadour gallantry lay not the passion and skill of a seasoned voluptuary, but probably the unstudied, matter-of-fact sexuality of a man whose primary expectation of a woman was that she should bear his children. Far from being an insatiable Bluebeard, at root Henry may have been sexually cool, if not timid. It was the severely unromantic, politically urgent need to beget progeny in sufficient quantity to prove himself and assure his dynasty which drove him through his long and colourful matrimonial career; and if he was infatuated now with Catherine Howard he had taken her to wife, rather than kept her as a mistress, first because he was innocent of amorous heroics and secondly because her function was the same as that of her predecessors, namely, to multiply his offspring.

Catherine probably found Henry a good deal less exciting than those paramours who had enlivened her adolescence, like Henry Manox, her music-teacher, and Francis Dereham, a dashing gallant with whom she had romped and made love at Lambeth before she was translated to the royal court; for she was now tied to a physically probably repugnant and often inexplicably moody lover, and before long the first raptures were spent. She became suspicious of Henry's affection and was bold enough to put it to him that he was about to turn from her to Anne of Cleves after all, a suggestion which the king brushed aside. She was jealous of Princess Mary and squabbled with her. Worst of all, the mercurial girl inevitably became the centre of male attraction in the Court and, led by a mixture of vanity, boredom and appetite, succumbed to its allurements. Like her cousin, Anne Boleyn, but less innocently, Catherine drew round herself a coterie of flirtatious courtiers, like Thomas Paston and Thomas Culpeper junior, two gentlemen of the Privy Chamber; and as if the court's own supply of dalliance were not enough, she was persuaded in early 1541 to find a place for none other than Francis Dereham, her lover of yore.[15]

She had been unchaste before her marriage; she took to adultery soon after it. By the time she set out with Henry on his progress to York in the late summer of 1541 she and Culpeper were hopelessly compromised. They had been meeting frequently in secret places for some months and she had bestowed obvious favours upon him. Now, as Henry and his massive entourage ground their way northwards during August and September 1541, Culpeper, aided by Catherine and lady Rochford, matron of the queen's suite and wife of Anne Boleyn's brother, broke into her apartment at almost every stopping-place. While Henry hunted and triumphed and brought his royal radiance to the North, he was being cuckolded by an audacious courtier.

Meanwhile the Council which had remained in London had been told by an informer about Catherine's misconduct, before marriage, with Dereham. After considerable hesitation, they sent Cranmer to Henry on his return to Hampton Court to present their information. The archbishop came to the king while he was at Mass on All Souls' Day and handed him a written document. Henry read it and unexpectedly denounced it as a pack of lies. He refused to believe the allegations against his queen and, instead, ordered that the informer should be quashed. Further investigation, however, brought confirmation of the allegations, including a full confession by Dereham. But still Henry refused to believe. Only when he met Wriothesley

15. For this and the next two paragraphs, see Smith, op. cit., 54 ff., 146 ff.

and Norfolk secretly, in a field outside Hampton Court, whither he had gone (so he said) to hunt, and accompanied them by boat to an all-night meeting of the Council at Gardiner's palace in Southwark, was the truth borne in upon him. First he raged and threatened Catherine with violence; then he wept, bemoaning his misfortune in meeting 'such ill-conditioned wives'; then he turned on the Council and tried to blame them; finally he departed and for days thereafter solaced himself in hunting.[16]

Henry's reaction, though doubtless one which contemporary society would have applauded unanimously, was harsh. Catherine had been accused of and, after her first hysterical denials, had admitted, incontinence before her marriage to Henry. But her sinfulness, objectively, was no greater than his. Had not he had mistresses? Had not he, for over twenty years, been the unlawful partner of Catherine of Aragon and lived, albeit innocently, in 'abominable sin'? But Catherine was a woman, and a masculine world required that she must overlook in him what he must denounce in her. Even so, she might yet have escaped the full penalty. Perhaps Henry might not have required her death, especially if it could have been proved that, as report had it, she and Dereham had years before pledged themselves to one another in marriage – in which case she would have been guilty of bigamy, but Henry could have divorced her on the ground that her first contract nullified the second, and thus perhaps spared her further disaster. But Catherine refused to agree that there had ever been a promise of marriage exchanged by her and Dereham and, much worse, quick fingers pulling at threads of information, soon drew out the main strands of the story of her dealings with Dereham and Culpeper in recent months. Torture and the threat of torture wrung no confession of adultery, though the parties concerned confessed in the end, but elicited sufficient evidence to establish intent thereto and, at law, the intention of adultery by or with the queen was treasonous.

16. *L.P.*, xvi, 1426. Smith, op. cit., 178 ff.

Culpeper and Dereham went to their death first. Several of the Howard dynasty were found guilty of misprision of treason a few weeks later. In January 1542 a bill of Attainder was introduced into Parliament against Catherine (then languishing under armed guard at Syon).[17] On 11 February it received royal assent, not by the king in person, but, to spare his hearing once more the 'wicked facts of the case', by a commission appointed by letters patent. Two days later she and lady Rochford were beheaded on Tower Green. The second niece whom the duke of Norfolk had seen mount the throne of England as royal consort had ended her life, as the first had done, in ignominy. Small wonder that the duke himself, who had escaped the recent purge of his family and thereafter (until he followed his two nieces to the Tower) retained the position which Catherine had been so useful in allowing him to recover, should have discreetly absented himself from the execution of his 'lewd sister' and preferred the country air.

Henry meanwhile was apparently a broken man. He grieved more over Catherine than any previous wife, so much so that the French ambassador thought he had gone mad. He had called for a sword to kill her whom he had loved so much and spent Christmas (1541) morosely moving around from palace to palace. But on the day that the queen's attainder received its first reading his spirits picked up and he celebrated his recovery with a great banquet at which twenty-six ladies sat at his table; and within a week of Catherine's death he marked the pre-Lenten carnival with massive feasting. Rumours were already flying about concerning his next fancy; and it was noted that he and Anne of Cleves had exchanged New Year presents.[18] Would he, after all, take that lady back?

For the moment, however, he was sated with matrimony.

17. 33 Hen. VIII, *c.* 21 (*Statutes of the Realm*, iii, 857). This act also made it treason for an unchaste woman to marry the king, and misprision of treason for anyone to conceal her unchastity.

18. *L.P.*, xvi, 1426; xvii, 63, 92, 124.

He would wait sixteen months before making his last and, in some ways, his best choice – a woman as different from Catherine Howard as the latter had been from Anne of Cleves, a sober, godly spouse to accompany him through the last three and a half years of his earthly life. But before he turned to Catherine Parr he had appointments with the French and the Scots.

If the North had been won over by the king's visit there in the autumn of 1541 (and there was talk next year that Henry would progress to Wales),[19] Scotland had not. James V would not act on his uncle's suggestions about hammering monks and kirkmen, and his Council would never have allowed him to be lured down to York by the king of England. James's infant sons had just died; there was a clear risk that he might be kidnapped on English soil; the churchmen who dominated the Scottish Council had no affection to spare for their schismatic and iconoclastic neighbour. After Henry had been sent away from York empty-handed and indignant, raids and arson on the Scottish Borders multiplied. Both kings wrote to each other complaining of these incidents and warning of their possible consequences.[20] In August 1542 Henry petulantly decided to send troops to the North, including some mercenaries hired in the Low Countries, under the duke of Norfolk.[21] At the same time he agreed that ambassadors of England and Scotland should meet at York, the very place to which James had refused to come to meet him last year, in order to patch up relations between their countries.[22] He would even yet bring the Scots to heel, therefore, if necessary by a show of force on their frontier; and having frightened them, would be able to turn his back on them and face the French.

On 10 July Francis and Charles went to war once more. Once more the peace of Western Europe was ruptured by a

19. So Marillac said. *L.P.*, xvii, 415.
20. *L.P.*, xvi, 1270, 1279.
21. *L.P.*, xvii, 661. Cf. ibid., 650–51. 22. ibid., 765.

renewal of that conflict between the Valois and the Habsburgs which had allowed Henry to make his forays into Europe in the earlier part of his reign and so conveniently shielded him during much of the 1530s; and once more their belligerence would be Henry's opportunity. For months Francis I had been manoeuvring for advantage and, in particular, had been trying to do to Henry exactly what Henry had been trying to do to James V, namely, drug him with diplomacy, not least by proposing the marriage of Princess Mary to his son. Negotiations for this match went ahead during the first months of 1542, but were continuously impeded by Henry's absolute refusal to allow Mary to be declared legitimate. He held his ground now just as he had done four years ago when Mary had been suggested as bride for a Portuguese prince. He would not allow the invalidity of his first marriage to be doubted, however obliquely.[23]

While the arguments about Mary's status (and her dowry) dragged on, Henry secretly conspired with Charles to unleash a double attack upon France. Since the end of 1541 he had repeatedly asked for a closer alliance with the emperor.[24] In June of the next year he sent the bishop of the new, and short-lived, see of Westminster to Charles to settle plans for a joint invasion of France in 1543, and lent Chapuys, the Imperial ambassador in England, his own sedan chair and a ship to enable him to cross quickly to the Netherlands to clinch agreement with the Regent there.[25] Meanwhile, at home, ships, guns and money were gathered in preparation for campaigning.

But Henry's tactics were necessarily fluid because his continental venture depended on Scotland. In the middle of September (1542) English commissioners met their Scottish confrères at York and presented a list of heavy demands. These, so Henry said, they quickly accepted. Moreover, they

23. *L.P.*, xvii, 145, 164, 167, 182, 415.

24. See the letter from Chapuys to Charles of 29 January 1542, in ibid., 63.

25. ibid., 441, 447. Cf. ibid., 595.

agreed that James would come to England for a meeting
with Henry at Christmas and make amends for his defection in the previous year.[26] The Scots were in no belligerent
mood. Maybe this conference had never been anything more
than a sham, as the French ambassador thought;[27] maybe
Henry's memory of the Scots' attack in 1513 was still so
green that he refused to trust them. Anyway, he now sent off
violent instructions to his commissioners that, if the Scots
did not at once agree to deliver some English prisoners held
in Scotland and give pledges that James would come either
to London or York at Christmas-time to conclude a treaty
of amity, the army should be sent in to do 'some notable exploit' against them.[28] Six days later news came from York
that, since the Scots hedged and wavered, the English
army would march. Three weeks after this decision had been
announced, Henry wrote a bellicose letter to Norfolk and
his fellows, upbraiding them for having delayed for lack of
carriages, which should have been gathered from 'Yorkshire,
Holderness and Hullshire', and ordering Suffolk to go on
ahead to devastate the Borderland.[29] But even before he had
finished correcting this letter, Norfolk had led his whole
army from Berwick via Coldstream towards Kelso. The duke
had set out with desperately little food and after six days of
burning and spoiling was back at Berwick; but his savage
rout left a trail of wreckage behind it.[30] As soon as he heard
the news of Norfolk's expedition, Henry wrote to his commander eagerly. Had Norfolk now dissolved his army?
What had he done to defend the borders against sudden
Scottish incursions? An army of up to five thousand was to
be held in readiness under Suffolk and Norfolk for this purpose; and there were enough victuals in the North and
Lincolnshire to feed them.[31]

Norfolk's raid had been intended to shock and intimidate

26. *L.P.*, xvii, 818, 852–3.　　　27. ibid., 770.　　　28. ibid., 862.

29. ibid., 987. The letter was corrected by Henry. The quotation is
of his words.

30. ibid., 994, 996, 998.　　　31. ibid., 1016.

the Scots. As has been said, it was probably an unnecessary piece of violence since James was neither ready for war nor anxious to expose himself to a repetition of the immense disaster of Flodden. Moreover, Henry's bullying stirred rather than stunned him. Faced with a violent enemy on his Border, James appealed to Rome and his fellow-princes for aid, and prepared a counter-attack.[32] On 23 November a Scottish force of up to twenty thousand which had entered the Debateable Ground in the west was put to flight by the English at Solway Moss after a skirmish – leaving a considerable body of prisoners behind them, the chief of which were quickly dispatched to the Tower. Solway Moss was no Flodden, but a little over three weeks later James V suddenly died (from grief it was said),[33] vacating his throne to a week-old daughter, Mary. The terrible combination of a military defeat and the premature death of the king at this moment seemed to lay Scotland prostrate before her aggressive neighbour as completely as had the disaster of twenty-nine years before.

Had Henry now marched in with the forces which were gathered in the North he must surely have conquered. But because he had never intended to do more than contain the Scots and because his major interest lay elsewhere, he tried to exploit Scotland's incredible misfortunes in a circuitous and improbable way. He would take Scotland and her infant queen into his hands and thus set about uniting the two realms, yes; but he would do so indirectly, relying primarily on those prisoners who had been taken at Solway Moss and were now to be turned into the core of an 'English' party in Scotland. Accordingly, the prisoners were quickly released, brought to court for a festive Christmas and sent home. But before they departed they were required to swear to the following design whereby Henry would gain control of Scotland's affairs: that the infant Mary should be betrothed to Henry's son; that the prisoners, returned to Scotland, should have Mary brought to England, build up a following for

32. *L.P.*, xvii, 1060.   33. *L.P.*, xviii, i, 44.

Henry, seize strongholds for him and thenceforth be his agents in their homeland. Furthermore, ten of the most trustworthy swore a secret article that Henry himself should receive the Scottish crown if Mary died. Confident that others would do the essential work for him, Henry sent the captives back to Berwick to wait until the hostages which he prudently required for the performance of their undertakings had arrived.[34] They were back in Edinburgh by the end of January 1543.

But in the meantime events had taken place in Scotland which threatened to frustrate all Henry's plans. On 3 January the earl of Arran, heir presumptive to the throne, was proclaimed governor of Scotland during the minority with right of succession if Mary died – and with the possibility, so rumour ran, that, if she did not, she would marry his son. Thus, just as Henry prepared to take Scotland and her princess into his hands, there had been set up in Edinburgh a leader who might at least exclude him and even rally Scotland against him. But again, Henry did not strike. Instead he bade the ex-prisoners who were now at Berwick and about to return home to have Arran and the cardinal seized and Mary brought to England.[35] He was still confident that he could control Scotland through the prisoners – all the more so when Arran, whom he had heard was 'a great favourer of the Scripture' and no friend of the kirkmen, himself soon arrested Cardinal Beaton and wrote disarmingly about reforming the Scottish Church and negotiating a peace and marriage treaty with England. On 10 February Henry sent safe-conducts for Scottish envoys to negotiate a treaty; and ten days later the offer of a three-month truce was accepted by Arran in the name of Mary Queen of Scots.[36]

35. *L.P.*, xviii, i, 7, 22 44. At first Henry had been told that Mary Stuart was also dead after premature delivery. So Chapuys in ibid., 44.
35. ibid., 22.
36. ibid., 139, 155, 188–9. Meanwhile Lord Lisle (in Edinburgh) had promised to procure Arran a supply of Bibles in the vernacular which were to be 'let slip' and thus break the kirkmen, ibid, 157.

Precious weeks were slipping by. By mid March, when Henry sent Ralph Sadler to Edinburgh post-haste to 'grope out' the situation, to see to Mary's removal to England and to bolster the 'English' clientele,[37] the French had already begun to send ships and munitions there, and the party of the dispossessed Cardinal Beaton was forming. But Henry still hoped that Arran would declare for the Reformation and sent him via Sadler), as he had sent James, a full-length manual on how to carry it out – how to set forth the Scriptures, how to do down the kirkmen, how to destroy Scottish monasticism. He announced in this letter, which was so full of cynical worldliness that it was understandably held up as fatal evidence against the quality of Henry's own zeal for reform,[38] that he had prepared a confession of faith (i.e. the *King's Book*) which could serve for Scotland as well as England and be published in the two kingdoms simultaneously. If the governor would agree to this plan for the union of the two peoples in a common doctrine and by royal marriage, then, as compensation for submitting to Henry's design, he could have the princess Elizabeth for the son whom he so ambitiously intended to marry to Mary Queen of Scots herself.[39]

At the best of times, Scotland was *terra ignota* to the English king. Shortly after James's death, he had asked the earl of Angus – an exile in England since 1528 – to come to court to tell him about his native land and to bring a map of Scotland with him. Angus had not come, but had suggested to Henry that he should consult his own physician, Dr Cromer, who was a Scot.[40] How much Cromer told him we do not know, but it cannot have helped him much to grasp

37. *L.P.*, xviii, i, 270.
38. By Knowles, *Religious Orders in England*, iii, 204. But it is fair to remark that this letter, like the instructions sent to James (which have been noted above), was a calculated appeal to a politique and not necessarily a complete and honest statement of royal ideals. Nonetheless it is a letter which few reputations could easily survive.
39. *L.P.*, xviii, i, 364.
40. *L.P.*, xvii, 1194.

the intricate confusion of factions which now jostled for
power in the kingdom. As Sadler tried to explain, three main
parties had emerged – one called 'the heretics and English
lords', that is, the governor and his 'partakers'; another,
'which is called the scribes and pharisees', who looked to
France, namely, the clergy and their allies; and a third
which was neutral 'and will take the stronger side in any
business'.[41] Henry had pinned his hopes on the first, believing that the oaths of the prisoners, English money and the
promise of English troops to help them put down a *coup
d'état* backed by France would not only hold them true to
him but enable him to control Scotland's destiny. But he
misjudged the situation. Arran and his fellows were fighting
no one's battle but their own. The governor would take
Henry's money, convince him of his anticlericalism and
anti-papalism, and allow him to think that he would immediately give Henry the signal to send in an army whenever affairs got out of hand – an army which he and the
'English' lords would join; but all this was to hold off the
English king and to abet his own jockeying for power. Cardinal Beaton was released from prison, and then a papal
legate, whom Henry ordered his ships to intercept before
he landed, was dispatched to Scotland.[42] This time Rome
had acted quickly. Arran pretended to disown the legate, but
he had already placed Scotland under papal protection[43] –
he, the man to whom Henry had addressed a long lecture on
how to overthrow popery in his land and who had fed Henry
with assurances that he thought the pope was no more than
a bishop, 'and that a very evil bishop'. Shortly before this,
the earl of Lennox had landed from France with French
gold and an envoy who came to promise French aid against
an English invasion. More than once, Henry had been told

41. *L.P.*, xviii, i, 425.

42. ibid., 535. The governor was also to arrest the cardinal and his
fellow bishops during the meeting of the Scottish Convocation, on the
excuse that it had assembled without his licence.

43. ibid., 324, 542–3, 572. For a useful summary of this complex
story, see Donaldson, *Scotland: James V to James VII*, Edinburgh
Hist. of Scotland (1965).

that he could not have his way in Scotland 'without strokes';[44] but the moment for swift military action had passed. He must now face the possibility that the young queen whom the Scots had refused to deliver to England would be carried off to France (the homeland of her mother, Marie de Guise, whom Henry had once wanted to marry but whom James had snatched from him)[45] and that, if his forces moved north, they would run into stiff resistance.

However, for the moment, Arran continued to hold Henry at bay with compliance. At Greenwich, on 1 July 1543, the Scottish ambassadors swore a treaty of peace with England (but one which did not commit them to the renunciation of France which Henry had wanted) and a treaty of marriage between Edward and Mary, their queen.[46] Henry had always demanded that Mary should be delivered to England immediately, but the Scots had resolutely resisted this and now had their way. Hostages for her delivery would be sent at once; but Mary herself would not come to England until she was ten. Six months of hesitation and confused anxiety, therefore, ended with Henry agreeing to terms of highly questionable value to himself and imposing a solution which, predictably, turned out to be no solution. Henry had not only overreached himself with this qualified success but, once again, misjudged the situation. Quite wrongly he reckoned that the governor and lords of Scotland had now submitted to him and that the way was clear to proceed against France.

Henry's original intention had been that the invasion of France should take place in the summer of 1543,[47] but Scot-

44. *L.P.*, xviii, i, 425. This is what the 'English' party said and Sadler, reporting their verdict, agreed.

45. See above, p. 462. In January 1543, when the news of James's death arived, Chapuys speculated whether Henry would now resume the quest for Marie de Guise's hand. *L.P.*, xviii, i, 44.

46. ibid., 804.

47. So his instructions to Thirlby on his embassy to Charles in July 1542 had stated. See *L.P.*, xvii, 447. Cf. ibid., 353, in which Chapuys reported Henry's intention to make war 'this year'. The letter was written in April 1543.

tish affairs had so engulfed him that this had proved impossible. Furthermore, negotiations with Charles for an offensive
alliance had been tripped up by one of those ironical consequences of Henry's past life which had already, more than
once, given him trouble. The difficulty was this: that
Charles, who was already embarrassed at the prospect of
concluding an alliance with a schismatic, could neither
accord Henry the title of Supreme Head of the Church in
any treaty document nor undertake to defend England
against attack of any kind, including that by 'spiritual persons'; while the English insisted that the king should receive
his full style and be protected against sudden isolation if the
pope should decide to join her enemy and turn the war into
a crusade. Europe was about to witness an alliance of the
emperor and a schismatic king against the Most Christian
king and his ally, the infidel Turk. Francis was reported,
scarcely credibly, to be troubled in his conscience about his
liaison; whereupon Henry remarked jovially that, whoever
gave him absolution, he and the emperor would impose the
penance.[48] But he could not easily lift Charles over his
scruple. The Imperialists would commit Charles to defending Henry against temporal princes only. When Henry
angrily observed that Charles had not always been so sensitive about papal rights (in 1527, for instance, when his troops
had sacked Rome), they were unmoved; and when he proposed that the text should speak of common defence against
'any person of any status, grade or dignity' they still objected. It took weeks to find an acceptable formula. And then
there was the matter of the royal style – a no less delicate
problem, which was eventually settled when both sides
agreed that Henry should be described as 'Defender of the
Faith, etc.' (not the last time that this innocent adjunct
has covered a multitude of disquiets).[49]

48. *L.P.*, xix, i, 84.
49. On these negotiations see esp. *L.P.*, xvii, 1017, 1044. On the
inwardness of a later use of 'etc.' in the royal style and its disappearance (in 1800), see Maitland, 'Elizabethan Gleanings, I, "Defender of
the Faith and so forth" ', *E.H.R.*, xv (1900), 120 ff.

Henry agreed to the new Anglo-Imperial treaty on 11 February 1543. It was kept secret until the end of May. By 15 June the English were convinced that Scotland was in their grasp[50] and a week later, in the presence of his Council at Westminster, Henry delivered an ultimatum to the French ambassador threatening war within twenty days for the recovery of the realm of France unless certain impossible conditions were fulfilled.[51] Shortly afterwards about five thousand English troops crossed to Calais under Sir John Wallop to aid the defence of the Low Countries; and on 6 June the first engagement between English and French ships took place in the Narrow Seas. No major enterprise would take place this year, but before it was out plans had been laid for its successor. Henry and Charles were each to put an army of 42,000 into the field before next 20 June. Charles would enter France through Champagne, while Henry led his troops along the Somme – to Paris.[52] Henry was to return to campaigning in the grand manner, after the fashion of thirty years ago.

In the meantime, however, things had gone seriously awry in Scotland. Only a few days after the treaties had been signed at Greenwich, Sadler was sending home alarming reports of imminent rebellion, led by Cardinal Beaton and Lennox against a governor who was plainly in the greatest difficulty.[53] Henry was soon in a frenzy of anxiety. Five thousand troops were made ready to aid Arran, with the promise of 'a greater furniture' if the cardinal and his fellows were not daunted by this first contingent. Sadler was told to bid Arran keep the closest watch on Beaton 'and his angels' and, astonishingly, to promise him that, if Mary were carried off and married elsewhere, Henry would make him king of Scotland if he remained loyal.[54] Sadler must

50. On that day the Privy Council reported to Harvel (in Venice) that 'the governor of Scotland, with the rest of the lords there, have wholly committed themselves unto his majesty'. *St.P.*, xi, 411 (*L.P.*, xviii, i, 707). This was typical optimism.

51. *L.P.*, xviii, i, 754, 759.

52. *L.P.*, xviii, ii, 526.

53. ibid., xviii, i, 880, 897, 905 etc.

54. *L.P.*, xviii, ii, 9.

keep Arran in hand, hold off Beaton, guard the infant queen,
stir the governor to strike down the cardinal, lure the latter
with the promise of richer rewards in England than anything the French or the bishop of Rome could ever provide,
watch for French penetration, have the pledges for the
observance of the recent treaties dispatched.[55] But the
stream of advice was ineffective. Though on 29 August
Sadler could write to Henry that the governor had at last
taken action against the cardinal and had sent an envoy to
ask for English help – having previously told Henry that
he wanted £5,000, not his five thousand troops[56] – three days
later came the report that the English grip on Scotland was
almost gone, that civil war was inevitable and that sooner
or later Henry must use force.[57] In fact he had already
decided to do so. On 31 August the Privy Council ordered
Suffolk to gather a large army to enter Scotland in aid of
Arran as he struggled for his life.[58] But on 4 September
Sadler reported that the governor had suddenly and un-
accountably ridden out of town. Next day came the crushing
news that he had gone over to the cardinal and joined him
at Stirling.[59] The man on whom Henry had pinned his hopes
had deserted the English cause.

'Under the sun live not more beastly and unreasonable
people than here be of all degrees,' wrote Sadler.[60] Henry,
outraged by Arran's perfidy, now picked up a reed no less
fragile than the governor – the earl of Angus, hitherto
regarded as the backbone of the 'English' party. Angus
would now become the object of his 'entire trust', the king-
pin of his Scottish policy. The new agent was quickly briefed.
He must now capture not only the wretched cardinal but
also the governor. He must capture the queen. He might
have what money and men from England he required.
Indeed, Henry wanted to send Suffolk with eight thousand
men to Edinburgh there and then, to sack the city and seize

55. *L.P.*, xviii, ii, 33, 46, 68, 75, 100.   56. ibid., 22, 94.
57. ibid., iii.   58. ibid., 118–19.
59. ibid., 128, 132.   60. ibid., 175.

the governor and his ally[61] – until the news that these two had flown to St Andrews forced him to hold over the enterprise for the moment and resume his former activity of shouting vain instructions, at Angus now, in the hope of controlling a situation which was so swift-moving, complex and remote that his chances of success were never rosy.

It was already months since the treaties of Greenwich had been signed and the Scots had done nothing to implement them. Arran had persistently stalled, though he had at least ratified them (on 25 August). Ignoring the warnings of Sadler that his grip on Scotland was so fragile that he must proceed stealthily, Henry disquieted even the pro-English Scots with his demand that they should abandon France, had himself failed to ratify the treaties of Greenwich and, despite the peace, seized some Scottish ships. Moreover, at the end of September he announced that he considered himself at open war with the Scots since the treaties had been 'annihilated' by their failure to observe them.[62] Again, however, he took no direct action, but waited in vain for Angus and his brother to strike for him. Then, on 11 December 1543, the Scottish Parliament solemnly annulled those treaties with England concluded five months previously; and four days later all former treaties between Scotland and France were renewed. In the twelve months since a double catastrophe threw the Scots at his feet Henry had not only failed to secure the marriage of their infant queen to his son, but had so mishandled his opportunity that the Scots were now rallied against him and the Auld Alliance refurbished.

Henry's first reaction to the news of Scotland's defiance was to order two violent raids on the lands of Angus and his supporters. But the latter persuaded him that they had not betrayed him, that they were still his good friends, that he should dispatch his main army elsewhere and then not until the spring.[63] To this Henry eventually agreed. In the previous autumn, the young earl of Lennox, who had re-

61. *L.P.*, xviii, ii, 169, 184, 256. Cf. 314, 442, 450 – similar calls for action.

62. ibid., 235.   63. *L.P.*, xix, i, 33, 51, 58.

turned from exile in France in the previous April, had
joined the English party. Since Lennox stood next to Arran
in the succession, he provided Henry with a powerful and,
as it proved, constant satellite. Accordingly, the king
swallowed his desire to flail clients whom he had thought
had betrayed him and, in March 1544, agreed to work
through the earl, Angus and others to gain control of Scottish affairs. If Lennox and his fellows, he promised, would
have the word of God preached in their kingdom, serve
England, secure Mary until the time of her delivery for
marriage, have him named protector during her infancy
and give hostages for the performance of their undertakings,
he would send an army which would set them up as a
puppet government, with Lennox at their head as governor.
His troops, aided by this English party, would so capture
Scotland that she would never again aid France or worry
England;[64] and to make doubly sure, he would call upon
the emperor to join in the struggle.[65] But within a few weeks
it became clear that Lennox could not fulfil his side of the
bargain and Henry promptly reverted to his policy of direct
violence. His commander-in-chief, Edward Seymour (Lord
Hertford), was commanded to attack Edinburgh and so de-
face it as to leave behind a fearful monument to the divine
vengeance of falsehood and treachery. He was to sack the
castle, put men, women and children to the sword, and
thence go to Leith and St Andrews and so punish the latter
that 'the upper stone may be the nether and not one stick
stand by another'; and as he went he would set up the proclamation (corrected by Henry himself) declaring the king
chief governor of the queen and protector of the realm.[66]
Henry sought bloodthirsty revenge for the Scots' renuncia-

64. *L.P.*, xix, i, 243; *St.P.*, v. 363–5, 386 f.
65. ibid., 92, 147, 168.
66. ibid., 314. A few days before this was written, the Privy Council
had told Hertford that Henry himself had corrected the draft of the
proclamation which was to be brought to Scotland by his army, ibid.,
249.

tion of what had been undertaken at Greenwich last summer, and he also wanted to knock Scotland out of the
Anglo-French war.

He believed that a stunning blow of this kind would intimidate his neighbour and keep out the French or any others
who might give them aid against him, like the Danes. But
Hertford, the man who was to lead the royal forces, rightly
questioned the wisdom of Henry's plan, suggesting that it
would exasperate rather than quell, that Scotland would
quickly recover from such a raid, that Henry should stand
by his original intention to occupy some strategic towns,
especially the port of Leith, possession of which would enable
him to re-enter Scotland later when a full invasion took place
and exclude the French in the meantime.[67] Hertford's
reappraisal of strategy was rejected. 'For a final resolution'
Henry, having carefully weighed his arguments, ordered the
commander to carry out a swift raid and not to seize and
fortify Leith or any other place, however many tempting
opportunities to do so presented themselves in the course of
the campaign.[68] This was to be a punitive expedition only,
designed to hold off the Scots while Henry was in France.

The plan was that a small force should ride overland from
the East and Middle Marches to Edinburgh where they
would meet the main army, under Hertford, which had
come by sea to Leith. Ships from London, Ipswich, King's
Lynn and Hull arrived at Newcastle on 20 April (a month
late and carrying quite inadequate supplies).[69] Fearful lest
food and money should run out before the expedition was
half done, Hertford boarded quickly and sailed for Scotland.
By 6 May he had landed, thrust aside a force led by Arran
and Beaton and taken Leith. Next day he met the horsemen
who had come by land and assaulted Edinburgh. The main
gate was blasted and much of the city burnt. After

67. *St.P.*, v, 371 (*L.P.*, xix, i, 319).
68. *L.P.*, xix, i, 348. Cf. 342, 386, 389, 405 for further evidence of
Henry's tight control of detailed planning of the expedition.
69. ibid., 355, 366.

despoiling the capital and the neighbouring countryside,
Hertford withdrew to Leith, sacked it and took to his ships
for home.[70] Henry was delighted by Hertford's exploits, and
doubtless still trusted that they would beat submissiveness
into the Scots and commend the 'English' party to their
opponents. But Scottish affairs did not respond as obediently
to the royal touch as that. Hertford's raid may momentarily
have taken some of the confidence out of England's enemies
and helped to bring about the appointment of the dowager
Marie de Guise in Arran's place; but Henry was thereafter
further away from securing control across the Borders,
even though Lennox remained loyal. Moreover, exactly as
Hertford had foretold, in the long run ten days of violence
only made the Scottish problem more bitter and more tenacious. Far from smoothing the way for the French campaign,
it stretched England's resources and disturbed her ally,
Charles, with the alarming thought that Rome might send
to lead a Franco-Scottish invasion of England that same
Cardinal Pole who had twice been sent to rally the emperor
against the heretic.[71] There was apparently no limit to the
discomfiture which his alliance with the English was to bring
in its train.

Preparations for the combined assault on France were
now far advanced. For weeks the ships and the men had
been gathering, and even before Hertford set sail for home
the Privy Council had written to him to dispatch some four
thousand of his men immediately to Calais.[72] The agreed
Anglo-Imperial strategy was that Henry and Charles should
lead their armies towards Paris. Though some of the Council
urged that it would be better if Henry were not to go in
person – for fear of some mishap, and lest his great bulk

70. *L.P.*, xix, i, 472, 483, 508, 533.

71. ibid., 497. Such an embassy by Pole never materialized. But in
August 1544 Paul III wrote sternly to Charles upbraiding him for
several things, including his alliance with a schismatic king who had
maltreated his aunt and was an enemy of Holy Church. *L.P.*, xix, ii,
134.

72. *L.P.*, xix, i, 508.

and dubious health should seriously slow down his army's progress – Henry clung to this agreement.[73] He had been preparing enthusiastically for this campaign[74] and was determined to heave his huge body into armour. As the time drew near for the expedition to begin, it was clear that his presence would be an encumbrance, and the emperor was told directly by his ambassador that Henry would so obviously not be able to endure the exertions of the campaign (though no one dared to tell him so) that every means should be used to keep him at home or at least to prevent him from travelling further than Calais. Chapuys went on to say that the only way Henry could be dissuaded from joining his army would be if Charles stayed away also. He made this suggestion, he later said, at the intercession of Paget and others of the Privy Council.[75] Charles himself had apparently already seen the desirability of keeping the king out of the campaign, not merely for the sake of the king's health and the army's progress. A special envoy had been sent to England not long before to dissuade him, but had found the king so adamant that he dared not try. Then, when the emperor heard that Henry was ill once more, he sent a second envoy to plead with him and again met no success.[76]

However, by the end of May, Henry had changed his mind and was clearly using Chapuys to alter the agreed strategy without damaging his reputation as a military captain. It was now proposed to the emperor that he and Henry should send their lieutenants with armies of about thirty thousand to capture Paris, hold it to ransom and then return, while Henry himself came to Calais with a smaller force for a local campaign – for the somewhat opaque reason that it was not fitting for a prince to take part in a rapid foray of the kind proposed and that Henry had won

73. *L.P.*, xix, i, 529, 530.
74. Chapuys wrote that the Privy Council had told him how Henry thought of nothing else, night and day, but the invasion of France.
75. ibid., 529, 603.   76. ibid., 619, 626.

renown from the recent raid on Edinburgh precisely because
he had not been there in person.[77] Charles wanted English
troops and money to come – but without the king. He was
not impressed, therefore, by these new proposals, arguing
that he was a younger man than Henry and had no honourable excuse for turning back after having come to Germany
from Spain expressly for the purpose of leading his army
into France. But as long as Charles insisted on campaigning
in person, Henry could not withdraw himself without loss
of face. It was all an unhappy muddle, full of promise of
future squabbling and recrimination between the allies.

While the strategy was still in debate, a vast English
army had crossed to Calais, led by those veteran war-lords,
the dukes of Suffolk and Norfolk. By the middle of June it
had moved eastwards into French territory, with its objective
still undefined. Though the king had answered a query from
Lord Cobham that Calais would need no special garrison
because his army would never stray far from it,[78] he wrote
to Charles shortly afterwards that he would wait until he
had arrived at Calais before deciding whether his men
should march further forward into France. Think again
about the plan to attack Paris, he begged the emperor. Let
raison de guerre and the supply of victuals determine tactics
as the campaign unfolded. The emperor's gout was a more
serious affliction than his bad leg, he argued. It would be
better to seize frontier towns than expose their flanks to the
enemy on a march to Paris – and so on.[79] But Charles would
not surrender and, meanwhile, the English army waited
aimlessly in enemy territory. Small wonder that a week or
so after setting out from Calais with the vanguard, Norfolk
should have written tartly to the Privy Council that he had

77. *L.P.*, xix, i, 619.

78. ibid., 691. This letter, from the Privy Council, suggests that
Henry was in close control of policy. Cf. the letter from the Council
to the royal agents who were raising mercenaries, and to Norfolk
(ibid., 682, 690), which are full of such phrases as 'the king orders
... wills ... desires ... thinks'.

79. ibid., 714.

expected to know, before this, where he was supposed to be going.[80]

The king had finally made up his mind about strategy two days before this letter was written. Norfolk was to lay siege either to the town of Montreuil (which the English troops had reached so easily in 1523) or else to Ardres, just outside the Pale.[81] However, this decision (made on 20 June) left open the burning question of whether the attack on Paris would take place. Had Norfolk succeeded quickly, at Montreuil or Ardres, another plunge 'into the bowels of France' as, long ago, Wolsey had called this tactic, might have been practicable. But, ever since he set out, the duke had sent up a wail of complaints about his army's disorganization and urgent shortage of bread, beer, guns and shot; and before long he had to confess that his siege of Montreuil (for thither he had turned, not to Ardres) was a shambles. On 14 July 1544, after several postponements, Henry arrived at Calais for the fourth time in his life and the second time in war. Shortly after he arrived, the duke of Suffolk set out to survey the lie of the land around Boulogne and assess the problem of laying siege to that town, a project which Henry had apparently been entertaining at least since he arrived in France.[82] On 19 July the siege began. The Imperialists protested to Henry that their programme had been to march forward, not to get bogged down in these two sieges of Montreuil and Boulogne; to which Henry retorted that, unless both were taken, an advancing army could not be supplied. But it was now becoming clear that he had broken the agreement and, if he undertook any major campaign, it would be directed at Normandy, not Paris.[83] As in 1523, he was not willing to let his men stray far from home, far from their supply-depots and their ships. A week after he arrived at Calais, he set out to the siege of

---

80. *L.P.*, xix, i, 758.   81. ibid., 741.   82. ibid., 932.

83. ibid., 955–6. But Henry assured Chapuys that, once Montreuil and Boulogne were taken (which would be soon, he would go forward with his army in person.

Boulogne. His army was now split in two: one half, under
Norfolk, battled on forlornly outside the walls of Montreuil;
the other, under Suffolk and now the king, prepared to take
Boulogne. Bad weather and shortage of powder had held up
both forces, and it was not until early August that the full
battery was opened up against the walls of Boulogne. Henry
lay to the north of the town, by the sea. He enjoyed the
siege hugely, supervising every move and appearing to be in
better spirits and health than had been seen for years.[84] On
11 September the castle was blown up, three days later the
English delivered their terms for the town's capitulation, and
on 18 September Henry entered it in triumph. He stayed
there a dozen days, supervising its fortification by its con-
querors (which included pulling down the church of our
Lady to make room for a bastion) and then, having knighted
some companions-in-war, departed.[85] Secret preparations for
his return to England had been in hand for two weeks, when
the Council with the queen, which had remained in England to attend to domestic affairs during Henry's absence,
was ordered to have ships sent to Calais and Boulogne, on
the pretence of bringing thither supplies, to carry him back
to England.[86] He embarked from Boulogne and returned
home quietly with a few companions on 30 September.[87]

It had been a rather dismal campaign. The splendid
strategy agreed months before had not been executed and,
though Henry had won a notable trophy in Boulogne, this
scarcely justified the huge expenditure of men and money
which the expedition had cost. Furthermore, the allies had
fallen apart as easily and quickly as previous discord concerning strategy had suggested they would. For weeks the
French had been making moves for peace and dangling
their terms before their enemies. Though doubtless Henry
was as ready to abandon Charles if it suited him as Charles
was to do the same to him, the king had behaved honourably and kept the emperor informed of all the French offers.

84. L.P., xix, ii, 35, 174, 424.   85. ibid., 424, App. 10.
86. St.P., x, 75 (L.P., xix, ii, 258).   87. L.P., xix, ii, 336.

Hence it was galling news that, unbeknown to Henry, on the day that the latter entered Boulogne the emperor had come to terms with the French at Crépy. Charles's army was in difficulty and he himself anxious to end the fighting. Accordingly, he accepted the unfavourable terms offered to him and abandoned England. True enough, he had written to Henry some days before suggesting that he should damp down his martial ardour, cut his losses and run,[88] but Henry had not expected to be left in the lurch quite so precipitately. Charles's withdrawal was a humiliation and exposed him to the full weight of the French army. The situation was quickly very serious. The dauphin moved across swiftly to relieve Montreuil and threatened to wipe out the unhappy Norfolk. He and his men – not the inhabitants of the besieged town – were starving, his horsemen, Imperial mercenaries, were now likely to quit, his supply line would be cut if the dauphin swung round to Étaples.[89] For a moment Henry thought of sending Suffolk to Montreuil with reinforcements. But he dared not risk a pitched battle and eventually ordered Norfolk to withdraw – which was scarcely a less perilous manoeuvre. Had the dauphin caught him and smashed his army, Henry would have been in peril at Boulogne. But Norfolk extricated himself from Montreuil without mishap and was back at Boulogne by the time the king left. For the last few days Henry had been in extreme anxiety and full of bitter complaints against the emperor;[90] but he returned home now with his army safe. He had evaded final disaster and held his captured town securely.

88. *L.P.*, xix, ii, 198. But the English ambassador with the emperor, Nicholas Wotton, had been kept fully informed about Franco-Imperial peace negotiations. See his dispatches of 20 September, ibid., 267–8.

89. ibid., 278, 285.

90. ibid., 304. The Imperial ambassadors reported that Henry delayed his departure, against the wishes of all the Council, in case there should be a major battle with the dauphin's force. Paget was said to have begged them to plead with him to leave, especially since the French king was not at the head of the French army, ibid., 318.

But three days after he landed in England, as he was
moving through Kent towards London, the astounding news
came that Suffolk and Norfolk had disobeyed orders and
led the bulk of their men out of Boulogne to Calais. The
excuse was that Henry's directions for building impregnable
defence-works in the captured town were impracticable and
that Calais was in need of aid against the dauphin.[91] Henry
angrily ordered his men to return to his appointed post.
Their 'light coming away' from Boulogne, the Council
would complain, showed that they were 'too well minded
to come homeward'. The king's affairs were being 'very
loosely handled many ways';[92] or, as Henry himself would
state more directly in a stinging letter, 'their bolstering and
unapparent reasons ... enculk a feigned necessity, to cloak
and maintain faults too much apparent to indifferent eyes'.[93]
They had effectively scuttled Boulogne and abandoned most
of their victual and guns, all because of an unconfirmed
rumour about the dauphin's movements. They must return
to their posts. But this they could not do, because the enemy
now had some 50,000 men in the field, their own horsemen
(mercenaries from the Low Countries) had, as expected,
followed Charles out of the fight, and they themselves were
exhausted. They were trapped in Calais and quickly started
shipping men homewards, while the dauphin raided freely
about them and a frantic Council lambasted them for in-
activity and rank disobedience.[94] It was a fitting end to this
disordered expedition. Norfolk and his men had had a
miserable, aimless time ever since they first set out from
Calais in the rain some fifteen weeks ago, and few of his
fellows had fared better. It had been different thirty-odd
years past, when the king's almoner, Thomas Wolsey, was in
control. At the best of times erratic supply, inadequate maps,
often wildly erroneous information about the opponent's
position and strength, sudden desertion and equally sudden
diplomacy made sixteenth-century warfare a haphazard

91. *L.P.*, xix, ii, 353.   92. *St.P.*, x, 104 (*L.P.*, xix, ii, 374).
93. *L.P.*, xix, ii, 383.   94. ibid., 377, 399, 414.

business, full of unexpected victories and defeats, unlooked-
for engagements and withdrawals. But the English campaign
of 1544 was a muddle even by the generous standards of the
times.

Once he was home, Henry had agreed to negotiate with
the French and had appointed commissioners to begin talks
at Calais. Seymour and Paget headed the English delegation
– not Norfolk and the others, who, as Henry pointed out to
them roughly, should not have been at Calais at all.[95] The
French party arrived on 16 October and started talking two
days later (by which time Henry had forgiven his disobedient generals and commissioned them to join the negotiations).[96] The discussions made no progress. Henry insisted,
as he had insisted ever since he captured the place, that
Boulogne must remain his and that Francis must abandon
the Scots. Neither of these demands was acceptable, and in
early November the French ambassadors finally left the
conference room.[97] Henry had won himself a little breath-
ing-space and was now about to be shielded by the winter.
The war was still on, because Boulogne would never be
surrendered. Indeed, that town was to be heavily fortified,
even though Henry had to send thither a large stock of
mattresses and tents, and nails and tiles to mend houses
before the troops at Calais would return to that inhospitable
place.[98] Like its generals, the army was near mutiny.

Charles had not only abandoned Henry, but was appointed
mediator between England and France. Henry poured out
bitter complaints about the emperor's defection, but the
latter merely replied that it was the English who had broken
faith. They had evaded the march on Paris. The siege of

95. *L.P.*, xix, ii, 383.
96. *St.P.*, x, 116 (*L.P.*, xix ii, 432). On 14th October Henry had
written to them to announce his pardon, but ordering them to send
reinforcements to Boulogne as soon as possible and return home themselves with the rest of the army. *L.P.*, xix, ii, 436.
97. *L.P.*, xix, ii, 443, 456, 470, 546, 561.
98. ibid., 489. On Henry's command the men were also to be
'comforted' with good words.

Montreuil was a sham, the attack on Boulogne had been
intended from the start and was needlessly prolonged. If
Henry had not been so insistent on taking part in the
campaign, Charles would never have taken the difficult route
through Champagne nor denied himself, for Henry's benefit,
supplies from the Low Countries. Moreover – and this was
the piece which most riled the king – at Calais, Henry had
himself agreed that Charles should be free to end hostilities
unilaterally. This the latter had done for the good of
Christendom and now generously offered his services as
arbiter of the Anglo-French dispute. Henry should accept
reasonable terms and return Boulogne, perhaps by handing
it over to a third party during the negotiations.[99] In reply,
Henry swung back with counter-accusations – that Charles
had been guilty of manifest treachery, that at Calais it had
been agreed that either side might negotiate independently
but not that either might conclude a treaty without the
other, that, far from being free to act as 'honest broker'
between disputants, Charles was bound by treaty to resume
the war as England's ally.[1] Each pelted the other with
recriminations for months, through the winter of 1544–5
and the following spring. By July 1545 Anglo-Imperial relations were not so much unrepaired as near breaking-point.
To his former grievances (which were still green) Henry had

99. *L.P.*, xix, ii, 507, 532, 577; xx, i, 7, etc.
1. *L.P.*, xix, ii, 517, 577; xx, i, 7, 54, 227, etc. The intensity of
Henry's bitterness towards Charles and his insistence that the latter
should return to the campaign are well illustrated by the many trenchant corrections in his own hand which he made to the following
three dispatches: a signet letter to Norfolk Suffolk and others at
Calais (dated 20 October) instructing ambassadors about to go thence
to the emperor (*St.P.*, x, 134 ff.); a letter of the Privy Council to
Hertford and others with the emperor (dated 31 October) which,
interestingly, Henry obviously went over minutely and corrected
heavily (ibid., 161 ff.); a letter from Henry to Charles (dated 5
February), full of savage complaints about the emperor's 'inhumanity',
disloyalty, etc. (*L.P.*, xx, i, 146). Henry was clearly much involved
in affairs, as he was also in the defence-works at Boulogne and in
Scottish matters.

added new ones: that Spanish troops had entered French employment; that English merchants in Spain were man-handled by the Inquisition; that gunpowder bought in Brabant could not be fetched away.[2] For his part, Charles too had gathered a new crop of complaints: that the English had seized Imperial ships and cargoes; that 700 Spanish arquebusiers who landed by chance in England had been lured to the Scottish Borders to join a very heterogeneous army (which already contained Albanian horsemen and mercenaries from Italy and Cleves); that Henry had defiantly resumed negotiations with the Lutherans whom Charles was now preparing to crush (and on whom, in the following year, he would inflict a great defeat at the Battle of Mühlberg).[3]

Henry had lost his ally and was in serious trouble. In the first place, he was no nearer mastery of Scotland than he had been a year ago. His motley army had been making on the average a dozen raids across the Borders per month and he and his Council had given incessant attention to finding a quick, cheap route through the rapids of the Scottish faction-struggle. Now Henry thought of ambushing Angus and his brother,[4] now he held out a friendly hand to them and offered them safe-conducts to come to England to negotiate once more;[5] now he agreed to sponsor the assassination of the cardinal, provided that Sadler had the work done without implicating him in business which was 'not meet' for a king.[6] But the truth was that he had made no progress towards imposing the treaties of Greenwich or securing the young queen. If anything, matters had gone from bad to worse. Early in 1545 English troops had raided Melrose and desecrated the tombs of Angus's ancestors, an action which allegedly so stirred the patriotism of Angus, Henry's erst-

2. *L.P.*, xx, i, 1087, 1203.
3. ibid., 933, 1202, etc.
4. ibid., 4, the Privy Council to Shrewsbury and others (dated 1 January 1545), reporting the king's wishes.
5. ibid., 218.
6. *St.P.*, v, 499 f. (*L.P.*, xx, i, 834). For other examples of Henry's close direction of Scottish affairs, see *L.P.*, xx, i, 466, 468, 481.

while client, that on 27 February he led a Scottish force to
victory at Ancrum, a few miles south-east of Melrose. This
was no large-scale engagement, but it was the first undeniable success for Scottish arms for generations and served
as an ominous prelude to what quickly became a grave crisis
engulfing England. For, by the spring of 1545 France was
apparently about to send a force to Scotland via the north-
west and another to just south of the Borders in the east,
and thence launch a Franco-Scottish invasion of England.
Moreover, since her forces were released by the peace with
the emperor, she could strike at Boulogne, invade England
from the south-east and perhaps land in Ireland or the West
Country.[7] Thirdly, Henry's attempts to find new allies and
mercenaries abroad had not met much success. In April
1545 his desperate isolation had driven him to send Christopher Mont (and one John Bucler) to Germany once more to
beg aid from Saxony, Bremen, Württemberg, Denmark –
indeed from as many as would respond. The agents took
with them an offer of an offensive and defensive alliance
with the Protestant League after the old manner, as well as
the now-familiar bait of a marriage treaty. They went to
Worms to attend a Diet (as before) and to negotiate with
the Protestants between sessions. After much pleading they
wrung no more from the Lutherans than the promise of a
defensive league which would provide Henry with 4,500
troops at his own expense, but only on condition that the
latter first deposited 200,000 crowns at Bremen for their use
if they were attacked. Hamburg refused to supply mercenaries and expressed the hope that the ships for which Henry
asked would never be needed; Bremen and Lübeck answered
the call for aid with a short *non possumus*.[8] Though the mer-
cenary captain Frederic van Rieffenberg had been hired,
with nearly 10,000 men, to succour a Boulogne whose line of

7. *St.P.*, v, 432 (*L.P.*, xx, i, 513); *L.P.*, xx, i, 619. The Imperial ambassador at Rome reported that Paul III promised men for the French
invasion of England. ibid., 457.

8. *L.P.*, xx, i, 677, 715, 808, 1047, 1135, 1207; ii, 46, 67–9, 102.

supply from England was threatened by French ships, the scramble for allies had achieved very little, and certainly not enough to cover Henry's nakedness. French power was closing in on him. Charles and the Protestant world stood aloof; and meanwhile it was becoming increasingly clear that the papal General Council, so often postponed and so long feared, would indeed assemble (as it did) at Trent in the following December.

Finally, Henry was desperately short of money. The campaign of 1544 had cost him, not the expected £250,000, but some £650,000, and between Michaelmas of that year and the following 8 September a further £560,000 was spent.[9] The demands of massive campaigning (the total cost of which from 1542 to Henry's death exceeded two million pounds) beggared him and drove him to drastic expedients. Benevolences, i.e. forced gifts, in 1542 and 1544 had been accompanied by forced loans and heavy subsidies, lay and clerical, in 1543 and 1545. Since 1542, a stream of sales of ex-monastic lands had grown into an avalanche which carried away land to the value of about a third of a million pounds in the two years which ran from Michaelmas 1543 to Michaelmas 1545.[10] Meanwhile the great debasement of the English coinage had been launched with the object of making quick profit, regardless of long-term consequence, by re-minting coin which contained an ever-increasing proportion of base-metal – an enterprise which probably yielded a good deal more than the known figure of a quarter of a million pounds. On top of this, there was a new, though small, burst of dissolution of a class of religious establishment which had hitherto escaped suppression, namely, colleges of secular priests and free chapels served by secular clergy, like Tattershall in Lincolnshire, St Elizabeth's Col-

9. Dietz, *English Public Finance, 1485–1558*, University of Illinois Studies in the Social Sciences, ix (1920), p. 149. The cost of garrisoning, fortifying and feeding Boulogne between September 1544 and October 1545 came to some £133,000. *L.P.*, xx, ii, 558.

10. Dietz, loc. cit.

lege in Winchester and Brundish chantry in Suffolk.[11] In 1545, Henry began to consider how to 'borrow' church plate – a project which, in reply to Henry's query, Hertford applauded on the ground that 'God's service, which consisteth not in jewels, plate or ornaments of gold and silver, cannot thereby be anything diminished, and those things better employed for the weal and defence of the realm'.[12] All this money-raising, it should be remembered, came on top of an 'ordinary' income of the crown which had been greatly expanded during the 1530s, particularly by the arrival of a new source of income in the shape of the first fruits and annual tenths of the secular Church. Even so, Henry was now desperate for cash and, having tightened every screw on his people, was trying to raise money on the Antwerp money-market. Such was the inexorable appetite of war.

And such too were the gruelling circumstances amidst which he stood in the summer of 1545 – circumstances of his own making. England now faced a threat greater than that of 1539, greater than any, perhaps, she had known for generations, or would know again until Philip II threatened her. She awaited invasion from three or four quarters by two powers whom she had drawn against herself and whose common cause she had herself largely re-fashioned. In the South, three armies of over 30,000 men were drawn up; one in Kent under the duke of Suffolk, one in Essex under the duke of Norfolk, one in the West under the earl of Arundel. The earl of Hertford stood at the head of an army on the Scottish Borders, the lord admiral was at sea with 12,000 men, waiting to grapple with an invasion fleet; and at Boulogne, whose commander, Lord Poynings, suddenly died in August, to be followed soon after by the duke of Suffolk, another army was drawn up.[13] None too soon, on 10 August Henry ordered processions throughout the realm with

11. See *Eighth Deputy Keeper's Report*, App. ii, 7 ff.
12. *L.P.*, xx, i, 1145. Cf. ibid., 984, 996 for Henry's sale of lead taken from churches, presumably ex-monastic churches.
13. ibid., 958.

prayers and hymns in English to intercede for victory.[14] At least, this is what the Council said the purpose was. But Providence might more suitably have been begged for mere survival.

In the middle of June Francis I had been near Rouen to see his invasion fleet of over 200 ships before it set forth for England. On the evening of Sunday 19 July it entered the Solent at the very moment when Henry, who had travelled south to inspect fortifications, was dining on board his flagship, *Great Harry*. As soon as the French armada was sighted, the king hurried ashore.[15] That night a chain of warning fires carried the news of the enemy's coming across England. There was fighting next day, and on the day after the French landed on the Isle of Wight – only to withdraw after twenty-four hours. They landed again near Seaford shortly afterwards, and again withdrew. Eventually, on 9 August, the lord admiral received orders to put out from Portsmouth, where Henry had previously bidden his ships to lie passively at anchor, and do battle with the French.[16] Six days later the English came close to their quarry – indeed, spent a night anchored hard by – but after a quick skirmish the French departed and left their pursuants becalmed off Beachy Head. Shortly afterwards a north-easterly gale blew up which kept Lord Lisle and his ships trapped on the same Beachy Head for a further forty-eight hours and allowed the French to escape into the Narrow Seas towards home. Probably Francis had never intended that his large fleet should carry out more than a few swift landings of the kind which Lisle was soon to make in Normandy, and to cut supply lines between England and Boulogne.

By early September, therefore, the threat of invasion seemed miraculously to have lifted. But Henry had been, and in part remained, in extreme difficulty. His enemies stood about him, he had no friends, his mercenaries had swindled him, his packed ships were soon stricken with plague which carried off hundreds of men.

14. *L.P.*, xx, ii, 89. 15. *L.P.*, xx, i, 1263. 16. *L.P.*, xx, ii, 82, 94.

We are at war with France and Scotland, [wrote Stephen Gardiner in a mood of deep gloom] we have enmity with the bishop of Rome; we have no assured friendship here with the emperor and we have received from the landgrave, chief captain of the Protestants, such displeasure that he has cause to think us angry with him. . . . Our war is noisome to our realm and to all our merchants that traffic through the Narrow Seas. . . . We are in a world where reason and learning prevail not and covenants are little regarded.

England had run herself into an impasse: she could not continue this crippling war, but had little chance of any but the 'worst peace', which, though 'better than the best war' in his reckoning, might be an insupportable disappointment to a king who already faced 'adversity in age'. Gardiner's survey of the scene[17] was baleful enough; to it we must add Wriothesley's.

In early November 1545 he reported how he had just been able to scrape together £20,000 for the wars – £15,000 in profits from the mints, 'our holy anchor', £3,000 from the Court of Augmentations, and £1,000 each from the duchy of Lancaster and the Court of Wards; but 'the Tenths and First Fruits hath nothing, the Surveyors nothing, nor the Exchequer about £1,000'.[18] A few days later, he wrote to Paget, 'I assure you master Secretary, I am at my wits' end how we shall possibly shift for three months following, and especially for the two next.'[19] The 1530s had brought the crown immense wealth and given it a financial security which few kings of England, or of anywhere else, had ever enjoyed. By the end of 1545 Henry was near bankruptcy.

It was in July 1543 that Henry's marriage to his last wife, Catherine Parr, took place.

17. To quote it I have conflated two letters written by him to Paget in November 1545. See Muller, *The Letters of Stephen Gardiner* (Cambridge, 1933), 185 ff. and 198 f. 'Thus be things entangled. Thus we be in a labrynth,' he wrote (ibid., 190). One is inclined to concur with him.

18. *St.P.*, i, 835 (*L.P.*, xx, ii, 729).   19. ibid., 840 (*L.P.*, xx, ii, 769).

Catherine, the daughter of a Northamptonshire knight and courtier of good estate, had been married and widowed twice already and was now thirty-one years old. When her second husband, Lord Latimer, died in 1543, it seemed that she would marry Hertford's brother, Thomas Seymour, a dangerous and lecherous man whose gallantry had won her. But Seymour was thrust aside (until he would be her fourth husband) by the king, who married her at Hampton Court on 12 July 1543, with Stephen Gardiner officiating. Despite her esteem for Seymour, Catherine was an impressive and agreeable woman. During her last widowhood, she had received Reformers like Coverdale and Latimer into her home and was now of a moderate Protestant persuasion which ran hand in hand with a cultivated Erasmianism.[20] Henry's last wife was almost as remarkable a figure as his first and, like the first, became the centre-piece of a humanist circle. It was probably thanks to her genial influence that in December 1543 all three of the royal children came together, for the first time, in their father's household; and it was certainly she who reorganized and directed the royal nursery, which was intended to provide a highly enlightened education for noble children as well as royal. It was she who brought in as tutors Anthony Cooke (whose daughter was the mother of Sir Francis Bacon) and the notable Cambridge humanist, John Cheke, together with one William Grindal, probably a relative of the great Elizabethan archbishop of Canterbury. It was her influence which led Princess Mary to take up the translation of Erasmus's *Paraphrases* on the New Testament and Elizabeth to translate both Marguerite of Navarre's *The Mirror of Glass of the Sinful Soul*, a classic of Erasmian pietism, and Erasmus's own *Dialogus Fidei*; and to the works of her stepdaughters and their tutors whom she patronized, Catherine added her own contribution: *The Prayers stirring the Mind unto Heavenly Meditations*, published in 1545 and quickly expanded, and *The Lamentation of a Sinner*, a work which appeared some

20. On this see McConica, op. cit., 215 ff.

months after Henry's death. Despite what Henry may have said and thought, marriage had served him well. He had spent the first twenty years or so of his reign in the company of an admirable woman and he passed its final years with an elevated, purposeful queen at his side who, riding above those who jockeyed for position as the old king neared his end and would have liked to undo her, did much to take away some of the bleakness of his last days.

[14]

The Last Months

HENRY spent the last eighteen months of his life in a jungle of diplomacy. It was more than a quarter of a century since the three leading monarchs of western Europe had taken up the struggle for international prestige and mastery, and all three may have thought that they now approached the climax of their careers: Henry with perhaps a final success against France and a bloody assault on Scotland; Francis with a last lunge against the Habsburgs; Charles, after years of waiting, with the crushing of Protestantism in Germany and the vindication of his Imperial authority. But over the years the cards had become so dog-eared, the players' features and tactics so familiar to their fellows that high diplomacy had to be played as it had never been played before. As a result, the three veteran rivals wove so dense a web of *détente* and *démarche*, anticipated, crossed and double-crossed with such ingenuity that it is a good deal easier now to admire their energy than to decipher their precise purposes.

Throughout, it may be said at once, Henry thrust and parried like a master. Until the last few days of his life, there was no sign of loss of grip or flagging enthusiasm. On the contrary, he now looked more confident and more formidable than perhaps he had ever been and held more in his hands than perhaps ever before. His first purpose was to retain his precious prize of war, 'our daughter' Boulogne, as he called it. Here, at least, was one fixed point in the plethora of feints and uncertainties. By September 1545 the Council was eager to end hostilities with France, cede the captured port and deliver England from the crippling expense of war. But Henry would have none of this – and was strongly abetted in his belligerence by his commander in France, the

earl of Surrey. 'Animate not the king too much for the keeping of Boulogne,' wrote Norfolk angrily to his son, 'for who
so doth at length shall get small thanks'; what progress the
father and his fellow-councillors had made in six days in
advancing their plan to render Boulogne and conclude peace,
'ye with your letters set back in six hours, [of] such importance by your letters in the king's opinion at this time'.[1]
Though the Council, after much ado, had prevented him
from sending 1,500 pioneers and 3,000 troops to reinforce
Boulogne, there was no sign of an Anglo-French accord by
the end of 1545. However, if Henry were to hold that town
against the full weight of Francis's army and perhaps use it
as a base for a further campaign in France, it was imperative
to dislodge the emperor from his sudden neutrality and haul
him back into the war on England's side. Charles must
abandon France, return to the treaty which he had so flag-
rantly disowned and give aid to an ally whom the common
enemy had invaded thrice and still threatened. Henry
would placate Charles with the assurance that he would refuse no reasonable offers and was ready to accept a truce of
several months in order to lick his own wounds,[2] but sooner
or later Charles must rally to the cause and honour his
treaty obligations. He wrestled with the emperor for months.
He offered all his children to any Habsburg princes and
princess, but met no enthusiasm. He secretly proposed that
he and Charles should meet, say, at Calais, as soon as possible, in the hope that he might thus recapture his ex-ally,
but Charles first parried the proposal by urging that it
would overtax Henry's health and be very difficult to fit in
before the Diet which he, the emperor, must attend in
Regensburg in January (1546), and then turned it against the
inventor by agreeing to meet Henry, very briefly, at Bruges
or Dunkirk or some such, provided that the latter had already come to terms with the king of France. The emperor
would gladly meet his 'uncle' if the 'uncle' had first done

1. *L.P.*, xx, ii, 455, 738; letters dated 27 September and 6 November.
2. ibid., 178, 376.

what the 'nephew' required of him. Though Henry then tried to out-manoeuvre Charles by agreeing to a truce with France only on condition that the interview took place, the point went to Charles.[3] There was no interview. Then, in mid October 1545, Stephen Gardiner was sent post-haste to Charles at Bruges on an embassy whose first purpose was to accomplish the 'eclarishment', i.e. clarification, of the old Anglo-Imperial treaty, which the Imperialists were now saying was ambiguous, and to bring Charles to heel. Gardiner was about as zealous a pro-Imperialist and accomplished a diplomat as man could hope for, but not even he could lay hands on his quarry. First he was headed off with complaints about English customs charges, then swept aside by days of celebration of the order of the Golden Fleece, then baulked by the emperor's gout and finally made to ride in the wake of the Imperial entourage as Charles moved off to his appointment at Regensburg[4] – all of which must have reminded him of that ordeal he had undergone in the king's service some seventeen years before, when he had been sent to Rome to batter Clement VII into compliance.

Through the winter of 1545–6, as Henry fretted at home, full of 'marvel' at how the Imperialists resisted him[5] and worrying over the draft 'capitulations' which Gardiner had presented, the bishop fought on. He must persuade Charles to find mates for Mary, Elizabeth and Edward, break with the perfidious French, join the English against them, allow the English to scour the Low Countries for the food, copper, saltpetre, leather, anchors and pikes of which they were in dire need. But Charles would do none of these things. As 1546 wore on, so he gathered his full weight to destroy German Protestantism. He was not particularly interested in Henry's children, had little time for Henry's affairs and needed all the food and munitions he could find. In theory his plans might have been well served if France and England

3. *L.P.*, xx, ii, 460, 547, 561, 586, 625, 667, 669, 737, 764, 830.
4. ibid., 714, 903, 1006; xxi, i, 8, 51, 65, 83, 87.
5. *L.P.*, xx, ii, 999.

had been at each other's throats while he was at the Protestants', but he judged it safer not to turn against the latter
until he had brought the French to peace and perhaps
drawn them into an anti-Lutheran league. Shortly after
Gardiner arrived at the Imperial court, the admiral of France
came there too. Charles had tolerated the Englishman's importunity only because he hoped that, under his aegis,
Gardiner and the admiral would settle the differences between their two countries and enter his grand alliance.

But he had enough worldly wisdom and experience of
both Francis and Henry to know that each would as easily
stab him in the back as they would one another. His fear of
Francis and, probably, of Henry was well-founded. Last
August (1545) Francis had sent a message to the emperor
via a Spanish friar who seems to have been cast in the mould
of the future Père Joseph, warning of plans for a league of
France, England and the Lutherans against him (and offering to abandon this in favour of an alliance with Charles
against Henry),[6] and, by the time Gardiner was with him,
Charles was sufficiently anxious about England to be careful
not to repulse her ambassador out of hand. She must be
kept dangling on half-promises, not thrust into the arms of
France. Accordingly, at Utrecht in January 1546, he agreed
to a partial 'eclarishment' of the former Anglo-Imperial
treaty.[7]

Just as Charles suspected that the two monarchs whom he
wanted to bring concord would turn against him, and just
as Francis suspected that Gardiner would swing Charles
back against France, so Henry was full of anxiety lest there
was a third conspiracy afoot which had him as its intended
victim. What was the real meaning of the French admiral's
coming to the Imperial court? Was it only to meet Gardiner?
Was Charles putting himself to all this trouble merely to
bring his brothers to peace? Had he signed at Crépy a
second treaty 'more secret than the first' which would leave

6. *L.P.*, xx, ii, 417.
7. *L.P.*, xxi, i, 71.

France free to sweep the English back to the Channel while he dealt with the Lutherans? Though officially Gardiner went to Bruges to negotiate peace with France, in reality he went both to resuscitate an offensive alliance against France and, at the same time, to 'decipher' the meaning of the admiral's coming.[8] Much as Henry might pine for campaigning against the French and Scots after the old style, he had to face the prospect of Charles and Francis uniting against him; and it was almost certainly in order to keep a grip on Francis and to secure a lever against Charles that, when Gardiner went to the emperor, Henry agreed to a proposal made by the Protestants that they should mediate between him and the French king independently of Charles.

In the middle of 1545, as we have seen, Henry had turned to the North Germans for military aid and met meagre response. By the autumn the Germans had need of him. About mid September a delegation from Hesse, Saxony and Württemberg arrived, having travelled via France and left two of their party there. They came to mediate between Francis and Henry, not out of zeal for the cause of international peace, but to prepare these two kings to aid them against an emperor who was clearly bent on their destruction.[9] Henry received them cordially and quickly decided to turn their embassy to his own ends. They left England in early October, having apparently won the king to their proposal to arbitrate between him and his enemy; shortly afterwards they and their colleagues had manipulated Francis into cooperation and, by 21 November, Paget and Tunstal were sitting in a tent near Guines hard at work with a French delegation.[10] Thus, at the same time as Gardiner was taking part in Anglo-French peace talks under the emperor's guidance at Bruges and discussing a meeting between Henry and Charles, Paget and Tunstal were at another Anglo-French conference by Guines, presided over by Ger-

8. *L.P.*, xx, ii, 714, 801, 999.
9. ibid., 431, 490, 553–5, 647–9, 693, etc.
10. ibid., 809–10, 836, 856.

man Protestants and with a meeting between Henry and
Francis on its agenda.

To their bitter regret, the Lutherans' attempt at mediation failed. After six weeks of wrangling over the future of
Boulogne and the Scots, Henry, who had watched the bargaining minutely, bade his agents come home. The French
had not offered acceptable terms, the emperor was proving
less recalcitrant. The Lutheran intervention had therefore
lost its value, or served its purpose, and the war with France
need not be halted.[11] There had been skirmishing around
Boulogne and Calais on and off throughout the past few
months, and the impetuous Surrey, a few days before, had
been worsted in a sudden engagement with a French force
on its way to succour a fortress overshadowing the English
lines. On 17 January, in conference with the Council, Henry
decided to send the earl of Hertford to France to take over
the lieutenancy and launch a major enterprise in the spring.
He would have 16,000 English, 4,000 Italians and Spaniards,
6,000 Germans and 4,000 horse, while the admiral put to sea
with a fleet of forty-five sail. The counties were to be mustered once more, while to Antwerp, Middelburg, Bremen,
Hamburg and Danzig went English agents in search of
corn, naval stores, munitions, money and mercenaries.[12]

Hertford landed at Calais on 23 March and immediately
set about fortifying the port of Ambleteuse, near Boulogne,
according to a 'plat' (i.e. plan) approved by Henry. The king's
idea was that, from this base, his army should at once move
out to strike at Étaples and Ardres. But this was regarded as
too risky, and after a swift exchange with his lieutenant he
withdrew his plan.[13] His large force lay in wait, therefore,
under the most accomplished English commander; and all
the indications were that the war with France would blaze
up once more when the spring had matured.

Yet within a few weeks Henry had decided to put an end

11. *L.P.*, xx, ii, 1011; xxi, i, 37, 173–4.
12. *L.P.*, xxi, i, 85, 91, 122, 124, 218, 221, 251–2, 272.
13. ibid., 507–8, 527, 577, 586.

to the struggle. It is not clear why he changed his mind. Perhaps the burden of war had crippled him; perhaps the desperate shortage of food which bad harvests brought in their train and his failure to raise victuals and enough munitions on the continent drove him to peace; perhaps Charles's evident intention to strike in Germany and thus ignore his erstwhile ally pulled him up; perhaps it was all of these things which now made imperative the discretion which the Council had urged upon him with great vigour months before and had probably continued to urge thereafter. Since late March a mysterious Venetian merchant, one Francisco Bernardo, had been passing to and fro between England and France carrying proposals for peace talks.[14] On 17 April Paget, Lisle (John Dudley, the future duke of Northumberland) and Hertford were commissioned to treat with envoys from France at Calais or Guines, or on some 'indifferent ground'.[15] Talks started nervously on 24 April. The matters to be settled were formidable. The English demanded vast sums of money, Boulogne and its surrounding area, and a free hand against the Scots; the French could concede none of these. The English relented somewhat, agreed to allow the Scots to be comprehended in the treaty if Queen Mary were delivered to England, or at least hostages for her delivery were forthcoming, and if Boulogne were ransomed by payment of all the arrears of the French pension and 8,000,000 crowns to reimburse English war expenses – an impossible sum. 'Eight millions! quoth they, you speak merrily. All Christendom have not so much money.'[16] The bargaining ran on for weeks, with Henry keeping a detailed watch on every move. By 15 May, after several threats to break off negotiations, the French had come to terms – whereupon Henry intervened from Greenwich requiring his commissioners to go with one Rogers (whom he was sending at once) to check the boun-

14. *L.P.*, xxi, i, 515, 550.
15. ibid., 610.
16. ibid., 749.

daries of the area of Boulogne, as defined by the French and,
in particular, make a 'plat' of the river Dèvre which marked
one extremity and whose source and course he did not
know.[17] Frantic days were spent waiting for this to be done
and for Henry to give his assent to the minutiae of the
treaty. By 3 June he was still not satisfied. Paget wrote
humbly apologizing for his lack of sufficient 'wit' to satisfy
the king and protesting that 'stoutness' had not been wanting. At last, on 6 June, the king finally agreed to the articles
of the treaty (having tightened them up at the last moment
when he heard that the French had shown more 'conformity
than they have used heretofore').[18] Late next day, in a tent
between Ardres and Guines, a treaty of peace between England and France was signed. A formula had been found for
dealing with the Scots, a solution for the future of Boulogne.
England would not make war on the former unless they
broke the peace, which was a feeble article; Boulogne would
be returned to France in eight years' time on payment of
2,000,000 crowns. When the Imperial ambassador saw Henry
six days later and observed that on those terms Boulogne
would remain his for ever, Henry smiled knowingly.[19] He
had won his point. He would keep his 'daughter'.

Outwardly France and England were quickly basking in
warm friendship. Henry stood as godfather (by proxy) to
Francis's grandson within a few days of the signing of the
treaty and, when the French admiral (at last) arrived to
attend Henry's ratification, he was magnificently received.
A few years ago, when the Anglo-Imperial treaty was drawn
up, Charles had refused to accord Henry his full style of
Supreme Head of the Church and had taken refuge behind
a diminutive 'etc.'. When Francis ratified this treaty at Fon-
tainebleau on 1 August 1546, though he pardonably denied
his brother the title of king of France, he swore amity with
the Defender of the Faith and the Supreme Head of the

17. *L.P.*, xxi, i, 849, 877.
18. ibid., 926–7, 974, 989, 995, 1007.
19. ibid., 1058.

Church of England and Ireland without a blush -- and this in the presence of no less than half a dozen cardinals.[20] But behind the screen of gallantry stood a good deal of well-judged suspicion. Months ago, when the peace talks were begun, Henry had told Hertford that, if they did not proceed briskly, he was to encourage the French by smashing Étaples (as he had always wanted him to do).[21] As soon as the Anglo-French treaty was first signed the garrison at Boulogne was reduced and the mercenaries (who had mutinied not long before) sent home, but by September, because the French had continued fortifications nearby, the king was sending reinforcements thither and had decided that Hertford should return to his command. One of the fortresses which the French were building, called Chatillon, would have controlled the harbour of Boulogne. Lord Grey, the English governor there, anxiously inquired what he should do about it. When the Privy Council unanimously ruled that any attempt on it would be an overt breach of the recent peace, Henry, having signed a letter forbidding Grey to act, gave the messenger oral instructions to 'impeach the fortification of Chatillon, and raze it if it be possible'. Grey did so. An armed band slipped out of Boulogne by night and in a few hours had undone two or three months' work. On hearing of Grey's action Henry confronted the Council, saying, 'How say ye, my lords? Chatillon the new fort, is laid as flat as this floor'; and to one of the Council who declared that the man responsible for this deserved to lose his head, he retorted 'that he had rather lose a dozen such heads as his that so judged'.[22] The Anglo-French peace was a loveless, rancorous affair.

In January 1546 Henry had peremptorily put an end to a

20. *L.P.*, xxi, i, 1405. In this letter, Lisle and Tunstal, Henry's commissioners at the ratification, report that six cardinals were present. But the official account in *Rymer*, xv, 98, mentions only five cardinals.
21. *L.P.*, xxi, i, 706–7.
22. *L.P.*, xxi, ii, Intro., xii fl. for a discussion of this story (told by Holinshed).

Lutheran attempt to halt his war with France and sent the mediators home deeply disappointed. Three months later he suddenly picked up once more the threads of Anglo-Lutheran diplomacy. One John Mason, clerk of the Privy Council, was dispatched to the new elector Palatine – who had recently declared for the Reformation – inviting him to send a secret embassy to England to discuss a marriage between Princess Mary and his nephew (who had been in England in March and now travelled back to Heidelberg with Mason), a league of Protestant princes and a conference of learned men from the two countries to draw up a common statement of faith. At the same time as Mason put these proposals to the elector Palatine at Heidelberg, the much-travelled Christopher Mont, who had long been resident agent in Germany, was to invite the landgrave of Hesse to join the holy league which Henry sought to erect.[23] It is difficult to plumb the exact depth of these proposals, but it is clear that they were primarily aimed against France. Now that he had lost the emperor, Henry was ready to offer his hand and money to the Protestants in return for aid against France. In particular he wanted to tap the Palatinate and Hesse for mercenaries and to deny the French these sources of military supply. The grandiose talk about a marriage and a religious agreement was probably merely bait with which to catch lanzknechts and perhaps lure two important German princes into some kind of anti-French engagement. It did not succeed. Neither the landgrave nor the nervous, gouty elector Palatine were willing to commit themselves against France at the very moment when they desperately needed that country to help them fend off the emperor, and Mason and Mont wrung nothing from them save a cautious consent to the idea of a doctrinal concord.[24]

But by the summer of 1546 England and France were at peace, as the landgrave had wished to God they had been when Mont was with him, and Charles had launched his attack on the German Protestants. Hence back to England

23. *L.P.*, xxi, i, 580, 582.   24. ibid., 796–9, 834 (2).

came the same nephew of the elector Palatine who had first stirred Henry to send Mason on his mission,[25] and at the same time there arrived in London one Dr Hans Bruno, a Protestant from Metz who had been a leading figure in the Lutheran attempt at mediation between France and England at Calais during the last winter, and had already paid a lightning trip to Henry in June. He had returned to London in August, apparently with precise proposals from the elector of Saxony for an Anglo-Lutheran *entente*. By the end of the month he was on his way home with the following promise from Henry to the Lutheran princes: if they would send commissioners quickly to England he would enter a defensive 'League Christian' with them against all-comers; if they would send the names of ten or a dozen divines he would select a team to be sent to England to settle the religious differences which still stood between them.[26]

What did this mean? We cannot know. But perhaps it was significant that the first article in the document with which Bruno now dashed home was an offer to the land-grave of an annual pension of 12,000 florins provided that he would supply Henry with troops on demand and forbid mercenaries of any other prince to cross his frontiers. Apparently the king had not changed since he sent Mason to Germany in April. As before, he wanted to exploit the Pro-testants' predicament in order to arm himself against the French. The defensive league which he proposed was to have him as its head and to admit no newcomers without his approval, and thus would exclude those to whom the afflicted Germans looked as a 'natural' ally against the emperor, namely, the French. As for the plans for a doctrinal con-ference, this was something that we have heard too often before to take seriously. Henry wanted troops, not theo-logians. Not surprisingly, the whole affair came to nothing. Moreover, all further appeal to put out a helping hand to the Lutherans was treated by the English with cynicism.

25. *L.P.*, xxi, i, 469, 582, 588, 1463.   26. ibid., 1526.

When Duke Philip of the Palatinate, the elector's brother, who was still in England, approached the English with new proposals for an Anglo-Protestant league Henry, 'to win time', as Gardiner reported, instructed Paget to tell the duke and his companion that nothing could be done until they had produced their commissions; and since these had been lost somewhere in Gravelines on their way hither, it would take weeks before any talking could begin.[27] When the French, following their own devious designs, proposed that Francis and Henry should form a league with the Lutherans, this – probably rightly – was immediately diagnosed as an elaborate trick whereby to recover Boulogne ahead of time, and refused out of hand.[28] By December 1546, when the Protestant cause was in the direst straits, indeed, faced annihilation by the emperor's forces, a new appeal for help came to Henry from Germany. For the third time that year Bruno, accompanied by the chancellor of Saxony, journeyed to London to implore succour. The two envoys visited Francis first and came away with the studied reply that he would do as Henry did in the matter.[29] But Henry had already decided that the French king must enter the league first lest, if he preceded Francis, the latter should 'slip to the emperor',[30] In other words, the fate of the Lutherans was entirely subordinate to England's obsession with the machinations of the perfidious French, and Henry was concerned only with making sure that Bruno and his companion were not used by Francis to double-cross him in much the same way as he wished to double-cross Francis.

What precisely Henry's diplomatic intentions were during the months which ran from the conclusion of the Anglo-French treaty in June 1546 to his death at the end of the following January only Heaven and Henry know. The lies,

27. *St.P.*, i, 881 (*L.P.*, xxi, ii, 256). Gardiner makes it clear that this was a device of Henry's devising.

28. *St.P.*, xi, 329 (*L.P.*, xxi, ii, 289).

29. *L.P.*, xxi, ii, 602, 638.

30. ibid., 619, 743.

the feints, the manoeuvring are so elaborate, the stealth so finely calculated, the evidence now so imperfect that perhaps half a dozen different interpretations may plausibly be put forward. But at least it does seem that, before all else, Henry was jockeying with a king of France whose every step was judged sinister and who was thought to be not only as bent on recovering Boulogne as Henry was on keeping it, but also a constant menace to the successful completion of the unfinished business in Scotland.[31]

Of course, Henry feared Charles too. He disliked the emperor's attack on the Protestants because it cost England an active ally against France, and no less because of the threat that, once Charles had destroyed the German heretics, he might lead a Catholic crusade against the English. Though the emperor swore that he had not played him false, Henry was convinced that he had entered an undertaking with the pope to destroy heresy everywhere. Charles said there was no such treaty, but the king had 'credible advertisement out of Switzerland, Almain, France and Rome itself of the said treaty and an authentic copy of the same' sent to him by the Lutherans. That Henry was 'not named therein expressly' was small comfort, for the Council of Trent was about its work, Luther had just died, Charles's armies were massed for the kill, the French were intriguing with Charles against him and, as the English pointed out to the Germans, had allowed their bishops to attend the papal pseudo-

31. I am not, therefore, wholly in accord with Smith, 'Henry VIII and the Protestant Triumph', *American Hist. Rev.*, lxxi (1966), 1237 ff. – a study of the meaning of the last months of Henry's reign – in which it is argued that, by late 1546, the paramount concern of English policy was to ward off, and prepare against, a Catholic attack led by the emperor. Professor Smith believes that Henry now feared, above all else, that Charles would turn against England once he had dealt with the Lutherans and that the English plans for a league with France and the Germans were therefore of primary importance. I do not deny that Charles was a worry, but I believe that France and Scotland probably still worried him even more. However, the evidence is so tangled that Professor Smith's interpretation may well be the better one.

Council at Trent.[32] But how seriously Henry expected that
the Catholic world would or could turn on him is difficult to
gauge. In public he complained bitterly of Charles's doings
and took pains to lie to the Imperial ambassador about the
purpose of one of Bruno's visits, saying that he had come
merely to report on the emperor's campaign in Germany.[33]
But at the same time he could arouse the French ambassador's suspicion by receiving an emissary from Charles with
especial cordiality and remark laconically to the latter, about
Charles's war, 'Well, God grant that good will come of
it.'[34]

The really alarming thing was what Charles might allow
the French to accomplish rather than what he threatened
directly himself. Henry's supreme fear was that Francis
might yet 'slip to the emperor' behind his back, or be won
over by an offer of Milan and leave him isolated.[35] The
happiest solution of the problem would have been to have
had France fling herself against the Habsburgs once more,
on the side of the Protestants, and thus leave him free to
go about his own business undisturbed. Alternatively, as he
secretly proposed to the Imperialists, he was ready to mediate between Charles and the Protestants and then join the
emperor in a war against the French.[36] Thus by the time
death overtook the king, the English were entertaining an
embassy from Germany and apparently talking boldly of
joining with France and the oppressed Lutherans against
the emperor,[37] and at the same time studiously working for
a renewal of that alliance against France which Gardiner
had tried to renovate during the previous winter and which
had been the foundation-stone of English policy since 1542.

32. *St.P.*, i, 857 (*L.P.*, xxi, ii, 27). Cf. *L.P.*, xxi, ii, 262, 315, 546.
33. *L.P.*, xxi, ii, 27.
34. *Sp. Cal.*, viii, 331.
35. *L.P.*, xxi, ii, 619, 725.
36. ibid., 546.
37. On 25 January 1547 the French ambassador could report that
Paget had told the Protestant embassy that England would join a
'league defensive' – if the king of France did likewise. ibid., 743.

Meanwhile Henry was massing forces against Scotland. Despite what happened on the Continent, England's 'rough wooing' of the Scots, her bloody flailing of a neighbour who had disowned treaties and refused to hand over the young queen to England's safe-keeping, continued. In September 1545 Hertford had led a violent raid from the East and Middle Marches which, it was jubilantly claimed, wrecked seven religious houses, sixteen castles and nearly 250 villages. Shortly before this, Henry had received the self-styled lord of the Isles and the earl of Lennox at court and planned an invasion of the Highlands which was to be launched from Dublin, under their leadership and with the king's backing. The expedition set out from Ireland in November and failed lamentably. But between then and the following July there were, on average, about half a dozen raids and incidents on the Borders.[38] Though Scotland was comprehended in the Anglo-French peace of June 1546, Henry did not relent in his determination to have his way. By November of that year he was rating Scottish ambassadors who had come to his court with charges of having broken the peace and so convinced them that he would attack once more that they immediately appealed to France for aid.[39] Henry may have been anxious about the emperor's victories, but through December and January of 1546–7 he was sufficiently sure of himself to be piling up forces in preparation for another assault against a Scotland which he had already savaged and mishandled.[40]

Such was some of the nervous, vigilant thrusting and parrying which occupied the last months of his life. But there remains one final ingredient to be added to this account thereof. In early August 1546 a man called Guron Bertano arrived in England to discuss terms for nothing less than a reconciliation of Henry to Rome. He came from a pope anxious to exploit the new Anglo-French peace and

38. *L.P.*, xxi, i, 1279.
39. *L.P.*, xxi, ii, 443.
40. ibid., 444, 675, 679, 702.

(perhaps) to secure some English representation at the Council of Trent. Once more, apparently, Paul hoped that the prodigal son might be won back, and was ready to accommodate everything that Henry had done – the divorce, the dissolution of the monasteries – if the king would but submit to the papal primacy.[41] Bertano received rather short shrift from his hosts. Henry told him that he would send English delegates to a council summoned by princes, say, in France (or did he merely demand that there should be a small, international conference of delegates from the Christian princes, a subsidiary to the Council of Trent? We cannot be sure);[42] and after waiting over seven weeks for a reply from Rome to Henry's very guarded response, Bertano was told to leave the country at once.[43] But he was received in audience by Henry and had two interviews with Paget. He was in the country nearly two months and initially had been optimistic about his chances of success. His embassy is a curious, intriguing episode. If Henry never intended to respond to him any more than he responded to the Lutherans, it is interesting that Bertano should have been able even to come, let alone to speak and to stay so long.

Would that Henry's diplomacy alone were difficult to unravel. Alas there is scarcely an event in the last year or so of his reign which is not enigmatic.

On Christmas Eve 1545 Henry came down to the Parliament house for the last time in his life to deliver the speech of prorogation, normally the work of a chancellor, and give the royal assent to the session's bills. He made a splendid, rolling oration which began as a vote of thanks to his loving subjects for their generosity – they had just, very reluc-

41. *L.P.*, xxi, i, 1215, 1309.

42. Paget told the French ambassador the former; Bertano told him the latter, ibid., 1412.

43. *L.P.*, xxi, ii, 192, 194, 203. Bertano says that he sent Henry's reply to Rome and that the latter's long, inexplicable delay in replying caused Henry to declare that he had been duped, and to order the papal envoy to depart.

tantly assigned the chantry lands to him[44] – and ended as a sermon on charity. He came to deliver an appeal for fraternal love and unity to a people stricken with religious discord. He blamed first the prelates who were now sitting before him, 'you, the fathers and preachers of the spirituality', who 'preach one against another, teach one contrary to another, inveigh one against another, without charity or discretion'. 'Some,' he said, 'be too stiff in their "mumpsimus", others be too busy and curious in their new "sumpsimus"' and sow doubt and discord among simple folk, who look to the clergy 'for light' and find only 'darkness'. 'Yet you of the temporalty,' he went on, moving the accusing finger round the assembly to point at the lay peers and the speaker and commons who crowded the back of the room, 'be not clean and unspotted of envy; for you rail on bishops, speak slanderously of priests, and rebuke the taunt preachers.' If the Scriptures have been given to the laity in their own tongue (but, since 1543, not for those under the degree of gentleman to read) this was 'only to inform your own conscience, and to instruct your children and family', not 'of your own fantastical opinions and vain expositions' to usurp the duty of judging what is truth and what is error – which is a function 'to us ... committed by God'. 'I am very sorry to know and hear,' sighed the Supreme Head, 'how unreverently that most precious jewel, the word of God, is disputed, rhymed, sung, and jangled in every alehouse and tavern ... of this I am sure, that charity was never so faint amongst you and virtuous and godly living was never less used, nor was God himself amongst Christians ever less reverenced, honoured or served.'[45] Such was Henry's last message to Parliament. It was a magnificent oration – of the kind that his daughter Elizabeth would emulate so well. It skilfully distributed its reprimand to every section of the assembly, so that none

44. According to Petre, the bill 'escaped narrowly' being 'dashed' and was 'driven over to the last hour, and yet then passed only by division of the house'. *L.P.*, xx, ii, 1030.

45. *Hall*, 864 ff.

could feel unduly hurt. It brought tears to many eyes – the
tears of loving, humble subjects.

He appealed for charity and godly unity, and spoke in the
loftiest tones about duty to sacred truth; but Caesar himself
dealt with the things of God with easy opportunism. Several
bills designed to recover that religious concord which he had
done so much to disrupt were on the agenda of the Parliament just prorogued – including one aimed against heretical
literature. At the beginning of the session, this and presumably the others had been 'set earnestly forward'. But the
Protestant Bruno, then about the business of bringing
France and England to peace, remonstrated with Paget, the
English commissioner at the peace conference, that this
legislation would encourage 'the common enemy', the pope,
as Bruno unfashionably called him. Paget wrote anxiously
to Henry to know how to reply to this.[46] The next thing we
hear is a message to Paget from Petre, then with the king,
announcing that 'the bill of books ... is finally dashed in the
common house, as are divers others, whereat I hear no[t]
that his majesty is much miscontent'.[47] Whether Henry had
signalled to the Commons that the bills which had been
hitherto 'set earnestly forward' were to be 'dashed' we cannot tell. The near-trouncing which the Chantries bill received suggests that, as Henry complained to them, the
Commons were in a surly mood. But he was not 'miscontent'
to have the attempt to discipline the 'fantastical opinions
and vain expositions' of his people pushed aside. In the following June, however, a proclamation appeared renewing
the ban on heretical vernacular books and imposing fresh
restrictions on printers – by which time 'Henry could diplomatically afford to be orthodox'.[48] In late 1545 he had
appointed Cranmer and two other bishops 'to peruse certain
books of service' which he presented to them, that is, to push
ahead with further liturgical changes. In January 1546 the
committee presented some minor recommendations – that

        46. *L.P.*, xx, ii, 985.   47. ibid., 1030.
        48. Smith, art. cit., 1257.

bell-ringing on Hallow E'en, the covering of statues in Lent and kneeling to the uncovered cross on Palm Sunday should cease. Henry accepted the suggestion that these 'enormities' should be suppressed. He went further. As we have seen, he commanded that there should be no kneeling to the cross at any time and that the yet 'greater abuse' of 'creeping to the cross' on Good Friday should 'cease from henceforth and be abolished'.[49] But scarcely had he raised his hand against these 'superstitions' than news came from Stephen Gardiner, then on that complex embassy to the emperor which has been discussed a short while ago, that he was making progress in his negotiations with the emperor; whereupon the king hastily countermanded his order. 'I am now otherways resolved,' he said when Denny brought him the letters which were to go out to Canterbury and York commanding the changes; for the moment 'any other innovation, change or alteration, either in religion or ceremony' must be set aside, even the abolition of enormities offensive to God and man, lest the emperor be alarmed and temporal advantages lost.[50]

Seven months later, in August 1546, Henry was standing in a pavilion specially erected at Hampton Court to celebrate the ratification of the Anglo-French peace treaty, leaning his huge, sick body on Cranmer and the French admiral, when he made a statement which astounded the archbishop and has led to much discussion ever since. He spoke about the decision which had been made not only to banish the usurped power of the bishop of Rome out of the kingdom of France, but to change 'the mass in both the realms into a communion service'. Henry was not now suggesting these things for the first time. Cranmer, who told the story in bated breath a few years later, when the Mass had at last been abolished in England, clearly understood that the two kings 'were thoroughly and firmly resolved in their behalf' already, that they had agreed to carry out these

49. *Miscellaneous Writings etc. of Thomas Cranmer*, p. 414 (*L.P.*, xxi, i, 109, 110).

50. *Foxe*, v, 562.

changes within six months and that they intended 'to exhort the emperor to do the like in Flanders and other his
countries and seignories'.[51]

When he spoke thus was Henry merely playing with
words or had he really decided to strike at the second tap-
root of the old religion, the sacrifice of the Mass? Should
we dismiss this story as further evidence of the deviousness
of his diplomacy[52] during his last months of life or was Foxe
right when he said that, had the king lived a little longer,
'most certain it is and to be signified to all posterity, that
his full purpose was to have repurged the state of the
Church, and to have gone through with the same, so that
he would not have left one Mass in all England'?[53]

Those who deny that Henry decided at this late hour to
plunge into such radical novelty and to do now to the Mass
what would eventually be done in his son's reign, can present
a formidable case. There is no sign of this intention before
the king's conversation with the admiral and no certain
evidence that he set about realizing it afterwards. Had
Cranmer not told his story years later no one could have
thought, as the archbishop himself said, that Henry 'had
been so forward' in the 'establishing of sincere religion'. In
the previous years he seems to have been assiduous in his
Mass-going; and his will provided for the customary profusion of Requiems. Moreover, in June 1546 one Dr Edward
Crome, an *enfant terrible* of the London clergy who had
already been in trouble with his ecclesiastical authorities no
less than four times since 1529 (and had on one occasion
been rescued by Henry himself), brought a spectacular series
of recantations to a close when he renounced his disbelief
in the sacrificial character of the Mass in a sermon at Paul's
Cross given before Bonner, Wriothesley, Norfolk and many
others.[54] This last attack on the vivacious Dr Crome, like the

51. *Foxe*, v, 568 f.
52. As Professor Smith argues forcefully (echoing others) in the
article already referred to.
53. *Foxe*, v, 692.   54. ibid., App. xvi (last document).

other heresy-hunts of these years, was not just an attack on one man but a ferreting out of a network of like-minded mischief-makers. It brought several to the Tower; it was supervised, if not spurred forward by the king.[55] Though Crome escaped surprisingly lightly, it may well be thought incredible that, at this very moment, Henry was prepared to deny what Crome had denied and assert what Crome had just been made to recant.

The belief that Henry was indeed about to plunge into Protestantism at the end of his reign, that Cranmer's story of what he said to the French admiral is, after all, to be taken as a momentous advance in the royal theology, is commonly buttressed by the following evidence: that the two men who were chiefly concerned with the education of the young Prince Edward, John Cheke and Richard Cox, were themselves of strong Protestant persuasion; that in the last few weeks of his life Henry struck down or thrust aside the leading conservatives, Norfolk and Gardiner, and excluded them and such as Bonner from the Council of Regency appointed in his will to administer the kingdom during his son's minority; that that Council was dominated by Protestants like Hertford and Dudley. If it was really Henry's intention that England should cling to the half-hearted doctrinal settlement which he had set up, the argument runs, then he set about it in a curiously inept way. Clearly he did not intend this. Clearly by the end of his reign he was changing his mind.

But this evidence is suspect. Cox and Cheke were celebrated humanists, deeply committed to Erasmian pietism and the cause of learning, but probably not yet to the Reformed faith, at least not overtly so. Dr Cox had taken a leading part in hounding those two arch-heretics, Crome and Anne Askew, and like Cheke's, his great days as a 'special advocate of Christ' lay in the future. Though their pupil eventually grew into a solid Protestant, during Henry's

55. *L.P.*, xxi, i, 790, 810–11 show the king being closely involved in Crome's affair – at least in a supervisory capacity.

reign these two men were obedient servants of the regime,
devoted to the cause of Greek and humanism.[56] Secondly,
the sudden assault on the Howards and the dismissal of
Gardiner from the inner circle of royal councillors – both
of which events are surrounded by a good deal of mystery –
cannot easily be seen as a deliberate purging of the Council
of Catholic influence. Conversely, the advance of such as
Hertford and Dudley may well have been due much more to
their loyalty and ability and, in the case of Hertford, to the
fact that he was uncle of the heir to the throne, than to their
religious allegiance. They were rising stars. They had
rendered the king notable service in war. Hertford had been
his leading captain since Suffolk's death in mid 1545 and
would have had the strongest claim to preferment, even if he
had not already been cast for primacy of place as future
royal uncle. If the Council of Regency which Henry left to
his son was possessed of a strange admixture of theological
hues, it is arguable that this merely reflected the complexity
of Henry's own allegiance; it is equally arguable that Henry
allowed the Protestant presence in the Council to expand not
so much for what it would positively do but primarily to
withstand a 'Catholic' counter-attack bent on undoing the
Royal Supremacy and betraying the cause.[57] We easily think
of Protestantism as offering the major threat to the Henrician settlement. But to Henry himself it may have been
popery, scotched but not killed, still present in high places
and waiting for him to die, which was the more obvious
danger. As well as this, the situation was so full of impon-
derables, the sands shifted so easily that, as the king peered
into the future, he may well have thought it prudent to
bequeath his son a group of men whose very variety would

56. See Smith, art. cit., 1243 ff. for a full survey of this matter.
57. This is a factor which is often overlooked. The fear that
Gardiner and those like him would throw off the Royal Supremacy
once Henry's weight was removed was both real and plausible. It
may well be that Henry was much more concerned to hold off a
resurgence of popery than to prevent a 'Protestant triumph'.

produce an equilibrium or stalemate – assuming, of course, that it was Henry's hand which drew up that fateful will.

In short, it seems prudent to dismiss the story of Henry's decision to abandon the Mass as part of the profusion of diplomatic chicanery of his last months and to reject Foxe's prognosis of what Henry would have done had he lived a little longer as the babbling of a hagiographer. Yet, a lingering doubt remains. Recently Henry had been picking at his religious settlement. It was he who, in late 1544, commissioned Cranmer and two fellow-bishops to 'peruse' the service books and he who added 'creeping to the cross' to the list of forbidden ceremonies which they drew up.[58] Though the royal decree prohibiting these ancient usages was halted by the demands of diplomacy, Henry sent a message to Cranmer to 'take patience herein, and forbear until we may espy a more apt and convenient time for that purpose'.[59] The latest attack on superstition was merely postponed until 'a more apt and convenient time', not abandoned. Shortly before this, Parliament had agreed to the dissolution of chantries. The act which passed sentence upon them had a financial purpose without doubt; but Dr Crome saw that to destroy chantries was at least to prepare the way to cracking the base of the Mass, and maybe Henry's mind was tracing the same course. The attack on the monasteries, a no less fiscal operation, had first been announced in 1536 as an attempt to weed out corruption and purify religion; it ended as an assault on monasticism as an institution and a denial of the theology thereof.[60] If chantries were likewise to be swept off the face of the land would it not have been expedient (because logical) to sweep away also the theology on

58. *Miscellaneous Writings etc. of Thomas Cranmer*, 414.

59. *Foxe*, v, 562.

60. As Philip Hughes pointed out in *Reformation in England*, i, 323. When the greater monasteries surrendered, the monks thereof denounced monasticism as merely a collection of 'dumb . . . papistical ceremonies', and explicitly denied that it was a way to Christian perfection. See e.g. *Rymer*, xiv, 611 ff.

which they stood? Is it possible that the chantries were not
now dissolved, despite the act, not only because the commissioners' work of surveying them had only just begun,
but also because that theology had not been discarded and
that, in August 1546, Henry was feeling his way towards
the moment, 'within half a year after', as Cranmer reported,
when the Mass and the chantries[61] might fall together and
financial necessity thus once more be the mother of theological invention? That Henry should have allowed Crome
to be harried shortly before he himself uttered that doctor's
very heresy, that he should have dealt so cynically with the
German Lutherans soon after he himself undertook to do to
the Mass exactly what Luther had done to it, and that he
should have pursued sacramentaries up to the last month of
his life does not make it impossible that what he said to the
French admiral was serious. The Supreme Head denied
theological initiative to his subjects, not to himself – and
Crome, as it happened, escaped lightly. Henry was his own
master, and if he had now lurched towards Lutheranism he
would not have seen his action as deriving from, or committing himself to, any moral allegiance to the cause of the
Gospel. Finally, the offence of the sacramentaries was their
denial of the Real Presence and this, as yet, stood firm in
Henry's mind.

Of course, when Henry said what he said in the pavilion
at Hampton Court this may have been no more than a piece
of kite-flying by an arch-tactician in the diplomatic game.
But it is not easy to see exactly what merely diplomatic
advantage he was seeking. If he wanted to bind Francis to
him why should it have been proposed to persuade the
emperor to join in the venture? True, it was suggested that
Charles should be invited to follow Francis in repudiating
the pope and gutting the Mass, or else the two kings 'would
break off from him'. This may support the thesis that Henry
was wanting to draw Francis towards him against Charles,
but it should be remembered that the emperor's alarming

61. And the doctrine of Purgatory, presumably.

victories did not come until the winter of that year and that, though Henry may already have been anxious about Imperial success, in all probability he still saw Francis as the major menace. Furthermore, it may be remarked that, even if Henry sought only diplomatic advantage from introducing radical change in the religion of his people this would not necessarily mean that the proposal was not seriously made. It was not so much that Henry kept 'religious conscience and diplomatic necessity' apart[62] as that the first was subservient to the second. Henry's religion could be moulded to any shape, as prestige, profit and power required. To few men did religion matter more than to Henry; but probably mainly because he could melt down the things that were God's and so easily imprint his own image on the newly-minted coin.

It is tentatively proposed, therefore, that Henry was seriously considering the momentous step which so astonished Cranmer when he heard about it that afternoon at Hampton Court. Perhaps the king's decision was a concomitant to the attack on the chantries and perhaps also as a means to draw Francis towards him. The chantries and Paris would together be worth the Mass. Perhaps the proposal had been put to the French to sound their reaction to, or gain support for, what he intended to do in his own kingdom. It is true that there was no clear sign in the next few months that Henry was preparing to carry out this great change; but Hertford and Dudley were known to be Protestants, they were indisputably advancing in power, and both the Imperial and the French ambassadors predicted that when Parliament reassembled in 1547 it would have a major agenda, including ecclesiastical business.[63] Ambassadors were often wrong in their forecasts. But by the time Parliament had found its

62. Smith, art. cit., 1263.
63. *L.P.*, xxi, ii, 546, 621, Van der Delft, in the first of these two documents, predicted that Parliament would deal with the proceeds of chantries. What this could mean is not clear. But at least he thought that something connected with chantries would be discussed.

feet, it would have been about 'half a year after' the strange
episode at Hampton Court.

By the 1540s religious heterodoxy had noticeably ceased
to be merely an affair of pockets of Lollard weavers and
husbandmen and merchants, or of individual clerics, but had
penetrated and silently taken root in every level of society,
including the Court. It had acquired powerful lay patrons;
like Puritanism and Catholic recusancy later, it had won
influential women to its cause who, more than any other
persons perhaps, could allow it to come out of the universities
and the avant-garde London churches to take possession of
lay, domestic life. It was probably because they perceived
how heterodoxy had thus advanced that such as Gardiner
launched a series of famous heresy-hunts during the last
years of Henry's reign which were aimed not merely at
rooting out individuals but uncovering the whole network
of friends, patrons and disciples who lay behind them. Thus
in 1543 the Protestant Thomas Becon, a man who had
connection with Thomas Lord Wentworth and several
gentry families of Kent, was run to earth and forced to
spend the rest of his life moving around the homes of Protestant gentry in the Midlands; at about the same time
Cranmer himself was nearly brought down; in July of that
year, Dr John London, a former visitor of the monasteries,
unleashed a major purge of the chapel royal of St George's
Windsor which ended with five members of the king's Privy
Chamber and the wives of three being implicated.[64] Three
years later, in 1546, Dr Crome was arrested and, under
Wriothesley's guidance, betrayed the names of allies at
Court, in the City and the country; and shortly afterwards
began the final ordeal of Anne Askew, who had been
arrested first in the previous year and now, after torture
administered, Foxe says, by Wriothesley and Rich in person,
went to her death at Smithfield. Anne was a sacramentary,

64. McConica, op. cit., 218 ff. for a good recent assessment of
several of these events.

but her real interest to Gardiner, Bonner and the others was her association with my Lady of Hertford and Lady Denny – and possibly other high-ranking women at Court, like the countesses of Suffolk and Sussex. Anne's persecution allowed orthodoxy to do what it had perhaps been preparing to do since the Windsor trials, namely, close in and pounce upon the knot of vipers at Court who were gathered around the queen herself.

It had become the habit of the godly queen, Catherine Parr, to hold daily Scripture classes with her ladies in waiting and, especially during Lent, to listen with them to sermons by her chaplains. Moreover, since her husband approved of all this, it was her wont to discuss religion with him also; and such was her charm and the esteem in which he held her, Foxe assures us, that a hot-tempered king who would allow few others to express any opinions on religious matters which were not his own gladly endured her passionate pleading with him that, 'as he had, to the glory of God and his eternal fame, begun a good and godly work in banishing that monstrous idol of Rome, so he would thoroughly perfect and finish the same, cleansing and purging the Church of England clean from the dregs thereof' (including perhaps the sacrifice of the Mass?). Eventually, as declining health robbed him both of mobility and some of his previous good nature, he ceased visiting her and, instead, she would come to him, but infrequently and only when either he sent for her or she judged the hour propitious to resume her crusade to have him 'zealously to proceed in the reformation of the Church'. One day when she was by him, somewhat to her amazement, he suddenly halted her flow (though he did so with 'a loving countenance') and, having rather pointedly changed the subject for a few minutes, let her take her leave. Gardiner had been present throughout the meeting, and after the queen's departure Henry turned to him and said, 'A good hearing it is, when women become such clerks; and a thing much to my comfort, to come in mine old days to be taught by my wife.' The bishop had long

wanted to quash this dangerous woman and, having opined
on the unseemliness of a woman presuming to impose her
views on the Supreme Head 'so malapertly', went on to
promise that, if the king gave him permission, he and others
of the Council would lay before him such evidence of
Catherine's treasonous heresy that 'his majesty would easily
perceive how perilous a matter it is to cherish a serpent
within his own bosom'. Henry at least pretended to be convinced by Gardiner's words and gave permission for 'certain
articles' to be drawn up against the queen; whereupon the
bishop and his friends quickly went to work to ferret out
the heresy that festered in her entourage, planning to charge
her sister and two of her Privy Chamber first, search their
rooms and coffers, and then carry Catherine off to the Tower
by night – to which plan Henry seemingly gave his assent.

Even as her accusers closed in on her and drew up a bill of
articles against her (which Henry signed), Catherine continued to visit Henry and plead with him to undertake
further reformation of the Church. One evening, after she
had been with him, Henry poured out complaints against
her to his physician, one Dr Wendy, and told him the whole
story of the plot against her, but bound him to secrecy.
Then, shortly afterwards, events took a strange turn. The
bill of articles fell 'from the bosom of one of the aforesaid
councillors' and was immediately brought to the queen.
When she read its contents and saw the king's signature
she collapsed. The king sent his doctors to her, including
Wendy, who broke the secrecy imposed on him and promised
the queen that, if she humbly submitted to her husband, he
would surely restore her to favour. Henry visited Catherine
soon after and the following evening she came to him to
seek pardon. Reverently and abjectly she threw herself on
his mercy, submitting herself 'to your majesty's wisdom, as
my only anchor, supreme head and governor here in earth,
next under God, to lean unto'; whereupon Henry replied,
'Not so by St Mary, you are become a doctor, Kate, to instruct us (as we take it), and not to be instructed or directed

by us.' And when Catherine disowned so 'preposterous' a purpose as that she, a mere wife, should presume to instruct her husband and professed that she would ever remain obedient in all matters of religion to her king, and had only talked theology to him to ease him during his infirmity, Henry made the famous response: 'And is it even so, sweetheart, and tended your argument to no worse end? Then perfect friends we are now again as ever at any time heretofore.' Next day Henry and Catherine, and the three ladies whom Gardiner intended to trap at the same time as he undid the queen, were taking the air in the garden of Whitehall when the lord chancellor arrived with some forty men to carry off the victims to the Tower. It was not Catherine who came to grief. Wriothesley knelt before the king to explain his coming. What he said was not overheard. But Henry broke in with 'Knave! arrant knave! beast! and fool!' and sent him and his train away forthwith.[65]

It is exceedingly difficult to know what to make of this incident. That Catherine was of Protestant persuasion seems beyond doubt. Gardiner and Wriothesley were so sure of themselves, Foxe was so confident of her godliness and in an only slightly later tradition so certain of her close association with Anne Askew that we must allow that her indisputable Erasmianism had a strongly heretical flavour. Whether or not Henry was ready at one point to throw her to the wolves and then changed his mind, whether or not he had all along only feigned assent to Gardiner's conspiracy, we cannot know. But why did he indulge in such elaborate subterfuge? Was it to teach Gardiner and the others a macabre lesson, or to frighten Catherine, or to break her evident independence of mind? Did it spring from that strange preference for the devious which was apparently now a trait of the man?

Something similar had happened three years before when Cranmer was under attack. Henry had been told that the archbishop was a heretic and had agreed that he should be seized at the Council table, like Cromwell, and taken to the

65. All this story comes from *Foxe*, v, 553 ff.

Tower. But that same night he summoned Cranmer to
Whitehall to warn him of the plot and explain that, once
he was in prison, 'three or four false knaves will soon be
procured to witness against you and condemn you'. Having
thus revealed a true insight into the machinations of his servants, Henry gave Cranmer his ring and told him to produce
it when he was arrested and appeal to be heard by the king
himself. Next day, when the Council pounced, Cranmer did
as the king had bidden and scattered his enemies, who, when
they then repaired to the king, were savagely rebuked.[66] Perhaps Henry had at least learned something from the fall of
Cromwell about the ways of his servants, but because he took
pleasure in intrigue or in confounding others, neither now
nor later was he capable, apparently, of the simple and direct
action of stamping out conspiracy when he first heard of it.
Maybe Cranmer and Catherine profited from this strange
manner of proceeding because they enjoyed his esteem and
affection; maybe because he could thereby gratify his taste
for circuitous stealth and humiliating his ministers. However, 'the greatest heretic in Kent', as Henry had jovially
described Cranmer,[67] survived; so did the greatest heretic at
Court; and so for a time did Gardiner. The latter had had a
desperate moment in 1544 when his nephew and secretary,
Germayne Gardiner, had suddenly been executed for upholding the papal primacy. Henry had prepared to strike at
the uncle in the belief that Germayne would never have
been so stiff in his treason without his encouragement. But,
while the vultures in the Council, led by Suffolk, circled glee-
fully over the Tower, a friend in the Privy Chamber sent
warning to Gardiner, who thereupon sped to the king's side
and, as could so easily happen, suddenly redeemed all just
when he seemed to be finally broken. Once more, when the
expectant victors assembled to arrest their quarry, they
found that the king had deserted them and that the
tenacious bishop had reinstated himself.[68]

66. *Foxe*, vii, 24 ff.; Ridley, op. cit., 236.
67. Ridley, 235.   68. *Foxe*, v, 526.

These were years of ruthless jockeying by ruthless men. But the picture which has sometimes been presented of Henry as a coarse, capricious tyrant striking wildly at his servants is wrong. The real bloodthirstiness was probably to be found among the contending factions in the Council who were locked in a power-struggle in which neither side had yet secured victory because neither side could capture and hold an inscrutable, volatile king. Henry remained his own master, playing with his puppets with as much devious skill as he did with the Lutherans and Francis and Charles, dashing the hopes of one group after another just when they thought they were about to taste victory, but, until violence fell unexpectedly on the Howards, refusing to draw blood himself. These were perilous times for a servant of the king; but this was not entirely the king's fault.

By the autumn of 1546 Hertford and Dudley were manifestly the leading figures in the Council. By late December, when the king fell so grievously ill that it must have been clear that the end was at hand, the Council sometimes met in Hertford's house;[69] and on the thirteenth of that month Henry Howard earl of Surrey, and his father the duke of Norfolk, after he had been stripped of his staff of office and his garter, were taken to the Tower.

The sudden assault on the great dynasty which had given so much to the king and whose history had been so entwined in the story of Henry's reign resists a definitive explanation. The rowdy, swaggering soldier-poet Surrey had marred his reputation in January of this year when he mishandled an engagement with the French outside Boulogne,[70] and had compounded his error subsequently by blandly asking that his wife should join him, a suggestion which Henry struck down with the retort that the tense situation at Boulogne was 'unmeet for women's imbecilities'.[71] Surrey had already been relieved of his command and was shortly back at Court – only to find himself summoned before the Council on a charge of 'indiscreetly' disputing of Scripture with other

69. E.g., *L.P.*, xxi, ii, 605.   70. *L.P.*, xxi, i, 33, 49.   71. ibid., 356.

young courtiers. Apparently he was caught in the purge of
Dr Crome's friends and the royal entourage which eventually fastened on to the queen herself; and though he seems
to have escaped with a warning, another courtier ended in
the Tower. Surrey had already been in trouble for eating
meat during Lent, he had been friendly with a notorious
sacramentary, George Blagge, and his brother, William
Howard, had been before the Council because of his suspect
views on religion. Though he may have had a particular dis-
like for Dudley, his eventual destruction can hardly have
been a 'Protestant' conspiracy against the conservative faction.

He died for treason, not heresy. He, the grandson of the
duke of Buckingham and descendant of Edward III, had
boasted of his Plantagenet blood and declared that, when
Henry died, his father would be 'meetest to rule the prince';
he had spoken truculently about the men of vile birth, 'foul
churls' like Cromwell and Wolsey, who had held power
about the king and ever sought the destruction of the
nobility; he had planned, it was said, to kill the Council,
depose the king and seize the young prince; he had suggested
to his sister that she should catch the king's eye and try to
become the royal mistress; finally – and this was the charge
on which he was tried and found guilty of high treason –
he had dared to quarter his own arms with those of Edward
the Confessor.[72]

Meanwhile, as interrogation built up the story of Surrey's
dangerous ambition and arrogance, ugly hints were made
about secret nocturnal visits by his father to the French ambassador Marillac in bygone days, and of letters written by
Surrey to him when the king was ill; and once he, too, was
in the Tower, Norfolk was being questioned about a secret
cipher he had used and about his loyalty to the Royal
Supremacy.[73]

At first sight, the son seems to have dragged down the
father; but it may well be that it was the duke, rather than

72. *L.P.*, xxi, ii, 555. Cf. ibid., 533, 546.   73. ibid., 554.

the earl, who was the primary quarry. Whether the attack came from a 'suspicious, ruthless and fearful old man who was determined to be master of his own kingdom even unto the grave',[74] or from a faction in the Council, headed perhaps by the prince's uncle, is very difficult to discover. But the interrogations of the duke in the Tower seem to have tried to pin popery on to him and to implicate him in Gardiner's strange dealings at Ratisbon in 1541, when undoubtedly there was some talk of 'a way to be taken between his Majesty and the bishop of Rome'. It is possibly significant that the duke's estates were not distributed among his opponents in the Council; but it is surely more significant that, having escaped execution by a hair's breadth thanks to Henry's own death, the duke was kept in the Tower during the next reign. This was a man whom, he dolefully confessed, Wolsey had hated and Cromwell tried for years to undo, whom the duke of Buckingham, his father-in-law, said at his trial he hated more than any other man, whose sister's husband had said he would like to run through with a dagger, who was hated by his two nieces, Anne Boleyn and Catherine Howard, who was hated by a wife (his second) from whom he had separated and whom his servants bound and sat on until she spat blood.[75] As he lay in the Tower and looked back over his grim life he rejoiced in his unfailing loyalty to his king amidst all these bitter passions; and, in truth, it is not easy to see what wrong Henry could have found in him. On the other hand it is not hard to imagine that there were several among the Council who hated him as heartily as had done many others who were better men than they were.

Henry's bullock body was a magnificent piece of nature's handiwork and, for the first thirty-five years or so of his life, had served him better than anyone sprung of such unpromising stock, exposed to so hazardous a thing as Tudor medicine and addicted to such dangerous sports as he was,

74. Smith, art. cit., 1243.   75. *L.P.*, xxi, ii, 554; xv, 443.

could reasonably have expected. Though in early 1514 he
had an attack of smallpox, and in 1521 the first of perhaps
several bouts of malaria, he showed no sign of the tuber-
culosis which carried off his father, his brother Arthur, his
illegitimate son the duke of Richmond, and his legitimate
son and heir Edward; and he never succumbed to the epi-
demics of either plague or sweating sickness which frequently stalked his reign. Three times, however, his immense
appetite for violent sports nearly cost him his life. First in
March 1524, the duke of Suffolk came within an ace of killing him in a tilt. Henry had forgotten to lower his visor and
thundered along the barrier on his charger heedless of the
warning shouts of onlookers, until the duke's lance struck
his helmet, shattered and filled the king's headpiece with
splinters; had it struck his face, it would have killed him.
It was an horrific moment, but Henry, though presumably
badly bruised, laughed off the incident and ran six more
courses.[76] Next year, while he was hawking near Hitchin, he
tried to leap over a wide ditch with a pole when the pole
broke and threw him head-first into the mud. Had not a
swift footman pulled his head out of the mud in which it
was stuck fast 'he had been drowned'.[77] But apart from the
headaches from which he suffered a good deal, especially in
the late twenties, no harm seems to have come of these bad
knocks – and the headaches may well have been due to
catarrh rather than them.

Nine years later came his third and most serious mishap.
One day in January 1536 he was running at the lists at
Greenwich when he was unhorsed by an opponent and fell
to the ground in his heavy armour with the mailed horse on
top of him.[78] He lay unconscious for two hours. For a cor-
pulent man of forty-four to fall thus was obviously very
dangerous. Whether it caused any brain damage is doubtful,
not least because it is difficult to see the deterioration of
character which, as has sometimes been argued, set in thereafter. Henry was not notably more cruel afterwards than he

76. *Hall*, 632.   77. ibid., 641.   78. *Sp. Cal.*, v, ii, 21.

had been before, nor more aggressive or appetitive. The tortuous and often moody hulk of the 1540s may seem a long way from the splendid youth of 1509, but it is very arguable that the first descended easily from the second and that there is no need to import the explanation of some sudden change of personality wrought by this fall. But the latter did affect him physically. Though he continued to ride and walk a great deal, he no longer rode to the hounds and, instead, shot from a stand or butt the game which beaters had brought to hand.

It was probably in 1528 that Henry was first afflicted with the ulcer on his leg (eventually on both legs) which was to plague him until he died. Some have thought that that ulcer was the result of syphilis, but since there is no sign of his ever having received the established treatment for this well-known secondary symptom of the disease, and no sign of other symptoms in him or in his children, it is more probable that the affliction was a varicose ulcer resulting from varicose veins. Inadequate and often savage treatment, together with lack of sufficient rest, would have caused the veins to become thrombosed, the leg to swell and an extremely painful chronic ulcer to develop on his thigh.[79]

By June 1537 both legs had been affected and Henry's condition was serious enough for him to confess confidentially to the duke of Norfolk that 'a humour which has fallen into our legs' was one of the reasons why he could not pay his promised visit to the North after the Pilgrimage of

79. See MacNalty, *Henry VIII. A Difficult Patient* (1952), on all this, especially 159 ff.: and Chamberlin, *The Private Character of Henry VIII* (1932). Shortly before this book went to press, Sir Arthur MacNalty suggested to me that Henry may have suffered from osteomyelitis, rather than a varicose ulcer. The scanty medical evidence will support either diagnosis. Osteomyelitis, a chronic septic infection of the thigh bone (in Henry's case) perhaps caused by an injury sustained while jousting, would have brought about a discharge of pus (as well as pieces of necrosed bone) and allowed the king those periods of remission which, we know, he enjoyed. No final verdict, therefore, can be passed on Henry's complaint. I am very grateful to Sir Arthur MacNalty for this communication.

Grace.[80] None the less, a month later he was on progress, travelling on horseback. In May of the next year a clot seems to have detached itself and caused a blockage to the lungs. For several days Henry was speechless and black in the face, and, as he appeared to be near death, two factions quickly sprang to life to dispute the succession, one backing Edward, the other Mary.[81] Had Henry died then there might have been a rehearsal of the events of 1553. But within a few weeks he had recovered sufficiently to resume the quest for a new wife, and to go on his usual progress in the late summer.

But ceaseless activity prevented the ulcer from healing. He was unwell again in September 1540 and, though able to enjoy his new marriage and a rigorous regime of early rising and a long daily ride by December, three months later, in March 1541, he was stricken with another serious attack of fever, derived from his ulcer and following a mild tertian, perhaps malarial, fever. His physicians, since his last fearful bout in 1538, had carefully kept the ulcer open, but now it suddenly closed. The danger was quickly dealt with and the crisis passed. But it left Henry in a black gloom for weeks.[82]

By now he was becoming a man of huge girth, eating and drinking prodigiously.[83] His great weight must have exacerbated his condition no less than did his dauntless zeal for riding. In March 1544 – just as he was about to set out on his last campaign – the ulcer flared up once more and the fever returned.[84] But in July of that year he crossed to Calais and rode a great courser to the siege of Boulogne. Though he was carried about indoors in a chair and hauled upstairs by machinery, he would still heave his vast, pain-racked body into the saddle to indulge his love of riding and to show himself to his people, driven by an inexorable will to cling to his ebbing life. In the following year he came down to the Isle of Wight, dined on *Great Harry* and toured fortifi-

80. *L.P.*, xii, iii, 77.   81. *L.P.*, xiii, i, 995.
82. *L.P.*, xvi, 558, 589.   83. As Marillac observed, ibid, 589.
84. *L.P.*, xix, i, 263.

cations. His fever returned again next February (1546) and struck him down for three weeks. But again he recovered. By 10 March he was reported as convalescing and spending his time playing cards with Dudley and other intimates (and perhaps listening to his wife's godly exhortations to continue the good fight).[85] Twelve days later he received newly-arrived envoys from the emperor amiably and told them that, though his leg still troubled him, his robust constitution had helped him overcome the attack. But the ambassadors reported to Charles that his face showed that it had been worse than he pretended.[86]

Even yet, he did not relent. The Imperial ambassadors found him remarkably *au fait* with current happenings in Europe, and in the next few months he received the brother of the elector Palatine, the ubiquitous Dr Bruno and the new French ambassador; and it was in the following August, during the celebrations of the Anglo-French peace at Hampton Court, that Henry held the conversation with the French admiral which we have discussed above, leaning on the admiral and Cranmer. Moreover, a short time before, he had announced his intention of going on a long progress to the extremities of his kingdom that year.[87]

By mid September he had set out to Guildford, where he received the French ambassador and thrashed him with complaints about French fortification around Boulogne, contrary to the treaty of peace. A few days later he was said to be ill, but Wriothesley crushed the report, saying that he had had a cold and was now better.[88] However, Henry had more than a cold. Van der Delft, the Imperial ambassador, heard that he had been very sick, though he had recovered quickly. He saw the king at Windsor in early October and found him graciousness itself. Indeed, with splendid *sang-froid* Henry offered him one of his physicians, since the ambassador, too, had been unwell. He seemed now to be full of vigour – arguing with the French ambassador, lam-

85. *L.P.*, xxi, i, 365, 391.   86. ibid., 439.
87. ibid., 447.   88. *L.P.*, xxi, ii, 129.

basting envoys from Scotland and hunting – even though
he was suddenly unwell on one occasion and had to commission Paget to receive de Selve, the Frenchman.[89] He had
come back to London in November 'for certain baths which
he usually has at this season' and then set out for Oatlands,
where he fell ill again about 10 December.[90] Van der Delft
saw Henry shortly afterwards and found him claiming to
be fully restored. But his looks told another story. Towards
the end of the month, as the attack on the Howards went
forward, he returned via Nonsuch to London. Catherine
had been sent away to Greenwich for Christmas, the Court
was closed to all but the Privy Council and some gentlemen
of the Chamber. It was van der Delft's opinion that the king
might not survive another attack of the fever which clearly
now possessed his body.[91] Though the Privy Council put it
out that he had completely thrown off the fever which 'some
grief of his leg' had caused and would be 'better for it a
great while',[92] the ambassador was right. Henry was a very
sick man; and a few days later his last will and testament
was drawn up.

Perhaps in the past Henry had used his will as a weapon
with which to discipline servants by holding over them the
threat of exclusion from the Council which would rule under
his infant heir.[93] The theory is, in itself, alluring, but it is
difficult to find evidence for it and even more difficult to believe that the king needed any such extra grasp on those
around him. Anyway, if hitherto his will had been an instrument for controlling the course of this reign rather than
for determining the destiny of the next, by late December
1546 it meant only one thing, namely, the nomination of
those who would inherit power on Henry's death – and inherit soon.

89. *L.P.*, xxi, ii, 139, 238, 315.   90. ibid., 382.
91. ibid., 605–6.   92. ibid., 619.
93. Such is the argument of Professor Smith in 'The Last Will and
Testament of Henry VIII: a Question of Perspective', *Journal of
British Studies*, ii (1962), 20 f.

On the night of 26 December 1546 Hertford, Dudley, Paget, Denny and two others were called to the royal presence. The sick king, who had rallied after his latest grave crisis, bade Denny fetch his will. But Denny produced the wrong document (presumably in honest error) and when Henry heard it read out he said 'that was not it, but there was another, of a later making, written with the hand of Lord Wriothesley being secretary', that is, the will which was drawn up in early 1544, shortly before the king set out for France. Denny fetched this document and it was read out. Either because he had forgotten its contents or because his mind was blurred by fever, Henry was surprised by its contents, saying that some had been put out from the list of executors and councillors whom 'he meant to have in, and some in whom he meant to have out'. Thereupon he ordered Paget to make the corrections: 'to put in some that were not named before, and to put out the bishop of Winchester's name'. When he came to the list of assistants to his executors he again added names, such as Northampton and Arundel, who had not been included in the list of executors and were now suggested to him by Paget and others; and again he refused to leave Stephen Gardiner on the roll, saying that 'he was a wilful man and not meet to be about his son', and that the bishop of Westminster should be put out also, because 'he was schooled by the bishop of Winchester'. According to Paget, not only he, but all who were with him, 'did earnestly sue to his majesty' to restore Gardiner, but Henry would not be moved, saying that 'he marvelled what we meant and that we all knew him to be a wilful man', that Gardiner 'should not be about his son, nor trouble his Council any more'.[94] That all of these men should have rallied on the bishop's behalf is scarcely credible

---

94. *Foxe*, vi, 163. Is it permissible to observe that if Henry really had used his will as means to discipline his servants – by threatening to omit their names from the Council of Regency – then it is surprising that he apparently did not know the contents of his latest will, that of 1544?

and astonished the king; but that is what we are told they did.

Moreover, probably soon after this interview, further efforts were made to reinstate him. According to a story which Sir Anthony Denny told Cranmer and which was passed to Foxe by the archbishop's secretary, Denny had knelt by Henry's bedside and, pretending to believe that Gardiner's name had been omitted from the final text of the will by accident, pleaded once more for the bishop. But Henry cut him short, crying, 'Hold your peace. I remembered him well enough and of good purpose have left him out; for surely, if he were in my testament and one of you, he would cumber you all and you would never rule him, he is of so troublesome a nature. Marry, I myself could use him and rule him to all manner of purposes, as seemed good unto me; but so shall you never do': and when Denny dared to raise the subject again later he was set upon by the king and told, 'if you will not cease to trouble me, by the faith I owe unto God, I will surely dispatch thee out of my will also'.[95] If we cannot accept every detail of these stories, nor fit them together exactly, we cannot escape the force of two separate testimonies which assert that it was Henry himself, of his own unshakeable volition, who struck Gardiner out of his will. Several times in recent years he had publicly voiced his suspicion of Winchester's loyalty to the Royal Supremacy, saying that he knew him to be 'too wilful in his opinions and much bent to the popish party', and excluding him from the committee which drew up the *King's Book* of 1543.[96] Gardiner believed that, as long as Henry lived, 'no man could do me hurt'.[97] There was some truth in this, for his unrivalled experience of royal affairs was not to be lightly thrown away; and, besides, the king probably had some admiration for this able, arrogant servant whom, he fondly

95. *Foxe*, v, 691 f.

96. So Paget, Somerset, Northampton, Warwick and others deposed in 1551. *Foxe*, vi, 162 ff.

97. Thus he wrote in a letter to Somerset in June 1547. ibid., vi, 36.

believed, only he could discipline. But it is also probably true that he 'misliked the said bishop ever the longer the worse' and might 'have used extremity against him' if he had lived longer. Several times he had asked Paget for 'a certain writing touching the said bishop, commanding him to keep it, save that he might have it when he called for it'.[98] The weapon lay at hand with which to destroy him; and he had enemies in plenty to persuade the king to use it. In late December 1546 the Protestant faction were openly proclaiming their hope that Winchester and fellow-adherents of the ancient faith would follow Norfolk to the Tower.[99] Seven weeks before, Dudley had struck Gardiner in the face at a Council meeting;[1] and not long before this, in early December, the bishop was seemingly on the brink of serious trouble in the shape of a charge that he had obstinately refused to agree to an exchange of some lands with the crown.

The episode is obscure. Gardiner insisted that he had 'never said nay' to this familiar form of land transaction which commonly disguised royal spoliation of episcopal temporalities, and had only begged to put his case in person to the king. But a stern reply was soon on its way accusing him of having 'utterly refused to grow to any conformity' when the proposal was put to him by Wriothesley, Paget and the chancellor of the Court of Augmentations, and accusing him of being more 'precise' than 'many of your own coat' who, though less indebted to the royal person than he, 'have yet, without indenting, dealt both more lovingly and more friendly with us'.[2] Perhaps he had seriously offended the king. Perhaps the incident was exploited by Seymour and his friends who, thinking the end to be at

98. *Foxe*, vi, 163.

99. *Sp. Cal.*, viii, 370. In a letter written at the end of January 1547, Chapuys recalled that when he was last in England, Dudley would have had Gardiner sent to the Tower if Norfolk had not interceded for him. ibid., 386.

1. *L.P.*, xxi. ii, 347.

2. *Foxe*, vi, 138 f. *St.P.*, i, 883 f. (*L.P.*, xxi, 487–8, 493).

hand, hustled the king into a conspiracy which would
finally unhorse Winchester and be completed with the
attack on the Howards. Gardiner was away from Court on
royal business at the time and was clearly all too aware that
'such as came now to Court were specially sent for'.[3] Maybe
he was about to be snared. The attack on Surrey and his
father succeeded. That on Gardiner did not – until the next
reign. The bishop temporarily escaped the clutches of his
pursuants, though the king remained convinced that he
should have no place in his son's Council of Regency. But
he made this decision not, probably, because of the recent
incident concerning the exchange of lands so much as because he had long since determined to exclude him.
Gardiner had neither been ruined nor reinstated.

It was on 26 December, therefore, when that knot of
councillors gathered around Henry to hear the will read
out, that the men were named to whom the future of Tudor
England was committed. Four days later, Hertford, Paget
and Sir William Herbert (a gentleman of the Privy
Chamber) came to the king once more. Henry held in his
hand a fair copy of his will which, apparently, was signed
there and then at the beginning and the end, witnessed by
a handful of Household officers and sealed with the signet;
which done, Henry delivered the document to Hertford,
revoking and annulling all former wills and testaments.[4]

Such (probably) were the events of 30 December, and in
telling them we have arrived amidst uncertainty and controversy. The will which Hertford had received from the
king's hands was indisputably signed by dry stamp, that is,
the outline of the royal autograph had been embossed on
the paper with a stamp and then inked in by a clerk empowered to commit what was technically the treasonous act
of forging the royal signature, and for which, to safeguard
himself, he had regularly to sue pardon. Such a method was

3. *St.P.*, i, 884. Cf. Muller, *Stephen Gardiner and the Tudor Reaction*
(1926), 46.
4. *L.P.*, xxi, ii, 770 (85).

commonly used for authenticating routine documents and was presumably used now because the king was too weak to subscribe with his own hand.

On 1 January the French ambassadors reported that Henry was stricken with fever once more and at the time of the ceremony of handing over his will he may already have been feeble.[5] But because the record of the clerk in charge of the dry stamp, one William Clerk, places the will as the penultimate entry in the list of documents stamped during the month of January 1547, when it would be expected to occur at the end of the December list, it has been argued that the will was not stamped, nor handed over to Hertford, until the very eve of Henry's death, 27 January; and that Henry had thus deliberately kept all the hawks who circled over his death-bed 'in a dither of apprehension' for four weeks.[6] This may have happened. It is certainly more credible than the theory that the will was not signed until after Henry's death. But the will itself states that it was signed on 30 December 1546.[7] Surely this statement must carry considerable weight. What motive could there have been for ante-dating it? And since Clerk wrote in his record that the will was signed (i.e. stamped), witnesed and sealed, and 'then, in our sights' handed over to Hertford, it cannot be that the will was signed on one day and delivered to Hertford weeks later. That Clerk listed it among the documents stamped in January 1547 is certainly strange, but this may have been an innocent mistake. After all, December was nearly ended and, since he presumably applied the stamp at the king's bedside, away from his office, he could easily have omitted to enter the event promptly in his record. Finally, that he placed it at the bottom of the January list cannot be proof that the document was stamped at the end of that month, for it is far from certain that his list observed chronological order. Clerk's concern was to keep a complete

5. *L.P.*, xxi, ii, 651, 662.
6. Smith, art. cit., 21, 24 f.
7. *Rymer*, xv, 117.

record of what had passed through his hands, not to provide evidence for the historian.

Whether the will which Hertford received on 30 December 1546 is the document which now lies among the royal wills in the Public Record Office is an open question, because the passage of time has made it impossible to determine whether the signatures thereon were applied by stamp or by the royal hand. Later on, in Elizabeth's reign, it was to be argued by supporters of Mary Queen of Scots that, because the will was stamped, not autographed, it did not fulfil the statutory requirements that it should be subscribed 'with your most gracious hand'[8] and that its exclusion of the Scottish line from the succession in favour of the daughters of Mary Tudor (by Charles Brandon) was therefore invalid.[9] Moreover, because it has seemed incredible that the king should have left behind, or been allowed to do so, an insufficiently authenticated instrument, there has been talk of a second will, validly subscribed, which was drawn up some time after the first and has since disappeared.[10]

Though there may have been such a document, it is not obvious that it would have been judged necessary for the reason alleged, for we cannot be certain that a stamped signature would not have qualified as subscription 'with your most gracious hand'. If the dry stamp did not authenticate acts of the royal will unimpeachably then, as Burnet observed, a large corpus of instruments drawn up and stamped by the king's death-bed, such as the endowment of Christ's Hospital in the City of London and the foundation of Trinity College Cambridge, would have been suspect.[11] When Norfolk's attainder was revoked in Mary's reign the grounds for the repeal were, among others, that the com-

8. So 28 Hen. VIII, *c.* 7.

9. Thus, for example, Maitland argued in a letter to Cecil, printed in *Burnet*, i, 549.

10. So Levine, 'The Last Will and Testament of Henry VIII; a Reappraisal Reappraised', *Historian*, 1964, 481 f. Mr Levine makes several points which challenge Prof. L. B. Smith's ideas.

11. *Burnet*, i, 549 f.

mission which gave royal assent to the act had been stamped, not signed, 'and that not [on] the upper but the nether part of it, contrary to the king's custom'.[12] The mere fact that the stamp had been used was not, therefore, regarded as conclusive evidence against the commission; the act of repeal felt it necessary to point to a second flaw, namely, that the stamp had not been affixed (as it was affixed to the will) to both the beginning and the end of the document. True, the statute which empowered Henry to devise the crown by will placed this instrument in a special category by explicitly requiring royal subscription, but it is surely arguable that, at the time, the dry stamp might easily have been considered sufficient, for neither Hertford nor Henry – assuming that he was *compos mentis* on 30 December 1546 – would have been eager to traffic in an obviously invalid document. The argument against the sufficiency of its subscription was a plausible, but later, invention by parties interested in asserting the claims of Mary Queen of Scots to the throne of England.

An Ockhamist antipathy to the multiplication of postulates leads one, therefore, to doubt whether the affair of the will was as involved as some have felt that it may have been, and to propose that there was only one will, that, probably because he was too weak at the time and his death seemed imminent, it was signed by dry stamp on 30 December,[13] that William Clerk recorded this stamping at the end of his January list for no sinister reason, that the parties concerned, even if they recalled the requirements of the statute as they stood around the king's bed probably believing that Henry's life was flickering out, would have judged the dry stamp as sufficient. Later on, in Mary's reign, Paget and Montague,

12. *Burnet*, i, 546.
13. In his letter to Cecil already quoted, Maitland asserted that Henry never ordered the stamp to be put on and that 'he had oft desired to sign it [*sc.* the will], but had always put it off'. But the writer gives no authority for this assertion and it is difficult to know how he could have learned all this.

chief justice of Common Pleas, swore that the will had been
tampered with in order to exclude Mary of Scotland from
the succession.[14] But it is not clear what they meant by this,
nor when this happened. In so far as, when Henry died,
Mary was still destined for the hand of Prince Edward, the
will did not exactly debar her. It is therefore difficult to see
exactly what skulduggery there could have been during the
last few days of Henry's life. Certainly it seems that it was
the king who determined the composition of his son's Council. It was he who excluded Gardiner and Thirlby, and thus
opened the way to Seymour's triumph; and, when he handed
the fateful document to the latter, this action must surely
have been a sign that the recipient was the man of the
future.

It has been argued that the failure of the will to provide
machinery for recruiting replacements to the Council of
Regency, its insistence that its decisions should have the
written consent of the majority and its omission of any
mention of a protector or governor not only show that it was
never designed to provide for the next reign but, over and
above this, expose Hertford to the charge of having violated
it egregiously when, hard upon Henry's death, he was proclaimed governor of the young king and lord protector of
his kingdom. But the will's lack of provision for replenish-
ing the Council may simply be evidence that it was drawn
up in a hurry or in the expectation that this was a matter
which that Council could deal with itself when the need
arose, like any body of executors. Secondly, the insistence
on the written consent of the majority was in respect of
anything appointed by this will, which is not the same as
making the impossible demand that all the political decisions
of the Council of Regency should have this consent.[15]
Lastly, the statute of 1536 had provided that a minor heir

14. Robert Persons, S.J., *Certamen Ecclesiae Anglicanae*, ed. Simons
(Assen, 1965), 171.

15. But this is only a suggestion, which does not pretend to solve
the problem fully.

should be under the guardianship of his mother and a
Council, or of a Council only, according as the king's last
will directed – without mention of a protector.[16] Why? Because he would be appointed, not by will, but by letters
patent. In 1544, before Henry departed to France, Catherine
Parr had been thus appointed governor and protector during the king's absence;[17] and it is possible that Hertford was
similarly elevated by the king shortly before his death. On
12 February 1547 van der Delft wrote that a few days before
he had seen with his own eyes Hertford produce letters
patent of the late king appointing him lord protector.[18] The
document is not on the patent roll. But van der Delft could
hardly have been mistaken about what he saw and so confidently reported. Either Henry at the last minute added to
the provisions of his will (as he was perfectly entitled to
do) and, of his own volition, named the royal uncle as the
man to whom he would bequeath mastery of his kingdom,
or Hertford snatched the prize for himself while the old
king was dying (or did so immediately after he died, presumably during those three days when Henry's death was
kept secret from the outside world – which we will discuss
shortly).

As has been said, Henry was gravely ill again in early
January. Despite announcements that he had recovered, few
– not even Catherine or Mary – had access to his chamber
and many were beginning to say that he was already dead.[19]
But his prodigious frame rallied once more and on 16 January he was able to receive both the Imperial and the French
ambassadors in audience. De Selve and his companion found
him well, gracious and in evident command of all about him.
He talked of a defensive league with France and the
Lutherans, listened to news from Germany and Genoa, and
promised to release the crew of a galley which had been

16. 28 Hen. VIII, *c.* 7, paragraph xiv.
17. *L.P.*, xix, i, 864, 1035 (78).
18. *Sp. Cal.*, ix, 31.
19. *L.P.*, xxi, ii, 675, 684.

seized.[20] The final relapse may not have come until ten or
eleven days later. On 27 January the royal assent was given
to Norfolk's attainder by commission, the chancellor explaining that the king was too ill to be present.[21] That evening it was clear that his end was very near, though his
doctors, fearful of being held guilty of that same treason of
foretelling the king's death which had cost Lord Hungerford his life six years before,[22] did not dare to say so. Eventually Sir Anthony Denny was bold enough to warn his
dying sovereign that he must prepare himself for his last
agony, and Henry, quieter now, began to think on his past
life and its shortcomings, saying, 'yet is the mercy of Christ
able to pardon me all my sins, though they were greater
than they be'. Denny then asked him if he wanted any
spiritual ministration, to which the king replied that, if he
wanted anyone, it would be Cranmer, but that 'I will first
take a little sleep and then, as I feel myself, I will advise upon
the matter'. After an hour or two asleep, he awoke and
bade Cranmer come. The archbishop was then at Croydon,
and by the time he reached the king's bedside Henry had
lost his speech. Had he not been near unconscious, doubtless Cranmer would have heard his confession and given him
the Viaticum. Instead he told the king to give him some
sign that he trusted in God; whereupon Henry, 'holding
him with his hand, did wring his hand in his as hard as he
could'. Shortly afterwards, in the early hours of Friday 28
January 1547, the king was dead.[23]

'The king is dead. Long live the king.' But the news that
Henry had come to his end was kept secret for three days,
primarily, it seems, because the king's death had halted the
execution of the duke of Norfolk, who had been due to suffer

20. *L.P.*, xxi, ii, 713.
21. *Lords Journals*, i, 283 ff.
22. Walter Lord Hungerford was attainted in 1540 for unnatural
vice and treasonously attempting to foretell the king's death by the
use of magic.
23. *Foxe*, v, 689.

that very morning, and threw his enemies into a bitter dilemma. Would they bluff the world and shed the blood of this dangerous man, or would they allow him to enjoy his miraculous reprieve? For three days, we may presume, the Council debated – while Henry's body lay secretly on its deathbed, awaiting its obsequies and Norfolk paced the Tower, unwitting of what was afoot – until counsels of prudence and mercy won, and the duke's life was spared.[24] What other dark scuffling took place during these three days we shall never know; but it is at least possible that the letters patent which conferred the office of protector on Hertford were drawn up then. At last, on Monday 31 January, the truth was revealed. Parliament had met on the 28th itself and the 29th, and had assembled on this Monday for its day's business when the chancellor rose and, with a voice choked with emotion, announced the king's death. Then Paget read Henry's will, and revealed the names of those who would inherit power in the land. Then was dissolved a Parliament whose life, in constitutional law, had expired with the king's three days before.[25]

Eight days later, on the night of 8 February, every parish church in the land held a solemn Dirge and tolled its bells. Next morning Requiem Mass was offered everywhere for the dead king's soul. On the 14th his embalmed body was carried by chariot towards Windsor in a procession four

24. Since the duke was earl-marshal it was also important to have his fate settled before the ceremonial of the coronation had to be organized. In the *Lords Journals* (i, 284) there is an intriguing *lapsus calami* of the clerk in the notice that the commissioners of the royal assent to the duke's attainder hastened about their work because of the imminence of Edward's *coronation* as prince of Wales. The clerk meant 'creation', not 'coronation', but he absent-mindedly used the wrong word. That the need for an earl-marshal was due to Edward's proposed elevation to the princedom of Wales rather than to his accession to the throne was presumably deliberate camouflage.

25. *Lords Journals*, i, 289 ff. The French ambassador, de Selve, heard the news on 31 January. *L.P.*, xxi, ii, 760. For the proclamation of Edward's accession (dated 31 January), see *Hughes and Larkin*, no. 275.

miles long. The corpse lay that night at Sion, under a huge
hearse; on the following day it came to Windsor and was set
down in the castle.[26] Next morning Stephen Gardiner celebrated the funeral Mass and delivered the panegyric in St
George's Chapel. After Mass came a fanfare of trumpets and
the solemn burial, between the stalls and altar of the chapel.
The king's will had directed that he should be buried, with
Jane Seymour, in the Lady Chapel which Henry VII had
once intended to be his final resting-place and in a costly
tomb which Wolsey had begun to prepare for his own use.
But that tomb was not yet finished and, instead, Jane Seymour's existing grave was opened and there Henry's huge
coffin set down – next to the remains of his beloved wife and
the mother of his heir.

Henry's magnificent tomb was never finished. Indeed, its
screen was taken down and its ornaments sold by order of
Parliament in 1646; and, over a hundred and fifty years later,
the empty sarcophagus and the base on which it stood was
used for Nelson's tomb in the crypt of St Paul's.[27] Nor, perhaps, did Henry's broken body find lasting rest in its borrowed home. Decades later there was persistent whispering
that the corpse had been taken out of its tomb and burned
during the reign of his elder daughter.[28] Moreover, Sir
Francis Englefield, sometime privy councillor to Queen
Mary and later a Catholic recusant exiled in Spain, told the
Jesuit Robert Persons that he had been present at Windsor
when Cardinal Pole, on Mary's command, had the tomb
opened and the embalmed corpse of the unrepentant
schismatic and heretic committed to the flames.[29] Thus, if we

26. Wriothesley, *A Chronicle of England*, Camden Society, n.s. xi
(1875–7), i, 181.
27. St John Hope, *Windsor Castle* (1913), 484 ff.
28. Fuller, *Church History of Britain etc.* (1665), v, 255.
29. Persons, *Certamen Ecclesiae Anglicanae*, ed. Simons, 273. It is
difficult to think that Englefield was telling an untruth or that Persons
would have had either the need or the desire to misrepresent him.
His story must be given some weight. It is corroborated by Fuller's
reports of 'whisperings' and by the fact that, on Edward VI's death,

are to trust this report, did Mary and Pole, with terrible
logic, finally strike down the man who had so ravaged their
lives and ravaged the people and the things that they most
loved.

'all work upon the tomb certainly came to an end' (St John Hope,
op. cit., 484). We may also recall how Hugh Weston, dean of Westminster, discovered the plan to exhume and burn Henry's remains,
but was disbelieved because he was a notoriously loose man. For
this story, see Simons's edition of the *Certamen*, 273, n. 1.

Henry the King

HE was in his fifty-sixth year when he died, and had reigned
for thirty-seven years and eight months. He had survived
pretenders, excommunication, rebellion and threats of invasion, died in his bed and passed his throne peacefully to
his heir. He had won a title, Defender of the Faith, which
English monarchs still boast, written a book which is still,
occasionally, read, composed some music which is still sung.
He had made war on England's ancient enemies and himself led two assaults on France. For nearly four decades he
had cut an imposing figure in Europe, mattering to its
affairs, bestriding its high diplomacy as few of his predecessors, if any, had done. He had defied pope and emperor,
brought into being in England and Ireland a national
Church subject to his authority, wiped about a thousand
religious houses off the face of his native land and of those
areas of Ireland under his influence, and bestowed on
English kingship a profound new dignity. He who had
broken the secular Church in England, hammered monks
and friars, and, recently, laid his hand on the chantries, had
brought the Scriptures in the vernacular to his people, hesitantly and partly unwittingly, but none the less decisively,
allowed his country to be directed towards the continental
Reformation into which it was to enter fully in his son's
and second daughter's reigns, and given to his people a new
sense of unity – the unity of 'entire Englishmen' rather than
that of 'Englishmen papisticate' or of those who were 'scarce
our subjects'. The England which he had led back into
European affairs and exposed to the immense creative
energies of continental Protestantism and which, at the same
time, had disowned allegiance to any external authority,
indisputably emerged from his reign with a new political

'wholeness', thanks to the destruction of the independent Church, the final incorporation of Wales, the pruning of many liberties and refurbishing of local Councils in the North and West, which lay under the surveillance of a Privy Council that, at least by the 1540s, had established itself as the supreme, omnicompetent executive body. Thanks above all to Thomas Cromwell, his reign had given England much 'good governance'. The administrative machine was more efficient and capacious than it had ever been – as was the legal (and this was largely to Wolsey's credit). A good deal probably had been done to discipline a society in which violence abounded and, in particular, to curb the peoples and their dangerous overlords in the re- moter parts of the land – the Marcher lordships in the North and West. Henry's own commanding presence, the prestige and evident significance of his Court, and the grow- ing authority of his servants in central and local government greatly strengthened the 'lines of force' which ran between king and subject, often (probably) swamping, always over- laying and, where necessary, checking, local loyalties. Again, never before had England felt the power of the 'state' so widely and deeply as in the 1530s and 40s. The compilation of the *Valor Ecclesiasticus* (a work cast on the scale of *Domesday Book*), the imposition of the oaths of Succession and Supremacy, the immense operation of dissolving the religious houses and distributing their property, the heavy taxation of the lay and clerical estates, the marshalling of large forces by sea and land, all this over and above the achievement of an ecclesiastical and doctrinal revolution, was a concentrated display of the power and ubiquity of central authority the like of which had not been seen hitherto; and if the major administrative developments of the years of Cromwell's dominance (and after) may be better described as a return to the medieval practice of building professional, bureaucratic government outside the royal household – after decades of intense concentration upon the latter – rather than a 'modern' event, it remains true that

the consolidation of the Council and the foundation of four
new financial courts gave the central government a new,
firm grip on the realm. Finally, never before had Parliament
been called upon to carry out so vast and consequential a
programme of legislation as that which came on to the
statute book between 1529 and 1545 – a programme which
ranged from the acts of Appeals and Supremacy, of Dissolution of Monasteries and Chantries, of Succession and Treason
to the act of Six Articles and the first Poor Law. Henry's
reign in many ways left a deeper mark on the mind, heart
and face of England than did any event in English history
between the coming of the Normans and the coming of the
factory.

Nor are there only great events in Church and State to
record. No survey of these years would be complete without at least a passing mention of the changes which they
brought to the navy. Henry inherited seven ships from his
father, had added twenty-four more by 1514 and, by the
early 40s, by purchase of Italian and Hanseatic vessels as
well as by increased home production, had built up a
nucleus of a powerful naval force. But it was not merely the
increase in the number of the king's ships which matters.
During the first French war, English shipwrights began ex-
perimenting with the Italian technique of mounting guns in
the waists of ships (to be fired through gunports), and thus
inaugurated what was to be little short of a revolution in
naval architecture and tactics. The medieval fighting ship
was a slow-moving, fat 'tub', high-charged with tall poop
and forecastle on which were mounted light-guns, man-
killers like the serpentine, and designed as an armed transport to be used for in-fighting, that is, grappling, boarding
and taking by hand-to-hand combat. It was a floating platform which could be moved up against an enemy ship and
from which the army-by-sea could launch an attack not
specifically different from many a land operation. Such had
been the tactics of naval warfare since time out of mind. The
new ship, however, was essentially a floating battery, a long,

slim vessel, with low poop and forecastle and marked tumble-home, pierced with one, two, three and eventually more rows of gunports; its gundecks carried increasingly heavy cannon; its fighting-strength consisted in the broadside. Sea-warfare, therefore, changed its character. Off-fighting replaced in-fighting, the broadside the hand-to-hand mêlée; and the army-by-sea, as such, disappeared.

This transformation of the English navy was far from complete by the end of Henry's reign. Ships of the old style continued to be built in the 1540s and the profound changes in naval tactics had, as yet, taken so little effect that the sea-fighting of the 40s was still based largely on time-honoured techniques. But the change in naval architecture had begun. Ships of the new design were being produced; old ones, like *Great Harry*, were rebuilt with tiers of gunports in their waists. The naval revolution, learned from Italian shipwrights and German gunfounders, was under way. Portsmouth dry-dock, constructed by Henry VII, was enlarged, Woolwich dockyard built in 1514, Deptford a little later. In 1546 the administration of the navy was reordered and the body which will eventually become the Navy Board set up.[1] How much of all this was due to Henry's own initiative is impossible to say, but it is likely that his marked interest in ships at least encouraged these developments. In 1514 he had licensed the incorporation of Trinity House of Deptford Strand, a body charged with the advancement of navigation and commerce, and the training of Englishmen in pilotage. He had been closely concerned with assembling the royal fleet for his first French campaign in 1513;[2] he had often visited his ships and, as on the occasion when he went to Southampton in June 1518, had had the guns of his galleys 'fired again and again, marking their range, as he is very curious about matters of

1. For an excellent introduction to all this, see Marcus, *A Naval History of England*, i, *The Formative Years* (1961). Cf. Oppenheim, *History of the administration of the royal navy* (1896).

2. *L.P.*, i, 1661.

this kind'.[3] He deserved his traditional title of 'Father of the English Navy'.

Henry was also a builder. He built in the grand manner, partly learned from Wolsey, partly copied from Francis I; and he built on a larger scale than any other Tudor monarch.

From the beginning of his reign he spent heavily on repairs and extensions to the royal palaces – new stables, a barn and gallery at Greenwich (besides considerable work on the chapel there), a new closet at Windsor and considerable repairs, a privy kitchen at Richmond, a gallery at Woking and numerous minor works at Eltham. He lavished thousands of pounds on Newhall in Essex, which he completed with a new gallery and decorated. He paled Windsor Great Park, spent £50 on lengthening the Star Chamber (in August 1517) and leaded its battlemented roof.[4] His first major enterprise, however, seems to have been rebuilding the decayed royal palace of Bridewell in order to provide the court with a new residence in London. The palace stood partly in the former garden of the Knights Hospitallers of St John and partly on land bought from the abbey of Faversham, on the west side of present-day New Bridge Street (by Ludgate Circus), in the parish of St Bride, from which it took its name. We know little about this building except that it was begun in May 1515, probably cost well over £20,000 and was finished in time to receive Charles V on his visit to London in 1522.[5] Henry occasionally stayed in it in subsequent years, but after his death it was abandoned by the crown and used to house some of London's vagrants. Thus, by a strange metamorphosis, an erstwhile palace was to give its name to a grim institution, the house of correc-

3. *L.P.*, ii, 4232. As Wingfield told Henry in April 1520, Francis I was not nearly his equal in knowledge of ships. See *L.P.*, iii, 748.

4. See the Chamber accounts for 1509 to 1523 in *L.P.*, ii, 1442 ff.; iii, 1537 ff. Details in the last sentence come from *L.P.*, ii, 1476 and *L.P.*, iii, 1544.

5. Stow, *Survey of London*, ed. Kingsford (Oxford, 1908), i, 70; ii, 44. For the building expenses see *L.P.*, ii, 1471 ff.; *L.P.*, iii, 1547.

tion. Bridewell suffered this fate probably not least because, within seven years of its completion, Henry had embarked on a rival project about three quarters of a mile due west in Westminster, where he constructed the most splendid home which English monarchy had yet built for itself.

It was perhaps typical of the man that he should not merely have owed to Wolsey the stimulus to embark on two major enterprises himself, but should have used the cardinal's own buildings as the nucleus of his own. He had probably long envied Wolsey his magnificent London residence, York Place (on the east side of modern Whitehall), and his country residence, Hampton Court, which had been begun in 1515. As we have seen, scarcely had Wolsey fallen from grace than Henry seized both. Wolsey had angrily protested that the former was the possession of the archbishops of York and was therefore not his to give; but his words were of no avail. Though York Place was not formally vested in the crown until early 1530, on 2 November 1529, only four days after its previous incumbent had been sentenced in King's Bench, Henry had come by boat from Greenwich and entered the cardinal archbishop's splendid riverside residence.[6]

Wolsey himself had repaired and enlarged the palace, adding (among other things) a great hall. Henry would complete what his servant had begun and turn York Place, a name which would soon be finally replaced by that of the palace of Whitehall, into a large-scale royal residence. He began the work quickly, and again at Wolsey's expense. Shortly after the latter had retired to Esher, that is, probably in early 1530, his enemies in the Council put it to Henry that a gallery of novel and elaborate design which Wolsey had lately added to that residence 'should be very necessary for the king, to take down and set it up again at Westminster'. A king who evidently felt no qualms in filching a palace was not likely to resist the temptation to pilfering this trifle. Before Wolsey's very eyes, as he lay

6. *Sp. Cal.*, iv, i, 323.

moping in his house at Esher, the gallery was dismantled
and carted away to embellish the king's new abode.[7] Thereafter Whitehall underwent elaborate development. Some of
the existing buildings were pulled down; by a complex
series of exchanges and purchases Henry acquired proper-
ties to the north and south of old York Place on both the
east and west side of the street which ran alongside it
roughly parallel with the river (and joining Westminster
to the Strand), on a line with modern Whitehall. To the
older buildings were added several galleries, privy lodgings,
a garden and an enclosed orchard. On the west side of the
street Henry built a large tiltyard (roughly on the site of the
Horse Guards' building today), an octagonal cockpit, bowl-
ing alleys and a great tennis court – enclosed, of course –
and what Stow described as a 'sumptuous gallery' for
spectators of the tournament. Between the two complexes
of buildings on either side of the street were erected two
gatehouses, King's Gate at the southern end, Holbein's
Gate (an erroneous attribution) at the northern, which
joined together the two sections and gave passage from one
to the other. The exact bounds of Henry's palace are difficult to determine. Perhaps it ran northwards into 'Scotland',
that is, the property where Scottish royal visitors to London
were customarily accommodated (and which is known today
as Scotland Yard) and southwards to near the Embank-
ment.[8] Certainly by the time that the main building was
complete, that is, by 1536, Whitehall had become the chief
London residence of the monarch. It was in the Queen's
Closet that Henry married Jane Seymour; it was in the
Great Hall, where seats had been set up on scaffolding for
those attending the spectacle, that in November 1538 Henry

7. *Cavendish*, 127.
8. For a full account of all this, see *Survey of London*, xiii, *St
Margaret's Westminster* (1930), pt i, 7 ff. and *passim*; pt iii, 1 ff.
Wolsey's gallery became the Privy Gallery continuing the Tiltyard
Gallery on the eastern side of Holbein's Gate, and running along the
north side of the Privy Garden to the private apartments.

presided over the trial for heresy of John Lambert and publicly argued with him; it was here that Henry was to die.

Moreover, the massive works at Whitehall were only part of a yet larger project. In 1531, Eton College surrendered to Henry the lands and buildings of the leper hospital of St James, which lay a few hundred yards to the west of York Place. Between 1532 and 1540, Henry built another palace, St James's, on the site of the hospital. The genesis of this undertaking (of which the gatehouse, chapel and other parts survive) is not clear; nor is it obvious why a second residence, so near Whitehall, was required. Presumably this was to be a subsidiary palace (perhaps for the use of royal children). So it remained until, in 1697, fire overtook Whitehall and thereafter St James's became the chief royal residence in the capital. With the hospital, Henry acquired some 185 acres of land, of which 55 acres were imparked. Furthermore, between 1531 and 1536, the crown acquired by exchange or purchase from Westminster Abbey, Abingdon Abbey, the hospital of Burton St Lazar and a number of individuals the whole stretch of largely open land which lay in the area today defined by St Martin's Lane, Oxford Street, Bond Street and Pall Mall – with Covent Garden (i.e. Convent Garden, for it had belonged to Westminster Abbey) added in the east. Thus, by the end of the 1530s the crown held a large spread of land, the bailiwick of St James, running from Westminster to Charing Cross and thence across modern Mayfair, in the southern section of which stood two new residences, the palace of St James and the collection of buildings which made up Whitehall, united by a walled park (which Charles II would embellish with an ornamental lake, an aviary – hence Birdcage Walk – and a track for playing the game of mall). Just north of Whitehall stood the royal Mews, that is, the home of the royal hawks and falconers, which was taken over by the king's horses when the royal

stables in Bloomsbury were burnt down in 1537 and thereby
gave their name, incongruously, to town stabling. South of
Whitehall lay the old palace of Westminster, long since
unsuitable as a royal residence, which Whitehall had now
superseded, and which was but 'a member and parcel' of the
king's palace at Westminster as, according to a statute of
1536, the whole complex of buildings was now officially to
be called. Thus had English monarchy been given a magnificent abode in the capital and London its first experience
of large-scale royal building.[9]

Henry had repaired the White Tower in the Tower of
London in 1532 and continued with additions and repairs
to Eltham, Windsor and his father's palace at Greenwich.
During the great invasion-scare of 1539 he began a run of
fortresses from the Thames estuary, via Sandgate, Deal,
Walmer and Dover to the Isle of Wight, Pendennis and
St Mawes, constructing heavily armed castles of foreign
style, largely under the direction of the German Stefan van
Haschenperg, Deviser of Buildings from 1537 to 1543;[10] and
in the early 1540s he built the castle and blockhouses at
Hull. It is possible that Henry himself helped to design
new fortifications at Calais, for we hear of 'splays [i.e.
firing-apertures] as the king's grace hath devised', to allow
an increased field of fire.[11]

But these military constructions were incidental to his
main purpose. It was above all in massive palace-building
– building which few English monarchs have rivalled –
that, in the 1530s and after, Henry was chiefly engaged.
During these years architecture was the handmaid of politics; for the monarchy which had been transfigured by the
assumption of the Royal Supremacy was now to be housed

9. *Survey of London*, xxix, *The Parish of St James, Westminster*
(1960), pt 1, 21 ff., Kingsford, *The Early History of Piccadilly,
Leicester Square, Soho, etc.* (Cambridge, 1925), 7, 15, etc.; Lambert,
The History of London and its Environs (1806), iii, 487 ff.

10. O'Neil, 'Stefan van Haschenperg, an Engineer to king Henry
VIII, and his Work', *Archaeologia*, 2nd ser., xci (1945), 137 ff.

11. *Chronicle of Calais*, Camden Society, xxxv (1845), 126.

in the hitherto unequalled splendour of palaces designed
for imperial kingship.

The programme had begun at Westminster. It was completed with the construction of a run of royal residences
some miles outside London, in Surrey. First, Wolsey's
country house, Hampton Court, which passed into the king's
hands in October 1529, was lavishly extended and embel-
lished. Between 1531 and 1536 Henry built the massive
Great Hall – 106 feet long and 60 feet high, and spanned
by a magnificent hammer-beam roof. So eager was the king
to see this hall completed that work went on in daylight
and by candlelight as well. He built the fine fan-vaulted
wooden ceiling of the Chapel Royal, constructed the Great
Watching Chamber (i.e. guard chamber) in 1535–6, the
Great Kitchen, the Close Tennis Court and a set of state
rooms which have since disappeared. He decorated the
building with his arms (having effaced Wolsey's), threw a
new bridge over the moat and, in 1540, had the splendid
astronomical clock placed in the main courtyard.

Then, in 1537, he acquired the manor of Oatlands, near
Weybridge (and soon Brooklands also), where he built a
new palace in the following year. At the same time he embarked on his most ambitious project – that monument to
ebullient kingship, the palace of Nonsuch. About six miles
south-east of Hampton Court and eight due east of Oatlands, an area of some 2,000 acres was chosen for the erec-
tion of a magnificent palace, obviously intended to outstrip
Francis I's Château de Chambord. The village of Cudding-
ton, together with its church (which stood on the most
attractive part of the site), was swept away to make room
for the king's works and hundreds of workmen and craftsmen, native and foreign, were brought in. The palace consisted of three courts forming the shape of a squared P;
much of its upper part was timbered, but covered with
slate and decorated with statuary and reliefs; at either
end of its 200-ft southern front stood 75-ft-high octagonal
towers. Italian, French and Dutch craftsmen executed prob-

ably the bulk of the lavish decoration within and without;
six French clockmakers erected the great clock; French
gardeners laid out the Privy Gardens, which boasted a
fountain, a maze and 200 pear trees brought from France.
At the southern end of the site stood a banqueting house
in a separately enclosed rectangle of five acres. This was a
two-storeyed building, the upper half of which was surrounded by a paved area, a timbered hall, the lower consisting of cellars.[12]

Nonsuch Palace was begun in April 1538. It was not quite
finished by the time of Henry's death. It had cost over
£24,000 by November 1545. Standing beside Hampton
Court, Oatlands and the old palace of Richmond and
athwart the royal honour of Hampton Court which ran
out as far as Epsom, Coulsdon, Balham, Battersea and
Mortlake, it was the climax of Henry's building.[13] Though
of basically traditional design, it was a large step beyond the
fortress-palace and showed forth Renaissance features far
more markedly than Hampton Court had done with its
famous medallions, or the gateway of Whitehall with its
classical pediment and pilasters. Nonsuch was not merely a
gorgeous home for imperial monarchy; it was of as much
moment in the history of English architecture as was

12. On all this, see the admirable work of Dent, *The Quest for
Nonsuch* (1962). A useful quick introduction to Henry's buildings,
including Nonsuch, is to be found in Summerson, *Architecture in
Britain 1530–1830*, Pelican History of Art (1958). Mr Dent refutes
the latter's suggestion (taken from Kurz, 'An Architectural Design
for Henry VIII', *Burlington Magazine* (1943), 81 ff.) that the pen and
ink cartoon once in the Louvre and reproduced in Sir John's volume,
was executed in the Presence Chamber of Nonsuch. Dent, op. cit.,
106 ff. See *V.C.H. Essex*, v, 99, 108 for Henry's imparkings and 'stand-
ings' (i.e. grandstands for shooting) in the area between Chingford
and Waltham Cross.

13. As Dent remarks, however, Henry does not seem to have frequented it much. He visited it in May 1545 and complained of the
slow progress which was being made; he came on a full-scale visit to
it in the following July. He apparently did not return. Dent, op. cit.,
136 f.

Henry's building at Whitehall and St James's in the evolution of London.

Henry was a huge, consequential and majestic figure. At least for some, he was everything that a people could wish him to be – a bluff, confident patriot king who was master of his kingdom and feared no one. By the end of his long reign, despite everything, he was indisputably revered, indeed, in some strange way, loved. He had raised monarchy to near-idolatry. He had become the quintessence of Englishry and the focus of swelling national pride. Nothing would ever be quite the same after he had gone.

Yet, for all his power to dazzle, for all the charm and bonhomie which he could undoubtedly sometimes show, and for all the affection which he could certainly give and receive, it is difficult to think of any truly generous or selfless action performed by him and difficult not to suppose that, even those who enjoyed his apparently secure esteem, like Jane Seymour or Thomas Cranmer, would not have been thrown aside if it had been expedient to do so, along with the many others who had entwined their lives around his, given him so much, and yet been cast away. He has sometimes been portrayed as one who, despite all that he was and all that he did to those who were close to him, retained a fundamental sense of the mood and mind of his people which, in the last resort, he would never transgress and with which he was always instinctively in accord. But it is not easy to substantiate this benevolent image. That Henry could be held back by his subjects' feelings is true. We have seen this happen in the years 1530 to about 1532.[14] But that he felt beholden to the mind of the political nation or would ever have expected it to thwart his will either seriously or for long may be doubted. He may indeed have declared to Parliament in 1543 'we at no time stand so highly in our estate royal as in the time of Parliament, wherein we as head and you as members are conjoined and

14. See above, pp. 380 ff.

knit together into one body politic',[15] but the simile of head
and members was an ambivalent one and in his scheme of
things, probably, the former commanded, the latter merely
obeyed. The sting, like many good stings, was in the head.
He used Parliament, of course, to legalize his momentous
programme and would never have thought of not doing so,
but he probably never expected Parliament, however difficult it might prove on occasion, to deny him what he seriously desired any more than the judiciary would refuse to
condemn an important political personage.

Three times he led England back into war with France,
wars that brought him little more than 'ungracious dogholes' and ephemeral international prestige. He left England's relations with Scotland, with which he had not dealt
dexterously – recently, at least – in bloody confusion. For
much of his reign he so completely ignored the new worlds
across the seas, preferring instead to pursue antique ambitions across the Channel, that for over a generation English
maritime expansion languished. Certainly he had once
tried (in 1521) to stir his people to follow up the pioneer
voyages of the Cabots and been rebuffed. It was no fault
of his that English foreign commerce had concentrated
upon the export of unfinished cloth to Antwerp and that
this trade expanded so fast during the reign that his merchants had little incentive to venture elsewhere. But the
English voyages of 1517, 1527 and 1536, as well as Robert
Thorne's pleas, suggest that the memory of the Cabots was
not dead.[16] Had Henry been so minded, he could surely
have roused it successfully.

It has been suggested in a previous chapter that he seriously mishandled his divorce suit. It is also arguable that, though
the need for a son was obvious, as things turned out, Henry
placed England in at least as great political jeopardy by repudiating his first marriage as he would have done if he had
accepted his lot and resigned himself to leaving behind a

15. Holinshed, *Chronicle* (1808), iii, 824.
16. See above, pp. 168 f.

mature heiress. Had he died during the ten years which ran
from 1527 to 1537, that is, between the time when the divorce
became public and Edward was born, there might well have
been an ugly crisis, with Mary, perhaps the duke of Richmond and (after 1533) Elizabeth, and maybe others, all finding their supporters and opponents. Had he died some time
between Anne Boleyn's death and Edward's birth, that is,
at a moment when he had no legitimate offspring, he would
have left a yet more perilous situation. For ten years the succession was desperately insecure; and, of course, despite
everything, he still left behind a minor heir. The grim upsets of his son's reign and the evident political success of his
younger daughter's both made something of a mockery of
his own matrimonial scramblings. Had Mary been the only
child, and had she ascended the throne in 1547 after a normal
youth and young womanhood – happily married, perhaps to
Pole – Henry might not have provided badly for the nation.
It is easy to appreciate that, by 1527, the king was sincerely
beset by a dynastic problem. The point is that his attempt
to solve it was dangerously unsuccessful for ten years, and
not notably happy thereafter.

A reign which accomplished an evident political integration of the kingdom at the same time saw the nation acquire
a religious discord of a kind which it had not known before
and which would soon become bitter and complex, sending
fissures down English society to its lowest strata and setting
neighbour against neighbour, father against son in a disunity from which that society has not yet fully recovered.
Of course, this would have happened in some form or
another anyway. Nothing could have insulated England permanently against continental Protestantism. But the fact
remains that this disunity first took root in Henry's reign –
despite his efforts to create a new national unity around the
Supreme Headship. He who had been made the richest king
in Christendom and seemed to have rescued the crown for
ever from any recurrence of those financial worries which
had beset it in the previous century left it in debt. He who

was always ready to parade his paternal care for the commonwealth was guilty of tampering seriously with that most delicate sinew of society, the currency, and embarking on a wholesale debasement of English coin, without parallel in English history, in order to raise quick money to feed his wars. It is true that the pollution of her silver coinage stimulated trade with Antwerp, and it is also true that the celebrated price rise of the sixteenth century – a European phenomenon – was due fundamentally to the growth of population and the increased velocity of money, itself a consequence of such things as heavy taxation and government spending, the quickened activity of the land-market and the expansion of trade. None the less, the sudden increase in the total volume of specie in circulation which debasement brought about inevitably hastened England into galloping inflation; and, in the long run, to tamper with the currency was a dangerous expedient.

He had proclaimed himself as one who would lead the English Church from bondage, but his overlordship was a good deal more stern than that of the popes had ever been. The acts in Restraint of Annates had spoken of the 'intolerable and importable' burden of papal taxation, but the act of First Fruits and Tenths of 1534 would bring to him perhaps as much as ten times the amount per annum which English churchmen had paid to Rome before he liberated them and multiplied about threefold the total amount which they had hitherto paid, as they had long since paid, to king and pope combined.[17] Popery, as it happened, was cheaper, if nothing else.

He had struck down incomparable men and women like Catherine of Aragon, More, Aske, Cromwell; he had sent the first cardinal to martyrdom, namely, Fisher, and would like to have done the same to another, namely, Pole. In a few years, hundreds of glorious buildings, 'one of the great beauties of this realm', as Aske said, the fruit of generations

17. Scarisbrick, 'Clerical Taxation in England, 1485–1547', *Journal of Ecclesiastical History*, xi (1961), 41 ff.

of piety and architectural accomplishment, and the many fellows of those few survivors, like Fountains, Rievaulx, Wimborne or Tewkesbury, which still stand glorious and defiant, disappeared off the face of the land which they had so long dominated and adorned. Nor was this the full toll of destruction which Henry unleashed; for, with the soaring stone, the vaults, towers and spires, went glass and statues, choirstalls and rood-screens, plate and vestments – the flower of a dozen minor arts. How much of the fair and precious almost every town of England and every corner of the countryside lost in three or four years from 1536 onwards, what it must have felt like to see and hear workmen set about their emptied, echoing spoil and reduce a great abbey to piles of lead and dusty stone, we shall never know. Nor can we know what marvels once awaited the pilgrim to St Thomas's shrine at Canterbury, or St Swithin's at Winchester, St Richard's at Chichester, or St Cuthbert's at Durham; for Henry bade them go. He who built more than any other Tudor (though little of his work survives) was responsible for more destruction of beautiful buildings and other works of art than the Puritans. Not since the coming of the Danes, and then on a much smaller scale, had so many sacred fanes been despoiled and so much treasure smashed.

Doubtless many rejoiced to witness all this and to see a nation walk out of so much of its past. The Erasmian had much to commend, as also did those who had so eagerly acquired ex-monastic land. Some lamented that England's steps towards true religion had so far been so hesitant and erratic, that so many of the old evils had scarcely begun to be rooted out. Clerical pluralism and non-residence had been lightly scotched, far from killed; the dumb-dogs, that is, ignorant clerks who neglected preaching, abounded; the paraphernalia, the lumber, the man-made superstructure of deans and archdeacons, commissaries and apparitors, bishops' courts and (to quote a later aphorism) 'filthy canon law' were yet to be hacked down, together with those 'popish dregs', like tithes, excommunications and the holy clutter of

trentals, dirges, godparents, holy oils, blessings, candles and
the rest. For some the true reformation had scarcely begun.
The vineyard cried out for labourers, but the honest
labourers were few and the Supreme Head showed little
sense of urgency for the godly work which had to be undertaken. Generations of Romish aberration had to be undone.
An ignorant, hungry people had at last to be fed.[18]

But there was another, and, for some, yet more serious
charge to be brought against the king. Undoubtedly Henry
roused hopes that, when he turned an avenging hand against
the English Church and, in particular, against English monasticism, he would use the wealth that had been locked up
therein to serious purpose, that is, for educational and social
ends. Never before had any Englishman had the power to
bestow such obvious and long-lasting benefit on the nation
as did this king when the vast landed wealth of English
monasticism came into his hands for him to dispose as he
willed. Out of the Dissolution could have come scores of
schools, hospitals and generous endowment of the universities, new highways, almshouses, and perhaps a major attack
on poverty. Wolsey himself, John Fisher, Richard Fox, to
name only Henry's contemporaries, had converted monastic
endowments to educational ends and, had Henry wanted to
follow them, these were precedents enough to guide him.
Again, Renaissance humanism was above all concerned with
education (at all levels) and social justice. Henry lived in a
world whose prophets, like Erasmus and More and their
successors, cried out for educational reform and protested
indignantly against the suffering of the poor at the hands of

18. See, e.g., a remarkable tract against the 'dregs of Rome' which
still clogged English Christian life, in P.R.O. S.P. 6/3, fols 106 ff. –
dated about 1534/5. This diatribe (whose main themes have been
summarized in this paragraph) anticipates quite remarkably many
of the latter complaints of the Puritans. By the end of Henry's reign
and the beginning of Edward's, men like Becon, Lever, Brinkelow
and Crowley will have launched a bitter attack on impropriations,
lay rectors, absentee clergy, 'lordly' bishops, 'filthy traditions and
beggarly ceremonies of Babylon'.

the grasping rich. For all its alleged materialism, Tudor society often showed a remarkable zeal for 'good works'; and the sixteenth century is only rivalled by the late nineteenth and twentieth in its importance in the history of English schooling. Moreover, it seems clear that the continental Reformation preserved a considerably higher proportion of monastic wealth for charitable purposes – schools, hospitals and the like – than the Henrician.

In 1533, Thomas Starkey had urged that clerical first fruits and tenths should be used for poor relief and proposed that some monastic revenues also be used to this end, as well as to support learning. Three years later he urged to Cromwell that the monasteries which still stood should be turned into little universities.[19] With the income from the secular church and from lands of suppressed monasteries let 'some notable charitable works be undertaken', an anonymous writer proposed.[20] Wriothesley had drawn up a paper listing what his king could do with the monastic wealth, including setting aside 10,000 marks p.a. to found new hospitals and refurbish old, 20,000 marks to support the army, 5,000 to build highways and the like, and thus provide employment for poor folk.[21] Indeed, Henry himself appeared to subscribe to these lofty aims. After the dissolution of the smaller monasteries in 1536, it had evidently been assumed by some that this was the end of the matter, that the remaining houses would stand unscathed – especially as the first act of Dissolution had declared that there were 'divers and great solemn monasteries of this realm wherein, thanks be to God, religion is right well kept and observed'.[22] It may well be that, at this time, Henry sincerely intended to go no further. In January 1538 Richard Layton crushed as 'vain babbling' and slanderous misrepresentation of the king a rumour which he had heard in Cambridge that all monasteries would fall;[23] and that rumour was solemnly disavowed in an official paper

19. *L.P.*, xi, 73. 20. *L.P.*, vii, 1065.
21. *L.P.*, xiii, ii, i.
22. *Statutes of the Realm*, iii, 575. 23. *L.P.*, xiii, i, 102.

produced some months later.[24] In July 1537 Henry himself re-founded Chertsey Abbey at Bisham and a nunnery at Stix-wold in Lincolnshire to pray for him and his queen; while as late as May 1538 a house for Cistercian nuns was re-founded 'in perpetuity' at Kirkless.[25] Though Layton's dis-avowal must have been disingenuous, for, even as he spoke it, he was about the business of bullying superiors of houses in Norfolk into surrender, Henry's curious refoundations may well have been further evidence of how untidy and, in the long term, often unpremeditated his campaign was. Any-way, by early 1538 the last phase was under way of the giant operation of abolishing the remaining monastic houses, together with the suppression of the friaries, a class of institution which had hitherto escaped attention; and in May 1539 Parliament passed the second act of Dissolution, which bestowed on the crown all monastic possessions sur-rendered since 1536 or to be surrendered in the future.

Thus was solemnly sanctioned what Henry's own actions and his own servants had recently argued would never happen. Parliament, however, had not yielded easily. On 20 May Marillac reported to Francis that the dissolution of the remaining monasteries was being discussed and that the members wanted to use 'certain abbeys' to provide for bishoprics and the foundation of schools and hospitals.[26] Parliament itself, therefore, was uttering concern that the wealth of English monasticism should not be wasted. It was almost certainly to placate (and to stifle) these dangerous ideas that, on the very day when the bill for the dissolution

24. *L.P.*, xiv, i, 402 – a very interesting, undated and unsigned apologia for Henry's Reformation. It is full of 'imperial' theory and, among other things, in the course of praising the king for deliver-ing England from superstition and idolatry by the suppression of shrines and relics, asserts that Becket was no martyr, but a profligate who was reconciled with Henry II years before his death and eventu-ally slain by a servant of the archbishop of York, with whom he was squabbling at the time.

25. Knowles, *The Religious Orders in England*, iii, 350.

26. *L.P.*, xiv, i, 998.

of the greater monasteries completed its journey through
the two houses of Parliament, there should have been rushed
through in a single day a further piece of legislation whose
grandiloquent preamble seemed to promise exactly those
things which, according to Marillac, the king's own subjects
desired; and interestingly enough, that preamble was written
by Henry himself, in his own hand.

The enacting clause of the bill which had thus suddenly
made its appearance empowered the king to create as many
new bishoprics as he might judge necessary – an obvious and
long-overdue reform, which Wolsey had been preparing to
effect shortly before his fall – and to endow them with ex-
monastic revenue. In the preamble of the act, the Supreme
Head wrote of his desire that, by this conversion of monastic
wealth, 'God's word might be the better set forth, children
brought up in learning, clerks nourished in the universities,
old servants decayed to have living, almshouses for poor folk
to be sustained in, readers of Greek, Hebrew and Latin to
have good stipend, daily alms to be ministered, mending of
highways, exhibition for ministers of the Church'.[27] That
out of the Dissolution should come some lasting benefit to
the community was not, therefore, the cry of a mere handful of day-dreamers. The king himself publicly proclaimed
numerous good causes to which monastic revenue was to
be turned, and publicly promised to endow them.

Shortly after the bill became law, a group of bishops,
which included Stephen Gardiner and Richard Sampson of
Chichester, set about elaborate plans for erecting a large
crop of new bishoprics.[28] Henry himself drew up his own
design for endowing thirteen new sees with the revenues of
some twenty large abbeys and so redrawing the diocesan
map of England that every major county or, in the case of
the smaller counties, neighbouring pairs thereof should be

27. B.M. Cleo. E, iv, fol. 366 (*L.P.*, xiv, i, 868 (2); printed in Cole,
King Henry the Eighth's Scheme of Bishopricks (1838), with a
facsimile of the text.

28. Cole, op. cit., *L.P.*, xiv, ii, 428–30.

the seat of a bishopric. Thus Waltham Cross would provide for the see of Essex, St Alban's for that of Hertford, Bury St Edmund's for that of Suffolk, Fountains for that of Lancaster, Peterborough for that of Northants and Huntingdon. Three houses were to be given to the new diocese of Cornwall, three to that of Nottingham and Derby, three to that of Bedford and Buckingham, etc.[29] But this plan was not to be implemented. Eventually only six new dioceses were set up and endowed with one abbey apiece, viz. Westminster, Gloucester, Bristol, Oseney, Peterborough, and Chester. Eight pre-Reformation cathedrals had been served by monks or canons – a practice almost peculiar to England – and though the monastic establishments were dissolved the new chapters of what now became secular cathedrals inherited the endowments of their monastic predecessors. Finally, the two abbeys of Thornton and Burton were converted into secular colleges. In all, therefore, sixteen former religious houses, having undergone a change of one form or another, either remained with, or were gained by, the secular Church. These sixteen included some of the wealthiest houses of all, with a total net income amounting to 'almost 15 per cent of the total income of all houses'.[30] But Henry's largesse was not as bounteous as this figure suggests. The new chapters of the ex-monastic cathedrals received only a small proportion of the revenues of the convents which they had supplanted; and, thanks to careful cheese-paring, the six new cathedrals were 'considerably more modest than ... even the smallest and poorest of the old secular cathedrals'.[31] As a result, less than a quarter of the total wealth of these sixteen houses was restored by the crown to the Church. Henry's re-endowments were niggardly; and time was to make them more niggardly yet. By forcing bishops to sell and exchange land, a tactic which seems usually to have given the crown the better of the bargain, Henry was able to begin a programme of fleecing the secular Church which his successors would elaborate, and to take back with one

29. B.M. Cleo. E, iv, fol. 365 (*L.P.*, xiv, i, 868).
30. Knowles, op. cit., 389.   31. ibid., 390.

hand some of the little which he had given with the other. Furthermore, in 1544 and 1546 respectively the two colleges which he had re-founded, Burton and Thornton, were judged 'superfluous' and joined the many other colleges which were then being sacrificed.

Six new bishoprics, meanly endowed, and eight secular-ized cathedral chapters to whom but a fraction of previous revenue had been restored – this was all that Henry spared for the Church of which, under God, he was Supreme Head. In some places canons' churches which had hitherto been either wholly or partly parochial survived the Dis-solution and continued to serve the neighbourhood. Else-where, as at Bolton, Malmesbury and Malvern, the dis-appearance of the local religious house could cause sufficient hardship for the townsfolk to buy back the church for use as a parish church; and at Tewkesbury, too, the monks' church was saved thus. But there may have been many other places, less enterprising than these, where the religious life of local layfolk was seriously upset by the disappearance of monastic churches in which they had hitherto worshipped.

The religious houses were certainly not the generous homes of refuge and succour of legend, but it is indisput-able that they supported, directly or indirectly, a large number of those institutions which are collectively styled 'hospitals' – hospices and hostels, almshouses, hospitals in the modern sense, leper-houses and asylums, etc. A con-siderable number of these, especially almshouses attached to houses of the old orders, survived. Bristol kept perhaps as many as nine out of its eleven houses for the old and sick; Exeter four out of seven; Newcastle thirteen; Norwich per-haps fourteen; Winchester three out of five; Worcester two out of three.[32] But alongside the survivals there was un-

32. I have culled these figures from Knowles and Hadcock, *Medieval Religious Houses* (1953). The fate of many hospitals at the time of the Dissolution (as before) is often so obscure that it is not possible to present exact statistics of suppressions and survivals. Cf. Clay, *Medieval Hospitals of England* (1909), a pioneer work, whose treat-ment of hospitals at this time is sketchy.

doubtedly widespread, patchy destruction. Sometimes the
houses suppressed may have been the least flourishing institutions; sometimes, as at St Nicholas's in Pontefract, the inmates received pensions. But elsewhere the suppressions
must have been a serious affliction. The hospitals belonging
to Bermondsey abbey, Bury St Edmunds, Hexham priory,
Peterborough and Whitby, and the large hospice at Walsingham were swept away; York lost its St Leonard's, the greatest
of all English hospitals, as well as the house of St Nicholas;
Worcester its St Wulstan's. If York was sorely hit, so too
was London. The hospitals of St Thomas (of Acon), St
Bartholomew, St Mary within Cripplegate (Elsing Spital, a
house for the blind), St Mary without Bishopsgate (which
had some 180 beds for the sick), St Giles in the Fields and St
Thomas at Southwark – all were suppressed, despite the
petition of the lord mayor that the houses which had been
closed should be restored and the survivors spared. At the
end of his life Henry yielded to entreaty and, as his letters
patent claimed, 'divine mercy inspiring us', restored St
Bartholomew's and endowed it with an income of 500
marks per annum, a sum which the citizens, 'thinking it for
their parts rather too little than enough', promptly doubled.[33]
Two years later the citizens bought back and reopened St
Mary's. The story of English hospitals and their fate at
the time of the Reformation awaits definitive study. When it
is made, the king who is honoured as the founder of the
College of Physicians in 1518, whose reign (in 1540) saw the
incorporation of the united companies of Barbers and Sur-
geons of London, and who had so keen a personal interest
in medical lore and his own health, will probably not occupy
an exalted place in it.

Nor can he in the history of education. Early in his reign,
John Fisher had struggled hard to secure sufficient revenues
from the lands of the late Lady Margaret Beaufort to
complete the building and equipping of her college of St

33. Stow, *Survey of London*, i, 318 f. Henry also parted with the
London Grey Friars, which became Christ's Hospital, ibid., ii, 24.

John at Cambridge, but had found himself so 'straitly handled and so long delayed and wearied and fatigate' that he gave up the fight and allowed the king, as Lady Margaret's heir at law, to enter his inheritance. Thereupon Henry apparently promised Fisher £2,800 to complete the foundation, but less than half, about £1,200 to be precise, ever came from the king into the building fund, with the result that Fisher had to embark on the dissolution of three small, largely derelict monasteries to make good the deficit;[34] an inauspicious beginning, this, both to Henry's dealings with the cause of learning and to his relations with Fisher. Moreover, despite the praise which Erasmus and others lavished upon this golden prince, despite the proximity of educational zealots such as Catherine of Aragon, Richard Fox and More, and despite the example of Wolsey, the king showed little interest in the academic life. He gave no more than conventional patronage to any scholar (and, indeed, presided over a Court in many ways less open, less cosmopolitan and interesting than his father's); he inherited none of his grandmother's interest in higher education; until he turned to the universities for support in the divorce he had little care for them and, in the whole of his reign, seems to have visited only one, namely Oxford, once. Within a few days of Wolsey's fall he was threatening the two educational establishments which the cardinal had founded, that is Cardinal's College at Oxford and the grammar school in his native Ipswich. By 22 November 1529 royal agents had sped to the last-named and, under the pretence of searching for hidden treasure, had stripped the school of its plate, vestments and sacred vessels, and set to work on its suppression. Thus perished a grammar school upon which its founder had lavished much imaginative and enlightened care; a school which, had it not been snuffed out, might well have rivalled St Paul's as a landmark in Tudor educational history. Instead, its stone was carried to London to supply the royal building at Whitehall. However, after many

34. *V.C.H. Cambridge*, ii, 438.

anxious months, the college at Oxford was saved. From his exile, Wolsey wrote to Henry beseeching him to remember his 'painful and long-continued service' and spare his foundation; and he wrote to More, Norfolk, Arundel and others, begging them lend their voice to his. In August 1530 a deputation came from the college, headed by the dean, to plead with the king. 'Surely we purpose to have an honourable college there,' said Henry to his visitors with something less than complete honesty, 'but not so great and of such magnificence as my lord cardinal intended to have.' Norfolk had reported that the king would dissolve the college and allow its inmates no more than the lands of St Frideswide's, the core of its endowments. But at length, thanks, it was said, to the duke's advocacy, the college survived – though with its establishment reduced and its offensive name changed.[35]

The monasteries had not provided a large-scale network of schools throughout the kingdom, but many of them were useful places of education. Evesham, Reading and Glastonbury, for example, supported schools of some considerable size, St Mary's, Winchester took in twenty-six daughters of the local squirearchy, some nunneries taught small boys, many other houses provided schooling on varying scales to outsiders, as well as to the boarders in almonry and songschools. When the crash came a good deal lived on in one form or another. Thus many of the secularized cathedrals, for example Canterbury, Worcester and Ely, received their 'King's Schools', nearly all of them refoundations rather than the fruit of royal bounty, and smaller than originally planned. Elsewhere schools survived or appeared as the result of local private enterprise. At Sherborne the town not only bought the abbey church from the royal grantee, but rented the schoolhouse and retained the former master to teach there. Likewise the townsfolk of Abingdon kept a

35. *L.P.*, iv, 6574–8, 6579, 6688. Before its apparently sudden reprieve, More thought that Henry would seize the college. See ibid., 6679.

former monastic school alive, and Cirencester, having lost
('to the great discommodity' of the town) a school dependent
on Winchcombe abbey, resuscitated it a few years later by
turning a chantry endowment to new purpose; and, at least
for a while, schools continued at Reading and Bruton. At
Warwick and Ottery St Mary townsfolk bought back some
lands hitherto held by suppressed colleges in order to
endow and re-found parish schools.[36] The worst damage to
schooling was, therefore, often avoided or made good. None
the less the Dissolution brought losses and upsets. Similarly
the passing of English monasticism and all that went with it
brought tempestuous times to the universities. Queens' College Cambridge joined in the scramble and successfully
petitioned Cromwell for the neighbouring Carmelite friary;
in 1546 Henry founded Trinity College, rolling together
three existing establishments, Michaelhouse, King's Hall
and Physwick Hostel, and endowing the new college with
the revenues of no less than twenty-six dissolved religious
houses. Buckingham College was re-founded and re-named
Magdalene College in 1542; much later Sir Walter Mildmay
gave the site of the Dominican friary to his new college,
Emmanuel, and part of the Greyfriars convent (which had
been quarried for stone for Henry's Trinity College) passed
into the possession of Sidney Sussex. Likewise Oxford
acquired, directly or indirectly, a few pickings, such as the
Cistercian hall of residence, St Bernard's, which went to
King's, formerly Cardinal's College (and eventually Christ
Church). Finally, in 1540 Henry endowed five regius professorships at Cambridge – out of the revenues of Westminster
Cathedral, however – in Greek, Hebrew, civil law, divinity
and medicine.[37] Yet all this was probably small recompense
for the buffeting which higher learning had suffered at his
hands. Heads of colleges had been purged and two chancel-

36. For all this see Simon, *Education and Society in Tudor England*
(Cambridge, 1966), 179 ff.

37. ibid., 202 ff.; Porter, *Reformation and Reaction in Tudor
Cambridge* (Cambridge, 1958), 10 ff.; *V.C.H. Cambridge*, iii, 177.

lors of Cambridge (Fisher and Cromwell) beheaded, royal injunctions had upset curricula by banning the teaching of scholastic theology and canon law, Richard Layton and his fellow royal visitors had unleashed gross vandalism when they visited Oxford to 'set Duns Scotus in Bocardo [the local prison] and ... utterly banished him for ever', leaving him and 'all his blind glosses ... a common servant to every man, fast nailed up upon posts in all common houses of ease- ment'. A little later, so Layton reported delightedly to his master, he had seen the quad of New College bestrewn with leaves ripped from the works of Scotus and doubtless others, and watched 'the wind blowing them into every corner'.[38] Both universities lost their friaries and monastic halls of residence, of which there had been twelve in Oxford, and both suffered decline in numbers when the supply of students from the religious orders was halted. Though Cromwell's *Injunctions* were seriously aimed at amending university life and teaching, and Dr Leigh's visitation of Cambridge fruitful of much sound advice, the 1530s on the whole brought upsets and dislocation to the universities – so much so that, in 1539, Cambridge reported to Cromwell that the number of students had been halved.[39] Moreover, scarcely had the colleges emerged from the stormy years of the Dissolution of the religious houses proper than they had to face the Chantries act of 1545 which gave the king the power to dissolve any institution at either University and seize its possessions. As Matthew Parker, then vice-chancel- lor, said later, the real threat probably came from folk about the king who were 'importunately suing to him to have the lands and possessions of both universities surveyed, they meaning afterwards to enjoy the best of their lands and possessions by exchange of impropriated benefices and such other improved lands'.[40] Ravening 'wolves' who stood near the king and who, so the high-minded Dr Cox would soon warn Paget,[41] would devour the endowments of colleges,

38. *L.P.*, ix, 117 f.   39. Simon, op. cit., 203.
40. ibid., 211.   41. *L.P.*, xxi, ii, 260.

chantries, cathedrals, churches and universities – these were
the real predators.

The university lands were surveyed, but surveyed by commissions headed by university men. Fearful of what the
recent act might bring them, Parker and the University of
Cambridge wrote urgently to Henry and Paget for protection, and turned also for help to Catherine Parr, who not
long before had looked to them to supply the chief lumin-
aries of her school for the royal children. Catherine proved
a good friend. She 'attempted the king's majesty' and reported her consort inclined rather to 'advance learning and
erect new occasion thereof, than to confound those your
ancient and godly institutions'. When the commissioners presented their report to Henry at Hampton Court in the spring
of 1546, the king was struck by the good husbandry of the
colleges and the leanness of their endowments, adding 'that
pity it were these lands should be altered to make them
worse'. Thus were '*lupos quosdam hiantes*' disappointed
and thus did a king who may only have been finally dissuaded from pruning Cambridge's colleges by the appeal
of Sir Thomas Smith, the first Regius professor of civil law,
deliver the universities from spoliation.[42]

It is impossible to believe that Henry ever intended to
inflict any serious damage on the universities. Indeed, his
lavish endowment of Trinity College and his foundation of
the Regius professorships mark him as one of the most
generous royal patrons in Cambridge's history; and all in
all he could claim to have given more to education than
any other king of England. Yet though this is true, though
many medieval hospitals survived, though he restored a few
others, though some monastic schools were re-founded by
him and others redeemed by private individuals and enterprising townsfolk, and though, sooner or later, a good deal
of ex-monastic wealth found its way back into educational,
civic and charitable undertakings, the fact remains that

42. *V.C.H. Cambridge*, iii, 177. *L.P.*, xxi, i, 68, 204, 279. See also
Dewar, *Sir Thomas Smith. A Tudor Intellectual in Office* (1964), 24 f.

Henry destroyed, damaged or dislocated scores of institutions which were actually or potentially of great value to the community. Furthermore, the most grievous charge which some were to raise against him was concerned not with what he did, but with what he failed to do. Six new episcopal sees, five Regius professorships, a college at Cambridge and a handful of other endowments – though impressive in themselves – were not much to show for the immense fortune which had flowed into his hands and with which he could have created a unique monument to enlightened kingship.

At the time, a number of voices cried out to him to do so. No less a person than Dr John London, himself one of the royal visitors to the religious houses, pleaded in vain that the church of the Franciscan friary at Reading be given to the township for use as a guildhall and a little later begged that the revenue of the houses of Northampton should succour the poor and unemployed of that town, which was passing through a period of economic distress.[43] Bishop Latimer asked Cromwell unsuccessfully that the income of the two friaries of Worcester be given to the upkeep of the city's school, bridge and wall, and pleaded (also unsuccessfully) that the priory of Great Malvern be allowed to survive, 'not in monkery, God forbid', but to serve the cause of 'learning, preaching, study, and hospitality'.[44] The mayor and aldermen of Coventry asked that the two friars' churches be allowed to stand as 'isolation' churches, for use of the sick in time of plague.[45] The reformer Robert Ferrar interceded in vain for the house of which he had been made prior, St Oswald's, near Pontefract, that it should stand as a

43. *L.P.*, xiii, ii, 367; xiv, i, 3 (5), 42. Dr London's reputation, hitherto lamentable, has been much repaired by Professor Knowles (op. cit., 354 ff.). London was far from being the salacious iconoclast of legend.

44. *L.P.*, xiii, ii, 543, 1036. Latimer promised Cromwell that the prior of Great Malvern would pay the king 500 marks and Cromwell 200 for such a reprieve.

45. ibid., 394. (Cf. xiv, i, 34.)

college 'for the nourishment of youth in virtue and learning';[46] and the abbot and community of Evesham likewise
begged to be allowed to stand as a college providing much-
needed education and hospitality to their neighbourhood –
and likewise met no success.[47] Similarly the University of
Cambridge besought Henry that monasteries hitherto given
over to superstition be turned into colleges of learning.
Meanwhile, no less a person than Lord Audley, who himself
acquired a fortune in monastic spoils, had appealed to Cromwell to save two great abbeys in Essex, St Osyth's and St
John's Colchester, not as monasteries, but as colleges where
poor folk could continue to have 'daily relief' and hospitality.
Despite his offer of £200 to Cromwell if the latter would
press his suit, the plea went unanswered.[48] Colchester Abbey
fell (and its abbot went to the gallows); St Osyth's became
one of Cromwell's many ex-monastic trophies.

'Our posterity will wonder at us', the illustrious Dr Cox
would later write to Paget, as he saw all about him nothing
but unconcern for learning and good works, and watched
the 'wolves' devour their prey.[49] Henry himself set them
a telling example. He had built St James's Palace on the
site of a lazar house; he used the chapel of the London
Charterhouse, whose inmates he had purged so bloodily, as
a store for tents and garden equipment; Chertsey Abbey
and Merton Priory supplied stone for Nonsuch Palace,
which itself stood on the site of a parish church; God's
House, Portsmouth, became an armoury; Maison Dieu,
Dover, a victualling yard. Small wonder if his subjects fell
upon the booty with zeal.

The 'wolves' were no doubt a large, influential number,
and no doubt, by responding to their clamour and shedding
the great wealth of medieval English monasticism among
them by gift, lease and sale, Henry not only yielded to widespread appetitiveness, but created an invaluable vested interest in the new regime. If, however, he had chosen to heed

46. *L.P.*, xiii, ii, 285.
47. ibid., 866.
48. *St.P.*, i, 587 f. (*L.P.*, xiii, ii, 306).
49. *L.P.*, xxi, ii, 282.

the cry of that positive, creative anticlericalism of which we spoke some time ago,[50] if he had wanted to follow English precedent, if, indeed, he had honoured his own high-flown promises, then at least a large proportion of the monastic wealth would have been used as such as Fisher and Wolsey had used it, and men like Starkey, Dr London and Bishop Latimer had begged him to use it. Had the king given his weight to the cause of righteousness, a nation to which the humanists and 'Commonwealth men' made such urgent appeal and which, for all its greed, showed itself ready to endow good causes with remarkable generosity, would have applauded him.[51] But Henry virtually ignored that cause. He was not one of the enlightened. He had taken hold of little of what Tudor humanism stood for and was a stranger to the fire that consumed an Erasmus or a Latimer. The disposal of the monastic lands, particularly the sales thereof, was skilfully enough done. Grantees paid a fairly high price, the land they received was subject to the annual tenth due from all ecclesiastical possessions and was held by knight service in chief – and therefore exposed the whole of the recipient's lands to feudal incidents levied by the Court of Wards.[52] The avalanche of sales during the 1540s which had carried away about two thirds of the monastic lands by Henry's death guaranteed, therefore, some income for the

50. See above, p. 319 f.
51. As must be the conclusion after pondering the contents of Jordan's *Philanthropy in England, 1480–1660* (1959), and its companion studies of charities in London, etc. Professor Jordan's contention that the volume of bequests for schools, civic improvements, etc. expanded during this period may not be acceptable in view of his neglect of the contemporary decline in the purchasing power of money, but the large-scale and widespread concern of testators of all degrees for these causes is, as he demonstrates, incontestable.
52. Youings, 'The terms of the disposal of the Devon monastic lands, 1536–58', *E.H.R.*, lxix (1954), 18 ff. Hurstfield, *The Queen's Wards* (1958), 18 ff., shows that the feudal tenure was quickly evaded by means of the fiction that ex-monastic land was held of the king as lord of the manor of East Greenwich – and held in common socage, and therefore free of most incidents.

crown despite the fact that the need for quick money had driven it to apparently reckless alienation of its capital assets. But the tactics of the operation were one thing; the strategy another. Not only did Henry fail to use the wealth that came to him in generous service to the cause of education, social justice or religion; worse, he squandered it to pay for the very cause which an Erasmus or a More most hated, namely, the fruitless war of prestige and amour-propre waged by vainglorious monarchy. Like so much else that was precious to England, the wealth of centuries of piety (or much of it) was poured out on the fields of northern France. It was a shrewd, bold subject who had written, probably in the 1530s, that it would be better to convert monastic revenue to building towns and providing better justice than ever to allow the king to take hold of them.[53]

It was not long before bitter cries of disappointment rose from the lips of those who had expected too much. The freer pulpit and the freer press in the first years of Edward's reign finally released the angry voice of the so-called 'Commonwealth men' – men like the tireless Hugh Latimer, the ex-friar Henry Brinkelow (alias Roderyck Mors), the social critic Robert Crowley, preachers and divines like Thomas Lever and Thomas Becon, and John Hales, a mere clerk of the Hanaper. As these men flailed the ungodliness and inhumanity of their fellow-men, trouncing every iniquity from merciless landlordism which oppressed the poor with fines, rack-rents, evictions and enclosures, to the tyranny of bishops and the bizarre, costly mysteries of the law (and much in between), so did they indignantly lament the betrayal of the Reformation from which they had hoped for so much. In the past, writers from Langland onwards had denounced worldly prelates, grasping clerks, 'abbey-lubbers' and above all the friars, so many of whom had manifestly fallen away from their founders' ideal of humble poverty; but it was now beginning to seem that the active greed of the new 'possessioners', the laymen who had taken over

53. *L.P.*, xiii, ii, 1204 – an anonymous, undated tract.

from the clergy, was more disgraceful than the parasitism of those whom they had supplanted. The critics of the old order were to lay about the new with yet greater violence and even to begin to speak about the monasteries with the same regret that Robert Aske had once voiced. As Becon lamented in his *The Jewel of Joy*, the Dissolution allowed the rich to oppress the poor on a larger scale than hitherto. The new 'Caterpillars of the Commonweal', i.e. those who had entered the monastic lands, 'abhor the name of monks, friars, canons, nuns, etc., but their goods they greedily gripe. And yet, where the cloisters kept hospitality, let out their farms at a reasonable price, nourished schools, brought up youth in good letters, they did none of these things.' 'The state of England', he cried, 'was never so miserable as it is at present.'[54] Said Thomas Lever, taunting the recipients of the monastic booty with bitter indignation, 'in the great abundance of lands and goods taken from abbeys, colleges and chantries for to serve the king in all necessaries and charges, especially in provision of relief for the poor and maintenance of learning, the king is so disappointed that both be spoiled, all maintenance of learning decayed and you only enriched'.[55] The poor commons, another savage broadside exclaimed, had expected to be delivered from their suffering, but 'alas they failed of their expectation and are now in more penury than ever they were. . . . Then they had hospitals and almshouses to be lodged in, but now they lie and starve in the streets.'[56] These outpourings are certainly not to be taken as well-informed, scientific analyses either of prevailing conditions or of their causes. Becon, Lever and the others exaggerated (probably wildly) the decay of learning and the collapse of relief for the poor.

54. Quoted by Simon, op. cit., 195.
55. White, *Social Criticism in Popular Religious Literature of the Sixteenth Century* (New York, 1944), 92. This work contains a good deal of interest concerning the development of 'Piers Plowman' and Utopian literature, as well as 'straight' religious and social criticism.
56. Quoted, ibid., 93.

What they denounced as mere greed and heartlessness was probably more often than not a legitimate desire of landlords struggling to hold their own against inflation to improve their circumstances by raising rents, enclosing, etc. Becon's rosy picture of the kindly monks of yore made good pamphleteering, but, alas, was quite misleading; and there is no reason to suppose that, if the religious had survived, they would not have been as oppressive as their lay successors. Nonetheless, they voiced a just, bitter disappointment at finding that a dream had become damnably like a nightmare.

Some years before, Henry Brinkelow had uttered that most interesting diatribe *The Complaynt of Roderyck Mors*, in the course of which he called on Parliament, among other things, to complete the destruction of the wealth of the Church that had been begun with the attack on the religious. 'Ye must first down with all your vain chantries, all your proud colleges of canons and specially your forked wolves of bishops,' he declaimed. But he then quickly remembered what had happened to the monastic property. 'For the goods of these chantries, colleges and bishops,' he therefore added, 'for the Lord's sake take no example at the distribution of the abbey goods and lands; but look for your erudition to the godly Christian Germans in this case, which divided not such goods and lands among the princes, lords and rich people, that had not need thereof, but they put them into the use of the commonwealth and unto the provision of the poor according to the doctrine of the Scripture.'[57] If Brinkelow overestimated the virtue of the continental Reformation, he had a sound suspicion that it had been a good deal more godly than Henry's. And what was it that that great Lutheran, Robert Barnes, wanted to say as he addressed the crowd which had come to see him burn at Smithfield, and was prevented from saying by the sheriff? He had begged to be allowed to make five requests of the

57. *The Complaynt of Roderyck Mors*, ed. Cowper, E.E.T.S. (1874), 47 f.

king. The first began: 'whereas his grace hath received into
his hands all the goods and substance of the abbeys' – but
then the sheriff stopped him and, in the confusion, Barnes
was not able to do more than exclaim, 'Would to God it
might please his grace to bestow the said goods, or some of
them, to the comfort of his poor subjects, who surely have
great need of them.'[58] He was able to continue with the remaining items of his appeal – that Henry would strike
down adultery and fornication, punish swearing and 'set
forth Christ's true religion'. But his first plea, concerning
the monastic lands, was stifled by a nervous sheriff. Had
Barnes prepared for his prince some clarion-call to enlightened benefaction?

Perhaps Crowley might speak last – Crowley, a man of
burning compassion from whose pen came pages of re-
morseless denunciation of greed and covetousness, and who
deserves to stand with Langland, More, the Diggers and
Marx as one of the great apostles of social justice. It is
appropriate to end, not with some thunderous passage from
a major work setting forth the familiar theme of Christian
stewardship and calling upon the rich to 'repent the oppres-
sion wherewith they vex the poor commons and show themselves, through love, to be brothers of one father and
members of one body with them';[59] but, rather, with a so-
called 'epigram' – a quiet, meditative piece of execrable
verse:

> As I walked alone
> and mused on things,
> That have in my time
> been done by great kings,
> I bethought me of abbeys
> that sometime I saw,
> Which are now suppressed
> all by a law.

58. *Foxe*, v, 436.
59. Crowley, *Select Works*, ed. Cowper, E.E.T.S. (1872), 159.

O Lord, (thought I then)
what occasion was here
To provide for learning
and make poverty clear.

The lands and the jewels
that hereby were had
Would have found godly preachers
which might well have led
The people aright
that now go astray
And have fed the poor
that famish every day.[60]

Haunting words. 'He is a wonderful man and has wonder-ful people around him', a French ambassador in England once wrote of Henry, 'but he is an old fox.'[61] 'Junker Heintz will be God and does whatever he lusts,' said Luther.[62] Maybe Henry was no more unaware and irresponsible than many kings have been; but rarely, if ever, have the unawareness and irresponsibility of a king proved more costly of material benefit to his people. All the same, it was the grief of a stricken man that overtook the lord chancel-lor on Monday 31 January 1547, when he announced to the lords that the monarch whom he and they had both feared and revered was dead.

60. Crowley, *Select Works*, 7.
61. *L.P.*, xiii, i, 56. Castillon to Francis I, January 1538.
62. *L.P.*, xvi, 106.

Manuscript Sources

British Museum, London

1. State papers in:
   a. Cotton MSS, Caligula D vi, vii, viii, ix
      Cleopatra C v; E iv, v, vi; F ii
      Galba B v; D v, vii
      Nero B vi
      Otho C x
      Titus B i
      Vespasian C vii
      Vitellius B ii, iii, iv, vi, xi, xii, xix, xx, xxi
   b. Additional MSS 15,387, 19,649, 25,114, 48,044 (not in L.P.).
2. Treatises on Henry VIII's divorce in Cotton MS, Otho C x; Harley MS 417; Additional MSS 4,622, 28,582.

Public Record Office, London

1. State Papers of Henry VIII (S.P. 1) 13, 16, 17, 19, 21, 22, 23, 54, 57, 59, 70, 74, 135, 178, 236, 238, 241.
2. The same, folio volumes (S.P. 2) C, L, N, P.
3. Theological Tracts (S.P. 6) 3, 5, 8, 9.
4. Exchequer records:
   a. Treasury of Receipt, Miscellaneous Books (E. 36) 215, 217.
   b. King's Remembrancer, Memoranda Rolls (E. 159) 309–14.
5. King's Bench records:
   a. Ancient Indictments (K.B. 9) 518.
   b. *Coram Rege* Rolls (K.B. 27) 1080–91.
   c. Controlment Rolls (K.B. 29) 164–7.
6. Treatises on Henry VIII's divorce in S.P. 1/42, 59, 63, 64.

House of Lords Record Office

Original Act, 32 Henry VIII, *c.* 60.

Haus-, Hof- und Staatsarchiv, Vienna
England Ber., Fasz. 5, Varia 2.

Vatican Archives, Rome
Arm. xxxix, 23, fo. 689.
Lettere di Principi ii.

Bibliography

(For a comprehensive bibliography of the reign of Henry VIII the reader is referred to *Bibliography of British History. Tudor Period, 1485–1603* (second edn, Oxford, 1959), ed. Conyers Read. What follows below is a list of works cited in the course of this biography. Unless otherwise noted, the place of publication is London.)

Primary Works

(Contemporary writings, chronicles, printed collections of documents, calendars, etc.)

Abel, Thomas, *Invicta Veritas* (Luneberg, 1532).

Acta Curiae Romana in causa matrimoniale Regis cum Catherina Regina (1531).

André, Bernard, *Annales Henrici* (printed in *Memorials of King Henry the Seventh*, ed. Gairdner).

Bekinson, John, *De Supremo et Absoluto Regis Imperio* (1547).

Brinkelow, Henry (*alias* Roderyck Mors), *The Complaynt of Roderyck Mors*, ed. Cowper, E.E.T.S. (1874).

Brown, Rawdon, *Four years at the court of Henry VIII* (2 vols, 1854).

Cajetan (Thomas de Vio, Cardinal), *De Coniugio regis Angliae cum relicta fratris sui* (Rome, 1530).

Calais, The Chronicle of, Camden Society, xxxv (1845).

Calendar of Papal Registers (1893–   ).

Calendar of Patent Rolls, Henry VII (1914–16).

Calendar of State Papers, Milan (1385–1618), ed. Hinds (1912).

Calendar of State Papers, Spanish, ed. Bergenroth, Gayangos and Hume (1862–   ). (*Supplement to the Calendar of State Papers, Spanish*, ed. Bergenroth. *Further Supplement to the Calendar of State Papers, Spanish*, ed. Mattingly.)

Calendar of State Papers, Venetian, ed. Rawdon Brown (1864–   ).

Caporella, Petropandus, *Questio de Matrimonio Serenissimae Reginae Angliae, etc.* (Naples, 1531).

Cavendish, George, *The Life and Death of Cardinal Wolsey*, ed. Sylvester, E.E.T.S. (1959).

Cochlaeus, Johannes, *De Matrimonio Serenissimi Regis Angliae, etc.* (Leipzig, 1535).

Cranmer, Thomas, *Articuli Duodecim* (printed in *Pocock*, 1, 334 ff.).

—, *Miscellaneous Writings and Letters of*, ed. Cox, Parker Society (1846).

Crowley, Robert, *Select Works*, ed. Cowper, E.E.T.S. (1872).

Determinacions of the moste famous and mooste excellent universities of Italy and France (1531).

Ellis, Henry, *Original Letters illustrative of English History* (1824; 1827; 1846).

Epistle of the moste myghty and redouted Prince Henry the VIII ... to the Emperours maiestie, to all Christen Princes and to all those that trewly and syncerely profess Chrystes religion (1538).

Erasmi, Desiderii Roterodami, *Opus Epistolarum*, ed. P. S. and H. M. Allen (12 vols, Oxford, 1906–58).

Fisher, John, *Defensio Assertionis Regis Angliae de Fide Catholica adversus Lutheri Captivitatem Babylonicam* (1524).

—, *De Causa Matrimonii Serenissimi Regis Angliae, etc.* (Alcala, 1530).

—, *The Earliest English Life of*, ed. Hughes (1935).

Fox, Richard, *The Letters of*, ed. P. S. and H. M. Allen (Oxford, 1929).

Foxe, John, *Acts and Monuments (The Book of Martyrs)*, ed. Pratt (8 vols, 1874).

Fuensalida, Gutierre Gomez de, *Correspondencia de*, ed. Duque de Berwick y de Alba (Madrid, 1907).

Gardiner, Stephen, *De Vera Obedientia* [printed in Janelle, *Obedience in Church and State* (Cambridge, 1930)].

Gee, Henry and Hardy, W. J., *Documents Illustrative of English Church History* (1896).

Glasse of the Truthe, A (printed in *Pocock*, ii, 385 ff.).

Hall, Edward, *Chronicle* (edn 1806).

Harpsfield, Nicholas, *A Treatise on the Pretended Divorce between Henry VIII and Catherine of Aragon*, ed. Pocock, Camden Society, 2nd ser., xxi (1878).

—, *The life and death of Sir Thomas Moore, knight*, ed. Hitchcock and Chambers, E.E.T.S. (1932).

Henry VIII, *Assertio Septem Sacramentorum*, ed. O'Donovan (New York, 1908).

Holinshed, Raphael, *Chronicles* (edn 1808).

Hughes, Paul L. and Larkin, James F., *Tudor Royal Proclamations*. I : *The Early Tudors (1485–1553)* (1964).

Journals of the House of Lords (1846).

Keilway, Robert, *Reports d'ascuns cases, etc.* (1688).

King's Book etc., The, ed. Lacey (1932).

Letters and Papers, Foreign and Domestic, of the reign of Henry VIII, 1509–47, ed. Brewer, Gairdner and Brodie (21 vols, 1862–1910). *Addenda* vol. i (1929–32).

Letters and Papers Illustrative of the reigns of Richard III and Henry VII, ed. Gairdner, Rolls Series (2 vols, 1861–3).

Lettres du Roy Louis XII (4 vols, Brussels, 1712).

Little Treatise against the mutterings of some Papists in corners (printed in *Pocock*, ii, 539 ff.).

Lloyd, C., *Formularies of Faith put forth by authority during the reign of Henry VIII* (Oxford, 1856).

Loazes, Ferdinand, *Tractatus in causa Matrimonii Serenissimorum Dominorum Henrici et Catherinae, etc.* (Barcelona, 1531).

Martene, Edmond and Durand, Ursin, *Veterum Scriptorum et Monumentorum amplissima collectio* (9 vols, Paris, 1724–33).

Materials for a History of the reign of Henry VII, ed. Campbell, Rolls Series (2 vols, 1873).

Memorials of King Henry the Seventh, ed. Gairdner, Rolls Series (1858).

Migne, J.-P., *Patrologiae Cursus Completus, etc.* (Paris, 1844–).

Monumenta Hapsburgica etc. (Vienna, 1853–8).

More, Thomas, *The Correspondence of,* ed. Rogers (Princeton, 1947). *V.s.* Harpsfield and Roper.

Nozarola, Ludovico, *Super Divortio Caterinae ... Disputatio* (?, 1530).

Paston Letters, 1422–1509, The, ed. Gairdner (6 vols, 1904).

Persons, Robert, *Certamen Ecclesiae Anglicanae,* ed. Simons (Assen, 1965).

Pocock, Nicholas, *Records of the Reformation, the divorce 1527–1533* (2 vols, Oxford, 1870).

Pole, Reginald, *Apologia ad Carolum Quintum, in Roccaberti, Bibliotheca Maximorum Pontificium, etc.* (Rome, 1698), vol. xviii.

—, *Pro Ecclesiasticae Unitatis Defensione*, printed *ibid.*

Previdelli, Hictonymus, *Concilium pro Invictissimo Rege Angliae, etc.* (Bologna, 1531).

Protestation made for the moste mighty and moste redoubted Kynge of England, etc. (1538).

Roper, William, *The Lyfe of Sir Thomas Moore, knight*, ed. Hitchcock, E.E.T.S. (1935).

Rymer, Thomas, *Foedera, Conventiones, Litterae, etc.* (edn 1704–35).

Sanuto, Marino, *Diarii* (Venice, 1879–   ).

Skelton, John, *Works*, ed. Dyce (1843).

State Papers of Henry VIII (11 vols, 1830–52).

Statutes of the Realm (11 vols, 1810–28).

Strype, John, *Ecclesiastical Memorials* (3 vols, Oxford, 1820–40).

Treatise proving by the King's laws that bishops of Rome had never right to any supremitie within this realm (1534).

Trefusis, Lady Mary, *Ballads and Instrumental Pieces composed by King Henry the Eighth etc.*, Roxburghe Club (1912).

Tyndale, William, *Works*, ed. Walter, Parker Society (3 vols, 1848–50).

Vergil, Polydore, *The Anglica Historia of*, ed. Hay, Camden Society, lxxiv (1950).

Vives, Luiz, *Apologia siva Confutatio etc.* (1531).

Wilkins, David, *Concilia Magnae Britanniae et Hiberniae* (4 vols, 1737).

Wriothesley, Charles, *A Chronicle of England*, ed. Hamilton, Camden Society, n.s. xi (2 vols, 1875–7).

Secondary Works

Andreae, Johannes, *Solemnis Tractatus de Arbore Consanguinitatis et Affinitatis* (edn Lyons, 1549).

Anglo, S., 'Le Camp du Drap d'Or et les Entrevues d'Henri VIII et de Charles Quint'. *Fêtes et Cérémonies au Temps de Charles Quint* (Paris, 1959).

—, 'The *British History* in Early Tudor Propaganda', *Bull. John Rylands Library*, xliv (1961).

Aquinas, Thomas, *Summa Theologiae*.

—, *Commentary on the Sentences of Peter Lombard*.

Baumer, F. le van, *The Early Tudor Theory of Kingship* (New Haven, 1940).

Behrens, Betty, 'A note on Henry VIII's divorce project of 1514', *B.I.H.R.*, xi (1934).

Bellarmine, Robert, *De Controversiis etc.*, in *Opera Omnia* (Naples, 1872).

Bonaventure, *Commentary on the Sentences of Peter Lombard*.

Brillaud, P. J., *Traité Pratique des Empêchements et des Dispenses de Mariage* (Paris, 1884).

Burnet, Gilbert, *History of the reformation of the Church of England*, ed. Pocock (7 vols, Oxford, 1865).

Busch, Wilhelm, *Drei Jahre englischer Vermittlungspolitik: 1518–1521* (Bonn, 1884).

Butrio, Anthony de, *Lectura super Quarto Libro Decretalium* (edn Rome, 1474).

Butterworth, C., *The English Primers, 1529–1545; their publication and connection with the English Bible and the reformation in England* (Philadelphia, 1953).

Cajetan (Thomas de Vio, Cardinal), *Commentaria super Summam Theologicam etc.*

Caspari, Fritz, *Humanism and the Social Order in Tudor England* (Chicago, 1954).

Chamberlain, S., *Hans Holbein the Younger* (1913).

Chamberlin, F., *The Private Character of Henry VIII* (1932).

Chambers, D. S., *Cardinal Bainbridge in the Court of Rome, 1509 to 1514*, Oxford Historical Series (Oxford, 1965).

—, 'Cardinal Wolsey and the Papal Tiara', *B.I.H.R.*, xxviii (1965).

Cheney, A. D., 'The Holy Maid of Kent', *T.R.H.S.*, 2nd ser., xviii (1904).

Clavasio, Angelus de, *Summa Angelica de Casibus Conscientiae* (edn Strasbourg, 1513).

Clay, R. M., *Medieval Hospitals of England* (1909).

Cokayne, (G. E. C.), *Complete Peerage* (1913).

Cole, H., *King Henry the Eighth's Scheme of Bishopricks* (1838).

Cooper, J. P., 'The Supplication against the Ordinaries Reconsidered', *E.H.R.*, lxxii (1957).

Costa, Stephen, *Tractatus de Affinitate, in Tractatum ex variis iuris Interpretibus Collectorium* (Lyons, 1549).

Creighton, M., *History of the Papacy* (edn 1901).

Dauvillier, J., *Le mariage dans le Droit Classique de l'Eglise* (Paris, 1933).

Dent, J., *The Quest for Nonsuch* (1962).

Devereux, E. J., 'Elizabeth Barton and Tudor Censorship', *Bull. John Rylands Library*, 49 (1966).

Dewar, M., *Sir Thomas Smith: A Tudor Intellectual in Office* (1964).

Dickens, A. G., *Lollards and Protestants in the Diocese of York, 1509–1558* (Oxford, 1958).

—, *Thomas Cromwell and the English Reformation* (E.U.P., 1959).

—, *Heresy and the Origins of English Protestantism* (1962).

—, *The English Reformation* (1964).

Dictionnaire du Droit Canonique, ed. Naz (Paris, 1924–   ).

Dictionnaire de la Bible, ed. Vigoroux (Paris, 1895–1912).

Dietz, F., *English Public Finance, 1485–1558*, University of Illinois Studies in the Social Sciences (1920).

Dix, G., *The Theory of Confirmation in relation to Baptism* (1946).

Dodds, M. H. and Ruth, *The Pilgrimage of Grace, 1536–7, and the Exeter Conspiracy, 1539* (2 vols, Cambridge, 1915).

Doernberg, E., *Henry VIII and Luther* (1961).

Donaldson, G., *Scotland: James V to James VII*, Edinburgh History of Scotland (Edinburgh, 1965).

Ehses, Stefan, *Römische Dokumente zur Geschichte der Ehescheidung Heinrichs VIII von England, 1527–1534* (Paderborn, 1893).

Elton, G. R., *The Tudor Revolution in Government* (Cambridge, 1953).

—, 'The Evolution of a Reformation statute', *E.H.R.*, lxiv (1949).

—, 'The Commons' Supplication of 1532: Parliamentary manoeuvres in the reign of Henry VIII', *E.H.R.*, lxvi (1951).

—, 'Thomas Cromwell's Decline and Fall', *Cambridge Hist. Journal*, x (1951).

—, 'King or Minister? The man behind the Henrician reformation', *History*, xxxix (1954).

—, 'The political creed of Thomas Cromwell', *T.R.H.S.*, 5th ser., vi (1956).

Esmein, A., *Le Mariage en Droit Canonique* (Paris, 1891).

Ferguson, A., *The Indian Summer of English Chivalry* (Durham, N. Carolina, 1960).

Ferrajoli, 'Un breve inedito di Giulio II per la Investitura del Regno di Francia ad Enrico VIII d'Inghilterra', *Arch. della R. Società Romana di Storia Patria*, xix (Rome, 1896).

Fiddes, Richard, *The Life of Cardinal Wolsey* (1724).

Flügel, J. C., 'On the Character and Married Life of Henry VIII' in *Psychoanalysis and History* (Englewood Cliffs, N.J., 1963).

Freisen, J., *Geschichte des canonischen Eherechts* (Tübingen, 1888).

Friedmann, Paul, *Anne Boleyn, a chapter of English history, 1527–1536* (2 vols, 1884).

Fuller, Thomas, *Church History of Britain etc.* (edn 1665).

Gairdner, James, 'New Lights on the Divorce of Henry VIII', *E.H.R.*, xi (1896).

Ganz, P., 'Holbein and Henry VIII', *Burlington Magazine*, lxxiii (1943).

Greenlaw, E., *Studies in Spenser's Historical Allegory* (Baltimore, 1932).

Guasti, 'I manoscritti Torrigiani donati al R. Archivio Centrale del Stato di Firenze', *Arch. Storico Italiano*, 3rd ser., xxv (1887).

Hamy, A., *Entrevue de François 1er avec Henry VIII à Boulogne-sur-Mer en 1532* (Paris, 1898).

Harris, J., *John Bale*, Illinois Studies in Language and Literature, xxv (1939).

Harriss, G. I. and Williams, P., 'A Revolution in Tudor History?', *Past and Present*, 25 (1963).

Herbert, Lord Edward of Cherbury, *The life and raigne of King Henry the eighth* (1672).

Hughes, A. and Abraham, F., *Ars Nova and the Renaissance*, New Oxford History of Music, iii (Oxford, 1960).

Hughes, Philip, *The Reformation in England. I: 'The King's Proceedings'* (1954).

Hurstfield, Joel, *The Queen's Wards* (1958).

Jacobs, H. E., *A Study in Comparative Symbolics: the Lutheran Movement in England during the reigns of Henry VIII and Edward VI, and its literary monuments* (Philadelphia, 1890).

Jacqueton, *La Politique extérieure de Louise de Savoie* (Paris, 1892).

Jordan, W. K., *Philanthropy in England, 1480–1660* (1959).

Joyce, G. H., *Christian Marriage, etc.* (1948).

Kaufman, 'Jacob Mantino', *Rev. des Études Juives*, xxvii (1893).

Kelly, M. J., 'The Submission of the Clergy', *T.R.H.S.*, 5th ser., xv (1965).

Kingsford, C. L., *The Early History of Piccadilly, Leicester Square, Soho, etc.* (Cambridge, 1925).

Knowles, M. D., ' "The Matter of Wilton" in 1528', *B.I.H.R.*, xxxi (1958).

—, *The Religious Orders in England*. III: *The Tudor Age* (Cambridge, 1959).

— and Hadcock, R. N., *Medieval Religious Houses* (1954).

Knox, D. B., *The Doctrine of Faith in the reign of Henry VIII* (1961).

Koebner, R., ' "The imperial crown of this realm": Henry VIII, Constantine and Polydore Vergil', *B.I.H.R.*, xxvi (1953).

Lambert, B., *The History of London and its Environs* (1806).

Lamont, W. M., *Marginal Prynne 1600–1669* (1963).

Law, E., *England's First Great War Minister* (1916).

Lebey, A., *Le Connétable de Bourbon, 1490–1527* (Paris, 1904).

Leeming, B., *Principles of Sacramental Theology* (1956).

Levine, M., 'The Last Will and Testament of Henry VIII: a Reappraisal Reappraised', *Historian* (1964).

Livius, Titus, *The First English Life of King Henry the Fifth*, trans. anon., ed. Kingsford (Oxford, 1911).

Lopez, Ludovicus, *Instructorium Conscientiae* (Salamanca, 1594).

McConica, J. K., *English Humanists and Reformation Politics under Henry VIII and Edward VI* (Oxford, 1965).

McNalty, A. S., *Henry VIII, a difficult patient* (1952).

Macquereau, R., *Histoire Générale de l'Europe* (Louvain, 1765).

Mainwaring Brown, J., 'Henry VIII's book . . . and the royal title of "Defender of the Faith" ', *T.R.H.S.*, 1st ser., viii (1880).

Maitland, F. W., 'Elizabethan Gleanings. I: "Defender of the Faith and so forth" ', *E.H.R.*, xv (1900).

Mansella, G., *De Impedimentis Matrimonium Dirimentibus* (Rome, 1881).

Marcus, G. J., *A Naval History of England*. I: *The Formative Years* (1961).

Mattingly, G., 'An early non-aggression pact', *Journal of Modern History*, x (1938).

—, *Catherine of Aragon* (1950).

—, *Renaissance Diplomacy* (1955).

Merriman, R. B., *The Life and Letters of Thomas Cromwell* (Oxford, 1902).

Milis de Verona, Johannes, *Repertorium, etc.* (edn Cologne, 1475).

Millican, C. B., *Spenser and the Round Table* (Cambridge, Mass., 1932).

Muller, J. A., *Stephen Gardiner and the Tudor Reaction* (1926).

Nelson, W., *John Skelton Laureate* (New York, 1939).

Nitti, F., *Leone X e la sua Politica* (Florence, 1892).

O'Neil, B. H. St. J., 'Stepan van Haschenberg, an engineer to King Henry VIII and his work', *Archaeologia*, 2nd ser., xci (1945).

Oppenheim, M., *History of the administration of the royal navy* (1896).

Oxley, J. E., *The Reformation in Essex, to the death of Mary* (Manchester, 1965).

Paludanus (Petrus de la Palu), *In Quartum Sententiarum etc.*

Panormitanus, *Commentarius in libros Decretalium, etc.* (Venice, 1588).

Pastor, L. von, *History of the Popes*, trans. Antrobus and Kerr (1891–1933).

Paul, J. E., *Catherine of Aragon and her friends* (1966).

Pollard, A. F., *Henry VIII* (edn 1951).

—, *Wolsey* (1929).

—, 'Thomas Cromwell's Parliamentary Lists', *B.I.H.R.*, xi (1931–2).

Porter, H. C., *Reformation and Reaction in Tudor Cambridge* (Cambridge, 1958).

Prierias, Silvester, *Summa Summarum etc.* (edn Antwerp, 1581).

Prueser, F., *England und die Schmalkaldener, 1535–40* (Leipzig, 1929).

Reed, A. W., *Early Tudor Drama* (1926).

Reese, Gustave, *Music in the Renaissance* (1954).

Reynolds, E. E., *St John Fisher* (1955).

Richard of Middleton, *In Quartum Sententiarum* (edn Venice, 1512).

Ridley, Jasper, *Thomas Cranmer* (Oxford, 1962).

St John Hope, *Windsor Castle* (1913).

Sanchez, Thomas, *Disputatio de sancti Matrimonii Sacramento* (edn Antwerp, 1620).

Sawada, P., 'The Abortive Council of Mantua and Henry VIII's Sententia de Concilio, 1537', *Academia*, xxvii (Nagoya (Japan), 1960).

—, 'Two anonymous Tudor Treatises on the General Council', *Journal of Ecclesiastical History*, xii (1961).

Scarisbrick, J., 'The Pardon of the Clergy, 1531', *Cambridge Hist. Journal*, xii (1956).

—, 'Clerical Taxation in England, 1485–1547', *Journal of Ecclesiastical History*, xii (1961).

—, 'The first Englishman round the Cape of Good Hope?', *B.I.H.R.*, xxxiv (1961).

—, 'Henry VIII and the Vatican Library', *Bibl. d'Humanisme et Renaissance*, xxiv (1962).

Scotus, Duns, *Questiones super quattuor libros Sententiarum etc.*

Simon, Joan, *Education and Society in Tudor England* (Cambridge, 1966).

Smith, Lacey Baldwin, *A Tudor Tragedy: The Life and Times of Catherine Howard* (1961).

—, 'The Last Will and Testament of Henry VIII: a question of perspective', *Journal of British Studies*, ii (1962).

—, 'Henry VIII and the Protestant Triumph', *American Hist. Review*, lxxi (1966).

Soto, Domingo de, *Commentarius in Quartum Sententiarum etc.* (edn Salamanca, 1561–79).

Steinbach, W., *Gabrielis Biel Supplementum* (—, 1521).

Stow, John, *Annals* (edn 1601).

—, *A Survey of London*, ed. Kingsford (2 vols, Oxford, 1908).

Sturge, C., *Cuthbert Tunstall* (1938).

Summerson, J., *Architecture in Britain, 1530–1830*, Pelican History of Art (1958).

Survey of London – vol. xiii, *The Parish of St Margaret's Westminster* (1930); vol. xix, *The Parish of St James's Westminster* (1960).

Thomson, J. A. F., *The Latter Lollards, 1414–1520*, Oxford Historical Series (1965).

Thomson, P., *Sir Thomas Wyatt and his Background* (1964).

Tierney, B., *Foundations of Conciliar Theory* (Cambridge, 1957).

Tjernagel, N. S., *Henry VIII and the Lutherans* (St Louis, 1965).

Torquemada, Johannes, *Commentaria super Decreto* (edn Lyons, 1519).

Ullmann, W., *Principles of Government and Politics in the Middle Ages* (1961).

Victoria County History. Bedfordshire; Essex; Cambridge.

Vittoria, F., *Relecciones Telógicas* (edn Madrid, 1933–6).

Wegg, Jervis, *Richard Pace* (1932).

Wernham, R. B., *Before the Armada: the growth of English foreign policy, 1485–1588* (1966).

Whatmore, L. E., 'The Sermon against the Holy Maid of Kent, delivered at Paul's Cross, 23 November, 1533, and at Canterbury, Dec. 7', *E.H.R.*, lviii (1943).

White, Helen, *Social Criticism in Popular Religious Literature of the Sixteenth Century* (New York, 1944).

Wilks, M. J., *The Problem of Sovereignty in the Later Middle Ages* (Cambridge, 1963).

Williamson, J. A., *The Voyages of the Cabots and the English Discovery of North America under Henry VII and Henry VIII* (1929).

Youings, Joyce, 'The terms of the disposal of the Devon monastic lands, 1536–58', *E.H.R.*, lxix (1954).

Zeeveld, W. G., *Foundations of Tudor policy* (1948).

(*Note*. Those Patristic and other writings cited in Chapter VII which are noted there as being found in *Migne* have not been separately listed in this Bibliography.)

Index

The following abbreviations are used: amb.=ambassador; archbp=archbishop; bp=bishop; k.=king; q.=queen.

MORE ABOUT PENGUINS
AND PELICANS

Penguinews, which appears every month, contains details of all the new books issued by Penguins as they are published. From time to time it is supplemented by *Penguins in Print*, which is a complete list of all titles available. (There are some five thousand of these.)

A specimen copy of *Penguinews* will be sent to you free on request. For a year's issues (including the complete lists) please send 50p if you live in the British Isles, or 75p if you live elsewhere. Just write to Dept EP, Penguin Books Ltd, Harmondsworth, Middlesex, enclosing a cheque or postal order, and your name will be added to the mailing list.

In the U.S.A.: For a complete list of books available from Penguin in the United States write to Dept CS, Penguin Books Inc., 7110 Ambassador Road, Baltimore, Maryland 21207.

In Canada: For a complete list of books available from Penguin in Canada write to Penguin Books Canada Ltd, 41 Steelcase Road West, Markham, Ontario.

THE PELICAN BIOGRAPHIES

Other Volumes in this Series

Queen Elizabeth I   *J. E. Neale*

Sir John Neale's study of Queen Elizabeth I has easily held its place for nearly forty years as the best and most readable biography of the great Tudor queen

'A masterly book, scholarly, wise and witty' – *English Historical Review*

Baudelaire   *Enid Starkie*

'It is a remarkable study where scholarship though profound is worn lightly and it remains completely readable ... Miss Starkie combines an analytical study of the life, with a critique of the poems ... The portrait of the man and his work here is honestly given in a brilliant narrative. He comes before us very vividly as a character' – *Sir Ifor Evans*

Joseph Conrad   *Jocelyn Baines*

'That this is the definitive life there can be little doubt ... here is Conrad as we have never had him before ... rarely has there been so enthralling and minute a study' – *The Times*

*Tolstoy   *Henri Troyat*

'Nothing less than this magnificent, massive, 700-page biography could even begin to do justice to one of the most complex, baffling and grand men that ever lived ... a masterly book' – *Sunday Telegraph*

*Richard Wagner: The Man, His Mind, and His Music
Robert W. Gutman

'A most serious and substantial contribution' – Robert Donington in the *Musical Times*

NOT FOR SALE IN THE U.S.A.

*NOT FOR SALE IN THE U.S.A. OR CANADA

PELICAN BIOGRAPHIES

Other volumes in the series:

NOT FOR SALE IN THE U.S.A.
*NOT FOR SALE IN THE U.S.A. OR CANADA